The Annotated and Illustrated

JOURNALS
of
MAJOR ROBERT ROGERS

The Annotated and Illustrated
JOURNALS
of
MAJOR ROBERT ROGERS

Annotated and with an Introduction
by Timothy J. Todish

Illustrated and with Captions
by Gary S. Zaboly

PURPLE MOUNTAIN PRESS
Fleischmanns, New York

The Annotated and Illustrated Journals of Major Robert Rogers
First edition 2002

Published by
PURPLE MOUNTAIN PRESS, LTD.
1060 Main Street, P.O. Box 309
Fleischmanns, New York 12430-0309
845-254-4062, 845-254-4476 (fax)
purple@catskill.net
http://www.catskill.net/purple
A free catalog of Purple Mountain Press books is available.

Library of Congress Control Number: 2002101418

Cover: *The Advanced Guard*, see page 163.
Back cover and frontispiece: *Rogers at Detroit*, see page 8.

Manufactured in the United States of America on acid-free paper.

Dedication

To American Rangers
who have bravely, courageously, and selflessly
"Led the Way" for the cause of American freedom

And especially to the soldiers of the
U.S. Army's 75th Ranger Regiment,
who are carrying that commitment
into the uncertain waters of the
twenty-first century

Table of Contents

Gary Zaboly Illustrations

A Note on the Frontispiece: *Rogers at Detroit, 1760*

THE LAST EXPEDITION of Major Robert Rogers in the French and Indian War began on September 12th, 1760, when, at recently surrendered Montreal, he received secret orders from General Amherst. These directed him to take 200 Rangers, in fifteen whaleboats, westward along the St. Lawrence River, and across lakes Ontario and Erie to Detroit. Not only would Rogers accept the surrender of that distant French trading post, but he would also relieve the garrisons of the other French forts on and near the lakes, make peace with the various Indian tribes in the vicinity, as well as carefully document his passage for the benefit of future English expeditions.

Reaching the western end of Lake Erie on November 20th, Rogers sent forward emissaries to announce his arrival and his terms. The French commandant of Detroit, Captain Bellestre, according to local Indians who greeted Rogers" had set up an high flag-staff, with a wooden effigy of a man's head on the top, and upon that a crow; that the crow was to represent himself, the man' s head mine, and the meaning of the 'whole, that he would scratch out my brains. This artifice, however, had no effect; for the Indians told him (as they said) that the reverse would be the true explanation of the sign."

Indeed, Captain Bellestre peacefully surrendered Detroit on November 29th; the garrison was disarmed and later sent as prisoners to Fort Pitt. Among the Indians who had formerly been allied with the French was the Ottawa, Pontiac, and with him several other chiefs. Rogers conferred to assure them of the peaceful intentions of the English in the region. The Canadians who owned farms surrounding Detroit were allowed to remain, as long as they swore an oath of allegiance to England.

Major Rogers is depicted a couple of days after the surrender. His silver-laced officer's jacket of wool, lined with green serge, includes cording on his right shoulder as rank designation, button-loops, and white metal buttons. Such a decorated uniform would undoubtedly have been worn only on formal occasions. A black ostrich feather decorates his green-painted leather cap. Red garters tie his green ratteen leggings. His arm cradles a fusil, and a cutlass hangs at his side.

In the middleground, Rangers remove trade goods from a few of his whaleboats. Bad weather is approaching, and worsening conditions will force Rogers, on December 16th, to abandon a side-trip from Detroit intended to receive the surrender of faraway Fort Michilimackinac. Parties sent to relieve other French posts were more successful.

Rogers made the report of his journey to General Amherst at New York on February 14th, 1761. At 29 years of age, he was one of the true heroes of the five-year conflict for control of North America (and certainly its most energetic); and, though in his later years he continually strove to revive the great fame he had once enjoyed, it would sadly forever remain for him an elusive object.

G.Z.

Acknowlegments

THIS BOOK is the result of five years of work from the point when Gary Zaboly and I actually decided to go ahead with it, and I was mentally planning it long before then. With any book, and especially with one of this magnitude, no one person can do it all by himself. So many people have contributed to this effort, and to all I offer my most sincere thanks. I also apologize to any whose names I have inadvertently omitted from this list.

First of all, both Gary and I would like to express our gratitude to all of the sponsors of the illustrations for the faith and support that they displayed for our project. To Wray and Loni Rominger and the staff of Purple Mountain Press we are also very grateful for their accepting this project, and also for their efforts in making the finished product turn out so well. Two research facilities and their entire staffs are also worthy of special mention. The William L. Clements Library at the University of Michigan in Ann Arbor, and the Thompson-Pell Research Center at Fort Ticonderoga, New York, are equally noteworthy for their tremendous collections and also for their user friendly attitudes towards visiting researchers. Together, they are to be credited with a very large share of the material that is presented in this book.

While space does not allow me to describe in detail the specific contributions of each of the following individuals, I say without hesitation that I never could have completed the project without their help: Dr. David A. Armour, of Mackinac State Historic Parks; Dr. Russell P. Bellico, of Feeding Hills, Massachusetts; Colonel Robert Black, Retired, of Carlisle, Pennsylvania; George A. Bray III, of Rochester, New York; Timothy J. Carlson, of Traverse City, Michigan; Dr. John C. Dann, of the William L. Clements Library; Mike, Judy, and Amy DeJonge, of Grand Rapids, Michigan; Brian Leigh Dunnigan, of the William L. Clements Library; Gerry Embleton, of Preles, Switzerland; William Farrar, of the Crown Point State Historic Site, New York; Gary L. Foreman, of Valparaiso, Indiana; Christopher Fox, of Fort Ticonderoga, New York; Richard & JoAnne Fuller, of Fort Edward, New York; Dr. Todd E. Harburn, of Okemos, Michigan; John Harriman, of the William L. Clements Library; John C. Jaeger, of Flat Rock, Michigan; Robert Lancaster, of Croton, Michigan; Father Barry A. Lewis, of Corunna, Michigan; Lieutenant Colonel John Lock, U.S. Army; Christopher Matheney, of the Ohio State Historical Society; Scott Mann, of Laingsburg, Michigan; Lieutenant Colonel Ian McCulloch, C.D. of the Directorate of History and Heritage, Canadian Armed Forces, and his wife Susan A. Johnson McCulloch (formerly of Fort Ticonderoga), of Ottawa, Ontario, Canada; Tom McElroy, of North Branch, Michigan; Father Dennis Morrow, of Grand Rapids, Michigan; Frank Nastasi, of Muttontown, New York; John-Eric Nelson, of Milford, Connecticut; Thomas Nesbitt, of the Crown Point State Historic Site; Jerry Olson, of Dearborn, Michigan; Ian Pedler, of Bristol, England; Robert J. Rogers, of St. Albert, Alberta, Canada; Ted Spring, of Nicoma Park, Oklahoma; Dr. David R. Starbuck, of Chestertown, New York; the late Earl Stott, former owner of Rogers' Island, New York; Charlie Sum, of Orlando, Florida; Timothy Titus, formerly of the Crown Point State Historic Site, New York; my wife Colleen, son Tim R., and brother, Terry Todish, all of Grand Rapids, Michigan; Michael Tracy, of Mackinaw City, Michigan; and last alphabetically, but certainly not least in contribution, Nicholas Westbrook, of Fort Ticonderoga, New York.

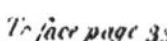

To face page 33.

Engrav'd for Mr. Mants History of the War in America. By J. Lodge.

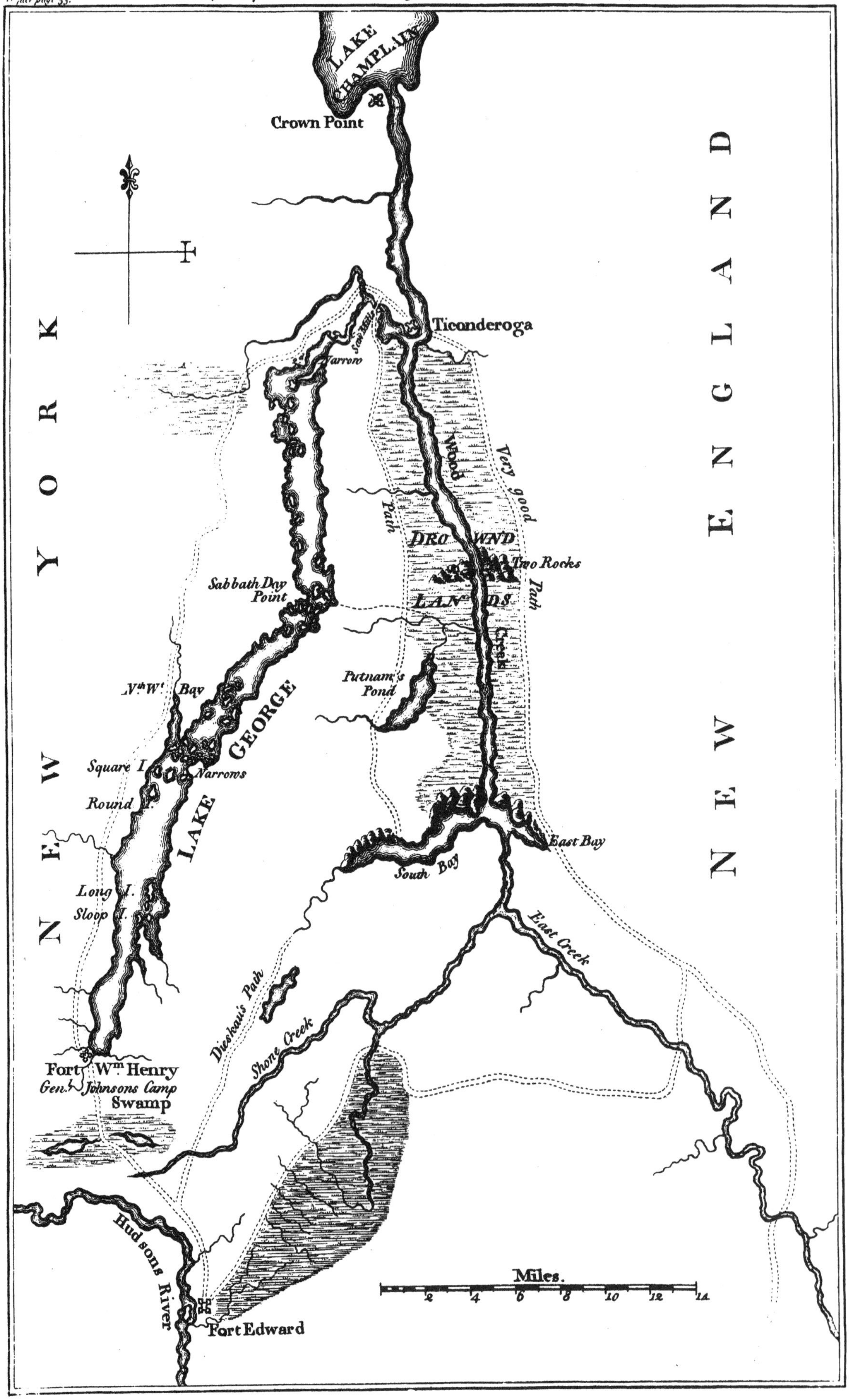

LAKE CHAMPLAIN
Crown Point
Ticonderoga
Saw Mills
Narrows
NEW YORK
NEW ENGLAND
Wood
Very good
Path
DROWND LANDS
Two Rocks
Path
Creek
Sabbath Day Point
Putnam's Pond
N.th W.t Bay
LAKE GEORGE
Square I.
Narrows
Round I.
Long I.
Sloop I.
East Bay
South Bay
East Creek
Dieskau's Path
Shone Creek
Fort Wm. Henry
Genl. Johnsons Camp
Swamp
Hudsons River
Fort Edward
Miles.
2 4 6 8 10 12 14

Preface

THIS BOOK is the result of five years of intense effort on the part of myself and my good friend, artist/historian Gary Zaboly. I consider Gary to be an equal partner in this project in every sense of the word. We both have a nearly lifelong interest in Robert Rogers and his famous corps of French and Indian War Rangers. For a quarter of a century, we have shared not only information and ideas about the Rangers, but a strong friendship as well. This book is the culmination of that interest, and that friendship.

My job has been to prepare Rogers' writings for publication, as well as to select primary and secondary sources to use as annotations to amplify Rogers' own words. The purpose of these extensive notes is to give the reader a more in depth look at the events that Rogers is describing, through the eyes of a variety of witnesses and scholars. I have tried particularly hard to find good French sources so that his opponents' perspectives are also presented.

Gary's job, on the other hand, was to do the original artwork and captions that really bring this book to life. I am extremely grateful that Gary was willing to be a part of this project. There can be no doubt that much of whatever success this book attains will be the result of his outstanding work. In today's world of historical art, Gary is one of the standard setters—both in terms of the artistic nature of his work, and also for its well-documented historical accuracy.

We hope that through our efforts, our readers will gain a deeper appreciation and respect not only for Major Robert Rogers, but also for bravery and sacrifices of the Rangers, Regulars, Provincials, and Native Americans who fought alongside him. We also hope that our effort does the same for their counterparts on the other side who were fighting just as hard for what they believed in.

Tim J. Todish
Grand Rapids, Michigan
December 2001

Map of Lake George and environs originally published in Thomas Mante's *History of the Late War in North-America* (London, 1772). Note the dotted line from the vicinity of Sabbath Day Point eastward to Wood Creek—the path used by Rogers and his men to carry the five whaleboats over the mountains in 1756 and subsequently employed as a short cut by other British scouts. The swampy area between Fort William Henry and Hudson's River marks the general location of Halfway Brook, scene of many French and Indian ambushes.

JOURNALS
OF
Major ROBERT ROGERS:

CONTAINING

An Account of the ſeveral Excurſions he made under the Generals who commanded upon the Continent of NORTH AMERICA, during the late War.

FROM WHICH MAY BE COLLECTED

The moſt material Circumſtances of every Campaign upon that Continent, from the Commencement to the Concluſion of the War.

TO WHICH IS ADDED

An Hiſtorical Account of the Expedition againſt the Ohio Indians in the Year 1764, under the command of Henry Bouquet, Eſq; Colonel of Foot, and now Brigadier General in America, including his Tranſactions with the Indians, relative to the Delivery of the Priſoners, and the Preliminaries of Peace. With an Introductory Account of the Proceeding Campaign, and Battle at Buſhy-Run.

DUBLIN:

Printed by R. ACHESON, at HORACE's-HEAD, William-ſtreet,
FOR
J. MILLIKEN, No. 10. in Skinner-row.
M,DCC,LX,IX.

From an original of the Dublin Edition
in the Clements Library

Introduction

The Rangers were representative of a young and vibrant nation on the move: their discipline was of the forest rather than the parade ground, and they attracted leaders of initiative and daring, leaders who set a standard of going beyond the expected.

Ranger Colonel Robert W. Black, Retired
Rangers in Korea

MAJOR ROBERT ROGERS of the Rangers is not only one of the most famous men to come out of Colonial America, he is also one of the most fascinating. He was born in Methuen, in the Massachusetts Bay Colony, on November 7, 1731. Rogers was a man of great physical strength, charisma, intelligence, ambition, and vision. Like all men, he also had his flaws and weaknesses.

Although he was born to a frontier family, Rogers did not come from abject poverty. In fact, for much of his youth, his family appears to have been relatively well off by frontier standards. He received little formal schooling, but that does not mean he was uneducated. While he probably had help with his published writings, the majority of the content is undoubtedly his own. Surviving letters and other documents show that he had a mastery of writing skills that was at least adequate for his time. In a nineteenth-century essay on Rogers, Joseph B. Walker wrote, "Rogers laid no claims to fine writing, but his own manuscript reports, written mostly in camp and hastily, attest to his possession of a fair chirography, a pretty good knowledge of grammar and spelling, together with a style of expression both lucid and simple."[1]

It is not my purpose to retell the story of Robert Rogers' life. That has been done a number of times already. On the other hand, there are a few things about him that I must mention for the reader to have a proper appreciation of this book.

Probably the first serious biography of Rogers was by Allan Nevins. It was published as part of the 1914 Caxton Club edition of Rogers' play, *Ponteach or the Savages of America.* While Nevins generally gives Rogers his due for his military exploits, he takes a rather negative approach to him as a person, particularly in his later years. Although there is certainly a basis for his criticisms, Nevins' account was written many years ago, and he did not have access to much of the information available today. Unfortunately, many later writers have repeated Nevins' conclusions, without attempting to verify them independently, or use the latest available research.

John Cuneo's *Robert Rogers of the Rangers* remains *the* definitive biography of Rogers. Dr. Russell Bellico has compiled an admirable though shorter account of his life in *Chronicles of Lake Champlain: Journeys in War and Peace,* as well as a more specialized essay in *Chronicles of Lake George: Journeys in War and Peace.* Canadian Forces lieutenant colonel Ian McCulloch's *Beaver* Magazine article is also a good summary of his career, written with a soldier's perspective. Robert J. Rogers, a retired Canadian naval intelligence officer, and descendant of James Rogers, has recently published *Rising Above Circumstances: The Rogers Family in Colonial America.* This book looks at Robert's life, but perhaps its most important contribution is its treatment of his older brother James. James Rogers served as an officer in Roberts' Ranger corps during both the French and Indian and Revolutionary Wars. Unlike Robert, James was as successful in peace as he was in war. He went on to become one of the founding fathers of Upper Canada, and through him we see some of the details of Robert's decline in his later years. Until the publication of *Rising Above Circumstances,* James Rogers had never received his due from any biographer.

To fully understand Robert Rogers, a knowledge of the history of his Rangers is also desirable. The most in depth work on them still is Burt Loescher's three volume *History of Rogers' Rangers.* Long out of print, the two main volumes are now available once again. Lieutenant Colonel John Lock's *To Fight with Intrepidity . . . The Complete History of the U.S. Army Rangers 1622 to Present,* is an excellent study of the entire history of the Ranger concept, with considerable emphasis on the colonial period.

My purpose in presenting this book is to allow Robert Rogers to tell portions of his life in his own words. To supplement his accounts, I add numerous annotations to give a broader picture of the events described. Most will be from eyewitnesses, or at least contemporaries of Rogers. Later secondary sources are used sparingly. Occasionally an annotation, or series of annotations, will be used to give a broader picture of what was happening, but for the most part I stick to the events actually being described in the *Journals.* When I quote from a journal or diary, I am giving that individual's personal outlook and opinion. When something is taken from an orderly book, it means it was part of the official orders of the day. While I may give numerous journalist's views describing the same incident, orderly book entries are usually alike, so only one is quoted.

Keep in mind that even though these are for the most part primary source accounts, the person being quoted is not always an eyewitness, and there is no automatic guarantee that the account is accurate and truthful. At times, some readers may think that the minute detail that I include is trivial, while others will find it interesting and useful. My challenge was not in finding enough material to include, but rather in deciding what *not* to use.

Gary Zaboly's wonderful original illustrations, along with his well-written captions, add an invaluable dimension to this edition of Rogers' *Journals.* They also fill in some gaps in his life that are not specifically covered in the text of the *Journals.*

This book is a reprinting the 1769 Dublin edition of Rogers' *Journals.* Although the type has been reset, as much as possible the original spelling, punctuation, and grammar have been retained for both Rogers' text and my annotations. There are two main exceptions. The first is that the eighteenth-century "hard s," (ſ) has been replaced by the modern "s". The second is where another editor has already made changes in a passage that I am quoting, I reproduce it the way it is written in that source. While sometimes it requires a little more care in reading, retaining the original format gives the reader a real appreciation of the flavor of the original writings.

This rare Dublin edition contains all of Rogers' French and Indian War exploits as first published in the more common 1765 London edition, plus additional material added to the later version. The bibliography will give more information on the publishing history of the *Journals,* as well as other titles mentioned in this book.

There were actually two versions of the Dublin edition of the *Journals.* The first was published by R. Acheson in 1769, and there was a second, virtually identical version by J. Potts in 1770. Victor Hogo Paltsits, who edited Rogers' *Journal on His Expedition for Receiving the Capitulation of the Western French Posts,* claims that both Dublin printings were "pirated," but does not explain why.[2]

The reader is cautioned that additional material in the Dublin Edition, commonly titled *An Historical Account of the Expedition Against the Ohio Indians,* was not actually written by Rogers. It was authored by the Reverend William Smith, an Anglican priest and educator who had a keen interest in military affairs. Father Smith's ideas show a good understanding of the unique characteristics of North American warfare. Those interested in Rogers and his Rangers will find Father Smith's narrative interesting reading, which is probably why it was added to the Dublin Edition of the *Journals.* It was first published on its own in Philadelphia in 1765, and several times thereafter.

Through the courtesy of the William L. Clements Library at the University of Michigan, a *Journal of the Siege of Detroit* that is attributed to Robert Rogers is also added here, even though it was not in either edition of his published *Journals.*

To the best of my knowledge, this Detroit journal has not been published since 1860. There is some question whether this work was actually written by Rogers. Allan Nevins accepts it as authentic, while John Cuneo flatly states that it is the work of Jehu Hay, a lieutenant in the 60th, or Royal American Regiment, who also served at Detroit.[3] However, a comparison of this document to the Hay Diary clearly shows they are different. The Rogers journal was supposedly found among the papers of Sir William Johnson in the New York Public Library. The Hay diary is believed to have been purchased from an English book dealer in the 1850s, and eventually made its way into the collections of the William L. Clements Library.

Rogers' Detroit journal begins on May 6, 1763, and, unfortunately, ends before the Battle of Bloody Run. It is clear that Rogers was not an eyewitness to all of the events that he writes about, since he did not even arrive at Detroit until July 26. The opening sentence of the journal states that it was "taken from the Officers who were then in the Fort, and wrote in their Words. . . ." Nineteenth-century historian Franklin B. Hough, who first edited the journal for publication, theorizes that Rogers was writing down the accounts of others to combine with his own experiences for a follow-up volume to his French and Indian War *Journals*. The last entry in the Detroit journal is on August 8. Hough believes that it was then forwarded to Sir William Johnson when two ships were sent to Niagara for supplies and reinforcements on August 13. It is not known if more of the journal was ever completed, but if it was, it has not been located.

Some people claim that Rogers' *Journals* are "boastful," and "self promoting." Others, including this author, disagree. Distinguished historian William L. Clements says that Rogers "recited his experiences in a modest way."[4] J. A. Houlding, the author of one of the classic works on the British army in the eighteenth century, says that Rogers' *Journals* convey "a striking realism and a consummate professionalism . . . ."[5]

Franklin B. Hough, who also edited a nineteenth-century edition of Rogers' French and Indian War *Journals*, said this, "The general tenor of the narrative, and details in abundance, are however well verified by independent authorities, and justify the belief that the accounts of services here given, are in the main reliable, and that the work fairly presents the conditions of affairs, as they existed, and the events, as they occurred, in the time and manner described."[6]

I think that by the time most readers see how others recorded the same incidents that Rogers describes, they will agree that his *Journals* are anything but boastful. It must be recognized that in war, both sides always tend to report things in the most favorable light possible. This often makes it difficult to resolve discrepancies in terms of troop strength, casualties, prisoners, and the like. In some instances, it will be up to the reader to decide between differing accounts of the same incident.

The "self promoting" part about the *Journals* I do have to agree with, but in a positive way. Rogers was a great visionary and definitely ambitious, but so are most great men. His dream was to discover the Northwest Passage. He wanted to open the way to the Pacific Ocean and the trade that lay beyond, and also saw the advantages of British development of the Great Lakes region. In order to realize his dreams, he had to sell people on his ideas and raise the necessary funds to accomplish them. Capitalizing on his past accomplishments was one way to achieve his goal. This technique has, and continues to be, used by many other great men.

One of Rogers' greatest strengths was his ability to accept and work with all kinds of people. His Ranger corps was very diverse, and his men were judged on their abilities and dedication to the ranging service. Rogers enlisted several companies of Stockbridge Mohican Indians into his Rangers, and gave their Indian officers the same status as white Ranger officers. He repeatedly defended them against the criticism, at times justified, that they received from superior officers. Two of his early companies, commanded by Humphrey Hobbs and Thomas Speakman, were made up of a high percentage of Irish Catholics and even some Spaniards.[7] Boston Burn, a black slave belonging to James Burn of Westford, Massachusetts, served as a Ranger in the 1758 campaign.[8]

The only surviving personal possession that definitely can be connected to Robert Rogers is his powder horn, now in the collections of Fort Ticonderoga. It was made for him by John Bush, a free black who is highly regarded for his beautifully engraved horns. Bush served in a Massachusetts Provincial regiment, was captured at Fort William Henry, and tragically died aboard a ship while being transported to France as a prisoner of war.[9]

Many people have made the assumption that because Rogers was so good at fighting Indians, he hated them. Nothing could be further from the truth. When it was time to fight the Indians, Rogers fought them with a skill and determination that few men possessed. At the same time, he had great empathy for them and treated them fairly. His ability to deal effectively with Indians made him a threat to Sir William Johnson, the Northern Superintendent of Indian Affairs, and was the cause of much of Johnson's animosity towards him. At the same time, Rogers' mastery of the techniques of wilderness warfare made his military superior, Thomas Gage, equally jealous of him. Although never fully successful, Gage wanted to replace the Rangers with his own 80th Light Infantry Regiment. Rogers' problems with these two powerful men were the cause of many difficulties that he later faced.

While governor of Michilimackinac, he negotiated an important treaty between two traditional enemies, the Ojibwa and the Sioux. His play, *Ponteach, or the Savages of America,* was very sympathetic to the Indians' plight, and harsh on the British traders and government officials who took advantage of them. As a result of Rogers' fairness towards Indians, he was well liked and respected by them.

When he was arrested at Michilimackinac on December 6, 1767, the local Ojibwa protested by throwing their British flag into the lake, and then tried to get the Ottawas to assist them in helping Rogers escape.[10]

One thing that must be made clear is that Robert Rogers did not invent the "Ranger." John Lock, a Ranger qualified U.S. Army officer, gives an excellent summary of the history of the ranger concept:

"The term 'Ranger' evolved as far back as thirteenth century England, when it was used to describe a far-ranging forester or borderer. By the seventeenth century, the term emerged to serve as a title for irregular and unique military organizations, such as the 'Border Rangers' who defended the troubled border between England and Scotland. The term crossed the Atlantic to the North American continent with England's early settlers."[11]

From the earliest days of forest warfare in North America, groups of Rangers performed scouting duties and made swift attacks on the bands of Indians that were endangering the frontier settlements. Captain Benjamin Church's Rangers during King Philip's War practiced tactics that Rogers would make famous some seventy-five years later. By the time of the French and Indian War, it was common for every Provincial regiment to have a "scouting" or "ranging" company. In fact, Rogers got his start as captain of the ranging company of Blanchard's New Hampshire Regiment. So although Rogers did not invent the ranger concept, he definitely refined it and brought it into prominence. He was one of the first to reduce his tactics to writing, and to formally train promising young officers and volunteers so that they could go back and share their knowledge with their own units. Through the exploits of his Ranger corps, he certainly gained a lasting place in history.

As a soldier, Robert Rogers had no formal military training. He applied his common sense and learned from experience. In many ways, this worked to his favor, as it allowed him to see solutions to problems that eluded his more rigid peers, particularly Regular British officers. At other times, he paid a high price for his lack of formal training. He and his Rangers always had difficulty in accepting what they viewed as the unnecessary parts of disciplined military life. There are even a few instances where they appear to have let their guard down while in the field, but these are rare.

Retired Marine Corps colonel and author Anthony Walker gives an interesting evaluation of Rogers and his command of the Rangers: "Rogers embodied the Ranger fighting spirit but also their carelessness and lack of discipline. This dichotomy seems quite logical for a man raised on the New Hampshire frontier, where individualism flourished, providing also an explanation for the Rangers' apparent lack of training in the art of woods fighting. *We already know how to fight in the woods, so why train?* Rogers' tactical errors seemed to reflect inattention rather than ignorance or perhaps a certain laziness, which led him to follow the easy way out rather than insist on more rigorous measures. He was a consummate woodsman, completely at home in the forests winter or summer and expected his subordinates to show the same skills, which frequently they could not."[12]

Colonel Walker is mistaken about the Rangers' "lack of training," for there are numerous examples of Rogers "exercising" his men in Ranger tactics. On June 25, 1758, a Massachusetts Provincial officer heard firing in the woods at Fort Edward. He learned that "ye General had given leave for four or five hundred Rangers to go out and hold a bush fight for 1/4 of and hour." On another occasion, a surgeon recorded that, "Major Rogers this Day exercised his men in Bush Fiteing which drew a great Number out of ye Camp, to view them." In yet another instance, this same surgeon wrote, "the Rangers exercised in Scout marches and Bush fighting which make a very pritty figure."[13]

The rest of Colonel Walker's observations, however, are worthy of consideration, especially since they are made by an experienced military officer. One thing that must be remembered though, is that nearly all of Rogers' defeats came when he was deep in enemy territory, when he was outnumbered and fighting under very trying circumstances. Biographer John Cuneo identifies two of Rogers' most valuable characteristics: "One was his aggressiveness: he carried the fight to the enemy. The other was his uncanny woodsmanship: he conquered the wilderness under the most adverse circumstances, including the rigorous limitations imposed by warfare. Time and time again Rogers carried out his orders in the heart of the enemy's territory in stormy, freezing weather under combat conditions and returned with his unit intact."[14]

In spite of the myth created in the movie *Northwest Passage* that Rangers who were too ill or too badly injured to keep up were left behind, Rogers showed a genuine concern for his men, and in return earned their affection and loyalty. On a winter scout to Crown Point in early 1756, one of his men became ill. Not wanting to endanger the entire party, he sent most of them ahead to safety. Rogers and seven men stayed with the ill Ranger, finally bringing him in twenty-two hours later. In the very difficult Battle on Snowshoes in March 1758, Rogers only narrowly escaped himself, yet he put the welfare of his men first. A Provincial soldier noted, "About 5 o'Clock I se ye Maj'r Com in Him Self Being in Ye Rear of ye Whol—"[15]

Perhaps the best example of Rogers caring for his men is after the Saint Francis Raid. When they arrived at the Cohase Intervals, everyone, Rogers included, was near death from exhaustion, exposure, and starvation. Still, he managed to find the strength and determination to build a raft and float down the Connecticut River to obtain food, promising that he would have it to them in ten days. Rogers and his three companions arrived at Fort No. 4 on October 31, and immediately dispatched provisions. They arrived just as he had promised—on the tenth day after the major had started down the river. Just sending the food was not enough for Rogers, however. Despite his own weakened physical condition, he allowed himself only two days to rest and write his report to General Amherst. Then he started back up the river himself, to "seek and bring in as many of our men as I can find . . . ."[16] No one would have criticized Rogers if he had allowed himself time to recover, or if he had gone directly to see Amherst to receive the well-deserved recognition for his raid. Instead, with barely any recuperation, he went back to see to his men's welfare.

When Rogers was first jailed for debt in January 1764, a group of soldiers from the 60th (Royal American) and 42nd (Royal Highland) Regiments actually stormed the jail and released him, although he protested, "Indeed I am afraid, gentlemen, you will ruin me." Even more telling of the extreme loyalty that he inspired in the soldiers—and remember, these were Regulars, not his own Rangers—is that this first party had no more than spirited him away before a second group appeared on the scene, intent on the same purpose.[17]

For the most part, Rogers' military weaknesses showed up in the area of administration. It must be remembered that later in the war, Rogers was placed in command of a corps of Rangers that amounted to roughly a thousand men, and he was often also in command of mixed forces of Rangers, Regulars, and Provincials. Without formal training to prepare him for these positions of relatively high command, it is remarkable that he did as well as he did.

Another factor that must be considered is that, as the size of the Ranger corps increased, the quality of the recruits decreased. At first, Rogers was able to restrict his recruiting to men who were much like himself—experienced woodsmen, hardened in the ways of forest warfare. As his corps grew, Rogers was forced to accept recruits, and even volunteers from other units, who had far less knowledge and experience than his original Rangers.

When the war ended and the Rangers were disbanded, Rogers obtained commissions in South Carolina, and then later, the New York Independent Companies. He returned to Detroit as part of the relief force during the 1763 Pontiac Uprising, and fought with distinction in the Battle of Bloody Run.

For all of his success, Rogers' life was also plagued with failure. Financial problems that began during his military service plagued him for the rest of his life. While some of it may have been due to faulty record-keeping abilities that technically justified his accounts not being paid, more often he was just a victim of the system that was in place at the time. It was not uncommon for an officer to advance his own funds or to borrow to pay his men or to meet their other needs. The officer would then submit a request for reimbursement from the government. A voucher to General Gage, signed by Rogers at Crown Point on March 1, 1760, is a good example:

"The abstracts for the pay of the Rangers are sent down to Mr. Benjamin Lyon, to whome I beg that the Warrents may be made out payable to, as he has advanced all the Money to me, except what I had in Albany of Mr. Abraham Dow which is to be Deducted, *Lyons Receipt for the Amount of the Warrent shall be equally binding on me*—" (Emphasis added)[18] Here Rogers is clearly taking personal responsibility for the funds advanced by Mr. Lyon to pay his Rangers. The problem is, these vouchers could be disallowed for a variety of technical reasons, such as requiring unrealistic substantiation for funds due to soldiers captured or killed. When many of his accounts were disallowed, he incurred a personal debt that contributed significantly to his later downward spiral. After the war, failed trading ventures, which he had hoped would help his financial position, added to his problems.

While sometimes the rejection of Rogers' expenses was *technically* correct, at other times it clearly shows a conspiracy to ruin him. General Amherst specifically requested that he serve in the relief force bound for the besieged Fort Detroit in 1763. Yet after Amherst's return to England, Gage refused to pay him, saying that he had served as a volunteer. He totally ignored the written orders that Amherst had left behind, which directed that, "Captain Rogers, who is Serving with Major Gladwin, must have his Half pay made up *full pay*, so long as he is kept on that Service." The fact that Amherst used the word "must," and underlined "full pay," had no affect on Gage.[19] For those readers with a deeper interest, John Cuneo, a lawyer by profession, does a thorough study of Rogers' financial difficulties in his book *Robert Rogers of the Rangers*.

In 1765, Robert went to England to try to settle

his financial affairs and to try to win support for an expedition to find the Northwest Passage. While in London, he published his *Journals,* and two other works, *A Concise Account of North America,* and the play *Ponteach, or the Savages of America: A Tragedy.* The *Journals* was well received, and if anything, *Concise Account* was even more popular, because of the interest in Britain's newly won territory in North America. *Ponteach,* though not as successful, does have the distinction of being the second play ever written by an American to be published.

While Rogers was able to raise considerable support, circumstances worked against him, and he was never able to fulfill his dream of finding the Northwest Passage. The route he proposed was very similar to that followed by Lewis and Clark years later. Had he received the necessary backing, he very likely would have been successful—not in finding a water route, for one does not exist anywhere near that latitude—but in being the first European to reach the Pacific Ocean through the heart of the continent.

While in London, Rogers did manage to secure an appointment as governor of the militarily and economically important post of Michilimackinac, located at the strait where lakes Huron and Michigan meet. Many of Rogers' actions and business activities have been subject to criticism. He was motivated by his desperate need to repay the debts incurred while he was in military service. Some actions that appear questionable by our standards today were widely acceptable practices at the time.

While he was at Michilimackinac, Johnson and Gage deliberately tried to undermine Rogers' ability to succeed. Again Gage showed his desire to deny Rogers any chance of success, when he wrote to Sir William Johnson, "Be So good to Send me your Advice in what manner he may be best tied up by Instructions and prevent doing Mischief . . . ."[20] What Johnson and Gage undoubtedly feared was Rogers' ability to interfere with their own control of the highly lucrative fur trade. Although it is a very complicated issue, there is little doubt that what Johnson and Gage were doing was at least partially illegal. Johnson wanted to funnel all of the western fur trade through only two posts, Niagara and Oswego, and from there down the Mohawk Valley to New York City, effectively cutting Canada out of the picture. Rogers, who was a partner in two unsuccessful trading ventures himself, was one of those who challenged the legality of this, which naturally increased his troubles with the powerful Johnson and Gage.[21]

Rogers' ambitious and basically unrealistic proposal to establish an independent government at Michilimackinac did not help matters. In the end, he was never given his promised commission as a captain in the 60th Regiment, and Gage even refused to pay him his salary. His arrest and court-martial on charges of treason was clearly the result of their political maneuvering. The infamous letter from Captain Joseph Hopkins inviting him to defect to the French was in Gage's possession before Rogers' Michilimackinac orders were ever issued, yet nothing was said or done at the time. Also there were actually *three* letters, but the only recipient ever identified by Gage was Rogers. He declined to name the other two, saying that they were "Gentlemen of good Character."[22] During the siege of Detroit, a large number of British officers had signed a petition requesting that Hopkins be court-martialed. Robert Rogers' signature was *first* on the list, and he became president of the resulting board of inquiry. Yet when the time came, both Gage and Johnson at best ignored the possibility that Hopkins might be trying to set Rogers up, and at worst, were willing to use him in their own scheme to destroy Rogers once and for all.

Even the charge of Rogers spending extravagant sums on gifts to the Indians shows a double standard. At his trial, Rogers introduced a statement from both the British and French traders at Michilimackinac stating that his gifts were necessary. They in fact were so concerned that the government's presents were not adequate that they donated additional gifts from their own supplies.[23]

Colonel Edward Cole, Rogers' counterpart at

Fort DeChartres, who was appointed by Johnson, spent considerably more than Rogers during the same time period. The conference that Rogers held at Michilimackinac was attended by over seven thousand Western Indians, and was the largest ever held up to that time. The resulting peace saved the Crown costly military expenses and also advanced British trade. Colonel Cole had no similar accomplishments, yet Rogers was charged, and Cole's similar "extravagances" were overlooked.[24]

Rogers was arrested on December 6, 1767, but was not brought to trial until the following October. He received extremely harsh treatment while in custody. He was allowed only one day, October 26, 1768, to prepare for his own defense. He was denied evidence and the testimony of witnesses that would have helped his cause. Still, his arguments were eloquent and well reasoned. Trial testimony eventually showed how weak the case was, and he was found innocent of all charges. Even after being acquitted in October, Gage did not order his release from custody until the following February.[25]

Robert J. Rogers, in his book *Rising Above Circumstances* writes, "From the treatment Robert received, it seems probable that his accusers had little intention of going through with the formality of a trial. Death in custody would have removed the requirement, and any suggestions of harsh treatment would soon be forgotten; an attempted escape, though to relieve his torment, would have firmly established his guilt. A lesser man might have tried to escape and died in the attempt. Robert was a strong individual, however, and had the respect and support of a large number of officers and friends."[26]

Despite Rogers devoting over half of his lifetime fighting to get out of debt, other than being suspected of passing counterfeit notes as a youth, there is no strong evidence that he was ever involved in any clearly illegal schemes. One very important fact, I believe, is that there are no negative comments about Rogers' character in General Jeffrey Amherst's *Journals*. Amherst was a man of high principles, very difficult to please, and extremely candid in his *Journals*. The fact that Rogers escaped his censure, while so many others did not, is significant.

Rogers returned to England in 1769 to find a means to pay his debts and rebuild his life. The funds that he was able to procure were inadequate, and went to his creditors. For part of 1771, and again in 1772, he found himself in debtor's prison. In 1774, he tried unsuccessfully to sue General Thomas Gage for twenty thousand pounds. Then a new bankruptcy law led to his release on August 4, 1774, after almost twenty-two months in the fleet prison. Shortly thereafter, his pay as a retired captain was restored, and in the spring of 1775, he managed to secure a pension as a retired major.

Roger returned to America in 1775 at the outbreak of the Revolutionary War. The fact that he was a retired British officer who had spent considerable time in England caused him to be looked upon with suspicion by the colonists. Eventually, both he and his brother James cast their lot with the Loyalists. Initially, though, Robert offered his services to the Americans. Although he was rebuffed, for awhile the British thought that they had lost a valuable ally. The *Hibernian Magazine* reported that, "After such usage and indignities, we cannot wonder that Major Rogers is now high in command in the American army: But we may lament that a man of his abilities and experience has been forced to take an active part against the British arms, which he so often and so nobly defended."[27]

Robert formed two units called the King's Rangers and the Queen's Rangers, but neither attained the fame that his French and Indian War Rangers had. His most notable accomplishment was probably the capture of the American spy and hero Nathan Hale. Captain William Bamford, of the 40th Regiment of Foot, noted in his diary, "Nathan Hale, a Cap't in ye Rebel Army, and a spy was taken by Maj'r Rogers and this m'g hang'd."[28] Meanwhile, many of his former Rangers, including John Stark and Moses Hazen, served with distinction in the American army.

In 1778, his wife Elizabeth, whom he had married in 1761, divorced him. Although he was not active in the field, Rogers' name and reputation were still valuable recruiting tools for the British army. Apparently he had started drinking heavily. His old superior, Frederick Haldimand, wrote that "he at once disgraces the Service, and renders himself incapable of being depended upon." Even his brother James, who had always stood loyally by him, remarked, "I am sorry his good talents should so unguarded fall a prey to Intemperance."[29]

In 1782, after the Revolution, Rogers sailed to England, never to return to North America. Once again, he tried desperately to settle his financial matters. Sadly, his last days were spent in declining health, in and out of debtor's prison. He was drinking excessively. There is no doubt that in his final years, he was a mere shadow of his former self. A doctor who visited him found him "very ill with a slow fever and a hammer-like pulse that no Medicine could touch." Rogers informed the doctor that, "his brother [James] was a gentleman of good fortune in British Canada, and he wished him, and the patient's heirs, to be informed of his condition, requesting the Return to the Climate in which he had been brought up, would restore him back to Normal Health."[30] He would never get his wish to return to North America. Robert Rogers died in London on May 18, 1795. A London newspaper reported his passing:

> Lieutenant Col. Rogers, who died on Thursday last in the Borough, served in America during the late war, in which he had the command of a body of Rangers with which he performed prodigious feats of valor. He was a man of uncommon strength, but adversity, and a long confinement in the Rules of the King's Bench, had reduced him to the most miserable state of wretchedness.[31]

Clements Library Director John Dann summarizes Roger's life in a manner that is both accurate and succinct: "Robert was not a saint, but there is no concrete evidence that he was an extraordinary sinner, either."[32]

Regardless of his personal weaknesses, Rogers' military abilities secured him a lasting place in history. Of all the Ranger leaders of colonial times, his fame has been the most enduring, and his influence survives to this very day. Units like Darby's Rangers and Merrill's Marauders of Word War II, the Ranger Infantry Companies (Airborne) of Korea, and the Special Forces and Ranger units of Vietnam, all informally trace their heritage back to Rogers' Rangers. Their tradition and spirit continues to live in today's 75th Ranger Regiment and the "Tab Rangers"of the modern U.S. Army, who still incorporate many of Rogers' maxims in their training.

In spite of such a dismal end for one who was once such a great man, there is evidence that even in his latter years, his old Ranger spirit was not entirely dead.

One of Rogers' biggest nemeses during his tenure at Michilimackinac, and later during his trial, was Lieutenant Benjamin Roberts. Roberts seems to have been a man sorely lacking in virtue. Kenneth Roberts, author of the famous novel *Northwest Passage*, had this to say about Benjamin Roberts: "The facts . . . seem to me to indicate that he was thoroughly unprincipled: that he would stoop to anything to accomplish his ends: that he was petulant, hot-headed, unreliable, a sycophant, a tale-bearer, devoid of good judgement, and a liar, in addition to having other grave faults."[33]

In his personal notes, Cuneo records a tale fully worthy of the indomitable Ranger of old. One day in the summer of 1787, Rogers was walking down a London street when he met Roberts. Rogers "carried the latter, struggling and kicking, and dumped him in an open grave in St. Michael's Churchyard and started to shovel earth on top of him."[34]

Cuneo, regrettably, offers no documentation for this story other than it is one of the "traditions of old London." That may be why it did not make it into the published edition of his book. True or not, it certainly is befitting of the spirit of Robert Rogers. As has been said about the inspiring movies of the great director John Ford: *If that's not the way it was, then that's the way it should have been!*

Notes

1. Walker, *Life and Exploits*, p. 12.
2.. Rogers, *Journal to the Western French Posts*, p. 264.
3. Rogers, *Ponteach*, p. 90; Cuneo, *Notes*, p. 104.
4. Rogers, *Michilimackinac Journal*, p. 5.
5. Houlding, p. 222.
6. Rogers *Journals*, Hough Edition, p. 4.
7. Cuneo, *Rogers*, p. 42.
8. Padeni, p. 165.
9. Padeni, pp. 162-163.
10. Cuneo, *Rogers*, p. 230; Lewis, p. 233; and Armour, *Colonial Michilimackinac*, p. 74.
11. Lock, *To Fight with Intrepidity . . .*, p. 1.
12. Walker, *The Woods Fighters*, pp. 46-47.
13. Cuneo, *Rogers*, p. 82.
14. Cuneo, *Rogers*, p. 30.
15. Cuneo, *Rogers*, pp. 31 and 79.
16. Cuneo, *Rogers*, p. 115.
17. Cuneo, *Rogers*, pp. 170-171.
18. Gage Papers, American Series, Collections of the William L. Clements Library.
19. Cuneo, *Rogers*, pp. 171-172.
20. Cuneo, *Rogers*, p. 183.
21. Cuneo, *Rogers*, pp. 195-199.
22. Roberts, Volume II Appendix, p. 77, and Cuneo, pp. 187-188.
23 Armour, *Treason? At Michilimackinac*, p. 87.
24. Roberts, Volume II Appendix, p. 146-147.
25. For a thorough study of Rogers' court-martial, Dr. David A. Armour's *Treason? At Michilimackinac* is highly recommended.
26. Robert J. Rogers, p. 160.
27. *Hibernian Magazine*, September 1776, p. 579.
28. Cuneo, *Rogers*, p. 270.
29. Cuneo, *Rogers*, p. 277.
30. Cuneo, *Notes*, p. 186.
31. *London Morning Post and Fashionable World*, May 25, 1795.
32. Dann, p. 26.
33. Roberts, Volume II Appendix, pp. 76-77.
34. Cuneo, *Notes*, pp. 184-185.

About the Annotations

A wide variety of information from numerous sources is presented in this book. The following information is designed to help the reader better understand the way the book is laid out.

1. Except in a few instances, the original spelling, punctuation, capitalization, and grammar have been retained for the *Journals* and the other primary sources that are quoted. It is hoped that by seeing these documents reproduced as closely as possible to the way they were initially written or published, the reader will gain a better appreciation not only for the unique flavor of the documents themselves, but also for the people who originally composed them.

2. The text of the original Dublin Edition of the *Journals* is printed as the widest columns, in 11-point type.

3. The footnotes to the original Dublin Edition, as written either by Robert Rogers (in the first section) or Father William Smith (in the second section) are set at the bottom of the page, as footnotes normally are, in 8-point type.

4. The extensive annotations include quotations from various historical sources, as well as my own comments. It order and to keep these annotations clearly distinct from the original footnotes, and to avoid tedious and constant page turning to the back of the book, they have been merged into the text as close to the place where they are relevant as possible. The column width has been narrowed, and the type size reduced to 10 point, so that it is easy to visually differentiate the annotations from the original text. The citations for sources in the annotations are briefly listed directly following the passage quoted and are fully identified in the bibliography.

5. Gary Zaboly's artwork is distributed appropriately throughout the book, with the captions in shaded gray boxes. Gary's footnotes and citations appear at the end of each his captions.

6. Both the bibliography and index are designed to help the reader get a better understanding of the material presented. Brief explanations of their design appear at the beginning of each.

7. Differences in text between the 1765 London edition and the 1769 Dublin edition of the *Journals* are also generally noted. Most of these appear to be typesetting errors, and the London edition version usually reads more clearly.

Tim J. Todish

Artist's Introduction

LIKE most of my contemporaries who have been gripped by the incredible story of Rogers' Rangers and the no less extraordinary life of their leader, Major Robert Rogers, I can attribute my earliest interest in them to a novel by Kenneth Roberts. I first became familiar with his 1937 historical epic, *Northwest Passage*, in a roundabout way when, as a child of eight, I viewed episodes of NBC's early color television series of the same name, starring Keith Larsen as Rogers. In the early 1960s I saw the vivid and exciting 1940 MGM movie version of *Passage*, with Spencer Tracy enacting the Ranger leader. It was an epiphany of sorts for me, and led to a reading of Roberts' book, the first of perhaps a dozen readings since. The exploits of Rogers' Rangers had hooked me.

Before he began writing his huge novel about Rogers, Kenneth Roberts, as he recalled in *I Wanted To Write*, was of the opinion that his intended protagonist "beat any character I had ever encountered." A more succinct summary of Robert Rogers is hardly possible, considering the life he had led—one so eventful, checkered and intense that it would have worn out ten ordinary men. Over the course of it he was a frontiersman, farmer, hunter, trapper, militiaman, Indian fighter, Ranger leader, celebrity hero, explorer, land and mine speculator, merchant, London socialite, America's earliest playwright, mapmaker, author of his published military journals as well as a geography of North America, commandant of the most important fur trading post in the West of the 1760s, and colonel of a Loyalist regiment during the Revolution. But his successes were counterbalanced by enormous personal challenges and difficulties: the scheming of envious rivals; heavy debt, infidelity, and divorce; accusations of counterfeiting, treason and spying; imprisonment, gambling, and alcoholism.

These *Journals*, by themselves, reveal a man who, in his heyday, had tireless stamina, enormous courage in battle, and the audacity to take tremendous risks in dealing with a very dangerous enemy; yet they read very modestly, having none of the braggadocio Rogers is often accused of by those "historians" who have not done their homework. Rogers, in fact, severely *underplayed* his role in the battles and skirmishes he had led his men into. Thanks to Timothy J. Todish's annotations of the entries, Rogers' true role is revealed as it was viewed and recorded by his contemporaries, both friends and enemies. Though many envied him, none doubted his genius in the peculiar arena of wilderness warfare.

When Tim Todish approached me in 1996 with the idea of producing a fully-footnoted edition of *The Journals of Major Robert Rogers*, with illustrations by myself, I initially thought it would be unmanageable, since we had no funds to create it with; and, in the course of my career as a self-employed historical illustrator, the expected meager royalty split of such a huge project would do little to compensate for the great amount of time necessary to produce the drawings.

Very quickly afterwards I came up with a possible solution: why not solicit sponsors for the illustrations, with the originals given to the sponsors once the book was printed? Imagining that we might be able to attract five or six interested parties, Tim and I launched a mail campaign to enlist contributors to the project. The response, as things turned out, was more than quadruple our expectations. In fact, so many subscribers signed on that a number had to be turned away, or else the project—considering other work obligations I also had to fulfill—would require yet another year to complete. After more than four years, it became time to wrap things up.

To these sponsors, then, we owe the book's

ability to present visual interpretations of Rogers' words, with captions explaining each illustration, along with the main text and annotations. Here follows a list of each contributor, and the scene or scenes they commissioned:

James Butler Jr.
The Advanced Guard
Robert Rogers Meets General William Johnson

Stuart, Jack, and Ruth Christians
Young Robert Rogers
Bivouac Over Lake George
Ambush On the Ice

Dr. Todd E. Harburn
Ambush At Bloody Run

Randolph G. Flood
Rogers' Island, November 1, 1757

Tom and Cynthia Heyseck
The Renovated 55th
The Fighting Retreat

The Michigan Company of
Military Historians and Collectors
Rogers' Rangers' Cadet School

Edward Nash Jr.
Hauling the Whaleboats Ashore
At Missisquoi Bay

Dennis Nielsen
Montcalm Masses His Indians
The Ticonderoga Peninsula, July 8, 1758
Marin's Raiding Party

Robert J. Rogers
The Grand Council At Michilimackinac,
July 2, 1767

Harry Todish
Robert Rogers Launches the Northwest
Passage Expedition From
Fort Michilimackinac

Terry Todish
Rogers Meets Pontiac

Wayne Zurl
Rogers' Rangers and Their Uniforms

Tim Todish self-sponsored *Abercromby's Spearhead*, and I contributed *The Legend of Rogers' Slide*, as well as two past works published elsewhere, *The Fires of St. Francis* and *The Starvation March*.

Of course there were many more choices for scenes that might have been picked from the list of fifty-five suggested illustrations we sent out to prospective sponsors. We nevertheless feel that those selected here are representative enough in terms of time, place and subject matter to give the reader a true sense of the scope and importance of the Rangers' history, and of the leadership they received from Rogers. For enabling us to achieve at least that much, Tim and I are most grateful for the generosity and faith in our project shared by each and every sponsor. Thank you all.

Historical illustration requires that the illustrator himself become a researcher and scholar, or else the drawn or painted results would scream out with deficiencies. Many modern illustrators get around this roadblock by creating sketchy, graphic pieces that often decorate pages quite well; in doing so they offer no challenges to the educated eye of the historian or well-versed reader. The pen-and-ink drawings published here are intended to represent, in a more realistic way, what is currently known about the Rangers and their history, with the artist fully understanding that the subject will forever remain a work in progress because new information, however gradually, will continue to be unearthed.

For close to forty years the subject of Rogers' Rangers has intrigued and fascinated me. Over the course of thirty of those years I have been engaged in collecting notes, books, and other materials concerning both their adventures and the life of their commander, intending someday to write and illustrate a book-length study of my own. This edition is not my final "word" on the subject, by any means, but it does provide a stage allowing me to present the results of the processing of much of the material gathered. This has been culled from a vast number of institutions, both public and private, and I am greatly indebted to them for helping to provide me with so many of the answers. These places include:

The New York Public Library, the New York Historical Society, the Huntington Library, the Library of Congress, the Fort Ticonderoga Museum, the Public Archives of Canada, the National Museums of Canada, the Royal Artillery Institution, the Henry Francis DuPont Winterthur Museum, the War Office (London), The Public Records Office (London), the Connecticut Historical Society, the New Jersey Historical Society, the Massachusetts Historical Society, the Vermont Historical Society, the Brooklyn Historical Society, the Derby Historical Society, the Kenneth Roberts Centennial Commission, the Courtauld Institute of Art, the Royal College of Surgeons of England, Williams College, the Derby Museum and Art Gallery, the Wagner College Library, the Darien Historical Society, and the Old Dartmouth Historical Society Whaling Museum. There are many, many others.

The individuals who also deserve credit for their help are legion. My 29-year correspondence and friendship with the Rangers' pre-eminent historian, Burt Garfield Loescher, of San Mateo, California, has been valuable beyond measure. His three-volume *History of Rogers' Rangers* remains the single greatest contribution to the subject, and it pleases me to realize that not only are all three volumes currently being reprinted by Heritage Press of Maryland, but also his long-unpublished manuscripts on various aspects of Ranger history will also finally see the light.

The late Colonel John R. Elting also generously took time from his busy career as a noted military historian to answer in full each and every letter I wrote to him over the past 24 years. His loss last year leaves a great gap in the scholarship, since his opinions and conclusions were always of the bare-knuckles, common-sense variety—direct, frank, yet wholly erudite.

With other long-term friends such as George Alfred Bray and Timothy J. Todish, I have enjoyed sharing information and ideas about Rogers' Rangers as well as other areas of French and Indian War history. Russell P. Bellico, another good friend, remains master of the nautical history of lakes George and Champlain; his books in this category, published by Purple Mountain Press, have become instant classics.

Nicholas Westbrook, Executive Director of Fort Ticonderoga and its museum, deserves credit for most of the merits in the view of the Ticonderoga peninsula included herein. Nick, always helpful to a comprehensive degree, clearly pointed out to me the problems with many of the contemporary maps of Fort Carillon and vicinity that purport to depict the situation as it was on July 8, 1758. The favor I asked of him, to simply review my initial version of this scene, resulted in his sending me a hundred pages of correspondence and copies of his own unfinished history of the fort's construction, with everything fully documented and footnoted, which significantly corrected and improved the illustration.

Stephen Laurent of Intervale, New Hampshire, hereditary chief of the St. Francis tribe and tribal historian of the Abenaki people, unselfishly shared many of his thoughts and notes with me over a number of years late in his life.

I must also thank the Readex Microprint Corporation for having published so many early American newspapers in both microprint and microfilm form. Purchasing complete runs of some two dozen microprint colonial newspapers from them, in the mid-1980s, has enabled me to devote long, uninterrupted hours at home in perusal of them. They have proven to be a goldmine of information, providing answers to many questions, as well as being a virtual window into the period and its culture.

Others whose generosities over the decades have enriched my knowledge of the subject in so many different ways include Francis Back, Mrs. William A. Baker, Harrison K. Bird, Martha Briggs, Timothy J. Carlson, Jim Ciborski, John R. Cuneo, Robert Fatherley, Joanne and Richard Fuller, George "Peskcunck" Larrabee, Albert W. Haarmann, John and Marge Holmes, Ruth Keeler, Richard C. Kugler, Philip Leibfried, Hugh Charles McBarron, Frank D. Nastasi, Thomas L. Nesbitt, Jerry and Mary Olson, John H. Rhodehamel, Robert J. Rogers, Robert S. Scherer Jr., Earl Stott, Melvin Tucker, Gregory J. W. Urwin, and Ross M. A. Wilson. There are dozens more, among them my father, who first took my brother and me camping in the Narrows of Lake George in the early '60s; and my wife, Cora, who always enjoys sharing my enthusiasm for the subject, and my work in it.

Gary S. Zaboly
Riverdale, New York
January 2001

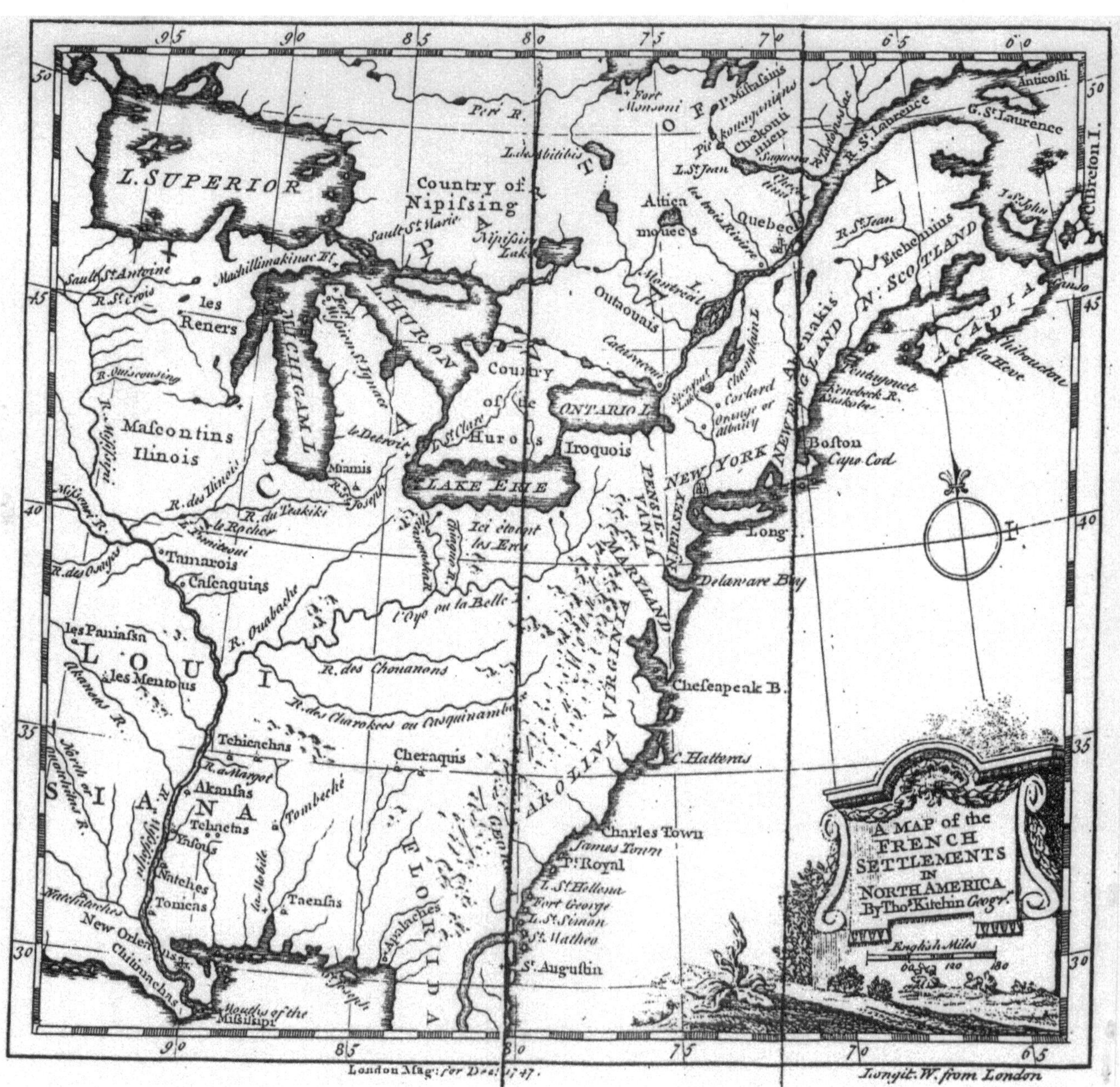

A Map of the French Settlements in North America by Thomas Kitchin.

Robert Rogers' Introduction

IT would be offering an affront to the public, should I pretend to have no private views in publishing the following Journals; but they will excuse me if I leave them to conjecture what my particular views are, and claim the merit of impartially relating matters of fact, without disguise or equivocation. Most of those which relate to myself can at present be attested to by living witnesses.

And should the troubles in America be renewed, and the savages repeat those scenes of barbarity they so often have acted on the British subjects, which there is great reason to believe will happen, I flatter myself, that such as are immediately concerned may reap some advantage from these pages.

Should any one take offence at what they may here meet with, before they venture upon exhibiting a charge, they are desired, in favor to themselves, to consider, that I am in a situation where they cannot attack me to their own advantage; that it is the soldier, not the scholar, that writes; and that many things here were wrote, not with silence and leisure, but in desarts and rocks and mountains, amidst the hurries, disorders, and noise of war, and under that depression of spirits, which is the natural consequence of exhausting fatigue. This was my situation when the following Journals or Accounts were transmitted to the generals and commanders I acted under, which I am not now at liberty to correct, except in some very gross and palpable errors.

It would perhaps gratify the curious to have a particular account of my life, preceding war; but though I could easily indulge them herein, without any dishonour to myself, yet I beg they will be content with my relating only such circumstances and occurrences as led me to a knowledge of many parts of the country, and tended in some measure to qualify me for the service I have since been employed in. Such, in particular, was the situation of the place in which I received my early education, a frontier town in the province of New Hampshire, where I could hardly avoid obtaining some knowledge of the manners, customs, and language of the Indians, as many of them resided in the neighbourhood, and daily conversed and dealt with the English.

Between the year's 1743 and 1755 my manner of life was such as lead me to a general acquaintance both with the British and French settlements in North America, and especially with the uncultivated desart, the mountains, valleys, rivers, lakes, and several passages that lay between and contiguous to the said settlements. Nor did I content myself with the accounts received from Indians, or the information of hunters, but travelled over large tracts of the country myself, which tended not more to gratify my curiosity, than to inure me to hardships, and, without vanity, I may say, to qualify me for the very service I have since been employed in.

About this time the proceedings of the French in America, were such as excited the jealousy of the English, especially in New-York and New-England; and as Crown-Point was the place from which, for many years, the Indians in the French interest had been fitted out against our settlements on the frontiers, a design was formed in the beginning of 1755 to dispossess them of that post; pursuant to which, troops were levied in the several provinces of New England, New York, and New Jersey. The general rendezvous was appointed at Albany in the province of New York, and the troops put under the command of Major General (since Sir William) Johnson, I had the honour of commanding a company in the troops furnished by the province of New Hampshire, with which I made several excursions, pursuant to special orders from the governor of that province, on the

Young Robert Rogers

THE LIFE of Robert Rogers prior to his exploits in the French and Indian War was never more than sketchily described by either himself or his contemporaries. In the introduction to his *Journals*, Rogers, in explaining how he came to be qualified for his Ranger captaincy, excludes any mention of his stints as a teenage militiaman back in 1746 and 1747, when he helped to defend the south-central New Hampshire frontier against French and Indian raiders. Instead, he remarks nebulously upon youthful experiences that led him into "a general acquaintance both with the British and French settlements in North America, and especially with the uncultivated desart" that was the wilderness between those settlements.

Much earlier in the eighteenth century, while New Englanders continued their slow expansion into the immediate frontier regions along the lower Merrimack and Connecticut rivers, bolder groups of fresh Scots-Irish immigrants ventured even farther beyond, impelled not only by the desire to claim new lands as their own, but also to escape the religious and secular prejudice they found in the homogeneous English towns. Distant major settlements such as Londonderry, Manchester and Pennacook (its name later changed to Rumford, and then again, finally, to Concord) were protected by stockades or rings of blockhouses. Near to these were the smaller, exposed hamlets such as Mountalona (later Starkstown, then Dunbarton), where Rogers' family eventually settled after living for about ten years in Methuen, Massachusetts.

Out from these new communities a few men dared to launch hunting and trapping expeditions into the unknown country far to the north, first canoeing along waterways edging the southern flanks of the White Mountains—perhaps even exploring for some distance into that range—and then up the Connecticut River to the broad intervales of both the lower and upper Coos regions. Beaver meadows abounded, and the game population was equally rich, for these lands sat in the very heart of the Abenaki's traditional hunting grounds. Although the Abenaki villages were hundreds of miles to the north and northwest of the New Hampshire frontier towns, the Indians were very sensitive about British encroachments onto their territory. It was no surprise, then, that while many white hunters and trappers returned home with bountiful harvests of skins and furs, there were probably a nearly equal number who found themselves skirmishing with their Abenaki counterparts, or being killed or captured by them.

These early eastern "mountain men" left behind almost no physical traces, and very few written records, of the time they spent in the wilderness pursuing their risky calling. Most of them remain shadowy figures remembered only by their names, applied to geographical features—Israel's River, John's River, Martin's Pond, and so on.

Robert Rogers' career as a hunter/trapper remains similarly lost to history, outside of some isolated clues and anecdotes. Certainly he would have been familiar with Baker's River, a major artery for travel deeper into the northern wilderness since it connected with the Merrimack forty miles above Pennacook. On this river in 1752 John Stark and three fellow hunters were ambushed by a party of Abenakis; one man was killed, one escaped, and Stark and the remaining man were captured. Rogers is said to have gone on at least one hunting trip with Stark; but once again the particulars are lacking. Had he, like Stark, been captured, history would have better recalled Rogers' time spent in the wilderness trapping beaver, otter, sable and mink, and hunting deer, bear, moose, wolves and catamount.

In his introduction, Rogers suggests that he early on developed an insatiable curiosity about the outlying territories he had not yet visited. Some descriptions of these lands he "received from Indians, or the information of hunters," but he was not content with merely listening to the accounts of others. In fact, he "travelled over large tracts of the country myself." At least one of these treks was in the form of a colony-sanctioned surveying expedition to the Coos meadows on the Connecticut in 1753, in official defiance of Abenaki claims.

The illustration shows Robert Rogers in about his nineteenth year of life, in early 1751, scrutinizing a rough map drawn in the snow by a French Canadian trapper in response to Rogers' questions about the country to the north. The scene (meant to be hypothetical) might be on the banks of Baker's

Gary Zaboly ©1998

River, or of another stream flowing near to the White Mountains. This was during the tenuous period of peace between King George's War, which had ended in 1748, and the real start of the final conflict in 1755.

At some point in his early adulthood Rogers began to learn enough of the French language to become conversant in it. This probably occurred during his northern excursions, when bands of Canadian and British hunters sometimes happened upon each other in the wilderness. Though these meetings were probably not always cordial, they were rarely as dangerous as encounters with Abenaki hunters proved to be.

In the illustration, Rogers wears a fur cap common to both Europe and North America in the mid-eighteenth century. His outer wear, however, is a bearskin "coat" of the rudest variety: simply a hide peeled from the carcass of the animal (its skin side dressed and dried), and worn belted like a short gown. (Rogers' father was shot because he was mistaken for a bear at a distance; it's possible he was wearing just such a coat with the hair side out, perhaps even with the hide of the animal's head still attached and worn like a hood). Underneath this he wears a lined jacket, and his neck is covered with a printed handkerchief. From his belt hangs a sheathed butcher knife. Coarse woollen leggings edged with "tape" (ribbon) are worn over durable buckskin breeches, while shoepacks, wrapped around his ankle, protect feet already snug in at least two pairs of socks and/or duffel or soft fur liners.

The Canadian wears a hood made of beaver skin, typical winter wear of many northeastern Indian tribes. His mittens are also of beaver, and hang from his neck by leather thongs. His capote, made from a brown blanket, is held around his waist with a sash, and has a shawl collar. Leggings of leather fall over his moosehide moccasins.

The seated Indian is the Canadian's partner. He is a survivor of the Pennacook confederacy of tribes that once populated the Merrimack valley, until King Phillip's War and subsequent conflicts with the English settlers drove the remnants into Canada and Maine. A meager few, however, remained here and there in the New Hampshire wilderness, especially along the upper Connecticut River intervales. His cowl-like hood is made of cloth and edged with ribbon, and his blanketcoat is decorated with rows of beads.[1] His mittens are of beaver, with the hair on the inside, and his leggings are of deerskin. The pouch hanging from his left shoulder is based on an actual Pennacook relic in the Peabody Museum of Salem, Massachussetts.

In middleground is the elm bark canoe of the Canadian and Indian, its construction the typical hunting pattern of Abenakis and Iroquois of the eighteenth century.[2]

Beyond the canoe stands the half-faced "encampment" of Rogers and his party, the most common form of hunters' shelter in the Colonial American forest. This was a quickly-erected, simple lean-to structure consisting of a framework of poles overlaid with panels of carefully stripped bark. Building it with brush and pine boughs instead of bark took far less time. It could be made large enough, if necessary, to hold 50 men or more.[3] Spruce, hemlock, or fir boughs made for a springy "mattress" over which a bearskin cover was placed, and then a blanket to complete the bed. With a fire going all night just beyond the open front of the shelter, and the hunters' feet positioned towards it, a fairly warm and comfortable sleep was generally had.

A surtout-wearing black servant, belonging to either Rogers or one of his partners, tends to his camp duties; beyond him two men return from a hunt, carrying their latest trophy bear on a pole. At right hang other recent game: two bucks and a catamount. On the wall of the shelter hang beaver skins, stretched for curing on hoops made of branches.

G.Z.

1. See sketch based on late seventeenth-century drawing of a blanket coat worn by a Canadian Indian, "The Canadian Capot (Capote)," by Francis Back, *The Museum of the Fur Trade Quarterly*, Vol. 27, Np. 3, Fall 1991, p. 12.
2. See photo of a model made by a St. Francis Abenaki, *The Iroquois: a Study in Cultural Evolution*, by Frank Gouldsmith Speck, Cranbrook Institute of Science, Bulletin 23, 1971 reprint, p. 17.
3. Gary Zaboly, "A Lodging For the Night: A Brief Study of Some Types of Wilderness Shelters Used During the French and Indian War," *Muzzleloader*, March/April 1989, p. 49.

northern and western frontiers, with a view to deter the French and Indians from making inroads upon us that way. In this manner I was employed till the month of July, when I received orders to repair to Albany, at which place I tarried till August 26th, and was then ordered with 100 men to escort the provision-waggons from thence to the Carrying-Place, then so called, since Fort-Edward. Here I waited upon the General, to whom I was recommended as a person well acquainted with the haunts and passes of the enemy, and the Indian method of fighting, and was by him dispatched with small parties on several tours towards the French posts, and was on one of these up Hudson's River on the 8th of September, when Baron Dieskau was made prisoner, and the French and Indians, under his command defeated, at the south-end of Lake George.

The 24th of September I received orders from the General to proceed with four men to Crown Point, and, if practicable, to bring a prisoner from thence; and with an account of the manner in which I executed these orders, I shall begin my Journals.

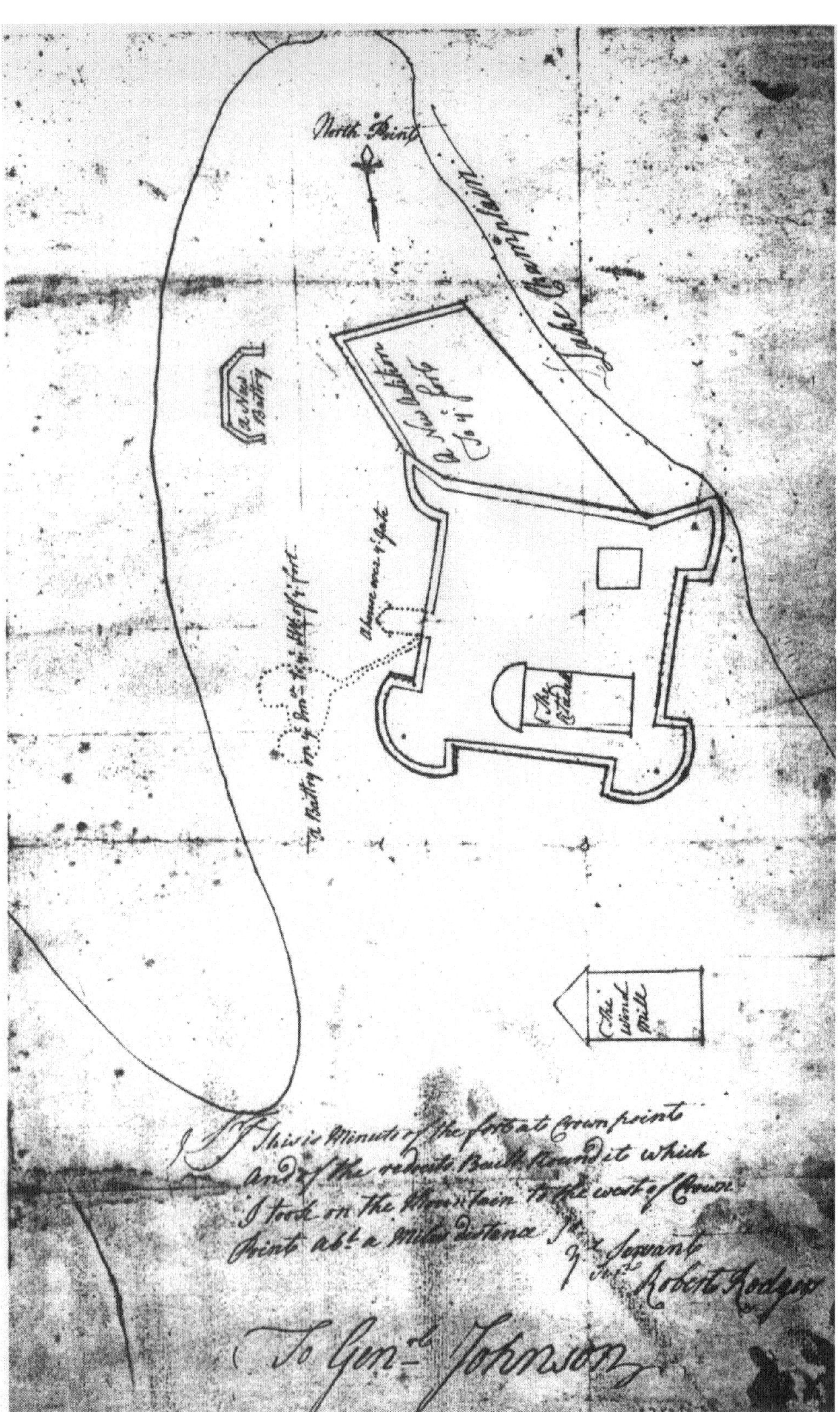

Robert Rogers' map of Fort Saint Frederick at Crown Point. He drew this map for General William Johnson on one of his first scouts in September 1755.

Courtesy of the Library of Congress and the Crown Point State Historic Site

A
JOURNAL, &c.

September 24, 1755.

PURSUANT to orders of this date from Major-General Johnson, Commander in chief of the Provincial Forces, raised for the reduction of Crown-Point, I embarked with four men upon Lake George, to reconnoitre the strength of the enemy, and proceeding down the Lake twenty five miles, I landed on the west side, leaving two men in charge of the boat, while I marched with the other two 'till the 29th, when I had a fair view of the fort at Crown-Point, and discovered a large body of Indians round the Fort, and from their repeated irregular firing, supposed they were shooting at marks, (a diversion much in use among the savages).

Thomas Mante, author of one of the first general histories of the war (1772) had this to say about the early contributions of Rogers and his men: "Captain Robert Rogers, of the new Hampshire regiment, a person well acquainted with the woods of North America, and with the Indians in the interest of the English, having by this time joined General Johnson, he was ordered on different scouts to discover the numbers of the enemy, and how they were employed. On the 24th of September he was sent to Crown Point, where he found the French were in number about five hundred, and were erecting a battery at the side of the fort." (Mante, p. 42)

The map that Rogers made for General Johnson on this date is reproduced on the opposite page. On the map he made the following notation: "Sr This is Minuts of the Fort at Crown Point and the redouts Built Round it which I took on the Mountain to the west of Crown Point ab't a Miles distance" Rogers signed the map "y'r Servant Robert Rodgers" Early in the war, he often spelled his last name "Rodgers."

The first French fort at Crown Point, called St. Frederic by the French, was built on the east shore of the lake in 1731. The fort that Rogers was sent to spy on was begun in 1734, and was on the west side of the lake. It took three years to complete, covered about one acre, and was described as being "on a Rock, having a very Strong Cittadel Arch'd with Stone three Storys high, the wall thereof is about Seven feet thick, it commands the Entrance into the Lake beforementioned [Lake Champlain] from the Southward & has four Regular Bastions, to the Southward is a Large plain." (Starbuck, p. 164, Titus, pp. 3, 14, *D.H.S.N.Y.*, Volume 4, p. 241)

Swedish traveler Peter Kalm felt that the fort was built in the wrong location. After a 1749 visit, he wrote: "Within one or two musketshots to the east of the fort, is a windmill built of stone with very thick walls . . . .This windmill is so constructed as to serve the purpose of a redoubt, and at the top of it are four or five small pieces of cannon . . . . Therefore the fort ought to have been built on the spot where the mill stands . . . . If it had been erected in the place of the mill, it would have commanded the river, and prevented the approach of the enemy; and a small ditch cut through the loose limestone, from the river (which comes out of the Lac St. Sacrement) to Lake Champlain, would have surrounded the fort with flowing water." (Kalm, p. 392)

At night I crept through the enemy's guard into a small village lying south of the fort, and passing their centries to an eminence south-west of it, from whence I discovered they were building a battery, and had already thrown up an entrenchment on that side of the fort. The next day, from an eminence at a small distance from the former, I discovered an encampment, which extended from the fort south-east to a wind-mill, at about 30 yards distance; as near as I could judge, their number amounted to about 500 men: but finding no opportunity to procure a captive, and that our small party was discovered, I judged it proper to begin a retreat homeward the 1st of October. I took my route within two miles of Ticonderoga, from whence I observed a larger smoak to arise, and heard the explosion of a number of small arms; but our provision being expended, we could not tarry to ascertain the number of the enemy there. On the 2d we arrived at the place where we left our boat in the charge of two men, but to our great mortification found they were gone, and no provisions left. This circumstance hastened us to the encampment with all possible speed, where we arrived the 4th, not a little fatigued and distressed with hunger and cold.

Massachusetts Provincial Lieutenant Colonel Seth Pomeroy noted Rogers' first scout in his journal, dated September 24: "Came in Capt. Rogers with 2 men yt [that] went with him 10 Days ago to vew Crown Point they ware within Fair Sight of Crown Point near 2 days Saw ye Eminence upon ye west Side there the Franch ware at worke making Tranch round ware we Intended to build Some works—" (Pomeroy, p. 19) However, Pomeroy's dates are in conflict with Rogers'.

There are numerous conflicts with the dates used in Rogers' *Journals*. These no doubt partially result from the fact that when Rogers was composing his *Journals* in London in 1765, he did not have access to all of his original reports, and he had to rely on his memory for events that had occurred up to ten years earlier. John Cuneo theorizes that the publisher of the journals also may have contributed to the problem by incorrectly assuming that the date the report was written was the date that the scout began, and adjusting the other dates for that particular incident accordingly. Other errors "can only be explained as erroneous reading of the written reports." (Cuneo, *Notes*, pp. 26-27)

One good example of this is a scout to Ticonderoga in September 1755. The original report indicates that this scout ran from September 27 through 29. Rogers wrote that he and his party crept to within sixty rods of the fort, which was still under construction. He estimated that there were about three thousand French troops there, and that the new fort "Commands the passage at the Carrying place, & (we tho't) the passage down Champlain from Wood Creek to Crown Point." On the last day, Rogers' party engaged a large canoe containing one Frenchman and nine Indians. After killing six, the Rangers pursued the survivors until three additional Indian canoes forced them to break off. (*D.H.S.N.Y.*, Volume 4, p. 261)

Seth Pomeroy also agrees that this scout began on September 27: "Capt Rogers with 2 others went of this Evening to vew Tinundorogo." (Pomeroy, p. 119) Then on September 30, he added, "Capt. Roger with 4 men yt went up ye Lake Last Saturday night in order to view Tiundorogo they took a good vew of yt Place & Found In there Judgement to be as many If not more Incampt there as we have In this Place & building a fort they Saw a battoe with ten men in In it Put off & Came up the Lake they hasten'd back & Plac'd themselves In a narrow Place on a Point of Land to wt there return ye Battos that went up to an Island ye men Laned Staid a little while & then Came back So Came by Capt Rogers & his 4 men within gun Shot they fired upon ye Battoe which had 9 Indians & a franch man in It they kill'd 2 ye first Shot So Continu'd firing till they had Shot 4- or 5 times apace kill'd or so Disabled Six of em yt they ware not abled to Paddle ye Battoe only 4 yt cou'd work they Put In there Canoe & Jumpt into it Persued em till they had all moust Come up with em Drawing So near ye Franch army they Sent out a number of there Battoes after them So our People ware oblig'd to turn and make ye best of there way off but they all arivd Safe with out any harm from ye Enemy & a bold adventure It was. (Pomeroy, pp. 120-121) Many of the details of this scout correspond to the next one described in the *Journals,* but which supposedly occurred from October 7-10.

For the most part, I will not attempt to further dissect these differences between Rogers' *Journals* and his original scout reports. Those interested in reading many of his early original reports are directed to a section of the *Documentary History of the State of New York,* Volume 4, Chapter XI, pp. 258-287, entitled *Journals of Sir Wm. Johnson's Scouts, 1755, 1756.*

October 7, 1755, I received orders of this date from General Johnson, to reconnoitre the French troops Ticonderoga. Accordingly I proceeded at night to a point of land on the west side of the lake, where we landed, hid our canoe, and left two men in charge of it.

The Indian canoe is the watercraft that people often picture the Rangers using on their scouts deep into French territory. While in truth they often used whaleboats and bateaux of European design, they also used canoes. On September 30, 1759, the Reverend John Cleaveland, a Massachusetts Provincial chaplain, described two birchbark canoes: "After Dinner took a walk down to ye Lake to see the two Birch-Canoes which were bro't in last Night; one is about Thurty-Feet long upon the Edges and Five Feet wide in the Widest Place, the other about Three or four and Twenty long, the outside made of Birch-Bark. The inside cieled with Cedar Clap-Boards thin as brown paper and laid length-ways of ye Canoe upon which crossways of ye Canoe is another laying of Cedar bent to the Shape of ye Canoe adzed down with young split Willow, They go with Paddles and The largest will carry 20 men. It is so light that four men might lift it up and carry it on their Shouldirss. Their Seams on ye Outside are patched to make them tite. (Cleaveland, September 30, 1759)

On October 7, 1759, Commissary Wilson noted in his orderly book that, "The Rangers and Indians are to take all the Canoes and as many more Whale Boats as may be wanted to carry their compleate Number and to have one Batteaux for their Sutler." (Wilson, pp. 175-176)

The next day, with the other three, I marched to the point at Ticonderoga, where we arrived about noon. I here observed a body of men, which I judged to be about 200 in number, who had thrown up an entrenchment, and prepared large quantities of hewn timber in the adjacent woods. We remained here the second night, and the next morning saw them lay the foundation of a fort, on the point which commands the pass from Lake George, to Lake Champlain, and the entrance of South Bay, or Wood Creek. Having made what discoveries we could, we began our return, in which we found that the enemy had a large advanced guard at the north end of Lake George, where the river issues out of it into Lake Champlain.

Mante, who almost certainly had access to Rogers' *Journals* when writing his book, says this about this particular scout: "On the 7th of October he was ordered to Ticonderoga, where he discovered about two thousand French, who had thrown up an intrenchment, and prepared a large quantity of hewn timber in the adjacent woods; he was even witness to their laying the foundations of a fort on the point which command the pass between Lake George and Lake Champlain." (Mante, p. 42)

While we were viewing these, I perceived a bark-canoe, with nine Indians and a Frenchman in it, going up the Lake. We kept sight of them 'till they passed the point of land, where our canoe and men were left, where, when we arrived, we had information from our people, that the above Indians and Frenchman had landed on an island six miles to the south of us, near the middle of the lake. In a short time after, we saw them put off from the island, and steer directly towards us; upon which we put ourselves in readiness to receive them in the best manner we could, and gave them a salute at about 100 yards distance,

Robert Rogers Meets General William Johnson

COLONEL JOSEPH BLANCHARD'S First New Hampshire Regiment began arriving at the Flats above Albany on August 11, 1755, too late to join Major General William Johnson's main army, which was already encamped at, or approaching, the Great Carrying Place, over 40 miles to the north.

Woefully under-equipped by their insolvent province's government, Blanchard's men could not march until many of them received "small brass kettles (one to five men)" as well as additional "blankets. . .shirts. . .jackets, shoes, stockings, caps, briches, axes and hatchets."[1] At Albany, Blanchard had many of these items generously supplied to him by private citizens, or out of the stocks of the other Provincial regiments.[2]

On August 18, Johnson sent an order to Blanchard to provide an escort for a provision train moving from Albany to the Great Carrying Place. Blanchard chose Robert Rogers, captain of the regiment's ranging company, for the assignment. Rogers left Albany on August 20 with his approximately 50 rangers, and one other New Hampshire company, to serve as guards for the wagons.[3]

Such a train would have taken five or six days to reach the Great Carrying Place, where Johnson's troops had already begun construction of the storehouse and stockade that were later expanded into Fort Edward. Rogers probably met Johnson on August 26, just as advance elements of the general's army were beginning the march up the newly-cleared road to Lake George. Before Johnson himself left, Rogers handed him a letter of introduction from Colonel Blanchard, who recommended the young captain, in Rogers' own words, "as a person well acquainted with the haunts and passes of the enemy, and the Indian method of fighting."

The illustration depicts this first meeting between two men who would figure prominently in each other's lives, and eventually engage in a fierce rivalry for political power and influence in the North American Indian trade. Johnson's general officer's attire and sash is augmented by a cutlass belt decorated with woven porcupine quills, and fringes of tinkling cones sprouting red hair. This belt is taken from a surviving relic known to have been either the property of, or a gift from, William Johnson.[4] It was natural, and not condescending, for him to frequently don articles of Indian dress to maintain his influence among his Iroquois neighbors and their allies.[5]

Rogers' clothing is typical of a hunter of the New England "back country" of the 1750s: hunter's cap with a back flap for inclement weather; a jacket of green or brown; tumpline supporting a bearskin-wrapped blanket-pack; bullet pouch hanging in front, with powder horn on his right side; knife and pistol stuck in his belt; and a tomahawk hanging at his left side. Indian-style leggings protect his legs from dense and thorny brush, and he wears moccasins of deer or moose skin. By a rope over one shoulder hangs a military-issue canteen. A leather cover keeps the lock of his fusil dry. Immediately below him, several of his rangers rest after their long, hot march from Albany.

To the right of General Johnson stands one of his Mohawk Indian "warrior chieftains," his rank distinguished by a gorget inscribed with Johnson's initials.[6] Red garters wrapped around the heads of all of Johnson's Native American forces marked them as allies of the Crown. Red ostrich feathers were also presented to important warriors. Cutlasses were weapons much desired by many Indians; some traded or given to them were "of the cymeter kind."[7] Bearskin was sometimes used to cover the locks of Iroquois guns.[8] The porcupine quill was a nasal decoration worn by some, though jewels were most often seen hanging from Mohawk noses.

At this stage in the expedition (August 26), Johnson had only about 60 Indians with him; 200 more, under old Chief Hendrick, arrived at the Lake George camp on August 30, firing their muskets into the air as a greeting at the entrance to the camp. The Provincial army drew into lines to receive them, discharging five of their cannon twice in a return salute.[9]

At far right stands one of Johnson's white officers serving among his Indians. Many of these men were from the Mohawk Valley Dutch settlements. Long experienced in trading, and sometimes even living, with the Iroquois, a few of them had also scouted against the French during "Governor Shirley's War" (1744-1749); thus their value went beyond the role of mere interpreters. Little is known of their military dress; it might have been green, the color, generally, of New York's Provincial

GARY ZABOLY
©1997

soldiers and in later years of the officers of Johnson's Indian Department. In actual field service they were often known to don Indian shirts, breechclouts, leggings and war paint, and sometimes even shaved their heads down to scalplocks.

Most of the 200 wagons in Johnson's expedition were of the "Dutch kind"—viz., Conestogas. The road axed through the forest—a forest along these flat and sandy sections replete with vast, ancient stands of white and red pines—averaged 30 feet in width; soggy stretches were corduroyed over, and stumps were pared down to earth level. Over the years this became known as the King's Road, or the King's Highway, or simply the Old Military Road.[10]

The setting is the northern edge of the clearing at the Great Carrying Place. At left is Hudson's River, and in the middle of it sits the upper end of what later became known as "Rogers' Island," headquarters for Rogers and his companies during most of the war.

G.Z.

1. Blanchard to Governor Benning Wentworth, Albany, August 26, 1755, *Provincial Papers of the Province of New Hampshire*, From 1749 to 1763, Vol. VI, p. 431.
2. "Many gentlemen in the city," wrote Blanchard, considered "my four hundred better than all the York and Rhode Island forces," Ibid., p. 430. *The Boston Gazette* of August 25, 1755 deemed his soldiers "all fine Fellows."
3. Rogers' dates in his Journals are often off by as many as ten days, due to the fact that many in the New World were still using the Old Style calendar.
4. Ted J. Brasser, *"Bo'jou, Neejee!" Profiles of Canadian Indian Art*, published by the National Museum of Man, the National Museums of Canada, Ottawa, 1976, plate 141, p. 143.
5. In 1757 and 1758, when he was not commander of the army on campaign, William Johnson frequently wore Native American dress from head to toe. Louis Antoine de Bougainville, aide-de-camp to General Montcalm, in a letter to a friend written in April of 1758, described a melodramatic scene he considered worthy of *The Iliad*, and in which Johnson was the main player. According to the tale told to him by the Caughnawaga Mohawks of Canada, who had heard it from their English-allied Mohawk brethren in New York, in August of 1757 Johnson had proposed to Major General Daniel Webb marching at once to the relief of Fort William Henry. When Webb refused, Johnson tore off one of his leggings and threw it at Webb's feet. "You won't do it?!" he exclaimed to Webb. As Webb continued to shake his head, Johnson threw his other legging at him, again saying, "You won't?!" He next threw garter, shirt, tomahawk and halberd down, until, stripped to his breechclout and moccasins, he turned to ride off with his mixed command of Indians and white men, "who had imitated his actions exactly." *Adventure In the Wilderness: The American Journals of Louis Antoine de Bougainville*, 1756- 1760, translated and edited by Edward P. Hamilton, University of Oklahoma Press, Norman, Oklahoma, 1964, p. 333.
6. These initialized gorgets were designed and issued by Johnson to his chiefs. This infuriated General William Shirley, the commander-in-chief, who wrote to Johnson on August 4 that, "as these presents are made with the King's money, Sir, and to create in the Indians a Dependence upon his Majesty, and not merely a personal Attachment to yourself, you will excuse me if I note the Impropriety of your omitting the King's Arms" from the gorgets. "The Papers of Sir William Johnson: Addenda," *New York History*, January 1979, p. 89.
7. James Thomas Flexner, *Lord of the Mohawk*, Little, Brown and Company, Boston and Toronto, 1979, p. 19.
8. *The Papers of Sir William Johnson*, James Sullivan, editor, Albany 1921, Vol. II, p. 619.
9. This somewhat remarkable moment was recorded in the diaries of Provincial soldiers Seth Pomeroy, John Burk, James Gilbert and Elisha Hawley.
10. See color "aerial" painting of the road ca. 1759, by Gary S. Zaboly, in *The Bulletin of the Fort Ticonderoga Museum*, Vol. XV, 1993 Number 5, facing p. 363.

which reduced their number to four. We then took boat and pursued them down the lake, till they were relieved by two canoes, which obliged us to retreat towards our encampment at Lake George, where we arrived the 10th of October.

Seth Pomeroy makes an interesting entry in his journal for October 1, 1755, were he talks about a discrepancy between information reported by Rogers and that learned from a French deserter: "a Franch man Decerted from ye army a Tinundorogo gave an acct. of about 400 men at ye Place which Seems to Contridict Capt. Rogers acct. But Capt. Rogers was there 2 or 3 Days after who gave acct of an army not Less then our army which must have Come there after ye Franch man had Left yt Place So yt It is Likely they Came & brought Cannon for Rogers Saw a battry there with Cannon Planted ye Deserter Sd there was none when he Came away So it is Provable they both Spoke true." (Pomeroy, p. 121)

On October 6, Pomeroy noted that Rogers and his company would be kept in service over the winter: "Collo. Blanchard Colo Williard Mr Emerson & ye whole of yt Rigement—(Except Capt Simes & Capt Rogers which are to Stay here at ye fort [Edward] all Winter with Each of them a Company of volentiers yt they think they Can raise for that Purpose) are gon home." (Pomeroy, p. 122) Captain Simes is William Symes, who commanded another Ranger company in Blanchard's New Hampshire Regiment.

On October 11, Pomeroy records information about another scout that is not mentioned in Rogers' *Journals*, "Capt. Rogers Came In yt went 4 Days ago to vew Tinundorogo found them building about 2 Miles this Side ye Carrying Place ye number apeard to be about a thoushand men . . . ." (Pomeroy, p. 124)

October 15, 1755. Agreeable to orders of this date from General Johnson, I embarked with forty men in five boats. Our design was to discover the strength of the enemy's advanced guard, and, if possible, to decoy the whole, or part of them, into an ambush; but tho' we were indefatigable in our endeavors for several days, yet all our attempts of this kind proved abortive; and, as an account of our several movements during this scout would little gratify the reader, I shall omit giving a particular detail of them. We returned safe to our encampment at Lake George on the 19th.

Seth Pomeroy gives this mention of Rogers' scout in his journal entry for October 15: "Capt. Rogers went Last night with a Small Scout to See If by any means Pick Some of ye Enemy . . ." (Pomeroy, p. 125)

October 21, 1755. I had orders from General Johnson of this date, to embark for Crown Point, with a party of four men, in quest of a prisoner. At night we landed on the west-side of Lake George, twenty-five miles from the English camp. The remainder of the way we marched by land, and the 26th came in sight of the fort. In the evening we approached nearer, and next morning found ourselves within about 300 yards of it. My men lay concealed in a thicket of willows, while I crept something nearer, to a large pine-log, were I concealed myself, by holding bushes in my hand. Soon after sun-rise the soldiers issued out in such numbers, that my men and I could not possibly join each other without a discovery. About 10 o'clock a single man march out directly towards our ambush. When I perceived him within ten yards of me, I sprung over the log, and met him, and offered him quarters, which he refused, and made a pass at me with a dirk, which I avoided, and presented my fusee to his breast; but notwithstanding, he still pushed on with resolution, and obliged me to dispatch him. This gave an alarm the enemy, and made it necessary for us to hasten to the mountain. I arrived safe at our camp on the 30th, with all my party.

November 4, 1755. Agreeable to orders from General Johnson this day, I embarked for the enemy's advanced guard before mentioned, with a party of thirty men, in four battoes, mounted with two wall-pieces each.

A bateau (plural bateaux) was the nautical

workhorse of both armies. Used to transport both troops and supplies, bateaux were flat-bottomed, double-ended vessels with a shallow draft, and had the ability to carry a large amount of weight for their size. Each bateau could carry approximately twenty-two soldiers plus provisions. They were made in varying lengths, generally twenty-five to thirty-five feet during the French and Indian War period. A thirty foot bateau generally was six to six and a half feet wide, and would have been slightly wider in the bow than at the stern. Bateaux were rowed, poled, or sailed. They averaged four to six oars set in thole pin rowlocks, plus a steering oar. The sides were almost perpendicular, and from twenty inches to two feet deep. Relatively heavy, they were not easily portaged. (Bellico, *Sails & Steam,* pp. 25-26, Zarzynski, p. 5, and Kalm, p. 333)

The next morning, a little before day-light, we arrived within half a mile of them, where we landed, and concealed our boats; I then sent out four men as spies, who returned the next evening, and informed me, that the enemy had no works round them, but lay entirely open to an assault; which advice I dispatched immediately to the General, desiring a sufficient force to attack them, which, notwithstanding the General's earnestness and activity in the affair, did not arrive till we were obliged to retreat. On our return, however, we were met by a reinforcement, sent by the General, whereupon I returned again towards the enemy, and the next evening sent two men to see if the enemy's centries were alert, who approached so near as to be discovered and fired at by them, and were so closely pursued in their retreat, that unhappily our whole party was discovered. The first notice I had of this being the case, was from two canoes with thirty men in them, which I concluded came out with another party by land, in order to force us between two fires; to prevent which, I with Lieutenant M'Curdy, and fourteen men, embarked in two boats, leaving the remainder of the party on shore, under the command of Captain Putnam—In order to decoy the enemy within the reach of our wall-pieces, we steered as if we intended to pass by them, which luckily answered our expectations; for they boldly headed us till within about an hundred yards, when we discharged the before mentioned pieces, which killed several of them, and put to rest to flight, in which we drove them so near where our land-party lay, that they were again galled by them; several of the enemy were tumbled into the water, and their canoes rendered very leaky. At this time I discovered their party by land, and gave our people notice of it, who thereupon embarked likewise, without receiving any considerable injury from the enemy's fire, notwithstanding it was for some time very brisk upon them. We warmly pursued the enemy, and again got an opportunity to discharge our wall-pieces upon them, which confused them much, and obliged them to disperse.—We pursued them down the lake to their landing, where they were received and covered by 100 men, upon whom we again discharged our wall-pieces, and obliged them to retire; but finding their number vastly superior to ours, we judged it most prudent to return to encampment at Lake George, where we safely arrived on the 8th of November.

Nov. 10, 1755. Pursuant to orders I received this day from Gen. Johnson, in order to discover the enemy's strength and situation at Ticonderago, I proceeded on the scout with a party of ten men on the 12th instant, and on the 14th arrived within view of the fort at that place, and found they had erected three new barracks and four store-houses in the fort, between which and the water they had eighty battoes hauled upon the beach, and about fifty tents near the fort; they appeared to be very busy at work. Having by these discoveries answered the design of our march, we returned, and arrived at our encampment the 19th of November.

From November 16-25, Robert Rogers' younger brother Richard, a lieutenant in the Rangers, led a successful scout past Ticonderoga to observe the French activity at Crown Point. His men suffered from the "Weather & Scarcity of Provisions" on this venture. (*D.H.S.N.Y.*,

Volume 4, pp. 281-283.)

December 19, 1755. Having had a month's repose, I proceeded, agreeable to orders from General Johnson, with two men, once more to reconnoitre the French at Ticonderoga. In our way we discovered a fire upon an island adjacent to the route we took, which, as we supposed, had been kindled by some of the enemy who were there. This obliged us to lie by and act like fishermen, the better to deceive them till night came on, when we proceeded and retired to the west-side of the lake 15 miles north of our fort. Here concealing our boat, the 20th we pursued our march by land, and on the 21st, at noon, were in sight of the French fort, where we found their people still deeply engaged at work, and discovered four pieces of cannon mounted on the south-east bastion, two at the north-east towards the woods, and two on the south. By what I judged, the number of their troops were about 500. I made several attempts to take a prisoner, by waylaying their paths; but they always passed in numbers vastly superior to mine, and thereby disappointed me. We approached very near their fort by night, and were driven by the cold (which now was very severe) to take shelter in one of their evacuated huts; before day, there was a fall of snow, which obliged us with all possible speed to march homeward, lest the enemy should perceive our tracks, and pursue us.

We found our boat in safety, and had the good fortune (after being almost exhausted with hunger, cold, and fatigue) to kill two deer, with which being refreshed, on the 24th we returned to Fort William Henry (a fortress erected in this year's campaign) at the south end of Lake George. About this time General Johnson retired to Albany, to which place commissioners were sent from the several governments whose troops had been under his command (New Hampshire only excepted) These commissioners were empowered by their respective constituents with the assent of a council of war, to garrison Fort William Henry and Fort Edward, for the winter, with part of the troops that had served the preceding year. Accordingly a regiment was formed, to which Boston government furnished a Colonel—Connecticut a Lieutenant-Colonel—and New York a Major: after which it was adjudged, both by Gen. Johnson and these Commissioners, that it would be of great use to leave one company of woodsmen or rangers under my command, to make excursions toward the enemy's forts during the winter; I accordingly remained, and did duty the whole winter, until called upon by General Shirley.

Thomas Mante has this to say about Rogers' scouting activities at this time: "Whilst preparations were making on both sides for the next campaign, Captain Robert Rogers, on that of the English, was constantly employed in patroling the woods about the Forts Edward and William-Henry, and observing the motions of the French at Ticonderoga and Crown Point; that this service he performed with so much alertness, that he made a great number of prisoners, and thereby procured very good intelligence of the enemy. The substance of this intelligence was, that M. de Montcalm intended to attack Fort William-Henry, as soon as the weather would permit him to take the field." (Mante, p. 78)

January 14, 1756. This day I marched with a party of seventeen men, to reconnoitre the French forts; we proceeded down the lake, on the ice, upon skaits, and halted for refreshment near the fall out of Lake George into Lake Champlain.—At night we renewed our march, and, by day-break on the 16th, formed an ambush on a point of land on the east shore of Lake Champlain, within gun-shot of the path in which the enemy passed from one fort to the other. About sun-rise, two sledges laden with fresh beef were presented to our view, we intercepted the drivers, destroying their loading, and afterwards returned to Fort William Henry, where I arrived with my prisoners and party in good health the 17th.

Since Rogers is sometimes confused on his dates, it is possible that Provincial captain Jeduthan Baldwin is referring to this scout when he writes in his journal for January 19, 1756: "In the morning about 6:30 we were alarmed by Capt. Rogers firing as he came in on the Lake (from ye Lake Champlain) where he took 2 prisoners & brot. them in with him. (Baldwin, p. 125)

January 26, 1756. Pursuant to orders of this date, from Colonel Glasier, I marched from Lake George with a party of fifty men, with a design to discover the strength and works of the enemy at Crown Point.

Colonel Beamsley Glazier, of the New York Provincials, who would soon be commissioned in the Royal Americans, showed interesting concern for the welfare of Rogers' men when he issued the orders for this scout: "you are to take Good Care of your men and not Expose them too much you are to use all Immaginable Protection not to Loos a man if it should Snow you are to Return Imedintly to this Fort . . . . I heartily wish you success" (*D.H.S.N.Y.*, Volume 4, p. 284)

On the 2d of February, we arrived within a mile of that fortress, where we climbed a very steep mountain, from which we had a clear and full prospect of the fort, and an opportunity of taking a plan of the enemy's works there. In the evening we retired to a small village, half a mile from the fort, and formed an ambuscade on each side of the road leading from the fort to the village. Next morning a Frenchman fell into our hands; soon after we discovered two more, but they unluckily got sight of us before they were in our power, and hastily retired to the fort. Finding ourselves discovered by the enemy by this accident, we employed ourselves while we dared stay in setting fire to the houses and barns of the village, with which were consumed large quantities of wheat, and other grain; we also killed about fifty cattle, and then retired, leaving the whole village in flames, and arrived safe at our fort, with our prisoner, the 6th of February.

Provincial captain Jeduthan Baldwin mentions this scout in his journal, with slightly different dates than Rogers: January 30, 1756: "Capt. Rogers with 50 men went a scout. 2 of them returned in evening." February 5, 1756: "Capt. Rogers came in with one prisoner. Left one sick." (Baldwin, p. 126)

February 29, 1756. Agreeable to orders from Colonel Glasier, I this day marched with a party of fifty-six men down the west-side of Lake George. We continued our route north-ward till the 5th of March, and then steered east to Lake Champlain, about six miles north of Crown Point, where, by the intelligence we had from the Indians, we expected to find some inhabited villages.—We then attempted to cross the lake, but found the ice too weak. The 17th we returned and marched round the bay to the west of Crown Point, and at night got into the cleared land among their houses and barns; here we formed an ambush, expecting their labourers out to tend their cattle, and clean their grain, of which there were several barns full; we continued there that and the next day till dark, when discovering none of the enemy, we set fire to the houses and barns, and marched off. In our return I took a fresh view of Ticonderoga, and reconnoitred the ground between that fort and the advanced guard on Lake George, approaching so near as to see their centries on the ramparts, and obtained all the knowledge of their works, strength, and situation, that I desired.

The 14th of March, we returned safe to Fort William-Henry.

Provincial captain Jeduthan Baldwin was a part of this scout, and recorded some interesting details that Rogers omitted, including a narrow brush with death for Rogers: February 29, 1756: "Capt. Putnam joined. Capts Rogers & Parker & I marched with 60 men toward Crown Point." March 1: "We sent back 5 of our men not well . . . Saw a wolf chase a deer into the water. Passed Capt. Putnam's *entreciel* [a search of several eighteenth- and twentieth-century English and French dictionaries has failed to provide a clear definition of this word] where the Indian town of trade, mass house, crop & camps, all standing. Very fine land." March 2: "Campt. on the low lands. Lodgd. not on feather beds but on hemlock boughs." March 5: "Lodgd. in sight of Crown Pt. without fire." March 6: "About 2 A.M. as we went across the Lake in order to way lay a road on the W. side (for by information we expected to find a village on the W. side abt. 10 or 15 miles down from Crown Pt. but there is none). Capt. Rogers fell off a ledge of rocks into the Lake, 26 ft. but with much difficulty he got out, but it prevented our crossing this morning as the ice was too weak." March 7: "Capt. Rogers went with 3 men abt. 3 A.M. to see if the ice would bear but found it too weak. We concluded to go and way lay from Crown Pt. to the Caralong [Carillon] . . . we lay just below the village till into the night." March 8: "Abt. 4 A.M. we marched to 1-1/2 miles of the upper village. We hid our packs in a barn on the Point. The fields were plowed, we went through making a large track. I stayed in a house with 23 men. Capts. Rogers, Parker & Putnam kept in a barn abt. 80 rods N. E. with 34 men, expecting every moment to take a prisoner. Capts. Rogers & Parker went a scout this day but could find nothing of the French, out of reach of their cannon. We kept very close till dark without victuals or drink. Abt. 9 P.M. we set fire to 9 barns & 2 houses. In the barns were large quantities of wheat, oats & pease. Then we came off abt. 4 miles. In the 2d barn set on fire was an. Indian asleep. He was so badly burned we had to carry him. Lodgd. in wet land. Lay cold." March 9: "Marched S. 15 miles, wading thro. a river and carrying the burnt Indian. We followed the enemy several miles. Lodgd. without fire." March 10: "We concluded to leave Capts. Putnam & Rogers & 6 men and the Indian, in order to find a good wagon road to or by the Caralong, and I was to lead the scout home and send down batteaux on the Lake for them. Travelled S. W. 6 miles, crosst. the notch of the mountains, mchd. W. 3 miles, came to Putnam's brook, & mchd. S. 6 miles. Crossed a road the Fr. & Indian scout of 160 men had made day before who were alarmed by the great fires seen at Crown Pt. on Monday evng. and embarked in their canoes at daybreak Tuesday morning. We lay abt. 1/2 mile from where the French campt on Tuesday night. They wrote on the trees 'if they catch us *they would burn us* or we should them directly.' Lodgd. this night without camp. March 11: Mchd. S. S. W. 18 miles & got to Ft. Wm. Henry abt. 2 P.M., the men very weak & faint, having had nothing to eat for some time." (Baldwin pp. 126-128)

The *Connecticut Gazette* also reported this scout: "Boston, March 29: On Tuesday Evening came to Town from Fort William Henry, at Lake George, Captain Robert Rogers, who has made himself famous in these Parts of America, by his [illegible] and Activity with his Scalping Parties near Crown Point. He informs, that on the first Inst. he went out with a Scout of 55 Men to distress the Enemy, and on the fifth came in Sight of the Fort, and continued round it undiscovered three Days, waiting an Opportunity to take some Prisoners, but without Success. On the 9th in the Evening they set Fire to 2 Dwelling-Houses and 9 Barns, which alarmed the enemy, upon which he return'd The next Morning they heard three Cannon fired at the Fort, which Capt. Rogers supposed were to alarm Ticonderago; and being within six Miles of it, he with six of his Party, went to view the Fort there, and came so near in the Evening, as to see the Centinels on the Walls: They afterwards joined their Companions, and made the best of their Way back to Fort William Henry, where they all arrived safe on the 15th, except an Indian (one of the Party) who was asleep in one of the Barns when they set Fire to it, and was so much burnt, that he died before they returned." (*Connecticut Gazette*, April 6, 1756, p. 4)

The next day, after my return from this scout, I received a letter, dated February 24, 1756, from Mr. William Alexander of New-York, who was secretary to Mr. Shirley, Commander in chief of the troops at Oswego the preceding year, and who now, upon the decease of General Braddock, succeeded to the chief command of all his Majesty's forces in North-America, and was now at Boston, preparing for the ensuing campaign, being previously recommended to this gentleman by General Johnson. I was desired by the above-mentioned letter to wait on him at Boston; of which I informed the commanding officer at the fort, and, with his approbation, I set out on the 17th of March, leaving the command of my company to Mr. Noah Johnson, my Ensign; my brother Richard Rogers, who was my Lieutenant, being sent to Boston by the commanding officer on some dispatches previous to this.

On the 23rd, I waited on the General, and met with a very friendly reception; he soon intimated his design of giving me the command of an independent company of rangers, and the very next morning I received the commission, with a set of instructions.

Rogers had already begun to make a name for himself. The *Connecticut Gazette* published a letter that he wrote, thanking the General Assembly for a monetary gift that they had given him: "I return you my hearty Thanks for the particular Instance of your Favour of the 12th February last, in bestowing One Hundred and Twenty Five mill'd Pieces of Eight on me, as you was pleased to say, For my good Services, done nigh and about Crown Point against the French and Indians. I know not how to make a sufficient Acknowledgment for this Act of Generosity, but shall, at all Times, exert my Utmost, in faithfully serving my God, my King, and Country, as an honest Soldier . . ." (*Connecticut Gazette*, April 3, 1756, p. 4)

According to the General's orders, my company was to consist of sixty privates, at 3s. New York currency per day, three searjents at 4s. an Ensign at 5s. a Lieutenant at 7s. and my own pay was fixed at 10s. per day. Ten Spanish dollars were allowed to each man towards providing cloaths, arms, and blankets. My orders were to raise this company as soon as possible, to inlist none but such as were used to travelling and hunting, and in whose courage and fidelity I could confide; they were, moreover to be subject to military discipline, and the articles of war.

Our rendezvous was appointed at Albany, from thence to proceed in four whale-boats to lake George, and, "from time to time, to use my best endeavours to distress the French and their allies, by sacking, burning, and destroying their houses, barns, barracks, canoes, battoes, & c. and by killing their cattle of every kind; and at all times to endeavour to way-lay, attack and destroy their convoys of provisions by land and water, in any part of the country where I could find them."

Whale boats were small, sturdy, easily maneuvered boats that were frequently used to transport troops and supplies. They were especially favored by the Rangers. On February 1, 1759, General Amherst laid down the specifications for the whale boats that he wanted Captain Joshua Loring to have built for the coming campaign: "Fifty Whaleboats, 20 feet in the Keel, 5 feet 2 Inches broad, 25 Inches Deep, 34 feet from Stem to Stern, and 7 Streakers [the fore-and-aft planks used to shape the hull of a boat] of a side from the Keel to the gunwale, all well put together, made light, & to row with Seven Oars besides the Steering Oar." (PRO 28511 84/64)

On July 17, 1759, Lieutenant Josiah Goodrich, a Connecticut Provincial, noted in his orderly book that, "ye Whale boats to be markt by ye cores [corps] they Are Delivered to In ye same manner As the Battoos Are the granidears to Receive theirs As soon As they are Ready for Which they Will Appli to Capt Lorin the Rangers will Receive After ye granidears all ye Whale Boats Are to be kept In ye Crick or other wise they will be split ye porpotion of whale bots And Battoos for Rangers are 42 Whale Boats . . . ." On the 12, Goodrich had previously noted that "Every commanding offir of A Rigt will take care to put water In ye boats or to have them hold In water every Day that they may Not be Leaky when Loaded" (Goodrich, pp. 52 and 47)

In this day of modern fiberglass and aluminum boats and canoes, it is easily forgotten how important it is to keep wooden vessels wet, so that the wood does not dry out and shrink, causing them to leak. "Capt Lorin" was

Joshua Loring, a Royal Navy officer who was in charge of shipbuilding and other naval affairs for Amherst's campaign of 1759.

With these instructions, I received letters to the commanding officers at Fort William-Henry and Fort Edward directing them to forward the service, with which I was now particularly charged.

When my company was completed, a part marched under the command of Lieutenant Rogers to Albany; with the remainder, I was ordered to march through the woods to No. 4, then a frontier town greatly exposed to the enemy; where,

April 28, 1756, I received orders to march from thence to Crown Point, in pursuance of which we travelled through desarts and mountains.

Although I will insert contemporary descriptions of Rangers' dress at appropriate places in the text, I will leave the in-depth discussion of the specific deatails of it to artist Gary Zaboly, who has studied this subject for years and has compiled an amazing body of information, which he shares in the captions to his illustrations and in the special appendix at the end of the book.

Fort No. 4, built in 1743 along the Connecticut River near present day Charleston, N.H., was so called because it was in township number four (of nine) established by the General Court of the colony of Massachusetts.

The second day of our march, my second Lieutenant, Mr. John Stark was taken sick, and obliged to return, with whom I sent six men to guard him Fort Edward.

We continued our march till the 5th of May, when I arrived with nine men at Lake Champlain, four miles south of Crown Point. Here we concealed our packs, and marched up to a village on the east-side, about two miles distant from Crown Point, but found no inhabitant there. We lay in wait the whole day following, opposite to Crown Point, expecting some party to cross the lake; but nothing appeared except about four or five hundred men in canoes and battoes, coming up the lake from St. John's to Crown Point. We kept our stations till next day, ten o'clock A.M. to observe the motions of the enemy, but finding no opportunity to trapan any of them, we killed twenty-three head of cattle, the tongues of which were a very great refreshment to us on our journey.

"Trapan" is probably "trappan," an old Saxon word meaning "to catch by snare or ambush; to take by stratagem," per Johnson's 1755 *A Dictionary of the English Language.*

We at this time discovered eleven canoes manned with a considerable number of French and Indians crossing the lake directly towards us, upon which we retired; and the better to escape our pursuers we dispersed, each man taking a different route. We afterwards assembled at the place where we concealed our packs, and on a raft crossed over to the west-side of the lake. In our way we had a view of the French and Indians, encamped at the old Indian carrying-place, near Ticonderoga, and on the 11th of May arrived safe at Fort William-Henry. Mr. Stark, with his party, arrived at Fort-Edward three days before. In their way they discovered a scouting party of three or four hundred Indians. Lieutenant Rogers with his party had arrived some days before this, it was at this time out upon a scout.

May 20, 1756. Agreeable to orders from the General, I set out with a party of eleven men to reconnoitre the French advanced guards. The next day, from the top of the mountain, we had a view of them, and judged their number to be about 300; they were busy in fortifying themselves with palisadoes. From the other side of the mountain we had a prospect of Ticonderoga fort, and from the ground their encampment took up, I judged it to consist of 1000 men. This night we lodged on the mountain, and next morning marched to the Indian carrying-path that leads from lake George to Lake Champlain, and formed an ambuscade between the French guard and Ticonderoga fort. About six o'clock 118 Frenchmen passed by without discovering us; in a few minutes after, twenty-two more came the same road, upon whom we fired, killed six, and took one a prisoner; but the large party returning, obliged us to retire in haste, and we arrived safe with our prisoner, at Fort William-Henry the 23rd.

> A French account of this incident is found in a diary believed to have been kept by Captain Gaspard-Joseph Chaussegros de Lery. In an entry for May 22, 1756, he wrote, "At 9 o'c. of the morning, there arrived 13 men of the Canadian Militia, who escaped from the portage where they were attacked by some 15 English, as they say. It is true that M. de Beaujeu had ordered M. de Fortenay, cadet, to go there with 20 armed men, each one with an axe, to work on the portage trail. They left their arms at one end of the said portage with a sentry to guard them, and came to the other end to work there. This portage is 3/4 of a league across. The English killed one man and scalped him, after which they left more promptly than they had come, without taking the trouble to follow the fleeing men; they could have captured these 20 men without firing a shot if they had wanted, as they were all sitting in a circle smoking their pipe. There is still missing from this detail only sieur Fontenay and we are very anxious as to his fate." (Lery, pp. 131-132)

The prisoner we had taken reported, "that a party of 220 French and Indians were preparing to invest the out-parties at Fort Edward," which occasioned my marching the next morning with a party of 78 men, to join a detachment of Col. Bayley's regiment, to scour the words as far as South Bay, if possible to intercept the enemy; but we could not discover them.

> On June 1, at Albany, Charlotte Brown, the Matron of the British army's General Hospital, noted in her diary, "Captain Rogers came from Lake George with a french Prisoner and 1 Scalp." (Charlotte Brown, p. 195)

June 13, 1756. Agreeable to orders this evening, I embarked with a party of 26 men in battoes upon Lake George, to revisit the French advanced guard; excessive thunder and lightning obliged us to land at about ten miles distance from our fort, where we spent the night. The next morning about sun-rise, we heard the explosion of upwards of twenty small arms, on the opposite side of the lake, which we supposed to be a party of French and Indians, cleaning their guns after the rain. In the evening we embarked again, and early in the morning of the 16th drew up our battoes about four miles distant from the advanced guard, and afterwards lay in ambush by a path leading from thence to a mountain, in order to surprize the enemy, who went there daily in parties, to take a view of the lake; but finding they were not at that place, we marched to the spot where the enemy had posted their advanced guard, but they had retired and demolished all their works there; we then continued our march towards Ticonderoga, near which place we ascended an eminence, and had a clear view of their works. I judged that their garrison and encampment consisted of about 3000 men: We then set out on our return, and arrived at Fort William-Henry the 18th instant, except one man, who strayed from us, and who did not get in till the 23d, then almost famished for want of sustenance.

About this time the General augmented my company to seventy men, and sent me six light whale-boats from Albany, with order to proceed immediately to Lake Champlain, to cut off, if possible, the provisions and flying parties of the enemy. Accordingly,

June 28, 1756. I embarked with fifty men and five whale-boats, and proceeded to an island in Lake George. The next day, at about five miles distance from this island we landed our boats, and carried them about six miles over a mountain to South Bay, were we arrived the 3d of July.

> This is the true life incident that inspired the scene in the 1940 movie *Northwest Passage,* where Spencer Tracy and his hardy Rangers carry their boats over a mountain to escape detection by French sloops on Lake Champlain while enroute to St. Francis. Actually, the

> Rangers carried the boats from Lake George to South Bay, which gave them access to Lake Champlain.
>
> In his journal, French Captain Louis-Antoine de Bougainville discusses the French surprise when these boats were later discovered: "one of the barges [whale boats] mounted with three swivels, and in it a barrel of powder, some balls and grenades, about forty oars, and many tracks on the shore at the edge of the woods . . . . The barges presumably belonged to a party which had for its object the capture or harrying of some of our convoys." The French were perplexed as to exactly how the Rangers had gotten their boats into Lake Champlain. Bougainville goes on to say, "It does not appear probable that they portaged these barges either from Lake George or even from La Barbue River." The French sent out at least two different parties to attempt to solve this mystery. (Bougainville, pp. 46-47)

The following evening we embarked again, and went down the bay to within six miles of the French fort, where we concealed our boats till the evening. We then embarked again, and passed by Ticonderoga undiscovered, tho' we were so near the enemy as to hear their centry's watch-word. We judged from the number of their fires, that they had a body of about 2000 men, and the lake and in this place to be near 400 yards wide. About five miles further down, we again concealed our boats, and lay by all day. We saw several battoes going and coming upon the lake. At night we put off again, with a design to pass by Crown Point, but afterwards judged it imprudent by reason of the clearness of the night, so lay concealed again the next day, when near a hundred boats passed by us, seven of which came very near the point where we were, and would have landed there; but the officer insisted, in our hearing, upon going about 150 yards further, where they landed, and dined in our view. About nine o'clock we re-embarked, and passed the fort at Crown Point, and again concealed our boats at about 10 miles distance from it. This day, being July 7th, 30 boats, and a schooner of about 30 or 40 tons, passed by us towards Canada. We set out again in the evening, and landed about fifteen miles further down; from which place I sent a party for further discovery, who brought intelligence of a schooner at anchor, about a mile from us; we immediately lightened our boats, and prepared to board her; but were prevented by two lighters coming up the lake, who, we found intended to land where we posted; these we fired upon, then hailed them, and offered them quarters, if they would come ashore; but they hastily pushed towards the opposite shore, where we pursued and intercepted them: we found their number to be twelve, three of which were killed by our fire, and two wounded, one of them in such manner that he soon died.

> "Lighters" were also called "shallops." These were probably small sailing galleys. (Bellico, *Sails and Steam*, p. 41)

> In his original report, Rogers says of this prisoner, "one of the wounded Could not March therefore put an end to him to Prevent Discovery . . . ." (*D.H.S.N.Y.*, Vol. XI, p. 286)

We sunk and destroyed their vessels and cargoes, which consisted chiefly of wheat and flour, wine and brandy; some few casks of the latter we carefully concealed. The prisoners informed us, that they were part of 500 men, the remainder of which were not far behind on their passage, which induced us to hasten our return to our garrison, where, with our prisoners, we safely arrived the 15th of July. These prisoners, upon examination, reported, "That a great number of regular troops and militia were assembling at Chamblee, and destined for Carillon, or Ticonderoga:* that great quantities of provisions were transporting there, and a new General** with two regiments lately arrived from France: that there was no talk of any design upon our Forts on this side; but that a party of 300 French, and 20 Indians, had already set out to intercept our convoys of provisions between Albany and Lake George: that 60 livres was the reward for an English scalp, and that the prisoners were sold in Canada for 50 crowns each: that their

*The former is the French, the latter the Indian name, signifying the meeting or confluence of three waters.
**The Marquis de Montcalm, who commanded in the reduction of Oswego this year, and of Fort William-Henry, the year following.

prospect of an harvest was very encouraging, but that the small-pox made great havoc amongst the inhabitants." About the time of my setting out upon this scout, Major General Shirley was superseded in his command by Major General Abercrombie, who arrived at the head-quarters in Albany on the 25th of June, and brought with him two regiments of regular troops from England. I therefore, upon my return, wrote his Excellency, desiring leave to lay before him the minutes of my last scout, and to recommend to his consideration an augmentation of the rangers.

> After this scout, Hospital Matron Charlotte Brown, at Albany, noted in her journal that, "News came that Capt. Rogers has taken eight Prisoners and four scalps." (Charlotte Brown, p. 196)
>
> On July 12, 1756, William Hervey of the 44th Regiment, stationed at Fort Edward, documented a recent scout by two of Rogers' Stockbridge Indians from Captain Jacob Cheeksaunkun's company. "Two Indians of Stockbridge, Captain Jacob's Company, arrived here from Crown Point, where they had been upon a scout. They brought us word that there were great numbers of French there, and that the woods were full of Indian scouts belonging to them; that they were obliged to leave their blankets and fly as fast as they could, being close pursued by the enemy; that on their return they struck out into the woods a good way, and coming again across the path of the west side of Lake George, they perceived a track of about two or three hundred of the enemy coming this way, and that when they came to the south end of the lake, they found that half of 'em had struck away to the west, and part to the east." (Hervey, p. 28)
>
> On July 16, Hervey records Rogers' return from the scout mentioned above in the *Journals*. "This evening Captain Rogers arrived from his scout from Lake Champlain, to which place he had been with his company of 60 men in 5 whale boats. He passed safe by the two French forts at the entrance into it. He went 25 miles down the lake, and falling in with two large boats, with six men in each, the 8th of this month at night, he fired upon 'em, and killed 4 and took the other eight, which he brought safe to Fort William Henry the 16th. He destroyed about 400 bushels of provisions and sunk the boats, and going six miles above the place where he took them, brought his whale boats ashore and hid them in a secure place, with a sufficient quantity of provisions and liquors against they returned, and came home by land." (Hervey, p. 29)
>
> On the 18, Hervey relates information about the prisoners from Rogers' scout: "Captain Rogers set forth with his prisoners for Albany. We got very little intelligence from them, being raw country men, just impressed from St. John's. They informed us that there were some forces landed from France this spring at Canada. Rogers informed us that they were strongly fortified at both Forts, and that they were about 9000 encamped about Ticonderoga, and that the prisoners had informed him that they talked of 8000 being to come there in all. Rogers informed us that there was a large schooner on Lake Champlain, which conveyed provisions between St. Jean's and Crown Point, and that after a portage of six miles, at St. Jean's the river Soirel was navigable for batteaus all the way to Montreal, and that there were great numbers employed in carrying provisions, of which they had plenty." (Hervey, pp. 29-30)

The General permitted me, with my brother Richard Rogers, to wait upon him at Albany. In this interview we discoursed on the subject of my letter, in consequence of which he immediately ordered a new company of rangers to be raised, and gave the command of it to my brother,* appointed Noah Johnson, my former Ensign, his First Lieutenant, Nathaniel Abbott his Second Lieutenant, and Caleb Page his Ensign. John Stark, formerly, my Second Lieutenant, was appointed my First, John M'Curdy succeeded to his place, and Jonathan Burbank was appointed my Ensign.

August 2, 1756. Agreeable to orders received of General Abercrombie at Albany, the 23d of July,

*He compleated his company in 28 days, and by the General's orders, went up Mohawke river, to serve as a scouting party for the troops that way.

I embarked this day at Fort William-Henry, on board one of the lighters built there this summer, with twenty-five of my company, in order to reconnoitre the enemy at Ticonderoga and Crown Point, and sixty men under Capt. Larnard of the provincials, who had General Winslow's* orders to proceed with his men to the French advanced guard; but he not being acquainted with the way thither, put himself under my command. We landed this morning about fifteen miles down Lake George, and proceeded with the party till the 4th in the evening, and encamped about a mile from the advanced guard. The 5th in the morning we mustered the whole party, and got to the summit of a hill, west of the advanced guard, where we discovered two advanced posts, which I then imagined was the whole of the guard, one of them on the west-side, half a mile southward of Lake Champlain, the other on the east-side of the Lake, opposite the former, at the old Indian carrying-place. We judged there were about 400 men on the east, and 200 on the west. After deliberating with Capt. Larnard upon the strength and disposition of the enemy, and the report of our advanced party we, concluded it unadviseable to continue there any longer. He returned towards Fort William-Henry, and I went on with my own party till we came within view of Ticonderoga Fort, where, from an eminence, I discovered the situation, but could not ascertain the strength of it to my satisfaction.

August 6, I went down towards Crown Point, by the west-side of Lake Champlain, and discovered several battoes passing from that place to Ticonderoga with troops on board. We then proceeded to the place where we burnt the village, as mentioned before, and there encamped, and perceived a party sallying out, driving a number of horses to feed.

The 7th we lay in ambush by the road, with a design to intercept such as might come out to drive in the cattle; but no one appearing for that purpose, we approached nearer, to within half a mile of the fort, where we were discovered by two Frenchmen, before they were in our power. This accident obliged us to make a retreat, in which we killed upwards of forty cattle. We arrived at Fort William-Henry, August 10.

> In his journal for August 11, William Hervey of the 44th Regiment, mentions another scout by members of Rogers' Stockbridge Indian Company: "This day Jacob with a party of Stockbridge Indians retirned from their scout. They had been to Tionderoga, where they said there were more men than all our army. About half a mile from the Fort they saw three Frenchmen, whom they fired at and killed two, and brought home their scalps." (Hervey, p. 34)

A company of Stockbridge Indians was this year employed in his Majesty's service, commanded by Indian officers, properly commissioned by General Shirley, before he was superseded in his command. General Abercrombie was somewhat at a loss how to dispose of this company, and applied to Sir William Johnson, who advised, that a part,** viz. thirty privates and a Lieutenant, should scout and scour the woods under my direction, which party had arrived while I was out upon my last scout, and Lieutenant Stark had strengthened their party with some of our people, and sent them out with particular directions what route to take, the day before I arrived.

About this time his Excellency the Earl of Loudoun arrived at Albany, and had taken upon him the command of the army, to whom I applied as I had done before to Gen. Abercrombie, transmitting to him an account of the Indian scout above mentioned (who returned the 13th with two French scalps, agreeable to their barbarous custom) and desiring that with them I might attempt to penetrate into Canada, and distress the inhabitants, by burning their harvest (now nearly ripe) and destroying their cattle.

Accordingly, August 16, we embarked in whale-boats in two departments, the one commanded by Lieutenant Stark, and the other by myself.—The next morning we joined each other, at which time also fell in with us a party of eight Mohocks, who had marched out from Fort

*General Winslow commanded the provincial troops this year by virtue of a commission from the several provinces, who were concerned in 1755, in the same expedition, and was now with the greatest part of the provincial troops at Lake George.

**The remainder of this Indian company, with their Captain, were sent to Saratoga, to be under the direction of Colonel Burton.

Bivouac Over Lake George

It is midsummer of 1756. Lake George and its mountain environs are being heavily watched and patrolled by scouting parties from both sides, the French in the north and the British in the south. Partisan activity is particularly busy this summer: enemy bateaux and canoes can often be seen on the lake, even from the ramparts of Fort William Henry; and the French at forts Carillon and St. Frederic sometimes observe bands of English Rangers looking down at them from surrounding heights.

In addition to spying on their respective enemies, the partisans conduct raids to destroy outlying buildings, crops, and livestock; ambush detachments of soldiers, work parties, and provision trains; and seize prisoners, generally lone sentries, for information. They also engage in explorations of the largely unmapped geography rimming both the lake and the Wood Creek/South Bay water corridor to the east.

The scene depicts a small scouting party of white Rangers from Captain Robert Rogers' company, and two Indians from the recently-arrived Stockbridge company, nearing the end of a pause for lunch high up the slopes of what is today called Black Mountain.[1] A small flotilla of enemy canoes commands the attention of two of the Rangers. Meanwhile, two Stockbridges are about to move on to do some advance scouting higher up.

A small and lightweight copper kettle has boiled the men's stew, perhaps pieces of salt pork mixed with rice and peas. A tamed wolf-dog accompanies the party. Because of the hot weather the Rangers are stripped to their shirts and leggings, most of them preferring Indian breechclouts to breeches, the clouts allowing for more suppleness in running (Rogers often cut the breeches from captured French soldiers to enable them to keep up with the Rangers as they made their swift return to their base).

Ranger shirts tended to be checked or plain, and no doubt often dyed green, brown or grey to match the colors of the forest. Leggings were similarly colored, generally made of frieze or ratteen, and on rarer occasion of natural deerskin. Ranger officers "usually carry a small compass fixed in the bottoms of their powderhorns," noted British Captain John Knox in 1757, "by which to direct them, when they happen to lose themselves in the woods".[2]

Small bullet bags of leather or sealskin, containing bullets and buckshot, hang down in front from a belt. Scalping knives were usually the clasp kind, and not carried in sheaths. Hatchets were generally carried slipped in the belt or in a frog attached to it, the blade often encased in a leather cover.

During these early years of the war Rogers' company was probably without an official "uniform," though judging by the Rangers' later documented attire it seems green would have been the most predominant color then as well. "They wear their cloaths short" was the way Knox summed up their "uniform" in 1757.[3] The Scotch bonnet was favored by many Rangers, but leather and felt jockey caps, cut-down hats, and caps of linen or wool were also worn. Moccasins were preferred for forest travel, allowing for swift and silent movement. Indian-style tumplines were also favored by scouting parties, though knapsacks were carried by some, and at times perhaps both were shouldered.

The Stockbridges were Christianized Indians of mostly Mahican parentage, but they were encouraged by the British high command to be "dressed and Painted like all other Indians."[4] Fashions among many northeastern Indians were copies of Mohawk dress.[5] These Indians are based mostly on figures in paintings made by Royal Artillery officer Thomas Davies that may very possibly represent Stockbridges: his view of Amherst's camp at Lake George in 1759, in the collection of the Fort Ticonderoga Museum, and one of his 1759 views of Ticonderoga as seen from Mount Defiance, owned by the New York Historical Society.

On a blazed section of the tree at right, a party of enemy Indians that had passed this way earlier has left painted figures to indicate what they would do to any Rangers they might encounter. In the lake beyond is the island-choked First Narrows, with part of Ganouski Bay (today's Northwest Bay) peeping just above it.

G.Z.

1. At an elevation of 2646 feet, Black Mountain is the highest peak among those immediately surrounding Lake George. From its summit one can see almost all of the 32-mile-long

GARY ZABOLY
©2000

lake; and it is reasonable to assume that Robert Rogers himself—always the mountain climber if critical intelligence of the area and the enemy's movements needed to be obtained—made the ascent to the top at least once.

As a teenager in the summer of 1968, long before I began to learn the intricate details about Rogers' activities around the lake, I climbed to the top of Black Mountain with some friends and cousins. I had been camping at the lake since 1964, and had long wanted to see the view from the top of this massive mountain, so foreboding-looking from the lake when its peak is darkened by heavy rain clouds (surely such a moment must have inspired its name). We slept overnight near the fire tower, and in the morning I explored the treeless, windswept summit. At the extreme northern edge, while I enjoyed the panoramic view, my eyes wandered for a second to the rock at my feet. What I saw was both unexpected and astounding: a carving, about a foot in length and quite weather-worn in appearance, reading "R ROGERS." Naturally I wanted to believe that it was the Real McCoy, though there was no way to prove it. I took photographs of it, and sent one to Adirondack Life magazine, along with a letter seeking from its readers any possible verification of the carving's authenticity, or any clues that might help point the way to either confirming or refuting same. Both the letter and the picture were published in the Winter 1973 issue, on page 46; but no reader ever replied to my enquiry.

In the summer of 1980, however, at a gathering of French and Indian War reenactors at Crown Point, I met a resident of the Black Mountain area who told me that he and many of his neighbors had long been aware of the "R ROGERS" carving, but cared not to publicize it. (A major coincidence of meeting this young man was that he was the son of the fire tower warden I had met that morning back in 1968). Since then, as far as I know, the carving remains as it has apparently long stood, unverified, its origin still a mystery.

2. Captain John Knox, describing Rogers' company in Halifax in July of 1757, in *An Historical Journal of the Campaigns in North America for the Years 1757, 1758, 1759 and 1760*, Toronto, 1914, p. 34.

3. Ibid., p. 34.

4. General Abercromby to Lord Loudoun, 2 January 1758, quoted in Loescher, I, footnote 250, p. 435.

5. *Memoirs of. . .the Captivity of John Gyles, Esq.* Boston, 1736, reprinted in America Begins, edited by Richard M. Dorson, Pantheon Books, New York, 1950, p. 221.

William-Henry the day before. We then marched directly to the place where we left our whale-boats the 7th of July, proceeding about twenty-five miles northward of Crown Point fort, on the west-side of Lake Champlain, where we all (excepting one man who strayed from us and returned) arrived safe the 24th. We embarked again in our boats, and steered down the lake toward St. John's. The 25th we proceeded twenty miles further, and about midnight discovered a schooner standing up the lake with a fair wind towards Crown Point; they passed us so swiftly that we could not possibly board her, as we intended.

The 26th we landed, and the Mohocks left us to join another party of theirs then out on a scout.

The 27th we got on a point, with a design to intercept the enemy's battoes, that might pass up and down the lake; but not discovering any, and our provisions growing short, we returned up the lake, and landed eight miles north of the fort at Crown Point, on the east-side of the lake.

The 29th in the morning we march to a village lying east of the fort, and in our way took prisoners, a man, his wife, and daughter, (a girl about fourteen years of age); with these prisoners we returned, and arrived safe at Fort William-Henry, Sept. 22, 1756.

> If the several previous dates given for incidents on this scout are correct, then Rogers could not have returned to Fort William Henry on September 22. The September 22 date is given in both the London and Dublin editions of the *Journals,* however.
>
> About this time (September 11) French Captain Louis-Antoine de Bougainville makes an interesting observation in his journal. He writes that,"They [the British] have little parties of Scottish Highlanders and a few Indians continually observing from the heights and the woods that surround Carillon. I suspect that they have established a flying camp behind the mountains north of the lake which supplies and shelters all these little parties." (Bougainville, p. 35) It is quite likely that these "Scottish Highlanders" described by Bougainville were actually Rogers' Rangers, or at least a mixed party of Rangers and Highlanders. The 42nd Highland Regiment had just recently arrived in North America, and probably would not have been assigned such critical scouting missions completely on their own. However, there is evidence that some of the Highlanders were working with the Rangers at the time. On August 29, 1756, Lord Loudoun wrote to the Duke of Cumberland, "I have given Orders to send Mr. Webb 250 of the Highland Regiment, with Rogers Company of Rangers of 50." (Pargellis, p. 233) This creates the possibility that by September 1756, at least some of the Highland Regiment was working out of Fort Edward and/or Fort William Henry, where the Rangers were stationed.

The man-prisoner, above-mentioned, upon examination, reported, "That he was born at Vaisac, in the province of Guienne in France: that he had been in Canada about fifteen years, and in the colonies service about six, and two years at Crown Point: that there were only 300 men at Crown Point, and those chiefly inhabitants of the adjacent villages; that there were 4000 men at Ticonderoga or Carillon, 1500 of which were regular troops, who had a sufficiency of all kinds of provisions: that he never was at Ticonderoga or at the advance guard, but heard there were only fifteen men at the latter: that the French had 600 Indians at Ticonderoga, and expected 600 more: that 1200 were arrived at Quebec for Carillon, which last 1800 were under the command of Mons. Scipio de la Masure: that they had a great quantity of cannon, mortars, shells, &c at Ticonderoga, but he did not know the number or quantity: that they expected the above re-inforcement in two or three days at Ticonderoga, having sent boats to Montreal to fetch them: that they understood by a letter that Oswego had fallen into their hands, but the news was not confirmed: that they had heard we intended to invest Carillon, but did not know what movements were intended on their side should we neglect it: that they had 150 battoes on Lake Champlain, which were kept at Carillon, thirty-five of which constantly plied between Montreal and that fortress: that Mons. Montcalm commanded at Frontiniac with 5000 men, but did not know whether these troops were regulars or provincials: that a great number of vessels had arrived at Canada with provisions and military stores: that they heard we had several ships in the river St. Lawrence: that Mons. le Conte de Levi commanded at Carillon, and came last May from France; and that, since the two last shallops or lighters (before-mentioned) were taken, they had augmented the number of men on board the large schooner in Lake Champlain from twelve to thirty."

Upon my return to the fort, I received orders from my Lord Loudoun to wait upon Col. Burton, of the 48th regiment, for instructions, he being then posted at Saratoga. By him I was ordered to return to my company at Fort William-Henry, and march them to the South Bay, thence east to the Wood Creek, then to cross it southerly, opposite to Saratoga, and return and make my report to him.

In this tour we apprehended four deserters from Otway's regiment, who were going to the enemy, and whom I sent back to Fort Edward, with a part of my detachment, under the command of Lieutenant Stark, and proceeded with the remainder to compleat my orders, after which I returned to Saratoga to make my report.

There I met my brother Capt. Richard Rogers with his company, he being ordered back from Mohock River, to join me with the remainder of the Stockbridge Indians; and I marched both companies to Fort Edward, where I was ordered to form an encampment. A part of the Indian company were sent out to the east-side of Lake Champlain to alarm the enemy at Ticonderoga, whilst I, with a detachment of my own, and Capt. Richard Rogers's company, was ordered on another party down Lake George, in whale-boats, and the remainder of the companies were employed in reconnoitering round the encampment, and also served as flankers to the parties that guarded provisions to Lake George. Capt. Jacob, who commanded the Indian party before-mentioned, returned two days before me with four French scalps, which they took opposite to Ticonderoga on the east-side.

Sept. 7, 1756. Agreeable to orders, I this day embarked on Lake George, with a party of fourteen men in a whale-boat, which we landed, and concealed the evening following, on the east shore, about four miles south of the French advance guard. Here I divided my party, taking seven men with me leaving the remainder in charge of Mr. Chalmer (a volunteer sent me by Sir John Sinclair) with orders, upon his discovering the enemy's boats going up the lake, &c. to make the best of his way with the intelligence to Fort William-Henry.

On September 8, William Hervey of the 44th Regiment notes another of Captain Jacob's Indian Company scouts in his journal: "This evening Captain Jacobs returned from his scout. He had been at the narrows of Tionderoga and brought away two scalps, one an officer's. His party brought advice that there were not then at that Fort half the number of tents that there were some time before when he was there." (Hervey, p. 39)

I was the 9th current within half a mile of Ticonderoga fort, where I endeavoured to reconnoitre the enemy's works and strength. They were engaged in raising the walls of the fort, and had erected a large block-house near the south-east corner of the fort, with ports in it for cannon. East from the block-house was a battery, which I imagined commanded the lake. I discovered five houses south of the fort close to the water-side, and 160 tents south-west of the fort, and twenty-seven battoes hauled upon the beach.

Next morning, with one private, I went to view the falls betwixt Lake Champlain and Lake George (where I had heard the explosion of several guns the evening before and had at that time sent Serjeant Henry to discover the reason of it) leaving the remainder of my party in charge of Mr. Gibbs, another volunteer, to wait our return. Sergeant Henry followed soon after me, and reported, "that the French were building a small fort at the head of the falls on the east-side of the lake; that he also discovered their guard to the westward, and imagined both consisted of 500 men." I returned, after finding the French were engaged in building a saw-mill at the lower end of the falls, and found my boats with provisions left, as I suppose, by Mr. Chalmer and his party, whom I waited for till seven o'clock next day; but he not returning, and I judging from their tracks that they were returned to Fort William-Henry, we likewise began our return, and arrived safe the 11th of September, where I found Mr. Chalmer and the party left with him, he having punctually obeyed the orders given him above. Upon my return, I communicated my observations upon the Lakes George and Champlain to my Lord Loudoun, giving him as just a description as I could of their situation.

September 24, General Abercrombie issued out orders, that three commissioned officers of the rangers, with 20 privates each, should reconnoitre the Wood Creek, South Bay and Ticonderoga; and these were alternately sent out, so that a continual scout was kept up for a considerable time.

October 22, 1756. The greatest part of the army was now at Fort-Edward, under the command of General Abercrombie, and Lord Loudoun arriving about this time with the remainder, it was generally expected that the army would cross the lake, and endeavour to reduce the French forts, notwithstanding the season was so far advanced; but his Lordship taking into consideration the probability that those lakes would freeze (which they generally do in the month of December) in which case no supplies could be had from, nor any communication kept up with Fort William-Henry; he determined to desist from this design, and contented himself with keeping the field till Mons. Montcalm retired to winter-quarters, and accordingly sought all opportunities to learn his situation and movements.

Agreeable to orders from his Lordship, I this day embarked in two whale-boats, with a party of twenty men, upon Lake George, with an intent to bring a prisoner from Ticonderoga. We passed the Narrows twenty miles from our embarkation, when Capt. Shephard (who was made a captive in August last and carried to Canada) hailed our boat; I knew his voice, and took him on board with three other men, one of whom was taken with him. He reported, that he left Canada fifteen days before. I went on my course till the 27th, towards Carillon, and landed that night on the west-side of the lake, concealed our boats, and travelled by land to within a mile of the fort. I kept spies out the day after to improve any opportunity that might offer, and the next day sent them still nearer, but to no good purpose: I at length discovered two men centries to the piquet guard of the French army, one of which was posted on the road that leads from the fort to the woods: I took five of my party, and marched directly down the road in the middle of the day, till we were challenged by the centry. I answered in French, signifying that we were friends; the centinel was thereby deceived, till I came close to him, when perceiving his mistake, in great surprize he called, Qui etes vous? I answered Rogers, and led him from his post in great haste, cutting his breeches and coat from him, that he might march with the greater ease and expedition. With this prisoner we arrived at Fort William-Henry, Oct. 31, 1756. Upon examination, he reported, "That he belonged to the regiment of Languedoc: that he left Brest last April was a twelve-month, and had served since at Lake Champlain, Crown Point, and Carillon, was last year with General Dieskaw in the battle at Fort William-Henry: that they lost in that engagement of regulars, Canadians, and Indians, a great number: and at Carillon were at this time mounted thirty-six pieces of cannon, viz. twelve eighteen pounders, fifteen twelve pounders, and nine eight pounders, that at Crown Point were eighteen pieces, the largest of which were eighteen pounders: that Mons. Montcalm's forces this year at Carillon were 3000 regulars, and 2000 Canadians and Indians: that Montcalm himself was drawn off with one battalion, and that the forces then in that neighbourhood consisted of five battalions and about 800 Canadians: that the Indians were all gone off, 200 of whom talked of returning to spend the winter at Carillon: that the advanced guard on the west-side above the falls were all drawn in, and that on the east consisted of 600 men, who were to decamp the 1st of November: that they had a camp of five battalions and sixty Canadians, about half a league from Carillon, and that the rest of the army were under the fort: that they had barracks sufficient for 500 men, which he understood were to quarter there: that they had one schooner and 200 battoes on Lake Champlain, and but five or six on Lake George: that Mons the Chevalier de Levi commanded in Mons Montcalm's absence, that the Canadians were commanded by Messieurs Le Corn and Columbie: that when Mons. Montcalm went off, he said he had done enough for this year, and would take Fort William Henry early in the spring; that the French had taken four of Captain Rogers's whale-boats in lake Champlain: that when he was taken prisoner, he imagined himself to be about a gun-shot and half from fort, and that the French camp was pretty healthy."

From this time we were constantly employed in patrolling the woods about Fort Edward till the 19th of November 1756, when I had his Lordship's orders to take another excursion down the Lake. Captain Abercrombie, Aid-de-camp and nephew to General Abercrombie, did me the honour to accompany me; but nothing material being in our power to effect, except taking a view of the fort and works of the enemy at Ticonderoga, we returned safe to Fort Edward the 25th in the evening.

About this time his Lordship drew off the main body of the troops from Fort Edward to be quartered at Albany and New York.

Both armies now being retired to winter-quarters, nothing material happened to the end of this year. The rangers were stationed at the Forts William-Henry and Edward, to which also two new companies of rangers were sent this fall, commanded by Captain Spikeman and Captain Hobbs, in one of which my brother James Rogers was appointed an Ensign.

These two companies were stationed at Fort William-Henry, mine and my brother Richard's at Fort Edward.

It should be noted that although their service to the British cause was essential, the Rangers did not always have the full acceptance or support of the Regular officers. Although recognized as being crucial to the war effort at this time, the long term goal of most high ranking British officers was to eventually replace them with specially trained light infantry, who although adept in Ranger tactics, would also have the discipline of Regular troops.

On August 20, 1756, Loudoun wrote to the Duke of Cumberland: "From the Indians, you see we have no support; some Rangers I shall be obliged to keep all the Winter, till I can make some of our own people fit for that Service. When I arrived here, I found there was a disposition in the Soldiers, to go out with Indians and Rangers, and that some of them were then out; I shall encourage it all I can, and if the parties that are now out, have success and escape, we shall soon get a knowledge of this Country, and be able to March with much more safety than at present; for I am convinced, that till we have every thing necessary, for carrying on the War here, within ourselves, Independent of Aid from this Country, we shall go on very slowly." (Pargellis, p. 224)

On October 22, 1756, the Duke of Cumberland wrote to Loudoun: "I hope that you will, in time, teach your Troops to go out upon Scouting Parties: for, 'till *Regular* Officers with men that they can trust, learn to beat the woods, & to act as *Irregulars*, you never will gain any certain Intelligence of the enemy, as I fear, by this time you are convinced that *Indian* Intelligence & that of *Rangers* is not at all to be depended upon." (Pargellis, p. 255-6) For an excellent account of the British Light Infantry in North America, see Lieutenant Colonel Ian M. McCulloch, CD. *"Within Ourselves . . ." The Development of British Light Infantry in North America During the Seven Years' War.*

On December 2, Cumberland again added: "I hope that you will, in time, teach your Troops to go out upon Scouting Parties: for, 'till Regular Officers with men that they can trust, learn to beat the woods, & to act as Irregulars, you never will gain any certain Intelligence of the Enemy & that of Rangers is not at all to be depended upon." (Pargellis, pp. 255-256)

Loudoun later wrote back to Cumberland, "I am afraid, I shall be blamed for the Ranging Companies; but as realy in effect we have no Indians, it is impossible for an Army to Act in this Country, without Rangers; and there ought to be a considerable body of them . . . for they will be able to deal with the Indians in their own way; and from all I can see, are much stronger and hardier fellows than the Indians . . . ." (Pargellis, p. 269)

It must be remembered that Rogers' companies were not the only Rangers in the British army, and that the different units came in varying levels of quality. Rogers' corps was generally perceived to be among the best, but they still shared in some of the criticism—criticism that was at times justified, and at other times based strictly on professional rivalry.

Rogers himself was generally excluded from this criticism. This is evidenced by a letter written by Captain James Abercrombie, a very active British Regular officer who served with Rogers on many occasions. See page 63 for the full text of this letter.

Captain Richard Rogers had leave go into New England for recruits to complete our two companies. He this winter waited upon the government of Boston, to obtain pay for our services in the winter 1755 before-mentioned, but could obtain none, notwithstanding Lord Loudoun, who was then at Boston, generously supported and enforced our solicitations with his interest.

January 15, 1757. Agreeable to orders from the commanding officer at Fort Edward, I this day marched with my own Lieutenant Mr. Stark, Ensign Page of Captain Richard Rogers's company, and fifty privates of said companies, to Fort William-Henry, where we were employed in providing provisions, snow-shoes, &c. till the 17th, when being joined by Captain Spikeman, Lieutenant Kennedy and Ensign Brewer of his company, and fourteen of their men, together with Ensign James Rogers, and fourteen men of Captain Hobbs's company, and Mr. Baker, a volunteer of the 44th regiment of foot, we began our march on the ice down Lake George, and at night encamped on the east-side of the First Narrows. The next morning, finding that some of the detachment had hurt themselves in the march the day before, as many were dismissed to return to the fort, as reduced our party to seventy-four men, officers included.

The 18th we marched twelve miles down the lake, and encamped on the west-side of it.

The 19th we marched three miles from our encampment further down the lake, and then took the land, and, upon snow-shoes, travelled northwest about eight miles from our landing, and three from the lake, where we encamped.

The 20th we marched north-by-east the whole day, and at night encamped on the western side, opposite to, and about three miles distant from lake Champlain.

The 21st we marched east, till we came to the lake, about mid-way between Crown Point and Ticonderoga, and immediately discovered a sled going from the latter to the former. I ordered Lieutenant Stark, with twenty men to head the sled, while I, with a party, marched the other way to prevent its retreating back again, leaving Captain Spikeman in the center with the remainder. I soon discovered eight or ten sleds more following down the lake, and endeavoured to give Mr. Stark intelligence of it before he sallied on the lake and discovered himself to them, but could not. They all hastily returned towards Ticonderoga. We pursued them, and took seven prisoners, three sleds, and six horses; the remainder made their escape. We examined the captives separately, who reported, "That 200 Canadians and 45 Indians were just arrived at Ticonderoga, and were to be reinforced that evening, or next morning, by fifty Indians more from Crown Point: that there were 600 regular troops at that fortress, and 350 at Ticonderoga, were they soon expected a large number of troops, who in the spring were to besiege our forts: that they had large magazines of provisions in their forts, and that the above-mentioned party were well equipped, and in a condition to march upon any emergency at the least notice, and were designed soon to way-lay and distress our convoys between our forts."

From this account of things, and knowing that those who escaped would give early notice of us at Ticonderoga, I concluded it best to return; and ordered the party, with the utmost expedition, to march to the fires we had kindled the night before, and prepare for a battle, if it should be a offered, by drying our guns, it being a rainy day, which we effected; and then marched in a single file, myself and Lieutenant Kennedy in the front, Lieutenant Stark in the rear, and Captain Spikeman in the center, Ensigns Page and Rogers were between the front and center, and Ensign Brewer between the center and rear, Serjeant Walker having the command of a rear-guard.

> Contrary to his usual practice, Rogers retreated by the same route that he came by. Ranger John Shute later stated that an officers' council recommended a different route but Rogers overruled them. (Loescher, Volume I, p. 340). There was some justification for Rogers' action, however. By returning to the fires of the night before, the Rangers were able to dry their guns so that they would be serviceable in the rainy weather. The snow was also very deep—four feet on the level one source reported—and by following their old tracks they were able to move much more quickly than if they had to break a new trail. This is a prime example of the closing statement to Rogers' Ranging Rules, where he warns, "Such in general are the rules to be observed in the Ranging service; there are, however, a thousand occurrences and circumstances which may happen, that will make it necessary, in some measure, to depart from them, and to put other arts and stratagems in practice; and which cases every man's reason and judgment must be his guide, according to the particular situation and nature of things . . . ."

In this manner we advanced half a mile, or thereabouts, over broken ground, when passing a valley of about fifteen rods breadth, the front having reached the summit of a hill on the west-side of it; the enemy, who had here drawn up in the form of a half-moon, with a design, as we supposed, to surround us, saluted us with a volley of about 200 shot, at the distance of about five yards from the nearest or front, and thirty from the rear of their party. This fire was about two o'clock in the afternoon, and proved fatal to Lieutenant Kennedy, and Mr. Gardner, a volunteer in my company, and wounded me and several others; myself, however, but slightly in the head. We immediately returned their fire. I then ordered my men to the opposite hill, where I supposed Lieutenant Stark and Ensign Brewer had made a stand with forty men to cover us, in case we were obliged to retreat. We were closely pursued, and Capt. Spikeman, with several of the party, were killed, and others made prisoners. My people, however, beat them back by a brisk fire from the hill, which gave us an opportunity to ascend, and post ourselves to advantage. After which I ordered Lieutenant Stark and Mr. Baker in the center, with Ensign Rogers; Serjeants Walter and Phillips, with a party, being a reserve, to prevent our being flanked, and watch the motions of the enemy. Soon after we had thus formed ourselves for battle, the enemy attempted to flank us on the right, but the above reserve bravely attacked them, and giving them the first fire very briskly, it stopped several from retreating to the main body. The enemy then pushed us closely in the front; but having the advantage of the ground, and being sheltered by large trees, we maintained a continual fire upon them, which killed several, and obliged the rest to retire to their main body. They then attempted to flank us again, but were again met by our reserved party, and repulsed. Mr. Baker about this time was killed. We maintained a pretty constant fire on both sides, till the darkness prevented our seeing each other, and about sun-set I received a ball thro' my hand and wrist, which disabled me from loading my gun. I however found means to keep my people from being intimidated by this accident; they gallantly kept their advantageous situation, till the fire ceased on both sides. The enemy, during the action, used many arts and stratagems to induce us to submit, sometimes threatening us with severity if we refused, assuring us that they every moment expected a large reinforcement, which should cut us to pieces without mercy: at other times flattering and cajoling us, declaring it was a pity so many brave men should be lost; that we should, upon our surrender, be treated with the greatest compassion and kindness; calling me by name, they gave me the strongest assurances of their esteem and friendship that words could do; but no one being dismayed by their menaces, or flattered by fair promises, we told them our numbers were sufficient, and that we were determined to keep our ground as long as there were two left to stand by each other.

After the action, in which we had a great number so severely wounded that they could not travel without assistance, and our ammunition being nearly expended, and considering that we were near to Ticonderoga, from whence the enemy might easily make a descent, and overpower us by numbers, I thought it expedient to take the advantage of the night to retreat, and gave orders accordingly; and the next morning arrived at Lake George, about six miles south of the French advanced guard, from whence I dispatched Lieutenant Stark with two men to Fort William Henry, to procure conveyances for our wounded men thither; and the next morning we were met by a party of fifteen men and a sled, under the command of Lieutenant Buckley, of Hobbs's company of Rangers, at the first narrows at Lake George. Our whole party, which now consisted of only forty-eight effective, and six wounded men, arrived at Fort William Henry the same evening, being the 23d of January 1757.

The nearest computation we could make of the number which attacked us, was, that it consisted of about 250 French and Indians; and we afterwards had an account from the enemy, that their loss in this action, of those killed, and who afterwards died of their wounds, amounted to 116 men.

Bougainville's account from his journal gives the French perspective on this same action: "M. de Lusignan, who commands there, [Ticonderoga] had sent off several sleighs escorted by a sergeant and fifteen men to go and get certain provisions from St. Frederic. At about halfway between the two forts an English detachment dashed out of the woods in four places, cut off our little convoy, took three sleighs and seven soldiers. The rest took off as fast as their legs would carry them for Carillon, and M. de Lusignan at once sent off one hundred men of the regulars and the colony troops, along with a few Indians and Canadian volunteers under the orders of M. de Basserode, captain of Languedoc, and M. d'Astrel, lieutenant in the same regiment. M. de La Granville, captain in the regiment of La Reine asked leave to go along as a volunteer. M. de Langlade, half-pay ensign of La Marine, was at the head of the Indians, almost all Ottawas. The detachment went to lay an ambush on the road of the English, whose advance guard appeared three hours after midday. After one discharge of musketry, which did not have the effect that one would expect, the rain which had been falling all day having wet the guns, our troops pounced upon the enemy with the bayonet and overwhelmed them. Their rear guard gained a height which overlooked that upon which our people were. They shot it out until nightfall, when the English seized the opportunity to retire in disorder, leaving food, snowshoes and forty-two dead, three of them officers, on the field of battle. Our people made eight prisoners and retook four of the seven they had taken that morning. They [the English] had killed the other three. We lost nine soldiers, one Indian and a Canadian killed in the action and twenty-seven wounded, three of whom died from their wounds. Our detachment passed the night on the field of battle and received a reinforcement of twenty-five men and a convoy of food and munitions, a surgeon and a chaplain. Our soldiers, who had no snowshoes, fought at a disadvantage, floundering in the snow up to their knees. M. de Basserode was wounded in the leg. Five commissary clerks who volunteered for the action behaved wonderfully. One of them got a musket ball through his throat and died the next day. In Canada everyone is a soldier, but every soldier is not equally brave."

The final portion of Bougainville's account is especially interesting, as it also gives us a look at how the French perceived Rogers' Rangers: "The English detachment consisted of seventy-three men, six of them officers, and ten sergeants, commanded by Robert Rogers, captain of one of the four companies of forest runners that the English call 'Rangers,' whose mission is to go scouting in the woods. The companies consist of fifty men, with three officers and four sergeants. Two are in garrison on a little island in the Hudson River, opposite Fort Lydius, or Edward. The other two in a little stockaded fort which is near the ditch of Fort George, or William Henry, to the south of this fort. The success of this affair cannot excuse M. de Lusignan from having weakened his garrison considerably and thus running the risk of being taken by a surprise attack." (Bougainville, pp. 81-82)

Both the officers and soldiers I had the honour to command, who survived the first onset, behaved with the most undaunted bravery and resolution, and seemed to vie with each other in their respective stations who should excel.

The following is the RETURN which was made of the Killed, Wounded, and Missing, in the above action.

Captain Rogers's Company.

Captain Robert Rogers, wounded
Mr. Baker, Volunteer, killed
Mr. Gardner, Volunteer, killed
Thomas Henson, killed
Serjeant Martin, wounded
Thomas Burnside, wounded
Serjeant Henry, missing
William Morris, missing
John Morrison missing

Sergeant Joshua Martin had an interesting history with the Rangers. Like Rogers, he first served in the scouting company of Blanchard's Provincial Regiment. On August 4, 1756, he enlisted in Richard Rogers' Ranging Company. He was seriously injured in this battle, suffering a shattered hip and a stomach wound. Still, he managed to catch up to the rest of the retreating Rangers, and eventually recovered. It appears that his promotion to sergeant actually came after the fight, on February 24, perhaps in recognition of his heroism. His Company was disbanded as part of the capitulation of Fort William Henry on August 9, 1757. On January 10, 1758, Rogers recommended him as second lieutenant in William Stark's Company, but Loudoun did not approve it because he was part of the capitulation. In 1759, after Amherst assumed command and disavowed the capitulation because of the massacre, Martin rejoined the Rangers as an ensign in Rogers' Own Company. He later served as an American officer during the Revolution. (Loescher, Volume III, p. 71)

Captain Richard Rogers's Company

Joseph Stephens, killed
Benjamin Woodall, missing
David Kemble, missing
Ensign Caleb Page, killed
David Page, wounded

Captain Hobbs's Company

Serjeant Jon. Howard, killed
Phineas Kemp, killed
John Edmonds, killed
Thomas Farmer, killed
Emanuel Lapartaquer, killed

Captain Spikeman's Company

Capt. Spikeman, killed
Lieut. Kennedy, killed
Robert Avery, killed
Thomas Brown, missing
Samuel Fisk, killed
Serjeant Moore, wounded
John Cahall, wounded

Total, 14 killed, 6 missing, 6 wounded

N.B. Those returned as missing, we afterwards found had been taken prisoner by the enemy.

Thomas Brown, a sixteen year old Ranger private from Massachusetts, was captured in the aftermath of this battle, and was held until November 1758. In 1760, he published a very vivid narrative of his captivity. The portion reprinted here deals with just the battle itself.

"I was born in Charlestown, near Boston, in New England, in 1740, and was apprenticed by my father to Mr. Mark White of Acton. In May, 1756, I enlisted in Major Rogers' Corps of Rangers, in the company commanded by Captain Spikeman. We marched to Albany, where we arrived the first of August, and from there to Fort Edward. I was out on several scouting patrols, on one of which I killed an Indian.

"On the eighteenth of January, 1757, we marched on a patrol from Fort William Henry. Major Rogers himself headed us. All of us were volunteers. Coming to the road leading from Ticonderoga to Crown Point, we saw about fifty sleighs on Lake Champlain, which was frozen over. The major thought it proper to attack them and ordered us all—about sixty in number—to lie in ambush. When they were close enough we were ordered to pursue them.

"I happened to be near the major when he took the first prisoner, a Frenchman. I singled one out, too, and followed him; some fled one way and some another, but I soon caught up with my man and took him prisoner. We captured seven in all—the rest escaped, some to Crown Point and some to Ticonderoga, where they had come from. When we had brought the prisoners to land, the major questioned them. They informed him that there were thirty-five Indians and five-hundred regulars at Ticonderoga.

"It was a rainy day, so we made a fire and dried our guns. The major thought it best to return to Fort William Henry by the same path we had come, as the snow was very deep. We marched in Indian file and kept the prisoners in the rear, in case we should be attacked.

"We went on in this order about a mile and a half. As we were going up a hill, and the center of our line was at the top, a party of about four hundred French and thirty or forty Indians opened fire on us before we had even seen them. The major ordered us to advance.

"At the first volley from the enemy I received a wound through the body. When I was able, I went to the rear, to the prisoner I had taken on the lake. I knocked him on the head and killed him—we did not want him to give information to the enemy.

"As I was going to take shelter behind a large rock, an Indian started up from the other side of it. I threw myself backward into the snow. It was very deep and I sank so low that I broke my snowshoes. In a moment I had pulled 'em off, but I was obliged to let my shoes go with them. One Indian threw his tomahawk at me, and another was just about to seize me, but I was lucky enough to escape and get to the center of our men.

"Hiding behind a large pine, I loaded and fired at every opportunity. After I had discharged my gun six or seven times, a ball came and cut it off just at the lock. About half an hour later, I received a shot in my knee. I crawled to the rear again and, as I was turning about, received a shot in my shoulder.

"The engagement lasted, as near as I could guess, five and one-half hours and, as I learned afterward, we killed more of the enemy than there were of us. By this time it had grown dark and the firing ceased on both sides. Taking advantage of the night, the major escaped with the well men without telling the wounded his plans, so they could not inform the enemy, who might pursue him before he was out of their reach.

"Captain Spikeman, a man named Baker, and myself, all very badly wounded, had made a small fire. After sitting about it for half an hour, we looked round and could not see any of our men. Captain Spikeman called to Major Rogers but received no answer, except from the enemy at some distance. We concluded our people had fled. All our hope of escape vanished now. We were so badly wounded that we could not travel; I could just barely walk, the others could scarcely move. We decided to surrender to the French.

"Just as we came to this decision I saw an Indian coming towards us over a small stream that separated us from the enemy. I crawled away from the fire so that I could not be seen, though I could see what happened there.

"The Indian came to Captain Spikeman, who was not able to resist, and stripped him and scalped him alive. Baker, who was lying by the captain, pulled out his knife to stab himself. But the Indian prevented him and carried him away.

"Seeing this frightful tragedy, I made up my mind to crawl into the woods if possible and die there of my wounds. But I was not far from Captain Spikeman and he saw me.

"For God's sake," he begged me, "give me a tomahawk so I can put an end to my life!"

"I refused him, and exhorted him as well as I could to pray, as he could not live many minutes in that deplorable condition on the frozen ground, covered with snow. He asked me to let his wife know—if I lived to get home—the dreadful death he died.

"I traveled on as well as I could. As I was creeping along, I found one of our people dead. I pulled off his stockings—he had no shoes—and put them on my own legs.

"By this time the enemy had made a fire and had a large number of sentries out on the Rangers' path. I was obliged to creep completely round them before I could get into the path again. Just before I came to it I saw a Frenchman behind a tree. He was within ten yards of me, but the fire was shining right on him and prevented him from seeing me. About every quarter of an hour they cried out in French, "All is well!" While the man that was so near me was calling out, I took the opportunity to creep away, so that he did not hear me and I got back into our path.

"I had no shoes, and the snow and cold put my feet into such pain that I soon could go on no longer. I sat down by a brook and wrapped my feet in my blanket. But my body became very cold from sitting still. I got up and crawled along in this miserable condition the rest of the night.

"The next day, about eleven o'clock, I heard the shouts of Indians behind me and I supposed they had seen me. Within a few minutes four of them came running towards me. I threw off my blanket, and fear and dread quickened my pace for a while. But I had lost so much blood from my wounds that my strength soon gave out.

"When the Indians were within ten or fifteen yards they cocked their guns and called me to stop. I refused, hoping they would fire and kill me on the spot; I preferred this to the terrible death Captain Spikeman had died.

"The savages soon came up with me, but instead of scalping me they took me by the neck and kissed me. On searching my pockets they found some money. They were so fond of it that they almost killed me in trying to see who could get the most. Then they took some dry leaves and put them into my wounds, and turned about and ordered me to follow them." (Thomas Brown, pp. 62-65 in Dover Press edition; pp. 3-9 in Ye Galleon Press edition)

Having laid this return before Major Sparks, commanding officer at Fort Edward, he transmitted the same to the General; and the 30th of January following, I wrote to Capt. James Abercrombie, then at Albany, recommending such officers as I thought most deserving, to fill up the vacancies occasioned by our late action, among whom were Lieutenant Stark to be Captain of Spikeman's company, and Serjeant Joshua Martin to be Ensign in Captain Richard Rogers's company; and I also mentioned several things in favor of the Rangers.

When word of this battle reached Albany, Hospital Matron Charlotte Brown made the following entry in her journal, "News came from the Lake that Capt. Rogers had ingaged with a Party of French and was much wounded and had lost 20 of his Men but he had taken 7 Prisoners and killed them all and retreated." (Charlotte Brown, p. 197)

In consequence of which I received the following answer.

Dear Sir,

Albany, Feb. 6, 1757.

"The General received your letter that was sent by Major Sparks, and returns you and your men thanks for their behaviour, and has recommended both you and them strongly to my Lord Loudoun, as also that they have payment for the prisoners they took. Upon receiving an account of your skirmish we sent an express to Boston, and, by the said opportunity, recommended, for Spikeman's company, your brother* for a Lieutenant. We expect the express back in a day or two, by whom I dare say, we shall have my Lord's approbation of the Rangers. Please to send me the names of the officers you would recommend for your own company, and also to fill up the vacancies in the others; as I am certain you have the good of the service at heart, your recommendation will be paid great regard to. I yesterday received your's of the 30th of January. You cannot imagine how all ranks of people here are pleased with your conduct, and your mens behavior; for my part, it is no more than I expected: I was so pleased with their appearance when I was out with them, that I took it for granted they would behave well whenever they met the enemy. When I returned I reported them as such, am glad they have answered my expectation.

I am heartily sorry for Spikeman and Kennedy, who I imagined would have turned out well, as likewise for the men you have lost; but it is impossible to play at bowls without meeting with rubs.

> "Rubs were any unevenness of the ground hindering (in the game of bowling) the motion of a bowl and hence any obstruction or difficulty." (Cuneo, *Notes,* pp. 42-43)

We must try to revenge the loss of them. There is few people that will believe it; but upon honour, I could be glad to have been with you, that I might have learned the manner of fighting in this country. The chance of being shot is all stuff, and King William's opinion and principle is much the best for a soldier, viz. 'that every bullet has its billet,' and that 'it is allotted how every man shall die;' and so that I am certain that every one will agree, that it is better to die with a reputation of a brave man, fighting for his country in a good cause, than either shamefully running away to preserve one's life, or lingering out an old age, and dying in one's bed, without having done his country or his King any service.

The histories of this country, particularly, are full of the unheard-of cruelties committed by the French, and the Indians, by their instigation, which I think every brave man ought to do his utmost to humble that haughty nation, or reduce their bounds of conquest in this country to a narrow limit. As soon as General Abercrombie receives my Lord's instructions in regard to the Rangers, I shall send you notice of it; in the interim, I hope you'll get the better of your wound. If I can be of any service to you or your men as long as they continue to behave so well, you may command

Your most humble servant,
To Capt. James Abercrombie,
Robert Rogers. Aid de Camp"

My wound growing worse, I was obliged to repair to Albany for better assistance, and there received the following instructions from General Abercrombie, viz.

Instructions for Capt. ROBERT ROGERS.

"His Excellency the Earl of Loudoun having given authority to me to augment the company of Rangers under your command, to one hundred men each, viz.

One captain,	upon an English pay;
Two Lieutenants,	" " " "
One Ensign,	" " " "

Four Serjeants at 4s. each, New York currency; 100 private men, at 2s. and 6d. each ditto per day; And whereas there are some private men of your company serving at present upon higher pay than the above establishment, you are at liberty to dis-

*James Rogers.

charge them, in case they refuse to serve at the said establishment, as soon as you have other men to replace them. If your men agree to remain with you and serve upon the above establishment, you may assure them they will be taken notice of, and be first provided for; each man to be allowed ten dollars bounty-money, and to find their own cloaths, arms, and blankets, and to sign a paper subjecting themselves to the rules and articles of war, and to serve during the war. You are to inlist no vagrants, but such as you and your officers are acquainted with, and who are every way qualified for the duty of Rangers; and you and your officers are to use your best endeavours to complete your companies as soon as possible, and bring them to Fort Edward.

James Abercrombie,
Major General."

About this time I again wrote to his Lordship, earnestly soliciting his friendly interposition and assistance, to obtain from the government here, an order for payment of what was due to me and my men, for our respective services during the winter 1755; but if that could not be obtained, that he would be pleased to direct me what method to take for the recovery thereof. Whereto his Lordship replied, that as these services were antecedent to his command here, it was not in his power to reward them. General Amherst, afterwards, on a like application, gave me much the same answer.

These applications not being attended with any success, and suits of law being afterwards commenced against me, by, and on behalf of those who served under me in that campaign, and verdicts obtained in their favour, I was not only obliged to answer their several demands, to the amount of 828 pounds, 3 shillings, 3 pence sterling, which I paid out of my private fortune, but also a considerable sum for law-charges, exclusive of what I ought to have received for my own services during that severe season. But for all of which I have not at any time since received one shilling consideration.

In the same letter I likewise informed his Lordship of the death of Capt. Hobbs of the Rangers who died a few days before, and recommended Lieutenant Bulkley of the same company, as a proper person to succeed him in that command.

March 5, I was taken ill with the small-pox, and not able to leave my room till the 15th of April following, during which time my officers were recruiting, agreeable to his Lordship's instructions. Not long after I received the following letter from Capt. Abercrombie.

Sir, *New York, April 22*, 1757.

"As there is another ranging company sent up to Albany, with orders to proceed to the forts, you will acquaint Colonel Gage, that it is my Lord Loudoun's orders, that the two companies at Fort William-Henry, and your own from Fort Edward, come down immediately to Albany, to be ready to embark for this place. Shew this letter to Colonel Gage, that he may acquaint Colonel Monro of his Lordship's orders, and that quarters may be provided for your companies in the houses about Albany. You will take particular care that the companies have provided themselves with all necessaries, and see that they are complete and good men. Since his Lordship has put it in your charge, I hope you will be very diligent in executing the trust, for, upon a review of the men, if any are found insufficient for the service, the blame will be laid upon you. If the officers of this ranging company that is gone up, are not acquainted with the woods about Fort William-Henry, your brother must send some officers and men of his company along with them, to let them know the different scouts.

I am, Sir,
Your most humble servant,
James Abercrombie,
Aid de Camp."

To Capt.
Robert Rogers
at Albany

Although specific information about the arms, equipment, and dress of the Rangers is elusive, occasionally small pieces of the puzzle are found. In the General Orders of 1757, the following order was issued on July 5, 1757, from Fort Edward: "The Men Belonging to ye Provensial Regts. who are Appointed to Do ye Duty of Rangers are to Be Emmediately Supplyd with Leather Shot Bags & Powder Horns to Carry their Ammunition in" (General Orders of 1757, p. 39)

There is a similar notation in the orderly book of Lyman's Connecticut Regiment for July 5: "The Men Belonging to the Provensial Regt who are appointed to Do the Duty of Rangers are to Be Immediately Supplyd with Leather Shot Bags & Powder Horns to." (Lyman, p. 31)

There is also evidence that the Rangers were at times allowed to practice their marksmanship skills: "The Ranging Companys Being to Fire at a Mark Between ye Hours of 4 & 6 oClock . . . ." (General Orders of 1757, p. 58, entry from Fort Edward, July 28, 1757).

Capt. Richard Rogers, with his own, and the new company of Rangers before-mentioned, which was raised in the Jersies, and commanded by Capt. Burgin, being left at Fort William-Henry, my own company from Fort-Edward, and Capt. Stark's and Capt. Bulkeley's from Fort William-Henry, agreeable to the above instructions, marched down to Albany, and from thence embarked for New York, where we were joined by another new-raised company of Rangers, under the command of Capt. Shephard from New Hampshire, and after some small stay there, re-embarked on board a transport, and left Sandy Hook on the 20th of June, with a fleet of near an hundred sail, bound to Halifax, where we soon arrived, and, according to orders, I encamped on the Dartmouth side of the harbour, while the army lay encamped on the Halifax-side. The Rangers were here employed in various services.

Captain John Knox gives another one of the rare descriptions of the Rangers in his journal entry for July 12-13, 1757: "A body of rangers, under the command of Captain Rogers, who arrived with the other troops from the southward, march out every day to scour the country; these light troops have, at present, no particular uniform, only they wear their cloaths short, and are armed with a firelock, tomahock, or small hatchet, and a scalping knife; a bullock's horn full of powder hangs under their right arm, by a belt from the left shoulder; a leathern, or seal's skin bag, buckled round their waist, which hangs down before, contains bullets, and a smaller shot, of the size of full grown peas: six or seven of which, with a ball, they generally load; their Officers usually carry a small compass fixed in the bottoms of their powder-horns, by which to direct them, when they happen to lose themselves in the woods." (Knox, Volume I, p. 34)

On July 3d, by orders, I commanded a party to Lawrence Town, and from thence to Schitzcook; some were left there to cut and make up hay in the meadows, for the horses intended to be used in an expedition to Louisbourg; others covered the haymakers, and others were dispatched on scouts, to make discoveries; in one of which two deserters from the 45th regiment were seized and brought in.

About the latter end of this month forty Rangers were sent across the isthmus of Nova Scotia, to the settlements on the Bay of Fundy, and a party down to the north-west arm, to scour the woods for deserters, &c. and brought in several, both from the army and navy.

About this time Admiral Holbourn arrived with a fleet from England, with several regiments of regular troops on board, which were landed, and likewise encamped at Halifax, upon which all scouting parties were called in; but certain intelligence being received that a French fleet of superior force had actually arrived at Louisbourg, the intended expedition against that place was laid aside, and thereupon the Rangers were remanded back to the western frontiers.

GARY ZABOLY
©1998

Montcalm Masses His Indians

In LATE JULY 1757 General the Marquis de Montcalm left Fort Carillon with his army of about six thousand French regulars, Canadian militia, and *coureurs de bois*, along with nearly two thousand Indians representing some nineteen different tribes. Their goal: besiege and capture the enemy's Fort William Henry, at the head of Lake George. The time was ideal for such a move, since Lord Loudoun had taken away the greater part of the British forces garrisoning northern New York to lay siege to Louisbourg, on Cape Breton Island. Among the forces removed were the Ranger companies captained by Robert Rogers, John Stark and Charles Bulkeley, the latter two having been stationed at Fort William Henry. In their absence the company of Robert's brother, Richard, had moved north from Rogers' Island to take over scouting duties at the fort. On June 22, however, Captain Richard Rogers died at the fort after a bout with smallpox.[1]

Montcalm's force eventually established its camp about three quarters of a mile west of Fort William Henry on August 3, and began advancing its saps and batteries. His Canadians and Indians were sent to occupy the rising ground south of the fort, thus covering the road leading to Fort Edward.

On August 7, after days and nights of heavy bombardment, the French sent into the fort a red flag of truce to induce Lieutenant Colonel George Monro to surrender. Montcalm had a trump card in his possession: a letter his Canadians and Indians had taken from the vest of a Connecticut ranger sergeant they had killed, written by General Daniel Webb at Fort Edward. In it Webb advised Monro that, since sufficient British and Provincial reinforcements could not be sent to his relief any time soon, he ought to consider surrendering Fort William Henry on the best terms possible.[2]

Montcalm's emissary was Captain Louis Antoine de Bougainville. He was taken blindfolded into the fort itself, and then escorted to the entrenched camp, on a hill 500 yards southeast of the fort. There Colonel Monro read Webb's letter, and soon comprehended that the Fates had decided against him.

While this was going on, the French-allied Indians made a spectacular display of themselves in full view of the English fort. An anonymous garrison member recorded in his diary, "During this interval the Enemy made a Shew of all their Indians, about 1200, on a Rising Ground about 250 yards distance bearing S:W: [while] their Engineers reconitred Our old Camp Ground which was afterwards a great Advantage to them."[3]

This display of Montcalm's Native American mercenaries was meant to further undermine the morale of the garrison, by suggesting the latter's possible fate if they persisted in their defiance and forced the French to take the fort by breach and storm. Well did the British remember what Indians had done to the wounded and other survivors of Braddock's field in 1755 and at Fort Ontario in 1756. It was obvious psychological warfare on Montcalm's part, at the very moment of the delivery of Webb's letter to Monro, even if Montcalm did not intend to have his Indians commit such atrocities here.

Never before had so many different tribes sent so many of their warriors to fight alongside the French. In the illustration a number of these tribes are represented. In left foreground, holding a war-club on one shoulder and a buffalo hide shield with his left arm, is an Iowa Indian, with whom no French interpreter could speak, so far to the west did this tribe reside. To the right of him stands a heavily tattooed Fox warrior, this figure based on a mid-eighteenth century drawing; both he and the Iowa are armed with native weapons, not firearms. Right behind them are two Chippewas, one with a feather through his nose and a body decorated with streaks of white clay, the other's body covered with charcoal mixed with grease except for a white circle around each eye.

A shirt-wearing Abenaki of St. Francis raises his musket in salute just behind a Pottawattomie war chief in a buffalo horn headdress with long red-dyed hair falling behind.

Behind the Chippewas is a Micmac chief, far removed from his Nova Scotia homeland. His long hair is wrapped in a turban, and he waves a French spontoon. Just above the Micmac's arm is a sachem of the Delawares, with metal headband sporting a crest of feathers.

Warriors and chiefs from other tribes—Nipissings, Algonkins, Iroquois, Hurons, Amalecites, Tete de Boule, Ottawas, Menominee, Miami,

Winnebago and Sauks——comprise the rest of the crowd.

Montcalm, in right center, returns their salute, his general's coat worn over a metal cuirass, which the engineer officer to the right of him also wears. (Armor in eighteenth-century North America, including helmets, was often worn by artillerymen and engineers, and sometimes by general officers making tours of lines and siegeworks).

Just behind Montcalm is a young orderly, dressed in a hussar's outfit of pelisse, dolman and busby. This attire was frequently worn by orderlies of both sides in the Seven Years' War, especially in Europe. Two regular officers ride in the orderly's wake. Although Montcalm did not bring horses with his army to Fort William Henry, on the first day of the siege his Indians had made him a gift of 50 British mounts "which the enemy had not had time to put in safety [and which] were roving on the lowlands situated in the neighborhood of the fort."[4] Although French engineers did make their survey of this area during the truce, it is not known if Montcalm accompanied them; his inclusion here is hypothetical.

At right stand two of the three Jesuit priests with the expedition who ostensibly "led" the Mission Indian contingent. With them is an Abenaki war captain; behind them stand two *coureur de bois* officers, one completely attired *a la sauvage*.

The land for some distance immediately around the fort had been cleared the year before. Many trees still lay where they had been chopped down. Three large gardens were kept outside the fort walls. A stretch of swampy ground and streams sits between this hill and the fort. Just beyond the southeast bastion is a hornwork. Within the fort itself, the roofs—viz., the shingles— had been taken off the barracks by the garrison on August 4 to prevent them from catching fire from French hot shot. At far right is another hill, upon which the English actually had most of their force positioned during the siege (space did not allow the inclusion of the entrenched camp they occupied and defended). In far left background is the French battery and camp, and in center background lies Lake George.

Montcalm's flag of truce, and Webb's letter, did not have the immediate effect the Marquis had thought it would. The siege continued for another two days. By August 9 the French battery had moved into the large garden to the left (west) of the fort, which made the British position untenable; thus the surrender.

As things turned out, even the formal surrender of the British garrison could not restrain the Indians from reaping bloody compensation for their services rendered during the campaign. Some historians have attempted to minimize or even dismiss the "massacre" that resulted; but massacre it truly was, even if its numbers did not fall into the hundreds as folklore remembers it. Richard Rogers's scalp, dug up and removed by the Indians from his grave, had its posthumous retribution by igniting a smallpox epidemic among the Pottawattomies.

G.Z.

1. Loescher, Vol. I, p. 175.
2. "A Message to Fort William Henry: Drama of Siege and Indian Savagery," Chapter 6 in Wilbur R. Jacobs, *Dispossessing the American Indian*, Charles Scribners' Sons, New York, 1972, pp. 68-74.
3. "A Journal Kept During the Siege of Fort William Henry, August 1757," *Proceedings of the American Philosophical Society* 37, 1898, p. 148.
4. Father Pierre Roubaud's letter of October 21, 1757, in *The Jesuit Relations & Allied Documents*, Vol. LXX, 1747-1764, Cleveland, 1900, p. 153.

Great numbers of the Rangers having been carried off this summer by the small-pox, I sent several of my officers by his Lordships command, to recruit in New Hampshire, and the Massachusetts provinces, with orders to join me at Albany. I afterwards embarked with the Rangers under my command, on board the fleet which carried the regular troops to New York, and from thence proceeded in small vessels up Hudson's River to Albany, where I was soon after joined by the new-raised recruits.

I then proceeded to Fort Edward, which was the only remaining cover to the northern frontiers of New York, and the more eastern provinces, Fort William-Henry* having been taken by the French, under the command of Mons. Montcalm, the August before. General Webb was then commanding officer at Fort Edward, and by his orders we were continually employed in patrolling the woods between this fort and Ticonderoga.

> On September 21, 1757, Provincial soldier Jonathan French recorded Rogers' return to Fort Edward in his journal: "Maj. Rogers arrived from Albany with 400 Rangers who had been at Halifax with His Excelency the Earl of Lowden" (French, p. 17)
>
> Thomas Mante comments on one of the abovementioned scouting missions. "Captain Rogers was then dispatched on a scout to Ticonderoga, with orders to take some prisoners. Having succeeded, he then returned with them to Fort Edward. The account given by these prisoners was, that the garrison of Ticonderoga consisted of about three hundred and fifty regulars; and that of Crown-Point of about one hundred and fifty. The weakness of these posts naturally suggested the propriety of hazarding an attempt on the first by an escalade; but, after many preparations for that purpose, the project was abandoned." (Mante, p. 104)

In one of these parties, my Lord Howe did us the honour to accompany us, being fond, as he expressed himself, to learn our method of marching, ambushing, retreating, &c. and, upon our return, expressed his good opinion of us very generously.

> George Augustus, Lord Viscount Howe, at 33, was one of the most competent officers in the British Army. He was the eldest son of the second Lord Viscount Howe, and succeeded to the title upon his father's death in 1735. His brother William also served in the army, while another brother Richard, became a navy admiral. Howe came to America in 1757 as the colonel of the 60th (Royal American) Regiment, and in September was appointed colonel of the 55th Regiment. On December 29, he was made brigadier general in America. Howe respected his officers and men, and was genuinely admired by them. He was responsible for many modifications in the Regular soldiers' dress and tactics to better adapt to North American conditions. While some of these changes were already being undertaken before Howe arrived in America, his enthusiastic support of them, and his personal example in practicing them, makes him the Regular officer most commonly associated with these adaptations.
>
> Howe's fame spread even to the French, and perhaps the best summary of his efforts was written by Captain Pierre Pouchot about the time of the 1758 expedition against Ticonderoga: "In his army he [Abercromby] had a young aristocrat, Lord Ho or Hau, strong-willed and highly admired in the army in which he preeminently set the tone. In the month of April he had come with a detachment to reconnoitre our positions at Fort Carillon. He seemed entrusted with the direction of the entire plan of attack in this campaign. He had urged all the officers to wear the same uniforms as private soldiers for fear of what happened in the Braddock incident, in which we fired at the officers as a priority. He encouraged the whole army to cut off the brims of their hats leaving only two finger-breadths of material. All the officers & soldiers were equipped with a kind of gaiter like those worn by the Indians & the Canadians, which were called *mituzzes.* Their haversacks were enveloped in a flap which they carried like the Indians & the

*My brother Captain Richard Rogers died with the Small-pox a few days before this fort was besieged; but such was the cruelty and rage of the enemy after their conquest, that they dug him up out of his grave, and scalped him. In consequence of the articles of capitulation at the surrender of this fort, the two companies of Rangers there were disbanded, and dismissed the service.

Canadians. Each of them had 30 pounds of flour, one pound of gunpowder and four pounds of shot in addition to a full cartridge box. As a result, this army could last for a whole month without recourse to stores. Their canteens were full of rum. Both soldiers & officers mixed some flour with a little water. They kneaded it & cooked it into cakes on a stone or under embers. This arrangement was very good for a light expedition. The soldier has everything he needs & is not more laden than normal. Both officers & soldiers had only one shirt; doubtless they chose cotton ones of good quality. Lord Ho had set the example. He washed his dirty shirt himself, laid it out in the sun, and while waiting for it to dry, was perfectly satisfied with his waistcoat." (Pouchot, p. 139)

Provincial Jonathan French remarked about one of the above mentioned scouts in a journal entry for October 2, 1757: "Maj. Rogers Brought in a French Prisoner taken at Ticonderago from his Post as he Stud Centinell." (French, p. 18)

About this time Lord Loudoun sent the following volunteers in the regular troops, to be trained to the ranging, or wood-service, under my command and inspection; with particular orders to me to instruct them to the utmost of my power in the ranging-discipline, our methods of marching, retreating, ambushing, fighting, & c. that they might be the better qualified for any future services against the enemy we had to contend with, desiring me to take particular notice of each one's behavior, and recommend them according to their deserts, *viz.*

As noted earlier, Loudoun's real purpose was to eventually replace the Rangers with specially trained Regular troops, led by Regular officers. This was partly due to the occasional difficulty in controlling and disciplining the American born and bred Ranger companies. The excessive cost of maintaining them was another factor. In 1758, nine Ranger companies cost twice as much as a full regiment of Regulars. (Anderson, pp. 181 and 768-9 n. 4) Nevertheless, it is clear that Loudoun deemed Rogers himself to be a very competent and valuable officer, and considered his Rangers to be among the best of the numerous Ranger units in the service. As time would show, for all their faults, the American Rangers never could be fully replaced by Regular troops.

The Cadet Company existed as a formal organization only for this one campaign season. An entry in a Provincial orderly book on November 8, 1757, recorded the company's official end: "All ye Folen tears [volunteers] belonging to ye Regular Troops & now with ye Rangers are to join their Respective Corps as Soon as they can." (Cuneo, p. 60) However, Captain John Knox mentions a seemingly contradictory order in his journal for November 18: "the Earl of Loudoun has ordered all the cadets, or volunteers of the army, to serve among the rangers until the opening of the next campaign." (Knox, Vol. I, pp. 108-109) Regardless of their exact official status, the tradition of the Rangers training promising Regular and Provincial troops continued for the rest of the war.

Walter Crofton	of the 4th regiment of foot.
Mr. Lyshat	ditto
Mr. Roberts	ditto

My thanks to Brian Leigh Dunnigan of the William L. Clements Library, who through his curiosity and effort determined that this should really be the 46th Regiment of Foot, and that the "Mr. Roberts" listed is quite probably the same Benjamin Roberts who later caused Rogers so much trouble during his tenure at Michilimackinac. Roberts was definitely serving as a volunteer in the 46th Regiment at this time.

Charles Humbles	of the 22d ditto.
Richard Edlington	ditto
Andrew Crawley	ditto
Thomas Millet	ditto
John Wilcox	of the 27th ditto.

John Wrightson	ditto
Michael Kent	ditto
Mr. Monsel	ditto
Francis Creed	ditto
Alexander Robertson	of the 42d ditto.
William Frazier	ditto
John Graham	ditto
Andrew Ross	ditto
William Frazier, jun.	ditto
Archibald Campbell	ditto
Arch. Campbell, jun.	ditto
Augus. Campbell	ditto
Charles Menzies	ditto
John Robertson	ditto
Will. Ervin, or Irwin	of the 44th ditto.
Thomas Drought	ditto
William Drought	ditto
Francis Carruthers	ditto
John Clarke	ditto
Walter Paterson	of the 48th ditto.
Mr. Nicholson	ditto
Richard Boyce	ditto
Charles Perry	ditto
Mr. Christopher	of the 55th ditto.
Mr. Still	ditto
Mr. Hamilton	ditto
Mr. Young	ditto
Allen Grant	of the second battalion of Royal Americans
Jonathan McDougal	ditto
Mr. Frisborough	ditto
Nicholas Ward	of the 3d ditto.
James Hill	ditto
John Schloser	of the 4th ditto
George Wardoman	ditto
Francis Barnard	ditto
Engelbertus Horst	ditto
Ericke Reinhault	ditto
Andrew Wackerberg	ditto
Luhainsans Dekesar	ditto
Donald M'Bean	ditto
Henry Ven Bebber	ditto
John Boujour	ditto
Edward Crafton	Rangers.
James Pottinger	ditto
Simon Stephens	ditto
Archibald M'Donald	ditto
Hugh Sterling	ditto
Mr. Bridge	ditto

These volunteers I formed into a company by themselves, and took the more immediate command and management of them to myself; and for their benefit and instruction reduced into writing the following rules or plan of discipline, which, on various occasions, I had found by experience to be necessary and advantageous, viz.

I. All Rangers are to be subject to the rules and articles of war; to appear at roll-call every evening on their own parade, equipped, each with a firelock, sixty rounds of powder and ball, and a hatchet, at which time an officer from each company is to inspect the same, to see they are in order, so as to be ready on any emergency to march at a minute's warning; and before they are dismissed, the necessary guards are to be draughted, and scouts for the next day appointed.

II. Whenever you are ordered out to the enemies forts or frontiers for discoveries, if your number be small, march in a single file, keeping at such a distance from each other as to prevent one shot from killing two men, sending one man, or more, forward, and the like on each side, at the distance of twenty yards from the main body, if the ground you march over will admit of it, to give the signal to the officer of the approach of an enemy, and of their number, & c

III. If you march over marshes or soft ground, change your position, and march abreast of each other to prevent the enemy from tracking you (as they would do if you marched in a single file) till you get over such ground, and then resume your former order, and march till it is quite dark before you encamp, which do, if possible, on a piece of ground that may afford your centries the advantage of seeing or hearing the enemy some considerable distance, keeping one half of your whole party awake alternately through the night.

IV. Some time before you come to the place you would reconnoitre, make a stand, and send one or two men in whom you can confide, to look out the best ground for making your observations.

V. If you have the good fortune to take any prisoners, keep them separate, till they are examined, and in your return take a different route from that in which you went out, that you may the better discover any party in your rear, and have an opportunity, if their strength be superior to yours, to alter your course, or disperse, as circumstances may require.

VI. If you march in a large body of three or four hundred, with a design to attack the enemy, divide your party into three columns, each headed by a proper officer, and let those columns march in single files, the columns to the right and left keeping at twenty yards distance or more from that of the center, if the ground will admit, and let proper guards be kept in the front and rear, and suitable flanking parties at a due distance as before directed, with orders to halt on all eminences, to take a view of the surrounding ground, to prevent your being ambuscaded, and to notify the approach or retreat of the enemy, that proper dispositions may be made for attacking, defending, & c. And if the enemy approach in your front on level ground, form a front of your three columns or main body with the advanced guard, keeping out your flanking parties, as if you were marching under the command of trusty officers, to prevent the enemy from pressing hard on either of your wings, or surrounding you, which is the usual method of the savages, if their number will admit of it, and be careful likewise to support and strengthen your rear-guard.

VII. If you are obliged to receive the enemy's fire, fall, or squat down, till it is over, then rise and discharge at them. If their main body is equal to yours, extend yourself occasionally; but if superior, be careful to support and strengthen your flanking parties, to make them equal to theirs, that if possible you may repulse them to their main body, in which case push upon them with the greatest resolution with equal force in each flank and in the center, observing to keep at a due distance from each other, and advance from tree to tree, with one half of the party before the other ten or twelve yards. If the enemy push upon you, let your front fire and fall down, and then let your rear advance thro' them and do the like, by which time those who before were in front will be ready to discharge again, and repeat the same alternately, as occasion shall require; by this means you will keep up such a constant fire, that the enemy will not be able easily to break your order, or gain your ground.

VIII. If you oblige the enemy to retreat, be careful, in your pursuit of them, to keep out your flanking parties, and prevent them from gaining eminences, or rising grounds, in which case they would perhaps be able to rally and repulse you in their turn.

IX. If you are obliged to retreat, let the front of your whole party fire and fall back, till the rear hath done the same, making for the best ground you can; by this means you will oblige the enemy to pursue you, if they do it at all, in the face of a constant fire.

X. If the enemy is so superior that you are in danger of being surrounded by them, let the whole body disperse, and every one take a different road to the place of rendezvous appointed for that evening, which must every morning be altered and fixed for the evening ensuing, in order to bring the whole party, or as many of them as possible, together, after any separation that may happen in the day; but if you should happen to be actually surrounded, form yourselves into a square, or if in the woods, a circle is best, and, if possible, make a stand till the darkness of the night favours your escape.

XI. If your rear is attacked, the main body and flankers must face about to the right and left, as occasion shall require, and form themselves to oppose the enemy, as before directed; and the same method must be observed, if attacked in either of your flanks, by which means you will

GARY ZABOLY ©1999

Rogers' Rangers' Cadet School

ROBERT ROGERS' stock had risen in the wake of the abortive attempt against Louisbourg and the fall of Fort William Henry. Formal siege and defensive warfare had failed the British, for the time being anyway. Many months of inactivity lay ahead; and in order for the tired and dispirited army to maintain some sort of physically contributive role, while preparing for a possible winter campaign, the eyes of several British commanders turned towards the Rangers. The realization was sinking in, finally, that the informality of wilderness warfare demanded that the Regulars learn to adapt themselves to its peculiar nature. Who better, then, to teach them how, or to provide an example to follow, than Captain Robert Rogers?

Lord Loudoun, spurred on by rather enlightened suggestions made by the Duke of Cumberland, encouraged his subordinates along this line.[1] Lord George Augustus Howe became the greatest active protagonist for Rogers' methods, once even accompanying the Rangers on a patrol between Fort Edward and Ticonderoga. The most concerted manifestation of this more flexible approach, however, came with the establishment of a 55-man company of volunteers drawn from cadets already serving in a number of regiments (the 22nd, 27th, 42nd, 44th, 46th, 48th, 55th and 60th, as well as six drawn from Ranger ranks). These volunteers were not only expected to learn the arts and tactics of ranging and bush-fighting, but were also slated, if approved, to obtain ensigns' commissions in either the Rangers or the Regulars, as vacancies occurred.[2]

The company was officially launched in mid-September 1757 at Albany, where Loudoun's army had just returned from Louisbourg. Certificates were issued to those who volunteered to join it.[3] Rogers writes that he "took the more immediate command and management of them to myself." After arriving at Fort Edward, the volunteers built their camp next to the Ranger huts already on Rogers' Island.

Not only did Rogers begin training them personally, but he also wrote a compendium of 28 "rules or plan of discipline" that "Gentlemen Officers" in the Rangers had to learn before they could graduate, with the caveat noted that the rules were meant to be flexible if "occurrences and circumstances" required such departures.

The scene illustrated is meant to be hypothetical: something like it might very well have happened. Rogers sometimes organized maneuver-like displays of Ranger tactics for the edification of the army at large; presumably the volunteers were now and then also instructed in this manner.

At right, a group of the volunteers stands listening to Rogers describe the maneuver on the field—the plain just east of Fort Edward, and north of the outlying blockhouse—being performed by a company of Rangers. They are demonstrating Ranging Rule #VI, viz., if you are marching in a body of 300-400 men, march in three columns with flankers and guards out; and if attacked in front, deploy to meet the attack by forming a front while keeping out flanking parties to prevent the enemy from surrounding you. Even though one company of Rangers did not make 300-400 men, still 100 or fewer men would have sufficed to enact the particular tactic on a smaller scale.

Each of the volunteers has a copy of Rogers' ranging rules, either printed or hand-copied by military secretaries. This, too, is supposition; but since Rogers wrote the rules expressly for them, it seems likely that each man had his own copy for study and reference.

Eventually the volunteers were required to purchase clothing suitable for ranging afield;[4] and thereafter were taken out on actual scouts with veteran Rangers. By the end of the "school's" existence—barely seven weeks after it was founded—it was disbanded as the main army went into winter quarters. Twelve of the volunteers eventually obtained commissions in Rogers' Rangers, while twenty-three achieved berths in Regular regiments before the end of 1758.[5]

It is of no little significance that Rogers' ranging rules are still being issued, in one form or another, to American Special Forces units; and, by the testimony given this artist/author by two veterans of the Vietnam War, memorizing them has helped save lives in the process.

G.Z.

1. Stanley M. Pargellis, *Lord Loudoun in North America*, Yale Historical Publications, Archon Books, New York, 1968, p. 304.
2. Burt Garfield Loescher, *The History of Rogers' Rangers*, Vol. I, San Francisco, 1946, p. 184.
3. Ibid., p. 185.
4. Idem, p. 286. Loescher theorizes, quite logically, that this clothing would have been green in color.
5. Idem, p. 185.

always make a rear of one of your flank-guards.

XII. If you determine to rally after a retreat, in order to make a fresh stand against the enemy, by all means endeavour to do it on the most rising ground you come at, which will give you greatly the advantage in point of situation, and enable you to repulse superior numbers.

XIII. In general, when pushed upon by the enemy, reserve your fire till they approach very near, which will then put them into the greatest surprize and consternation, and give you an opportunity of rushing upon them with your hatchets and cutlasses to the better advantage.

XIV. When you encamp at night, fix your centries in such a manner as not to be relieved from main body till morning, profound secrecy and silence being often of the last importance in these cases. Each centry therefore should consist of six men, two of whom must be constantly alert, and when relieved by their fellows, it should be done without noise; and in case those on duty see or hear any thing, which alarms them, they are not to speak, but one of them is silently to retreat, and acquaint the commanding officer thereof, that proper dispositions may be made; and all occasional centries should be fixed in like manner.

XV. At the first dawn of day, awake your whole detachment; that being the time when the savages chuse to fall upon their enemies, you should by all means be in readiness to receive them.

XVI. If the enemy should be discovered by your detachments in the morning, and their numbers are superior to yours, and a victory doubtful, you should not attack them till the evening, as then they will not know your numbers, and if you are repulsed, your retreat will be favored by the darkness of the night.

XVII. Before you leave your encampment, send out small parties to scout round it, to see if there be any appearance or track of an enemy that might have been near you during the night.

XVIII. When you stop for refreshment, chuse some spring or rivulet if you can, and dispose your party so as not to be surprised, posting proper guards and centries at a due distance, and let a small party waylay the path you came in, lest the enemy should be pursuing.

XIX. If, in your return, you have to cross rivers, avoid the usual fords as much as possible, lest the enemy should have discovered, and be there expecting you.

XX. If you have to pass by lakes, keep at some distance from the edge of the water, lest, in case of an ambuscade or an attack from the enemy, when in that situation, your retreat should be cut off.

XXI. If the enemy pursue your rear, take a circle till you come to your own tracks, and there form an ambush to receive them, and give them the first fire.

XXII. When you return from a scout, and come near our forts, avoid the usual roads, and avenues thereto, lest the enemy should have headed you, and lay in ambush to receive you, when almost exhausted with fatigues.

Not only were the Rangers cautious as they returned from a scout, at least in the nighttime, the garrisons also had to be careful that the approaching force was friendly. An order issued at Fort Edward on August 19, 1757, directed that: "As Soon as any Patroles approach ye Camp, ye sentrys will be Perticularly carefull to Challing & hail them & then to give notis to ye Officer of ye Regt. Who will send out a Seargt. & file of men to Examin them before they Enter ye Camp." (Lyman, p. 56)

If the Rangers were already in the camp when an alarm was sounded, their orders were equally specific, as noted on August 13, 1757: "For the Future Upon any Alarm the Ranging Companys are only To Turn out at the Head of their Incampment. But they are Not To March out of the Lines, Unless By an order from the Genll or Lord Howe." (Lyman, p. 54)

XXIII. When you pursue any party that has been near our forts or encampments, follow not directly in their tracks, lest they should be discovered by their rear-guards, who, at such a time, would be most alert; but endeavour, by a different route, to head and meet them in some narrow pass, or lay in ambush to receive them when and where they least expect it.

XXIV. If you are to embark in canoes, battoes, or otherwise, by water, chuse the evening for the time of your embarkation, as you will then have the whole night before you, to pass undiscovered by any parties of the enemy, on hills, or other places, which command a prospect of the lake or river you are upon.

XXV. In padling or rowing, give orders that the boat or canoe next the sternmost, wait for her, and the third for the second, and the fourth for the third, and so on, to prevent separation, and that you may be ready to assist each other on any of emergency.

XXVI. Appoint one man in each boat to look out for fires, on the adjacent shores, from the numbers and size of which you may form some judgment of the number that kindled them, and whether you are able to attack them or not.

XXVII. If you find the enemy encamped near the banks of a river or lake, which you imagine they will attempt to cross for their security upon being attacked, leave a detachment of your party on the opposite shore to receive them, while, with the remainder, you surprize them, having them between you and the lake or river.

XXVIII. If you cannot satisfy yourself as to the enemy's number and strength, from their fire, &c. conceal your boats at some distance, and ascertain their number by a reconnoitring party, when they embark, or march, in the morning, marking the course they steer, &c. when you may pursue, ambush, and attack them, or let them pass, as prudence shall direct you. In general, however, that you may not be discovered by the enemy on the lakes and rivers at a great distance, it is safest to lay by, with your boats and party concealed all day, without noise or shew, and to pursue your intended route by night; and whether you go by land or water, give out parole and countersigns, in order to know one another in the dark, and likewise appoint a station for every man to repair to, in case of any accident that may separate you.

Such in general are the rules to be observed in the Ranging service; there are, however, a thousand occurrences and circumstances which may happen, that will make it necessary, in some measure, to depart from them, and to put other arts and stratagems in practice; and which cases every man's reason and judgment must be his guide, according to the particular situation and nature of things; and that he may do this to advantage, he should keep in mind a maxim never to be departed from by a commander, viz. to preserve a firmness and presence of mind on every occasion.

Rogers' Ranging Rules are rightfully remembered as one of the first *written* manuals for irregular warfare in North America. However, Ranger tactics had been evolving here for many years. Benjamin Church, who fought in King Phillip's War, 1675-76, practiced many of the same tactics used by Rogers, and his memoirs were published in Boston in 1716. Rogers certainly improved and perfected the concept, but he did not *invent* it, as others have sometimes claimed. Even the British (or at least some of them) understood the importance of using irregular tactics in certain situations. Prior to the French and Indian War, James Wolfe drew up a list of instructions for the 20th Regiment of Foot at Canterbury. A look at two of his maxims will show a similarity to American Ranging tactics:

- "There is no necessity of firing very fast; a cool well-levelled fire, with the pieces carefully loaded, is much more destructive and formidable than the quickest fire in confusion." (Entick, Volume IV, p. 92 n.)
- "All little parties that are intended to fire upon the enemy's columns of march upon their advanced guard or their rear, are to post themselves so as to be able to annoy the enemy without danger, and to cover themselves with slight breastworks of sod behind the hedges, or with trees or walls or ditches, or any other protection, that if the enemy return the fire, it may do no mischief. These little parties are to keep their posts till the enemy attack with a superiority; upon which they are to retire to some other place of the same kind, and fire in the same manner, constantly retiring when they are pushed." (Entick, Volume IV, p. 95-6 n.)

Although Rogers' cadet company was dissolved after the 1757 campaign, he did continue to instruct others in his tactics while training his own men. Connecticut Provincial Abel Spicer recorded in his journal for August 19, 1758: "This day in the forenoon Major Rogers took his men without the camp beyond the advance guard to exercise them in the woods to skulk and to fire as to engage the enemy. The General went to see them and several of the chief officers." (Spicer, p. 100)

A document entitled *Standing Orders* for Rogers' Rangers that starts out "Don't forget nothing" has been circulating for years, and copies have been distributed to many modern army personnel. I have been able to trace this document back to the August 1962 issue of *True: The Man's Magazine.* Lieutenant Colonel John Lock, the author of the fine Ranger history *To Fight with Intrepidity . . .* has found these same orders in a 1960 U.S. Army Ranger Training Manual. The folksy wording definitely has a foundation in the words of Sergeant McNott, a character in Kenneth Roberts' classic 1937 novel *Northwest Passage.* While they make for interesting reading and do bear some resemblance to Rogers' real Ranging Rules, the *Standing Orders* are definitely a modern creation.

My Lord Loudoun about this time made a visit to Fort Edward, and after giving directions for quartering the army the approaching winter, left a strong garrison there under the command of Colonel Haviland, and returned to Albany. The Rangers* with the before-mentioned volunteers, were encamped and quartered in huts on an adjacent island in Hudson's River, and were sent out on various scouts, in which my ill state of health at this time would not permit me to accompany them, till December 17, 1757, when, pursuant to orders from Lieutenant Colonel Haviland, commanding officer at Fort Edward, I marched from thence with a party of 150 men to reconnoitre Carillon, alias Ticonderoga, and if possible to take a prisoner.

This island, where the Rangers encamped, became known as "Rogers' Island." Some historians have questioned whether the name was applied during the Rangers' occupation. The *London Chronicle/Universal Evening Post* labels it as such in 1758: "We have advice from Roger's Island, near Fort Edward, that Lieut Holmes of the Rangers, returned the 6th ult. from a scout to Ticonderoga with about seven men; and reports that he lay very near the fort; that there is a very large encampment there; that the enemy have erected some block-houses at their breast-work, and that many Indians are there." (*London Chronicle/Universal Evening Post*)

Another period reference is in a scout report by Sergeant Phillip Wells, which records, "Leaving Rogers Island near Fort Edward on the 23d Janry 1759" (Wells Manuscript)

Rogers' Island was large for a river island, approximately 50 acres, and in addition to the Rangers' huts, it contained regular barracks, a military hospital, and a specialized smallpox hospital, which was located on the isolated southern portion of the island.

Fort Edward was one of the most important of the northern British posts, located in the strategic Hudson River about forty miles north of Albany. At its peak, with a garrison of fifteen to sixteen thousand men, it temporarily became the third largest "city" in the British colonies. Even when Fort William Henry was operational, Fort Edward retained its importance because it was possible for French and Indian parties to bypass Fort William Henry by coming down South Bay and Wood Creek. (Starbuck, pp. 54-56)

For a more complete description of both Fort Edward and Rogers' Island, see Gary Zaboly's detailed illustration with its accompanying caption.

The Rangers' duties included more than just scouting. On November 10, it was stated that, "Majr. Rogers is to order a Guard of Rangers to post proper sentery from it, on ye Live Stock Garden & Fire wood & no Sort of thing to be taken out of ye Garden without proper leave from Col: Haviland & no fire wood to be

*Several of them were dismissed with an allowance of thirteen days pay to carry them home, being rendered unfit for immediate service by their past fatigues, and several officers were sent recruiting in order to have the companies complete by the opening of the spring.

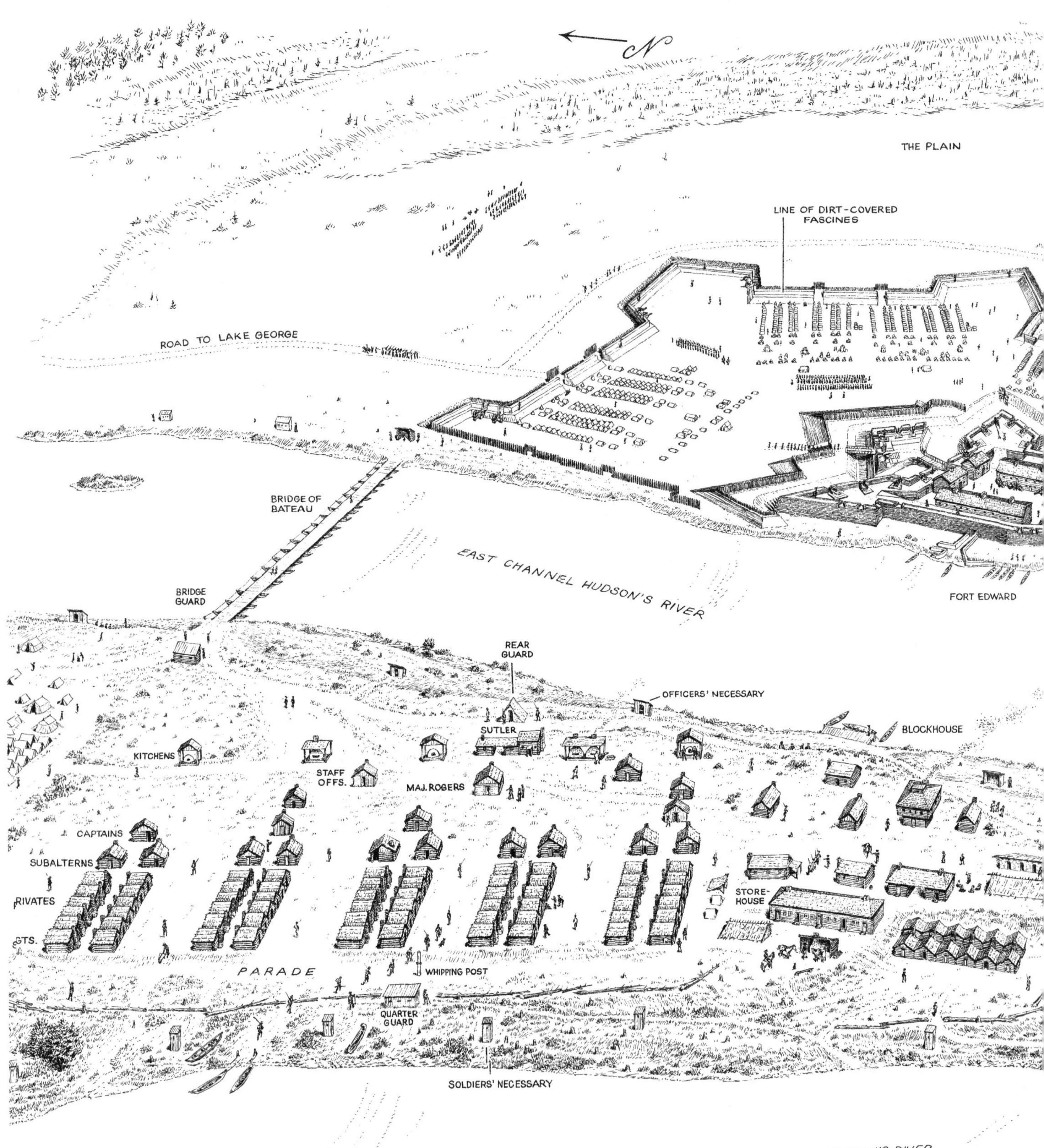
N
THE PLAIN
LINE OF DIRT-COVERED FASCINES
ROAD TO LAKE GEORGE
BRIDGE OF BATEAU
EAST CHANNEL HUDSON'S RIVER
BRIDGE GUARD
FORT EDWARD
REAR GUARD
OFFICERS' NECESSARY
BLOCKHOUSE
SUTLER
KITCHENS
STAFF OFFS.
MAJ. ROGERS
CAPTAINS
SUBALTERNS
RIVATES
GTS.
STORE-HOUSE
PARADE
WHIPPING POST
QUARTER GUARD
SOLDIERS' NECESSARY
WEST CHANNEL HUDSON'S RIVER

ROGERS' ISLAND, NOV. 1, 1757

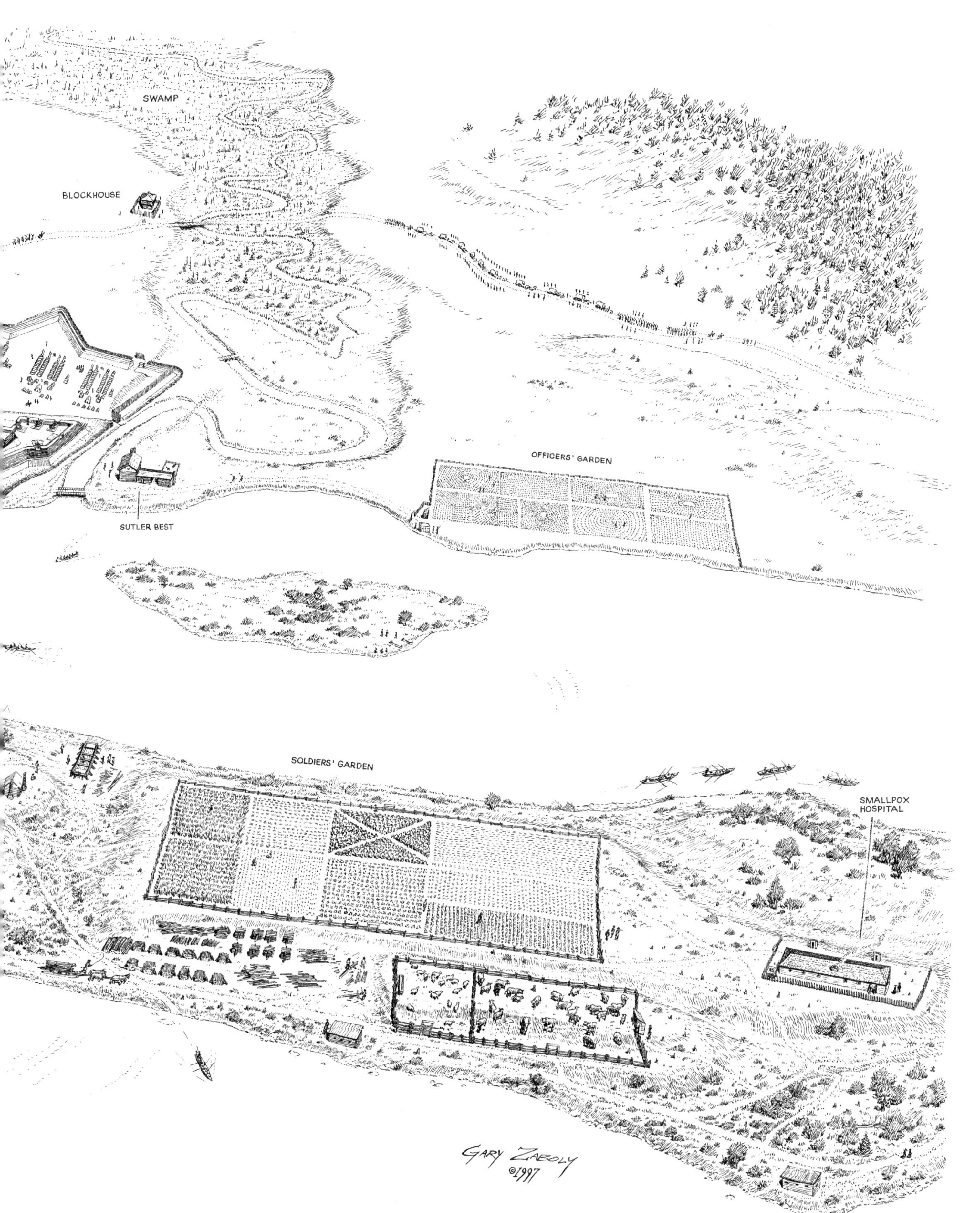
SWAMP
BLOCKHOUSE
OFFICERS' GARDEN
SUTLER BEST
SOLDIERS' GARDEN
SMALLPOX HOSPITAL
GARY ZABOLY
©1997

Rogers' Island, November 1, 1757

IN MID-SEPTEMBER 1757, Robert Rogers returned to Rogers' Island from Nova Scotia with the four companies of Rangers under his overall command: his own, Captain John Shepherd's, Captain John Stark's, and Captain Charles Bulkeley's. The latter two had been stationed at Fort William Henry since October of 1756 (albeit under different captains that first year of their existence). With William Henry now demolished by Montcalm, the men of Stark's and Bulkeley's made their new encampment on the island in the Hudson, alongside Rogers' and Shepherd's companies. In addition, 56 cadets out of the Regular regiments had volunteered to form a company "to be trained to the ranging, or wood-service," under Rogers' tutelage, and they, too, were newly billeted in huts on the island. (Tents were anathema to all Rangers; they preferred to live in even half-faced camps of brush rather than tents like the rest of the army).

How all these huts were arranged is not depicted on any contemporary map yet found. However, at Crown Point in 1759, Royal Artillery Captain Thomas Davies painted a watercolor showing rows of Ranger huts aligned perpendicularly to the large fort General Amherst had constructed on the peninsula. This disposition agrees somewhat with contemporary rules for military castrametation (i.e., "the art of measuring, arranging, and ordering camps"[1]), as delineated in Humphrey Bland's *A Treatise of Military Discipline*. Davies' bark-roofed log huts share common walls, and have their doors fronting onto company streets. Since archaeological evidence unearthed on Rogers' Island has, until recent years, been very poorly documented, it remains uncertain how scrupulously Rogers' Rangers adhered to Bland. The illustration is meant to offer plausible speculation regarding the hut question.

A large blockhouse had been constructed on the island in 1756 for the specific purpose of barracking the Rangers;[2] but Rogers' men felt more at home in bark lean-tos or log huts, echoes of their former days as hunters and trappers.[3] As a result, the blockhouse was relegated to service as a temporary hospital.[4] It might also be that the spacious blockhouse proved more difficult to heat in the winter months, the smaller huts being more efficient in keeping the Rangers warm.

By early June of 1757 a smallpox hospital had been constructed on an isolated knoll near the southern end of the island. Another significant building known to have been on the island was "a large Store House for Provisions."[5] Evidence of armories, workshops, various sheds and cabins has also been uncovered by archaeology; many of these were situated on the lower end of the ridge directly across the river from Fort Edward.

Access between island and fort during the summer months was possible by simply fording the river, which in that season averaged a depth of only two feet. Bridge-building became necessary as the waters rose with the approach of fall. In late September 1757 a pontoon bridge of bateaux, held together with a cable and covered by planks, was installed some 500 feet north of the fort.

The "front" of the Rangers' camp—that side facing a potential enemy attack—contained their parade ground; here also was located their whipping post. Several Rangers objecting to this mode of punishment chopped down the post on December 6, 1757, and were later tried for the offense.

"Necessary houses" were located on the riverbanks for obvious reasons—privates' privies along one side of the island, and officers' along the opposite one. Often mere holes were dug for the purpose, with ample dirt shoveled in after each use. When a Ranger said he was "easing himself on the riverbank" he was not referring to idle relaxation under the sun.[6]

The lower part of the island, aside from the smallpox hospital, seems to have been devoid of habitations at this time. Instead, a large, fenced garden to provision the private soldiers of all the regiments, pens for sheep and cattle, and piles of cordwood evidently occupied much of the landscape here.[7]

On November 7, "a Scow fifty feet long and 15 feet wide" was launched, according to Provincial diarist Rufus Putnam. Where the scow had been constructed is not known; in the illustration it is placed, arguably, on the lower ground just north of the garden. According to Lord Loudoun's diary, this scow could carry 150 barrels, and required six men to row it and one to steer.[8]

On September 16, all Provincial troops stationed across the river, in the lines surrounding Fort

Edward, were ordered to move onto Rogers' Island. Their tents seem to have populated much of the island's upper half (only the lower edge of their camp is shown here).[9]

All Regulars were concentrated within the fort, and in the lines that stretched beyond it to the north and east. These lines were built of dirt-covered fascines, and shaped into parapets with firing steps, with exterior ditches, and several batteries were positioned along their length. By November 5, the Regulars were ordered to pull down all the lines. Most of the British troops then marched into winter quarters at Albany, while a few remained garrisoned within the fort itself. Most of the American regiments also left, returning to their homes in the nearby provinces.

Immediately south of the fort, across a creek, were the home and storehouse of sutler Best, and beyond it a road led to the officers' garden. At least one blockhouse stood to the east (by 1759, six blockhouses guarded the approaches to the fort).

Through most of November and up to mid-December, Robert Rogers was rarely to be seen, recuperating from the effects of scurvy. Whether he was treated in his own hut, or in one of the hospitals on the island or in the fort, is not known.

Although references have been made in the foregoing to "Rogers' Island," it must be kept in mind that, in 1757, contemporary diarists and correspondents called it "the Great Island" or simply "the island." One of the earliest appearances of the term "Rogers' Island" is in *The New-York Mercury* of September 11, 1758 (which printed a "letter from Rogers' Island"), but it is reasonable to assume that Rogers' name had been applied to it long before this.

G.Z.

1. Lewis Lochee, *An Essay on Castrametation*, London, 1778.
2. According to the "Plan of Fort Edward" showing "Part of the Island," as drawn in July of 1757 by Royal Engineer Colonel James Montressor, the larger part of the blockhouse was some 40 feet square, suggesting a possible living capacity, in both the upper and lower apartments, for at least 200 men. See the reproduction of this map in the second edition of John R. Cuneo's *Robert Rogers of the Rangers*, published by the Fort Ticonderoga Museum, Ticonderoga, New York, in 1988. The several "Rangerss Hutts," also seen in the plan, immediately surrounding the blockhouse, have been included in our illustration. The occupants of these several huts are not known. Captain Israel Putnam's Connecticut Ranger company was also billeted on the island—in fact, his was one of the very few Ranger companies based at Fort Edward at the time this plan was drawn by Montressor—so these might represent the huts of his company.
3. Uncovered hut sites on Rogers' Island are generally eleven feet square, with a hearth of either stone or brick on one side. Earl Stott, *Exploring Rogers' Island*, Publication No. 2, The Rogers' Island Historical Association, Fort Edward, New York, 1969; and David R. Starbuck, *The Great Warpath: British Military Sites from Albany to Crown Point*, University Press of New England, Hanover and London, 1999, pp. 54-82. The walls of the huts might have been made of hewn logs, squared, like those of the blockhouse, straight enough so that they rested tightly on top of one another. If chinking was needed, clay was available from the riverbank. This was the common method of building log dwellings in northern New England. However, in Thomas Davies' "A South View of the New Fort at Crown Point," sketched in 1759, most of the log cabins are clearly of round logs. This would suggest that some cabins on Rogers' Island were also made of logs that were not squared, a construction method obviously requiring less time and effort.
4. Loescher, Burt Garfield, *The History of Rogers' Rangers*, Vol. I, San Francisco, 1946, pp. 91-92.
5. "Report of the Works Carried on in the Several Undermentioned places, with their present State, October 1st, 1757," Loudoun manuscripts, LO6754, The Huntington Library, San Marino, California.
6. Testimony of Ranger Private Aaron Burt in the trial of the whipping post "mutineers," Loescher, Vol. I., p. 306.
7. Noted *General Orders* for November 10, 1757, "Major Rogers is to order a guard of rangers to post proper sentries from it, on the live stock, garden, and firewood." This implies that these were probably situated near to one another. Lyman's orders, quoted in William H. Hill, *Old Fort Edward Before 1800*, privately printed at Fort Edward, New York, 1929, p. 151.
8. Loudoun's diary, in the collection of the Huntington Library. Entry of November 25, 1757.
9. That the Provincials were not camped south of the bridge is surmised by the *General Orders* for November 10, which required "the guard at the Island end of the Bridge not to suffer any man to pass over toard the Garden after the Retreat"—meaning, south of the island's bridge. Hill, *Old Fort Edward*, p. 151. Any remaining trees on the perimeter of the Provincials' camp were quickly felled; so devoid of wood did this section of the island become that the men resorted to hacking at the stumps for chips.

> touch.d as they will be answerable for it . . . ." (General Orders for 1757, p. 135) This order is notable for two reasons. Generally the Rangers did not have to perform routine garrison fatigue and sentry duties, but apparently the reduction in troop strength for the winter made this necessary. More importantly, it should be noted that in this order, Rogers is officially referred to as "Major," although his formal promotion would not take place until the following spring.
>
> Just before the above-mentioned scout, Captain-Lieutenant Henry Pringle and Captain Archibald Gordon, both of the 27th (Inniskilling) Regiment, entertained Rogers for dinner. Pringle described Rogers as "a very resolute and clever fellow" and says that he has, "several times, as he terms it, banged the French and Indians heartily." He then goes on to say of the Rangers, "They are created Indians & the only proper Troops to oppose them—They are good Men, but badly disciplined—They dress & live like Indians & are well acquainted with the Woods—There are many of them Irish . . . —They shoot amazingly well . . . and mostly with rifled barrels." (Henry Pringle *Entrybook*, December 16, 1757, quoted in McCulloch, *Men of the 27th*, p. 138) Pringle was a volunteer with Rogers during the March 1758 Battle on Snowshoes. A vivid account of his capture follows later in the *Journals.*

We marched six miles and encamped, the snow being then about three inches deep; and before morning it was fifteen: we however pursued our route.

On the 18th in the morning, eight of my party being tired, returned to the fort; with the remainder I marched nine miles further, and encamped on the east-side of Lake-George, near the place where Mons. Montcalm landed his troops when he besieged and took Fort William-Henry, where I found some cannon-ball and shells, which had been hid by the French, and made a mark by which I might find them again.

The 19th we continued our march on the west-side of the lake nine miles further, near the head of the north-west bay.

The 21st, so many of my party tired and returned as reduced our number to 123 officers included, with whom I proceeded ten miles further, and encamped at night, ordering each man to leave a day's provisions there till our return.

The next day we marched ten miles further, and encamped near the great brook that runs into Lake George, eight miles from the French advanced guard.

The 23d we marched eight miles, and the 24th six more, and then halted within 600 yards of Carillon fort. Near the mills we discovered five Indian's tracks, that had marched that way the day before as we supposed, on a hunting party. On my march this day between the advanced guard and the fort, I appointed three places of rendezvous to repair to, in case of being broke in an action, and acquainted every officer and soldier that I should rally the party at the nearest post to the fort, and if broke there to retreat to the second, and at the third to make a stand till the darkness of the night would give us an opportunity to get off. Soon after I halted, I formed an ambush on a road leading from the fort to the woods, with an advanced party of twenty men, and a rear-guard of fifteen. About eleven o'clock a serjeant of marines came from the fort up the road to my advanced party, who let him pass to the main body, where I made him prisoner. Upon examination, he reported, "that there were in the garrison 350 regulars, about fifty work-men, and but five Indians: that they had plenty of provisions, & c. and that twelve masons were constantly employed in blowing up rocks in the entrenchment, and a number of soldiers to assist them: that at Crown Point there were 150 soldiers and fourteen Indians: that Mons. Montcalm was at Montreal: that 500 Ottawawas Indians wintered in Canada, and that 500 Rangers were lately raised in Canada, each man having a double-barrelled fuzee, and put under an experienced officer, well acquainted with the country: that he did not know whether the French intended to attack any of the

English forts this winter or not; but that they expected a great number of Indians as soon as the ice would bear them, in order to go down to the English forts; and that all the bakers in Carillon were employed in baking biscuit for the scouts above-mentioned."

About noon, a Frenchman, who had been hunting, came near my party in his return, when I ordered a party to pursue him to the edge of the cleared ground, and take him prisoner, with this caution, to shoot off a gun or two, and then retreat to the main body, in order to intice the enemy from their fort; which orders were punctually obeyed, but not one of them ventured out.

The last prisoner, on examination, gave much the same account as the other, but with this addition, "that he had heard the English intended to attack Ticonderoga, as soon as the lake was froze so as to bear them."

> There had indeed been discussion of such an attack, but it was never implemented for a number of reasons. The plan called for a winter attack, led by Rogers and Howe. Rogers presented his version of such a plan to Lord Loudoun in New York on January 9, 1758. A swiftly moving, properly equipped force of four hundred men was to bypass Ticonderoga and capture the more vulnerable Fort St. Frederic at Crown Point. They would ambush some French sleighs, and make "their Drivers prisoners, after which he [Rogers] would put French Cloathing on his own Men & proceed with their Slays . . . before they Could Discover the Deceit he should have sufficient men in the fort to keep the Gates open & take it by surprise." (Bellico, *Chronicles of Lake Champlain,* pp. 147-148) Ticonderoga would then be cut off and starved into submission before it could be resupplied and reinforced when the weather broke in the spring. Even though the plan was not attempted, knowledge of it must have been common in the colonies. The March 1758 issue of the *Gentlemen's Magazine* from London reported from a "Letter from a Gentleman at New-York, dated Feb. 6," that "At the time you receive this, you will probably hear of a campaign in the snow, under my Lord How, and Captain Rogers, a famous partisan. If it succeeds, it will open us a passage, thro' the Lakes, into Canada, to Montreal or Quebec, which may perhaps be a summer expedition." (*Gentleman's Magazine,* March 1758, p. 144)
>
> If this plan had been implemented, and had it been successful, the heavy losses suffered at Ticonderoga in July would definitely have been prevented. It may have then been possible, as the letter suggests, to carry out an expedition into the heart of New France during the summer of 1758, which in turn could have significantly shortened the war.

When I found the French would not come out of the fort, we went about killing their cattle, and destroyed seventeen head, and set fire to the wood, which they had collected for the use of the garrison, and consumed five large piles; the French shot off some cannon at the fires, but did us no harm. At eight o'clock at night I began my march homewards, and arrived at Fort Edward with my prisoners the 27th.

> This scout illustrates both Rogers' daring and his sense of humor. It also shows that in most cases, he records his exploits in his *Journals* in a relatively modest manner. If he were truly the shameless self promoter that many of his detractors claim him to be, then this is certainly an incident that he would have recorded more dramatically. Captain Anne-Joseph-Hippolyte de Maures de Malartic, the "aide-major," or adjutant of the Bearn Regiment, tells the full story in his journal entry of January 2, 1758: "A courier from Carillon reports, that the English shewed themselves there on Christmas eve to the number of 150, with the design of setting fire to the houses under the curtain of the fort; that the cannon prevented them doing so; that they killed some fifteen beeves, to the horns of one of which the commander had affixed a letter couched in these words: 'I am obliged to you, Sir, for the repose you have allowed me to take; I thank you for the fresh meat you have sent me; I shall take care of my prisoners; I request you to present my compliments to the Marquis de Montcalm. (Signed)

ROGER, Commandant of the Independent Companies.' " (*D.R.C.H.S.N.Y.* Vol. 10, p. 837)

In his April 30 letter to Marshal de Belle Isle, Paymaster General Andre Doreil showed that he did not necessarily share Rogers' sense of humor: "Last January Captain Robert Roger, a great partisan, came roving in the neighborhood of Carillon with a detachment of 70 men. The artillery of the fort drove him away pretty quick. In his retreat he burnt a pile of timber and charcoal, took a wood-cutter prisoner (who afterwards escaped from him), and killed 18 oxen or cows, which he could not remove; they were found in the woods and have served to subsist the garrison. He had caused to be attached to the head of one of the oxen a letter addressed to the Commandant of the fort, the contents thereof were an ill-timed and very low piece of braggadocio." (*D.R.C.H.S.N.Y.* Vol. 10, p. 703)

Connecticut Provincial Jabez Fitch makes a brief mention of Rogers' return from this scout in his journal. It is significant in that it is another example of Rogers being referred to as "Major," even though his official promotion was still some months away: "This Day Majr Rogers Came in from His Scout to Tionderoge Brought in Two Prisoners &c." (Fitch, p. 40)

Even General Abercromby thought this action by Rogers was worthy of note. He wrote to the Earl of Loudoun that, "after killing all the live stock but three Bullocks, he left a Receipt for the Commandant as a Voucher to pass his Accounts, with the Agent Victualler; and stuck the same in a Cleft Stick in the Path; and by the two Deserters who followed him, he learnt that his Receipt came to the Commandants hand who was much provoked at it." (Cuneo, *Rogers*, p. 67)

In my return, I found at the north end of Lake George, where the French had hid the boats they had taken at Fort William Henry, with a great number of cannon-balls; but as the boats were under water we could not destroy them.

It was common practice for both sides to sink their boats in shallow water over the winter to preserve and protect them. They would then be raised again in the spring.

Upon my return to Fort Edward, I received a letter from Captain Abercrombie, informing me that the Earl of Loudoun, who was then at New York, had thoughts of augmenting the Rangers, and had desired General Abercrombie to command me down to receive his directions. I accordingly prepared for my journey, and upon my arrival was received by his Lordship in a very friendly manner; and, after much conversation upon the subject, he was pleased to inform me of his intentions of levying five additional companies of Rangers, desiring me to name the persons whom I thought fit for officers, and such as might be depended upon, to levy the men his Lordship desired; which I accordingly did, and then received from him the following instructions.

"By his Excellency John Earl of Loudoun, Lord Machline and Tairenseen &c. &c. &c. one of the sixteen peers of Scotland, Governor and Captain General of Virginia, and Vice Admiral of the same, Colonel of the 13th Regiment of foot, Colonel in chief of the Royal American regiment, Major General and Commander in Chief of all his Majesty's forces, raised or to be raised in North-America:

"Whereas I have this day thought proper to augment the Rangers with five additional companies, that is, four New England and one Indian company, to be forthwith raised and employed in his Majesty's service; and whereas I have an entire confidence in your skill and knowlege, of the men most fit for that service; I do therefore by these presents appoint you to raise such a number of non-commission officers and private men as will be necessary to compleat the said five companies, upon the following establishment, viz. each company to consist of one Captain, two Lieutenants, one Ensign, four Serjeants and 100 privates. The officers to have British pay, that is, the same as an officer of the like rank in his Majesty's regular forces; the Serjeants 4s. New York currency per day, and the private men 2s.6d currency per day.

And the better to enable you to make this levy of men, you shall have one month's pay for each of the said five companies advanced to you; upon these conditions, that, out of the first warrants that shall hereafter be granted for the substinence of these companies, shall be deducted the said month's pay now advanced. Your men to find their own arms, which must be such as upon examination, shall be found fit, and be approved of. They are likewise to provide themselves with good warm cloathing, which must be uniform in every company, and likewise with good warm blankets. And the company of Indians to be dressed in all respects in the true Indian fashion, and they are all to be subject to the rules and articles of war. You will forthwith acquaint the officers appointed to these companies, that they are immediately to set out to on the recruiting service, and you will not fail to instruct them that they are not to inlist any man for a less term than one year, nor any but what are able-bodied, well acquainted with the woods, used to hunting, and every way qualified for the Ranging service. You are also to observe that the number of men requisite to compleat the said five companies, are all to be at Fort Edward on or before the 15th day of March next ensuing, and those that shall come by the way of Albany are to be mustered there by the officer commanding, as shall those who go straight to Fort Edward by the officer commanding there. Given under my hand, at New York, the 11th day of January 1758.

Loudoun.

By his Excellency's command,

To Capt. J. Appy"

Robert Rogers.

While the companies that Rogers raised were "independent" companies under the regular establishment, they were also clearly part of a multi-company Ranger "corps" under his personal command. This concept is supported by a general order issued at Fort Edward on July 18, 1757: "When Ever Two or More of ye Independent Companys are Joind Together, they are to Look Upon them Selves as a Corp & not to act as Separate Companys & all Returns Reports &c. are to Be Made to & Signed By ye Commanding offr. of ye Whol." (General Orders of 1757, p. 46)

Not all American troops were highly thought of by Regular officers, but on December 30, 1757, General Abercromby wrote to Lord Loudoun that the Rangers were "useful and well behaved." (Cuneo, *Notes*, p. 46) An indication of this esteem is the fact that Rogers' Corps was taken into the Regular Establishment, while most other Ranging units (Gorham's is another exception) remained Provincial troops.

In pursuance of the above instructions I immediately sent officers into the New England provinces, where, by the assistance of my friends, the requested augmentation of Rangers was quickly compleated, the whole five companies being ready for service by the 4th of March.

Today, Rogers' corps is universally referred to as "Rogers' Rangers." It is worth noting that the same name was applied to them during the course of the French and Indian War. Connecticut Provincial Jabez Fitch notes in his journal for February 16, 1758 that "This Day Serjt Geer Listed with Roger's Rangers &c." (Fitch, p. 49)

Those Rangers who remained in service over the winter at Fort Edward were assigned a variety of duties, one of the more unique of which was noted by Fitch. On February 26, he recorded in his journal, "a Mighty warm Pleasant Day a Number of Majr Rogerss Men was over On this Side with their Snow Shoes To Tread Down ye Snow Round on the Glassea." (Fitch, p. 50) Fitch was saying that some of the Rangers came over from Rogers' Island to pack down the snowdrifts around the walls of the main fort with their snowshoes.

The heavy snows in January restricted the Rangers ability to scout the enemy. Captain-Lieutenant Henry Pringle recorded in his journal on January 27, at Fort Edward, that "we have had prodigious Snows which has employed all the Garrison in clearing the Works & when the first is removed a second two feet comes in the night—Our intercourse with the French is stop'd by it, as we have not had a deserter since, nor have we sent another Scout there yet." (Henry Pringle *Entrybook,* quoted in McCulloch, *Men of the 27th,* p. 140)

Four of these companies were sent to Louisbourg, to join the General Amherst, and one joined the corps under my command; and tho' I was at the whole expense of raising the five companies, I never got the least allowance for it, and one of the captains dying, to whom I had delivered a thousand dollars as advance pay for his company, which, agreeable to the instructions I received, had a right to do; yet was I obliged to account with the government for this money, and entirely lost every penny of it.

In a history of the war published in 1765, the Rev. John Entick gives an interesting description of the Rangers and light infantry that participated in the Louisbourg Campaign: "Our light infantry, Highlanders, and Rangers, the French termed the *English savages,* perhaps in contradistinction to their own native Indians, Canadians, &c. the true French savages. These light infantry were a corps of 550 volunteers chosen as marksmen out of the most active resolute men from all the battalions of regulars, dressed some in blue, some in green jackets, and drawers, for their easier brushing through the woods, with ruffs of black bear's skin round their necks, the beard of their upper lips, some grown into whiskers, others not so, but all well smutted on that part, with little round hats like several of our seamen.—Their arms were a fusil, cartouch-box of balls and flints, and a powder horn flung over their shoulders. The Rangers are a body of irregulars, who have a more cut-throat, savage appearance; which carries in it something of natural savages: the appearance of the light infantry has in it more of artificial savages." (Entick, Volume III, p. 277 n.)

It is known that at least for the 1758 campaign, Rogers' Ranging Companies were issued, for the first time, an official green uniform.The exact makeup and appearance of this uniform has been debated by historians and artists for years, and many of the exact details are still uncertain.

As noted in the above order of January 11, 1758, Loudoun instructed Rogers that his men were to, "find their own arms, which must be such as upon examination, shall be found fit, and be approved of. They are likewise to provide themselves with good warm cloathing, which must be uniform in every company, and likewise with good warm blankets. And the company of Indians to be dressed in all respects in the true Indian fashion."

Little specific information is known about the uniforms that Rogers had made for his men at this time. As with their drill and discipline, the Rangers combined the best of military and frontier styles in their clothing, mixing in some elements of American Indian dress that were especially well suited to their mode of wilderness warefare. Even after the regimental style coats were issued, it is questionable whether they were worn on an everyday basis, or reserved for cooler weather and formal occasions. It is also likely that the Rangers often continued to wear various types of dress that they previously favored.

To date, the most accurate screen portrayal of Ranger dress is in the "Rogers' Rangers" episode of the award-winning 1998 History Channel documentary series *Frontier: Legends of the Old Northwest.*

For a more complete discussion of this subject, including new evidence on the uniform that is being presented for the first time, see the detailed caption by artist Gary Zaboly for his illustration of the circa 1758 uniform in the appendix.

It has already been mentioned, that the garrison at Fort Edward, was this winter under the command of Lieut. Col. Haviland. This gentleman, about the 28th of February, ordered out a scout under the direction of one Putnam, Captain of a company of one of the Connecticut provincial regiments,with some of my men, given out publickly at the same time, that, upon Putnam's return, I should be sent to the French forts with a strong party of 400 Rangers.

This was known not only to all the officers, but soldiers also, at Fort Edward before Putnam's departure.

This officer is Revolutionary War hero Israel Putnam, who commanded a company of Connecticut Provincial Rangers during the French and Indian War and is mentioned frequently in Rogers' *Journals*.

While this party was out, a servant of Mr. Best, a sutler to the Rangers, was captivated by a flying party of the enemy from Ticonderoga; unfortunately too. One of Putnam's men had left him at Lake George, and deserted to the enemy. Upon Captain Putnam's return, we were informed he had ventured within eight miles of the French fort at Ticonderoga, and that a party he had sent to make discoveries had reported to him, that there were near 600 Indians not far from the enemy's quarters.

March 10, 1758. Soon after the said Captain Putnam's return, in consequence of positive orders from Col. Haviland, I this day began a march from Fort Edward for the neighbourhood of Carillon, not with a party of 400 men, as at first given out, but of 180 men only, officers included, one Captain, one Lieutenant, and one Ensign, and three volunteers, viz. Mess. Creed, Kent and Wrightson, one serjeant, and one private, all of the 27th regiment; and a detachment from the four companies of Rangers, quartered on the island near Fort Edward, viz. Captain Buckley, Lieutenants Philips, Moore, Crafton, Campbell, and Pottinger; Ensigns Ross, Wait, M'Donald, and White, and 162 private men. I acknowledge I entered upon this service, and viewed this small detachment of brave men march out, with no little concern and uneasiness of mind; for as there was the greatest reason to suspect, that the French were, by the prisoner and deserter above mentioned, fully informed of the design of sending me out upon Putnam's return: what could I think to see my party, instead of being strengthend and augmented, reduced to less than one half the number at first proposed. I must confess it appeared to me (ignorant and unskilled as I then was in politicks and the art of war) incomprehensible; *but my commander doubtless had his reasons, and is able to vindicate his own conduct.*

Rogers certainly undertook this scout with some legitimate concern. One must seriously question Haviland's motives here, especially considering that he reduced Rogers' strength from 400 to 180 men, knowing full well that the French must have received word of his scout and would be waiting for him. Rogers and Haviland often did not see eye to eye. Connecticut Provincial Jabez Fitch makes note in his journal on February 19, of an incident that occurred at Fort Edward shortly before this scout. "In ye morning Som of ye Rangers Went a Hunting & Fired Several Guns in Hearing of ye Garrison—About which Col. Haviland & Majr Rogers Had Som Difference &c." (Fitch, p. 49)

An interesting sidelight to this scout is a recent meeting at Fort Edward between Rogers and a noted French partisan officer, Lt. Wolff [also Wolf and Volf] of the Bentheim Regiment. Wolff was carrying official dispatches to the British at Fort Edward when he and Rogers had a chance to discuss the December Ranger raid on Fort Carillon. Captain Malartic, of the Bearn Regiment, recorded what transpired: "M. de Vaudreuil has had news from Carillon informing him that M. Wolff, sent with letters for Fort Lydius, [the French name for Fort Edward] has returned; he speaks in high terms of the civilities he has received; Captain Roger, whom he saw, quizzed him on the fresh meat they let him eat at Carillon; M. Wolff answered him to be careful of himself when he come again . . . " (*D.R.C.H.S.N.Y.* Volume 10, p. 837) As the reader shall see, this scout did not turn out to be as pleasant of an experience for Rogers as his December raid.

We marched to the half-way brook, in the road leading to Lake George, and there encamped the first night.

The 11th we proceeded as far as the first Narrows on Lake George, and encamped that evening on the east-side of the lake; and after dark, I sent a party three miles further down, to see if the enemy might be coming towards our forts, but they returned without discovering any. We were however on our guard, and kept parties walking on the lake all night, besides centries at all necessary places on the land.

The 12th we marched from our encampment at sun-rise, and having distanced it about three miles, I saw a dog running across the lake, whereupon I sent a detachment to reconnoitre the island, thinking that Indians might have laid in ambush there for us; but no such could be discovered; upon which I thought it expedient to put to shore and lay by till night, to prevent any party from descrying [to catch sight of; succeed in discerning] us on the lake, from hills, or otherwise. We halted at a place called Sabbath-day Point, on the west-side of the lake, and sent our parties to look down the lake with perspective glasses, which we had for that purpose. As soon as it was dark we proceeded down the lake. I sent Lieutenant Phillips with fifteen men, as an advanced guard, some of whom went before him on scates, while Ensign Ross flanked us on the left under the west-shore, near which we kept the main body, marching as close as possible, to prevent separation, it being a very dark night. **In this manner we continued our march till within eight miles of the shore, French advanced guards, when Lieutenant Philips sent a man on scates back to me, to desire me to halt;** upon which I ordered my men to squat down upon the ice.

> In the Dublin edition, pp. 74-75, this sentence in bold types makes no sense. It appears that a portion of the original text was left out. In the London edition, p. 82 the same passage reads: **"In this manner we continued our march till within eight miles of the French advanced guards, when Lieutenant Philips sent a man on scates back to me, to desire me to halt;"**

Mr. Phillips soon came to me himself, leaving his party to look out, and said, he imagined he had discovered a fire* on the east-shore, but was not certain; upon which I sent with him Ensign White, to make further discovery. In about an hour they returned, fully persuaded that a party of the enemy was encamped there. I then called in the advanced guard, and flanking party, and marched onto the west-shore, where, in a thicket, we hid our sleys and packs, leaving a small guard with them, and with the remainder I marched to attack the enemy's encampment, if there was any; but when we came near the place, no fires were to be seen, which made us conclude that we had mistaken some bleach patches of snow, or pieces of rotten wood, for fire (which in the night, at a distance resembles it) whereupon we returned to our packs, and there lay the remainder of the night without fire.

The 13th, in the morning, I deliberated with the officers how to proceed, who were unanimously of opinion, that it was best to go by land in snow-shoes, lest the enemy should discover us on the lake; we accordingly continued our march on the west-side, keeping on the back of the mountains that overlooked the French advanced guards. At twelve of the clock we halted two miles west of those guards, and there refreshed ourselves till three, that the day-scout from the fort might be returned home before we advanced; intending at night to ambuscade some of their roads, in order to trepan them in the morning. We then marched in two divisions, the one headed by Captain Buckley, the other by myself: Ensigns White and Wait had the rear-guard, the other officers were posted properly in each division, having a rivulet at a small distance on our left, and a steep mountain on our right. We kept close to the mountain, that the advanced guard might better observed the rivulet, on the ice of which I imagined they would travel it out, as the snow was four feet deep, and very bad traveling on snow-shoes.

In this manner we marched a mile and a half, when our advanced guard informed me of the enemy being in their view; and soon after, that they had ascertained their number to be ninety-six, chiefly Indians.

*A small party of the French, as we have since heard, had a fire here at this time; but, discovering my advanced party, extinguished their fire, and carried the news of our approach to the French fort.

We immediately laid down our packs, and prepared for battle, supposing these to be the whole number or main body of the enemy, who were marching on our left up the rivulet, upon the ice. I ordered Ensign M'Donald to the command of the advanced guard, which, as we faced to the left, made a flanking party to our right. We marched to within a few yards of the bank, which was higher than the ground we ocupied; and observing the ground gradually to descend from the bank of the rivulet to the foot of the mountain, we extended our party along the bank, far enough to command the whole of the enemy's at once; we waited till their front was nearly opposite to our left wing, when I fired a gun, as a signal for a general discharge upon them; whereupon we gave them the first fire, which killed above forty Indians; they retreated, and were pursued by about one half of our people. I now imagined the enemy totally defeated, and ordered Ensign M'Donald to head the flying remains of them, that none might escape; but we soon found our mistake, and that the party we had attacked were only their advanced guard, their main body coming up, consisting of 600 more, Canadians and Indians; upon which I ordered our people to retreat to their own ground, which we gained at the expence of fifty men killed; the remainder I rallied, and drew up in pretty good order, where they fought with such intrepidity and bravery as obliged the enemy (tho' seven to one in number) to retreat a second time; but we not being in a condition to pursue them, they rallied again, and recovered their ground, and warmly pushed us in front and both wings, while the mountain defended our rear; but they were so warmly received, that their flanking parties soon retreated to their main body with considerable loss. This threw the whole again into disorder, and they retreated a third time; but our number being now too far reduced to take advantage of their disorder, they rallied again, and made a fresh attack upon us. About this time we discovered 200 Indians going up the mountain on our right, as we supposed, to get possession of the rising ground, and attack our rear; to prevent which I sent Lieutenant Philips, with eighteen men, to gain the first possession, and beat them back; which he did, and being suspicious that the enemy would go round on our left, and take possession of the other part of the hill, I sent Lieutenant Crafton, with fifteen men, to prevent them there; and soon after desired two Gentlemen, who were there volunteers in the party,* with a few men, to go and support him, which they did with great bravery.

The enemy pushed us so close in front, that the parties were not more than twenty yards asunder in general, and sometimes intermixed with each other. The fire continued almost constant for an hour and a half from the beginning of the attack, in which time we lost eight officers, and more than 100 private men killed on the spot. We were at last obliged to break, and I with about twenty men ran up the hill to Phillips and Crafton, where we stopped and fired on the Indians who were eagerly pushing us, with numbers that we could not withstand. Lieutenant Phillips being surrounded by 300 Indians, was at this time capitulating for himself and party, on the other part of the hill. He spoke to me, and said if the enemy would give them good quarters, he thought it best to surrender, otherwise that he would fight while he had one man left to fire a gun.**

> Rogers' footnote below is in error because Lieutenant William Hendrick Philips was not killed in this battle. Philips, who was of Dutch, Indian, and French ancestry, was one of the most colorful of Rogers' officers. He was a veteran of the January 1757 First Battle on Snowshoes. Captured in the present battle, he later made his escape and rejoined the Ranging Service. During the Saint Francis Raid, he led the small party that included the captives, which made its way directly back to Crown Point. He died in 1819 at one hundred years of age. (Loescher, Volume II, p. 62, and Volume III, pp. 63-64)

I now thought it most prudent to retreat, and bring off with me as many of my party as I possibly could, which I immediately did; the Indians closely pursuing us at the same time, took several prisoners.

*I had before this desired these gentlemen to retire, offering them a Serjeant to conduct them; that as they were not used to snow-shoes, and were unacquainted with the woods, they would have no chance of escaping the enemy, in case we should be broke and put to flight, which I very much suspected. They at first seemed to accept the offer, and began to retire; but seeing us so closely beset, they undauntingly returned to our asssistance. What befel them after our flight, may be seen by a letter from one of the Gentleman to the commanding officer, which I have inserted next to this account of our scout.

**This unfortunate officer, and his whole party, after they surrendered, upon the strongest assurances of good treatment from the enemy, were inhumanly tied up to trees, and hewn to pieces, in a most barbarous and shocking manner.

GARY ZABOLY
©2000

Ambush on the Ice

THE WORK of Rogers' Rangers was often violent and dirty. Not infrequently did Robert Rogers find his best-laid plans going awry in the unpredictable and brutal arena that was forest warfare. Almost as often he found his own empirically-conceived Ranging rules failing him: on at least five different occasions during the war, Rogers led his men into enemy ambushes, or, as in the case of the March 13, 1758, "Battle on Snowshoes," a counter-ambush.

Most of these episodes were played out in distant and lonely corners of the wilderness. Such a place was the wide valley of a twisting brook about two miles west of the northern end of Lake George. The brook was then nameless to the English, but the French knew it as Bernetz Riviere. (At some undetermined time after the French and Indian War it was dubbed Trout Brook by Anglo-American settlers).

Today's Route 9N roughly follows the old Indian path that led from the shores of the lake—about where the Rogers' Rock campground now lies–northward along the valley of the brook. The path then turned east around the northern end of a small range of three peaks, and continued on to the Ticonderoga peninsula.[1] This was the route more or less traversed on March 13 by Rogers and his 183 snowshoed men, mostly Rangers, with eight Regulars of the 27th Regiment along for the experience—all of them volunteers. They had left the ice of the lake that morning and by 3:00 p.m., after a stop for a cold lunch, were still negotiating the path, unseen under four feet of snow. The brook lay some 100 yards to their left, paralleling their march. To their immediate right rose the steep slopes of the little mountain range. A French patrol from Fort Carillon was known to routinely scout the area every day, and Rogers wanted to ambush the next day's patrol at a position a little farther north. He was also certain that if any other enemy party was out, it would be traveling on the easiest road in the vicinity: the frozen brook.

When Rogers finally received word from his advanced guard that an enemy party of some 96 men, mostly Indians, was indeed moving southward on the brook, he deployed his detachment along the rivulet's high bank, crouching in hiding from the eyes of their foes. They waited in dead silence until, in Rogers' own words, the enemy's "front was nearly opposite to our left wing, when I fired a gun as a signal." At this, the Rangers rose up and blasted a volley into the flank of the meandering column, "which killed above forty Indians," according to Rogers, though he exaggerates considerably: early French accounts seem to agree on far fewer Indian losses—no more than eight killed and seventeen wounded, some very badly—in the course of the entire battle that afternoon.[2] (French prisoners taken in May would admit to a total of twelve battle dead[3]).

Half of Rogers' command then pursued the fleeing survivors of the enemy, with Ensign Gregory McDonald's advanced guard ordered to head them off if possible. The rest of Rogers' men remained to scalp the dead and dying on the brook. Rogers himself, as shown in the illustration, vigorously engaged in such trophy-taking on this occasion and no doubt on many another. Scalps meant bounty money, and the memory of the Fort William Henry bloodbath, just seven months before, was still very fresh in the Rangers' minds. (For Robert Rogers the event had struck home in a very personal way: the body of his brother, Richard, dead of smallpox, had been dug up and scalped by Montcalm's Indians after the fort's surrender).

Ironically, this one act of Rogers might have inadvertently caused the deaths of a number of his own men taken prisoner in the aftermath of the battle, an engagement lost by the Rangers when the enemy party they had fired upon turned out to be just the advanced guard of over 200 additional French and Indians. The Rangers, in turn surprised and decimated, retreated and reformed, and succeeded in twice driving back the reinforced enemy party; but by now they had lost both the initiative and their superiority of numbers. After losing scores of men over an hour and a half of combat, Rogers saw that further resistance was useless, and ordered a general retreat. However, one party of surviving Rangers under Lieutenant William Phillips, comprising Rogers' right-flank defense, had become completely surrounded by a large party of Indians. Phillips saw that further resistance was useless, and decided to surrender when the enemy assured him and his men that they would be given "good quarters," Shortly afterwards, in Rogers' own words, Phillips' men were inhumanly tied up to trees, and hewn to pieces, in a most barbarous and shocking manner."

What caused this overturning of the enemy offer of "good quarters"? In order to rid themselves of any extra weight and thus expedite their escape from the field after getting Rogers' order to retreat, the fleeing Rangers threw off their green uniform jackets. According to the account of Adjutant Malartic, "the Indians having discovered a chief's scalp in the breast of an officer's jacket, refused all quarter, and took 114 scalps."[4] This was confirmed by the publication of testimony from French prisoners in *The Boston News-Letter* of May 25, 1758, who related that "above 30 of the English. . .were killed and cut to pieces after they had capitulated, the Indians being enraged at finding a Number of Scalps in an Officer's Pocket which they took." That Rogers might have been the owner of the scalp-stuffed jacket is suggested in Jabez Fitch's diary entry for March 15, 1758, at Fort Edward: "In ye Majrs Last retreet he Lost all His Scalps Except one."[5]

Rogers, in his *Journals* account of this battle, leaves out any mention of scalp-taking by either himself or his Rangers;[6] and if he ever admitted to anyone that he suspected that most of the surrendered Rangers were hacked to death because of a war chief's scalp found by the Indians in his own jacket (possibly a fallen Caughnawaga's, considering that that tribe bore the brunt of losses that day), it has not been recorded by history.

Also seen in the illustration is a hypothetical situation: a Ranger wolf-dog, not unlike "Sergeant Beaubien," owned by Ranger Lieutenant William Stark, about to engage an Indian dog.

Dogs often accompanied the scouting parties of both sides, and had done so in the previous colonial wars in North America between Britain and France. They helped detect the presence of the enemy, sometimes even attacked him, tracked game, and in wintertime could assist in dragging the "traines" (toboggans) of the Indians and Canadians. In fact, Rogers had spotted "a dog running across the lake" to an island the day before the battle, and he had rapidly "sent a detachment to reconnoiter the island, thinking the Indians might have laid in ambush there for us; but no such could be discovered."

G.Z.

1. This path can be clearly seen on a map of Lake George and Wood Creek drawn in 1757, at the request of Major General James Abercromby, from information supplied by Rogers and his Rangers. (Chatham Papers, Public Record Office, London, Bundle 95).
2. Nevertheless, among Indian warriors, these numbers added up to a heavy loss. See extracts from the contemporary accounts of the battle by Montcalm, Malartic, and Doreil, pp. 384-386, Burt G. Loescher, *The History of Rogers' Rangers, Vol. I: The Beginnings, January 1755-April 6, 1758*, San Francisco, 1946. Malartic, for instance, asserts that only two Indians were killed in the Rangers' initial volley, which seems incredibly low.
3. Ibid., p. 381. Another version of the French prisoner testimony has them admitting to 27 Indian casualties. *The New-York Mercury*, May 22, 1758.
4. Ibid., p. 385.
5. The Diary of Jabez Fitch Jr., in the French and Indian War, Rogers Island Historical Association, Glens Falls, New York, second edition, 1968, p. 54.
6. In his official report to General Abercromby, Rogers does not refrain from mentioning scalping; the report was printed in toto in *The Boston News-Letter* of April 7, 1758.

An event that has become one of the greatest legends of Rogers' career supposedly occurred at this point. While making his escape, tradition has it that Rogers descended the steep face of a huge rock formation that even today is known as "Rogers' Rock," or "Rogers' Slide." Historian Benson Lossing wrote, "The whole height of Rogers' Rock is about four hundred feet, and the 'slide' almost a smooth surface, with a descent on an angle of about twenty-five degrees from meridian, is two hundred feet . . . . He [Rogers] was equipped with snow-shoes, and eluded pursuit until he came to the summit of the mountain. Aware that they would follow his track, he descended to the top of the smooth rock, and, casting his knapsack and his haversack of provisions down upon the ice, slipped off his snow-shoes, and, without moving them, turned himself about and put them on his feet again. He then retreated along the southern brow of the rock several rods, and down a ravine he made his way safely to the lake below, snatched up his pack and fled on the ice to Fort George. The Indians, in the mean while, coming to the spot, saw the two tracks, both apparently approaching the precipice, and concluded that two persons had cast themselves down the rock rather than fall into their hands. Just then they saw the bold leader of the Rangers making his way across the ice, and believing that he had slid down the steep face of the rock, considered him . . . under the special protection of the Great Spirit, and made no attempt at pursuit." (Lossing, Volume I, p. 116)

For a more complete, and far more accurate, discussion of this incident and whether or not it could be true, see the caption for Gary Zaboly's scene depicting this event.

We came to Lake George in the evening, where we found several wounded men, whom we took with us to the place where we had left our sleds, from whence I sent an express to Fort Edward, desiring Mr. Haviland to send a party to meet us, and assist us in bringing in the wounded; with the remainder I tarried there the whole night, without fire or blankets, and in the morning we proceeded up the lake, and met with Captain Stark at Hoop Island, six miles north from Fort William-Henry, and encamped there that night; the next day being the 15th, in the evening, we arrived at Fort Edward.

The number of the enemy was about 700, 600 of which were Indians. By the best accounts we could get, we killed 150 of them, and wounded as many more. I will not pretend to determine what we should have done had we been 400 or more strong; but this I am obliged to say of those brave men who attended me (most of whom are now no more) both officers and soldiers in their respective stations behaved with uncommon resolution and courage; nor do I know an instance during the whole action in which I can justly impeach the prudence or good conduct of any one of them.

The following is a LIST of the Killed, Missing, &c.

The Captain and Lieutenant of his Majesty's regular troops, volunteers in this party, were taken prisoners; the Ensign, another volunteer of the same corps, was killed, as were two volunteers, and a Serjeant of the said corps, and one private.

These volunteer officers were Captain-Lieutenant Henry Pringle and Lieutenant Boyle Roche, both of the 27th (Inniskilling) Regiment. Roche left the army after the Pontiac Uprising in 1763, and later served in Parliament. (McCulloch, *Men of the 27th*, p. 140 n. 42). Pringle eventually reached the rank of major-general in the British army.

Of Capt. Rogers's Company,
Lieut. Moore—-Killed.
Serjeant Parnell—-Ditto.
Thirty-six privates Ditto.
Of Capt. Shepherd's Company,
Two Serjeants
Sixteen privates
Of Capt. James Rogers's Company,
Ensing M'Donald—-Killed.
Of Capt, John Starks's Company,
Two serjeants—-Killed.
Fourteen privates Ditto.

GARY
ZABOLY
©2000

The Legend of Rogers' Slide

PERHAPS the one event most nearly approaching folklore in the life of Major Robert Rogers concerned a Munchausenesque feat that he might have performed during his flight from the scene of the near-annihilation of his detachment at the Battle on Snowshoes on March 13, 1758. His expedition of 175 Rangers and eight British volunteers from the 27th Regiment of Foot had encountered a superior force of French and Indians, and, despite gaining the initiative in the early stages of the battle, Rogers' men could not withstand the relentless enemy counterattack. Scores of Rangers fell, and after ninety minutes of combat in the valley of the little Bernetz Riviere (later called Trout Brook by the English), three and a half miles west of Ticonderoga, the Ranger leader ordered the survivors to run for their lives. They had left their hand sleighs and additional provisions at today's Friend's Point, five miles to the south, by the shores of frozen Lake George, and this would be their place of rendezvous.

To get there, they would have to follow their snowshoe tracks southward along the valley of the brook, roughly following the route of an old Indian path, until they reached what is today called Cook's Bay, where earlier that day they had removed their ice creepers or skates and donned snowshoes for the overland trek. This line of escape, however, would be the most hazardous, since the French and Indians would no doubt be soon swarming over the tracks in expectation of the fleeing Rangers. The only real alternative was to climb up and over the small mountain range of three peaks immediately behind the Ranger position, standing between themselves and the lake.

During this retreat the legend of Rogers' Slide was born, of his escaping the pursuing Indians by sliding down the steep naked precipice on the east face of Bald Mountain (today's Rogers' Rock): a nearly superhuman exploit that might be easily dismissed as pure fantasy were there not so many contemporary, or nearly contemporary, sources that suggested such an event might have indeed occurred.

In his *Journals* Rogers states only that he determined to make his retreat with "as many of my party as I possibly could, which I immediately did; the Indians closely pursuing us at the same time, took several prisoners. We came to Lake George in the evening ["at about eight o'clock," according to his actual post-battle report[1]], where we found several wounded men, whom we took with us to the place where we had left our sleds." No mention of any personal stunts or heroics, or that the retreat was anything but as he summarized it in those two sentences. Nevertheless, is it at all possible to flesh out the story of both his escape and that of his surviving Rangers, and thereby arrive at a chronology that might either support or completely debunk the legend?

The starting time and length of the battle must first be established. Rogers in his report says it was about "one hour and a half from the beginning of the Attack"[2] to the time of his decision to order a retreat. An account of the battle published in *The Boston Evening-Post* of April 13, 1758, noted that "The Engagement lasted from 3 oClock P.M. till half an Hour after 4." Fort Edward-based Provincial soldier Jabez Fitch somewhat concurs in his March 15th diary entry. "The Battle," he wrote, after obtaining details of the affair from survivors, "Begun at 3oClock. . .& Lasted Till Sunset".[3] In that shadowed, mountain-hemmed valley, choked with tall, thick primeval timber, winter twilight would indeed have begun closing in at about 4:30 P.M. Thus, Rogers spent nearly 3 1/2 hours—from about 4:30 to 8:00—making his way to the ice of Lake George.

The Ranger commander knew the area well after two and a half years of scouting the lake, especially its northern environs—the very edge of French occupation. He realized that the quickest route to the ice was directly south, along the western slopes of the small mountain range for about a mile and a half, and then east over a saddle that slightly notched the range, with the southernmost peak, Bald (then also known as Bare) Mountain, rising south of the saddle. The trail up and over this saddle was a little over a mile long, the generally gradual ascent of 250 feet above the valley, and equally gradual descent to the lake, making it traversable on snowshoes. (In 1973 I hiked this route with a 35-pound pack on my back, from the highway to Heart's Bay, trail's end, at a moderate pace, in only twenty minutes' time. Of course, it was early June and not snowbound March, but the ease and quickness of the trail makes it obvious why Rogers would have likely chosen it for his retreat).

That a number of the survivors made their way across this route is a logical conclusion; Rogers even offered Regular volunteers Captain Henry Pringle and Lieutenant Boyle Roche "a sergeant to conduct us thro' the mountain," in Pringle's own words from his letter printed in Rogers' *Journals*. "Thro' the mountain" could only have been a reference to the trail over the saddle. Unfortunately for Pringle and Roche, loosened and untied snowshoes prevented them from immediately joining in the general retreat, and they became lost for six days in the white forest.

Did Rogers himself get to the lake this way? He gives no clue as to the number of Rangers in his retreating party, if any. Toward the end of his official report, he writes, somewhat misleadingly—and certainly without intending to—that "Lt. Crofton got off with me in my party as did Mr. Creed the Volunteer, both of whom behaved exceedingly well."[4] What Rogers is really saying here is not that these two men actually made their retreat in his immediate company, but that they were the only survivors of note that General Abercromby would want to hear about ("my party" referring to the *entirety* of the survivors); all the other officers and Regular volunteers, with the exception of Ranger Ensign Joseph Waite, had been either killed or captured. In fact, no Ranger or volunteer survivor ever spoke of being with Rogers in the retreat, so his exact route and experiences along the way remain something of a mystery. Or do they?

Whether Rogers was alone when he retreated or with several others, he did record that fleeing Rangers were being captured or cut off from following his tracks by the superior numbers of the enraged enemy. His own servant was separated from him, and was later found wandering alone in the forest by Pringle and Roche. Observed *The New Hampshire Gazette* of March 24, 1758: " 'Tis hoped that many who were missing and dispersed in the woods, may in time return to the fort." *The Boston Gazette* of April 24 reported that "20 Men, which Major Rogers mentioned in his Journal, to be killed or Fallen prisoners, have since got safe in." It appears quite evident, then, that most of the men retreated singly, a tactic advised in Rogers' own Rule for Ranging #10: "If the enemy is so superior that you are in danger of being surrounded by them, let the whole body disperse, and every one take a different road to the place of rendezvous appointed for that evening." A few of the retreating men, like Pringle, Roche and Rogers' servant, out of necessity eventually joined together in small groups for survival. Thus, Rogers himself was probably alone for part, if not all, of the way back to the lake.

One other piece of evidence that points to his being alone is that the Ranger leader gives a much different version of his retreat in his official report. Instead of using the pronoun "we" to describe his flight to the lake, as he did in his published *Journals* seven years later, Rogers wrote to General Abercromby that "I came to Lake George in the evening about 8 o'Clock, & found there Several Wounded Men, which I took with me to the place where we left the Slays."[5] As he would refrain from mentioning in his Journals, for instance, any scalping of the enemy committed by either himself or his Rangers, in his original report Rogers is generally more forthright about things, less concerned about disguising the embarrassment of the total defeat he had suffered. The reality is that all the survivors, himself included, had been scattered over the wintry landscape and forced to run for their lives like lone, nearly helpless rabbits.

Rogers being alone is also found in the tradition that quickly arose in the aftermath of the battle. This tradition continues to be told in books, from histories of the French and Indian War to Adirondack Park travel guides. In a nutshell, it relates that he was closely pursued by Indians to the top of Bald Mountain, to a point on the cliff edge just above what has since been called "Rogers' Slide": a naked, smooth and steeply sloping (60 degrees) face of granite falling about 700 feet to the lake. By backtracking in his own snowshoe prints—or else reversing his snowshoes—and then escaping down the mountain via another way, he fooled the Indians into thinking he had actually slid down the rock face. Seeing him walking far below on the ice of the lake, and thus believing that Rogers was under the protection of an especially benevolent personal *manitou*, they gave up their chase of him. One version says that he let his pack slide down the precipice, to suggest the trail of his body–an easily dismissible version, since all of the Rangers' packs had been thrown off before the battle began.

The more sensational version has Rogers actually *sliding* down the precipitous, bald face of the mountain, and somehow surviving without debilitating injury. That Rogers does not hint at having performed such a feat, or even at having escaped his pursuers by taking another route down the mountain, is not reason enough to dismiss the legend as being without foundation. Rogers in his writings was not one for extraneous details; his accounts of scouting excursions, skirmishes and even full-scale battles are understated, almost matter-of-fact in their narrative, and often extremely hurried and sketchy. Indeed, General Abercromby, upon reading Rogers' report of his first Battle on Snowshoes, more than a year earlier, referred to it in a letter to Lord Loudoun, saying, "His relation by way of his journal is very modest."[6] This impression was echoed in a review of the first edition of the *Journals of Major Robert Rogers* in London's *Monthly Review*, in 1766, which observed that "The Author writes like an honest, a sensible and a modest man."

If Rogers had dared the incredible exploit of sliding down a huge rock face that evening, or even if he had eluded the "closely pursuing" Indians by choosing a less hazardous way down Bald Mountain, he would not have made an official record of it. In fact, admitting to such a desperate means of escaping capture or death might have done more harm than good to his reputation as a commander.

If Rogers did indeed leave the trail over the saddle and attempt to climb up Bald, the southernmost peak of the small range, could such an ascent have been possible on snowshoes? Would it also have made sense, with the Indians not far behind and with the light of a rising moon allowing his trail in the snow to be easily followed?

The answer to the first question is clearly yes. From the saddle to the summit of the mountain is an elevation gain of little more than 300 feet, and in most places the climb is gradual: not a difficult challenge for a 26-year-old Ranger officer like Rogers, whose lion-like strength and capacity for endurance were commonly known and respected by his contemporaries. Modern-day, middle-aged historians or even outdoorsmen who might attempt to duplicate this climb, under similar conditions of time and weather, will only experience inevitable frustration, and therefore think it not possible.

Another drawback for the modern hiker up Bald Mountain—now called Rogers' Rock—is that the second- and third-growth woods covering it today provide a false impression of its actual condition in 1758. Then, almost two and a half centuries ago, the forest was virginal, composed of "mostly pine woods. . .of red and white pine and cypress," noted traveler Peter Kalm of the land around that part of the lake. "Both white and red oak grew abundantly among the pines, but they were small."[7] The pines frequently grew in clumps, or stands, and the thickness of their intermingled limbs, sometimes beginning as high as 75 feet above the forest floor, allowed for the passage of only minimal sunlight, if at all; thus, underbrush was almost nonexistent in many places. Where today low-hanging branches and thickets will slow you down if you attempt to "bushwhack" your way across the Rock rather than use the existing trails, in Rogers' time the forest was frequently more open and accessible.

Nor was Rogers unaccustomed to climbing mountains in wintertime—even heights much steeper than Bald Mountain. On February 2, 1756, he and a party of Rangers "climbed a very steep mountain," as he notes in his *Journals*, a mile west of French Fort St. Frederic at Crown Point (either today's Coot's Hill or Bulwagga Mountain). In his official report to Major General William Johnson his revealing wording is that they "Clambrd up a great Mounton."[8] From the top of it he had a good view of the fort and its outworks, and there he sat down and drew a simple plan of them for his commander.

In early February 1758, Rogers led a party several miles down the ice of Lake George, and then quickly across the approximately six or seven miles of snow-draped mountain terrain to South Bay, albeit getting there too late to intercept a returning body of French and Indian raiders led by Langy.

On March 6, 1759, Rogers escorted Engineer Lieutenant Diederick Brehm to the top of Sugar Bush—today's Mount Defiance—to allow him to make observations and a map of Fort Carillon and its defenses. Conditions were so bad on this scout, and the air so cold, that a number of the men, Rogers included, suffered frostbite. No matter: the map was made, the mountain descended, and a battle was fought and won the next day with part of the French and Canadian garrison that sortied out.

Men other than Rogers and his Rangers were also climbing the snowclad mountains around Lake George. On February 12, 1756, Provincial soldier Jeduthan Baldwin, stationed at Fort William Henry, made a scout to the top of nearby Prospect Mountain, 2021 feet high, with 21 men. On March 2, Baldwin was out with Rogers on another scouting expedition to Crown Point, and noted rather casually, "We set out abt. Sunrise and marched over a large mountain called Parker's Mtn." The next day, they went "Over several large mountains."[9]On an expedition east of Lake George in February of 1758, Provincial officer Rufus Putnam and his party climbed a number of mountains despite five feet of snow on the ground.

There are other examples; but suffice to say

that consistent throughout these accounts is the fact that none of these men evidently found ascending a mountain while wearing snowshoes, even when the snow was extremely deep, so severe a challenge as to merit shirking from or complaining about it. Even after fighting a ninety-minute battle they remained stoic, hardy souls, most of them; and Rogers was arguably the hardiest of them all.

Thus, for Robert Rogers, climbing to the top of Bald Mountain on the night of March 13, 1758 would have been no impossible feat. And he seems to have had plenty of time to do it in, having fled the battlefield at 4:30 and eventually arriving on the ice of Lake George at 8 o'clock. This means he took about three and a half hours to traverse what should have been little more than a two-and-a-half-mile journey on snowshoes.

Clearly, Rogers made some kind of detour somewhere along the line of his retreat, for when he finally did arrive at the lake he "found there Several Wounded Men,"[10] who had somehow, inexplicably, outdistanced him.

Allowing, then, some credence to the legend that has Rogers reaching the cliff edge atop Bald Mountain, by understanding that he indeed *would* have had time enough to do it, we must next examine, with a combined mix of care and skepticism, the earliest sources of this romantic, incredible, and frequently-dismissed legend.

The first known reference of any kind relating directly to the legend occurred two and a half years after the battle, in the diary of British captain Christopher French, now in a private collection. While traveling on the waters of Lake George, he wrote, on October 23, 1760, "near [is] a place called Rogers' Leap from his having jumped down it to escape from Indians. I am surprised he did not break his neck, it is so dangerous a precipice."

A land petition submitted to the Governor-General of New York in 1766, by William Friend, a former officer in His Majesty's 1st Regiment of Foot, mentions "Rogers' Rock" as the northern boundary for the patent he sought. Rogers' name, then, had very quickly attached itself both to the mountain and to the slide; and mountains are not usually christened after people unless there are good reasons for doing so.

By 1777 American soldiers traveling on the lake were also noting "Rogers' Rock" in their journals. One of them, James M. Hadden, added that it was famous for Rogers' "descending a part of it with his Detachment (during the last War) where it appears almost perpendicular. This was his only alternative to escape falling into the hands of a superior Corps of Savages in the French Interest; It happen'd during the Winter which no doubt facilitated his descent by flakes of Snow &c. collected on the Rock, as in its present state one would doubt the fact if not so well authenticated,"[11]

Timothy Dwight, who went up the lake as a tourist in 1802, was given additional details about the Rock by his "guide," who said that Rogers "escaped down a narrow and steep valley at the South end of the rock, thirty or forty rods from the precipice which abuts upon the lake. The Indians supposed him to have fallen down the precipice, and therefore gave over the pursuit."[12] Dwight was also informed—evidently by someone else—that, as a young man, Vermont's Revolutionary War Lieutenant Colonel Robert Cochran had accompanied Rogers' expedition, and had made his escape on the Rock "in the same way, together with several others. This gentleman, being employed to run the line between the Counties of Essex and Washington, told his attendants, when he came to this rock, that he would show them a tree in which was lodged a musket-ball shot at himself between thirty and forty years before, in this encounter. Accordingly, he pointed out the tree, and his men cut out the ball."[13]

In 1831, Theodore Dwight Jr., nephew of Timothy Dwight, went on his own tour of Lake George, and contended in the eventual travel book he wrote that Rogers virtually skied down the Slide—on his snowshoes no less.

Francis Parkman, either unaware of or ignoring the evidence that suggested there might be some historical basis for the overall legend, wrote in his 1851 work, *History of the Conspiracy of Pontiac*, that Rogers' sliding down on his snowshoes is a story that "seems unfounded."[14] In his *Montcalm and Wolfe*, published in 1884, Parkman's opinion about Rogers' feat remains unchanged: "There is an unsupported tradition that he escaped by sliding on snowshoes down a precipice of Rogers' Rock."[15] The fantastic-sounding, snowshoe-skiing concept was repeated and accepted, however, in the 1917 monograph, *A Battle Fought On Snowshoes*, by the Major's own great-great-granddaughter, Mary Cochrane Rogers.

Perhaps it isn't really so fantastic-sounding. Expert modern snowshoers know very well how to use their *racquettes* as mock skis, generally sliding down slopes using one foot, then the other, one at a time, with the weight of the body kept back on the heels of the snowshoes. For truly steep slopes, it is suggested that the winter trekker can sit on the heels of his snowshoes and slide down, almost sled-like.[16]

If Rogers *had* made the frightening slide down

the steep and long rock incline, however the means, could he have survived without being killed or at least suffering serious injury? Other frontiersmen were known to have made cliff-edge (literally), hairbreadth escapes from Indians, and had survived intact. Daniel Boone is said to have jumped a high cliff over Dick's River, Kentucky, leapt onto the upper branches of a tall sugar maple, and climbed down it to safety, to the chagrin of his Shawnee pursuers far above him. Samuel Brady supposedly made a successful jump across an Ohio stream some 22 feet wide and 20 deep, while fleeing a war party. In September 1777, with Indians close behind him, Samuel McCulloch reportedly made a jump of over 150 feet from a cliff into Wheeling Creek, while seated on his horse; and both man and animal survived.

Perhaps the most extreme case of someone surviving a fall from a great height is to be found in *The Guinness Book of World Records*. In 1942, Russian pilot Lieutenant I. M. Chisov fell from his damaged plane, 21,980 feet in the air, *without a parachute*. He landed on the side of a snow-covered ravine and slid to the bottom. He lived to tell about it, albeit suffering a fractured pelvis and severe spinal damage.[17]

There have been many survivors of avalanches and bad ski falls, but what about those who *deliberately* chose to slide down a steep mountainside in wintertime? In 1916, British explorer Ernest Shackleton and two others, in order to reach the shelter of a whaling station on the opposite coast of South Georgia Island, in the Antarctic Ocean, slid down a steep, icy mountain slope some 2000 feet in length. They had locked themselves together, arms and legs, as if riding a bobsled; and, sitting on coils of rope, shot down the great incline at a speed of nearly a mile a minute. A snowbank cushioned their uninjured arrival at the bottom.[18]

Rogers himself had already slid down a slope in wintertime, though unintentionally, during the scout to Crown Point mentioned earlier that Jeduthan Baldwin had taken part in. In his diary entry of March 6, 1756, Baldwin notes that as they began to descend the high banks of icy Lake Champlain to cross to the eastern shore, "Capt. Rogers fell off a ledge of rocks into the lake, 26 ft. but with much difficulty he got out, but it prevented our crossing this morning as the ice was too weak."[19] Rogers himself, of course, does not mention the fall, merely stating in his *Journals*, "We then attempted to cross the lake, but found the ice too weak." Indeed he did; and once again Rogers decided that an event like falling into a lake and struggling to get back out was too irrelevant—and embarrassing—to report.

It is not the intention here to *prove* that Robert Rogers ventured, and survived, sliding down the eastern face of Bald Mountain on March 13, 1758. One can find no parallel in eighteenth-century American history that even comes close to such a feat. However, there does exist a nearly contemporary parallel feat, in a report in London's *Annual Register*, issue of December 1767, written almost ten years after the battle; nothing could better serve to point out the possibility that Rogers might have indeed made the slide, and survived it:

> They write from Newcastle, that one William Hodgson, aged twenty-two, labourer, at Sir Laurence Dundas' alum work, fell, during the late great snow, from the top of the cliff at the new work at Lofthouse, which from top to bottom measures just 155 yards. The precipice is somewhat slanting for about two-thirds from the top. He slid down that part of the rock on his breech with amazing velocity, carrying down with him a large quantity of snow, which preserved him in a great measure; and being thrown with great vehemence from a projecting crag, which turned him heels over head, he fell down perpendicular upwards of fifty yards into a snow drift at the foot of a cliff, where he lay above half an hour before his companions could get to him to take him up.[20]

Hodgson did survive the fall, although when the crag caused him to tumble uncontrollably, "heels over head," two-thirds of the way down, he began to suffer a series of injuries, including a broken right thigh and a dislocated left knee and right collar bone.[21] Up to that point, however, he had been somewhat cushioned by the snow that he carried "down with him. . .which preserved him in a great measure." Rogers' Slide has no such intervening crag, so conceivably Robert Rogers might have made the descent of nearly 700 feet "preserved" by the snow he accumulated under him (a theory somewhat suggested by James Hadden in 1777). Hodgson's entire fall was 155 yards, or 465 feet, about 235 feet less than the presumed descent by Rogers; but Hodgson's fall, thanks to the crag, was much more violent.

Could there have been enough snow on the steep slide to have effected such a snowy cushion? Rogers wrote that "the snow was four feet deep" in the valley of the Bernetz River as his men marched through it that afternoon; and the account of Captain Pringle also suggests a landscape buried under very heavy recent snowfalls; so it is quite possible that Rogers would have encountered an incline coated with at least several inches of snow, not a smooth rock face. This would certainly not have stopped his rapid fall, but it would have had the effect of decelerating it by degrees.

It isn't known if a snowdrift covered the ice at the base of Rogers' Slide on March 13, 1758, which would have certainly softened the impact of the Ranger leader's fall. But even if the snow had managed to cushion his descent, chances are that Rogers would nevertheless have experienced some sort of injury. A hint that this might have been the case is found in Jabez Fitch's entry of March 15. He noted that, after all the Ranger survivors and wounded of the March 13th battle had returned to Rogers' Island, "about 5 oClock I Se ye Majr Com in Him Self Being in ye Rear of ye Whol."[22] Some might attribute Rogers' "lagging behind" as the heroic thing to do following the near-annihilation of his party, or perhaps he was commanding a rear guard in the event of the enemy's possible follow-up attack on his column. But an alternate explanation might be that he was simply limping from an injury suffered during his retreat, or even on the slide. Rogers wrote his official report of the battle on March 17, and went to Albany within a week to confer with Lord Howe, so he had at least four or five days of rest following his return. The journey to Albany—even if he was not nursing an injured foot or leg—would probably have been made by sleigh.

Going down the slide, however, was not the only way open to Rogers to make his descent to the lake that night. In order to get to the very top of the slide to begin such a hazardous but speedy descent, you must first climb down from the summit edge some 50 feet until you reach a narrow ledge rimmed with trees. This ledge continues on in either direction, north and south; standing there, you can plainly see that you have other, more sensible ways of descending than by taking the slide itself. Perhaps this is what Rogers realized, too, if this is the route he took. On either side of the naked slide, the mountain slope, while no less steep, is more broken, split with narrow crevices and jutting with minute ledges, and is covered with enough trees and brush for one to cling to while descending in safer, much slower increments, as opposed to the unhindered, breakneck velocity the slide itself would have engendered.

We can see, then, that an escape via the slide by moving down its more maneuverable and brushy margins, was far from impossible, and much saner. But even an escape down the smooth slide itself cannot be entirely written off, if the conditions had happened to be just right for Rogers that night. Men and women often perform incredible feats of strength and daring when faced with sudden, seemingly insurmountable challenges, especially when the issue is life-and-death. With Rogers, it was an issue of almost certain death—one by slow torture or disembowelment no doubt—behind him, while the Slide at least offered him a chance roll of the dice.

If even this scenario is too improbable for many to accept, there remains the other Rogers escape route on the Rock that Dwight and Colonel Cochran mentioned: the "narrow and steep valley" at the southern end of the mountain.

In early July of 1972 I made my way to the top of Rogers' Rock, and eventually arrived at the open, rocky clearing at its most southeastern crest——the place where French advanced pickets were often posted because it gave them an unobstructed view of the lake all the way to the shoreline below Black Mountain, twelve miles away. It was about 6 P.M., and I decided it was time to return to my tent site at the Rogers Rock campground just south of the mountain. I had pretty much done my own pathfinding across the Rock, but the thin trail here was well worn and dusty, and so I followed it west, intent on making a gradual descent on the western slope of the mountain. It kept to the edge of the summit, allowing for fine views of lake and forest; but soon I saw another interesting thing. A ravine, or small valley, broke the southern flank of the mountain into two jutting abutments. The ravine itself was strewn with large boulders, and trees and ledges peppered its length. As a boy I had often climbed and played on the large granite cliffs in the parks that edge upper Manhattan Island, so it looked like a very doable, and obvious, shortcut. Indeed it was, and to my surprise I made it to the bottom of the mountain via the ravine in a matter of minutes.

At the time I was unaware of any account that had Rogers descending this way; it wasn't until a few years later, after engaging in more research on this battle, that I made the connection between my accidental discovery and the "folklore" about Rogers' alternate route. It all began to look to me more like historical reality, and my opinion about the legend of his escaping via Bald Mountain being pure invention was forever discarded.

The final question, perhaps, is *why* Rogers and some of his men would choose to climb up Bald Mountain that night, instead of taking the easier path across the saddle—or even following their own tracks made earlier that day and leading southward along the valley of the brook—to get to the ice of the lake.

Captain Henry Pringle offers probably the most graphic explanation, and this from the pen of one of the survivors: "such dispositions were formed by the enemy. . .it was impossible for a party so weak as ours to hope for even a retreat." When Pringle and Roche realized they could not retreat in time with their comrades, Pringle wrote that he "leaned against a rock in the path, determined to submit to a fate I thought unavoidable. . . Every instant we expected the savages; but what induced them to quit this path, in which we actually saw them, we are ignorant of, unless they changed it for a shorter, to intercept those who had just left us." No doubt this is exactly what the Indians had done.

Their backs to the mountain range, and their front and flanks either hemmed in or completely cut off, Rogers and his surviving men had no choice but to retreat southward and higher along the slopes behind them until they reached the saddle trail. That the Indians knew of this trail, and endeavored to "intercept" those Rangers fleeing toward it, is almost certain. Rogers and a handful of his Rangers, once they had arrived there, probably saw that they had been cut off—or were about to be—and so they turned instead to bypass the Indians by climbing the northern flanks of Bald Mountain.

Montcalm wrote to Minister M. de Paulmy, from Montreal on April 10, 1758: "I am fully persuaded that the small number who escaped the fury of the Indians, will perish of want."[23] This impression is one that is common to all the contemporary French accounts: the battle's aftermath had resulted in the utter dispersal of those English who had escaped the Indians' pursuit, and these survivors were given, if wrongly, little chance of returning to Fort Edward alive. Rogers himself was deemed among the slain.

Again, this has not been written to prove that any one of the above scenarios relating to Rogers' escape actually occurred; but rather to show that they very well could have, and that one of them probably did serve as the origin of the "legend." Real life is never pre-programmed like fiction, where characters must operate and behave in the logical ways we expect them to, and where plot and incidents must reflect a plausible reality and outcome.

Looking at the steep and exposed face of Rogers' Slide today, the word "impossible" comes to mind when the idea of the Ranger leader descending that way is proposed. Even the idea that Rogers and others could have, or would have, climbed up Bald Mountain that frozen night seems, at first glance, illogical and improbable. But such assumptions, especially when all the available evidence has not been carefully examined, are too obviously easy and arrogant opinions born of ignorance. In this case, at least, there might be more truth to the legend than many of us might be willing to concede.

G.Z.

1. Burt Garfield Loescher, *The History of Rogers' Rangers: Vol. I, The Beginnings, January 1755-April 6, 1758*, San Francisco, 1946, p. 368.
2. Ibid., p. 367.
3. *The Diary of Jabez Fitch Jr., in the French and Indian War*, Rogers Island Historical Association, Glens Falls, New York, second edition, 1968, p. 54.
4. Loescher, p. 368.
5. Ibid., p. 368.
6. Idem, p. 342.
7. Peter Kalm, *Travels Into North America*, Warrington, England, 1770, Dover Publications reprint, New York, 1987, p. 597.
8. E. B. O'Callaghan, ed., *Documentary History of the State of New York, Vol. IV, New York*, 1849-50, p. 184.
9. "The Diary of Jeduthan Baldwin," *Journal of the Military Service Institute*, Vol. XXXIX, July-August 1906, p. 127.
10. Loescher, p. 368.
11. Russell P. Bellico, *Chronicles of Lake George: Journeys In War and Peace*, Purple Mountain Press, Fleischmanns, New York, 1995, p. 184.
12. Ibid., p. 221.
13. Idem, pp. 221-222.
14. Francis Parkman, *History of the Conspiracy of Pontiac*, MacMillan Company, New York, reprint of 1929, p. 105.
15. Francis Parkman, *Montcalm and Wolfe*, Little Brown & Company, Boston, 1901, Vol. II, p. 19.
16. Carl Heilmann, "Snowshoe Trekking," *Harrowsmith Country Life*, Jan./Feb. 1993, p. 62.
17. Norris McWhirter, *The Guinness Book of World Records*, Bantam Books, New York, 1980, p.467.
18. Alfred Lansing, *Endurance: Shackleton's Incredible Voyage*, Avon Books, New York, p. 256.
19. Baldwin, p. 127.
20. The *Annual Register*, December 1767, pp. 72-73.
21. Ibid., p. 73.
22. Fitch, p. 53.
23. Loescher, p. 384.

Of Capt. Bulkley's Company,
Capt. Bulkley—-Killed.
Lieut. Pottinger—-Ditto.
Ensign White—-Ditto.
Forty-seven privates—-K. and Miss.
Of Capt. William Starks's Company,
Ensign Ross—-Killed.
Of Capt. Brewer's Company,
Lieut. Campbell Killed.

A Gentleman of the army, who was a volunteer on this party, and who with another fell into the hands of the French, wrote the following letter, some time after, to the officer commanding the regiment they belonged to at Fort Edward.

"*Carillon, March* 28, 1758.

"Dear Sir,

As a flag of truce is daily expected here with an answer to Monsieur Vaudreuil, I sit down to write the moment I am able, in order to have a letter ready, as no doubt you and our friends at Fort Edward are anxious to be informed about Mr.—— and me, whom probably you have reckoned amongst the slain in our unfortunate encounter of the 13th, concerning which at present I shall not be particular; only to do this justice to those who lost their lives there, and to those who have escaped, to assure you, Sir, that such dispositions were formed by the enemy, (who discovered us long enough before) it was impossible for a party so weak as ours to hope for even a retreat. Towards the conclusion of the affair, it was cried from a rising ground on our right, to retire there; where, after scrambling with difficulty, as I was unaccustomed to snow-shoes, I found Capt. Rogers, and told him that I saw to retire further was impossible, therefore earnestly begged we might collect all the men left, and make a stand there. Mr.———, who was with him, was of my opinion, and Capt. Rogers also; who therefore desired me to maintain one side of the hill, whilst he defended the other. Our parties did not exceed above ten or twelve in each, and mine was shifting towards the mountain, leaving me unable to defend my post, or to labour with them up the hill. In the mean time, Capt. Rogers with his party came to me, and said (as did all those with him) that a large body of Indians had ascended to our right; he likewise added, what was true, that the combat was very unequal, that I must retire, and he would give Mr.——— and me a Serjeant to conduct us thro' the mountain. No doubt prudence required us to accept his offer; but, besides one of my snow-shoes being untied, I knew myself unable to march as fast as was requisite to avoid becoming a sacrifice to an enemy we could no longer oppose; I therefore begged of him to proceed, and then leaned against a rock in the path, determined to submit to a fate I thought unavoidable. Unfortunately for Mr.——— his snow-shoes were loosened likewise, which obliged him to determine with me, not to labour in a flight we were both unequal to. Every instant we expected the savages; but what induced them to quit his path, in which we actually saw them, we are ignorant of, unless they changed it for a shorter, to intercept those who had just left us. By their noise, and making of fire, we imagined they had got the rum in the Rangers packs. This thought, with the approach of night, gave us the first hopes of retiring; and when the moon arose, we marched to the southward along the mountain, about three hours, which brought us to ice, and gave us reason to hope our difficulties were almost past; but we knew not we had enemies yet to combat with more cruel than the savages we had escaped. We marched all night, and on the morning of the 14th found ourselves entirely unacquainted with the ice. Here we saw a man, who came towards us; he was the servant of Capt. Rogers, with whom he had been oftentimes all over the country, and, without the least hesitation whatsoever, he informed us we were upon South-Bay; that Wood-Creek was just before us; he knew the way to Fort Anne extremely well, and would take us to Fort Edward the next day. Notwithstanding we were disappointed in our hopes of being upon Lake George, we thought ourselves fortunate in meeting such a guide, to whom we gave entire confidence, and which he in fact confirmed, by bringing us to a creek, where he shewed the tracks of Indians, and the path he said they had taken to Fort Anne. After struggling thro' the snow some hours, we were obliged to halt to make snowshoes, as Mr.——— and the guide had left theirs at arriving upon the ice. Here we remained all night without any blankets, no coat, and but a single waistcoat each, for I gave one of mine to Mr.——, who had a laid aside his green jacket in the field, as I did likewise my furred cap, which became a mark to the enemy, and probably was the cause of a slight wound in my face; so that I had but a silk handkerchief on my head, and our fire could not be large, as we had nothing to cut wood with.

While green clothing offers good concealment for most of the year, during the winter such is not the case. Some of the Rangers may have laid their green jackets aside because of the way they contrasted with the winter landscape.

An interesting testimonial to the value of green uniforms is contained in the journal of Colonel John Simcoe, who eventually took over the command of the Queen's Rangers, the unit that Robert Rogers started during the Revolutionary War. Simcoe writes, "green is without comparison the best color for light troops with dark accoutrements; and if put on in the spring, by autumn it nearly fades with the leaves, preserving its characteristic of being scarcely discernable at a distance." (Simcoe, p. 38)

Before morning we contrived with forked sticks and strings of leather, a sort of snow-shoes, to prevent sinking entirely; and, on the 15th, followed our guide west all day, but he did not fulfill his promise; however the next day it was impossible to fail; but even then, the 16th, he was unsuccessful; yet still we were patient, because he seemed well acquainted with the way, for he gave every mountain a name, and shewed us several places, where he said his master had either killed deer or encamped. The ground, or rather the want of sunshine, made us incline to the south-ward, from whence by accident we saw ice, at several miles distance, to the south-east. I was very certain, that after marching two days west of South Bay, Lake George could not be south-east from us, and therefore concluded this to be of the upper end of the bay we had left. For this reason, together with the assurances of our guide, I advised continuing our course to the west, which must shortly strike Fort Anne, or some other place that we knew. But Mr.——— wished to be upon the ice at any rate; he was unable to continue in the snow, for the difficulties of our march had overcome him. And really, Sir, was I to be minute in those we had experienced already and afterwards, they would almost be as tiresome to you to read, as they were to us to suffer.

"Our snow-shoes breaking, and sinking to our middle every fifty paces, the scrambling up mountains and across fallen timber, our nights without sleep or covering, and but little fire, gathered with great fatigue, our sustenance mostly water, and the bark and berries of trees; for all our provisions from the beginning was only a small Bologna sausage, and a little ginger, I happened to have, and which even now was very much decreased; so that I knew not how to oppose Mr.———'s intreaties; but as our guide still persisted Fort Anne was near, we concluded to search a little longer, and if we made no discovery to proceed next day towards the ice; but we fought in vain, as did our guide the next morning, tho' he returned, confidently asserting he the had discovered fresh proofs, that the fort could not be far off. I confess I was still inclined to follow him, for I was almost certain the best we could hope from the descending upon this ice to our left was to throw ourselves into the hands of the French, and perhaps not be able to effect even that; but from the circumstances I have mentioned, it was a point I must yield to, which I did with great reluctancy. The whole day of the 17th we marched a dreadful road, between the mountains, with but one good snow-shoe each, the other of our own making being almost useless. The 18th brought us to the ice which tho' we longed to arrive at, yet I still dreaded the consequence, and with reason, for the first sight informed us, it was the very place we had left five days before. Here I must own my resolution almost failed me, when fatigue, cold, hunger, and even the prospect of perishing in the woods attended us, I still had hopes, and still gave encouragement, but now I wanted it myself; we had no resource but to throw ourselves into the enemy's hands, or perish. We had nothing to eat, our slender stock had been equally shared amongst us three, and we were not so fortunate as to ever to see either bird or beast to shoot at. When our first thoughts were a little calmed, we conceived hopes, that if we appeared before the French fort, with a white flag, the commanding officer would relieve and return us to Fort Edward. This served to palliate our nearest approach to despair, and determined a resolution, where, in fact, we had no choice. I knew Carillon had an extensive view up South Bay, therefore we concluded to halt during the evening, and march in the night, that we might approach it in the morning, besides the wind pierced us like a sword; but instead of its abating it increased, together with a freezing rain, that incrusted us entirely with ice, and obliged us to remain until morning, the 19th, when we fortunately got some juniper berries, which revived, gave us spirits, and I thought strength. We were both so firmly of that opinion, that we purposed taking the advantage of its being a dark snowy day, to approach Carillon, to pass it in the night, and get upon Lake George. With difficulty we persuaded the guide to be of our opinion, we promised large rewards in vain, until I assured him of provisions hid upon the lake; but we little considered how much nature was exhausted, and how unequal we were to the task: however, a few miles convinced us, we were soon midway up our legs in the new-fallen snow; it drove full in our faces, and was as dark as the fogs upon the banks of Newfoundland. Our strength and our hopes sunk together, nay, even those of reaching Carillon were doubtful, but we must proceed or perish. As it cleared up a little, we laboured to see the fort, which at every turn we expected, until we came to where the ice was gone, and the water narrow. This did not then agree with my idea of South Bay but it was no time for reflection; we quitted the ice to the left, and after marching two miles, our guide assured us we ought to be on the other side of the water. This was a very distressing circumstance, yet we returned to the ice and passed to the right, where, after struggling through the snow, about four miles, and breaking in every second step, as we had no snow-shoes, we were stopped by a large water-fall. Here I was again astonished with appearances, but nothing now was to be thought of only reaching the fort before night; yet to pass this place seemed impracticable: however, I attempted to ford it a little higher, and had almost gained the opposite shore, where the depth of the water, which was up to my breast, and the rapidity of the stream, hurried me off the slippery rocks, and plunged me entirely into the waters. I was obliged to quit my fuzee, and with great difficulty escaped being carried down the fall. Mr.———, who followed me, and the guide, though they held one another, suffered the same fate; but the hope of soon reaching a fire made us think lightly of this: as night approached we laboured excessively through the snow; we were certain the fort was not far from us, but our guide confessed, for the first time, that he was at a loss. Here we plainly observed that his brain was affected: he saw Indians all around him, and though we have since learned we had everything to fear from them, yet it was a danger we did not now attend to; nay we shouted several times to give information we were there; but we could neither hear nor see any body to lead us right, or more likely to destroy us, and if we halted a minute we became pillars of ice; so that we were resolved, as it froze so hard, to make a fire, although the danger was apparent. Accidentally we had one dry cartridge, and in trying with my pistol if it would flash a little of the powder, Mr.——— unfortunately held the cartridge too near, by which it took fire, blew up in our faces, almost blinded him, and gave excessive pain. This indeed promised to be the last stroke of fortune, as hopes of a fire were no more; but although we were not anxious about life, we knew it was more becoming to oppose than yield to this last misfortune. We made a path around a tree, and there exercised all night, though scarcely able to stand, or prevent each other from sleeping. Our guide not withstanding repeated cautions, straggled from us where he sat down and died immediately. On the morning of the 20th, we saw the fort, which we approached with a white flag: the officers run violently towards us, and saved us from a danger we did not then apprehend; for we were informed, that if the Indians, who were close after them, had seized us first, it would not have been in the power of the French to have prevented our being hurried to their camp, and perhaps to Montreal the next day, or killed for not being able to march. Mons. Debecourt and all his officers treated us with humanity and politeness, and are solicitous in our recovery, which returns slowly, as you may imagine, from all these difficulties; and though I have omitted many, yet I am afraid you will think me too prolix; but we wish, Sir, to persuade you of a truth, that nothing but the situation I have faithfully described could determine us in a resolution which appeared only one degree preferable to perishing in the woods.

"I shall make no comments upon these distresses; the malicious perhaps will say, which is very true, we brought them upon ourselves; but let them not wantonly add, we deserved them because we were unsuccessful. They must allow we could not be led abroad, at such a season of snow and ice, for amusement, or by an idle curiosity. I gave you, Sir, my reasons for asking leave, which you were pleased to approve, and I hope will defend them; and the same, would make me again, as a volunteer, experience the chance of war to-morrow, had I an opportunity. These are Mr. ———'s sentiments as well as mine; and we both know you, Sir, too well to harbour the least doubt of receiving justice with regard to our conduct in this affair, or our promotion in the regiment; the prospect of not joining that so soon as we flattered ourselves has depressed our spirits to the lowest degree, so that we earnestly beg you will be solicitous with the General to have us restored as soon as possible, or at least to prevent our being sent to France, and separated from you, perhaps, during the war.

"I have but one thing more to add, which we learned here, and which perhaps you have already observed from what I have said, that we were upon no other ice than that of Lake George; but by the day overtaking us, the morning of the 14th, in the very place we had, in coming, marched during the night, we were entirely unacquainted with it, and obliged to put a confidence in this guide, whose head must have been astray from the beginning, or he could not so grossly have mistaken a place where he had so often been. This information but added to our distress, until we reflected that our not being entirely lost was the more wonderful. That we had parted from South Bay on the 14th, was a point with us beyond all doubt, and about which we never once hesitated, so that we acted entirely contrary to what we had established as a truth; for if, according to that, we had continued our course to the west, we must inevitably have perished; but the hand of Providence led us back contrary to our judgment; and though even then, and often afterwards, we thought it severe, yet in the end it saved us, and obliged us to rest satisfied that we construed many things unfortunate, which tended to our preservation. I am, & c."

Canadian historian Ian McCulloch has established that Captain Henry Pringle of the 27th Regiment is the author of this letter. He discovered a copy of the letter in Pringle's *Entrybook,* which is in the National Archives of Canada. (McCulloch *Men of the 27th*, p. 141)

Connecticut Provincial Jabez Fitch gives a clear and fairly accurate account of this battle in his journal. On March 14, he writes, "About Noon Som of Marj Rogerss Scout Came in & inform yt [that] they Have Had a hot Ingagment Such as Scarce Ever was Know in ye Country & Most of His Party are Distroyd—Capts Stark Shepperd & Durke with all ye Rangers yt Could By any Means Be Spaird Was Emmediately Sent out To Help in those yt were Left Alive as there were Many Wounded &c—This afternoon Som others Came in & Inform Much Like ye Former—I went Down to Capt: Durkes & Got Information yt Capt: Bulkley Lieuts More Camble McDanll & Som other offrs were Sartainly Kild—Lt Tracy Tells Me yt Josh Johnson is Dead & that Josh Chequipes Has Got a Ltcy In ye Ranging Corp—"

On March 15, Fitch continues, "In ye

Morning there was 3 Hors Slays Sent to Meet ye Majrs Party in order To Help in His wounded Men &c—About 3 oClock I Se ye Majr Com in Him Self Being in ye Rear of ye Whol—This was a Vast Cold & Tedious Day Especially for ye Wounded Men—In This Action Capt: Buckley was Kild & 3 offrs of ye Ragls was Either Kild or Captavated—I Am Informd yt of ye Sub: Belonging To ye Ranging Corp & No offr Escaped Except ye Majr & 2 Lts—The Whol Scout Consisted of 180 & About 40 Returnd 5 of which were wounded—Corpl Shamon of Capt: Putnams Company was Lost in this Action—& Sarjt Humphrys of ye Ragls—The Battle was Fought about 4 Mils west from Tianderoge it Began at 3 oClock on ye 13th of March—& Lasted Til Sunset—ye Majr Drove ye Enimy from ye Ground 3 Times & Got a Number of Scalps—But ye Enimy were Cheefly Indions But I am Informd yt they Gave our People Vary Good Quarter—In ye Majrs Last Retreet he Lost all His Scalps Except one—" (Fitch, pp. 53-54)

In April, General James Abercromby gave this account of the action in a letter to William Pitt in England: "I received an Account, of a Skirmish, between Capt. Rogers, and a Superior party of the Enemy, on the 13th of last Month, within five Miles of Tienderoga, in which, the Captain and His Command, distinguished themselves, but for a more particular Detail thereof, I must beg leave to refer you to His own Journal." (Pitt, Volume I, p. 232) This is not particularly revealing as to the details of the battle, but it does indicate that Rogers was keeping suitably complete records of his activities as they occurred.

In his 1772 history of the war, Thomas Mante gives this account: "As the operations of the English on the continent were once more to be directed against Ticonderoga and Fort du Quesne, Captain Rogers, being appointed a major in America only, and the corps of Rangers under his command being augmented, was ordered to discover the strength of the French at the first of these places. Accordingly, the Major issued from Fort Edward, on this service, with one hundred and seventy men, on the 10th of March; but, on the 13th, he unexpectedly fell in with a party of one hundred French, and six hundred Indians. A severe action was the consequence; in which both the Major and those under him did everything that could be expected from good officers and soldiers, killing about one hundred and fifty of the enemy, and wounding as many more; though not without losing five of his officers, and about one hundred rank and file killed. The enemy, therefore, still retaining their superiority in point of strength, and leaving him, of course, but very little hopes of succeeding better in a second attack, he thought it prudent to retreat. Lieutenant Philips, and a few men, who had surrendered, in this affair, to the French Indians, in consequence of a promise of protection, were inhumanly tied up to trees, and cut to pieces." (Mante, pp 111-112) Mante makes the same mistake that Rogers makes in stating that Lieutenant Philips was killed.

For comparison purposes, it is interesting to read the French accounts of this same action, which has become known as "The Second Battle on Snowshoes," or "The Battle of Rogers' Rock." Captain Malartic's account gives a hint that the French did indeed know that Rogers was coming: "A Cadet, detached from Carillon, came to inform the General that M. la Durantaye's party had arrived the 12th, on which day an old sorcerer had assured them that they would see the English before long; on the morning of the 13th, 5 or 6 Indian scouts came to say that they had discovered fresh tracks of 200 men, whereupon the chiefs raised the muster-whoop and set out immediately with their warriors, some soldiers and Canadians, who traveled nearly 3 leagues without meeting any one; suspecting that the English had taken the Falls road, they took the same course; M. la Durantaye, who had joined them at the Bald Mountain, was with the vanguard; he received the enemy's first fire, which made him fall back a little, and gave them time to scalp two Indians whom they had killed; meanwhile, M. de Langy, having turned them with a strong party of Indians, and having fallen on them when they felt sure of victory, had entirely defeated them; the Indians having discovered a chiefs scalp in the breast of an officer's jacket, refused all quarter, and took 114 scalps; the opinion is, that only 12 or 15 men escaped, and that this detachment was composed of 170 @. [sic] 180, commanded by Captain Roger, who is supposed to be among the killed." (*D.R.C.H.S.N.Y.* Volume 10, pp. 837-38)

On April 10, 1758, Montcalm wrote from Montreal to the Marquis de Paulmy: "Capt. D'hebecourt, [Captain Louis-Philippe Le Dossu d'Hebecourt] of the regiment of La Reine, who commands at Carillon, having been informed, on the thirteenth of March, that the enemy had a detachment in the field, which was estimated by the trail to number about two hundred men, sent a like detachment of our domiciliated Indians, Iroquois and Nepissings, belonging to the Sault St. Louis and the Lake of the Two Mountains, who had arrived on the preceding evening, with some thirty Canadians and several Cadets of the Colonial troops, under the command of Sieur de la Durantaye, of the same troops; Sieur de Langy, one of the officers of the Colony, who understands petty war the best of any man, joined the party with some of the Lieutenants of our battalions, who are detached at Carillon. The English detachment consisted of two hundred picked men, under the command of Major Roger, their most famous partizan, and twelve officers. He has been utterly defeated; our Indians would not give any quarter; have brought back one hundred and forty-six scalps; they retained only three prisoners to furnish *live letters to their father.* [Live letters is an Indian term meaning prisoners for interrogation].

"About four or five days after, two officers and five English surrendered themselves prisoners, because they were wandering in the woods, dying of hunger. I am fully persuaded that small number who escaped the fury of the Indians, will perish of want, and not have returned to Fort Lydius. We have had two Colonial Cadets and one Canadian slightly wounded, but the Indians, who are not accumstomed to lose, have had eight killed and seventeen wounded, two of whom are in danger of dying. The Marquis de Vaudreuil takes great care of the sick; has made presents in the name *of the Great Ononthio* (that is, the King), to the families of those who have been slain, and the dead on this occasion have been covered with great ceremony; [the practice of giving presents to the families of Indians slain in battle] the Indians are content and very anxious to avenge their loss. Lieutenant de Fouriet, of the la Sarre regiment, and Sieur d'Arenne, proposed to be employed in the regiment of Languedoc, have distinguished themselves on this occasion.

"*The live letters,* or, to use a more correct expression, the prisoners, do not as yet furnish us anything decisive regarding the project of the English . . . ." (*D.R.C.H.S.N.Y.* Volume 10, p. 693)

A document entitled "Bulletin of the Most important Operations during the winter of 1757-8," dated from Montreal, April 18, 1758, is similar, but gives some additional details:

"The English have had all winter the design to surprise and bombard Carillon, and have made their appearance before it several times. Captain d'hebencourt, of the regiment of La Reine, who has been appointed, after the campaign, Commandant of that post, and the garrison have been very alert, and the incursions of the English have always been bootless. Sieur d'hebencourt being informed that they had a party of 200 men in the field, profited on the 13th of March, by the fortunate arrival, on the preceding evening, of 200 Iroquois or Nepissings from Sault St. Louis and the Lake of the Two Mountains, with Sieur Durantaye and several Colonial Cadets, who were joined by Sieur de Langry, a very intelligent officer, some Lieutenants and sergeants of our battalions, whom zeal alone had induced to march thither. The English detachment, composed of picked men and of 12 officers, under the command of Major Roger, their best partizan, has been totally defeated. The Indians have brought back 146 scalps; few prisoners—merely some to furnish *their father with live letters*—an expression used by the Indians to designate prisoners. The remainder will have perished of want in the

The Renovated 55th

AS GENERAL WEBB in the early fall of 1757 consolidated his garrison at Fort Edward with the returning troops from the failed Nova Scotia expedition, he ordered, in Robert Rogers' own words, that Rangers be "continually employed in patrolling the woods between this fort and Ticonderoga. In one of these parties, my Lord How(sic) did us the honour to accompany us, being fond, as he expressed himself, to learn our method of marching, ambushing, retreating, &c, and, upon our return, expressed his good opinion of us very generously."

Irish-born Lord Viscount George Augustus Howe, Brigadier-General in the British army and Colonel of the 55th Regiment of Foot, was a commander with an almost unparalleled genius for leadership and innovation. Drawing from his experience with the Rangers, he began to revamp his regiment into a kind of light infantry, outfitted for wilderness marching and trained in bush-fighting tactics; it soon became a model for the rest of the army under Major General James Abercromby's overall command.

Being universally liked on a personal level by both the Regular and Provincial soldiers, Howe proved himself an easy convincer: his innovations were quickly and readily adopted by most. And these changes were quite radical, especially for the tradition-bound redcoats. By the early summer of 1758, Abercromby's soldiers, gathering for the final push against Fort Carillon, had been transformed, in the words of one of them, into a species of fighting men whose attire made them resemble "common Ploughmen."[1]

Hats were ordered trimmed down to narrow brims. Queues were snipped off, and hair cropped to within an inch of the skull. Coats were cut nearly to the waist, and all lace and "regimentals" (facings and cuffs) were removed to make the uniform as light as possible. Waistcoats were also deemed superfluous, and left behind with swords and hangers. Linen overalls or buckskin breeches were preferred over the army-issue breeches. Checked shirts were probably provided for field use.

Indian-style leggings (green being the favored color) protected their legs from brush and insects. They rolled up their provision-filled haversacks in their blankets, and these in turn were wrapped in bearskin mattresses or other covers, the bundles tied and carried with tumplines a la Rangers, Canadians and Indians.

The officers were not to wear sashes, but only gorgets to distinguish themselves while on duty. The deliberate shooting-down of Braddock's officers by the enemy at the Monongahela was not lost on Lord Howe (although, ironically, he would be one of the first men killed in the upcoming campaign). Officers generally carried fusils. The muskets of the men were cut down to make them lighter and more manageable in the woods, and their barrels were blackened to prevent sun glint. The ten best marksmen in each regiment received rifle-barreled carbines of an undetermined manufacture, equipped with iron ramrods and bayonets. Leather lock covers, and plugs for the gun muzzles, kept their weapons generally free from damp. Waistbelts carried the bayonets, and tomahawks in place of swords.

By more than one report, Howe was said to have had such a "soldier-like constitution" that he was able to "undergo all hardships."[2] Evidently two or three officers did not share his strength or spirit, for they refused to obey his demands for reform, and he had them arrested; "and it is very likely," wrote one observer, "they will be broke for setting a bad example to the army." [3]

The scene depicts Lord Howe, at left, on a training exercise with his regiment in the rugged country skirting the southern perimeter of Lake George. The man at right carries a rifled carbine. In truth, Howe's renovations had turned the British Army, in 1758 at least, into a force of carbon-copy Rogers' Rangers.

G.Z.

1. "Extract of a letter from Flat Bush, dated June 28, 1758," in *Boston Evening-Post*, July 3, 1758.
2. "Part of a Letter from New-York, May 31, 1758" in *London Chronicle*, August 19, 1758.
3. Ibid.

Note: Many of the details concerning Lord Howe's renovations were culled from reports printed in contemporary American and British newspapers. The recollections of Anne MacVickers, as excerpted in Norreys J. O'Conor, *A Servant of the Crown in England and in North America*, 1756-1761, New York: Appleton-Century, 1938, pp. 92-95, both support and enlarge upon the newspaper accounts. Captain Pierre Pouchot's *Memoirs on the Late War in North America Between France and England*, translated by Michael Cardy, edited and annotated by Brian Leigh Dunnigan, Old Fort Niagara Association, Inc., Youngstown, New York, 1994, p. 139, provides additional details on the accoutering of the men under Howe and Abercromby.

Gary Zaboly
©1999

woods. A few, including two officers of Bleknis' regiment voluntarily surrendered themselves prisoners at our fort at Carillon, at the end of five days, their guide having died the night before. [The regiment referred to was The 27th or Inniskilling Regiment. The officers were Captain Pringle and Lieutenant Roche.] We have lost in that action 8 Indians and have had 17 wounded; also two Cadets of the Colony and one Canadian. The dead have been covered with great ceremony; presents have been made to the families in the name of the King (the Great Ononthio). The Governor-General will reward the bravery of our Iroquois by a promotion and a presentation of some gorgets and medals to those who have distinguished themselves; they will be thereby more encouraged to revenge the loss they have suffered." (*D.R.C.H.S.N.Y.* Volume 10, p. 697)

Another account, written by the Paymaster General, Andre Doreil, to the Marshal de Belle Isle on April 30, is not as complete as those above, but does offer some different details:

"March 13. Robert Roger, the partisan, returning with 200 men to try to strike a blow in the environs of Carillon, was discovered by some Indians sent out by M. d'hebecourt, who came in all haste to advise him of the fact. This officer immediately dispatched a detachment of 200 Canadians and Indians who had arrived the evening before from Montreal. This detachment stopped Rogers' march and utterly defeated him. The Indians brought back 144 scalps and some prisoners; among the latter were two officers. There were 12 in the party. Robert escaped almost naked, with some fifteen men and two officers. There is reason to presume that he will have perished of cold and hunger in the woods, inasmuch as three days subsequently, the two officers, after having wandered in a vain effort to escape, came to surrender themselves prisoners at Carillon, having left two men dead of fatigue and hunger within two leagues of that place. This action has been brisk, and our detachment has performed wonders in it. We have had two Cadets dangerously wounded, four Indians killed and 16 wounded." (*D.R.C.H.S.N.Y.* Volume 10, p. 703)

Governor Vaudreuil's report to Marshal Duke de Noailles shows that at least some of the French thought that Rogers' scout was the prelude to the anticipated winter attack on Ticonderoga. It also shows Vaudreuil's tendency for self promotion: "[The British] laid their plan to scale Fort Carillon; their preparations were perfect; their ladders constructed, and their army ready to march . . . . I had been careful to send some parties of Canadians and Indians against them, who by their zeal and good disposition found resources for their support. I shall confine myself, my Lord, to that detachment, on whose return the enemy's army was to put itself in motion. 'Twas a detachment *d'elite* commanded by Major Robert Rogers, the most celebrated English partizan. He had orders from his officer to break up the ice, to lay down the route the army was to follow. But that detachment was entirely defeated by a party of soldiers of the Marine, Canadians and Indians, the command of which I had confided to a few simple Cadets belonging to our troops.

"In this way, my Lord, I protected the Colony, during the winter, from the menaces of our enemies." (*D.R.C.H.S.N.Y.* Volume 10, p. 809)

Bougainville recorded the battle in his journal entry for March 19: "News from Carillon of the fifteenth, Sieur de Hebecourt, commanding at this fort, having been warned by two Abnakis that they had discovered some fresh tracks, sent out scouts whose report was that there was a great English body marching from the direction of St. Frederic. M. de la Durantaye, arrived the night before, left with his two hundred Sault St. Louis Iroquois. MM. de Montegron, de Force, lieutenant of La Sarre, and d'Avesine, sub-lieutenant of Bearn, joined him. Our advance guard fell on the enemy, who then first discovered them, and delivered a discharge at point-blank range. But the main body having come up and M. de Langis having turned the enemy, the detachment under command of Captain Rogers was entirely defeated. The Indians brought back 144 scalps and took seven prisoners. We had two cadets wounded, a Canadian wounded, three Iroquois and a Nipissing killed, eighteen Iroquois wounded, almost all severely, [and] an Abnaki whose arm it was necessary to amputate." (Bougainville, pp. 198-199)

Pierre Pouchot adds some interesting additional information in his memoirs: "A few officers & soldiers of the garrison desired to participate in the raid. They set out in the direction of the lake. Three leagues further on, their scouts recognized numerous human footprints on the lake ice and returned to inform the main party of the fact. They immediately decided to go back into the woods through which the English had to pass. Our scouts, seeing the English company marching down a small hill, ran to warn their comrades who were close by. They arrived at the top of a small rise at the very moment when the English were at the bottom of the hill. They attacked & in an instant had killed 146 of them. Only about fifteen out of a company of 200 escaped. Robert Roger, in command of them, left behind his uniform, his commission & his orders the better to flee. Eleven officers or volunteers had joined this detachment, 4 of whom belonged to the regiments recently arrived from England. Five of them went to Carillon to surrender, having got lost in the woods where they were starving. In this skirmish, we had five Iroquois of the Falls killed and a Nepissin of the Lake & three other Iroquois fatally wounded. This was another action in which the Indians displayed great vigor. They had to engage a detachment of elite volunteers, who were called 'rangers.'" (Pouchot, pp. 130-131)

After the battle, the French had great hopes that Rogers was among the killed. Vaudreuil wrote to M. de Massiac that "Mr. Robert Rogers, who was at the head of the detachment defeated by our cadets, had the knack to escape when he saw his ruin imminent; he left on the field of battle, his coat, and even the order he received from his General, which gave me every reason to believe that he had been killed, the rather [sic] as an Indian assured me that he himself had killed him." (*D.R.C.H.S.N.Y.* Volume 10, p. 924) Despite their hopes, the French were soon to learn that even with the heavy casualties suffered by the Rangers, Rogers himself had survived. On May 27, Captain Malartic, of the Bearn Regiment, recorded in his journal that, "Captain Roger is not dead; 'twas he who took the 4 men belonging to the garrison of St. Frederic . . . . " (*D.R.C.H.S.N.Y.* Volume 10, p. 841)

Upon my return from the late unfortunate scout, I was ordered to Albany to recruit my companies, where I met with a very friendly reception from my Lord How, who advanced me cash to recruit the Rangers, and gave me leave to wait upon General Abercrombie at New York, who had now succeeded my Lord Loudoun in the chief command, my Lord being at this time about to embark for England. I here received a commission from the General, of which the following is a copy.

"By his Excellency James Abercrombie, Esq;
Colonel of his Majesty's 44th Regiment of Foot,
Colonel in Chief of the 60th or Royal American
Regiment, Major General and Commander in
Chief of all his Majesty's Forces raised or to be
raised in North America, &c.

"Whereas as it may be of great use to his Majesty's service in the operations now carrying on for recovering his rights in America, to have a number of men employed in obtaining intelligence of the strength, situation, and motions of the enemy, as well as other services, for which Rangers, or men acquainted with the woods, only are fit: Having the greatest confidence in your loyalty, courage and skill in this kind of service, I do, by virtue of the power and authority to me given by his Majesty, hereby constitute and appoint you to be Major of the Rangers in his Majesty's service, and likewise Captain of a company of said Rangers. You are therefore to take the said Rangers as Major, and the said Company as Captain, into your care and charge, and duly exercise and instruct, as well the officers as the soldiers thereof, in arms, and to use your best endeavors to keep them in good order and discipline; and I do hereby command them to obey you as their Major and Captain respectively, and you are to follow and observe such orders and directions from time to time as you shall receive from his Majesty, myself, or any other superior officer, according to the rules and discipline of war.

"Given at New York, this 6th day of April 1758, in the thirty-first Year of the reign of our Sovereign Lord George the Second, by the Grace of God, King of Great Britain, France and Ireland, Defender of the Faith, &c.

JAMES ABERCROMBIE.

By his Excellency's command,

J. Appy"

> Upon his promotion to major, Rogers received a letter from Col. Joseph Blanchard, his old commander in the Massachusetts Provincial Regiment. Blanchard encouraged Rogers to, "Wake up, and let your Companies be not only the Glory of the Continent, but an Honour to the Kingdom, for which in these Wars, they are adapted—in your Station never suffer your Invention to be at Ease until all is accomplished." (Blanchard to Rogers, March 10, 1758, published in the *Pennsylvania Gazette,* April 6, 1758)

I left New York April 8, and according to orders attended Lord How at Albany for his directions, on the 12th, with whom I had a most agreeable interview, and a long conversation concerning the methods of distressing the enemy, and prosecuting the war with vigour the ensuing campaign. I parted with him, having the strongest assurances of his friendship and influence in my behalf, to wait upon Colonel Grant, commanding officer at Fort Edward, to assist him in conducting the Rangers, and scouting parties, in such a manner as might best serve the common cause, having a letter from my Lord to him. Capt. Stark was immediately dispatched to Ticonderoga on the west-side of Lake George. Capt. Jacob, whose Indian name was *Nawnawapeteoonks*, on the east-side, and Capt. Shepherd betwixt the lakes, with directions to take if possible some prisoners near Carillon. About the same time I marched myself with eighteen men for Crown Point. Capt. Burbank was likewise dispatched in quest of prisoners. These scouts being often relieved, were kept out pretty constantly, in order to discover any parties of the enemy that might sally out towards our forts or frontiers, and to reconnoitre their situation and motions from time to time. The success of my own scout was as follows.

April 29, 1758, I marched from Fort Edward with a party of eighteen men, up the road that leads to Fort William Henry four miles, then north four miles, and encamped at Schoon Creek, it having been a very rainy day.

On the 30th we marched north-and-by-east all day, and encamped near South Bay.

The 1st of May we continued the same course and at night encamped near the narrows, north of South Bay.

The 2d, in the morning, made a raft, and crossed the bay over to the east-side, and having distanced the lake about four miles we encamped.

The 3d we steered our course north, and lay at night about three miles from Carillon.

The 4th we marched north-by-east all day, and encamped at night three miles from Crown Point Fort.

The 5th we killed one Frenchman, and took three prisoners.

The 6th, in the morning, began our return homeward, and arrived with our prisoners at Fort Edward the 9th.

One of the prisoners, who appeared to be the most intelligible, reported, "that he was born at Lorrain in France; that he had been in Canada eight years, viz. two at Quebec, one at Montreal, and five at Crown Point; that at the latter were but 200 soldiers, of which Mons. le Janong was commander in chief; that at Ticonderoga there were 400 of the Queen's regiment, 150 marines 200 Canadians, and about 700 Indians; and that they daily expected 300 Indians more; that they did not intend to attack our forts this summer, but were preparing to receive us at Ticonderoga; that they had heard that I, with most of my party, was killed in the conflict last March; but afterwards by some prisoners which a small party of their Indians had taken from Dutch Hoosyk, they were informed that Rogers was yet alive, and was going to attack them again, being fully resolved to revenge the inhumanity and barbarity with which they had used his men, in particular Lieut. Philips and his party, who were butchered by them, after they had promised them quarters; that this was talked of among the Indians, who greatly blamed the French for encouraging them so to do."

Captains Stark and Jacob returned the day before me; the former brought in with him six prisoners, four of which he took near Ticonderoga; they having escaped from New York and Albany, were in their flight to the French forts. The latter, who had but one white man with him, and eighteen Indians, took ten prisoners, and seven scalps, out of a party of fifty French. An account of these scouts, and the intelligence thereby gained, was transmitted to my Lord How, and by him to the General.

About the middle of May, a flag of truce was sent to Ticonderoga, on Col. Schyler's account, which put a stop to all offensive scouts, till its return.

May 28, 1758, I received positive orders from the General, to order all officers and men, belonging to the Rangers, and the two Indian companies, who were on furlow, or recruiting parties, to join their respective companies as soon as possible, and that every man of the corps under my command should be at his post at or before the 10th of next month. These orders were obeyed, and parties kept out on various scouts to the 8th of June, when my Lord How arrived at Fort Edward with one half of the army.

> This continuing series of scouts was very important in keeping the British high command informed about the movements of the French and their Indian allies. It also did much to increase the fame of the Rangers, whose exploits were widely reported in England as well as in the colonies. The *London Chronicle* mentions two such scouts:
>
> • "Albany June 1. There are 26 prisoners taken, and eight scalps, by the Rangers about Fort-Edward."
>
> • "Boston June 15. By an express that came in on Sunday from Albany, we learn, that an ensign in Capt. Jacob's company had been out on a scout with 24 men, and within about six miles of Ticonderoga were attack'd, by a number of French and Indians, and were obliged to retreat to Fort Edward, where the officer and 12 of his men got safe in, the others were missing when the express came away." (*London Chronicle*, July 29-August 1, 1758)

His Lordship immediately ordered me out with 50 men in whale-boats, which were carried over in waggons to Lake George, and directed me at all events to take a plan of the landing-place at the north-end with all possible accuracy, and also of the ground from the landing-place to the French fort at Carillon, and of Lake Champlain for three miles beyond it, and to discover the enemy's numbers in that quarter. Agreeable to these orders, on the 12th in the morning, I marched with a party of fifty men, and encamped in the evening at the place where Fort William-Henry stood.

> While Rogers was on this scouting mission, other members of his corps remained at Fort Edward, ready for any eventuality. Captain Goose Van Schaick, of Delancey's New York Regiment, recorded in his orderly book for June 10, "Capn Shepherds and Capn Burbanks Company of Rangers to be ready to march on the shortest notice." (Van Schaick, June 10, 1758)

On the 30th we proceeded down the lake in five whale-boats to the first narrows, and so on to the west end of the lake, where I took the plan his Lordship desired. Part of my party then proceeded to reconnoitre Ticonderoga, and discovered a large encampment there, and a great number of Indians. Well I was, with two or three others, taking a plan of the fort, encampment &c. I left the remainder of my party at some considerable distance; when I was returning to them, at the distance of about 300 yards, they were fallen upon by a superior number of the enemy who had got between me and them. Capt. Jacobs, with the

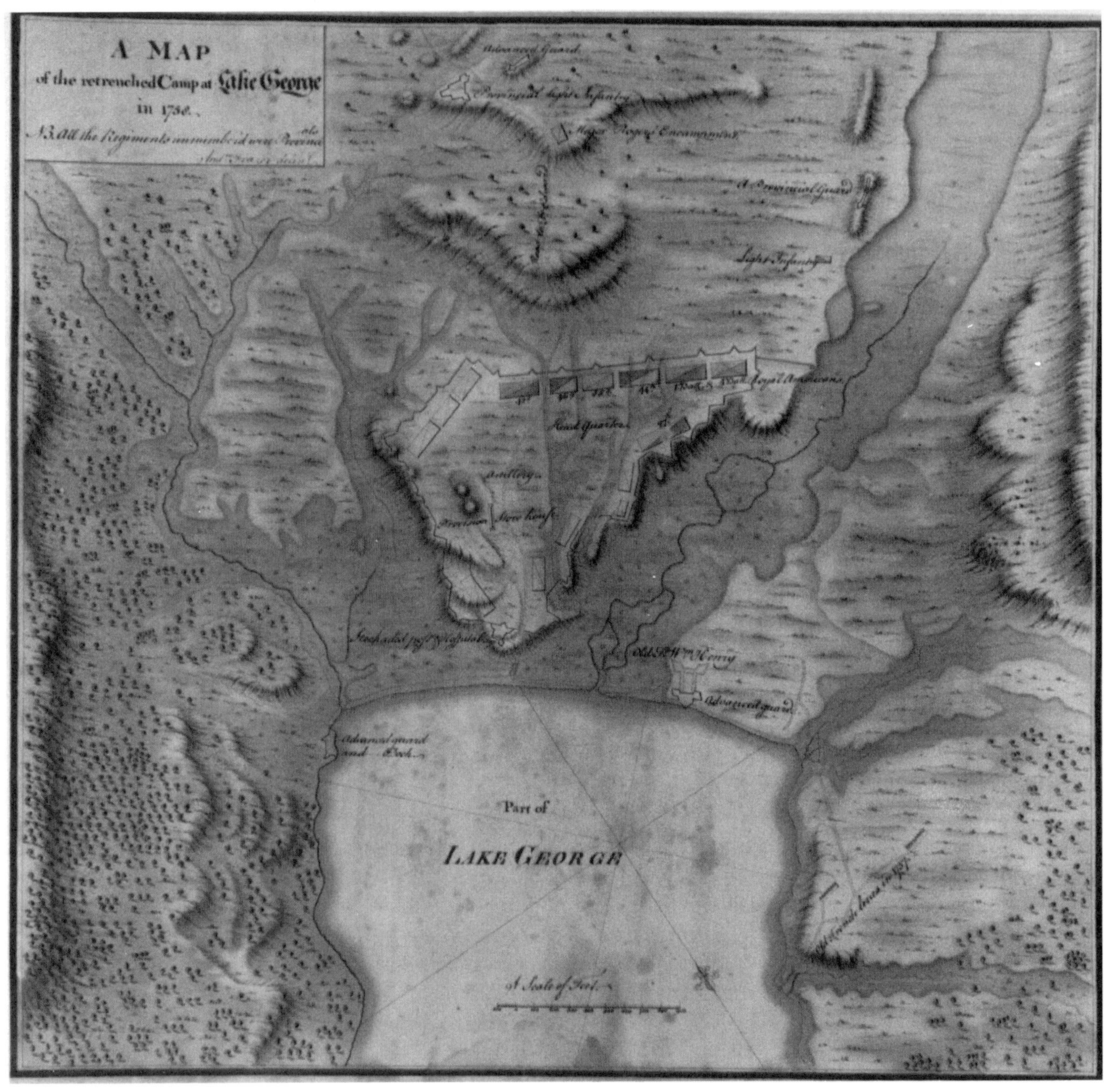

Andrew Frazer's map of Lake George in 1758 shows the construction of the retrenched camp at the head of Lake George, right after Abercromby's defeat at Ticonderoga in July 1758. It shows "Major Robert Rogers' Encampment" on the high ground at the top center of the map. Courtesy of the Fort Ticonderoga Museum.

Mohegon Indians, run off at the first onset, calling to our people to run likewise; but they stood their ground, and discharged their pieces several times, at last broke through the enemy, by whom they were surrounded on all sides except their rear, where a river divided them: they killed three of the enemy, but lost eight of their own party in this skirmish. My party rallied at the boats, where I joined him, and having collected all but the slain together, we returned homewards.

A June 18 entry in the journal of William Hervey of the 44th Regiment shows that once again there might be a discrepancy in Rogers' dates. More importantly, it shows that Rogers may have had a closer brush with death than his *Journals* imply. Hervey writes, "Rogers came in from a scout to the joy and surprize of all, as his Lieutenant Porter came in first and reported that Rogers must be either killed or taken." (Hervey, p. 49) It appears that by "came in," Hervey is referring to the camp at Half Way Brook.

Massachusetts Provincial James Henderson noted in his journal for June 18 that, "About this Time Major Rogers had a Scirmish with the French and Indians he was obliged to Retreat there is 12 or more of his men a Missing" (Henderson, p. 196)

In Albany, clothing agent John Macomb wrote that, "Yesterday we had an acc't of Major Rodgers party, to the number of 50 being all cut off save 5, & himself wounded in two places's." (Cuneo, *Notes*, p. 58)

This battle also resulted in some interesting comments from British officers involved in other theaters of the war. On June 27, 1758, General John Forbes, who was preparing for the Fort DuQuesne Expedition, wrote to General Abercromby, "I have just now heard some confused tale of Rogers having been worsted and mortally wounded—I shall be very sorry if it proves true, as I take him to be too good a man, to be easily spared at present." (Forbes, p. 127)

The same day, Forbes wrote the following advice to Colonel Henry Bouquet, his second-in-command: "I give this caution from hearing (altho perhaps false) that Rogers with a party of 50 men, had been surprised near Tunderoga, and that all were cut off but himself mortally wounded & five more. Guarding against surprizes must be inculated early amongst our now undisciplined troops, and the strictest orders to prevent any surprize must be daily enjoined them." (Forbes, p. 125, and Bouquet, Volume II, p. 136)

Two of Rogers' Indians who were captured returning from a scout to Ticonderoga about this time were taken to Quebec, sold as slaves, and transported to Haiti. There they were sold again, and set to hard labor until January 1759, when they managed to escape and eventually secure passage back to New England. (Frazier, pp. 125-126)

On the 20th at Half Way brook, we met my Lord How, advanced with three thousand men, to whom I gave an account of my scout, together with a plan of the landing-place, the fort at Carillon, and the situation of the lakes.

I obtained leave of my Lord to go to Fort Edward, were his Excellency Major General Abercrombie was then posted, who ordered me to join my Lord How the next day with all the Rangers, being 600, in order to proceed with his Lordship to the lake.

About this time, Massachusetts Provincial James Henderson records a tragic incident involving the Rangers. On June 23, he notes that "one of the centinels shot one of the Raingers Dead for not answering when hailed." (Henderson, p. 196) It is not known if this Ranger belonged to Rogers' corps or one of the Provincial Ranger units.

At the army's camp at Lake George, a call was put out for volunteers from the other regiments to join Rogers' corps. Captain Goose Van Schaick, of Delancey's New York Regiment, recorded in his orderly book that "Such of the provinchall Troops as are Willing and Fit to serve Major Rogers this campaign shall have an Encouragement over & above their present pay which Major Generall Abercrombie hereby promises to be Duly paid." (Van Schaick, June 20, 1758)

On the 22nd his lordship encamped at the lake where formerly stood Fort William-Henry, and ordered the Rangers to advance 400 hundred yards on the west-side, and encamp there, from which place, by his Lordship's orders, I sent off next morning three small parties of Rangers, viz. one to the narrows of South Bay, another to the west-side of Lake George, and a third to Ticonderoga Fort, all three parties by land. Another party consisting of two Lieutenants and seventeen men, proceeded down the lake for discoveries, and were all made prisoners by about 300 French and Indians. This party embarked in whale-boats.

In a letter to Prime Minister Pitt, General Abercromby stated that intelligence recently gained from some French prisoners was "in a great Measure confirmed by Captain Rogers, who returned on the 17th from a Scout. [Once again there is a conflict in dates.] Two days before he had a clear view of Tienderoga from the Hill between Lake-George & Wood Creek, which not only overlooks the Fort, but a Part of Lake Champlain—From this Eminence he perceived an Encampment of three Regiments & about 100 Batteaux coming up the Lake, as well as a good Number of Men lying on the Banks, just disembarked; Not content with this Discovery, & out of Zeal for the Service, He, contrary to his Instructions, proceeded with his Whale Boats too far down the Lake, and fell in with a superior Force, and was obliged to retreat, with the Loss of 5 Men killed & 3 taken—amongst the latter, Ensign Downing of the 55th who went out as a Voluntier. This was an unlucky Affair, as they must learn a great deal from these Prisoners . . . ." (Pitt, Volume I, pp. 286)

Although Abercromby criticizes Rogers for exceeding his orders on this scout, it would appear that this charge is unjustified. As Rogers notes on page 115, he was instructed to, "take a plan of the landing place at the north-end with all possible accuracy, and also of the ground from the landing-place to the French fort at Carillon, and of Lake Champlain for three miles beyond it, and discover the enemy's number in that quarter."

The French version of this incident is found in documents sent by Montcalm to M. de Cremille: "[June] 25th Sieur de Langy arrived in the evening from his scout with one officer and sixteen soldiers of Major Rogers' troop, who were taken within two leagues of the head of the Lake in an island where they had landed on perceiving our Indians; he reported that the English were at the Lake in great numbers with bateaux . . . . " (*D.R.C.H.S.N.Y.* Volume 10, p. 892)

The Rev. John Cleaveland, a Massachusetts Provincial chaplain, wrote in his journal at Schenectady, "Major Ingersol came to Town from Albany and brings word that they had advised there yt [that] Major Rogers had been out with a party of fifty men, some where [on] the lakes and had an engagement with ye Enemy in which he lost Six men and received a Slight wound himself in one of his legs." (Cleaveland, July 20, 1758)

About the 28th of June his Excellency Major General Abercrombie arrived at the lake with the remainder of the army, where he tarried till the morning of the 5th of July, and then the whole army, consisting of near 16,000, embarked in battoes for Ticonderoga.

The order of march was a most agreeable sight; the regular troops in the center, provincials on each wing, the light infantry on the right of the advanced guard, the Rangers on the left, with Colonel Broadstreet's battoe-men in the center. In this manner we proceeded, till dusk, down Lake George to Sabbath Day Point, where the army halted and refreshed. About ten o'clock the army moved again, when my Lord How went in the front with his whale-boat, Liutenant Col. Broadstreet's and mine, with Lieutenant Holmes, in another, whom he sent forward to go near the landing-place, and observe if any enemy was posted there.

Holmes returned about day-break, met the

army near the Blue Mountains within four miles of the landing place, and reported that there was a party of the enemy at the landing-place, which he discovered by their fires.

As soon as it as was light his Lordship, with Col. Broadstreet and myself, went down to observe the landing-place before the army, and when within about a quarter of a mile, plainly discerned that it was but a small detachment of the enemy that was there; whereupon his Lordship said he would return to the General, that the army might land and march to Ticonderoga. About twelve o'clock the whole army landed, the Rangers on the left wing. I immediately sent an officer to wait upon the General for his orders, and received directions from Capt. Abercrombie, one of his Aids de Camps, to gain the top of a mountain that bore north about a mile from the landing-place, and from thence to steer east to the river that runs into the falls betwixt the landing and the saw-mill, to take possession of some rising ground on the enemy's side, and there to wait the army's coming.

> Cuneo theorizes that Rogers was given this assignment in order to prevent a mistake that Braddock's army had made before the Battle of the Monongahela in 1755—failure to secure the high ground commanding their intended line of march. (Cuneo, *Notes*, p, 60)

I immediately marched, ascended to the top of the hill, and from thence marched to the place I was ordered, were I arrived in about an hour, and posted my party to as good advantage as I could, being within one quarter of a mile of where Mons. Montcalm was posted with 1500 men, whom I had discovered by some small reconnoitring parties sent out for that purpose. About twelve o'clock Colonels Lyman and Fitch of the provincials came to my rear, whom I informed of the enemy's being so very near, and inquiring concerning the army, they told me they were coming along. While this conversation passed, a sharp fire began in the rear of Col. Lyman's regiment, on which he said he would make his front immediately, and desired me to fall on their left flank, which I accordingly did, having first ordered Captain Burbanks with 150 men to remain at the place where I was posted, to observe the motions of the French at the saw-mills, and went with the remainder of the Rangers on the left flank of the enemy, the river being on their right, and killed several. By this time my Lord Howe, with a detachment from his front, had broke the enemy, and hemmed them in on every side; but advancing himself with great eagerness and intrepidity upon them, was unfortunately shot and died immediately.*

> The French party, a reconnaissance in force numbering about 350, had been sent to observe the British advance from on top of Mount Pelee, or Bald Mountain, or Rogers' Rock, as it is known today. It was led by two officers of sound ability, Captain de Trepezac of the Bearn Regiment, and Ensign Jean-Baptiste Levrault de Langis Montegron (often called Langy), of the Compagnies Franches de la Marine. Langis was an experienced partisan officer whose skills were on a par with Rogers' own. This incident is a good example of how war is truly an inexact science, and how even the most competent commanders can have a bad day. As incredible as it may seem, with all of their experience, and being basically on their "home ground," when Trepezac and Langis stumbled into Lord Howe's party they were lost in the woods. Perhaps not lost in the sense that they did not have a clue where they were, but certainly lost in the sense that, with the bridges destroyed and not being able to travel by their usual route, they became disoriented and were unable to avoid the larger British force.
>
> Captain Malartic, of the Bearn Regiment, recorded that "At four o'clock we heard several shots which we judged were fired at M. de Tropezec's detachment. A quarter of an hour afterwards we saw some soldiers wading, and M. de Tropezec arrive mortally wounded; he told us that he had lost his way through the fault of his guide, and that wishing to reach the Falls, he had got into the midst of a considerable party of the enemy." (*D.R.C.H.S.N.Y.*, Volume 10, p. 722)

*This noble and brave officer being universally beloved by both officers and soldiers of the army, his fall was not only most sincerely lamented, but seemed to produce an almost general consternation and langour through whole.

Abercromby's Spearhead

"A most agreeable sight," was the way Robert Rogers described General Abercromby's vast flotilla of over a thousand vessels as it moved northward up Lake George from its base camp on July 5, 1758. It was understatement typical of soldiers throughout history. "A very fine appearance they made," echoed Dr. Caleb Rea with the Massachusetts forces.[1] In Nova Scotia, Regular Captain John Knox received a letter from an officer with Abercromby, who noted that "our transports were batteaus and whaleboats, and in such numbers as to cover the lake for a considerable length of way. . . I think I never beheld so delightful a prospect."[2]

On the evening of the 5th the army encamped at Sabbath Day Point for several hours, eating supper and building large fires to intimidate the French down the lake. A few hours before dawn of the 6th, it moved on for the final leg of its voyage. The advance guard was composed of three sections of 100 whaleboats each: Major Rogers' Rangers rowing close to the western shore; Colonel John Bradstreet's bateaumen (not rowing bateaus on this expedition) in the center; and Major Gage's 80th Light Armed Infantry, near to the eastern shore. Each section was divided into four columns, 25 vessels long, each one rowed by five men.

Behind this advance guard came the main body of the army, preceded by a radeau, or floating battery. The main body was split into four parallel sections totaling sixteen columns of bateaus, each boat rowed with five oars and one paddle. The two outer sections were composed of Provincial troops, and the two middle ones of Regulars. In back of these sections came more boats carrying artillery stores, the hospital and commissary, as well as more guns on radeaus or rafts. Behind these vessels came the rear guard.

"In the narrow Places, they were obliged to form into Subdivisions to give themselves Room to row," noted a report in *The Pennsylvania Journal* of July 27, 1758. Sometimes "they extended from front to Rear full Seven Miles."

The illustration depicts Major Rogers in the foremost whaleboat of his column, passing the mountain on the eastern shore of the lake known today as Anthony's Nose. (Bald Mountain—and Rogers' Slide—would soon be coming up on Rogers' left, in the direction of the viewer.) He holds a spyglass as the pre-dawn greyness begins to make objects discernible all around him. Some three miles ahead of him lies the French advanced post of Contrecoeur, near the northern end of the lake.

Rogers' black servant, Prince, carries his master's fusil, and will accompany him into battle. The whaleboat is inscribed as one of the Rangers' own: evidence exists that the boats in Amherst's 1759 campaign were each marked according to their corps, and the same might have been the case in 1758.[3]

Rogers' first experience with whaleboats on the lakes came in June of 1756, when, he says, General Shirley "augmented my company to seventy men, and sent me six light whale-boats from Albany." These probably came from Cape Cod or Nantucket, like the sixteen sent to Albany in April of that year, primarily for use on Lake Ontario.[4] Whaleboats were also being built at Fort William Henry, according to Provincial diarist Jeduthan Baldwin, who noted on April 3, "Went after cedar for whaleboats."[5]

Bougainville's journal describes one of four of Rogers' whaleboats, found "abandoned in a little cove" on Lake Champlain, as being "mounted with three swivels".[6] He adds that "Several of the oars were bound with cloth."[7] Rogers' feat that year of carrying five whaleboats six miles over the mountains from Lake George to South Bay was probably not as herculean as it might sound, judging by Paul Dudley's 1725 description of the lightness of typical whaleboats:

> They are made of Cedar Clapboards, and so very light that two Men can conveniently carry them, yet they are twenty Feet long, and carry Six Men. . .These boats run very swift.[8]

Lord Loudoun noted in his diary on September 9, 1757, that in order to preserve whaleboats, "the Nantucket Men Place them on Crotches with their Bottoms up so that they may not touch the Ground."

From a number of French and Indian War sources we also learn that both bateaus and whaleboats, when carrying provisions, were layered with pine boughs to keep water in the bottoms of the boats from doing damage to them; that blankets

Majr ROGERS Compy 1

and even tents were often used to make improvised sails; and that muskets were sometimes stacked in the bows as the soldiers rowed.

The French garrison at the northern end of the lake retired after offering only minimal resistance, leaving behind a considerable hoard of provisions, livestock, fowl and miscellaneous plunder for Abercromby's men.

G. Z.

1. "The Journal of Dr. Caleb Rea," *Historical Collections of the Essex Institute*, April-June, 1881.
2. Captain John Knox, *The Siege of Quebec and the Campaigns in North America, 1757-1760*, edited by Brian Connell, The Folio Society, London, 1976, p. 78.3.
3. "Lake George Camp, Tuesday, 17th July 1759. . .The Whale Boats to be mark'd by the Corps they are given to, in the same manner as the Batteaus." "Extracts from Captain Moneypenny's Orderly Book," *Bulletin of the Fort Ticonderoga Museum*, Vol. II, July 1932, No. 6, p. 223.
Provincial soldier Josiah Goodrich added more about these marks: "Camp at Lake George, 12 July 1759: Every Rigt to mark And number their one [own] battoes." "The Josiah Goodrich Order Book," *Bulletin of the Fort Ticonderoga Museum*, Vol. XIV, Summer 1981, No. 1, p. 48.
4. *The New York Mercury*, April 26, 1756. "Upwards of 230 whaleboats capable of holding 16 men each" were expected at Oswego that summer. Ibid., July 12, 1756.
5. "The Diary of Jeduthan Baldwin," *Journal of the Military Service Institute*, Vol. XXXIX, July-August 1906.
6. *Adventure in the Wilderness: The American Journals of Louis Antoine de Bougainville, 1756- 1760*, translated and edited by Edward P. Hamilton, University of Oklahoma Press, Norman, Oklahoma, 1964. Entry of October 2, 1756, p. 46.
7. Ibid., p. 51.
8. Dudley quoted in William A. Baker, "The Whaleboat 'Middlesex,' Technical Notes," *Nautical Research Journal*, Vol. 29, September 1983, No. 3, p. 119.

In a later entry, Malartic clearly identifies Langis as the "guide" who led the party astray: "M. de Trepezee arrive next mortally wounded, who states that M. de Langy, who was guiding them, as he was acquainted with the way through the woods, had gone astray, and did not find out his mistake until three o'clock. . . ." (*D.R.C.H.S.N.Y.*, Volume 10, p. 845)

Of this action, Rev. John Entick says: "But, though we lost only two officers, and not above 18 men killed and wounded, our success cost us very dear, in the death of Lord Howe, who fell the first man in this skirmish, by a musket ball through his breast: of which he died instantly. Had our army been sufficiently provided with guides, this action might have become fatal to the enemy." Entick's remarks are interesting, for they show that even at this early date, historians recognized that one of Abercromby's biggest failings was in the proper use of his Rangers. Rogers and his men had been over the ground around Ticonderoga on countless occasions, yet they were not used to directly guide the less experienced troops. (Entick, Volume III, pp. 253-4)

Mante recorded the incident in this manner: "Lord Howe, at the head of the right-center column, supported by the light infantry, fell in with about five hundred French, who had likewise lost themselves in the woods. The action was maintained with great bravery on both sides; nor did the enemy give way, till they had near three hundred killed, and one hundred and forty-eight taken prisoners; the killed and wounded on the side of the English did not exceed forty. But this advantage was too inconsiderable to counterbalance the loss of Lord Howe, who, almost at the beginning of the action, received a musket-ball in the breast, of which he instantly expired." (Mante, p. 146)

Rogers' Rangers were not initially involved in this fight, but upon hearing the firing, they came to assist. A letter written at Fort William Henry on July 9, apparently by a Provincial officer, gives some interesting insight into the aftermath of the battle: "We soon routed this party & took 152 prisoners, killing near 300, some of whom were scalped by our people, but the most of them were left untouched till evening, when Major Roger's Indians paid them the compliment of the knife." (*Gentleman's Magazine*, September, 1758, p. 445)

Samuel Cobb, a captain in Preble's Massachusetts Regiment, noted in his journal for July 6, "at 1 oClock in the Morning Imbarked and Came at 8 oClock and Landed within 5 Miles of the fort the french Guard ran out at our appearance Majr. Rogers Rangers came up with part of the french Guard killed 7 of them lost 2 of our Men in the afternoon Ingaged the french took 180 of them Prisoners and killed 110 more. Lord Howe was kill'd in the Battle and about 60 of Our Men Amissing" (Cobb pp. 18-19)

Provincial Lemuel Lyon writes in his journal for July 7: "Majer Rogers went down to the mils and drove them of there from & kild and took upwards of 150 & at Son down the last of the Army marched down to the Mils and Major putnom made a Bridge over by the Landing place this night we lodged by the Mils." (Lyon, p. 22) It is interesting that Lyon makes no mention of the death of Lord Howe.

The French also suffered a considerable number of killed in this action. The author of an anonymous letter, believed written from the camp at Lake George on the army's retreat southward, estimated the French dead at "near 300." His prisoner estimate agrees closely with Rogers', but he adds one fact that the Major failed to mention: "Some [of the dead] were scalped immediately, but the Chief of 'em were left untouched till Evening when Majr Roger's paid 'em that compliment." (*B.F.T.M.*, January 1945, p. 16)

There were taken prisoners of the enemy in this action, five officers, two volunteers, and one hundred and sixty men, who were sent to the landing place. Nothing more material was done this day. The next morning, at six o'clock, I was ordered to march to the river that runs into the falls, a place where I was the day before, and there to halt on the west-side till further orders, with four hundred Rangers, while Capt. Stark, with the remainder of the Rangers, marched with Capt.

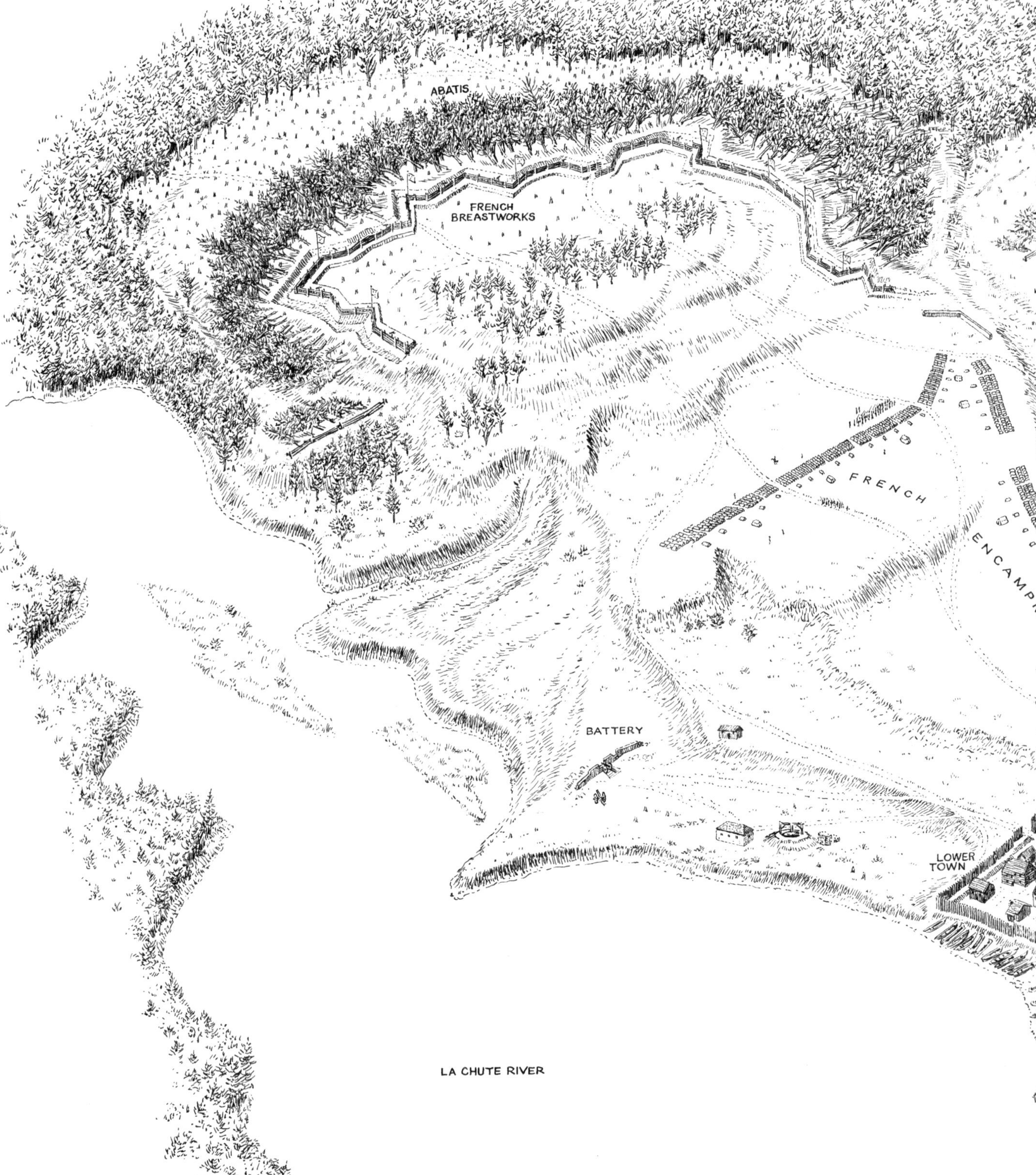
ABATIS
FRENCH BREASTWORKS
FRENCH
ENCAMPME
BATTERY
LOWER TOWN
LA CHUTE RIVER
GARY ZABOLY ©1999

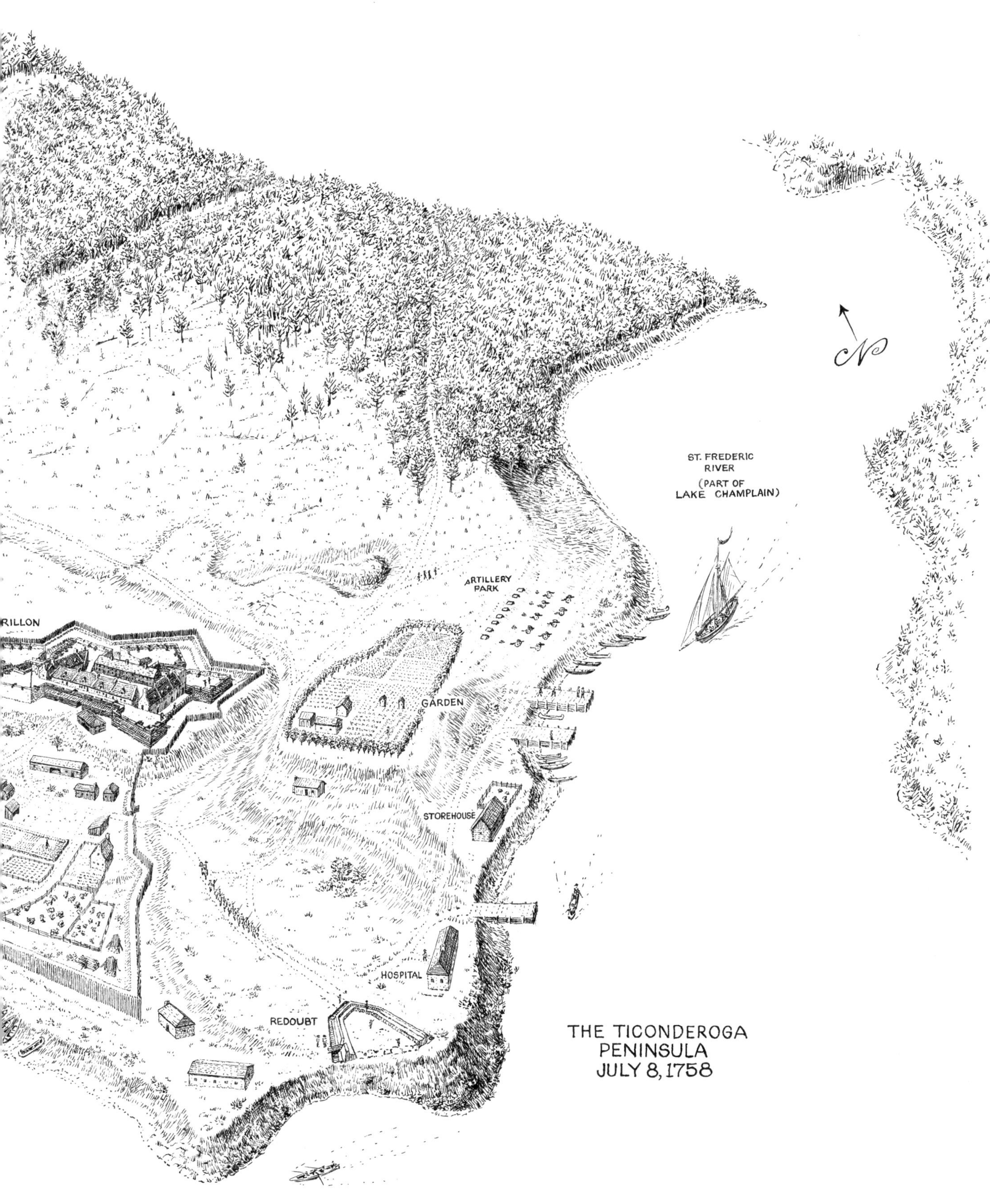

THE TICONDEROGA PENINSULA JULY 8, 1758

The Ticonderoga Penninsula, July 8, 1758

YOUNG Engineer Lieutenant Mathew Clerk looked down at Fort Carillon from the summit of the steep mountain to the south of it,[1] and he noticed an interesting thing. The French were working like desperate moles to complete an outerwork on the heights lying a half mile west of the fort, but, from what he could see, the entrenchments in their present condition were hardly formidable enough to stop General Abercromby's army from taking them by direct assault. Clerk rushed down the mountain and informed the general of this, adding that "the Attack should be forthwith made on the Entrenchments."[2]

It was the morning of July 8, 1758. Heeding the unanimous advice of both Clerk and those Regular officers who had accompanied him on the reconnaisance, General Abercromby agreed to launch an immediate attack. Clerk's additional advice, seconded by Ranger Captain John Stark, who had also gone up the mountain with him, was to set up a battery on the summit in order to bombard the French lines in the flank while the assault was being made. This, however, was deemed too time-consuming a task, and was pushed aside in the rush to commence the attack.[3]

Many of the soldiers in Abercromby's army were told that the enemy position on the heights was "not fortified, only a few Logs laid one on another as a breast Work."[4] It was a cruel and fatal deception. Lieutenant Clerk and his entourage had misjudged the height and extent of the French lines when they viewed them from the mountaintop, a full mile and a quarter distant. Even with the best spyglass, however, it was probably an understandable deception. Provincial John Brainerd later wrote that, as seen from the French side, the breast work of logs "was just up to a man's chin, on our side [when the depth of the outside ditch was added to the overall height of the work] it was about nine feet high."[5] So young Clerk saw only the interior of the French lines, and not the true height from the perspective of an attacker.

"Its Evident ye Conductors of ye affair were very Ignorant of ye French Intrenchment," wrote Massachusetts Colonel Oliver Partridge, for "they had not only yr. Ditches but Ranges of Trees with out them Resembling a Hurricane."[6] According to the account of one British officer, the assaulting columns learned only too late that the French had built "a strong intrenchment, consisting of a number of large trees, laid lengthwise one over the other, 7 or 8 feet in height and pierced with a double row of loop-holes. The upper side was covered with bags of earth, by which arrangement there was a triple fire. The intrenchment flanked itself perfectly well and was impregnable to musketry. A huge abbatis of trees which extended outside the entire length, rendered it more formidable. This was not ascertained until after our misfortune. . . . The French were invisible; nothing was to be seen of them but a small bit of their caps."[7]

Montcalm and his engineers had somehow managed to erect a last-minute breastwork which, combined with courage and rapid-fire volleys in the faces of the charging British, Provincials and Rangers, enabled the vastly outnumbered French to inflict enormous casualties and win the day, thus maintaining possession of the little Ticonderoga peninsula for another year.

They were fortunate that the lines held, for Fort Carillon itself, even after three years of construction work, was in no condition to withstand a formal, European-style siege. Begun in 1755 as a rectangular fort with four arrow-shaped bastions at each corner, its original construction was of timber cribbings filled with earth and stones. Gradually the northern and western walls were covered with mortared limestone. Parapets and embrasures were fitted with cannon. Four barracks were also built; by the time of Abercromby's attack only one of these—the northern barrack—remained as a wooden structure.

The southern wall, pierced by the main gate, also remained in its original wooden condition, with a fraise of sharpened stakes jutting out horizontally three feet from the top of the wall. There was still no eastern wall, only a puny line of earth-filled, wickerwork gabions. The western demilune had been largely completed, while the northern one was still partially wooden. Deep ditches covered the northern and western approaches; surrounding most of the fort was a palisade of pointed logs about eight feet high. Immediately outside the main gate stood a large wooden shed that also served as a blockhouse, containing an upper floor for artillery, its walls lined with gunports.

South of the fort was the "Lower Town," a stockaded collection of log huts, construction sheds, livestock pens, and probably a few mortared stone buildings. The fort garden lay to the east, near the artillery park.

Contemporary maps of the battle area are often flawed in one respect: many of them show defensive works that were not in place on the day of battle. The oft-reproduced 1768 map by Thomas Jefferys, for instance, first published in Thomas Mante's *The History of the Late War in North-America* (London, 1772), even shows a wharf on the southern shore of the point that did not exist. On July 8, 1758, the only exterior redoubt of any size that covered the fort was a U-shaped one, open toward the St. Frederic River, on the rocky promontory at the end of the peninsula. During the attack, batteries were being set up by the French at the eastern end of their lines, and near the point of land on the La Chute River, but they were not finished in time to play a role in the battle.

South of the western flank of the lines, and north of its eastern flank, smaller lines covered by abatis had been built. The southern line was manned by a mixed group of soldiers, the northern one by Canadians. A small, V-shaped redoubt had been begun near the eastern end of the "French lines" on the 8th, but evidently was not armed with guns during the assault.

Between the Lower Town and the unfinished battery on the La Chute River was a brick kiln and yard. The encampment arrangement of the French troops is based on the plan by Therbu, showing its location on the morning of July 8.

G.Z.

1. Today's Mount Defiance. In the 1750s the British knew it as Rattlesnake Mountain or Sugar Hill.
2. Major General James Abercromby to M. James Abercromby, Camp at Lake George, 19th August, 1758, *Bulletin of the Fort Ticonderoga Museum*, Vol. XVI, 1998, No. 1, p. 74.
3. Letter from Lake George, 10 July 1758, *Canadian Historical Review*, New Series II, 1921, p. 361; Caleb Stark, *Memoir and Official Correspondence of General John Stark*, published by Edison C. Eastman, Concord, New Hampshire, 1877, p. 26.
4. Letter of "J.B.," London, 25 August 1758, in *Bulletin of the Fort Ticonderoga Museum*, ibid., pp. 84-85.
5. Brainerd's letter to P. V. B. Livingston, Lake George, July 11, 1758, *New York History*, XVII, p. 206.
6. Oliver Partridge to his wife, Camp at Lake George, July 12, 1758, in *Acts and Resolves of the Province of Massachusetts Bay*, Vol. IV, Boston, 1881, p. 23.
7. E. B. O'Callaghan, *Documents Relative to the Colonial History of the State of New York*, Vol. X, Albany 1858, p. 734. The reference to the French "caps" is interesting. Does it mean that the French—at least those seen by this officer—wore their fatigue caps, or *bonnets du police*, rather than hats?

Abercrombie and Mr. Clerk the Engineer, to observe the position of the enemy at the fort, from whence they returned again that evening. The whole army lay the ensuing night under arms. By sun rise next morning, Sir William Johnson joined the army with four hundred and forty Indians. At seven o'clock I received orders to march with my Rangers. A Lieutenant of Captain Stark's led the advanced guard. I was within about three hundred yards of the breast-work, when my advanced guard was ambushed and fired upon by about 200 Frenchman. I immediately formed a front, and marched up to the advanced guard, who maintained their ground, and the enemy immediately retreated; soon after the battoe-men formed on my left and light infantry on my right.

There is some question about whether Rogers properly positioned his Rangers in preparation for the main assault. The author of the anonymous letter mentioned above also notes that "The Rangers Instead of taking Post to the Left imployed themselves in firing on the Enemy to the Right so that when our Regiment was going to take Post where we ought to be In ye Rear of our Friends we were surprized by ye Enemy about 200 yards from the Breast Work who fired on us . . . ." (*B.F.T.M.*, January 1945, p. 17) A very similar account, probably drawn from the same letter, was published in the *London Chronicle.* (*London Chronicle,* September 19-21, 1758).

Perhaps the ambush of his advance guard and the ensuing action made it impossible for Rogers to get his men into their proper position. There is a French account, sent by Montcalm to M. de Cremille, that suggests that this could be the case. "About one o'clock our detachments, and grenadiers, who were in advance, perceived the enemy approaching in three columns; they all came in without any confusion. The signal was given, and the following instant the three columns were seen defiling; the 1st towards the left of the intrenchment, the 2nd against the centre; the 3rd, which appeared the strongest, marching towards the bottom, on the right of the hill. Some Indians and Rangers went in front as guides. Chevalier de Levis, who perceived them, ordered M. de Raymond's troop to make a sortie by the wood, in order to outflank that column. It succeeded so perfectly that its fire, with that of La Reine and Bearn on the right of the hill, obliged that column to throw itself on the right, in order to avoid a double flank fire." (*D.R.C.H.S.N.Y.*, Volume 10, p. 909)

There is another interesting factor in the equation. Just before the army embarked, Captain Hugh Arnot, of Gage's (80th) Light Infantry, noted in his journal that "Roger's Rangers were augmented by Draughts from the Provincials to 700." He had previously recorded on June 17 that the Rangers' strength at Fort Edward was three hundred men. Thus, it is possible that when Rogers moved his men into position for the attack on the French breastworks, he was leading a force that was made up of half or more Provincial "draftees" who he had had little or no time to train as Rangers. It is also worth noting here that in these instances, Arnot uses the terms "Rogers Rangers" and "Roger's Rangers." This, and other similar instances, clearly establish that Rogers' corps was known as *Rogers' Rangers* during this time. (Arnot, pp. 30 and 33)

This fire of the enemy did not kill a single man. Soon after three regiments of provincials came up and formed in my rear, at two hundred yards distance. While the army was thus forming, a scattering fire was kept up between our flying parties and those of the enemy without the breast work. About half an hour past ten, the greatest part of the enemy being drawn up, a smart fire began on the left wing, where Col. De Lancey's, (the New Yorkers,) and the battoe-men were posted, upon which I was ordered forward to endeavour to beat the enemy within the breast-work, and then to fall down, that the pickets and grenadiers might march through. The enemy soon retired within their works; Major Proby marched through with his pickets within a few yards of the breast-work, where he unhappily fell, and the enemy keeping up a heavy fire, the soldiers hastened to the right about, when Col. Haldiman came up with the granadiers to support them, being followed by the batalions in brigades for their support. Col. Haldiman advanced very near the breast-work, which was at least eight feet high; some of the provincials with the Mohocks came up also.*

We toiled with repeated attacks for four hours, being greatly embarrassed by trees that were felled by the enemy without their breast-work, when the General thought proper to order a retreat, directing me to bring up the rear which I did in the dusk of the evening. On the ninth in the evening, we arrived at our encampment at the south-end of Lake George, where the army received the thanks of the General for their good behaviour, and were ordered to entrench themselves; the wounded were sent to Fort Edward and Albany. Our loss both in the regular and provincial troops, was somewhat considerable. The enemy's loss was about five hundred, besides those who were taken prisoners.

July 8, 1758. By order of the General, I this day began a scout to South Bay, from which I returned the 16th, having effected nothing considerable, except discovering a large party of the enemy, supposed to be near a thousand, on the east side of the lake.

> In the period following the disaster at Ticonderoga, Rogers and the other Ranger officers were engaged in a continuing series of scouts designed to detect the movements of the French and their Indian allies. In an August 1 journal entry, French Captain Malartic observed that, "Captain Roger is out every day scouting; sometimes North, at other times, South . . . . " (*D.R.C.H.S.N.Y.*, Volume 10, p. 850)
>
> An interesting document in the Gage Papers, in the collections of the Clements Library, is a "list of scouts to be performed" dated July 24, 1758. In the left margin of the list, the names of the Ranger units assigned are written, and some are crossed out, which seems to indicate completion of the assignment. The list of assignments is reproduced here as closely as possible to the way it is written in the original manuscript.

"Scouts to be performed

Sr

Rogers — It is my Opinion that a Party, ought to be sent out dayly to reconnoitre on the West side of Lake George about ten Miles North. who may return again in the Evening---

Rogers — A Second party on the West side to go across the Mountains to Hudsons River, & return again in the Evening---

N:W Partridge offr 30
N E Putnam Do — A Party should reconnoitre round Encampment every Morning and Evening

The Advanced Guard on the Island is sufficient to keep a good Look out on the Lake, who ought to be cautioned to be very careful in the night as well as the Day---

Putnam — That a constant Scout ought to be kept out to Deskau's Landing, & the Entrance to Wood Creek into the Bay

Rogers
~~Hampshire & Rogers~~ — Another to the high Rock betwixt South Bay and the Narrows on said Bay—also

Partridge
~~Partridge (7 or 8)~~
~~Rogers~~ — A small party to be sent out as far as the East Pond on Scoon Creek---

From the Halfway Brook, Capt. Burbank is to keep out Scouts to reconnoitre from the East Pond to Fort Anne along Scoon Creek—and a constant Scout to the Falls on Wood Creek.---

Rangers Encampment — The Rangers that may be quartered at Fort Edward ought constantly to keep out a party to East Bay and another east to the Indian Road leading from East Bay to Hoosuck---

To Head or cut off any party of the Enemy, that may come out by way of Wood creek, South, or East Bay, (if discovered seasonably) 'twould be

*This attack was begun before the General intended it should be, and as it were by accident, from the fire of the New Yorkers in the left wing; upon which Col. Haviland being in or near the center, ordered the troops to advance.

> advisable to go down the Lake in Boats, & cross over the Mountains to the Narrows North of South Bay & Lay there in Ambush for them against their return.

Lake George, July 24th, 1758
To Brig.dr Genl. Gage---"
(Gage Papers 1, July 24, 1758)

This party the next day, viz. the 17th, fell upon a detachment of Col. Nicholl's regiment at the half-way brook, killed three captains, and upwards of twenty private men.

Massachusetts Provincial James Henderson gives a detailed account of this incident in his journal entry of July 20: "there was 18 Killed nigh the half way Brook there is 5 more a Missing 6 of the slain were Commission officers viz Capt Deacon of Sudbury and Lieut Samll Curtis Capt Laurance of Groton and Capt Jones of Wilmington and Ensign Davis the others Name I am not informed of certainly our Men that Was in the Fort at the halfway Brook Issued out and Beat the Enemy off the Bloody Wretches Cut the Throats of some of the men they Likewise Murdered some poor Women that was there" (Henderson, pp. 197-198)

The 27th another party of the enemy fell upon a convoy of waggoners between Fort Edward and Half-Way Brook, and killed 116 men, sixteen of which were Rangers.

There is a unique sidelight to this engagement. Scalping was a fairly common practice by both sides, but it took an interesting twist here. Captain-Lieutenant Henry Skinner of the Royal Artillery makes the following comment in his journal on July 17, 1759, nearly a year later: "The commanding Officer of this party [Pierre {or Louis} St. Luc de la Corne] is the man who butchered our bullock escort last campaign; at which affair they were so wanton in their barbarities, that they scalped an ox." Gary Zaboly has found information indicating that the ox survived and was eventually sent to England and put on exhibit, where it became quite a curiosity. (Skinner, p. 380, and p. 380 n42)

In pursuit of this party, with a design to intercept their retreat, I was ordered to embark the 18th with 700 men; the enemy however escaped me, and in my return home on the 31st, I was met by an express from the General, with orders to march with 700 men to South and East Bay, and return by way of Fort Edward, in the prosecution of which orders nothing very material happened till the 8th of August; in our return, early in the morning of which day, we decamped from the place were Fort Anne stood; and began our march, Major Putnam with a party of Provincials marching in the front, my Rangers in the rear, Capt. Dalyell with the regulars in the center, the other officers suitably disposed among the men, being in number 530, exclusive of officers (a number having by leave returned home the day before.)

In both the Dublin and London editions, Rogers says the 18th, but just above that he says the 27th, so he must really mean the 28th here.

Captain Henry Champion records this incident in his journal on July 27: "This day was killed and missing 25 men between Fort Edward and halfway brook, one Lieut—Stephens, one teamsman, one Sargt.—Wells of Windsor, ye regt. provost and 30 women and children, 38 teams and waggons destroyed with their carts and loading, which was letters, stores, officers' baggage and money to pay ye Regulars' Regiments. Found 12 dead bodies of men: one woman sprang out of ye waggon and ran back and escaped, one little child, a girl, ran back in the path like a quail, a waggoner who cut his horses' ropes and cleared him from ye waggon rode back ye path, took her by ye hand, catched her up before him and saved her." (Champion, p. 422)

James Henderson also gives a vivid account of this attack in a July 28 journal entry: "The French and Indians waylaid our teams between Fort Edward and the half way Brook and Killed 136 oxen or more that was in the teams and destroyed a great part of the provisions and other valuable Goods as Rum and Money and as near as I can learn there was about 30 or 35 Killed and taken three or 4 women Killed in a barbarous manner striping them naked and cutting them after a cruel manner."

On July 29, he continued: "Major Rogers went out with about 700 men and the next day he was Reinforced with about 1500 more they went to the South Bay thinking to Intersept the Enemy but they were gone before they come to Bay our men heard them shooting as they Went down the Bay in their Battoes They made no discovery more at this time" (Henderson, pp. 198-199)

Massachusetts Captain Samuel Cobb recorded in his journal for July 27, "the Indians Waylaid the Road between fort Edward and halfway Brook and they killed and took about 80 of our Men and women and Destroyed about 80 Teams Oxen and Loading" (Cobb, p. 21)

Massachusetts Provincial Chaplain John Cleaveland recorded the incident this way on July 29: "Last night about midnight an express being bro't from Half-way Brook that the Enemy had fell upon our Team, Waggons and Guard and cut off the Teams, etc. upon the arrival of this report there was an alarm made and a Thousand men sent away to South Bay if possible to intercept the Enemy upon their return; God seems to be against us by suffering these Barbarous Enemy to prey upon us: it is said that the Enemy took or killed 13 or 14 women, that the Regulars of the Guard were all killed except one, and that the Provincials turned their backs and ran, that the Indians got drunk with ye liquor in ye carts and officers of the Regulars perceiving it sent to Col. Hart, who was on the way with about half of his Regiment, to joyn him and he refused." (Cleaveland, July 29, 1758)

Cleaveland then continues the next day: "This morning before Day a man came in from Rogers at South Bay. He found Eighteen or twenty of ye Enemy's Boats and imagined that there were yet more. Immediately orders were given that General Lyman, Col. Whitcomb and Major Spencer with 600 men go immediately after Rogers to joyn him and they all were on board of Boats before Sun-rise. . . .the Boats I have spoken of above were not in South Bay but in Lake George." (Cleaveland, July 30, 1758)

On July 31, he adds more details to the attack on the supply train: "The account we now have of the affair of the Teams last Friday between Fort Edward and Half-way Brook is that there were five and Thirty ox-Teams coming from Fort Edward with an escort of 45 men and there were some passengers 12 or 14 Women, and that when they had got about 5 miles this side of Fort Edward the Enemy fired upon ye advance guard and killed some of them; ye rest turned and ran back to the Teamsters. The Enemy pursued and killed Twenty odd, one carter and 7 or 8 women. Some of these yt [that] got clear of the enemy being overheated with running dyed as soon as they got back to the Fort. That Col. Hart of ye New-Hampshire, Commandant at that Fort, turned out with a party of men upon hearing the guns, but when he had got nigh the enemy he made a halt; but Capt. Burbanks who from Half-way Brook with about 45 men coming upon the Enemy almost drunk with the Liquor they had got out of the carts, sent twice to Col. Hart to join him or let him have 100 men, but he refused either (for which he is now under arrest) whereupon he attacked the Enemy and drove them off, but took no Scalps nor prisoners . . . . Came this Day from Major Rogers a Battoe with a Deserter from us they took near the South-Bay belonging to Lord Howe's regiment who deserted before we went down the Lake. These men say that if Rogers had been an Hour sooner he would have been able to cut off ye Enemy returning with our prisoners and spoils from in ye rear of them being but just set off when the advanced guard of Rogers came in sight." (Cleaveland, July 31, 1758)

In a journal entry for July 28, Connecticut Provincial Abel Spicer records: "This day here was 93 men drafted from Colonel Whitings regiment for rangers and was paraded about four o'clock in the afternoon and they was ordered to keep in readiness so that if there should be any alarm they might turn out immediately. And in the night we was alarmed, for the French and Indians had cut off about 40 teams and killed 10 or 12 men and several women. The chief of the teams had sutlers stores and 3 of the men that was killed was sutlers. And as soon as the news came the rangers and some more was drafted out of the other regiments and some of the light infantry and Major Putnam and Rogers went [as] chief commanders and in less than one hour from the time that we was first rallied we got our provisions and put aboard the bateaux, and got on our way." (Spicer, p. 105)

On the same day, Joseph Smith of Groton, Connecticut, noted in his journal, "a nomber of teams was going from fort Edward to the lake and the french and Indians fell upon them and kild 17 men and five women and 137 oxen they Cut off the oxens horns and Cut ought there tongues and went of" (Joseph Smith, pp. 3-4)

Abel Spicer goes on to give a more complete account of this scout than Rogers does:

"Saturday, 29th. - In the morning, sun about two hours high, we landed on the east side of the lake and there we had our provisions and rum dealt out to us and marched off immediately to go to the South Bay. . .at night, we got so near to the bay that we could hear them fire and halloo as they was going up the bay and then we shifted our course to try to get ahead of them, and we travelled till night and then lay down on the side of a mountain, the ground being very wet by reason of the great amount of rain that we had before, which made bad lodging.

"Sunday, 30th. - This morning about sunrise we marched on again, and just as we got on our march we heard the Indians halloo again and we marched on towards the noise, and about 8 o'clock we came to the place where they encamped and the shouting that we heard in the morning was supposed to be the time when they marched off, and they wrote on the trees that they had got seven prisoners and 2 of them was women. And they wrote that their scout was 1800 strong. And after we had been there a little while there was a man hallooed several times on the other side of the bay and Major Rogers answered him, and continued hallooing and two men swam over the bay to see if they could find what was the matter. But Major Rogers did keep hallooing to him and asked him why he did not come to the water side, and he said he was so weak he could not. And these men that swam over came back again for fear that he was sent to lead them into some snare. And Major Rogers still hallooed to him to come to the water side and at last he got there and Major Rogers did climb into the top of a large tree and then he examined him from where he came, and he said that he was taken by three Indians at the Bloody Pond, which was between Lake George and Half Way Brook, and the Indians carried him away by the South Bay almost to Ticonderoga, and they all lay down and went to sleep and while they was asleep he run away from them, and they did not take his provisions from him and he had five days allowance when he was taken, and he had been five weeks in the woods and nothing else to eat but what he could find in the woods, sometimes goose berries and huckle berries and some sort of roots, but he was almost dead and begged for help. And then they made a raft and brought him over and he was so weak that he could not travel and then they made a bier and we brought him about 11 miles and then we came to our bateaux [at Lake George]. And while we was gone the men that was left to take care of the bateaux was surprised in the night and thought that they spied some French bateaux and put back to the camps. And they immediately sent out one thousand regulars and as many provincials to the same place where we left our bateaux and we came to them at night, and we all encamped on a small island a small distance from the shore. And it blew very hard and it rained almost all night and in the morning there was several of the bateaux stove in by the seas tossing them one against another.

"Monday, 31st. - This hath been a very wet month. We lay here this day till almost night and then we pushed off and came down to the island where the advance guard was kept and there was stopped about midnight. Some lay in their bateaux for the island would not contain them all. But what it was for was not known, but in the morning we heard that there was a number of Indians and French seen between Fort Edward and Half Way Brook and there was a large scout sent after them.

"Tuesday, August 1st. - This morning by sunrise we all pushed off and landed on an island about 10 or 12 miles down the lake and lay there till about noon. And Major Rogers landed on another island about 100 rods from the island where Major Putnam landed, and they had their provision dealt out to them for four days scout and then they pushed off to the shore and the Major Putnam went on the same island and there was not provisions enough for them and they sent back after more provisions. And they was not to go till the next day.

"Wednesday, 2d. - This morning Major Putnam's men had ten days rations dealt out to them and Major Rogers had as much for his men. And there was about 100 of the regulars and about 150 of the light infantry and about 400 of the rangers and they got their men served with provisions and landed them on the shore and marched off about 9 o'clock. And they was drawed up in three columns when they marched and Major Rogers marched in the front and Major Putnam on the rear. And the counter sign for the scout was Boston. That was, if any man should hail you, you must answer Boston, and if you hailed anybody and they did not answer Boston, you must take them to be an enemy. And we marched till we came to a place where Rogers encamped with a scout about a month before, which was about half way from the lake to South Bay.

"Thursday, 3d. - This morning they sent out two small scouts a little ways round to [see] if they could discover any enemy and to return in two hours. And after they had returned we marched again about South Point as we did the day before. And about 3 o'clock we came within about half a mile of the head of South Bay and made a halt. And Major Putnam went to the bay to see if he could spy any enemy and returned again before night. And then we came to the head of the Bay and encamped there that night, and there was sheds made of bark that looked as though they had been made four or five days.

"Friday, 4th. - This morning it rained and had rained all the latter part of the night. And about 8 o'clock in the morning it cleared off and they sent a small scout round and one scout back in the path where we came but they came back and discovered nothing. And then we went upon a small hill which was close by the head of the bay and made a small breast work with old logs that we could pick up without chopping so that it might be done without making much noise. And Major Rogers went with his men and the regulars and the light infantry to Wood Creek and encamped there, which was about 4 or 5 miles from the head of the bay. This night here was one of the light infantry died that was left with Major Putnam when Rogers went to Wood Creek.

"Saturday, 5th. - This morning Major Putnam gave liberty for some of them to go away some distance from the bay and build some fires but they had no liberty before. Here was some men sick that was sent back to the camps today and a few well ones sent to take care of them.

"Sunday, 6th. - This morning Major Putnam sent off ten more men that was not well. And about noon there was a bateau came up the bay and was discovered and they put back again as fast as they could. And then Major Putnam ordered all his men to pack up and go to Major Rogers at Wood Creek, and we marched off and joined Major Rogers about 5 o'clock in the afternoon. And Roger's men spyed a bateau in the creek. A regular spyed it first and hailed it and then they made off as fast as they could." (Spicer, pp. 105-109) Spicer's account will continue after Rogers' own account of the Battle of Fort Anne.

Connecticut Provincial captain Henry Champion gives more details about the man rescued by the Rangers, and also some of the women captives: "About 12 of ye clock came in from ye party one of Rogers' Sarg'ts in a whale boat with one of Lord How's men who was taken at bloody pond five weeks past—ran away the second night with five days provisions as he saith, was lost, taken up yesterday by Major Rogers up against Ticonderoga just starved.

"Said Sargt. Says they saw ye party of enemy going down South Bay that did ye mischief the 28th, said party about 300; they saw three women alive in one batteau, but our men were about half an hour too late to give them fire.

"Some say the starved man was a deserter from Lord How's Regt." (Champion, p. 423)

William Hervey, of the 44th Regiment, records in his journal that "Rogers, with 650 men came in the evening; he had been at South Bay to cut off the enemy returning, but was 2 hours too late. (Hervey, p. 51)

The Putnam referred to here is, of course, Israel Putnam, who was captured in the opening moments of this battle, and then later exchanged.

James Dalyell of Gage's Light Infantry, also referred to above, was a brave and talented, but overly ambitious young officer who would later be killed in the Battle of Bloody Run during the Siege of Detroit in Pontiac's Uprising of 1763.

After marching about three-quarters of a mile, a fire begun with five hundred of the enemy in the front; I brought my people into as good order as possible, Capt. Dalyell in the center, and the Rangers on the right, with Col. Partridge's light infantry; on the left was Capt. Gidding's of the Boston troops with his people, and Major Putnam being in the front of his men when the fire began, the enemy rushing in, took him, one Lieutenant, and two others, prisoners, and considerably disordered others of the party, who afterwards rallied and did good service, particularly Lieutenant Durkee, who notwithstanding two wounds, one in his thigh, the other in his wrist, kept in the action the whole time, encouraging his men with great earnestness and resolution. Capt. Dalyell with Gage's light infantry, and Lieutenant Eyers of the 44th regiment, behaved with great bravery, they being in the center, where was at first the hottest fire, which afterwards fell to the right where the Rangers were, and where the enemy made four different attacks; in short, officers and soldiers throughout the detachment behaved with such vigour and resolution, as in one hour's time broke the enemy and obliged them to retreat, which they did with such caution in small scattering parties, as gave us no great opportunity to distress them by a pursuit: we kept the field and buried our dead. When the action was over, we had missing fifty-four men, twenty-one of which afterwards came in, being separated from us while the action continued. The enemy's loss was 199 killed on the spot, several of which were Indians.* We arrived at Fort Edward on the 9th, being met at some distance from it by Col. Provost, with a party of 300, and refreshments for the wounded, which I had desired by an express sent before.

This engagement is generally known as the "Battle of Fort Anne," since it occurred near the ruins of the old fort. William Hervey of the 44th Regiment sets the stage with this August 1 entry to his journal: "Rogers and Putnam with 700, including 50 volunteers of Regulars, went out; end of South Bay; Dieskaw's path, east of Wood Creek, by the falls, to Fort Edward or Halfway brook." (Hervey, p. 51)

Abel Spicer's account continues, with this vivid account of the battle and its immediate aftermath:

"Tuesday, 8th. - Our officers shot at a mark thinking there was no danger. And about 7 o'clock we marched off in a single file and the reserves were near a mile behind but the rear wheeled to the right which brought us into a half circle and then we began to drive them. And Major Rogers sent a party of a hundred men for a small hill and the right flank to take

*By a detachment that went out afterwards, fifty more of the enemy were found dead near the place of action.

advantage of the ground and the rest of them was in a half circle. And then Major Rogers sent off to Fort Edward for a recruit of men and then he hallooed to the French and said, 'Come up you French dogs like men.'And then he hallooed to the officer on the hill and asked him if he wanted more men, if he did he should have 500, which was to frighten the French. And they did not stand it but a little while longer but hallooed to get together and run off as fast as they could. The fight lasted about two hours but after they had gone off we buried the dead and brought off the wounded. And about sunset the party from Fort Edward met us about half way from Fort Edward to Fort Ann and then the recruits carried the wounded and we traveled till 9 or 10 o'clock and then we halted and built fires. And they brought out doctors. . .and they dressed some of the wounds in the night. And two men died of their wounds before morning.

"Wednesday, 9th. - This morning about sunrise we marched off and came to Fort Edward about 8 o'clock in the morning and carried the wounded men to the hospital. And Colonel Fitch took an account of all wounded and missing to send by the post to be put in the prints [newspapers]. Out of Colonel Whitings there was almost half wounded and missing, they being in the front. There was not but one commissioner [commissioned officer] went from the regiment, and he was an ensign, and he was shot in the body with five bullets and one in the arm, and he was scalped and stripped, and but one sargeant from the regiment, and he was killed, and but two corporals and they was both wounded, one shot through the thigh and one through the hand, so that we had no officer left.

"Thursday, 10th. - This day we intended to go to the lake but there was no guard going and Major Rogers was going the next day and we concluded to stay until he went.

"Friday, 11th. - This morning here was 30 teams going to the lake and a guard of about 400 men to guard them but Major Rogers did not go with them as he did intend, for there was Indians seen between Fort Edward and Fort Miller the day before and he went out with about 4 or 500 men and returned the next day and discovered no enemy." (Spicer, p. 109)

Massachusetts Provincial James Henderson tells of the battle in his journal entry for August 8: "Major Rogers went out with a large scout of men near 600 in their Return from the South Bay near to Fort Ann the French and Indians laid an Ambush for them and fired upon them but the Major Bravely resisted them and after some hours fighting mad them leave the ground our men got 54 scalps and two prisoners it is reported that our men found many of them dead in the woods since there is nigh 100 of our men Killed and a missing Major Putnam is missing also" (Henderson, p. 199)

The Reverend John Cleaveland, a Massachusetts Provincial chaplain, gave this account in his journal entry for August 9: "This morning hear that Major Rogers has fell in with the Enemy at Wood-Creek and has got the better of them. The Lord send us Success and give us hearts to give Him the glory of all . . . . This Evening heard that Maj'r Rogers and Major Putnam have had a Brush with the French and Indians at Wood-Creek near Fort Ann, that our men were marching in an Indian File. that Maj Rogers and a Regular officer in the Front were firing at marks upon a wager, the Enemy were marching in the Road towards them and hearing the fire at marks posted themselves in ambush and when our troops has passed by, 12 or 14 with Major Putnam in the rear, the Enemy fell on these, killed scalped the most of them. Upon this the Troops as soon as they could be formed in a Front made a stand for about an Hour and then the Enemy drew off. It is said Rogers got 9 scalps and two prisoners, a Frenchman and a Dutchman; that two of our men scalped by ye enemy are got into Fort Edward like to do well. Putnam is missing but how many are killed and wounded on our side I can't hear, some say above 20. O when will men be wise?"

On August 11, Cleaveland added some additional information, and corrected his earlier incorrect statement about the relative positions of Rogers and Putnam: "Hear that Major

GARY ZABOLY
© 1997

Marin's Raiding Party

FOLLOWING the debacle of Abercromby's defeat at Ticonderoga on July 8, 1758, and the retreat of his army back to its main camp at the southern end of Lake George, the galvanized French seized the moment to send large raiding parties out of Fort Carillon. They fell upon work parties, patrols, pickets, and supply trains along the military wagon road between the lake camp and Fort Edward, with the overall strategic intention of forcing Abercromby to abandon his position on the lake.[1] Led by such partisan leaders as La Corne de St. Luc, Courtemanche, and Joseph Marin, these parties drew out equally large pursuit detachments from the British posts, composed mostly of Rangers and light infantry units.

Robert Rogers, and Captain Israel Putnam of the Connecticut Provincials, had attempted to cut off La Corne's party after its destruction of a supply train on July 28, by rushing halfway up Lake George and then trekking overland to Two Rocks on Wood Creek, but they were too late by mere minutes. The supply train ambush had been particularly brutal, even by frontier standards: dozens of men, women and children had been slaughtered—some of the women being obviously raped and tortured before being killed—and even the oxen had been killed and scalped.[2] Unfortunately, LaCorne and his party got away unmolested. Returning to Lake George, Rogers and Putnam encamped on Sloop Island until the 31st, when they received orders from Colonel Haviland, at Fort Edward, to try to intercept yet another large enemy party that had been detected near Halfway Brook. Once again Rogers and Putnam crossed the mountains east of the lake, but this time, on August 4, they set up ambuscades at the northern and southern ends of South Bay.

Meanwhile, that very day, Canadian partisan Captain Joseph Marin left Fort Carillon with over 300 men, mostly Canadians and Indians, but including about 50 troops of the French Marines. The Indians no doubt represented most of the various bands then present at Fort Carillon: Canadian Iroquois (Caughnawaga), Algonkins, Nipissings, Abenakis, Hurons, Ottawas, and Missisaugas.[3] By the 6th the hidden Rangers and light infantry spotted bateaus and canoes on Wood Creek and South Bay, no doubt advance elements of Marin's party.

Rogers and Putnam joined forces again and, observing no further signs of the enemy, on the 7th they marched south toward the decaying ruins of old Fort Anne. Near there, on the 8th, Marin's force ambushed them; but the tables were eventually turned in the savage bushfight that followed, and Marin was forced to withdraw after enduring considerable casualties. The French and Indians, however, had taken Israel Putnam captive.

Evidently, after leaving Fort Carillon on August 4, Marin's party had rowed and paddled down Wood Creek toward its junction with South Bay. When its advance scouts were spotted by Rogers and Putnam, Marin landed the detachment somewhere along the swampy western edge of the creek, and hid his boats in the brush and woods. From here they marched toward the British outposts in the south, bent on doing mischief and mayhem around them.

The scene illustrates several leaders of the French and Indian party, including Marin himself, as they deploy to survey the country ahead of them. At left is a voyageur officer; his breed Bougainville considered the "good kind" of Canadian, at least where bushfighting was concerned. "One recognizes them easily by their looks," said Bougainville, "by their size, and because all of them are tattooed on their bodies with the figures of plants and animals. The operation is long and painful. The figure is outlined by pricking the skin with a needle and printed in by burning powder in the holes. One would not pass for a man among the Indians of the Far West if he had not had himself tattooed."[4]

He wears a wool cap, the favored headgear of the *voyageurs* in their travels. These were either red or blue, and sometimes had tasselled ends. His war attire is all Indian: breechcloth, leggings and moccasins. Three knives are carried "as a precaution or safeguard."[5] Though well tattooed, Canadians rarely painted their faces like Indian warriors.[6] Despite traditional depictions of bearded *voyageurs*, in the eighteenth century shaved faces were the rule among the Canadians.[7] This officer carries his musket in a sealskin gun case.[8]

To the *voyageur's* right is 39-year-old Joseph Marin, who, like his late father, Paul, was long experienced in dealing with Indians, and in recruiting many western tribes into the French sphere of influence. Long before Robert Rogers' own attempt, Marin had already dabbled in efforts to discover the Northwest Passage water route across the continent.[9] He had commanded French trading posts in the Mississippi Valley. In 1756, he was called east to participate in the theater of war in the Ohio Valley, and later in upper New York Province, including the campaign against Fort William Henry. His reputation and deeds became known to the English, who regarded him as "a Person noted for going among the Indian Settlements, and bringing them a great Distance to War, and was by way of Distinction called the Indian General."[10]

No known portrait of Marin has come to my attention. His dress on this occasion can, however, be surmised from various evidences. Typical of French partisan fighters in charge of Indians, he would certainly have dressed largely as they did. Ruffled shirts, a favorite dress of Indian war chiefs, were also known to distinguish some Canadian officers on campaign.[11] Since his influence among the western tribes was of paramount importance, doubtless he would have flattered them by adopting some items of their native clothing and accouterments (for instance, a cloth or fur turban surrounding hair done up with feathers). Like the voyageur, his pack is carried by a beaded and quilled tumpline. His weapons include knife, pistol carried in the multi-colored sash around his waist, and double-barreled carbine. Partisan officer La Corne carried one of the latter on his Saratoga raid in 1747.[12] With information obtained from a prisoner in December of 1757, Robert Rogers noted in his *Journals*, "500 Rangers were lately raised in Canada, each man having a double-barrelled fuzee."

The tall Indian to Marin's right is the six-foot four-inch Caughnawaga Mohawk chief who would both startle and wreak havoc among Rogers' and Putnam's men in the August 8th engagement, until Rogers himself dropped him with a well-aimed bullet.[13] Indian chiefs were often designated by gorgets or medals and carrying spears, or, in this case, the gift of a French spontoon which he has decorated according to his own taste. The split outer rims of his ears are tied behind his neck for traveling in the woods, with feather tufts partially covering them. His beaded burden strap is based on an actual Caughnawaga relic in the collection of the Memorial Hall Museum, Deerfield, Massachusetts. The pack itself is the party's "war bundle": made of woven reeds, it contains protective amulets, Indian medicines, wampum, and other important items. A tasseled wooden stopper keeps the barrel of his French musket dry. In his beaded waistbelt at back rests a tomahawk.

To his right is an officer of the *Compagnies Franches de la Marine*, regulars raised in Canada and trained, to some degree, in bush warfare. The clothing distributed to Marine troops on such expeditions can only be theorized. Bougainville speaks of "coats, breeches, *mitasses* [leggings]" in the Fort Carillon stores in August of 1758 as being "of poor material, too short, too tight."[14]

This officer wears sturdy buckskin breeches, unlike most of his men. The blue fatigue cap with *fleur-de-lys* usually associated with the Marines might not always have been available; this officer instead wears a plain cap. He carries his supplies in a knapsack instead of a tumpline pack. Under his Marine cartridge box is a brass-mounted horn powder flask. At his left hip hangs a bayonet and tomahawk. His gun is a Model 1728 infantry musket. Gold lace trims his sleeved *veste* of blue serge.

At far right is a chief of the Missisauga tribe, one of several western Indian nations that sent its warriors east to fight with Montcalm against the British. The Missisauga were particularly vigorous in the cause. This man has no European weapon of any kind, outside of the metal lance-head on his spear, and the gunstock he has converted into a painted war club. A wooden nose plug, fur turban, and skin breechcloth add to his primitive appearance. He is also very deadly with the bow; in the abovementioned 1757 raid led by Marin,[15] four American Provincials were killed by arrows that might have flown from Missisauga bows. The rumor afterwards spread among the Anglo-American soldiers that the western tribe that fired them "not only kill, but if they have the Opportunity, suck the Blood out of the Bodies of the Dead."[16]

In the background, canoes and bateaux of Marin's party are being brought ashore. Much of the area immediately surrounding Wood Creek was known as "the drowned lands," and for good reason: the water channel itself was mostly narrow, hemmed in by muddy swamps and inundated grassland, with muskrat and beaver lodges and dams frequently hindering transportation.[17]

Rogers' defeat of Marin's party effectively put an end to the French attempts to dislodge Abercromby's army by incessant raiding. Instead, in the latter months of 1758, activity was relegated mainly to reconnoitering parties, and to the light skirmishing that resulted when enemy parties encountered each other in the no-man's land between the French and British positions. As things turned out, the British did abandon their

Lake George camp in the fall, pulling back to Fort Edward for winter quarters.[18]

G.Z.

1. *Adventure in the Wilderness: The American Journals of Louis Antoine de Bougainville, 1756- 1760*, translated and edited by Edward P. Hamilton, University of Oklahoma Press, Norman, Oklahoma, 1964. Entry of July 25, 1758, p. 249.
2. One of Putnam's Rangers, named Jones, later recalled the scene as he accompanied a party of Provincials to assist in the burial of the slain: "Following up the trail, he soon found the corpse of a woman which had been exposed to the most barbarous indignities and mutilations, and fastened in an upright position to a sapling which had been bent over for that purpose." A. W. Holden, *History of the Town of Queensbury, in the State of New York*, Albany, 1874, p. 324. Provincial diarist James Henderson recorded much the same in his entry of July 8, 1758: "there was. . .three or 4 women killed in a barbarous manner, stripping them naked and cutting them after a cruel manner." "James Henderson's Journal," *The First Half Century of the Society of Colonial Wars in the Commonwealth of Massachusetts, 1893-1943*, Boston, 1944, p. 199. Revisionist historians often take Rogers' Rangers to task for their destruction of the Abenaki village at St. Francis, likening it to racial genocide. But LaCorne's ambush at Halfway Brook clearly provides additional evidence that neither side in the war could claim a monopoly in savagery. In fact, it can be said, when the "tally" is made, that the French and Indians committed such acts more frequently than did the Anglo-Americans and their own Indian allies.
3. Ibid., p. 255.
4. Idem, p. 288.
5. J.C.B. (otherwise anonymous), *Travels in New France*, Pennsylvania Historical Society, 1941, p. 147.
6. Peter Kalm, *Travels in North America*, Dover, New York, 1987, reprint of 1770 edition, p. 577.
7. "Canadian Militia, 1750-1760," plates nos. 553 and 554, by Francis Back and Rene Chartrand, Military Uniforms in America series, The Company of Military Historians, 1984.
8. Captain John Knox found a sealskin gun case of a Canadian partisan in Nova Scotia in May, along with "several haversacks of the same skin." John Knox, *The Siege of Quebec, and the Campaigns in North America*, 1757-1760, Folio Society Edition, London, 1976, p. 170.
9. *Journal of Joseph Marin, August 7, 1753 - June 20, 1754*, edited and translated by Kenneth P. Bailey, The Henry E. Huntington Library, 1975, p. xv.
10. *Boston Evening-Post*, August 28, 1758.
11. During Marin's raid on Fort Edward on July 23, 1757, one killed Frenchman was presumed by the British "to be an Officer, as we have his ruffled Shirt." *Boston Gazette*, August 4, 1757.
12. E. B. O'Callaghan, *Documents Relative to the Colonial History of the State of New York*, Albany, New York, 1858, p. 79.
13. Wrote Lt. Thomas Barnsley to Colonel Henry Bouquet on September 7, 1758, "this Sachem was 6 foot 4 inches high proportionably made, in Short he was the Largest Indian Ever Rogers Saw." *The Papers of Henry Bouquet*: Vol. II: The Forbes Expedition, edited by S. K. Stevens, D.H. Kent, and A. L. Leonard, The Pennsylvania Historical and Museum Commission, Harrisburg, Pennsylvania, 1951, p. 481.
14. Bougainville, p. 257.
15. See note 10.
16. *Boston Gazette*, August 8, 1757.
17. Wood Creek was called the Chicot River by the French; this was actually the southernmost arm of Lake Champlain.
18. The British, before leaving their Lake George camp, had buried there those munitions they did not take back to Fort Edward, and had deliberately sunk all their vessels—row galleys, two radeaus or floating batteries, a sloop, whaleboats and bateaus—in hidden places under the southernmost waters of the lake, to be retrieved during the 1759 campaign. According to Bougainville, however, Montcalm "sent a detachment with some specialists to try to unearth their artillery caches, to find and haul out the bark and the barges. This detachment found . . .the location of the bark, fifty sunken barges, and several other caches in a neighboring swamp." (Bougainville, p. 292). When Amherst's engineers came on the scene in 1759, they could not find the large radeau, a seven-sided, flat-bottomed vessel designed to carry at least seven big guns. It had been unofficially dubbed *Land and End* or *Land Tortoise* by Abercromby's men. The vessel's missing status was ascribed, correctly, to the activity of the French between the campaigns. Although the Provincials had had some trouble in sinking the radeau before they broke camp in 1758 (see Russell P. Bellico, *Sails and Steam in the Mountains: A Maritime and Military History of Lake George and Lake Champlain*, Purple Mountain Press, Fleischmanns, New York, 1992, p. 85), it was not reported lost, and evidently everybody knew precisely where *Land Tortoise* should have been, because in 1759 Royal Artillery Captain-Lieutenant Henry Skinner noted in his journal, "Most of the things which were buried here last campaign have not been discovered by the enemy; the only thing of any consequence that they have found is a floating battery, which mounted eight battering-pieces, and was sunk in the Lake." "A Royal Artillery Officer With Amherst: The Journal of Captain-Lieutenant Henry Skinner, 1 May - 28 July 1759," introduction and footnotes by Gary S. Zaboly, *Bulletin of the Fort Ticonderoga Museum*, Volume XV, 1993, Number 5, p. 375. *Land Tortoise* was rediscovered by side- scan sonar and divers in 1990, in about a hundred feet of water. (See Bellico, pp. 84-85). Clearly, Montcalm's "specialists" had indeed discovered her, lifted her, and sunk her again where no eighteenth-century technology could ever find or lift her again.

Rogers is got into Fort Edward and that he with Capt. Giddings and about 300 men set off this morning to Fort Miller having heard the evening before that a Body of the Enemy were set there on the East Side of the River. The Good Lord enable them to go forth in His Name and crown them with remarkable Success and wipe off the Reproach which lies upon us and Defend our Land and Privileges Amen. and Amen. Those that came into the camp this Evening yt [that] were in Rogers' late Fight sat [said] that Putnam was in the Front and the Enemy ambushed them and attacked our Front, that Rogers got fifty odd scalps and that the killed, wounded and missing on our side exceed a 100, and that they had the advantage of us by hearing our men firing at marks in the morning, this is a judg't of God upon us." (Cleaveland, August 9 and 11, 1758)

Connecticut captain Henry Champion gives this account in his journal for August 8: "This day near Fort Ann Major Rogers and Major Putnam who went out with about 800 men about a week ago had a fight, before ye fight they had sent in about 100 who were poorly, so our party were about 700, ye enemy about 400. Our party lodged at Fort Ann over night, in ye morning fired at marks, then Major Putnam marched off in ye front for Fort Edward, ye men in a single file.

"Major Rogers brought up ye rear, but before ye rear were all moved, ye front were a mile on and were ambushed by ye enemy, who lay in a half moon and fired before they were discovered on our front, and ran on and cut off about 12 or 20 with whom was Major Putnam; he is killed or taken as we hear from a letter.

"Major Rogers brought up ye rear with a litter, had a smart skirmish, drove off ye enemy, got about 50 scalps and took two prisoners. We have killed and missing about 40 or 60, wounded about 40 or 60. . . . Major Rogers went towards Saratoga with 300 next day scouting after a number of the enemy who was suspected to be there, but found not." (Champion, pp. 424-425)

Doctor Thomas Haynes Sr., a Provincial surgeon, left an account that was compiled after the fact, rather than as an eyewitness, but it has some interesting details:

"July 29 there was a number of the enemy came down by the way of South bay and unaware fell upon a small part of our people about four miles north of Fort Edward upon the wagon Rode. In this Disaster we lost 32 men and forty teams loaden with provisions, rum, wine, brandy and some money. The men were all slain.Viz. 139 only one escaped with life. The same day or about midnight we received the melancholy account which made a universal alarm throughout the whole incampment and a detachment was made in the following manner: eight out of each company to go to South Bay under Majors Putnam and Rogers which they effected by morning light, the whole of the schout [scout] was about 1400. They went in Batteaus to East Bay and then by land to South Bay. July 29 there was an augmentation of the scout, seven hundred to follow Putnam and join him.

"July 30th Eleven hundred more were drafted and sent the same way under Gen Lyman to go to South bay which they did, but two days after Gen Lyman came back with most of the schout. Putnam and Rogers staid with about 1000 men to clear the wood of the enemy—

"July 31 in the morning our scout came across a party of the enemy three miles south of Fort Ann. Maj. Putnam marching in the front of the scout, and Maj. Rogers brought up the rear. whereupon Rogers and one Lieut. of the light infantry laid a wager to shoot at a mark and discharged their pieces at an old tree which gave the enemy timely notice to discover our corps and ambushcade them in their return home which they did, and took them at as good advantage as they could they fired upon our scout. Putnam immediately ordered the party under him to return the fire which was effected. The enemy prest upon our men and took Major Putnam and Lieut. Tracy with two more the Provincials, charged their pieces and rushed on upon the enemy with precipatation and discharged their fire locks with great advantage. The fire lasted about two hours.

Major Rogers being in the rear he advanced up as fast as he could with advantages equal to his Generals and heroic Good Conduct &c. Here Rogers surrounded the enemy and obliged them to quit the field with the loss of their chief and 200 men killed and missing, 80 left upon the field and three prisoners. We lost killed 53, wounded 50, taken four. They returned the same night to Fort Edward, brought in the wounded and the most of them slightly wounded. After this our forces went to build Fort Edward and make it stronger by throwing up a glacis all round the fort and fashioned the same with two rows of pickquets one in the ditch and another between the glacis and main ditch for a breastwork of defence in time of besiegement this work was carried on till the middle of November which hereafter &c." (Haynes, entries for July 29, 30 and 31, 1759)

Joseph Smith's journal for August 8 notes that: "majer Rogers and majer Putmon was coming in from a scout to 10 Days and majer Rogers and another offissor shot at a mark for a wager upon which the Enemy Discovered them and Enambushed them majer Putnom being in front and majer Rogers being in the rear with about Six hundred men with them the Enemy fired the first they fought for about two hours then beat the Enemy of soon as the nuse came in at fort Edward our regement sallyed ought to help them in they went ought about three of the Clock in the afternoon and came in just before the brake of the Day majer Putnom and Leut. Trase [Tracy] is missing and nobody knows what is become of them there was about 80 men kild wounded and mising." On August 12, he added, "Colo Fitch received a letter from majer Putnom which gave an account that he was taken and carried into tinindinoge fort [Ticonderoga] and Leuit trasy with him and both was Prisinors there" (Joseph Smith, pp. 4-5)

On August 9, Captain Samuel Cobb made the following entry in his journal, "Infermation that Major Rogers has had an Ingagement with 15 hundred french and Indians at South bay he bing out with 7 hundred Men and a party of Provinl. Troops. Lieut Jacob Brown and 5 privates out of my Company out with the party." (Cobb, p. 22)

An "*Extract of a Letter from* Albany, August 14" reprinted in the *London Magazine*, gave this account of the battle: "Major Rogers and the enemy, the 8th instant, had a brush near fort Anne, near the Wood Creek. All that we know of the affair is, that the enemy, about 150 Indians, and 300 Canadians, designed to cut off our escort between Saraghtoga and fort Edward; but were met by Rogers with about 600, who received the first fire, which killed and wounded several of his men. The engagement lasted above two hours. We had killed of our own men, some say 50, others 80. The French 60 or 70 at least. We took two prisoners, who say, the enemy lost several persons of note, particularly M. Morrier, one of the principal directors of Indian affairs, a person noted for going among the Indian settlements, and bringing them a great distance to war; he was called the Indian general. [This report is most likely in error. The French are not known to have lost anyone fitting that description, certainly not Marin]. Rogers pursued the enemy two miles, but could not come up with them. The next day he buried his dead, and scalped the enemy. Next post it is probable I may be able to send you further particulars of this affair." (*London Magazine*, October, 1758)

The *Gentleman's Magazine* had this to report: "*Philadelphia, Aug 24.* We have letters by yesterday's post which say that a party of 700 of *Roger's* Rangers, with Puttnam in the front, fell in on the 8th instant near fort *Anne* with a party of 170 *Indians* and 280 *Canadians* and colony troops. *Roger's* party was then in an *Indian* defile which took up a long while before the rear came up. A scout has been out since from Half-way brook to the place of action, and found upwards of 40 *Indians* bodies, 20 scalped; They counted upwards of 100 dead bodies and believe there might be many more, but the stench was so great they could not stand it. *Rogers* buried all his dead.

"The enemy carried off Major *Puttnam*, Lieut. *Tracy*, and three provincials. A flag of truce came to the camp at *Lake George* the 12th;

and we learn, *Vaudreuil* will agree to an exchange of prisoners. Major *Puttnam, &c,* are at *Ticonderoga. Roger's* party consisted of 65 regulars soldiers volunteers, and two officers, 80 light armed infantry, and 80 rangers, the rest were made up of provincials. (*The Gentleman's Magazine,* Volume XXVIII, October, 1758, pp. 498-499)

General Abercromby's report to William Pitt contains some interesting additional information: "permit me to inform you of the Steps I took upon the first Intelligence of this Disaster, which did not reach me till 9 at night, by one of the Officers that had been detatched from the Half-Way Brook, and had continued on the Spot till the Enemy were retired, who assured me, that great Part of them were drunk, which, together with being loaded with Spoils, must greatly retard them in their Retreat. Upon this, I immediately ordered a Detachment of 700 Men, from among the Light Infantry, Rangers, & Provincials, whom I put under the Command of Rogers and Putnam, to proceed with them to a narrow Pass at the Wood Creek, by which, if the Enemy came that way at all, and were not already passed, we cou'd not fail of intercepting them; accordingly, I saw them all off, by two o'clock in the Morning.

"But as the Place Rogers and his people were to land at, is within view of the Enemy's Look-Out, whence they might discover our Batteaus, & guess at the Number of our Men, as well as at our Design, & probably endeavour to prevent the Execution of it, by sending a larger Party against them, I order'd out another Detachment, of 1000 Men, from the whole Line, under the Command of Colo. Haviland, to Cover & sustain Rogers and his Party, in Case of Necessity; This Detachment went off next morning, . . .

"On the 30th Colo. Haviland sent to acquaint me, that Rogers and his Party, without any opposition whatsoever, had got to their Place of Rendez-vous, but unfortunately too late by two Hours, the Enemy being already far on the Lake in their Canoes when they came up.

"Several other Scouting Parties of Ours, having returned, about this Time, and reported, that they had tracked several small ones of the Enemy, from Half Way Brook down to Still Water, which were supposed to come by the Way of South Bay; I immediately directed Colo. Haviland, to detatch Rogers & Putnam, from whence they were, with 700 chosen Men and ten Days' Provisions, to sweep all that back Country & come in by Fort Edward . . . .

"Pursuant to the Directions, I sent, Colo. Haviland, Rogers & Putnam made choice of their 700 Men, consisting in Light Infantry, Rangers, Provincials, and about 60 Voluntiers from among the Regulars, with whom they crossed over, from the first Narrows, (twelve Miles below this) towards South Bay, where Putnam, with 400, took up his Station, and Rogers, with the Remainder of his Party, lay in Ambush, a little above where the Wood Creek discharges itself into the South Bay.

"On Sunday the 6th Instant, a Canoe, with 6 Indians, was discover'd coming up the Creek, and notwithstanding all previous Enjunctions to the Contrary, one of the Provincials challenged them, upon which the Indians tacked, and got off: — About the same time, two boats were in with Putnam's advanced Guard, and by a like Stupidity escaped also. — Upon these unlucky discoveries, Rogers and Putnam joined, edging away towards Fort Edward.

"When, on the 8th, within two Miles of Fort Ann, they fell in with a Party of the Enemy, consisting of about 450 Indians, Canadians, and Marine Companies, under the Command of Mor. Marin, one of their most famous Patizans; after a Dispute of two Hours, the Enemy gave way, with the Loss of about 150, two of which were brought in Prisoners, the Remainder Killed or scalped; of the latter they reckon 56, and at least 15 of them Indians Scalps. Our Loss is trifling; a few scalped or killed, which our People buried; Putnam and one of His Lieutenants are taken Prisoners, and must have fallen into the Enemies Hands very early, as he was missed for a long Time, which proved the more unlucky, as 300 of the Connecticut Troops, which were under His

Command, and of His own choice, scatter'd so, that there was no possibility of collecting them to pursue the Enemy, which might easily have been effected, with a visible Prospect of an entire Success.

"I must not omit, doing Rogers the Justice to say, that he merits much to be commended, he having, by Report of a very good Officer in the Light Infantry, who was on this Party, acted the whole time with great Calmness and Officer-like. . . ." (Pitt, Volume I, pp. 319-322)

Mante gives a fairly clear and concise picture of the battle: "Whilst the intrenchments of General Abercromby inclosed him in security, [after his stinging defeat at Ticonderoga] M. de Montcalm exerted his usual activity in harassing the frontiers, and in detaching parties to attack the convoys of the English. On the 17th of July, one of these parties destroyed three provincial officers and upwards of twenty men, at Half-way-brook; and on the 27th of the same month, one hundred and sixteen waggoners and sixteen rangers met with the same fate between that place and Fort Edward. Major Rogers was then detached with a party of seven hundred men, in quest of the enemy; but they had the good fortune to escape him. On his return, he met an express from the General, with orders to proceed to south and east Bay, and return by Fort Edward. Whilst the Major was pursuing the route prescribed him by these orders, he was attacked on the 8th of August, near the spot where Fort St. Anne stood, by about five hundred of the enemy, his own number being reduced to five hundred and thirty men. Both he and his men behaved with so much spirit, that, in an hour, they broke the assailants, and obliged them to retreat, though (such was the enemy's caution) without any prospect of being able to distress them by a pursuit. In this action there fell one hundred and ninety of the French; and the English lost about forty, the missing included. Major Putnam and two lieutenants were made prisoners. (Mante, pp. 158-159)

The French perspective is given in Doreil's report to Marshal de Belle Isle: "Since the great day of the 8th, the Mis de Montcalm has always had some detachments in the field to harass and watch the enemy. These detachments had likewise for object to place themselves between the enemy's intrenched camp on the ruins of Fort William Henry and Fort Edward, to attack and destroy their convoys. They have had divers success. The first, which marched on the 16th of July under the orders of a Colonial Captain, returned the 21st with 10 prisoners and 24 scalps. The impatience of the Indians prevented this detachment destroying a party of 300 English which had taken refuge in a stockaded inclosure lately erected to serve as a depot on the Fort Edward road.

"The second, likewise under the command of a Colonial Captain, which left the camp the latter part of July, fell in also on the Fort Edward road, at the enemy's camp, with a convoy of 40 carts, each of which had from 4 to 6 oxen yoked to it; these carts were loaded with provisions, effects, merchandise, &ca. They destroyed them entirely. The oxen were killed; the carts burnt; the property pillaged by the Indians; 110 scalps were secured and 84 prisoners taken; of these, 12 are women or girls. The escort, which was defeated, consisted of 40 men, commanded by a Lieutenant, who has been taken; the remainder of the men, who were killed or taken prisoners, consisted of wagoners, suttlers, traders, women and children. The English, 'tis known, feel this loss very sensibly. Some baggage and effects belonging to General Albercrombie, as well as his music, were among the plunder.

"On the news of this defeat, the English General sent a very considerable force in pursuit, under the command of the partisan Robert Rogers, but he was too late. He was on the point of returning, when, on the advice of a Colonial gunner, a deserter, he received orders to lay in ambush to surprise a third detachment which the Marquis do Montcalm had just dispatched under the orders of M. Marin, a Colonial officer of great reputation. This detachment was composed of 50 Regulars, 100 Canadians and 150 Indians. That of the enemy, of about 700 men. They met in the woods, about seven o'clock in the morning of the 8th of

August, and in spite of superior numbers, M. Marin made his arrangements to fight the enemy. He forced them to waver by two volleys, which killed a great many; but having been supported by the Regulars, they rallied and the firing was brisk on both sides for nearly an hour. M. Marin, perceiving that they were receiving a reinforcement, and the Indians, who feared that they would not be able to carry off some wounded, demanding to retire, he was obliged to think of retreating, which he did in good order, and without being pursued, after having, for an hour longer, kept up a fire with such picked men as he had, who performed prodigies of valor. The Indians, in general, have also behaved well; but of 100 Canadians, more than 60 deserted M. Marin, no one knows wherefore, at the very moment when the English were wavering. This somewhat astonished the Indians, and prevented that brave officer deriving all the advantage he could from the circumstance.

"Meanwhile, our loss is but trifling in comparison with that the enemy must have suffered, which is estimated at over 200 men. Scouts, sent on their trail, have seen a great many wounded, whom they were carrying on litters, and a great many dead on the field of action. M. Marin took some prisoners, 2 of them officers, now here. On our side we have had 3 soldiers, 3 Canadians and 4 Indians killed; two Cadets, one soldier, 5 Canadians and 4 Indians wounded—the majority of them very slightly." (*D.R.C.H.S.N.Y.*, Volume 10, pp. 818-819)

Captain Malartic had this to say about the Battle of Fort Anne: "[August] 10th M. Marin has come back with his detachment, and reported that on his way towards Fort Ann, where he expected to strike a blow on a road very much frequented by the English, he heard the report of three shots; that the scouts came in to inform him that they had seen 100 English who were coming towards him; whereupon he immediately ambushed his party, who fired two volleys at the English; the latter scattered themselves in the woods and behind trees, where they kept up a very brisk fire, and had been joined by Captain Roger with 500 men, and a Major of Militia with 200; that he had taken 5 prisoners; that seeing the English were too numerous to be forced, he ordered his wounded to be removed and retreated in very good order, leaving thirteen men on the field; that some Indians had returned thither in the course of the night to try and take some scalps, and found the English drinking and singing." (*D.R.C.H.S.N.Y.*, Volume 10, p. 851)

Bougainville adds the following: "M. Marin returned the tenth. He encountered Rogers with five hundred men, supported by Major Putnam at the head of 250 men, of a new corps composed of picked men, called light infantry, under the command of Sieur Gage, brigadier general. The game was not even. Our people withdrew in good order, leaving on the field of battle thirteen dead, five of them Indians, and bringing off their wounded to the number of ten. They took five prisoners, including Major Putnam. A large part of the Canadians in M. Marin's detachment were of the bad sort. They claim that the militia commander gave him these because of professional jealousy." (Bougainville pp. 261-262)

And Pierre Pouchot says: "A raiding party led by M. Marin, a colonial captain, came upon a corps of their troops, made up of 7 to 800 troops commanded by Roger. M. Marin captured a major of the English militia and a few others & took only two scalps. The losses of the English were estimated at 100 men by the French, who had four Indians killed & four wounded and six Canadians killed and six wounded, among them an officer & a cadet." (Pouchot p. 152)

The following entry appears in the orderly book of Brigade Major Alexander Moneypenny on August 12, 1758: "The Genll. [Abercromby] returns his Thanks to the officers & Men, who were lately out with Majors Rogers, Putnam & Capt Dalzell, for their good Behaviour on that Occasion, and he now hopes they are satisfy'd that Indians are a Despicable Enemy, against Men who will do their Duty. (*B.F.T.M.*, Volume XIII, Number 1, December 1970, p. 91)

Miraculously, one of the officers wounded

in the battle and scalped by the Indians survived. "Lieutenant Wooster of the Connecticut Forces, who was wounded in Rogers' skirmish, is yet alive and likely to recover, no pains being spared to effect it, as the surgeons are extremely fond of making a cure of so extraordinary a case, which is this, he being in the front with Major Putnam, or not far in his rear, the enemy fired upon him, and 8 bullets lodged in him, 3 of which are taken out; he had also three wounds by a tomahawk, two of which were on his head, and the other in his elbow, his head was flayed, almost the hair part off. He was sensible all the while the enemy were scalping him, and finding himself wounded in so many places that he could not run, and the enemy close upon him, he fell on his face and feigned himself dead, and no doubt but the enemy thought he actually was; however they gave him two blows on his head, but not so hard as to deprive him of his senses, and then scalped him, during all which time he made not the least resistance." (*New Hampshire Gazette*, September 8, 1758, quoted in Bray, p. 56)

An interesting result of Rogers' victory in the Battle of Fort Anne was later noted by Lieutenant Thomas Barnsley of the Royal American Regiment, in a September 7 letter to Colonel Henry Bouquet: "The French Indians are not so forward in scouting as they us'd to be, before Major Rogers had the last skirmish with them . . . ." Barnsley goes on to tell his version of this fight: "it is Remarkable in that Attack of Rogers' that he was Surpris'd by about 600 of the French who lay in Ambush watching of Rogers party which Consisted of About the same Number Shooting of Pidgeons as they went along the woods for thier diversion that upon the first fire all the provincials Commanded by Major Putnam, and most of Rogers own Rangers ran away when about Sixty Regulars with 100 Light Infantry stood the Brunt of four Fires from the French before Rogers could Rally them again and that A party of the French & Indians who had taken post behind a Tree that had fallen down; the Regulars and Light Infantry Advanc'd and Flank'd the Tree; beat them off and took possession of the Contrary Side, then some fresh Troops came up close to the tree, and After their Fire was discharg'd on Each side they fell on with the Butts of thier Firelocks and pulling one another for prisoners, when Major Rogers came up with the troops he had Rallied. A stout Engagement issued for some time till the French Retired Leaving behind them About 100 Kill'd on the spot 40 of which was Indians one of Which was a Sachem who had behav'd in very Extraordinary manner during the Attack at the tree as Soon as our people had fired he Leap'd upon it and Kill'd two men himself upon which A Regular officer belonging to Young Murrays Struck at his head with his Fuzee, but could not knock him down though he made his head bleed, and as he was going to kill the officer with his Tomahawk he was shot by Major Rodgers after Standing on the Tree a Considerable time, had several blows with Firelocks which could not move him, this Sachem was 6 foot 4 inches high proportionably made, in Short he was the Largest Indian Ever Rogers Saw, this affair has been of great service to us as one of the Leadingst Partisans belonging to the French was kill'd at the same time and has made them very back ward in their Scouting ever Since." (Bouquet, Volume II, pp. 480-481)

I remained at Fort Edward till the 11th of the month, when I received orders from Col. Provost, who now ranked as Brigadier, and commanded at Fort Edward, to march and pursue the tracks of a large party of Indians, of which he had received intelligence, down the east-side of Hudson's River, in order to secure our convoys from them, and intercept their retreat; but this report which the Colonel had heard being groundless, my scout was ineffectual. I returned to Fort Edward on the 14th, and went with a detachment directly to the encampment at Lake George.

On August 19, Connecticut Provincial Abel Spicer noted in his journal that: "This day in the forenoon Major Rogers took his men without the camp beyond the advance guard to exercise them in the woods to skulk and fire as though engaged by the enemy. The General went to see them and several of the chief officers. (Spicer, p. 110)

Aug. 20, 1758. By orders from the General I embarked with five men in a whale-boat, to visit and reconnoitre Ticonderoga, in which excursion I obtained several articles of intelligence concerning the enemy, their situation and numbers at different posts, and returned the 24th to the encampment at Lake George.

I was employed in various other excursions towards the enemy's forts and frontiers, and in pursuit of their flying parties till the campaign for this year ended, and our army retired to winter quarters.

Notwithstanding little was effected by our late campaign to Ticonderoga; yet the British army in America were not every where unsuccessful: for Col. Broadstreet, with a detachment of 2000 men, reduced the French fort at Cataraqua, called Fort Frontenac,* and General Amherst, who commanded the British troops at Cape Breton, had succeeded in the reduction of that important fortress, and now returned from his conquest, with a part of the troops that had been employed there, and it was appointed commander in chief to his Majesty's forces in North America (General Abercrombie embarking for England).

The capture of the French Fortress at Louisbourg is the victory at Cape Breton that Rogers is referring to. Edmund Munroe (Monroe), sergeant-major of the Rangers, recorded in his orderly book from the camp near Lake George on August 28, 1758: "The Rangers to be under arms at six o'clock this evening to illuminate the rejoicing for the success of his Magisty's arms at Louisbourg at which time Major Rogers gives to his Ranging Company a token of his dependence on their loyalty and bravery, a barrell of Wine treat, to congratulate this good news to them, and the good behaviour of the four Companies of Rangers at Louisbourg."

Munroe goes on to describe in detail how the "fire of rejoicing" is to take place, "The firing to begin with 21 guns from the Royal Artillery, and then from the right of the 27th Reg. Round the line & to finish with the left of Col. Bayley's Reg. This to be repeated till the whole shall have fired three rounds. The Commanding Officers of Regiments to order a review of the their Regiments at 12 O'clock, and the balls to be drawn, and to have cartridges without balls made up for the rejoicing fire." (Munroe, p. 217)

Munroe's orderly book gives more interesting details about the activities of the Rangers in the late summer and fall of 1758:

"Lake George Camp, Aug. 29 . . . Maj. Rogers Rangers to discharge their pieces between 4 and 6 this evening, beyond the advanced guards."

"Lake George Camp, Aug. 31 . . . One Capt. One Subaltan, two Serjeants, two Corporals, and forty men from the Rangers to hold themselves in readiness to embark on the sloop tomorrow."

"Camp at Lake George, Sept. 1 . . . A detachment of 4 subaltans and 100 volunteers from the Regulars, three Companies of light infantry, 100 of Major Rogers Rangers, 100 of Col. Partridges Rangers, 100 of Connecticut Rangers to march tomorrow morning at 9 O'clock, with seven days provisions under the command of Capt. Dalzell [Dalyell] of the light infantry. This detachment to be under arms this afternoon at 4 O'clock, on the ground near the old Fort." [The ruins of Fort William Henry.]

"Camp Orders:

"Lieut Brewer with a sergeant and 30 men to Parade immediately for the half-way Brook.

"One Capt 4 Subaltans, 4 sergeants, and 150 men from the Rangers to be ready to proceed on a scout tomorrow morning. The Captain to take care that his party are provided with seven days provisions.

"A subaltan of each Company to see that huts, tents, and encampments are kept clean and in good order, and this order to be complied with every morning.

"The Sergeant Major to attend at the adjutant's tent at half an hour after nine in

*This fort was square faced, had four bastions built with stone, and was near three-quarters of a mile in circumference. Its situation was very beautiful, the banks of the river presenting on every side an agreeable landscape, with a fine prospect of the Lake Ontario, which was distant about a league, interspersed with many islands that were well wooded, and seemingly fruitful. The French had formerly a great trade at this fort with the Indians, it being erected on purpose to prevent their trading with the English; but it is now totally destroyed.

the morning, and at six in the afternoon to receive such orders as may be given to the Rangers." (Munroe, pp. 218-219)

On September 7, Massachusetts Provincial chaplain John Cleaveland notes a scout that Rogers was involved in: "Major Rogers returned from down the Lake this afternoon and have like to have been taken by ye Enemy, an Indian first Spying him give intelligence to their co'y that give them an opportunity to way-lay him but He with the small party taking to their Heels got clear; it is said they discovered the French Camp to be much larger than ours and saw about 70 Battoes in the Lake and some halled up upon ye Shoar." (Cleaveland, September 7, 1758)

The *New Hampshire Gazette* mentioned two other scouts that occurred in the late summer of 1758: "Extract of a letter from Rogers' Island, near Fort Edward, September 11. The 6th Instant a small party of our men (who were sent forward to acquaint them at Halfway Brook, that the teams with an escort were coming down the lake to Fort Edward) were fired upon by a party of Indians, and one Sergeant belonging to Captain Lovell of the Rangers was killed.

"The same day in here came Lieutenant Holmes of the Rangers from a scout to Ticonderoga with about 7 men; who informs, that he lay very near the fort, and says, that there is a very large encampment there, and that the enemy have erected some blockhouses at their breastwork.—Many Indians are there.—He waylaid opposite the fort, where came along a canoe with two Indians in it; he being forward of his party fired upon him that paddled and shot him through the body; upon which the other cried for quarters; but the first recovering a little said No Quarters, and tumbled into the water, and swam ashore; they fired upon the other, who did the like: One of the party swam and fetched the canoe, in which was a beautiful gun and sundries.—There is no doubt but both the Indians received their death wounds. The party being near and in plain sight of the fort, who beat to arms, they thought it prudent to retire as fast as possible, and came in all well." (*New Hampshire Gazette,* October 6, 1758)

In a journal entry for September 9, James Henderson of the Massachusetts Provincials mentions the scout in the first *New Hampshire Gazette* article reprinted above: "There was an Ecort a Going from the Lake to the half way Brook there was a few men Sent before the guard the Indians fired upon them and killed one of them and scalped him and wounded another the man slain belonged to Major Rogers it was near the Bloody Pond" (Henderson, p. 200)

The Reverend John Cleaveland also gives a good description of this incident in his journal entry for September 9: "This morning as ye escort were going from hence to Half-way-Brook five Rangers were sent word to give notice to the Teams to be ready to meet them and when they got about half a mile from the escort a small party of the enemy fired upon them, killed and scalped one, took another prisoner and wounded the Third. The Enemy left a Tomahawk and spear sticking in the man killed above; a proud and cruel Enemy! N.B. the person supposed to be taken captive is got into camp so that the enemy this Time have got only one scalp." (Cleaveland, September 9, 1758)

As another example of these late summer and fall scouts, on September 24, Abel Spicer noted that, "in the afternoon Major Rogers went with 200 men up the lake." (Spicer, p. 112) Actually, it should read "down" the lake, as Rogers undoubtedly headed north towards French territory. On the 29, he added, "This day Roger's scout came in and brought two bark canoes that the Frenchman that was with them told them of." (Spicer, p. 113)

Of the same scout, Captain Champion recorded on September 24, "Major Rogers went out with 150 men on 8 days scout down ye

Facing page: Thomas Kitchen's map shows Fort Edward and Rogers' Island in 1759. There are some changes from 1757 (as depicted in Gary Zaboly's illustration). Editor's collection.

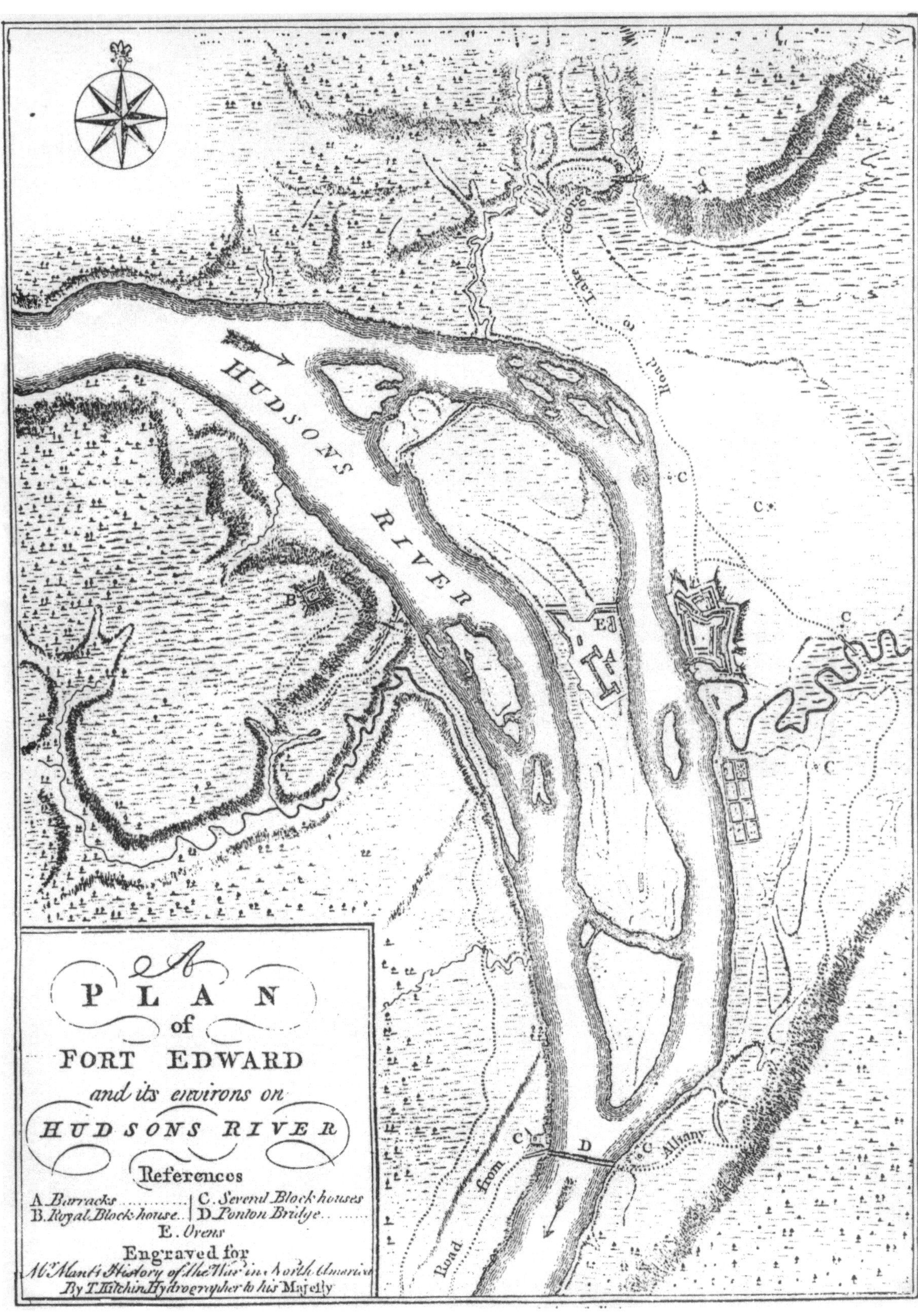
A PLAN of FORT EDWARD and its environs on HUDSONS RIVER
References
A. Barracks
B. Royal Block house
C. Several Block houses
D. Ponton Bridge
E. Ovens
Engraved for Mr. Mant's History of the War in North America
By T. Kitchin Hydrographer to his Majesty
HUDSONS RIVER
Road to Lake George
Road from Albany

> lake." On their return on the 29, he added, "Ye chief of Major Rogers scout came in. Capt. Staunton says they have brought in ye bark canoes that ye 20 French and indians came in, that ye French deserter gave account of, who came in on ye 25th instant. Ye party that went with said deserter to cut off said 20 joined Major Rogers' scout laid wait for said 20, but were discovered by them." Then on October 1, he noted, "Ye remaining part of Major Rogers' scout came in, made no further discovery." (Champion, p. 430)
>
> James Henderson writes the following about this scout. On September 25: "there Went 55 Men out of our Battalion down the Lake with Major Rogers a Scout for 8 Days" He then records their return on October 1: "the above Scout Returned They Went down as far as the Landing place at Tyconderoga our men fired at the Enemy and the Enemy at them there is nothing more Remarkeable at present." (Henderson, p. 200)
>
> On September 29, Reverend Cleaveland notes the return of Rogers' scout, "Rogers returned and it is said He went to ye Battoe-Island and fired upon ye French-Advance-Guard kept there. I don't learn yet what Discoveries he made of ye Numbers and Situation of ye Enemy . . . ." (Cleaveland, September 29, 1758)
>
> On September 30, Champion said that he "Went with 107 of ye Rangers on fatigue, cutting trees." (Champion, p. 430)

The head quarters were now fixed at New York, and I had now new commanders to obey, new companions to converse with, and, as it were, a new apprenticeship to serve.

> While Rogers was involved with these administrative duties, over the winter of 1758-59, his Rangers were still very active in their scouting duties. The following excerpts from a scout report by Sergeant Philip Wells, of Rogers' Own Company, gives some of the flavor of a winter patrol:
>
> "Leaving Rogers Island near Fort Edward on the 23d Janry 1759"
>
> "Febry 3d: This morning I concluded to return___the Snow Being So Deep That it was Impossible to march in the Snow, Being then___Two feet and a Half Deep In the Woods, and Lay so Light that the Snow Shoes Sunk almost knee Deep . . . ."
>
> " 7th . . . this morning Swung Packs And march'd An East Course and Arrived at Fort Edward about three o'clock in the Afternoon___the Party all well and in Good Health___this Being the Sixteenth Day of our Scout___the men was very much Beat out By Reason of the Weather Being Excessive Cold, and travelling on Snow Shoes." (*Wells' Manuscript*)

From Albany where I was settling some accounts with the Paymaster, I began my acquaintance by the following letter to Col. Townshend, Deputy Adjutant General to his Excellency.

"Sir, *Albany, Jan.* 28, 1759.

"Inclosed I send you the present state of his Majesty's companies of Rangers at Fort Edward, together with a list of the officers, now recruiting in the different parts of New England, who have lately advised me, that they have already inlisted near 400 men, which recruits are much wanted at Fort Edward, as it may be expected that the enemy will soon send their Indians, to endeavour to intercept our convoys between here and Fort Edward.

"To be seasonably strong to prevent their playing their old pranks, I would humbly propose, were it consistent with the service and agreeable to General Amherst, my setting out for New England, in order to dispatch such Rangers as are there with all possible speed to Fort Edward, or otherwise, as his Excellency shall direct. If it should be agreeable to the General that I should go to New-England, I should be glad it might be by way of New York, that I might have an opportunity to wait upon the General myself, and represent to him the necessity of an augmentation of the Rangers now at Fort Edward, and the desire of the Stockbridge Indians to re-enter the service.

"The arms of the Rangers are in the hands of Mr. Cunningham at New York, which will be soon wanted at Fort Edward; I should therefore be glad they might be forwarded as soon as may be. I have wrote to Mr. Cunningham, to make application to you for convenient carriages for the same, which I should be glad you would furnish him with. And till the time I have an opportunity of paying you my respects in person, I beg leave to subscribe myself, Sir,

Your most obedient humble servant,
Robert Rogers."

"*P.S.* General Stanwix informs me, that a subaltern officer, and about twenty Rangers, are to be stationed at No. 4; the officer I would recommend for that post, is Lieut. Stephans, who is well acquainted with the country thereabout. He is now recruiting."

To Col. Townsend.

Soon after this I returned to Fort Edward, where I received the Colonel's answer, as follows.

"Sir, *Feb.* 5, 1759.

"I received your letter, with the inclosed return. The General commands me to inform you, he can by no means approve of your leaving Fort Edward.

"Your recruiting officers are all ordered to send up their recruits to Fort Edward. They are not only wrote to, but an advertisement is put in all the papers, which was the only method the General had of conveying his intentions to them, as you had not sent me any return of the officers names, and places where they were to recruit at. In obedience to that order, the recruits will be up sooner than if they waited your coming down. I have likewise repeated the order to every officer, according to your return, by this post, and if you are complete by the returns they make, I shall order up every individual officer to their posts.

"Any proposals for the augmentation of the Rangers, or proposals from the Stockbridge Indians, you would chuse to offer to the General, he desires may be immediately sent down to him.

"The arms for the Rangers, which you mention are in the hands of Mr. Cunningham, shall be sent up to you immediately.

"I have wrote to Lieut. Samuel Stephans, to acquaint him with the General's intentions of leaving him at No 4.

"If the enemy send out any scouting parties this year to pick up intelligence, or attack our convoys, the season of the year is now coming on that we may expect them; you therefore must see the necessity of your remaining at Fort Edward. Your officers and men should join you as fast as possible. The General would at another time comply with your request.

Your obedient humble servant,
R. Townshend, D.A.G."

Feb. 15, 1759.

To Major Rogers.

I wrote to the Colonel, proposing an addition of two new companies of Rangers upon the same footing as those already in the service, and the raising of three companies of Indians to serve in the ensuing campaign; and lest the Indians should be gone out on their hunting parties, and so be prevented from joining us, I wrote to three of their Sachems, or chiefs; one of which to King Uncus, head Sachem of the Mohegan Indians (which in substance is like the others) I will here insert, as a specimen of the method in which we are obliged to address these savages.

"Brother Uncus,

"As it is for the advantage of his Majesty King George, to have a large body of Rangers employed in his service the ensuing campaign, and as I am well convinced of the sincere attachment you have to him, I therefore carefully obey General Amherst's orders to me, to engage your assistance here early in the spring.

The Fighting Retreat

IT is shortly after sunrise on March 7, 1759. A skirmish line composed of Rogers' Rangers and a number of Iroquois allies halts in their withdrawal from the south arm of Lake Champlain to turn and fire on 80 pursuing Canadians and Indians. Rogers' party of 92 men has just ambushed an enemy wood-cutting detail on the eastern shore, directly across from Fort Carillon (the latter can be seen in center distance). Hearing the initial firing, the fort's commandant, Captain Le Dossu d'Hebecourt, immediately sent out 150 regulars in support.[1]

The volley from the rising ground position of the Rangers and Iroquois stopped the Canadians and Indians in their tracks, and allowed Rogers and his men to continue their withdrawal through the forest, still "in a line abreast." Twice more the enemy attacked, and were engaged in similar fashion, until the Rangers and their Indian allies finally made a countercharge, thus putting an end to the enemy's pursuit. Rogers then led his men over the steep, snowclad slopes of the mountains that ranged between Lake Champlain and Lake George, to Sabbath Day Point, where the other half of his expedition waited for them around welcoming campfires.

Rogers brought back five prisoners, four of whom remained in the hands of the Iroquois. This Indian detachment, when it had left Fort Edward with Rogers' main column on the 3rd, was composed of 52 "Mohawks, Conojohery's, Schoharry's, Dilliways, Oneidas, and Senneekees,"[2] and not just Mohawks, as Rogers writes. In the foreground, a Mohawk (left) and an Oneida (right) hurry away one of the luckless French woodcutters. The Mohawk wears a leather shirt and is draped in a laced stroud matchcoat of English manufacture. The Oneida wears largely native attire: beaverskin hood,[3] short bearskin cape, and a long bearskin tunic (hair on the inside) with pelts attached to cover the arms.[4]

This action marked the successful close of Rogers' overall expedition to make observations of the French defenses on the Carillon peninsula, and to seize prisoners there to gain intelligence that would assist in the planning of General Amherst's attack later that year.

Before they swooped down on the woodcutters, Rogers notes, both he and his men "stripped off our blankets," an indication that the Rangers probably wore their blankets matchcoat-fashion, like the Indians, or like cloaks. Ranger blankets were often striped, no doubt English blankets with multiple stripes near the edges. Though warmly dressed and well experienced in winter trekking, the veteran Rangers had encountered extremely cold weather on this outing, and many of them, Rogers included, eventually suffered frostbite.[5]

G.Z.

1. Burt Garfield Loescher, *Genesis: Rogers' Rangers, The First Green Berets*, San Mateo, California, 1969, p. 39.
2. "Particulars of Major Robert Rogers's last Scout against the Enemy," *The Boston Gazette*, April 9, 1759.
3. Based on an artifact in the collection of the American Museum of Natural History, New York City.
4. Prior to receiving the white man's trade coats, Native Americans living in cold climes made sleeves of animal pelts as separate attachments, tying them to the shoulders of their skin tunics or "gowns."
5. "The weather being so severe," wrote Rogers to General Haldimand, "that it is almost impossible to describe it."

GARY ZABOLY
©2000

"I hope you'll continue to shew that ardent zeal you have all long expressed for the English, ever since you have been allied to them, by raising a company of your men with the utmost expedition.

"Should you chuse to come out a Captain, General Amherst will readily give you the commission for it; if not, I shall expect Doquipe and Nunnipad. I leave to you the choice of an Ensign and two sergeants; but I hope you'll engage the fittest men for their stations. I would have the company consists of fifty private men, or more, if you can get them; and if those men that deserted from Capt. Brewer will join you, the General will pardon them. You may employ a Clerk for the company, to whom General Amherst will allow the usual pay.

"I heartily wish you success in raising your men, and shall be exceeding glad that you join me with all the expedition you possibly can. I am,

Brother Uncus,
Your most obedient humble servant,
To King Uncus. *Robert Rogers."*

With this letter, or any other wrote to them, in order to give it any credit or influence, must go a belt of wampum, suitable to the matter and occasion of it, and upon which the bearer, after having read the letter, interprets it, and then delivers both to the Sachem, or person they are directed to.

The latter end of February, about fifty Mohocks, commanded by Captain Lotridge, came from Sir William Johnson to join me, and proceed to Fort Ticonderoga on a scout.

March 3, 1759, I received the following orders from Col. Haldiman: "An officer being chosen by the General to make observations upon the enemy's situation, and the strength of their forts upon Lake Champlain, you are ordered to march with your Rangers, and the Mohock Indians, under the command of Capt. Lotridge, and take all the measures and precautions possible, that he may execute his intentions, and perform the service, which the General has much at heart; and to effect this with more security, a body of regulars is likewise ordered to join with you, and you are to have the command of the whole. Lieut. Brheem is to communicate his orders to you; and the service being performed, you will endeavour to take a prisoner, or prisoners, or strike such a stroke on the enemy, and try to bring us intelligence.

An account of this scout in the *Gentleman's Magazine* identifies the engineer as Lt. Diedrich Brehm of the 60th Regiment. (*Gentleman's Magazine*, May 1759, p. 203)

"He recommends it in the strongest manner, that if some of the enemy should fall into your hands to prevent the Indians from exercising their cruelty upon them, as he desires prisoners may be treated with humanity.

Fred. Haldiman,
Commander at
Fort Edward."

Fort Edward,
March 3, 1759.

Pursuant to the above orders, I marched the same day with a party of 358 men, officers included, and encamped the first night at Half-Way-Brook.

Robert Rogers' original report of this scout offers more details than are contained in his *Journals.* This and several subsequent annotations are taken from his original report. This first excerpt gives a much more detailed picture of who participated in the scout, and contains some significant names. "Parsuant to an Order from Colonell Haldimand of the above date Marched from this Place for Ticonderoga being joyned by Capt. Lotteridge and fifty Two Indians Composed of Mohawsh Coonajaharys Schoharys Delewares Onidas and Senechas and the following Detachment———viz,
The Royall or First Regiment Lieutenants West and Cook four Sergeants one Corporall and forty Privates Royal Americans Light Infantry Capt. Willyamoz Lieut. McKay Ensigns Brown Monins four Sergeants Four Corporalls and one hundred and ten Private Volunteers of the americans Lieut Turnbull three Sergeants two

> Corporalls and forty one private. And Lieut Bream Engineer: of the Rangers Lieutenants Toot Holmes Brewer and [William] Stark: seven Sergeants and Seventy nine Privates————
> "The Total Officers Included three hundred fifty eight————" (Robert Rogers, *Scout Report March 3, 1759)*

One Indian, being hurt by accident, returned to Fort Edward. The 4th marched to within one mile and a half of Lake George, and halted till evening, that we might the better pass undiscovered by the enemy, if any were on the hill reconnoitering. We continued our march till two o'clock in the morning, and halted at the first narrows. It being excessive cold, and several of our party being frost-bitten, I sent back twenty-three, under the charge of a careful serjeant, to Fort Edward. We continued here till the evening of the 5th, then marched to Sabbath day Point, where we arrived about eleven o'clock, almost overcome with the cold. At two o'clock we continued our march, and reached the landing place about eight. I sent out a small party to observe if any of the enemies parties went out.

> Here, in his original report, Rogers gives a more detailed picture of how he planned to deal with the enemy: "I intended to Form my Ambuscade and Draw a Party out of the Fort by Scalping Stragglers With a Small Party and retire again to the main body . . . ." (Robert Rogers, *Scout Report March 3, 1759)*

They returned and reported, that none were to be seen on the west-side of the lake, but on the east were two working parties. It now appeared to be a suitable time for the engineer to make his observations. I left Capt. Williams to remain at this place with the Regulars, and thirty Rangers, while I, with the engineer, forty-nine Rangers, and Capt. Lotridge, with forty-five Indians, went to the isthmus that overlooks the fort, where he made his observations. We returned to our party, leaving five Indians and one Ranger to observe what number crossed the lake in the evening from the east-side to the fort, that I might know the better how to attack them next morning. At dark the engineer went again, with Lieut. Tute, and a guard of ten men, to the entrenchments, and returned at midnight without opposition, having done his business to his satisfaction. On which I ordered Capt. Williams with the Regulars back to Sabbath-day Point; the party being extremely distressed with the cold, it appeared to me imprudent to march his men any further, especially as they had no snow-shoes. I sent with him Lieut. Tute and thirty Rangers, with directions to kindle fires on the aforesaid point. At three o'clock I marched with three Lieutenants and forty Rangers, one Regular, and Capt. Lotridge with forty-six Indians, in order to be ready to attack the enemy's working parties on the east-side of the lake early in the morning. We crossed South-Bay about eight miles south of this fort;* from thence, it being about six o'clock, bore down right opposite the fort, and within half a mile of where the French parties agreeable to our expectations, were cutting of wood. Here I halted, and sent two Indians and two Rangers to observe their situation. They returned in a few minutes, and brought intelligence that the working parties were close to the banks of the lake, and opposite the fort, and were about forty in number; upon which we stripped off our blankets, and ran down upon them, took several prisoners, and destroyed most of the party as they were retreating to the fort, from whence being discovered, about eighty Canadians and Indians pursued us closely, being backed by about 150 French regulars, and in a mile's march they began a fire in our rear; and as we marched in a line abreast, our front was easily made; I halted on a rising ground, resolving to make a stand against the enemy, who appeared at first very resolute: but we repulsed them before their reinforcement came up, and began our march again in a line abreast; having advanced about half a mile further, they came in sight again.

> Rogers originally recorded that they "took Seven Prisoners and four Scalps Killed Several others as they were retreating to the Fort . . . ." (Robert Rogers, *Scout Report March 3, 1759) The Gentleman's Magazine* account previously mentioned relates that they "took 7 prisoners, 4 scalps, and killed several others as they were

*Here we found that a party of the Indians had gone up the bay towards our forts.

retreating . . . ." (*Gentleman's Magazine*, p. 225) It is quite obvious that the *Gentleman's Magazine* account is based on Robert's original report.

As soon as we could obtain an advantageous post, which was a long ridge, we again made a stand on the side opposite the enemy. The Canadians and Indians came very close, but were soon stopped by a warm fire from the Rangers and Mohocks. They broke immediately, and the Mohocks with some Rangers pursued, and entirely routed them before their Regulars could come up.

In his original report, Rogers wrote that the enemy "behaved with great bravery for Some time, but soon found they could not stand against our Marksmen . . . ." (Robert Rogers, *Scout Report March 3, 1759)*

After this we marched without any opposition. In these several skirmishes we had two Rangers and one Regular killed, and one Indian wounded, and killed about thirty of the enemy.

Here, in his original report, Rogers also credits his own men with their good performance: "Both officers and men Behaved with Great Bravery, in Particular Capt. Lotterige and Lieut Holmes, who endeavored to Exceed; both of which behaved with great Courage and Coolness During the whole affair." (Robert Rogers, *Scout Report March 3, 1759)*

We continue our march to 12 o'clock at night, and came to Capt. Williams at Sabbath-day Point (fifty miles distant from the place we set out from in the morning.) The Captain received us with good fires, than which scarce any thing could be more acceptable to my party, several of which had their feet froze, it being excessive cold, and the snow four feet deep.

Rogers' original report contains this additional detail, "this Days march tired two prisoners we was oblidged to kill them . . . ." (Robert Rogers, *Scout Report March 3, 1759)*

Next morning marched the whole detachment as far as Long-Island in Lake George, and there encamped that night. On our march from Sabbath-day Point to this Island, I gave leave to some of the Rangers and Indians to hunt near the side of the lake, who brought us in great plenty of venison for our refreshment.

I sent Lieut. Tute, with the following letter, to Col. Haldiman, fearing lest a party of Indians we had some notice of might have gone up South-Bay, and get an opportunity of doing mischief before I could reach Fort Edward with the whole detachment.

Camp at Sabbath-day Point, Friday, eight, o'clock in the morning.

"Sir,

"I send this to let you know that sixty Indians, in two parties, are gone towards Fort Edward and Saratoga, and I fear will strike some blow before this reaches you. Mr. Brheem is satisfied he has done his business agreeable to his orders; since which I have taken some prisoners from Ticonderoga, and destroyed others of the enemy, of the particulars of which the bearer will inform you.

As a result of this scout, Engineer Lieutenant Diedrick Brehm wrote an excellent report on conditions at Ticonderoga, which became a major tool in the formation of Amherst's strategy for the 1759 campaign. The original manuscript is in the Gage Papers at the Clements Library, and was reprinted in the *B.F.T.M.*, Volume XI, Number 1, December 1962, pp. 35-48.

"The Mohocks behaved with great bravery; some having been within pistol-shot of the French fort.

"Two-thirds of my detachment have froze their feet (the weather being so severe that it is almost impossible to describe it) some of which we are obliged to carry. I am, &c.

R. ROGERS."

In his report to William Pitt, General Amherst wrote of Rogers' scout: "on the 3rd of this month, Major Rogers went from Fort Edward with a party of 32 Indians 84 Rangers & 200 Regulars to Tienderoga, he returned on the 10th took near the Fort seven Prisoners and four Scalps, was obliged to kill two of the Prisoners in his return who could not keep up with the Party; he supposed he killed near thirty of the Enemy with the loss of two Rangers, one Regular, and one Indian badly wounded, several of the party frostbitten: on this Occasion the Engineer who went with the party has taken the best draft of the Fort & Intrenchment, that the Snow on the ground and the time he had, would permit him to do, by which and the Information of the Prisoners the lines are new-made since the Attack of last year . . . ." (Pitt, Volume II, p. 79)

On March 12, 1759, Thomas Barnsley of the 60th (Royal American) Regiment, wrote to Colonel Henry Bouquet: "There was a Scout went from Fort Edwd: the 4th Inst Consisting of 300 Men Viz. Capt. Williamoz 3 Subs [subalterns] & 120 men of Col Prevost Battn [of the Royal Americans] 2 Subs and 40 Men of the Royal Scots Fifty two Mohawk Indians the Rest was Major Rogers and his Rangers; Lieut Brehm went by order of Genll Gage who gave him in writing what observations he was to make; They fell in with a French Scout of 10 men five of which they Scalp'd the other five they have prisoners; the prisoners have told Them that there is a Scout of 50 Indians about Fort Edward and Saratoga. Wee Expect our Scouts Return Every day and of Course more News . . . ."

At the bottom of the letter, Barnsley added the following postscript: "since I wrote the Above there is an Express from Coll Haldiman to Genll Gage Acquainting him that Rogers had shew'd a small party at Ticonderoga Which intic'd them out of the Fort and that he had fall'n upon them Kill'd 40 on the spot & taken five prisoners. The Loss on our Side was three Kill'd on the spot and one Indian Wounded. This Acc't Rogers sent to Col. Haldiman by one of his Rangers but the Scout is not come in yet." (Bouquet, Volume III, pp. 190-191)

Mante also gives an account of this scout: "In the mean while, Major Rogers had been ordered, with Lieutenant Brheme, an assistant engineer, with a party of three hundred and fifty men, to make what observations they could on the enemy's forts of Ticonderoga and Crown-Point. They left Fort-Edward on the 3rd of March. Lieutenant Brheme having executed his orders, returned. Major Rogers fell in with a working party of the French, killed some, and took several prisoners, near Ticonderoga, with the loss of three or four men. The weather was so intensely cold during this expedition, that it froze the feet of two-thirds of the detachment; some to such a degree, that the rest were obliged to carry them." (Mante, p. 204)

In his journal of Amherst's 1759 Campaign, Captain-Lieutenant Henry Skinner of the Royal Artillery noted, "One grand scout went out from Fort Edward, this winter (under the command of Major Rogers) with 60 Mohawk Indians, a detachment of regulars, with several volunteer Officers and one Engineer, to Fort Carillon; the Indians fell upon a party on the other side of the river, who were cutting wood, and took 11 prisoners. The regulars remained some miles from the fort, intended for an ambuscade; but the enemy did not pursue the Indians to the place, who made a very good retreat with their prisoners, but were obliged to scalp six of them. The Engineer having reconnoitred the lines, as much as he desired, the scout returned, and, through the intenseness of the cold, many of them were frost-bitten, and lost their limbs, and these chiefly rangers." (Skinner, p. 366)

The *London Chronicle* for May 8-10, 1759, reported the scout in this manner: "Extract of a Letter from Albany, March 12: By an express from Fort Edward last Saturday night, we have an account, that Major Rogers was on his return from a grand scout, with upwards of 300 men; that he has taken five prisoners and six scalps, and killed about 30 of the enemy; our loss, it is said, is three men killed, one Mohawk wounded, and about 14 men frost-bitten. The prisoners give an account, that 70 French Indians were sent out from Ticonderoga to cut off our convoys between Stillwater and Saraghtoga. All the posts above Albany are put upon their guard, so that it is to be hoped no mischief will ensue from these savages." (The *London Chronicle: or, Universal Evening Post,* May 8-10, 1759).

Fort Edward, March 10, 1759.

"Dear Sir,

"I congratulate you heartily on your good success, and send you twenty-two sleys to transport your sick. You will by this opportunity, take as many boards as you can conveniently.*

My best compliments to Capt. Williams, and to all the gentleman. I am, Sir,

Your most humble Servant,
FRED. HALDIMAND.

"P.S. I had the signal guns fired to give notice to the different posts. Nothing has appeared as yet."**

We were met by the sleys, and a detachment of 100 men at Lake George, and all arrived safe at Fort Edward, were I received the following letters upon my arrival.

"Sir,

"I yesterday received your letter by Mr. Stark. The General approves of raising the Indian companies; but as he has not heard the Rangers are complete, he cannot agree to the raising more companies, till the present ones are complete at Fort Edward. Mr. Stark sets out to-morrow for New England. I have ordered him to hurry up the recruits of your corps, and repeat my orders to the officers, to join their companies if they are complete. Your arms have been tried and proved by the artillery; they answer very well, and are ordered to be sent to you as fast as possible: the general has sent to you by Capt. Jacobs. We have chose out one hundred men from each regiment, and pitched upon the officers to act this year as light infantry; they are cloathed and accoutred as light as possible, and, in my opinion, are a kind of troops that has been much wanted in this country. They have what ammunition they want, so that I don't doubt but they will be excellent marksmen. You may depend upon general Amherst's intentions to have you; I heard Brigadier Gage mention you to him. From what knowledge I have of the General, I can only say that merit is sure to be rewarded; nor does he favour any recommendation, without the person recommended really deserves his promotion. You will return your companies to me as soon as complete.

Your obedient humble servant,
New-York R. TOWNSHEND.
Feb. 26, 1759.
To Major Rogers.

"Sir, *New-York, Feb 13, 1759.*

"This will be delivered to you by Capt. Jacob Nawnawampeteoonk, who last campaign commanded a company of Stockbridge Indians, and who, upon hearing that you had wrote to me concerning him, came to offer me his service for the ensuing campaign: But as you have not mentioned to me the terms and conditions on which he was to engage, I have referred him to you to give in his proposals, that you may report to me thereupon, and inform me if you think his service adequate to them; after which I shall give you my answer. I am, Sir,

Your very humble Servant
JEFF. AMHERST.

To Major Rogers.

Before I received this letter from his Excellency, I had wrote to him, recommending several officers to the vacancies in the ranging companies, and inclosed a journal of my late scout; soon after my return from which I went to Albany, to settle my accompts with the govern-

*Boards left at the place where Fort William Henry stood, and now wanted at Fort Edward.

**The explosion of these signal-guns (as we afterwards heard) was heard by the party of the enemy, then near Fort Millar, eight miles below Fort Edward, who thereupon supposing themselves discovered, returned with precipitation.

ment, were I waited upon his Excellency the General, by whom I was very kindly received, and assured that I should have the rank of Major in the army from the date of my commission under General Abercrombie.

I returned to Fort Edward the 15th of May, where I received the melancholy news, that Capt. Burbank, with a party of thirty men, had in my absence been sent out on a scout, and were all cut off.

> This fight occurred near the ruins of Fort William Henry on May 11, 1759. Captain Jonathan Burbank was killed, and at least twenty-six Rangers were captured. (Loescher, Volume II, pp. 216-217; and Volume III, p. 19) The Indians scalped Burbank, thinking that he was Rogers. When the captured Rangers informed them that they were wrong, they said that they were sorry that it was Burbank. Apparently he had previously shown them some kindness, and they said that he was a "good man." (Roby, p. 82n in original edition; p. 141, n59 in reprint)

This gave me great uneasiness, as Mr. Burbank was a gentleman I very highly esteemed, and one of the best officers among the Rangers, and more especially as I judged the scout he was sent out upon by the commanding officer at the fort was needless, and unadvisedly undertaken.

Preparations for the campaign were hastened by his Excellency the General in every quarter; the levies from the several provinces forwarded, the companies of Rangers compleated, and disciplined in the best manner I was capable of, and of which the general was pleased greatly to approve.

> Amherst apparently did not fully approve of the discipline of all of the Ranger companies, for on May 27, 1759, he recorded in his journal: "I tried to get the second Jacobs Company of Indians out of Town but Rum stopped them." (Amherst, p. 112)
>
> While it is often assumed that individual marksmanship was not a high priority in eighteenth- century armies, Amherst did show concern for it in the 1759 campaign. Massachusetts Provincial Major John Hawks notes in his orderly book on June 17, 1759: "All the men returned by the provential Regts. not to be marksmen, are to assemble tomorrow morning in the front of their Regt. They will then march to the left of the ground where the Massachusetts fired this evening and will fire five rounds a man; Major Rogers will take care the grounds in front is clear. Officers of each Regt. to attend to see that the men level well . . . ." (Hawks, p. 17)
>
> Not only did the Rangers and the Provincials recognize the importance of accurately aimed fire, so did the British Regulars. In 1755, before even coming to North America, James Wolfe wrote, "We fire bullets continually . . . and let me recommend the practice, you'll soon find the advantage of it. Marksmen are nowhere so necessary as in a mountainous country; besides firing balls at objects teaches the soldiers to aim incomparably, makes the recruits steady, and removes the foolish apprehension that seizes young soldiers when they first load arms with bullets. We fire, first singly, then by files 1, 2, 3 or more, then by ranks, and then by platoons; and the soldiers see the effects of their shot especially at a mark, or upon water. We shoot obliquely, and in different situations of ground from heights downwards and contrarywise . . . ." (Harper, p. 14)
>
> Captain-Lieutenant Henry Skinner of the Royal Artillery noted in his journal, "The commanding Officers of cantonments received the General's orders, in the winter, to practise their men at firing at marks, whenever the weather permitted." (Skinner, p. 365)
>
> Skinner goes on to describe the formation of light infantry companies in the various regiments for the upcoming campaign. They are "to form a company of men from each regiment, and those to be the most active, with proper Officers: These to be called the light infantry of the regiments they belonged to, and to be dressed agreeable to the pattern given by the General, and armed with a carbine and bayonet only." (Skinner, p. 365)
>
> The orderly book of the 42nd Royal

Highland Regiment gives us a look at some of the technical details of this practice firing:

April 3: "The regiment to be under arms at half an hour after 9 o'clock to-morrow, each man to have a good flint in his pocket as they are to fire at marks." (Wallace, p. 11)

April 4: "The regiment to be out to-morrow at the same hour and place as to-day. All the shooting boards are to be covered with paper and a black spot made in the middle." (Wallace, p. 11)

April 9: "The cartridges with ball to be taken from the men forthwith and kept in store until further orders. 15 cartridges with powder only to be delivered and made up ready for the field on Wednesday morning." (Wallace, p. 11)

April 10: "The regiment to be out to-morrow at the usual time and place. The officers are strictly to examine before the regiment leaves barracks and take particular care that the men have no cartridges with ball in their cartridge boxes or have any of their fire-locks loaded." (Wallace, p. 11)

April 11: "Such of the men of the different companies that fired before the word of command in the field this day and were observed either to talk or to be in any way careless to be out this evening and twice to-morrow with the acquart men; [*awkward men* were those who were having difficulty with some aspect of their drill, and were slated for extra training] and such of them as for the future will be guilty of the same are to be drilled twice a day when there is an opportunity through the whole summer." (Wallace, p. 11)

June 9: "The Light Infantry of the Royal Highland Regiment is to practice firing ball to-morrow morning at 6 o'clock near the Royal Blockhouse [at Fort Edward] on the other side of the river, the camp not to be alarmed.

"It is a Standing Order that no dropping shots are to be fired. Whenever there are any firelocks that cannot be drawn, a report to be made thereof that they may be collected together and fired off when the camp is advertised of it that there may be no unnecessary alarms. The Indians to be particulary acquainted with this order which if they disobey they shall be severely punished." (Wallace, p. 16)

June 11: "The picquets and guards to load with a rinning [running] ball that there may be no waste of ammunition."

"*Regimental Orders.* When any guard or piquet returns to camp with their arms loaded, the officer of that guard or piquet is to see them draw their ball in the Front before they are dismissed for which he is to be answerable." (Wallace, p. 16)

There are a number of examples of accidental firearm discharges killing or wounding both Regular and Provincial soldiers. There are also numerous references to soldiers being ordered to "draw" their charges after being relieved from sentry duty or other assignments that required loaded weapons. It seems that the issuance of powder-only cartridges and the strict control of lead musket balls is an attempt to prevent such accidents, as well as save valuable ammunition. The editor of this orderly book, Colonel Wallace, speculates that a "running ball" is one that is "not rammed home with a wad, so that it could be withdrawn without firing the charge." (Wallace, p. 16) From my own long experience with black powder firearms, this seems like a reasonable assumption, provided that the ball is slightly undersize and the barrel is clean. I have never seen the term officially defined in a period source, nor have I been able to find a clear description of what is meant by "dropping shots."

About this time, we also get another rare look at the dress of the Rangers. However, this one must be taken with a great deal of caution. It is from a May 5 entry in the journal of Captain John Knox. The dilemma is that Knox was part of Wolfe's army destined for Quebec. While his description most certainly does not apply to the Ranger companies under Robert Rogers' direct command on the Lake George front, it does fit the widely accepted dress of Gorham's Rangers from Nova Scotia, who were a part of the Quebec Campaign. It is also *possible,* but not certain, that the companies of Rogers' Rangers that were sent to take part in the Quebec Campaign were similarly uniformed for this season. Companies commanded by James Rogers (Robert's older brother), William Stark (John's older brother), Moses Hazen, and Jonathan Brewer, all were detached from Robert's corps to serve with Wolfe. In addition, independent Ranger companies commanded by Joseph Gorham and Benoni Danks were a part of Wolfe's ranging force, which amounted to a total of 576 officers and men. (Robert J. Rogers, p. 37)

Captain Knox describes the dress of the Rangers in the Quebec Campaign as follows: "The Rangers have got a new uniform cloathing; the ground is black ratteen or frize, lapelled and cuffed with blue; here follows a description of their dress: a waistcoat with sleeves, a short jacket without sleeves; only arm-holes, and wings to the shoulders (in like manner as the Grenadiers and Drummers of the army) white metal buttons, linen or canvas drawers, with a blue skirt, or short petticoat of stuff, made with a waistband and one button; this is open before, and does not extend quite to their knees: a pair of leggins of the same colour with their coat, which reach up to the middle of their thighs (without flaps) and, from the calf of the leg downwards, they button like spatterdashes; with this active dress they wear blue bonnets, and, I think, in a great measure resemble our Highlanders." (Knox, Volume I, p. 307)

In the month of June, part of the army marched with General Gage for the lake. I was ordered to send three companies there with Capt. Stark, and to remain with the General myself with the other three companies, till such time as he marched thither.

On June 13, Commissary Wilson recorded that, "Captain Stark, with his Company of Rangers, will Joyn the Detachment from the Four-Mile Post; a Company of Indians will likewise be ordered to Joyn them." (Wilson, pp. 23-24)

In this interval, pursuant to his Excellency's orders, I sent out several parties to the French forts, who from time to time discovered the situation of the enemy, and brought satisfactory intelligence.

About the 20th of June, the General with remainder of the army marched to the lake, the Rangers being in the advanced guard; and here his Excellency was pleased to fulfil his promise to me, by declaring in public orders, my rank of Major in the army, from the date of my commission, as Major of the Rangers.

On June 21, 1759, Amherst recorded in his journal: "The Rangers commanded by Major Rogers and Gages Light Infantry by Major Gladwin were the advanced guard . . . ." This passage was the inspiration for Gary Zaboly's cover illustration for this edition of Rogers' *Journals*. (Amherst p. 124)

Commissary Wilson also records this order on June 20, and gives further details about the security of the march: "Major Roggers with the Rangers, and Major Gladwin with Gages Light Infantry will form the Advanced Guard, and are to take great Precaution in keeping out Flanking Partys, to the Right, as far as Half-way Brook, from there to the lake will have Advanced Partys and Flanking Partys, to the Left as well as the Right." (Wilson, p. 38; see also Knox, Volume 1, pp. 474-475)

On June 22, in the "After Orders" for the day, Connecticut lieutenant Josiah Goodrich entered, "Major Roggors Is on All commands to Rank as major According to ye Date of his Commishons As shock next After ye majors who have ye Kings commishons or one from Majeties Commande In cheaf" (Goodrich, June 22, 1759) This is undoubtedly an attempt to clarify Rogers' status among the other officers, as he had been officially promoted to major more than a year earlier. There are entries similar to this one in nearly every orderly book from Amherst's army from this period that I have examined.

We continued here collecting our strength together; and making necessary preparations, and get-

The Advanced Guard

IN the late afternoon of June 21, 1759, the forward elements of General Jeffrey Amherst's army, marching on the road cut through the forest four years earlier by General William Johnson, cautiously approach the vicinity of Lake George. Early that morning they had left Fort Edward; and it has been a long, hot march. The army's ultimate mission: capture Fort Carillon and the other French posts on Lake Champlain, just beyond the northern end of Lake George. First, however, they have to reoccupy General Abercromby's old campsite at the southern end of the lake.

A report of a large enemy party lying in possible ambush had been sent back to Amherst; and the advanced guard is on high alert.[1] Like the rest of the army on this day, the advanced guard marches in two columns, each two ranks wide. The Rangers under Major Robert Rogers comprise one column, and Gage's Light Infantry (the 80th) the other. Two of the Ranger companies are made up of Stockbridge Indians, captained by Jacob Cheeksaunkun and his son.

In the foreground of the scene, Major Rogers and "Captain Jacobs" pause to scrutinize the forest ahead of them. Their dress is largely based on figures seen in the foreground of Captain Thomas Davies' painting of Amherst's camp as it appeared two or three weeks later. In the left background is the beginning of the Ranger column, with Gage's brown-clad men marching along the opposite side of the road. In between ride a British Regular officer and a lieutenant colonel of a Provincial regiment. Beyond these men rides Major Henry Gladwin of the 80th. Flank guards slink through the surrounding timber.

On this campaign, as decreed in Amherst's General Orders, British officers were allowed to take fusils, gorgets, swords or hangers, and colors, but no sashes; sergeants were to carry firelocks and cartouch boxes, but no halberts. British infantrymen were to leave all swords behind.[2]

Most of the stumps in the road had been pulled out during previous campaigns. Two weeks after he had established his camp at Lake George, Amherst "sent out 400 Axemen to clear each side of the road 30 yards to the right and left of it, leaving a few trees for the border of the road as a security to those that pass."[3]

Two bald eagles eye the progress of the column. Davies' painting shows these birds, which were still numerous around the lake when Reverend Timothy Dwight visited it in 1802.[4] Rattlesnakes, wolves, deer, bears, beavers, and great flocks of pigeons were also common to the area in the mid-eighteenth century. Now and then wild horses, sometimes in small herds, roamed the nearby meadows and forests.

G.Z.

1. Jeffrey Amherst, *The Journal of Jeffrey Amherst*, edited by J. Clarence Webster, Chicago, Illinois, 1931, entry of June 21, 1759.
2. "The Amherst Expedition Against Ticonderoga, 1759: Extracts from the General Orders of the Army," *The Bulletin of the Fort Ticonderoga Museum*, Vol. VI, January 1942, Number 3, pp. 89-91.
3. Amherst, entry of July 6, 1759.
4. Timothy Dwight, "First Journey to Lake George," in Russell P. Bellico, *Chronicles of Lake George: Journeys in War and Peace*, Purple Mountain Press, Fleischmanns, New York, 1995, p. 217.

ting what intelligence we could of the strength and situation of the enemy, till July 21, 1759, when the army embarked for Ticonderoga.

On June 28, some of the Rangers were involved in an interesting decoy mission. Commissary Wilson recorded the details in his orderly book on the 27th: "2 Companies of Grenediers with 2 Companys of Light Infantry ordered this morning with as many Rangers and Indians as Majr Roggers can furnish, under the Command of Capt. Johnson, the whole commanded by Majr Campbell, to march to-morrow two Hours before Daybreak, by the same route Colo. Haviland took: which Post Captain Johnson will show, and to remain there whilst the Boats are fishing. They are to take one Days Provision, and to go as light as possible, as they are not only a covering Party to ye Boats, but to attack any Body of the enemy they may find. One Boat will be allowed each Battalion in Camp, one Artillery, one Rangers, one Light Infantry, one Grenediers. The General will have an Officer in each Batteau. Captn [John] Stark will have a red Flag in his Batteau, and every Batteau must be near enough to call each other, and ready to follow Capt. Stark immediately, as he knows where the covering Party is posted, and will row in at a proper Time. The Fishermen will take their Arms Capt Lorring will deliver, and great Care must be taken they are not so much crowded. Capt Stark will receive his Orders when the whole is to return from Majr Campbell. Every Battoe to be returned to the same Place that it is taken from, and to be well fastened." (Wilson, p. 49) The wording here is confusing, but from comparison with other orderly books, it is evident that Captain Loring was supposed to supply the boats for this effort. The plan was to use the fishing boats as decoys, and if attacked, they would draw the enemy into an ambush set up by the rest of the force.

On June 28, an order was issued regarding the provisions drawn by the Rangers: "When ye Rangers and Indians Draw provision each company must Make A Return of their Effective present And Maggor Rogers Will sign ye Whole As It Is A standing order that they Always Receive It two Days before It Is Dew that their may be A sufficence In their Camp to supply Scouting" (Goodrich, June 28, 1759)

On June 29, Commissary Wilson noted an order that, "The Companys of Rangers and Indians incamp'd are to be under Arms to-morrow Morning at 5 o'clock, to be inspected by Brigr Gage." (Wilson, p. 52)

On July 2, about 18 men of the New Jersey Regiment (The Jersey Blues), out collecting bark, were attacked and all but four were killed or captured. Rogers pursued the marauders, but could not catch them.

Major John Hawks, a Massachusetts Provincial officer, recorded an order on July 4 that gives an interesting look the behavior, and expected behavior, of the army. While not directed specifically at the Rangers, they were undoubtedly worthy of inclusion. "As it is notoriously true that profane cursing and swearing prevails in the camp [at Halfway Brook]. It is not only very far from the Christian soldiers duty and very displeasing to the Lord of Hosts & God of Armies but dishonorable before men.

"It is, therefore, required and expected, that for the future the odious sound of cursing and swearing is turned into a profound silence. If after the publishing these orders, any is found guilty in the violation of these orders they may expect such punishment as A Court Marshel judge for disobedience." (Hawks, p. 27)

On July 4, Captain Jacobs was sent out on a scout with 30 men. Thomas Mante later wrote that, "Captain Jacobs of the Stockbridge Indians, with about thirty others, having been sent to hover about Ticonderoga, was not so successful as the French Indians; but it was, in a great measure, his own fault. He had received orders not to appear on the lake in the daytime; but was so imprudent as to disobey them; in consequence of which he was attacked by a superior force, and only ten of his party returned to the camp; Jacobs himself being taken prisoner." (Mante, pp. 208-209)

Captain-Lieutenant Henry Skinner records

information about another Ranger scout in a journal entry from Lake George on July 7: "This evening a party of rangers returned from a scout to Crown-Point; say that very few of the enemy are to be seen at that place, but there is a great number of tents at Ticonderoga; that they saw Jacobs and his party closely pursued ashore by the enemy in birch canoes, and that they fired on Jacob's party before they were able to get on shore; and they heard a firing for some time." (Skinner, p. 374)

On the 12th, although not specifically mentioned in his *Journals,* Rogers was part of a large scout of four hundred to five hundred men, depending on the source. They located and engaged a party of French and Indians on an island in the lake, suffering one sergeant killed and one Indian wounded. The French also suffered a number of casualties in this fight, and three of their bateaux were sank. (Webster, pp. 130- 131, and Henshaw, p. 211) Captain-Lieutenant Skinner wrote, "This morning Major [John] Campbell [newly promoted and transferred from the 42nd to the 17th Regiment the day before], with 400 grenadiers, rangers, and Indians, went in battoes and whale-boats attended by the proe [a row galley] with the 18 pounder in her, and one serjeant and six men of the artillery, to drive the enemy from the islands on the Lake. About eight in the morning the enemy fired on our advanced boats with the rangers, and killed one serjeant and wounded an Indian; upon which a smart firing began on both sides: The Major ordered these boats to retire, and the cannon to be fired, which made so good a shot at a great distance, that the enemy's Indians returned to their birch canoes with the greatest precipitation; but, finding that we could not come up with them, they lay on their oars when we did: We fired several shots at them, and it is thought sunk one of their canoes. After the Major found that he could not come up with them, he returned to the islands, and destroyed the huts which they had built, and then came to the camp." (Skinner, p. 375)

Massachusetts Provincial Lemuel Wood recorded in his journal for July 12: "This morning Major Rogers went down the lake with a party of the Rangers, some Indians, light infantry, Royal Scots and regulars, about 400 in all. [They] carried down with them a row galley with a field piece in it. About 8 o'clock in the morning we heard the report of several cannon down the lake and saw smoke at the mouth of the Narrows. All the pickets of the lines were ordered out and down the lake to their aid, some by land and some by water. About 12 o'clock there was a whale boat came in from the party and said that there was a large number of French and Indians down at the first Narrows that our men had driven them off and killed some of them. The French run off left their bateaux and what little they had. A little after sunset Major Rogers came in with the party he had left [with]. A sergeant of the Rangers & a regular were killed, and Indian wounded. He destroyed some of the enemy but how many he could not tell." (Wood, p. 131)

On July 14, Skinner makes another very interesting note in his journal: "General Amherst acquainted the commanding Officer at Carillon that, if any of his Indians scalped or killed any women or children belonging to his Britannic Majesty, he would scalp all the prisoners that might fall into his hands, as he had ordered his Indians not to do it, on pain of death." (Skinner, p. 378) Scalping was widely practiced by both sides, especially by, but not limited to, the Indian Allies. Mistreatment of women and children, however, was looked upon with disfavor. Amherst never forgot, or forgave, the atrocities that were committed after the surrender of Fort William Henry in 1757.

On July 15, Wood recorded that, "The Rangers were ordered to clear their pieces this morning which they did."

On the 16, he recorded another scout by the Rangers, "Last night there was a large party of regulars, Rangers and light infantry went down the lake in bateaux to see what they could discover. They went down as far as the first Narrows but found no enemy so they returned home again." (Wood, p. 132)

Rogers and his Rangers were obviously

more active in gathering intelligence for Amherst's campaign than they had been for Abercromby a year earlier.

It is also interesting to note that volunteers, and if necessary, draftees, were being sought from the Provincial regiments for service with the Rangers. Brigade Major Alexander Moneypenny's orderly book contains the following entry for July 16, 1759: "Eight of the Provincial Battalions are to give Thirteen Men each & two of the Provincial Battns. 14 Men each for the Ranging Service. The Men are to be told that they will be paid the Difference betwixt the Provincial Pay & that of the Rangers. Commanding Officers of those Battns. to turn out all Volunteers, willing to serve in the Rangers, tomorrow at One o'clock. Major Rogers will attend and choose the Number each Regiment is to furnish out of such Volunteers." (*B.F.T.M.*, Volume II, Number 6, July 1932, pp. 222-223. See also Hawks, p. 36)

On the 17, Lemuel Wood made note of more men being drafted into the Ranging Service, "This day there was a draft out of each provincial regiment to go into the Rangers to fill up Major Rogers' company. The men to draw Rangers pay and be dismissed at the time the other provincial are." (Wood, p. 132)

On July 18, Major John Hawks adds another interesting detail about the new Ranger recruits: "The men that have been chose to serve with the Rangers are to join them this evening att 5 o'clock & follow such orders as they shall receive from Major Rogers. They are not to take tents but live in huts in the same manner as the Rangers do." (Hawks, p. 39) While most of the army that was not quartered in actual barracks during the campaign season generally lived in their tents, Rogers' Rangers stayed in wooden huts at their main posts. This was most likely due to the fact that a good portion of the corps remained in service on the frontiers the year around. The majority of the Provincials were released for the winter, and most of the Regulars went into warm and secure winter quarters in places like Albany and New York.

I was in the front with the Rangers on the right wing, and was the first body that landed on July 22, at the north end of Lake George, followed by the grenadiers and light infantry, which Col. Haviland commanded.

Captain-Lieutenant Skinner noted that the first boats were under way by 6:00 a.m., and that for awhile, "the wind being fair, the army made use of their blankets for sails, ..." Over night, the wind came up and made the lake very rough. When the army made their landing the following day, it was so warm that the men "only landed in their waistcoats." Skinner continued, "The advanced guard of the army, composed of light infantry, rangers and Indians, attacked Mr. Bournie, with 200 Indians and near the same number of regulars, who retreated after their first fire, as his Indians behaved very dastardly; we scalped four of them, and took two prisoners who were of Berry's regiment; the wounded not known. This attack was near the saw-mills . . . ." (Skinner, pp. 381-382)

I marched, agreeable to orders from the General, across the mountains in the isthmus; from thence, in a by-way, athwart the woods to the bridge at the Saw-mills; where finding the bridge standing, I immediately crossed it with my Rangers, and took possession of the rising ground on the other side, and beat from thence a party of the enemy, and took several prisoners, killed others, and put the remainder to flight, before Colonel Haviland with his grenadiers and light infantry got over.

Massachusetts Provincial Lemuel Wood wrote that, "Major Rogers with his men went over the flats at the mills to the west side of the lake. The enemy met them there and they had a little engagement. Major Rogers soon drove them back, killed some, and took 2 or 3 prisoners . . . . The regulars and Rangers went over the river at the mills and went to clearing a road for the cannons as fast as possible. The French and Indians came out and kept firing and yelling most part of the afternoon." (Wood, p. 134)

Robert Webster, of the Fourth Connecticut Provincial Regiment, reports that Rogers killed four French and took two prisoners at about three o'clock in the afternoon. (Webster, p. 132)

The army took possession that night of the heights near the Saw-mills, where they lay all this evening.

The enemy kept out a scouting-party, with a body of Canadians and Indians, which killed several of our men, and galled us prodigiously.

July 23rd, The General, early in the morning, put the army in motion; at the same time ordered me in the front, with directions to proceed across the Chesnut Plain, the nighest and best way I could, to Lake Champlain, and do my endeavor to strike it near the edge of the cleared ground, between that and the breast-work, where I was to halt till I received further orders. Having pursued my orders, and halted at the lake, I informed the General of my situation, and that nothing extraordinary had happened in our march.

The General by this time had appointed and formed a detachment to attack their main breastwork on the hill, and had got possession of it. I was ordered to send two hundred men to take possession of a small entrenchment next to Lake Champlain; and Captain Brewer, whom I had sent to take possession of this post, happily succeeded.

From the time the army came in sight the enemy kept up a constant fire of cannon from their walls and batteries at our people.

Captain-Lieutenant Skinner noted in his journal on July 25, "Four men killed by a shell from the enemy, who have got the distance to the camp, and kill and wound many of our men." (Skinner, p. 384)

The General at this time had left several provincial regiments to bring the cannon and ammunition across the Carrying Place, together with provisions, which they did with great expedition.*

July 24. All this day the engineers were employed in raising batteries, as was likewise a great part of the army in that work, and in making and fetching fascines, till the 26th at night; all which time I had parties out to Crown Point to watch the motions of the enemy there; by which means the General had not only daily, but hourly intelligence from those posts.

This intelligence of French activity north of Ticonderoga is in marked contrast to General James Abercromby's lack of knowledge of the same during his campaign a year earlier. It shows that Amherst knew how to effectively utilize his Ranger force.

Gathering intelligence was not the only duty assigned to the Rangers. The "After Orders" for July 25 state that "Sixty of Major Roger's rangers will march, with their Commanding Officer, into the trenches this night, and will be employed, at a proper time, to alarm the enemy, by firing into the covered way, to keep their attention from the workmen." The next paragraph indicates that this might have been a task reserved for Rogers' Indian Companies: "we have carried our approaches within six hundred yards of the fort, and Major Rogers, with his Indians, are advanced, endeavoring to amuse the besieged from our works by popping into theirs." (*B.F.T.M.*, January 1942, p. 101; see also Knox, Volume I, pp. 506-507)

Along the same lines, Captain-Lieutenant Henry Skinner wrote on July 25 that, "Rogers with his rangers, amused the besieged by continually firing into the covered-way." On the 26, he added, "Major Rogers ordered to fire into the covered-way, as the night before, which drew their attention on his parties." (Skinner, pp. 384-385)

In contrast to the 1758 assault on Ticonderoga, Amherst was proceeding very deliberately, taking the time to set up formal siege lines and leaving nothing to chance. The heavily outnumbered French really did not expect to be able to hold out indefinitely. French commander Colonel Francois-Charles de Bourlamaque had orders to abandon the fort and flee north to Isle aux Noix before the British had him completely sealed off.

*About this time some of the Provincial regiments were sent to Oswego, to assist in building a fort there.

I this day received orders from the General to attempt to cut away a boom which the French had thrown across the lake opposite the fort, which prevented our boats from passing by, and cutting off their retreat. For the completion of this order I had sixty Rangers in one English flat-bottomed boat, and two whale-boats,* in which, after night came on, I embarked, and passed over to the other side of Lake Champlain, opposite to the Rangers encampment, and from that intended to steer my course along the east-shore, and privately saw off their boom, for which end I had taken saws with me, the boom being made with logs of timber.

On July 25, Massachusetts Provincial James Henderson recorded Colonel Roger Townshend's death in his journal, as did many other soldiers: "This Day Colo Townsend was slain By a Cannon Ball he was a gentleman much esteemed by the Genl." (Henderson, p. 205)

Amherst did indeed think highly of Townshend, and viewed his death as a great loss. On July 25, 1759, he wrote in his journal: "Colonel Townshend killed by a Cannon ball. The loss of a friend is not made up by all the success that a Campaign can give ones self personally." (Amherst, p. 145)

About nine o'clock, when I had got about half way from the place where I had embarked, the enemy, who had undermined their fort, sprung their mines, which blew up with a loud explosion, the enemy being all ready to embark on board their boats, and make a retreat. This gave me an opportunity to attack them with such success as to drive several of them ashore; so that next morning we took from the east-shore ten boats, with a considerable quantity of baggage, and upwards of fifty barrels of powder, and large quantities of ball. About ten o'clock I returned, and made my report to the General.

Amherst recorded this incident in his journal as follows: July 26, 1759: "I had ordered Major Rogers to go to night and cut the boom, and I put up three tents and made a fire on the eastern side which had a good effect for the Enemy kept firing at it as much as if there had been a real Camp there. About ten o'clock a Deserter came in & said the Garrison was to get off and blow up the Fort. I wrote to Major Rogers immediately to attack them, and soon we saw the Fort on fire and an Explosion but as the Deserter said a Match was laid to blow the whole up I would not order any men into it. However some volunteers went & brought away the Colours and I sent two other Deserters with some volunteers to try to cut the Match, who on their arrival found that there was no more danger . . . ." (Amherst, p. 146)

On July 27, the daily orders as recorded by Commissary Wilson directed that, "Major Roggers will send a Company of Rangers tomorrow Morning with all the Boats to the Fort. The Companies posted on the Lake Side from Collo. Haviland's Corps will joyn their Corps at Revallie Beating, after which Major Roggers will put Trees across the Foot Path that has been made by the Lake Side. Major Roggers will receive his orders from the Generall . . ." (Wilson, p. 101)

Massachusetts Provincial lieutenant William Henshaw recorded in his orderly book for July 28, at Fort Edward: "News by Colo. [William] Amherst that Ticonderoga is in the Hands of the English. The 26th Inst. in the Night the French Deserted it after Blowing up one End & Setting it on Fire but the English soon Extinguish'd the Fire; the French made their Escape in Battoes. Information thereof: Rogers Raingers Pursued them, took about Twenty Prisoners & some Plunder." (Henshaw, p. 216)

Provincial soldier William Gavit also wrote of the incident in a letter to his brother Ezekiel: "In the night they [the French] Abandoned their fort Carrying of the Best of their Effects Seting on fire their fort and the Rest Our Rangers Lying By the Lake Spyed them on their march fired on them and Persued and kild a Considerable Number took about 20 Prisoners With Much of their Valuable Effects." (Gavit, p. 217)

*These boats were carried across the land from Lake George to Lake Champlain, on which day the brave and worthy Colonel Townshend was killed by a cannon ball from the enemy, whose fall was much lamented by the General.

The 27th I was ordered with my party to the Saw-mills (to wait the flying parties of the enemy which were expected that way) were I lay to the 11th of August,* on which the I received the following orders from General Amherst.

"Sir,

"You are this night to send a Captain, with a proper proportion of subalterns, and two hundred men, to Crown Point, where the officer is to post himself in such a manner as not to be surprised, and to seize on the best ground for defending himself; and if he should be attacked by the enemy, he is not to retreat with his party, but keep his ground till he is reinforced from the army.

I am, Sir,
Your most obedient,
To Major Rogers. *Jeff. Amherst."*

Lemuel Wood noted in his journal on August 1 that, "We had some news by some Rangers that came from Crown Point this morning that the fort was actually on fire that they had went into it and walked round on the walls that the French were all gone. Lieutenant Flatcher who was out with party declared that he set his name on the flag staff this morning." (Wood, p. 137)

The officer who led this party was Lt. John Fletcher of Moses Brewer's Company. The Rangers were unable to raise the English colors over Fort St. Frederic, as the French had cut the flagpole's halyard. Fletcher wrote his name on the pole, and when he made his report to General Amherst, he brought him some cucumbers and apples from the French gardens. (Loescher, Volume II, p. 48)

Connecticut Provincial Robert Webster recorded in his journal that on August 3 " there was a regular hanged for deserting. He deserted to the French and Rogers' men brought him in yesterday with a French coat on him, and [he] was hanged immediately and his French coat was buried with him and a label on his breast." (Webster, p. 135)

Capt. Brewer went with a party, and the General followed the 12th with the whole army, and the same day arrived at Crown Point, where it was found that Captain Brewer had executed his orders extremely well.

Captain John Knox notes in his journal for August 1 that the Rangers also had an additional duty: "A detachment of Rangers were sent this day by land to Crown Point, in order to intercept any skulking parties of the enemy who may occupy the woods, with an intent to surprise our people here, after the departure of the army." (Knox, Volume II, p. 181)

This evening I had orders for encamping, and the ground for each corps being laid out, my camp was fixed in the front of the army. Immediately after the General had got the disposition of his camp settled, he began to clear ground, and prepare a place for erecting a new fort, in which service great part of the army was employed.

This new fort, when completed, would be one of the two largest British forts in North America, Fort Pitt being the other. Constructed slightly south of the ruins of the French Fort St. Frederic, the main British fort was in the shape of a pentagon. The walls were forty feet high, thirty feet thick at the base, and one half mile in circumference, with five massive bastions. Among its buildings were two magnificent Georgian style limestone barracks, one for officers and one for soldiers. There were three substantial outer redoubts to add to the fort's defenses. As at Forts Edward and William Henry, Rogers' Rangers lived in wooden huts located to the south of the main fort. (Starbuck, p. 164, and Titus, p. 14)

I had orders to send Capt. Stark, with two hundred Rangers, to cut a road to No. 4. which party was immediately sent.

Building this road was not a typical Ranger assignment, but it shows what a versatile military unit they were. Amherst documented the road building effort as follows: August 8, 1759: "I . . . sent 200 Rangers to cut a Road to open a communication from New England & New

*About this time a party of my people discovered that the enemy's Fort at Crown Point was likewise blown up, and the enemy fled.

Hampshire to Crown Point." (Amherst, p. 153) On September 9, he added: "Capt Starks returned with his Party from No 4; fourteen of his men deserted, six left sick behind. He said he had made the Road & that there were no mountains or swamps to pass & as he came back it measured 77 miles. It may be much shortened." (Amherst, p. 166) Fort No. 4 was located near the site of modern Charleston, New Hampshire.

During these transactions I sent out (by the General's approbation) several scouting parties against the enemy,* which brought in prisoners from St. John's Fort, and others penetrated into the back country, the better to learn the nature and situation of it.

Rogers himself took part in at least one of these scouts. Amherst's journal entry for August 1, 1759 notes: "I sent Major Rogers and Capt. Abercromby sixteen mile up South Bay [meaning south from Ticonderoga] to cross from thence to Lake George and reconnoitre the shortest and easiest passage for making a Road; by this Ticonderoga will be as good a Post for us as it was for the Enemy." (Amherst, p. 149)

Not every scout by the Rangers met with Amherst's approval. On August 23, 1759, he wrote in his journal: "Capt Tute arrived, the Indians firing & making the yell of having Scalps and a very great noise for a very little they have done. Capt Tute lay opposite to the Enemys Sloops some time but nobody came on shore; he then crossed to the east side & finding a canoo with some things left with it, knew a Scouting Party must be out & so resolved to wait for them. His Party of 40 men behaved ill or they should have taken the six Enemy Indians, three French men & two men of Prideaux's, instead of killing one Indian; one of Prideaux's escaped & joined him. They supposed they wounded two more Indians, and our own Rangers firing at they knew not what, wounded two of their Comrades, a pretty opportunity lost of taking all that Scouting Party. The luck of finding the canoo waiting for them, and attacking them properly (if it had been executed); could not have failed of taking the whole and there was no Risk." (Amherst, p. 160)

Amherst did give Tute another chance. In his journal for August 26, 1759, he recorded: "I sent Capt Tute of the Rangers with nine men and a man of Gages to go down about half way the Lake, and to go up the Riviere de Sable, steering a west course as far as they could and then lay the whale boat up & proceed by land to Swegatchi to make what discoveries he could . . . ." (Amherst, p. 161)

Thus we were employed till the 12th of September, when the General, exasperated at the treatment which Capt. Kennedy had met with, who had been sent with a party as a flag of truce to the St. Francis Indians, with proposals of peace to them, and was by them made a prisoner with his whole party; this ungenerous inhumane treatment determined the General to chastize these savages with some severity, and, in order to it, I received from him the following orders, viz.**

There is some question about Amherst's true motives for sending Kennedy on this mission. While officially he was supposed to be traveling under a flag of truce to seek peace with the Indians, there is strong evidence that his real purpose might have been to carry dispatches to General Wolfe who was besieging Quebec. On August 8, 1759, Amherst confided in his journal: "As it is of consequence that I should hear from Gen Wolfe as well as he should likewise hear from me I concluded to send Capt Kennedy with Lt Hamilton, Capt Jacobs, and four Indians to go through the settlements of the Eastern Indians with a proposal from me & take their answer to Mr Wolfe whom I have directed to treat them accordingly." (Amherst, p. 153) Later, on September 10, after the party was captured, he wrote: "One [letter] from Mons Montcalm of no date, acquainting me that Capt Kennedy and Hamilton were Prisoners, an excuse to send to see what we are about and to send several Letters to their officers who are Prisoners. . . ." (Amherst, p. 167) This is an interesting reaction, considering the

*Captain Tute, and Lieutenant Fletcher, in two different scouting parties, were taken and carried to Canada.

**That this expedition might be carried on with the utmost secrecy after the plan of it was concerted the day before my march, it was put into public orders, that I was to march a different way, at the same time I had private instructions to proceed directly to St. Francis.

strong possibility that Kennedy's party was on a spy mission itself.

In his journal, Connecticut Provincial Robert Webster recorded, "Still at Crown Point. This day the scout set out for Suagothel 500 in number. They took thirty days provisions with them under the command of Major Rogers." Note that Webster identifies the destination as "Suagothel," just as Kenneth Roberts does in his novel *Northwest Passage.* (Webster, p. 141)

"You are this night to set out with the detachment as ordered yesterday, viz. of 200 men, which you will take under your command, and proceed to Misisquey Bay, from whence you will march and attack the enemy's settlements on the southside of the river St. Lawrence, in such a manner as you shall judge most effectual to disgrace the enemy, and for the success and honour of his Majesty's arms.

"Remember the barbarities that have been committed by the enemy's Indian scoundrels on every occasion, where they had an opportunity of shewing their infamous cruelties on the King's subjects, which they have done without mercy. Take your revenge, but don't forget that tho' those villains have dastardly and promiscuously murdered the women and children of all ages, it is my orders that no women or children are killed or hurt.

"When you have executed your intended service, you will return with your detachment to camp, or to join me wherever the army may be.

Your's, & c.
Jeff. Amherst."

Camp at Crown Point,
Sept. 13, 1759.
To Major Rogers.

Mante wrote the following about Rogers' mission: "Captain Kennedy, who had been sent by the General with a flag of truce, to offer peace to the Indians of Saint Francois, was detained by them with his whole party. This insult exasperated the General to such a degree, that he immediately determined to chastise them with a severity equal to the offence. With this in view, the more effectually to distress the enemy, he ordered a party of two hundred men under Major Rogers to march and attack them on the south side of the river St. Lawrence; the barbarities and infamous cruelties which those dastardly villains, in particular, had promiscuously committed on women and children, merited the most exemplary punishment. The troops sent against them were, however, forbid to use any retaliation against women and children; in a spirit truly becoming an English enemy." (Mante, pp. 218-219)

In pursuance of the above orders, I set out the same evening with a detachment; and as to the particulars of my proceedings, and the great difficulties we met with in effecting our design, the reader is referred to the letter I wrote to General Amherst upon my return, and the remarks following it.

Copy of my Letter to the General upon my return from St. Francis.

"Sir,

"The twenty-second day after my departure from Crown Point, I came in sight of the Indian town of St. Francis in the evening, which I discovered from a tree that I climbed, at about three miles distance. Here I halted my party, which now consisted of 142 men, officers included, being reduced to that number by the unhappy accident which befel Capt. Williams,* and several since tiring, whom I was obliged to send back.

The Indian village of St. Francis was also known as Odanak. It was located on the St. Francis River, near present day Pierreville, Quebec, Canada. It was inhabited by the Abenaki tribe, who were Christianized by the French. By 1759, the Abenakis were fiercely anti-English.

In 1721, the French missionary Father Pierre Charlevoix wrote that the Abenakis "now live on the banks of the St. Francis, two leagues from its discharge into Lake St. Peter. This spot is very delightful, which is pity, these people having no relish for the beauties of a fine situation, and the huts of Indians con-

*Capt. Williams of the Royal Regiment was, the fifth day of our march, accidentally burnt with gun-powder, and several men hurt, which together with some sick, returned back to Crown Point, to the number of forty, under the care of Capt. Williams, who returned with great reluctance.

tributing but little to the embellishment of a prospect. This village is extremely populous, all the inhabitants of which are Christians. The nation is docile, and always much attracted to the French." (Charlevoix, Volume I, p. 191)

Gordon Day gives this description of the village: "Perhaps this is the time to correct the common impression that the village of 1759 was an irregular assembalge of squalid bark huts. The engineer, Franquet, who visited St. Francis seven years before Rogers, counted 51 houses arranged in a square. They were made of squared timbers covered with either bark or boards. Twelve more houses were built after the French style, by which we might assume frame construction. James Johnson of Charleston, who was a captive there in 1754 mentioned some houses of stone. There are to this day three or four houses in the village whose construction under their sheathing is log, but I do not know that any of them go back to 1759. Yet it will be remembered that Rogers did leave three houses unburned for the sake of the corn in them." (Day, *Rogers' Raid*, p. 15)

The word Abenaki comes from "Wobanaki," which means "land or country of the East," or "an Indian from where the day-light comes." (Laurent, p. 205) Today the Abenakis are a proud and industrious people, who maintain a small museum and several monuments to Rogers' raid at the present day village of Odanak.

While he was writing his famous novel, *Northwest Passage,* Kenneth Roberts corresponded with Stephen Laurent, the son of Chief Joseph Laurent who authored the Abenaki dictionary cited above. Laurent wrote to Roberts, "The situation of the old town of St. Francis, today known as Odanak, was and still is on the easterly bank of the St. Francis River, a little northwest of the French-Canadian village of Pierreville. St. Francois-du-Lac, which appears on the maps, has no relation to the Indian village. St. Francois is on the westerly bank: Odanak on the easterly . . . . The houses were for the most part close to the bank of the river . . . . It is a high bank all along; in some places as high as sixty feet . . . . I have always understood that Rogers and his men forded the St. Francis River midway between the present Pierreville and Drummondville, perhaps near the small town of St. Joachim." (Roberts, Volume II Appendix, p. 17)

On a visit to Odanak in 1986, this writer had the great pleasure to meet Bernadette Laurent, a daughter of Chief Joseph Laurent, and sister of Stephen Laurent. She was a most charming and gracious lady who made us feel very welcome. It was from her that I obtained my copy of the Abenaki dictionary written by her father.

At eight o'clock this evening I left the detachment, and took with me Lieut. Turner and Ensign Avery, and went to reconnoitre the town, which I did to my satisfaction, and found the Indians in a high frolic or dance. I returned to my party at two o'clock, and at three marched it to within five hundred yards of the town, where I lightened the men of their packs, and formed them for the attack.

Kenneth Roberts determined that there was a full moon on October 6, 1759, so depending on exactly what the date of the Rangers' attack was, the moonlight probably worked to their benefit. (Roberts, Volume II Appendix, p. 17)

There is a discrepancy as to the actual date of the attack. By Rogers' figures, it would have taken place on the early morning of October 6, given his departure from Crown Point on September 13. Gary Zaboly has researched it thoroughly, and believes that it actually took place on October 4. The Abenaki monument at Odanak also lists the date as October 4.

"At half an hour before sun-rise I surprised the town when they were all fast asleep, on the right, left, and center, which was done with so much alacrity by both the officers and men, that the enemy had not time to recover themselves, or take arms for their own defense, till they were chiefly destroyed, except some few of them who took to the water. About forty of my people pursued them, who destroyed such as attempted to make their escape that way, and sunk both them and their boats. A little after sun-rise I set fire to all their houses, except three, in which there was corn, that I reserved for the use of the party.

"The fire consumed many of the Indians who had concealed themselves in the cellars and lofts of their houses. About seven o'clock in the morning the affair was completely over, in which time we had killed at least two hundred Indians, and taken twenty of their women and children prisoners, fifteen of whom I let go their own way, and five I brought with me, viz. two Indian boys and three Indian girls. I likewise retook five English captives, which I also took under my care.

It is impossible to say for sure exactly how many Indians were actually killed in the raid. Rogers' estimate is probably too high, but I did find one Abenaki oral history source that agrees there were about two hundred killed. (Roberts, Volume II Appendix, p. 50) Loescher says that the number killed was sixty-five to one hundred forty. (Loescher, Volume II, p. 59) Rogers' number was probably influenced by the number of warriors estimated as living in the village, and by the fact that many of the Indians were trapped in their burning houses. He had no way of knowing how many of the warriors were away, either searching for him or hunting, but it appears that a considerable number of them were. On the other hand, it is hard to believe that, knowing Rogers was in the area, and that his two most likely targets were either Saint Francis or Wigwam Martinique (Yamaska), the Abenakis would have left the village full of women and children without a sufficient force of warriors to protect them. One thing can be said with certainty, however. From the time of the raid on, the Abenakis ceased to be a threat to the New England frontier, and from that standpoint, the expedition was a tremendous success.

A New York newspaper gave the following account of the attack: "It was performed with such Alertness by the Officers and Men, that the Enemy had not Time to recover themselves, or to take their Arms for their Defence, til they were mostly destroyed, excepting some who took to the Water; and they were pursued by 40 of our People, who dispatched many of them, and sunk their Boats, etc . . ." (The *New York Mercury* #380, November 26, 1759)

The Abenaki oral tradition, while it cannot be conclusively verified, should at least be considered. This is a summary of their accounts, drawn from a number of sources. On the night before the attack, the Abenakis were having a celebration, possibly a wedding party or a harvest dance, in the large council house, which was next to their Catholic chapel. When one young woman was outside taking a rest from the party and the dancing, she was approached by a strange Indian who was not an Abenaki. (This Indian is identified as a Stockbridge Ranger named Samadagwas, and is probably the same one killed in the attack; Obomsawim gives his name as Schaghticoke). Samadagwas told the young woman that he belonged to a party that was going to attack the village in the morning. She went inside and warned her people. Some families took heed and hid their women and children in a large ravine nearby; others did not believe her and remained in the village. A number of the warriors were away from the village, either hunting or assisting in the search for Rogers' party, whose boats had been discovered at Mississquoi Bay.

When the Rangers attacked the next morning, the warriors that remained fought tenaciously in defense of their village. They fortified themselves in the council house where the celebration was held the night before. (This council house survived into the twentieth century, and is shown in a 1915 photograph of the village. When it was torn down, many lead musketballs were found in the window and door frames). Only about thirty Abenakis were killed, some of them women and children. Two boys and three girls or women were taken prisoner. The Rangers looted and burned the village before beginning their retreat. On the return march, when the food ran out, one of the boy prisoners was killed and eaten by his captors.

Abenaki warriors joined the French in pursuit of Rogers' party. After the Rangers split into small groups, several were overtaken. A number of Rangers were killed, and others were taken captive. Some of the captives were brought back to Odanak, where they were turned over to the women for torture. One group overtook the party that had killed and eaten part of the Abenaki boy. Two Rangers who were still carrying part of his flesh were killed outright. Three others were brought back to the French post at Isle aux Noix. They also freed one of the women captives.

One part of the Abenaki tradition that doesn't fit is the story that the day before the attack some women washing clothes saw wood chips floating down the river, presumably from rafts that the Rangers were making. The women reported this, but nothing was done. Gordon Day speculates that Rogers may have actually made rafts to cross the river, then later covered up that fact and claimed that they just forded it when he learned that the wood chips cost him the element of surprise. Day further suggests that in *Northwest Passage,* Kenneth Roberts had Rogers specifically forbid the making of rafts in order " not to diminish the glory of his hero." (Day, *Rogers' Raid*, p. 8)

The Abenaki women may well have noticed the wood chips as their oral tradition implies, but they could have come from any number of sources, the *least* likely of which, I feel, was from Rangers building rafts. If rafts were built, it would have been much more logical for the cutting to have been done up on the riverbank, where there would be no danger of wood chips floating down river. The true danger would have been from the sound of the chopping being heard and giving away their presence. Anyone familiar with the woods knows how far a sound like this carries, and it would have been a legitimate concern. Another question that needs to be addressed is where would the Rangers have gotten the axes or saws necessary to prepare the logs for these rafts. The small tomahawks that they carried would have been quite ineffective for such a task, yet for them to have carried large felling axes and/or saws on the difficult march through the swamp seems unlikely. Building rafts for so many men also would have taken time—time during which the Rangers would have increased their risk of discovery. I believe that they crossed the river as quickly and quietly as possible, just as Rogers said, by fording it. (This summary account of the Abenaki oral tradition was composed from a variety of sources. Except for my disagreement with Gordon Day over the raft building, his accounts and analysis are by far the best. See: Day, *Rogers Raid*, pp. 3-17; Day, *Oral History*, pp. 99-108; MacLoed, pp. 147-149; Loescher, Volume II, pp. 57-64; Frazier, pp 133-136; and Pierce/Obomsawim, pp. 37-38. One account, known as the *Pennoyer Narrative*, reprinted in Roberts, Volume II Appendix, pp. 49-55, is so full of known errors that it was not considered).

Marie-Jeanne Gill, wife of the village chief, Joseph Gill, was one of the women captured. Their son, Antoine Gill, was also taken, but according to Abenaki tradition, was returned to his village the next year. Both Joseph's and Marie-Jeanne's parents were reportedly British captives who were brought to Saint Francis years earlier.

The following year, a Boston newspaper reported this information about the fate of the prisoners, "Major Rogers was returned from New-York, having left the young Indian Lad (one of the prisoners he bro't off from st. Francois) to be put to School to be instruckted in the English Language; that the young girls which he also bro't off, died lately with the Small-Pox at Albany: These Children, it is said, were relatives to Mrs. Williams, who was taken Captive when in her infancy and educated and married in Canada." (*Boston News-Letter,* No. 2058, February 7, 1760)

"When I had paraded my detachment, I found I had Capt. Ogden badly wounded in his body, but not so as to hinder him from doing his duty. I had also six men slightly wounded, and one Stockbridge Indian killed.

As noted above, if Abenaki tradition is correct, this Stockbridge Indian was probably Samadagwas, the same one who warned the village of the impending attack.

"I ordered my people to take corn out of the reserved houses for their subsistence home, there being no other provision there: and whilst they were loading themselves I examined the prisoners and captives, who gave the following intelligence: 'That a party of 300 French, and some Indians, were about four miles down the river below us; and that our boats were way-laid, which I had reason to believe was true, as they told the exact number, and the place where I left them at: that a party of 200 French and fifteen Indians, had, three days before I attacked the town, gone up the river Wigwam Martinic, supposing that was the place I intended to attack; whereupon I called the officers together, to consult the safety of our return, who were of opinion there was no other way for us to return with safety, but by No. 4 on Connecticut River. I marched the detachment eight days in a body that **day**; [In the London edition this word is "way."] and when provisions grew scarce, near Ampara Magog [Memphremagog] Lake, I divided the detachment into small companies, putting proper guides to each, who were to assemble at the mouth of Amonsook River,* as I expected provisions would be brought there for our relief,** not knowing which way I should return.

This is near the modern towns of Wells River, Vermont, and Woodsville, New Hampshire.

"Two days after we parted, Ensign Avery, of Fitche's, fell in on my track, and followed in my rear; and a party of the enemy came upon them, and took seven of his party prisoners, two of whom that night made their escape, and came in to me next morning.

Two of the five of Avery's men who remained prisoners were later exchanged. One of them, Frederick Curtiss, left this account: "After nine days travail in an unknown Wilderness . . . [we] were at the close of the Ninth Day Surprised by a party of Indians about Twenty or Thirty in Number that had pursued us & watching an opportunity when we were Resting our Selves being much Enfeebled by travail & destitute of provision save mushrooms & Beach Leaves for four or five days then past Came upon us unperceived till within a few foot of us. Some with their guns presented while others Seised upon us that we had no opportunity for defense or flight & So made us all prisoners Stript us of our Cloathes & tyed us to trees save one Ballard whom after binding they stabb'd & killed. afterwards they loosed us from ye tree & carryed us about two mile: Two of ye prisoners Escaped vis. Hewet & Lee. The rest of us was Carryed back & we travail'd together or in Light ye next Day to the place they went about building their Canoes which was the last place that I saw my fellow prisoners Excepting Moses Jones. as they Got their Canoes Ready they went off one Canoe Load after another, ours was the Last . . . at the End of five days we got Back again to St. Francis at night, having lived nine days on mushrooms and Beach leaves. These prisoners that was Carryed in the day Time was killed outright five of whom Lay there dead on the Ground . . . ." (Cuneo, *Rogers*, pp. 109-110) Moses Jones is the other surviving member of this party. (Cuneo, *Notes*, p. 75)

Avery, with the remainder of his party joined mine, and came with me to the Cohase Intervals, where I left them with Lieut. Grant, from which place I, with Capt. Ogden, and one man more, put down the river on a small raft to this place, where I arrived yesterday; and in half an hour after my arrival dispatched provisions up the river to Lieut. Grant in a canoe, which I am pretty certain will reach him this night, and next morning sent two other canoes up the river for the relief of the other parties, loaded with provisions, to the mouth of the Amonsook River.

"I shall set off to go up the river myself tomorrow, to seek and bring in as many of our men as I can find, and expect to be back in about eight days, when I shall, with all expedition, return to Crown Point. As to other particulars relative to this scout, which your Excellency may think proper to inquire after, I refer you to Capt. Ogden, who bears this, and has accompanied me all the time I have been out, behaving very well. I am, Sir, with the greatest respect,

Your Excellency's most obedient servant,

No. 4. *R. Rogers."*
Nov. 5, 1759.
To General Amherst.

*Amonsook River falls into Connecticut River about sixty miles above No. 4.

**An officer upon some intelligence that I had when going out, was sent back to Crown Point from Misisquey Bay, to desire that provisions might be conveyed to this place, as I had reason to believe we should be deprived of our boats, and consequently be obliged to return this way.

Hauling the Whaleboats Ashore at Missisquoi Bay

WE have Provincial diarists to thank for giving us an idea of what the weather was like on the night of September 23, 1759, when Rogers drew his seventeen whaleboats out of Lake Champlain for the last time while en route to St. Francis. Back at Crown Point, a storm of rain was recorded as falling all day and night, with warm temperatures. At Quebec, the latter part of the day was noted as being moderate and rainy. Thus, it can be assumed that rain also fell on Rogers and his men as they disembarked on the eastern shore of Missisquoi Bay; and perhaps lightning accompanied the warm-weather storm. In fact, rain fell in the regions adjacent to the territory the expedition would march through for twenty-five of the approximately sixty days of its round-trip duration, with frost and snow adding more misery in its latter stretches.

Concrete evidence for the foul-weather garb of the Rangers under Rogers' direct command has not yet been found, beyond the probable use of blankets worn Indian fashion when nothing else was available; and, in fort and camp, surtouts and greatcoats, for men on sentry duty, on daily patrols, and engaged in other local outdoor assignments. (For their muskets, lock covers and plugs for the barrels would have been requisite in such weather). However, a reasonable supposition might be drawn by examining the rainwear of other lightly-equipped units of the war in North America.

Colonel James Prevost, commander of the 4th Battalion of the Royal American Regiment, proposed clothing and equipping certain Regular troops as Rangers in mi-1757, and among his recommendations for uniforming them was "a cloak of good cloth, well cut and light which the soldier would carry rolled and tied".[1]

Nine months later, Captain George Scott, who would command Ranger and light infantry companies at Louisbourg in 1758 and at Quebec in 1759, suggested to Lord Loudoun that North American Rangers be issued "a short Cloke made of light, thin, painted Canvas lin'd with Bays, which will keep the Rangers Arms, Ammunition and Body dry let it rain ever so hard," an additional advantage being that the Ranger could load his musket under the protection of the cloak in bad weather. It would also be much lighter than a greatcoat, and would have a hood to pull over the soldier's cap. He further stated that troops operating in trenches and batteries would find it "of great utility."[2] Indeed, volunteers serving with light infantry and Rangers at Louisbourg *were* provided with both cloaks and blankets.[3]

Many of the men in this illustration wear short, light cloaks with hoods and capes. The man at right wears a kind of improvised surtout or light "watchcoat": a checked shirt cut and altered into something resembling a loose bedgown, and then coated with oil as a preservative against the rain. This type of improvised foul weather garment was among the suggested wear for light troops in William Smith's *Reflections on the War with the Savages of North America*, first published in 1765. In lieu of a hood, a piece of oiled linen was recommended to be "put under the hat or cap to carry the rain down to the watchcoat or surtout, otherwise whatever [is] wet soaks through the hat or cap, will run down the neck, and thereby in some measure defeat the design of the watchcoat." These garments were further recommended to be coated "some dark or greenish colour. . .to make them less remarkable in the woods."

It is probable that the men of Rogers' St. Francis expedition wore several types of rainwear, representing as they did a number of diverse units—Rangers, Provincials, Light Infantry, Regular volunteers, and Indians——who were unarguably not all equipped with the same clothing and accouterments. Cloaks were apparently in short supply back at Crown Point, at least among the Provincial troops, that September of 1759.[4]

In the foreground of the illustration, Major Rogers directs "two trusty Indians to lie at a distance in sight of the boats, and there to stay till I came back, except the enemy found them; in which latter case they were with all possible speed to follow on my track, and give me intelligence."

Indeed, a French patrol did discover the boats on September 24, burned some of them, and took the remainder by portage trail north to St. Jean, on the Richelieu River. These boats almost certainly had pointed bows and sterns, and steering oars rather than rudders. Rowing was done by three oarsmen at starboard and two at port. The boats might have been painted green or brown to facilitate their concealment, and their oars muffled with sheepskin or pieces of blanket to enable them to row silently in the night past the French forts and patrols on Lake Champlain.

Most of the whaleboats probably had masts; and if sails were lacking, blankets could be improvised to serve almost as well. Those of the Rangers' provisions left behind in the boats were no doubt covered with oilcloths.

The discovery and loss of Rogers' boats and the reserve provisions in them played no small role in dooming many men of the expedition to starvation, exhaustion, and even death from same, on the long march back from St. Francis—that, combined with the paucity of game, the rugged terrain of lower Quebec Province and northern Vermont and New Hampshire, and the bad weather that plagued them for over half the journey.

G.Z.

1. Prevost to the Duke of Cumberland, May 12, 1757, *Military Affairs In North America*, edited by Stanley Pargellis, Archon Books, Hamden, Connecticut, 1969, p. 337.
2. George Scott to Lord Loudoun, Halifax 13th February 1758, LO6927, Loudoun Papers, Huntington Library, San Marino, California.
3. Captain John Knox, *An Historical Journal of the Campaigns in North America For the Years 1757, 1758, 1759 and 1760*, edited by Arthur G. Doughty, Vol. I, Books for Libraries Press, Freeport, New York, 1970, p. 211.
4. "The Provincials begin to grow sickly and lose some men. . .They want Cloaks to keep them warm." *The Journal of Jeffrey Amherst*, edited by J. Clarence Webster, Toronto and Chicago, 1931, entry of September 22, 1759.

I cannot forbear here making some remarks on the difficulties and distresses which attended us, in effecting this enterprize upon St. Francis, which is situated within three miles of the river St. Lawrence, in the middle of Canada, about half way between Montreal and Quebec. It hath already been mentioned, how our party was reduced by the accident which befel Capt. Williams, the 5th day after our departure, and still farther by numbers tiring and falling sick afterwards. It was extremely difficult while we kept the water (and which retarded our progress very much) to pass undiscovered by the enemy, who were then cruizing in great numbers upon the lake; and had prepared certain vessels, on purpose to decoy any party of ours, that might come that way, armed with all manner of machines and implements for their destruction; but we happily escaped their snares of this kind, and landed (as hath been mentioned) the tenth day at Misisquey Bay. Here, that I might with more certainty know whether my boats (with which I left provisions sufficient to carry us back to Crown Point) were discovered by the enemy, I left two trusty Indians to lie at a distance in sight of the boats, and there to stay till I came back, except the enemy found them; in which case they were with all possible speed to follow on my track, and give me intelligence. It happened the second day after I left them, that these two Indians came up to me in the evening, and informed me that about 400 French had discovered and taken my boats, and that about one half of them were hotly pursuing on my track.

> French General Bourlemaque wrote to Governor Vaudreuil after Rogers' boats were discovered: "Three days ago I learned, Monsieur, through my scouts, that there were 17 whaleboats in Missicoui Bay . . . . I sent a courier to M. deRigaud. 300 men, whom I sent on the tracks of the English, found that they were heading for Chambly, Maska [Yamaska] or St. Francis. They thought there might be 200 or 240 men . . . . The English left the Bay of Missicoui the morning of the 23rd . . . . I have 360 men who are waiting for them in the place where the whaleboats are." (Roberts, Volume II Appendix, pp. 19-20)

This unlucky circumstance (it may well be supposed) put us into some consternation. Should the enemy overtake us, and we get the better of them in an encounter; yet being so far advanced into their territory, where no reinforcement could possibly relieve us, and where they could be supported by any numbers they pleased, afforded us little hopes of escaping their hands. Our boats being taken, cut off all hope of a retreat by them; besides the loss of our provisions left with them, of which we knew we should have great need at any rate, in case we survived, was a melancholy consideration. It was, however, resolved to prosecute our design at all adventures, and, when we had accomplished it, to attempt a retreat (the only possible way we could think of) by way of No 4; and that we might not be destroyed by famine in our return, I dispatched Lieut. M'Mullen by land to Crown Point, to desire of the General to relieve me with provision at Amonsook River, at the end of Cohase Intervals on Connecticut River, that being the way I should return, if at all, and the place appointed being about sixty miles from No. 4. then the most northerly English settlement. This being done, we determined if possible to outmarch our pursuers, and effect our design upon St. Francis before they could overtake us. We marched nine days through wet sunken ground; the water most of the way near a foot deep, it being a spruce bog. When we encamped at night, we had no way to secure ourselves from the water, but by cutting the boughs of trees, and with them erecting a kind of hammocks.

> The *Boston News-Letter* reprinted this account of the march through the swamp. Rogers "went through a swamp 50 of miles in length, at least; and at Night, when he and his Party wanted Rest, they were obliged to fell saplins, and to lay them a-cross each other, in Form of a Raft, and cover them over with Boughs and Leaves to keep themselves from the Wet: Several of his party perished in this swamp . . . ." (*Boston News-Letter,* No. 2058, February 7, 1760)

We commonly began our march a little before day, and continued it till after dark at night.

The tenth day after leaving Misisquey Bay, we came to a river about fifteen miles above the town of St. Francis to the South of it; and the town being on the opposite or east side of it, we were obliged to ford it, which was attended with no small difficulty, the water being five feet deep, and the current swift. I put the tallest men up the stream, and then holding by each other, we got over with the loss of several of our guns, some of which were recovered by diving to the bottom for them. We had now good dry ground to march upon, and discovered and destroyed the town as before related, which in all probability would have been effected with the loss of no man but the Indian who was killed in the action, had not my boats been discovered, and our retreat that way cut off.

This nation of Indians was notoriously attached to the French, and had for near a century past harassed the frontiers of New England, killing people of all ages and sexes in a most barbarous manner, at a time when they did not in the least suspect them; and to my own knowledge, in six years time, carried into captivity, and killed, on the before-mentioned frontiers, 400 persons. We found in the town hanging on poles over their doors 600 scalps, mostly English.

The circumstances of our return are chiefly related in the preceding letter; however it is hardly possible to describe the grief and consternation of those of us who came to Cohase Intervals. Upon our arrival there (after so many days tedious march over steep rocky mountains, or through wet dirty swamps with the terrible attendants of fatigue and hunger) to find that here was no relief for us, where we had encouraged ourselves that we should find it, and have our distress alleviated; for not withstanding the officer I dispatched to the general discharged his trust with great expedition, and in nine days arrived at Crown Point, which was an hundred miles through the woods, and the General, without delay, sent Lieut. Stephans to No. 4, with orders to take provisions up the river to the place where I had appointed, and there wait as long as there was any hopes of my returning; yet the officer that was sent being an indolent fellow, tarried at the place but two days, when he returned, taking all of the provisions back with him, about two hours before our arrival. Finding a fresh fire burning in his camp, I fired guns to bring him back, which guns he heard, but would not return, supposing we were an enemy.*

Our distress upon this occasion was truly inexpressible; our spirits, greatly depressed by the hunger and fatigues we had already suffered, now almost entirely sunk within us, seeing no resource left, nor any reasonable ground to hope that we should escaped a most miserable death by famine. At length I came to a resolution to push as fast as possible towards No. 4, leaving the remains of my party, now unable to march further, to get such wretched subsistence the barren wilderness could afford,** till I could get relief to them, which I engaged to do within ten days. I, with Captain Ogden, one Ranger, and a captive Indian boy, embarked upon a raft we made of dry pine trees. The current carried us down the stream in the middle of the river, where we endeavoured to keep our wretched vessel by such paddles as we had made out of small trees, or spires split and hewed. The second day we reached White River Falls, and very narrowly escaped being carried over them by the current.

Near present day Wilder, Vermont. (Roberts, Volume II Appendix, p. 28)

Our little remains of strength however enabled us to land, and to march by them. At the bottom of these falls, while Capt. Ogden and the Ranger hunted for red squirrels for a refreshment, who had the good fortune likewise to kill a partridge, I attempted forming a new raft for our further conveyance. Being not able to cut down trees, I burnt them down, and then burnt them off at proper lengths. This was our third day's work after leaving our companions. The next day we got our materials together, and compleated our raft, and floated with the stream again till we came to Wattockquitchey Falls, which are about fifty yards in length: here we landed, and by a weath made of hazel bushes, Capt. Ogden held the raft, till I went to the bottom, prepared to swim in and board it

*This Gentleman, for this piece of conduct, was broke by a general court-martial, and rendered incapable of sustaining any office in his Majesty's service for the future: a poor reward however, for the distresses and anguish thereby occasioned to so many brave men, to some of which it proved fatal, they actually dying with hunger.

**This was ground-nuts and lily roots, which being cleaned and boiled will serve to preserve life, and the use and method of preparing which I taught to Lieut. Grant commander of the party.

when it came down, and if possible paddle it ashore this being our only resource for life, as we were not able to make a third raft in case we had lost this.

> Now called Ottauquechee Falls, at the junction of the Ottauquechee and Connecticut Rivers, near North Hartland, Vermont. (Cuneo, *Notes*, p. 77)

I had the good fortune to succeed, and the next morning we embarked and floated down the stream to within a small distance of No. 4, where we found some men cutting timber, who gave us the first relief, and assisted us to the fort, from whence I dispatched a canoe with provisions, which reached the men at Cohase four days after, which (agreeable to my engagement) was the tenth after I left them.

Two days after my arrival at No. 4 I went with other canoes, loaded with provisions, up the river myself, for the relief of others of my party that might be coming in that way,* having hired some of the inhabitants to assist me in this affair. I likewise sent expresses to Suncook and Pennecook upon Merrimack river, that any that should chance to straggle that way might be assisted; and provisions were sent up said rivers accordingly.

On my return to No. 4, I waited a few days to refresh such of my party as I had been able to collect together, and during my stay there received the following letter from General Amherst, in answer to mine of No. 5.

"Sir, *Crown Point, Nov.* 8, 1759.

"Captain Ogden delivered me your letter of the 5th instant, for which I am not only to thank you, but to assure you of the satisfaction I had on reading it; as every step you informed me you have taken, has been very well judged, and deserves my full approbation. I am sorry Lieut. Stephens judged so ill in coming away with the provisions from the place were I sent him to wait for you.

"An Indian is come in last night, and said he had left some of your party at Otter River. I sent for them; they are come in. This afternoon four Indians, two Rangers, a German woman, and three other prisoners; they quitted four of your party some days since, and thought they had arrived here.** I am in hopes all the rest will get in very safe. I think there is no danger but they will, as you quitted them not till having marched eight days in a body; the only risk after that will be meeting hunting parties. I am, Sir,

Your humble servant,

To Major Rogers. JEFF. AMHERST."

> Kenneth Roberts, while writing *Northwest Passage,* extracted all of the weather related information that he could find from the journals of Jeffery Amherst and Robert Webster. He then submitted the information to W. R. Gregg, chief of the United States Weather Bureau in Washington. Mr. Gregg concluded that a series of storms advancing up the Atlantic coast produced "general gales and widespread precipitation," leading to similar conditions along Rogers' line of march. The result was that the weather was probably unseasonably cold, wet, and generally miserable for the entire march to and from Saint Francis. (Roberts, Volume II Appendix, pp. 25-26) Since General Amherst was both commander in chief, and the officer who ordered the St. Francis Raid, his comments about it are extremely important. All of his journal entries pertaining to the raid are included here in their entirety.
>
> September 11, 1759: "Capt Disserat of the Regt de la Reine who came with the Flag of Truce said Kennedy was taken by some St Francois Indians who were hunting." (Amherst, p. 167)
>
> September 12, 1759: "As Capt Kennedy's Journey was now over I ordered a detachment of 220 chosen men under the command of Major Rogers to go & destroy the St Francois Indian Settlements and the French settlements on the South side of the River St Lawrence, not letting any one but Major Rogers know what about or where he was going." (Amherst, p. 168)
>
> September 13, 1759: "Major Rogers set out with his Party." (Amherst, p. 168) September 14, 1759: "One Indian came back sick from M Rogers Party." (Amherst, p. 169)

* I met several different parties; as Lieut. Curgill, Lieut. Campbell, Lieut. Farrington, and Serjeant Evans, with their respective divisions, and sent canoes further up for the relief of such as might be still behind, and coming this way. Some I met who escaped from Dunbar's and Turner's party, who were over-taken (being upwards of twenty in number) and were mostly killed or taken by the enemy. [Cuneo claims that Dunbar, Turner, and ten of their men were killed, while the rest escaped. (Cuneo, *Rogers*, p. 110)]

**Upon our separation, some of the divisions were ordered to make for Crown point, that being the best route for hunting.

GARY ZABOLY 1985 ©

The Fires of St. Francis

"THE twenty-second day after my departure from Crown Point,"[1] wrote Robert Rogers in his letter to General Amherst of November 5, 1759, "I came in sight of the Indian town St. Francis in the evening, which I discovered from a tree that I climbed, at about three miles distance."

Not surprisingly, Rogers seems to have been as expert at tree climbing as he was at quickly ascending and descending steep mountains. It was a skill he no doubt perfected as a boy and young man growing up in the frontier settlements of Methuen, Massachusetts and Mountalona (later Dunbarton), New Hampshire. Provincial soldier Abel Spicer, who had taken part in Rogers' and Putnam's pursuit of La Corne's raiders after they had massacred the supply train at Halfway Brook on July 28, 1758, recorded an earlier example of Rogers' tree-climbing ability. Although the enemy party had managed to barely elude their pursuers, Rogers and Putnam continued their chase north along the shores of South Bay until "a man hallooed several times on the other side of the bay." Spicer added that "Major Rogers did climb to the top of a large tree and then he examined him" by shouting across the bay.[2]

Once Rogers had sighted the Abenaki town that October night in 1759, he went to reconnoiter it, and found "the Indians in a high frolic or dance."[3] In his terse, modest way, he neglects to mention, as several contemporary reports do, that he had shaved off his facial hair, disguised himself as an Indian, and "went through the Town, and was spoken to several Times by the Indians, but was not discovered, as he was dress'd like one of them."[4]

Samuel Williams, in his *Natural and Civil History of Vermont*, published fifty years after the raid, says that Rogers went to reconnoiter the town with "two Indians who understood the language of the St. Francois tribe."[5] Rogers himself only mentions that he took Lieutenant Turner and Ensign Avery, both of them, not coincidentally, officers of the Mohegan Indian company. The St. Francis Indians were not all pure Abenakis in the sense of their ethnic homogeneity. To no small degree they were composed of refugees, and the descendants of refugees, from several New England tribes defeated in earlier wars with the English. Thus, Turner and Avery, and no doubt Rogers to a lesser extent, would have been able to communicate with the essentially Algonkian-speaking inhabitants.

At 2:00 A.M. Rogers, Turner and Avery returned to the detachment, and prepared for the attack on the village. Despite the fact that his whaleboats had been discovered at Missisquoi Bay, and that the disguised trio of officers probably warned some of the village's women and children to seek refuge from the coming attack, the Rangers achieved a nearly complete surprise. Only a handful of Indian men had heeded the warnings of the mysterious strangers by preparing a defense in the village's council house.[6] When the attack finally came, it was far from being a complete annihilation. French accounts agree on no more than 40 Indians killed, some of them women and children—perhaps an unavoidable result considering the darkness and confusion that prevailed during the pre-dawn attack, and the subsequent firing of the lodges, which "consumed many of the Indians who had concealed themselves in the cellars and lofts," in Rogers' words.

Secrecy had been paramount all throughout the launching of the expedition. General Amherst had ordered Rogers "to go and destroy the St. Francois Indian Settlements and the French settlements on the South Side of the River St. Lawrence, not letting any one but Major Rogers know what about or where he was going."[7] Rogers himself notes in his *Journals:*

"That this expedition might be carried on with the utmost secrecy after the plan of it was concerted the day before my march, it was put into public orders, that I was to march a different way, at the same time I had private instructions to proceed directly to St. Francis."

What was this "different way"? *The Boston Gazette* of October 8, 1759 provides the answer. In reporting the Rangers' expedition leaving Crown

Point on September 13, the paper mentions its supposed destination, "Rogers having tis said set out with a design to join General Johnson who had march'd with 3000 Men to attack Oswegatchi."

It was the perfect ruse: at Oswegatchie, on the St. Lawrence River, stood both the French post of La Galette and Abbe Piquet's Iroquois mission village, a prime target of the overall British campaign of 1759. Had it been the actual destination of Rogers and his men, they would have been required to cross 100 miles of uncharted Adirondack mountain terrain, strange geography even to the Rangers. The landscape of gloomy timber, bogs, ridges and gorges would have swallowed them up, and they would not have been heard from for weeks. That the Oswegatchie deception worked among the Anglo American forces is revealed in Connecticut soldier Robert Webster's diary entry of September 13: "Still at Crown Point. This day the scout set out for Suagothel 500 in number. They took thirty days provisions with them under the command of Major Rogers."[8]

Webster, like many of his fellow Provincials, was a terrible speller, writing "Sllatoga" when he meant "Saratoga," "Albone" for "Albany," and so on. Because "Oswegatchie" was often shortened to "Swegatchie" by Amherst himself, or "Soegatzy" by the French, Webster's corruption of the name into "Suagothel" is understandable.[9] Another Connecticut Provincial, Christopher Comstock, wrote it as "Ca Chochee." Other men throughout the years penned equally distorted versions: "Swegatsy" (Captain Stoddard in 1753[10]), "Sweegassie" (a Commissioner of Indian Affairs at Albany in 1754),[11] "Swagochea" (Peter Pond in 1760),[12] "Suergachy" (Daniel Claus in 1758);[13] and, in the one version sounding the most like Webster's, "Swagotha," in *The New Hampshire Gazette* of June 8, 1779.

Unfortunately, historians such as John Cuneo and novelists such as Kenneth Roberts never made the Oswegatchie/"Suagothel" connection. In Ranger history, "Suagothel" became a deliberately mythical place invented by Robert Rogers, rather than the deplorable misspelling of Robert Webster it actually was.[14]

G.Z.

1. Actually October 3, 1759.
2. "The Diary of Abel Spicer," in *History of the Descendants of Peter Spicer*, compiled by Susan Spicer Meech and Susan Billings Meech, F. H. Gibson, Boston, 1911, entry of July 30, 1758.
3. Called "Odanak" by its Indian population.
4. *The Boston Gazette*, November 25, 1759.
5. Samuel Williams, *A Natural and Civil History of Vermont*, Burlington, 1809, p. 430.
6. Gordon M. Day, "Rogers' Raid In Indian Tradition," *Historical New Hampshire*, Vol. XVII, June 1962, p. 9.
7. Jeffrey Amherst, *The Journal of Jeffrey Amherst*, edited by J. Clarence Webster, Chicago, Illinois, 1931, entry of September 12, 1759.
8. "The Diary of Robert Webster, April 5th to November 23rd, 1759," *The Bulletin of the Fort Ticonderoga Museum*, Vol. II, Number 4, July 1931.
9. E. B. O'Callaghan, *Documents Relative to the Colonial History of the State of New York*, Vol. X, Albany, New York, 1858, p. 203.
10. E.B. O'Callaghan, *The Documentary History of the State of New York*, Vol. II, Albany, New York, 1849, p. 626.
11. Ibid., p. 559.
12. "The Journal of Peter Pond," in *The Journal of American History*, Vol. I, No. 1, 1907, p.93.
13. *Daniel Claus' Narrative of His Relation with Sir William Johnson*, Society of the Colonial Wars in the State of New York, 1904, p. 5.
14. For a further look at this issue, see Gary S. Zaboly, "What Was Suagothel?," *French and Indian War Magazine*, Vol. 3, No. 1, July 1986, pp. 5-10.

WAITE
GARY ZABOLY
1993

The Starvation March

AT least forty-nine of Rogers' men died during the St. Francis expedition: nineteen killed by the French and Indians, and about thirty dying from starvation and exposure in the wilderness during the long retreat back. Another ten men had been taken captive by the pursuing enemy, and of these only two are known to have made it back home in 1760.

That so many—a good number of veteran Rangers among them—died during the retreat should not be surprising: the Rangers were constantly on the move through a trackless country choked with mountains and swamps, and strangely devoid of game. Such was southeastern Quebec Province and northern Vermont and New Hampshire in the fall of 1759. A great part of the march took place in cold, rainy weather, the men racing in vain against the oncoming frost and snows while a vengeful enemy nipped at their heels. Exhaustion, lameness, sickness, hunger and starvation were inevitable.

Rogers' men had long been used to stretching their usually meager trail rations. At their base camps they were supplied with any number of eatables, among them: chunks of dried and salted beef and pork, rice, peas, corn meal, sausages, biscuits (hardtack), chocolate, sugar, ginger (thought to prevent scurvy and purify water), and rum. Ranger excursions generally allowed little time for hunting: what they ate they had to carry on their backs, or obtain by raiding the enemy's livestock or food supplies.

When the Rangers' reserve provisions were seized by the French and Indians in the hidden whaleboats at Missisquoi Bay, Rogers knew that St. Francis would have to supply his men with the food they would need for the return trek. However, all that the Rangers could find at the Abenaki village were stores of corn, most of it undoubtedly in kernel form. Among these was probably a quantity of parched corn, a powdery substance that was a common, lightweight trail food for Indian warriors. A spoonful of this, combined with a drink of water, would expand in the stomach and give one the sensation of having digested a full meal.[1] This "food" was called "roheeheg," "yohicake," or "no-cake" by the New England Indians. Mexican Indians called it "pinole."[2] Sometimes it was mixed with dried maple sugar or honey, or spiced with roots, herbs, or salt.

A mix of cornmeal and water was also used to make round cakes, about six inches in diameter, usually referred to as "Indian bread" or "ash cake. "These were cooked on flat stones, under ashes, the dough sometimes protected from dirt by wrapping it in green leaves.

Unfortunately, after the raid a lot of room in the Rangers' packs was filled not with corn but with St. Francis loot. By the time they had reached Lake Memphremagog, eight days after leaving the destroyed Abenaki village, their provisions had nearly run out, and they were forced to split into "small companies of twenties" in order to hunt and forage.[3]

What they found was a wilderness unusually barren of wildlife. Bears, squirrels, pigeons and other animals had been strangely flocking to the New England coastal towns all throughout 1759, especially in September, the very month Rogers' expedition had left Crown Point.[4] Some prognosticators saw these migrations as omens of a very hard winter coming on; and indeed this turned out to be the case, with the victorious British army particularly suffering in its winter quarters in occupied Quebec. Blame might also be laid on an environment still affected by the ecological disruptions of earlier natural disasters, such as the drought and vast forest fires in northern New England in 1754, and a severe earthquake the following year.

It became so desperate for the Rangers that the mere sight of an owl made the mens' mouths water, as one veteran of the retreat later recalled: "Instantly the bird was brought down by the eager shot of several of the men, dissected and distributed by the well known method of 'Who shall have this?'

"He shared a leg, which he devoured without cooking, and by this refreshment the party were enabled to continue the march, and at length arrived without the loss of a man."[5]

Another detachment, whittled down to ten men, considered itself lucky when it shot and divided a partridge. Muskrats, beavers, frogs, fish, beech leaves, tree bark, roots, lily pads, and mushrooms helped sustain other parties. Leather from the straps of their knapsacks, bullet pouches, and powder horns, or from their moccasin flaps, as well as lumps of tallow, provided temporary nourishment for many.[6] Some of the Rangers even cooked the Indian scalps they had taken at St. Francis, for the little circles of flesh they carried.

Cannibalism, in fact, became part of the folklore of Rogers' raid and retreat; but it had a real grounding in fact. For instance, some of the Rangers in the party led by Lieutenant George Campbell had "lost their senses; whilst others, who could no longer bear the keen pangs of an empty stomach, attempted to eat their excrements. What leather they had on their cartouch-boxes, they had already reduced to a cinder, and greedily devoured. At length, on the 28th of October, as they were crossing a small river, which was in some measure dammed up by logs, they discovered some human bodies not only scalped but horribly mangled, which they supposed to be those of some of their own party. But this was not a season for distinctions. On them, accordingly, they fell like Cannibals, and devoured part of them raw; their impatience being too great to wait the kindling of a fire to dress it by. When they had thus abated the excruciating pangs they before endured, they carefully collected the fragments, and carried them off.

"This was their sole support, except roots and a squirrel, till the 4th of November, when Providence conducted them to a boat on the Connecticut river which Major Rogers had sent with provisions to their relief, and which rendered tolerable the remainder of their journey to No. 4, where they arrived on the 7th of November."[7]

One lone Ranger eventually limped out of the White Mountains, the sole survivor of a party that had unfortunately strayed into it, and came to the settlements below, "and in his bloody knapsack was a piece of human flesh, of which for the last eight days he declared he had eaten to support the flickering spark of light that now but faintly burned within him."[8]

Ranger Sergeant David Evans, with one of the parties back on the Connecticut, was still plagued with guilt when he told his own particular story to an historian many decades later. One night, he said, he stole a peek into another Ranger's knapsack and discovered it held three human heads. He cut a piece from one of them, broiled it and ate it. He swore "that he would die with hunger, before he would do the same again. He said that when their distresses were greatest, they hardly deserved the name of human beings."[9]

When Rogers arrived at the junction of the Wells and Connecticut rivers, and found none of the food he had requested General Amherst to send there in anticipation of the Rangers' arrival, he had no choice but to hurry on himself to Fort Number Four to get relief. The rest of his command would have to fend for themselves at the junction, hunting what game they could find, and forage for "ground-nuts and lilly roots."

Ranger Peter Lervey went two miles up from the mouth of the Wells River and killed a bear and some smaller animals. A dozen miles to the south, Captain Joseph Waite had pushed on with a small squad, and "was so fortunate as to kill a deer, which gave good refreshment to himself and his famishing men; and having reserved a small portion for themselves, he hung up the remainder conspicuously on a tree, or trees, for the relief of their suffering associates, who were expected soon to be passing that way. That there might be no misunderstanding, he cut his name, Waite, on the bark of a tree from which he had suspended a portion of his life-saving venison; and as this tree stood on the bank of a small river, just above its union with the Connecticut, the grateful men, in remembrance of their kind benefactor, called it Wait's River, by which name it has ever since been known."[10]

Another Ranger settled down for "a very good breakfast" of a cooked small trout and the hand of a deceased black Ranger.[11]

After four grueling days of rafting down the Connecticut, Robert Rogers, barely able to stand on his feet, finally made it to Fort Number Four on October 31, 1759, and ordered provision-laden canoes to be sent back up the river to relieve his weak and hungry Rangers.

"A Ballad of Rogers' Retreat" was written by an anonymous New Englander not long after the event; and two of the stanzas grimly describe the fate of the Rangers after they had escaped the wrath of the pursuing French and Indians:

> "The rest there fled into the wood
> where they did dy for want of food
> these men did grieve and mourn and cry
> wee in these howling woods must dy
>
> few of these men rogers there fore
> conducted safe to numbr four
> the rest behind did their remain
> wheir they with Hunger firce were slain"[12]

G.Z.

1. John Heckewelder, *The Travels of John Heckewelder in Frontier America*, edited by Paul A. W. Wallace, University of Pittsburgh Press, Pittsburgh, 1985, p. 117.
2. Horace Kephart, *Camping and Woodcraft*, MacMillan, New York, 1917, p. 153.
3. *South Carolina Gazette*, December 1, 1759.
4. *Boston Evening-Post*, September 10, 1759.
5. Epaphras Hoyt, *Antiquarian Researches*, Greenfield, Massachusetts, 1824, p. 306.
6. Nathaniel Bouton, *The History of Concord, New Hampshire*, Concord, 1856, p. 200.
7. Thomas Mante, *The History of the Late War in North America*, 1772, Research Reprints, New York, 1970, pp. 223-224.
8. John H. Spaulding, *Guide to the Historical Relics of the White Mountains*, New Hampshire, 1858, p. 36.
9. Luther Roby, *Reminiscences of the French War*, Concord, New Hampshire, 1831, pp. 180- 181. Kenneth Roberts' *Northwest Passage* manages to excuse the Rangers' cannibalism by attributing it to only one man of the party, Corporal Crofton, who, in the novel, is caught with an Abenaki's head in his knapsack. Crofton is deemed insane, and Rogers eventually has him tied up and led like a bear. The 1940 movie version has Crofton leaping over a cliff edge rather than face the wrath of Rogers (Spencer Tracy), who has just discovered him gnawing at the head.
10. Silas McKeen, *A History of Bradford, Vermont*, Montpelier, Vermont, 1875, p. 39.
11. *The Vermont Quarterly Gazette*, edited by Abby Maria Hemenway, No. III, Vermont, April 1862, p. 272.
12. "A Ballad of Rogers' Retreat, 1759," edited by Seymour Bassett, *Vermont History*, 1978, p. 22.

September 18, 1759: "At night Capt Butterfield of the Provincials who went with Major Rogers returned to the opposite Shore with seven men who were taken ill. He left Major Rogers on the 15th in Otter River waiting for a dark night or an opportunity to pass the two french Sloops & a Schooner which were laying off the Otter River; they sailed toward Crown Point. At night Capt Williams who was taken very ill returned with two men of the Royals, 2 Gages, 3 Rangers, 2 Provincials & 13 Indians." (Amherst, p. 170)

September 19, 1759: "A man of the Royal Highlanders and one of Montgomerys were brought in by seven Rangers, this makes 40 men returned of Rogers, two officers included, the two men wounded by a firelock accidentally going off. The Royal Highlander dyed soon after he was brought in." (Amherst, p. 170)

October 3, 1759: "Lt McMullin came in with six men from Major Roger's Party whom he left nine days since, he imagines, about forty miles beyond Mischiscove Bay. The Lt had lamed himself so Major Rogers had to send him back and intended to pursue the orders I had given him and thought of returning by No 4." (Amherst, p. 174)

October 4, 1759: "Sent Lt Stevens to No 4 to take up some provisions to Well's River, in case Major Rogers should return that way." (Amherst, p. 175)

October 25, 1759: "Capt Brewer returned with the 100 Rangers I had sent with Capt Dalyel. He had been to look for M Rogers' boats; found them all burned by the Enemy." (Amherst, p. 184)

October 30, 1759: "Lt Stevens who I had sent to meet Mr Rogers returned. Said there was no probability he would ever come back that way, but he should have waited longer." (Amherst, p. 185)

November 2, 1759: "Mons de Cadillac said M Rogers Party had burnt the settlement at St Francis, killed some Indians, women & children. I fancy he is mistaken about the women & children & that some Indians & Canadians had assembled & attacked M Rogers in his retreat at night." (Amherst, p. 186)

November 7, 1759: "Capt Ogden of Schuylers arrived from Mr Rogers Party bringing me a Letter from the Major of the 1st November from No 4 acquainting me that the 22nd day after his departure from Crown Point he got to the Village of St. Francis, reconnoitred it, attacked it next morning before sun rise. On the right, left, & center found all asleep; some tryed to get off by water whom forty of his party demolished & drowned. About seven the Affair was over, the Houses burnt, & he killed about 200, took 20 women & children, 15 of which he let go, & brought away 2 Indian boys and 3 girls, & retook five English Prisoners. Capt Ogden was wounded & six men were slightly wounded, one Stockbridge Indian killed. He then consulted with his officers as he knew his boats were way laid & all determined to return by No 4. He marched the whole body together 8 days and then separated. One of his Partys was attacked two days after they separated & had seven men taken, but two got off again at night. He arrived at No 4 with Capt Ogden & one man on the 31st Oct and immediately sent away Provisions in Canoes to meet the others who were behind. In the Afternoon an Indian came in with a Scalp & some hours after he had been in Camp, Indian like, he said he had left 16 of Mr Rogers party at the Otter River. I immediately sent away an officer of Rangers with three whale boats." (Amherst, p. 188)

November 8, 1759: "The officer of Rangers returned from Otter River; brought in four Indians, two Rangers, a German woman who had been taken at German Flats, two young Squaws, and a young Indian boy. They were loaded with wampum & fine things they took at St Francis." (Amherst, p. 189)

November 21, 1759: "Lt Campbell brought me a letter from Mr Rogers, he had got only 51 men of his party in but expected more." (Amherst, p. 193)

When Amherst submitted his official reports to Prime Minister Pitt, he obviously drew heavily on his daily journal. For all of the previous entries, the information in the report to Pitt is less detailed than that in the journal.

However, for this date (November 21), Amherst adds some information that is not in the journal: "Lt. Dunbar, of Gage's, was attacked two days after they separated, by a Party that pursued, the Lieut: was supposed to be killed, with Lt. Turner of the Indians, who was his Guide, & ten Men of Gages; eight men of his Party made their Escapes . . . ." (Pitt, Volume II, p. 224)

News of Rogers' attack traveled quickly. On October 8, Brigadier Robert Monckton wrote to William Pitt from Quebec, "I am this day informed that a Party from His [Amherst's] Army, have fallen upon, and destroyed a French and Indian Settlement called St. Francis in Lake St. Pierre, as some of the Indians were not returned home from the French Army, they escaped." (Pitt, Volume II, p. 178)

On November 7, Massachusetts Provincial lieutenant William Henshaw, encamped "near Crown Point," also made note in his orderly book of Rogers' return. "News that Majr. Rogers is come into No. 4 with his party, Lost but 1 Man." (Henshaw, p. 251)

On November 19, Ensign Ebeneezer Dibble of Connecticut wrote of Rogers return, "number 4. An account of the Skout of mager Rodgers at Sant fransways from Crownpint 22 day one oure and 3 quars distroying the Plase and Takeing the Plonder 30 days in the martching Back to numr 4 The Indans that was kild 140 Savadgs and Burt the houses and—& in them 6 Prisners and one of our Capt Tinas and 20 lost By the way Coming Back and 20 the Enymis disstroy[ed]." (Dibble, p. 322)

In his book published in 1772, Thomas Mante included some interesting details of the raid: "On the 8th of November, whilst the General was still at Crown-Point, he received the following account of the expedition on which he had sent Major Rogers, against the Indians of Saint Francois. It was not till the twenty-second day after his departure that the Major came in sight of the place; and, by this time, his party, from various accidents in the march, was reduced to one hundred and forty-two men. However, he reconnoitred the town about eight in the evening, in hopes of discovering an opportunity suitable to his numbers; and, agreeably to his wishes, finding the Indians in a high dance, returned to his party at two, and marched them to within five hundred yards of the town; where he eased them of their packs, and formed them for the attack. At half an hour after sun-rise the next morning he surprised the town, when the inhabitants were all fast asleep, and fell on them so instantaneously, that they had not time to recover themselves and take arms for their defence. Some attempted to get to the waters, and, by that means, make their escape; but they were quickly pursued by about forty of the Major's people, who sunk them and their boats. The remainder, in the mean time, set fire to all the houses except three, in which there was corn, which Major Rogers thought proper to reserve for the use of his party; and the flames consumed many of the Indians, who had concealed themselves in the cellars and lofts. By seven o'clock in the morning, the business was completely over. In this short period the English killed at least two hundred Indians, and took twenty of their women and children; but they brought away but five. The rest were permitted to go where they pleased. Five English captives were likewise delivered from slavery, and taken under the protection of their countrymen; and all this with the loss of only one Indian killed, and Captain Ogden and six men wounded. Major Rogers being informed by his prisoners that a party of three hundred French, with some Indians, were about four miles below him on the river, and that his boats were, besides, waylaid, and having reason to believe this information was true, as they told him the exact number of his boats, and named the place where he left them, he thought proper to consult with his officers concerning a retreat, especially as he had the same reason to believe that a party of two hundred French, and fifteen Indians, had, three days before he attacked the town, gone up the river to Wigwam Martinique, on a supposition of its being the place he intended to attack. The result of this deliberation was, that there was no safe way to return but by No. 4, on the Connecticut river: upon this he marched his detachment that rout for eight days successively, in one body, till, provisions growing scarce, near Amparamagog-Lake, he thought best to divide his people into small parties, giving guides to each, with orders to rendezvous at the discharge of the Amansook river into the Connecticut river, as he there expected to receive a supply of provisions from the army, in consequence of a request he, on his setting out, had made to the General for that purpose; for it was impossible for him, at that time, to tell which way he should be obliged to return. He then continued his march, and arrived at No. 4, on the 5th day of November; fatigue, cold, and hunger, with the continual prospect of starving, being his constant attendants. But great as the sufferings of this party were, they were nothing when compared with those of another, commanded by Lieutenant George Campbell, then of the Rangers. These were, at one time, four days without any kind of sustenance, when some of them, in consequence of their complicated misery, severely aggravated by their not knowing whither the route they pursued would lead, and, of course, the little prospect of relief that was left them, lost their senses; whilst others, who could no longer bear the keen pangs of an empty stomach, attempted to eat their own excrements. What leather they had on their cartouch-boxes, they had already reduced to a cinder, and greedily devoured. At length, on the 28th of October, as they were crossing a small river, which was in some measure dammed up by logs, they discovered some human bodies not only scalped but horribly mangled, which they supposed to be those of some of their own party. But this was not a season for distinctions. On them, accordingly, they fell like Cannibals, and devoured part of them raw; their impatience being too great to wait the kindling of a fire to dress it by. When they had thus abated the excruciating pangs they before endured, they carefully collected the fragments, and carried them off. This was their sole support, except roots and a squirrel, till the 4th of November, when Providence conducted them to a boat on the Connecticut river, which Major Rogers had sent with provisions to their relief, and which rendered tolerable the remainder of their journey to No. 4, where they arrived on the 7th of November." (Mante, pp. 221-224)

There are also a number French accounts of the raid which add further perspectives. Perhaps the most succinct is that contained in an *Extract of a journal kept at the army commanded by the late Lieutenant-General de Montcalm*: "Towards the fore part of October a detachment of about 200 men of Mr. Arebert's army, headed by Captain Rogers, having had the boldness to traverse a pretty extensive tract of country, covered with timber, succeeded, under cover of the surprise, in burning the Indian village of St. Francis; M. de Bourlamaque was fully advised of his march; he had caused the removal of the canoes which Rogers had been obliged to abandon beyond Isle aux Noix, and expecting him to return by the same route, had him watched, at the passage, by a strong detachment of Canadians and Indians; but Rogers had anticipated all that, and had, in consequence, resolved to reach Orange by another way; he could not, however, escape the pursuit of a party of 200 Indians who rushed to vengeance. Want of provisions rendered it necessary for him to divide his force in small platoons, in order more easily to find subsistence; the Indians massacred some forty and carried off 10 prisoners to their village, where some of them fell a victim to the fury of the Indian women, notwithstanding the efforts the Canadians could make to save them." (*D.R.C.H.S.N.Y.*, Volume 10, p. 1042)

Pouchot adds the following information about the St. Francis Raid: "Major Rogers . . . formed a raiding party of about 400 men, who had been to our mission of St. Francois on Lac St. Pierre. He found this Abenaki village entirely denuded of its warriors. He killed around thirty women & old people and brought back a number of young men prisoner. Since he lacked provisions, he divided his troops into several bands to return to Fort George. They all perished of exposure or hunger in the forest, except that of Rogers himself, who fortunately had a Loup Moraigan as a guide. He only returned with 21 men, however, all of them haggard & emaciated." (Pouchot p. 249) Brian Dunnigan, editor of Pouchot's *Memoirs,* states that Pouchot uses the term "Loup Moraigan" to describe Rogers' Stockbridge Mohican Rangers. (Pouchot p. 249)

The French missionary, Abbe Maurault, left this account of the destructions of Saint Francis: "Rogers left Crown Point, the evening of the 4th September, with a detachment of 200 men. He headed toward Missisquoi Bay, which was about 100 miles from St. Francis. As there were always Abenaki scouts and Canadians on Lake Champlain, he proceeded with caution in order to escape being surprised. The 9th, in the evening, he was camped on the right bank of the river when an accident occurred which forced him to part with some of his troops. A barrel of powder having taken fire, Captain Williams and seven soldiers were wounded. Therefore he sent 50 men from his detachment to accompany the wounded to Crown Point, while he continued his journey. On the 24th he reached Missisquoi Bay. He hid his whaleboats stocked with food against the return of the expedition, left two Iroquois to guard them, and entered the forest heading for St. Francis.

"Bourlamarque was very much absorbed by General Amherst's activities on Lake Champlain and often sent detachments to make reconnaissance. On the 25th one of these detachments entered Missisquoi Bay and discovered Rogers' whaleboats; they seized these and carried the news to their commander at Isle aux Noix. Bourlamarque, knowing that by this route one could easily reach the Abenaki village of St. Francis, informed M. de Vaudreuil of the fact. The governor, however, completely absorbed by the misfortune which was about to descend on the colony, neglected this matter.

"On the 26th, the two Iroquois, who had been left to guard the whaleboats, rejoined Rogers and informed him that 400 men, French and Abenakis, had seized the whaleboats, and that 200 men were pursuing him. This news was a bit upsetting, for he saw it would now be impossible to return by Lake Champlain. He immediately sent Lieutenant McMullen and ten men through the forest to Crown Point, to inform General Amherst of what had happened, and to ask him to send provisions to the head of the Connecticut River, at the junction of the Ammonoosuc River, so that he might return by that route. Then, with all haste, he continued his march toward St. Francis. The evening of the 3rd he arrived at the St. Francis River, about fifteen miles above the Indian settlement. He forded the river to the right bank, and at eight o'clock, on the evening of the 4th, he was about one mile from the village. He halted at this point to rest his troops, and with Lieutenant Turner and Ensign Avery went out to examine this section.

"On this day the village was celebrating the arrival of some warriors who had returned from an excursion against the English. The savages had organized a grand ball. They danced until four o'clock when they retired to their houses completely exhausted, never dreaming that the enemy was at their gates.

"Since 1754, the hatred of the Abenakis for the English had redoubled. They attacked them constantly and had taken many scalps. On this day one saw 600 or 700 English scalps hanging from poles.

"Rogers returned to his troops at two in the morning and had them advance to within five or six hundred yards of the village. Then he prepared for the attack. He divided his men into several parties, and, a half hour before sunrise, he burst upon the village while all the savages were deep in sleep. The soldiers rushed into the houses and killed all who fell into their hands, without regard to age or sex. This was a frightful massacre. When the sun rose the scene was terrifying. Rogers himself would have been touched with compassion had it not been for the scalps of his compatriots, which filled his heart with rage and made the soldiers continue to slaughter the women and children. About 200 savages were killed; 20 women and several children were taken prisoners. [*Note by Abbe Maurault:* Among these prisoners was the wife of Joseph-Louis Gill and her two children, Antoine and Xavier. This woman was killed by the soldiers during the journey; later the two children were set free and returned to St. Francis.]

"After the massacre the soldiers set fire to the village. All the lodges, the greater part of the houses and the church were destroyed by fire.

"This was the first church of the Abenakis at St. Francis; it had existed for more than fifty years; it possessed many priestly ornaments, magnificent sacred vases and many precious objects. All was destroyed as well as the Mission records and a rich collection of manuscripts. The little silver statue, which had been given to the mission in 1701 by the canons of Chartres, was saved and taken to New England. The silver shirt in a reliquary *(la chemise d'argent en reliquaire)* also given by the same canons, was destroyed.

"The booty taken by Rogers consisted of $933, a great quantity of Wampum necklaces and some provisions.

"Rogers left St. Francis the 5th, and started for New England by going up the St. Francis River. After marching eight days his provisions were exhausted. Therefore he divided his troops into various bands so that they could more easily find game and sustain life, ordering them all to meet at the junction of the Ammonoosuc.

"However, after Rogers' departure from St. Francis, several Abenaki warriors returned to the village and decided to pursue the English. Two days after the English had separated into bands, the savages fell upon one led by Ensign Avery. Seven soldiers were taken prisoner, but two of them soon escaped. Another band of twenty men, led by Lieutenants Turner and Dunbar, was also attacked. These twenty men were all killed or taken prisoner.

"Rogers, after a difficult and fatiguing march of many days, reached the Connecticut River with the men that remained. Unfortunately he did not find the provisions at the spot agreed upon. Several men from Charlestown had come there with provisions, on the order of General Amherst, and, after waiting there several days, had returned to Charlestown.

"In this desperate situation, Rogers had recourse to roots to appease their hunger. This meagre nourishment saved the soldiers' lives. He built a raft of dry wood, on which he embarked with Captain Ogden, a soldier and a young captive. In this way he was able to reach Charlestown. Some canoes, loaded with provisions, were at once sent to the head of the river for the detachment, who with this aid was able to reach Charlestown, after having lost several men in the forest." (Roberts, Volume II Appendix, pp. 43-46)

As soon as my party were refreshed, such as were able I marched to Crown Point, where I arrived Dec. 1, 1759, and upon examination found, that, since our leaving the ruins of St. Francis, I had lost three Officers, viz. Lieut. Dunbar of Gage's Light Infantry, Lieut. Turner of the Rangers, and Lieut. Jenkins of the Provincials, and forty-six serjeants and privates.

In a letter to General Amherst dated December 12, 1759, Rogers adds some additional thoughts and insights on the Saint Francis Raid: "The Misfortunes attending my Retreat from Saint Francois causes me great uneasiness, the Brave men lost I most heartily lament, and fear your Excellency's censure as the going against the place was my own proposal, and that I shall be disappointed of that Footing in the Army which I have long endeavor'd to merit.

"Lieut. Stephen's Misconduct in coming off with the Provisions hurt me greatly, and was the cause of so many perishing in the woods, I put him under an Arrest, & also confined a Serjeant of Genl. Gage's Regiment for aspersing my Character by spreading a False Report that I took away from Dunbar's party Provisions and gave it away to others who had loaded themselves with Plunder after the Place was destroyed.

"I hope Your Excellency will be pleased to order a Court Martial that I might have justice done me as I have nothing to depend on but my character." (Roberts, Volume II Appendix, p. 12)

On December 24, Amherst wrote two letters to Rogers in response to his above remarks: "I am Sorry to see you have so many Men Missing; this will, I hope, be a Lesson to all other Partys to Secure Provisions and themselves, instead of loading themselves with Plunder, by which they must be Lost, if an Enemy pursues."

In response to Rogers' request to try Stephens and the sergeant from Gage's, Amherst wrote: "I Disapprove entirely of Lieut. Stephen's Conduct, and I have Wrote to Brigr. General Gage, that if the Evidences can be Collected without prejudicing the Service, it would be but right that a Court Martial should sit for his Trial.

"I Have no Objection neither to One on Mr. Gage's Serjeant, if You absolutely Chuse it, but the Evidences are so dispersed, that before they can be Assembled, a great deal of time must Elapse . . . but to tell you the truth, I do not think there is any Occasion for One, as, from anything I have heard of the Affair, it is not in the power of that Serjeant to hurt your Character." (Roberts, Volume II Appendix, p. 35)

On April 1, 1760, Rogers wrote to General Gage asking him to expedite Stephen's court-martial, which had not yet been convened:

"Lieut Stephens that was in A Rest and went to Number four from Albany is Come Here to have his Tryal, the Evidences are all Present.

"I beg Sir you would please to order a Court Martial for that purpose the Evidences belongs to Number four wants to Return as soon as possible to Plant their Grain." (Clements Library Collection: Gage Papers, American Series)

Several of the witnesses were deposed on April 3, and on April 23, the court-martial itself was finally held. Lieutenant Stephens testified that he had halted at the "Cohass," or Cohase Intervals. He was afraid that his provisions might be lost if he ventured farther north, due to rough water in the Connecticut River. This was three miles by land and five miles by water from the junction with the Wells River, where he was ordered to meet Rogers' party. Ranger Andrew Wansant testified that there was no rough water between the Cohass and the junction with the Wells River. Stephens further testified that he had sent parties overland to the appointed spot every day to await Rogers' arrival. There was a conflict in the testimony about how long Stephens actually waited once they reached the Cohass—between three days and five days. The court found Stephens "Guilty of a Neglect of Duty, in not taking his Canoes up to Wells Rivers according to his Orders from General Amherst & that therefore he be suspended during the General's pleasure." (Roberts, Volume II Appendix, p. 39)

The trial transcript is reproduced in the special Appendix to *Northwest Passage* on pages 35-39. Kenneth Roberts feels that at least part of the blame for Lieutenant Stephens' early departure is due to Lieutenant McMullen's estimate of how fast Rogers' party would be traveling, and suggests that McMullen should have been court-martialed as well.

The Rangers at that place were all dismissed before my return, excepting two companies, commanded by Captains Johnson and Tute,* with whom I found orders left by the General for me to continue at that garrison during the winter, but had leave, however, to go down the country, and to wait upon his Excellency at New York.

On November 23, 1759, Amherst noted in his journal: "I reduced the six companies of Rangers to two. Shall keep the officers on pay in case they may be wanted." (Amherst, p. 193)

After giving my return to the general, and what intelligence I could of the enemy's situation, he desired me, when I had leisure, to draw a plan of my march to St. Francis; and then by his order, I returned by the way of Albany; which place I left the 6th of February 1760, with thirteen recruits I had inlisted; and the 13th, on my way between Ticonderoga and Crown Point, **my party was attacked by about sixty Indians, who killed five, and took four prisoners. I with the remainder,**

*Capt. Tute who had been taken prisoner, was returned by a flag of truce, while I was gone to St. Francis.

made my escape to Crown Point, from whence I would have pursued them immediately; but Col. Haviland, the commanding officer there, judged it not prudent, by reason the garrison at that time was very sickly,* I continued at Crown Point the remainder of the winter.

> The passage in bold letters was omitted from the Dublin edition, but appears in the London edition. Without it, the sentence makes little sense.
>
> Of this incident, Amherst wrote to Pitt in a letter of March 8: "on the 12th Feby. Major Rogers was going from Tionderoga to Crown Point, fourteen Sutlers Slays were passing, and were attacked five miles from Tionderoga, by about 70 Indians, or French dressed like Indians, the Major pushed on and got to Crown point, most of the others returned to Tionderoga, two Indians and a Squaw who were with Rogers, were killed, four Rangers and a Slay-man carried off, one Slay broke and four Horses destroyed, a Chest of Arms broke open, and some taken away, with some Money of Major Rogers's. There was no escort with the Slays, Rogers had sixteen Men, but were unarmed . . . ." (Pitt, Volume II, pp. 263-264)
>
> These unarmed Rangers were the new recruits, under the command of Sergeant Thomas Beaverly, who was among the captured. Rogers himself did not start out with the convoy, but caught up with it just prior to the attack. He hurried on to Crown Point, where he asked Colonel Haviland for permission to organize an immediate pursuit. Haviland refused, saying that he did not have enough manpower to risk it. This action took place near the same spot where Rogers had ambushed the French sleighs during the opening phase of The First Battle on Snowshoes in January, 1757. (Cuneo, *Rogers*, pp. 119-120)

On the 31st of march, Capt. James Tute, with two regular officers and six men, went out a scouting, and were all made prisoners; the enemy was not pursued, on account of the sickness of the garrison.

The same day I received from General Amherst the following letter.

"Sir, *New York, March 1*, 1760.

"The command I have received from his Majesty, to pursue the war in this country, has determined me, if possible, to complete the companies of Rangers that were on foot last campaign; and as Captain Wait called upon me yesterday, and represented that he could easily complete the one he commands in the colony of Connecticut and the Province of the Massachuset's Bay, I have furnished him with beating orders for that purpose, as also with a warrant for 800 dollars on account of that service.

"This day I have wrote to Capt. John Stark in New Hampshire, and Capt. David Brewer in the Massachuset's Bay, inclosing to each of them a beating order for the respective provinces; and I herewith send you a copy of the instructions that accompany the same, by which you will see they are ordered, as fast as they get any number of men, to send them to Albany. I am, Sir,

Your humble servant,

To Major Rogers. *Jeff. Amherst."*

My answer to the above.

"Sir, *Crown Point, March* 15, 1760.

"I received your Excellency's letter, dated the 1st instant, together with a copy of your instructions to Capt. John Stark and Capt. David Brewer, whereby I learn that they are to be at Albany by the 1st of May next with their companies. Since I received intelligence from your Excellency that the Rangers are to be raised again, I have wrote to several of my friends in New England, who will assist them in compleating their companies; and as many of the men belonging to the two companies here were frost-bitten in the winter, and others sick, many of whom I judged would not be fit for service the ensuing campaign, I employed Lieut. M'Cormack, of Capt. William Stark's company (that was with Major Scott) Lieut. John Fletcher, and one Holmes, and sent them recruiting the 20th of February for my own and Captain Johnson's company, and advanced them 1100 dol-

*My own sley was taken with 1196 £. York currency in cash, besides stores and other necessaries; 800 £. of this money belonged to the crown, which was afterwords allowed me, the remaining 396 £. was my own, which I entirely lost.

lars. These three recruiters I do not doubt will bring good men enough to complete to us here; so that those who are frost-bitten may be sent to hospitals, and those unfit for duty discharged, or otherwise disposed of, as your Excellency shall direct.

There being so few Rangers fit for duty here, and those that are much wanted at this place, has prevented me from proposing any tour to the French and Indian settlements in pursuit of a prisoner, which may, I believe, be easily got at any time, if sent for. I am, Sir,

Your Excellency's
most obedient humble servant,
To General Amherst. *R. Rogers."*

A letter from General Amherst,

"Sir, *New York,* 9th *March,* 1760.

"As I have not heard that either of the Jacobuses, who each commanded a company of Stockbridge Indians the last campaign, are returned from their captivity, I would have you write (if you think Lieut. Solomon capable of and fit for such a command) to him, to know if he chooses to accept of the same; but it must be on condition of bringing to the field none but good men, that are well inclined, and that are hale and strong. Whatever number he or any of his friends can raise that will answer this description, I will readily employ this summer, and they shall meet with all the encouragement their services shall merit. All others that are to old or too young, I shall reject, nor shall I make them any allowance of payment, altho' they should join the army; so that, in order to prevent his having any difference with these people, it will behove him to engage none but what shall be esteemed fit for the service; he must also observe to be assembled with them at Albany by the 1st of May at furthest, from which day he and they shall be entitled to their pay, that is, for so many as shall be mustered there, and for no more; he must likewise take care that every man comes provided with a good firelock, and that they be always ready to march at a moment's warning, wherever they are ordered to, in default of which they shall forfeit their pay that shall be due to them at that time. All this you will explain to him particularly, and so soon as you receive his answer, inform me thereof. As an encouragement to enter the service upon the foregoing conditions, you may assure him also, that if he conforms to them in every respect, and that he and his men prove useful, they shall be better rewarded than they have yet been.

"Captain Ogden having solicited me for a company of Rangers, assured me that he could raise and complete a very good one in the Jersies; I have given him a beating order for that purpose, and instructions similar to those I sent you a copy of in my last for Captains Stark and Brewer, and have also granted him a warrant for four hundred dollars, on account of the bounty-money, to be as usual stopped out of the first warrants for the subsistence of that company. I am, Sir,

Your humble servant,
To Major Rogers. *Jeff. Amherst."*

This Captain Ogden is the same one who, as a member of the New Jersey Provincials, volunteered for the St. Francis Raid, was shot through the body, and recovered enough to accompany Rogers to No. 4 on the raft. As a reward for his heroic service, he was commissioned to lead a company of Rogers' Rangers in the 1760 campaign."

My Letter to the General.

Crown Point, 20th *March,* 1760.

"Sir,

"I observe the contents of your Excellency's letter of the 19th, and shall take particular care to let Lieut. Solomon know every circumstance relative to his being employed the next summer, and to advise your Excellency as soon as I hear from him. He has already informed me he would be glad to engage with some Indians.

"Mr. Stuart, the Adjutant of the Rangers, who is at Albany, I have desired to go to Stockbridge, to deliver Solomon his orders, and to explain them properly to him.

"I am heartily glad that your Excellency hath been pleased to give Captain Ogden a company of the Rangers, who, from the good character he bears, I doubt not will answer your expectations.

"Inclosed is a sketch of my travels to and from St. Francis. I am, Sir,

Your Excellency's most humble servant,

To General Amherst. *R. Rogers."*

This map still survives in a private collection. David Bosse, former curator of maps at the Clements Library, says that it is a "Highly detailed manuscript map showing relief and drainage in the area of northern Vermont and southern Quebec. Rogers' route from Missisquoi Bay to the Odanak village and return to the British post on the Connecticut River (No. 4) is shown." (Bosse, p. 58)

The General's Letter to me.

"Sir, *New York*, 9th *April*, 1760.

"I am to own the receipt of your letters of the 15th and 20th ultimo, and to approve what you therein mention to have done for completing your and Capt. Johnson's company; as also your having sent Adjutant Stuart to Stockbridge, to deliver Solomon his orders, and to explain them properly to him. This will avoid all mistakes, and enable you the sooner to inform me of Solomon's intentions, which I shall be glad to know as soon as possible.

"I thank you for your sketch of your travels to and from St. Francis, and am, Sir,

Your very humble servant,

To Major Rogers. *Jeff. Amherst."*

Soon after this I had the pleasure of informing the General that the Stockbridge Indians determined to enter the service this year; but as many of them were out a hunting, that they could not be collected at Albany before the 10th of May; and that the recruits of the ranging companies began to assemble at Crown Point.

May 4, 1760. This day Serjeant Beverly, who had been taken prisoner, and made his escape, came in seven days from Montreal to Crown Point. He had lived at the Governor's (Monsieur de Vaudreuil) house, and brought the following intelligence, which I immediately transmitted to the General, viz.

"That about the 10th of April, the enemy withdrew all their troops from Nut Island, excepting 300, which they left there to garrison the place, under the command of Monsieur Bonville: that the enemy also brought from the island one half of the ammunition they had there, and half of the canon: that the enemy had two frigates, one of 36 guns, the other of 20 guns, that lay all winter in the River St. Lawrence, and some other small vessels, such as row-galleys, & c. that all the troops of France and Canada went down to Jecorty the 20th of April, except those left to garrison their fort, which was very slenderly done, together with all the militia that could be spared out of the country, leaving only one man to two females to sow their grain, where they were assembled by Monsieur Levy, their General, with an intent to retake Quebec:* that ninety six men of the enemy were drowned going down to Jecorty: that he saw a man who was taken prisoner the 15th of April, belonging to our troops at Quebec: that this man told him our garrison there was healthy; and that Brigadier General Murray had 4000 men fit for duty in the city, besides a post of 300 hundred men at Point Levy, which the enemy attempted to take possession of in the month of February last, with a considerable body of troops, and began to fortify a church at or near the Point, but that General Murray sent over a detachment of about 1000 men, which drove the enemy from the post, and took a Captain, with about thirty French soldiers, prisoners, and fortified the church for his own conveniency: that the General has another post on the north-side of the river at Laurat, a little distance from the town, in which he keeps 300 men: that there is a line of block-houses well fortified all round the land-side of the town, under cover of the cannon: that the breast-work of fraziers is extended from one block-house to another, as far as those houses extend: that they heard at Quebec of the enemy's coming, but were not in the least concerned: that a detachment from Quebec surprised two of the enemy's guards, at a place called Point de Treamble, each guard consisting of fifty men, and killed or took the most part of them. One of those guards were all grenadiers."

*This place, the capital of all Canada, had been taken by the English troops last year, under the command of General Wolfe.

He moreover reports, "That two more of our frigates had got up the river, and that two more men of war were near the Island of Orleans: that the French told him that there was a fleet of ten sail of men of war seen at Gaspee Bay, with some transports, but put back to sea again on account of the ice; but as they had up different colours, they could not tell whether they were French or English: that the beginning of May the enemy was to draw off 2000 of their men to Nut Island, and as many more to Oswagotchy: he heard that they did not intend to attack Quebec, except the French fleet gets up the river before ours: that 100 Indians were to come this way, and set out about the fifth of May; the remainder of the Indians were at present gone to Jecorty: that General Levy, the Attawawas, and Cold Country Indians, will all be in Canada by the beginning of June, ten Sachems being sent by the French last fall, to call those nations to their assistance: that of great number had deserted to the French from the battalion of Royal Americans at Quebec, which the French have engaged in their service:; but that they were to be sent off, under the care of Monsieur Boarbier, up to Attawawas River, to the French colony betwixt the lakes and the Mississipi River: that the most part of the enemies Indians are intent on going there; and that a great number of French, especially those who have money, think to save it by carrying it to New Orleans: that he saw at Montreal two Rangers, Reynolds and Hall, that were returned by Col. Haviland deserted last fall: that they were taken prisoners near River-head Block-house, when after cattle: that two more Rangers are to be here in ten days with fresh intelligence from Montreal, if they can possibly make their escape: that Monsieur Longee, the famous partisan, was drowned in the River St. Laurence, a few days after he returned with the party that took Captain Tute: that the Indians have a great eye to No. 4. roads, as they say they can get sheep and oxen coming here from that place: that he heard Gen. Murray had hanged several Canadians lately, that were carrying ammunition out of Quebec to the enemy: that the two Captains Jacobs are still in Canada; the one taken with Captain Kennedy is on board a vessel in irons, the other ran away last fall, but was returned, having froze his feet, and is at Montreal."

The famous partisan refered to was Ensign Jean-Baptiste Levrault de Langis de Montegron, Rogers' old adversary from the Battle on Snowshoes. It was a truly unfortunate end for such a brave and active soldier.

A few days after this, I went down the Lake Champlain, to reconnoitre Nut Island, and the garrison there, the landing places, & c. On my return from that service to Crown Point, I had an order from General Amherst to repair to Albany, the head-quarters, as fast as possible.

I set out, in obedience to this order, the 19th of May, and waited upon the General at Albany the 23rd, and gave him all the information I could, in regard to the passage into Canada by the Island de Noix, or Nut Island, and likewise that by Oswego and La Galette.

The General being acquainted by an express, that Quebec was then besieged by the French, informed me of his intentions of sending me with a party into Canada, and if the siege of Quebec was continued, to destroy their country as far as possible, and by constantly marching from one place to another, try to draw off the enemy's troops, and prolong the siege till our vessels got up the river. He strongly recommended, and ordered me to govern myself according to the motions of the French army; to retreat if they had raised the siege, and in case, by prisoners or otherwise, I should find the siege still going **me**, to harass the country, tho' it were at the expence of my party. I had at the same time the following instructions from him in writing.

In the London edition of the *Journals*, page 173, the word "me" is written as "on," which makes much more sense.

"Major Rogers, you are to take under your command a party of 300 men, composed of 275 Rangers, with their proper officers, and a subaltern, two serjeants, and twenty-five men of the Light Infantry regiments; with which detachment you will proceed down the lake, under convoy of the brig, where you will fix upon the safest and best place for laying up your boats, which I imagine one of the islands will best answer, while you are executing the following services.

"You will with 250 men land on the west-side, in such manner that you may get to St. John's (without the enemy at the Isle au Noix having any intelligence of it) where you will try to surprize the fort, and destroy the vessels, boats, provisions, or whatever else may be there for the use of the troops at the Isle au Noix. You will then march to Fort Chamble, were you will do the same, and you will destroy every magazine you can find in that part, so as to distress the enemy as much as you can. This will soon be known at the Isle au Noix, and you must take care not to be cut off in your retreat; for which reason, when you have done all you think practicable on the western-side; I judge your best and safest retreat will be, to cross the river and march back the east-side of Isle au Noix. When you land on the west-side, you will send such officer with the fifty Rangers, as you think will best answer their intended service, which is, to march for Wigwam Martinique, to destroy what he may find there and on the east-side of the river, and afterwards to join you, or to retreat in such manner as you will direct him. You will take such provisions as you judge necessary with you, and fix with Capt. Grant (who shall have orders to wait for your return) the places where he may look out for you when you come back.

"You will take your men as light with you as possible, and give them all the necessary caution for the conduct, and their obedience to their officers; no firing without order, no unnecessary alarms, no retreating without an order; they are to stick by one another and nothing can hurt them; let every man whose fire-lock will carry it have a bayonet; you are not to suffer the Indians to destroy women or children, no plunder to be taken to load your men, who shall be rewarded at their return as they deserve.

May 25, 1760. *Jeff. Amherst."*

By giving Rogers this mission, Amherst hoped that "This may alarm the Enemy & may force some of their Troops away from Quebec." (Amherst, p. 203) As for Rogers' prospects for success, he wrote "If he can get by Isle au Noix without some of their Party discovering him he will effect this easily." (Amherst, p. 204)

With the above instructions the General delivered me a letter directed to General Murray at Quebec, desiring me to convey it to him in such manner as I thought would be quickest and safest.

Having received these instructions I returned to Crown-Point as fast as possible, and about the beginning of June set out from thence with a party of two hundred and fifty men* down Lake Champlain, having four vessels, on board of which this detachment embarked, putting our boats and provisions into them, that the enemy might have less opportunity of discovering our designs.

Colonel Haviland reported to Amherst that Rogers departed on June 1 with a party of 303 officers and men. (Amherst, p. 207)

The 3rd, I landed Lieut. Holmes with fifty men at Misisquey Bay, and gave him proper directions agreeable to my orders from the General, informing him that one of the sloops should cruise for him till his return, which upon signals that were given him would take him on board, upon which he was to join me or wait on board 'till my return, as the situation of affairs might direct him. Here likewise I sent the letter I had received from the General to Brigadier Murray, through the woods, and gave the following instructions to the Officer I intrusted with it, viz.

Instructions for Sergeant Beverly
of his Majesty's Rangers.

"You are hereby directed to take under your command, these three men, viz. John Shute, Luzford Goodwin, and Joseph Eastman, and march them from Misisquey Bay, to which place

*The Stockbridge Indians who had been mustered at, and now marched from Albany, and who were to be part of the detachment of 300, agreeable to the General's orders, had not arrived at Crown Point at the time of my embarkation, but were ordered to follow after and join me.

you will be convoyed by Lieut. Holmes with a party I have sent there for a particular purpose; you are to land there in the night time, as otherwise you may be discovered by a party from the Isle au Noix; you will steer your course about north-east, and make all the dispatch you possibly can with the letter in your charge to Quebec, or to the English army at or near that place, and deliver it to Brigadier Murray, or to the officer commanding his Majesty's forces in or upon the river St. Lawrence. A sketch of the country will be delivered you with these orders, that you may the better know the considerable rivers you have to cross, betwixt Misisquey Bay and Quebec. The Distances are marked in the draught, as is the road I travelled in last fall, from Misisquey Bay to St. Francis, which road you will cross several times, if you will keep the course I before directed. The rivers are so plainly described in the plan, that you will know them when you come to them. The River St. Francis is about half way of your journey, and is very still water, and may be easily rafted where you cross it; but lower down it is so swift and rapid that you must not attempt it. Shedoir River you will likewise be obliged to pass on a raft; it is swift water for some miles from its mouth; you had better examine it well before you attempt to cross it. As soon as you pass this river, steer your course about east, leaving Point Levy on your left hand, and fall in with the River St. Lawrence, near the lower end of the island of Orleans, as it may be possible that General Murray may have encamped the army either at the isle of Orleans or the isle of Quodoa; therefore you are not to depend on finding at once the exact place of his encampment, but are positively ordered to look out for the English fleet, and the first line of battle ship you see, you are to venture on board, as I think it not possible the enemy should have any large ships there, and whatever English ship you get on board of, will convey you directly to General Murray, when you will deliver him the verbal message I told you. You may apply to the general for fifty pounds who will pay it to you, and also give you proper directions to join me as soon as you have rested yourself from your march. I wish you a good journey, and am, Your's, & c.

To Serjeant Beverly. *Robert Rogers."*

As soon as I had dispatched the two parties beforementioned, I, with the remainder, crossed Lake Champlain to the west-side, and the 4th in the morning got into my boats, and landed with about 200 men, about twelve miles south of the island Noix, with an intent to put in execution the General's orders to me of May 5th with all speed. Capt. Grant sent the two sloops to attend, which I ordered to cruise further down the lake than where I landed, and nearer to their fort, to command the attention of the enemy till I could get into their country. I lay still all the 5th, there being a heavy rain, and the bushes so wet that both we and our provisions would have been greatly exposed by a march.

In the afternoon of this day, several French boats appeared on the Lake, which were discovered by the two sloops, as well as by my party on the shore. These boats continued as near as they could to our vessels without endangering themselves, till after dark. Concluding their boats would cruize the whole night to watch the motions of our sloops, I imagined it would be a prudent step to send the sloops back to Capt. Grant, the commander of these vessels, who lay near Mott Island; I accordingly went to the sloops in a boat after dark, and ordered them to return. The enemy, who kept all night in their boats, having a strict look-out, discovered where I landed, sent a detachment from the island next morning to cut off my party. I discovered their intentions by my reconnoitring parties, who counted them as they crossed from the fort in the morning in their boats, to the west-shore, and informed me that they were 350 in number. I had intelligence again when they were about a mile from us. Half after eleven they attacked me very briskly on my left, having on my right a bog, which they did not venture over, thro' which, however, by the edge of the lake, I sent seventy of my party to get round and attack them in the rear. This party was commanded by Lieut. Farrington. As soon as he began his attack, I pushed them in the front, which broke them immediately. I pursued them with the greatest part of my people about a mile, where they retired to a thick cedar swamp, and divided into small parties. By this time it rained again very hard. I called my party immediately together at the boats, where I found that Ensign Wood of the 17th regiment was killed, Capt. Johnson wounded through the body, a second shot thro' his left arm, and a third in his head. I had two men of the Light Infantry, and eight Rangers, wounded, and sixteen Rangers killed. We killed forty of the enemy, and recovered about fifty fire-locks. Their commanding officer, Monsieur la Force, was mortally hurt, and several of the party were likewise wounded. After the action I got the killed and maimed of my detachment together in battoes, returned with them to the Isle a Mot, near which the brig lay. I dispatched one of the vessels to Crown Point, on board of which was put the corpse of Mr. Wood, but Capt. Johnson died on his passage thither; this vessel I ordered to bring more provisions. I buried the rest of the dead on an island, and then began to prepare for a second landing; being joined about this time by the Stockbridge Indian Company, I was determined at all adventures to pursue my orders, settled the plan of landing, and left the following instructions with Capt. Grant, viz.

"You will be so good as to fall down the lake with your vessels as soon as possible, as far as the Wind Mill Point, or near where you lay at anchor the last time I was with you, and cruize near it for two or three days, which will be the only method I can think of that has any appearance of attracting the attention of the enemy till I get into their country; as soon as I observe or think you pretty near the Wind Mill Point, I shall land with my party on the west side opposite to the north-end of the Isle a Mot, in the river that runs into the bay which forms itself there, and from thence proceed to execute the General's orders. If they do not attack me in my march till I compleat my design, you may be certain I shall come back on the east-side, and endeavor to join you near the Wind Mill Point, or betwixt that and the Isle a Mot. When I arrive, the signal that I will make for your discovering me, will be a smoak and three guns, at a minute's interval each from the other, and repeated a second time, in half an hour after the first; but if the enemy should attack me on my march before I get to the place I am ordered, which I believe they will do, in case I am worsted I shall be obliged to come back on the west-side, and shall make the before mentioned signals betwixt the Isle a Mot and the place where I had the battle with the enemy the 6th instant. It is uncertain when I shall be at either shore; so that I would recommend it to you not to come back south of the Isle a Mot till my return, as a contrary wind might prevent your getting in with your vessels to relieve me. I send you Sergeant Hacket and ten Rangers, to be with you in my absence, as we this day agreed. If Lieutenant Darcy comes down in season to go with me, I shall leave Ensign Wilson with you; but if Darcy should not come till after I land, you'll be pleased to take him under your direction, as well as all those that may come with him to join me; tho' I would recommend it not to send any party to the island, to take a prisoner, till the fifth day after my landing, as the loss of a man from us may be of very bad consequence. Lieut. Holmes has appointed between the eleventh and sixteenth day after his landing for his return to Misisquey Bay, and from the eleventh to the sixteenth, as before mentioned; I should be glad the sloop might cruize for him at the place he appointed to meet her. I am, Sir,

Your humble servant,

R. Rogers."

I cannot but observe with pleasure, that Mr. Grant, like an able officer, very diligently did all that could be expected of him for the good of the service, carefully attending with his vessels till my return from this second excursion, on which I embarked with two hundred and twenty men, officers included, and landed the 9th of June, about midnight, on the west shore opposite the Isle a Mot, from thence marched as fast as possible to St. John's, and came to the road that leads from it to Montreal, about two miles from the fort, the evening of the 15th. At eleven o'clock this night, I marched with an intent to surprise the fort, to within four hundred yards of it, where I halted to reconnoitre; which I did, and found they had more men than I expected. The number of the centries within the fort were seventeen, and so well fixed, that I thought it was impossible for me to take the place by surprise, especially as they had seen me, and fired several guns accordingly. I left it at two o'clock, and marched down the river to St. d'Etrese; at break of day I reconnoitred this place, and found that the enemy had in it a stockaded fort, defensible against small arms.

> This is Fort Saint Therese, located on the Richelieu River at the point where the river became navigable into Lake Champlain without further rapids or portages. (*D.H.S.N.Y.*, Volume 1, p. 59). When first constructed in 1665, it was described as being rectangular in shape, approximately 150 feet by 90 feet. The walls were fifteen feet high, and there was a bastion in each corner. Fort Saint Therese was three miles from Fort Saint Jean (Saint Johns) and nine miles from Fort Chambly. (Cadieux, p. 18)

I observed two large store-houses in the inside, and that the enemy were carting hay into the fort. I waited for an opportunity when the cart had just entered the gate-way, run forward, and got into the fort before they could clear the way for shutting the gate. I had at this time sent different parties to the several houses, about fifteen in number, which were near the fort, and were all surprised at the same instant of time, and without firing a single gun. We took in the fort twenty-four soldiers, and in the houses seventy-eight prisoners, women and children included; some young men made their escape to Chamblee. I examined the prisoners, and found I could not proceed to Chamblee with any prospect of success; therefore concluded my best way was to burn the fort and village, which I did, together with a considerable magazine of hay, and some provisions, with every battoe and canoe, except eight battoes which I kept to cross the river, and these we afterwards cut to pieces: we also killed their cattle, horses & c. destroyed their waggons, and every other thing which we thought could ever be of service to the enemy.

> Ensign Donald Stuart of the 27th Regiment, who was behind the French lines under a flag of truce at the time, reported that before burning the houses, Rogers allowed the inhabitants to remove their bedding. (Cuneo, *Notes*, p. 82)
>
> A document in the Bouquet Papers entitled *Intelligence Received at Presque Isle* dated June 26, 1760, records, "Major Rogers has destroyed St Therese, a Village of 14 or 15 Houses, between St. Jeane and Chambli; none of the Enemy were killed, as he surprised, and by that means had an opportunity of saving the Women and Children, whom he set at Liberty, bringing of the Men, 34 or 35 Prisoners." (Bouquet, Volume IV, p. 611)

When this was done, I sent back the women and children, and gave them a pass to go to Montreal, directed to the several officers of the different detachments under my command. I continued my march on the east side of Lake Champlain, and when passing by Misisquey Bay, opposite the Isle au Noix, my advance-party, and the advance-party of about 800 French, that were out after me from their fort, engaged with each other; but the body of the enemy, being about a mile behind their advance-party, retreated, to my great satisfaction. I pursued my march with all possible speed: and the same day, being the 20th day of June, arrived at the lake opposite where the vessels lay; and as I had sent a few men forward to repeat the signals, the boats met us at the shore. We directly put on board, the enemy soon after appeared on the shore where we embarked. I had not at this time any account from Lieutenant Holmes, either by prisoners or otherways.

Upon examination the prisoners reported (some of them had been at the siege of Quebec) "that the French had lost five hundred men there; and that they retreated after twelve days bombarding and cannonading, and came to Jack's quarters, where General Levy left five hundred men, being composed of a picquet of each battalion of the army, and that there were four hundred Canadians who staid voluntarily with them; that the rest of the army was quartered by two's and three's on the inhabitants, from there to St. John's. In Montreal there are about a hundred and fifty troops, and the inhabitants do duty. That in Chamblee Fort are about one hundred and fifty men, including workmen; and the remnants of the Queen's regiment are in the village. That there are twelve cannon at St. John's, and about three hundred men, including workmen, who are obliged to take arms on any alarm. That at the Isle au Noix there are about eight hundred stationed, besides the scouts between that and Montreal. That there are about an hundred pieces of cannon there." This is the substance of their report, in which they all agree, and which, with an account of my proceedings, I transmitted to the General.

In his journal for June 10, 1760, Amherst recorded the following account of this scout: "I had a Letter from Major Rogers of the 7th that on the 3rd he landed Lt Holmes with 50 men on Mischiscoui bay, & a Sergt and 3 men with my letter for Br Murray. On the 4th he landed in the evening with 200 men on the West Side. The 5th he imagined he was discovered by the Enemy. Lay still all day as he was within 8 miles of Isle au Noix. On the 6th his Party came in & told him the Enemy being about 300 chiefly Indians were coming to him. About half an hour after eleven they attacked him briskly & he was not behindhand in returning it. About one the Enemy retreated & he pursued them half a mile to Cedar Swamp which he thought better not to engage in. He thinks he killed about 50, but they took their killed & wounded except three Indians, two of which he scalped, & the third the Enemy had saved him that trouble. He brought off Capt Johnson of the Rangers very badly wounded, who afterwards dyed, and Ensign Wood of Moncktons with seven men of that Regt & three others were killed & nine wounded, all of which he brought off & returned in his batteaus to the Vessels. If the Enemy has not taken a prisoner, they will be greatly alarmed, and cant but tell it but it may be an advanced party of the Army that is on the lake." (Amherst, p. 208)

On the 21st I put the twenty-six prisoners on board one of the vessels, with fifty men of my detachment, and ordered her to proceed to Crown Point, and tarried with the other vessels to cover Mr. Holmes's retreat, who joined us the same evening, without having succeeded in his enterprise, missing his way by falling down a river that falls into Sorrel, instead of that called Wigwam Martinic, which empties itself into St Lawrence at Lake St. Francis. I arrived at Crown Point the 23rd of June, and encamped my Rangers on the east-shore, opposite the fort.

Thomas Mante gave the following account of this series of operations by Rogers' Rangers: "his Excellency, on the 25th of May, ordered Major Rogers, with a detachment of three hundred men, to enter Canada, that thereby the attention of the enemy might be drawn off, so as to prolong the siege of Quebec, till the men of war, expected to its relief, could get up the river St. Lawrence. As the most effectual method of executing this service, Major Rogers was ordered to fall down the Lake Champlain, under convoy of a brig; then, after laying up his boats, to proceed by land, with two hundred and fifty men, on the west side of the Lake; get to St. John's, if possible, without the knowledge of the enemy; surprise the fort at that place, and destroy the vessels, boats, provisions; in a word, all the stores he might find laid up there for the use of the French troops at the Isle-Aux-Noix. From hence he was to proceed to Fort-Chamble, on the same business. In short, he was to destroy every magazine he could meet with, and distress the enemy every other way as much as possible, particularly by sending fifty rangers against Wigwam-Martinique. But, as his arrival and operations must soon be known at the Isle-Aux-Noix, he had likewise directions to keep, in his return, on the east side of that island, in order to prevent his retreat being cut off. In the mean time Lieutenant Grant was to continue cruizing in the brig, to be ready to receive the Major on his return. To these orders was added a strong injunction, that neither women nor children should be injured.

"On the 4th of June, Major Rogers landed at the place he was ordered, and proceeded on his expedition by land; but, two days after, he was attacked by a party of about three hundred and fifty French, and had sixteen men killed, and ten wounded. The enemy had about forty killed and wounded. After this affair Major Rogers thought proper to return to the Isle de la Motte, where Lieutenant Grant was waiting for him in his brig. Here, being joined by the Stockbridge Indian company, he determined, at all events, to set forward again and pursue his orders; first agreeing with Lieutenant Grant upon the place where the latter should cruize to receive him, and on some signals, by which he might know him at his arrival there. On the 9th of June the Major landed, about midnight on the west shore opposite the Isle de la Motte, and from thence proceeded, as fast as possible, to St. John's; so that by the 15th, in the evening, he found himself but about two miles from the road that led to it from Montreal: the enemy, however, being too alert to be surprised, he marched down the river side to St. Therese, where there was a stockaded fort, defensible against small arms only. The French being carting hay, he seized the opportunity of a cart's being just entering the gate, and rushed into the fort before the carriage could be got clear enough of the gateway to let the gate be shut. The garrison, consisting of twenty-four soldiers, were made prisoners, with seventy or eighty inhabitants, women and children included. From the intelligence he gained here, the attack on Fort Chamble appeared impraticable. This determined the Major to burn the village and the fort, and destroy every thing in them that could be useful to the enemy. The women and children he sent to Montreal, with proper passes to protect them from any scouting party. He then continued his march on the east side of Lake Champlain; but, as he was passing by Missisquey-Bay, opposite to the Isle-Aux-Noix, his advanced party was attacked by an advanced detachment of the French, whose main body being about a mile in their rear, they thought proper to fall back upon it, whilst the Major seized the opportunity of pursuing unmolested his march with all possible expedition. On the 20th of June he arrived at that part of the banks of the lake, opposite to which Lieutenant Grant was to keep cruizing to receive him; and the lieutenant performed his duty on this occasion, so much like an officer, particularly by keeping a diligent look-out for the appointed signals, that the Major and his party were arrived but a few minutes before Lieutenant Grant had them on board, to the great mortification of a large body of French, who immediately after made their appearance. Lieutenant Holmes, who commanded the fifty rangers sent to Wigwam-Martinique, missed his way by going down a river which falls into the Sorel, instead of that called Wigwam-Martinique, which empties itself into the river St. Lawrence, at Lake Saint Francis." (Mante, pp. 297-300)

The following letter I received from General Amherst, dated at Canijoharry, June 26, 1760.

"Sir,

"Colonel Haviland sent me your letter of June 21, which I received last night, and saw with pleasure, you was returned without the loss of a man of your party, and that you had done every thing that was prudent for you to attempt with the number of men you had under your command. From the situation the enemy is now in, by being forced back to their former quarters, on Governor Murray's having obliged them to abandon their cannon, and raise the siege of Quebec, I hope Lieutenant Holmes will return with equal success as you have done. I am, Sir,

Your humble servant,

To Major Rogers. *Jeff. Amherst."*

I remained at Crown Point with my people without effecting anything considerable, more than in small parties reconnoitring the country about the fort, while every thing was got in readiness for embarking the army the 16th of August;

which was done accordingly, having one brig, three sloops, and four rideaus, which latter were occupied by the royal train of artillery, commanded by Lieut. Colonel Ord. Our order of march was as follows, viz.

In his orderly book on July 3, 1760, Massachusetts major John Hawks notes one incident that probably was looked upon with dismay by many of the Rangers: "A sutler of ye Rangers, and George Morris of the market who had their liquor stove in this day to quit Crown Point immediately. If they are thereafter found in camp or any post between this and Albany they will be whipped and drummed out. All sutlers and market people are desired to take notice that they will be served the same way or worse if they are found to make soldiers drunk or doing anything else contrary to orders." (Hawks, p. 81)

On July 11, Samuel Hodge, a New Hampshire Provincial, makes an interesting entry in his orderly book: "Majr Rogers will order piles of wood to be gathered about 60 yards in front of his Encampment and Set fire Every Evening at Picket mounting ye fires are to be kept till Day break" (Hodge, p. 304)

A radeau "was a wide, partially enclosed floating barge with both sails and oars, mounting heavy guns which would be used in defense of a fleet of bateaux." The lower sides inclined slightly outward, while the upper sides sloped inward at a steep angle. This made it impossible for an enemy to board, and at the same time enclosed and protected the crew. (Bellico, *Sails and Steam*, pp. 35 & 77) The Reverend John Cleaveland described a radeau as follows: "went to see the famous Rideaux to carry Cannon on ye Water, some call it Ord's Ark, it is planked up higher than a man's Head Shelving in or arching inwards to defend ye men's Bodys & Heads with Port-Holes for ye Cannon." (Cleaveland, October 9, 1758) Thomas Ord was Amherst's artillery commander.

The radeau "Land Tortoise," deliberately sunk by the British in the fall of 1758 to preserve it over the winter, has recently been discovered on the bottom of Lake George near Fort William Henry. Connecticut captain Henry Champion remarked in his journal for October 7, 1758, "A large floating thing has been building about three weeks, looks as if it would be done in one week more." He goes on to describe the Land Tortoise as "51 feet in length, about 16 or 18 feet wide, straight flat bottom, flaring waist about 5 feet high, then turns with an elbow . . . timber and covers over ye top all but a streak about 8 or 9 feet wide." (Champion, 431, Zarzynski, pp. 7-8, and Starbuck, pp. 187-191) A radeau was a truly unique looking vessel.

Six hundred Rangers and seventy Indians in whale-boats in the front, commanded by Major Rogers as an advance-guard for the whole army, all in a line a-breast, about half a mile a-head of the main body, followed by the light infantry and grenadiers in two columns, two boats a-breast in each column, commanded by Col. Darby.

On August 13, 1760, Amherst made the following comment in his journal about the Indians accompanying the expedition: "The Indians in the whaleboats made strange appearances." (Amherst, p. 229)

The right wing was composed of Provincials, commanded by Brigadier Ruggles, who was second in command of the whole army. The left was made up of New Hampshire and Boston troops, commanded by Col. Thomas. The seventeenth and twenty-seventh regiments, with some few of the Royals, that formed the center column, were commanded by Major Campbell of the 17th regiment. Col. Haviland was in the front of these divisions, between that and the light infantry, and grenadiers. The royal artillery followed the columns, and was commanded by Colonel Ord, who had for his escort, one Rhode Island regiment of Provincials. The sutlers, & c. followed the artillery. In this manner we rowed down the lake forty miles the first day, putting ashore where there was good landing on the west-side and there encamped.

The day following we lay by. The 18th, the wind blowing fresh at south, orders were given for embarking, and the same day reached a place on the west shore, within ten miles of the Isle a Mot, where the army encamped. It having blown a fresh gale most part of the day, some of my boats split by the violence of the waves, and ten of my Rangers were thereby drowned.

The 19th we set sail again early in the morning, and that night encamped on the north-end of the Isle a Mot.

The 20th, before day, the army was underway, with intention to land; having but twenty miles to go, and having the advantage of a fair wind, we soon came in sight of the French fort, and about ten in the morning Col. Darby, with the granadiers and Light Infantry, and myself with the Rangers, landed on the east-shore, and marched and took possession of the ground opposite the fort on that side, without the least opposition. Having done this, an officer was sent to acquaint Col. Haviland (who, with the remainder of the army, was at the place where we landed) that there was not the least danger to apprehend from the enemy. The next day we began to raise batteries, and soon after to throw some shells into the garrison. About the 24th a proposal was made for taking the enemy's vessels, three of which were at anchor a little below the fort, and some of their rideaus likewise. It was introduced by Col. Darby, who was ordered to take the command of the party appointed for this service, which consisted of two companies of Regulars, and four companies of my rangers, with the Indians. We carried with us two haubitzers and one six-pounder and silently conveying them along thro' the trees, brought them opposite the vessels, and began a brisk fire upon them, before they were in the least apprised of our design, and, by good fortune, the first shot from the six-pounder cut the cable of the great rideau, and the wind being west, blew her to the east-shore, where we were, and the other vessels weighed anchor and made for St. John's, but got all a-ground, in turning a point about two miles below the fort. I was, by Col. Darby, ordered down to the east-shore with my Rangers, and crossed a river about thirty yards wide, which falls into Lake Champlain from the east. I soon got opposite the vessels, and, by firing from shore, gave an opportunity to some of my party to swim on board with their tomahawks, and took one of the vessels; in the mean time Col. Darby had got on board the rideau, and had her manned, and took the other two; of which success he immediately acquainted Col. Haviland, who sent down a sufficient number of men to take charge of and man the vessels, and ordered the remainder of the Rangers, Light Infantry, and Grenadiers, to join the Army that night, which was accordingly done; and about midnight the night following the French troops left the island, and landed safe on the main; so that next morning nothing of them was to be seen but a few sick, and Col. Haviland took possession of the fort.

The second day after the departure of Monsieur Bonville and his troops from the island, Mr. Haviland sent me with my Rangers to pursue him as far as St. John's Fort, which was about twenty miles further down the lake, and at that place I was to wait the coming of the army, but by no means to follow further than the fort, nor run any risk of advancing further to Montreal. I went in boats, and about day-light got to St. John's, and found it just set on fire. I pursued, and took two prisoners, who reported, "That Monsieur Bonville was to encamp that night about half-way on the road to Montreal; and that he went from St. John's about nine o'clock the night before; but that many of their men were sick, and that they thought some of the troops would not reach the place appointed till the middle of the afternoon." It being now about seven in the morning, I set all hands to work, except proper guards, to fortify the log-houses that stood near the lake side, in order that part of my people might cover the battoes, while I, with the remainder, followed Monsieur Bonville, and about eight o'clock I got so well fortified, that I ventured our boats and baggage under the care of 200 Rangers, and took with me 400, together with the two companies of Indians, and followed after the French army, which consisted of about 1500 men, and about 100 Indians, they had to guard them. I was resolved to make his dance a little the merrier, and pursued with such haste, that I overtook his rear-guard about two miles before they got to their encamping ground. I immediately attacked them, who, not being above 200, suddenly broke, and then stood for the main body, which I very eagerly pursued, but in good order, expecting Monsieur Bonville would have made a stand, which however he did not chuse, but pushed forward to get to the river, where they were to encamp, and having crossed it, pulled up the bridge, which put a stop to my march, not judging it prudent to cross at a disadvantage, inasmuch as the enemy had a good breast-work on the other side, of which they took possession; in this pursuit, however, we considerably lessened their number, and returned in safety.

In the evening Mr. Haviland came in sight, and landed at St. John's. As soon as he came on shore, I waited upon him, and acquainted him with what I had done, & c. and that I had two prisoners for him; he said it was very well, and ordered his troops there that night, and next day went down the river Sorriel, as far as St. d'Etrese, were he encamped, and made a strong breast-work, to defend his people from being surprised. I was sent down the river Sorriel, to bring the inhabitants under subjection to his Britannick Majesty, and went into their settled country in the night, took all their priests and militia officers, and sent some of them for the inhabitants. The first day I caused all the inhabitants near Chamblee to take the oaths of allegiance, & c. who appeared glad to have it in their power to take the oaths and keep their possessions, and all were extremely submissive. Having obliged them to bring in their arms, and fulfilled my instructions in the best manner I could, I joined Col. Darby at Chamblee, who came there to take the fort, and had brought with him some light cannon. It soon surrendered, as the garrison consisted only of about fifty men. This happened on the first of September.

On the 2nd, our army having nothing to do, and having good intelligence both from Gen. Amherst and Gen. Murray, Mr. Haviland sent me to join the latter, while he marched with the rest of the army for La Pierre. The 5th in the morning I got to Longville, about four miles below Montreal, opposite where Brigadier Murray lay, and gave him notice of my arrival, but not till the morning of the 26th, [The London edition says the 6th, which is obviously correct.] by reason of my arrival so late.

By the time I came to Longville the army under the command of Gen. Amherst, had landed about two miles from the town, where they encamped; and early this morning Monsieur de Vaudreuil, the governor and commander in chief of all Canada, sent out to capitulate with our General, which put a stop to all our movements, till the 8th of September, when the articles of capitulation were agreed to, and signed, and our troops took possession of the town-gates that night. Next morning the Light Infantry, and Granadiers of the whole army, under the command of Col. Haldiman, with a company of the royal artillery, with two pieces of cannon, and some haubitzers, entered the town, retaking the English colours belonging to Pepperel's and Shirley's regiments which had been taken by the French at Oswego.

Thus at length, at the end of the fifth campaign, Montreal and the whole country of Canada was given up, and became subject to the King of Great Britain; a conquest perhaps of the greatest importance that is to be met with in the British annals, whether we consider the prodigious extent of country we are hereby made masters of, the vast addition it must make to trade and navigation, or the security it must afford to the northern provinces of America, particularly those flourishing ones of New England and New York the irretrievable loss France sustains thereby, and the importance it must give the British crown among the several states of Europe: all this, I say, duly considered, will, perhaps, in its consequences render the year 1760 more glorious than any preceding.

And to this acquisition, had we, during the late war, either by conquest or treaty, added the fertile and extensive country of Louisiana, we should have been possessed of perhaps the most valuable territory upon the face of the globe, attended with more real advantages than the so-much-boasted mines of Mexico and Peru, and would have for ever deprived the French, those treacherous rivals of Britain's glory, of an opportunity of acting hereafter the same perfidious parts they have already so often repeated.

On the 9th General Amherst informed me of his intention of sending me to Detroit, and on the 12th in the morning, when I waited upon him again, I received the following orders.

By his Excellency Jeffery Amherst, Esq; Major General and commander in chief of all his Majesty's forces in North America, & c. & c. & c.

To Major Rogers, commanding his Majesty's independent companies of Rangers.

"You will upon receipt hereof, with Capt. Waite's and Capt. Hazen's companies of Rangers under your command, proceed in whale-boats from hence to Fort William-Augustus, taking along with you one Joseph Poupao, alias La Fleur, an inhabitant of Detroit, and Lieut. Brehme, Assistant Engineer.

"From Fort William-Augustus you will continue your voyage by the north-shore to Niagara, were you will land your whale-boats, and transport them across the Carrying-place into Lake Erie, applying to Major Walters, or the officer commanding at Niagara, for any assistance you may want on that or any other occasion, requesting of him at the same time to deliver up to you Monsieur Gamelin, who was made prisoner at the reduction of said fort, and has continued there ever since, in order to conduct him, with the above-mentioned Poupao, to their habitations at Detroit, where, upon taking the oath of allegiance to his most sacred Majesty, whose subjects they are become by the capitulation of the 8th instant, they shall be protected in the peaceable and quiet possession of their properties and so long as they behave as becometh good and faithful subjects, shall partake of all the other privileges and immunities granted unto them by the said capitulation.

"With these, and the detachment, under your command, you will proceed in your whale-boats across Lake Erie to Presque Isle, where, upon your arrival, you will make known the orders I have given to the officer commanding that post; and you will leave said whale-boats and party, taking only a small detachment of your party, and marching by land, to join Brigadier General Monkton, wherever he may be

"Upon your arrival with him, you will deliver into his hands the dispatches you shall hearwith receive for him, and follow and obey such orders as he shall give you for the relief of the garrisons of the French posts at Detroit, Michlimakana, or any others in that district, for gathering in the arms of the inhabitants thereof, and for administering to them the oath of allegiance already mentioned; when you will likewise administer, or see administered, the same to the before mentioned Gamelin and Poupao; and when this is done, and that you have reconnoitered and explored the country as much you can, without losing time unnecessarily you are to bring away the French troops and arms, to such a place as you shall be directed by General Monkton.

"And when the whole of this service is compleated, you will march back to your detachment to Presqueisle, or Niagara, according to the orders you receive from Brigadier Monkton, where you will embark the whole, and in like manner as before, transport your whale-boats across the Carrying place into Lake Ontario, where you will deliver over your whale-boats into the care of the commanding officer marching your detachment by land to Albany, or wherever I may be, to receive what further orders I may have to give you.

"Given up under my hand at the head quarters in the camp Montreal, 12th Sept. 1760.

Jeff. Amherst."

By his Excellency's command.

J. Appy."

In his journal for September 12, 1760, Amherst noted his orders to Rogers: "Wrote to Br Gen Monckton & ordered Major Rogers with two Companys of Rangers to go to him to assist in relieving the Posts Myamis, Fort Detroit, St Joseph, Michimichinak, & c. I sent an Engineer Lt Brehme to explore the country & Lt Davis of

> the Artillery to take a view of Niagara Falls . . . ." (Amherst, p. 251)
>
> When he notified William Pitt of Rogers' mission in a letter of October 4, Amherst added a few additional details: "I sent Major Rogers with 200 Rangers to the Posts of Fort Detroit, Miames, St. Joseph, Michilimackinak &c, on the Frontiers of Canada, with Letters from Monsieur de Vaudreuil, to the commanding Officers, to give up those Posts according to the Capitulation, I sent an Engineer with Major Rogers to explore the Country, and I wrote to Br. General Monckton, as he is so much nearer, to send some Regular Troops with the Rangers to take possession." (Pitt, Volume II, pp. 336-337)

An additional order was given, which was to be shewn only to the commanding officers of the different posts I might touch at, the expedition being intended to be kept a profound secret for fear the march should be impeded by the enemy Indians through whose country I was obliged to march.

This order was as follows, viz.

"Major Walters, or the officer commanding at Niagara, will judge whether or not there is provision sufficient at Presque Isle; and Major Rogers will accordingly take provisions from Niagara. Eight day's provision will take him from Montreal to Fort William-Augustus; there he will apply to the commanding officer for a sufficient quantity to proceed to Niagara. Major Rogers knows where he is going, and the provisions he will want; some should be in store likewise at Presque Isle, for the party Brigadier General Monkton will send.

Jeff. Amherst.

Montreal, 12th Sept. 1760.

> After assigning Rogers and his detachment to take over the western French posts, on October 25 Amherst ordered the rest of the Ranger companies disbanded. "I ordered all the Rangers away to morrow, some by No 4, & the rest by Albany, to pay them off & get rid of the expense as soon as possible . . . ." (Amherst, p. 261)

In pursuance of these orders I embarked at Montreal the 13th of Sept. 1760 (with Captain Brewer, Captain Wait, Lieutenant Brheme, Assistant Engineer, Lieut. Davis [Thomas Davies] of the royal train of artillery, and two hundred Rangers) about noon, in fifteen whale-boats; and that night we encamped at la Chine; next morning we reached Isle de Praires, and took a view of the two Indian settlements at Coyhavagu and Cone-fadagu.

On the 16th we got up to an island in the Lake of St. Francis, and the next night encamped on the western shore, at the lower end of the upper rifts. We ascended these rifts the day following and continued all night on the shore, opposite a number of islands.

In the evening of the 19th we came to the Isle de Gallettes, and spent the 20th in repairing our whale-boats, which had received some damage in ascending the rifts.

This morning I sent off ten sick Rangers to Albany, by way of Oswego, recommending them to the care of Col. Fitch, commanding at Oswego, who was to give them suitable directions.

We left Isle de Gallettes on the 21st; about twelve o'clock, the wind being unfavourable, we passed Oswegachi, and encamped but three miles above it on the northern shore.

On the 22nd we continued our course up the river, the wind blowing fresh at south, and halted in the evening at the narrow passes near the islands; but, upon the winds abating at midnight, we embarked and rowed the remainder of that night, and the whole day following, till we came to the place where formerly stood the old Fort of Frontiniac, where we found some Indian hunters from Oswegachi. We were detained here all the next day by the tempestuousness of the weather, which was very windy, attended with snow and rain: we however, improved the time in taking a plan of the old fort, situated at the bottom of a fine safe harbour

There were about five hundred acres of cleared ground about it which, tho' covered with clover seemed bad and rocky, and interspersed with some pine-trees. The Indians here seemed to be well pleased with the news we brought them of the surrender of all Canada, and supplied us with great plenty of venison and wild fowl.

We left this the 25th, about ten in the morning, steering a south-course two miles, then west six miles, which brought us to the mouth of a river thirty feet wide, then south four miles, where we halted to refresh the party.

About four in the afternoon we rowed for the mountain bearing south-west, which we did not come up to till some time in the night, and found it to be a steep rock, about one hundred feet high. It now grew foggy, and mistaking our way about six miles, we rowed all night, and till 8 o'clock next morning, before we put ashore; which we then did on a point, where we breakfasted, and then proceeded on our voyage, rowing till 8 o'clock at night (being about one hundred miles, as we imagined, from Frontiniac) we landed. This evening we passed two small islands at the end of a point extending far into the lake; the darkness and fog prevented us from taking such a survey of them as to be able to give a particular description of them.

The 27th of September, being very windy, we spent the time in deer-hunting, there being great plenty of them there, tho' the land is rocky, the timber bad, chiefly hemlock and pine; and I believe it is generally so on the north-side of Lake Ontario.

We embarked very early on the 28th, steering south-west, leaving a large bay on the right, about twenty miles wide; the western side of which terminates in a point, and a small island: having passed both, about twenty miles on a course west by south we entered the chops of a river, called by the Indians *Grace of Man*; there we encamped, and found about 50 Messissagua Indians fishing for salmon. At our first appearance they ran down, both men and boys, to the edge of the lake, and continued firing their pieces, to express their joy at the sight of the English colours, till shall such time as we had landed.

They presented us with eight deer just killed and split in halves, with the skin on, but the bowels taken out, which, with them, in a most elegant and polite present, and significant of the greatest respect. I told them of the success of their English brethren, against their fathers the French; at which they either were, or pretended to be, very well pleased.

Some of us fished with them in the evening being invited by them, and filled a bark-canoe with salmon in about half an hour. Their method of catching the fish is very extraordinary. One person hold a lighted pine-torch, while a second strikes the fish with a spear. This is a season in which the salmon spawn on these parts, contrary to what they do in any other place I ever knew them before.

I found the soil near this river very good and level. The timber is chiefly oak and maple, or the sugar-tree.

At seven o'clock the next morning we took our departure from this river, the wind being a-head. About fifteen miles further, on a west-south-west course, we put into another river, called the Life of Man. The Messissaguas, who were hunting here, about thirty in number, paid us the same compliments with those we just before received from their countrymen, and instead of a deer, split up a young bear and presented me with it. Plenty of fish was catched here also. The land continued good and level, the soil of blackish colour, and the banks of the lake were low.

The wind being fair the 30th, we embarked at the first dawn of day, and with the assistance of sails and oars, made great way on a south-west course, and in the evening reached the river Toronto, having run seventy miles. Many points extending far into the lake, occasioned a frequent alteration of our course. We passed a bank of twenty miles in length, but the land behind it seemed to be level, well-timbered with large oaks, hickaries, maples, and some poplars. No mountain appeared in sight. There was a track of about 300 acres of cleared ground, round the place where formally the French had a fort, that was called Fort Toronto. The soil here is principally clay. The deer are extremely plenty in this country. Some Indians were hunting at the mouth of the river, who run into the woods at our approach, very much frightened. They came in, however, in the morning and testified the joy at the news of our success against the French. They told us "that we could easily accomplish our journey from thence to Detroit in eight days: that when the French traded at that place, the Indians used to come with their poultry from Michlimakana, down the river Toronto: that the partage was but twenty miles from that to a river falling into Lake Huron, which had some falls, but none very considerable: they added, that there was a carrying-place of fifteen miles from some westerly part of Lake Erie, to a river running without any falls thro' several Indian towns into Lake St. Clair.

I think Toronto a most convenient place for a factory, and that from thence we may very easily settle the north-side of Lake Erie.

We left Toronto 1st of October, steering south, right across the west-end of Lake Ontario. At dark we arrived at the south-shore, five miles west of Fort Niagara, some of our boats being now become exceeding leaky and dangerous.

This morning, before we set out, I directed the following order of march:

"The boats in a line. If the wind rose high, the red flag hoisted, and the boats to croud nearer, that they might be ready to give mutual assistance in case of a leak or other accident;" by which means we saved the crew and arms of the boat commanded by Lieutenant M'Cormack, which sprung a leak and sunk, losing nothing except their packs.

We halted all the next day at Niagara, and provided ourselves with blankets, coats, shirts, shoes, magassins, & c.

I received from the commanding officer eighty barrels of provisions, and changed two whale-boats for as many battoes, which proved leaky.

In the evening some of my party proceeded with the provisions to the falls, and in the morning marched the rest there and began the portage of the provisions and boats. Mess. Brheme and Davis took a survey of the great cataract of Niagara.

As the winter-season was now advancing very fast in this country, and I had orders to join Brig. Monkton from Presque Isle, wherever he might be, to receive his directions, I set out this evening, the 5th of October, in a bark-canoe, with Lieutenants Brheme and Holmes, and eight Rangers, leaving the command of my party to Capt. Brewer, with instructions to follow to Presque Isle, and encamped eight miles up the stream issuing out of Lake Erie. The land appeared to be good on both sides of the river.

Next morning embarked early, and steered a south-west course. About noon opened Lake Erie, and leaving a bay to the left, we arrived by sunset at the southern shore of the lake, we then steered west till eight o'clock at night, and drew up our boats on a sandy beach, forty miles distant from where we embarked in the morning.

The wind was very fresh next day, which prevented our setting out till 11 o'clock; so that we made no further progress than about twenty-eight miles on a west-south-west course. A little after noon, on the 8th of October, we arrived at Presque Isle, having kept a southerly course all the morning; I tarried there till 3 o'clock, when, having sent back my party to assist Captain Brewer, Mr. Brheme, Lieutenant Holmes, and myself, took leave of Colonel Bouquet, who commanded at Presque Isle, and with three other men, in a bark-canoe, proceeded to French Creek, and at night encamped on the road, half way to Fort du Bouf.

> On October 8, Colonel Henry Bouquet wrote to General Robert Monckton, "Major Rogers brings us the most welcome News of the surrender of all Canada . . . ." (Bouquet, Volume V, p. 58)

We got to this fort about 10 o'clock next day, and after three hours rest launched our canoe into the river, and paddled down about ten miles below the fort.

On the 10th we encamped at the second crossings of the river, the land on both sides appeared to be good all the way. The 11th we reached the Mingo Cabbins, and the night of the 12th we lodged at Venango; from thence went down the River Ohio; and on the morning of the 17th I waited upon Brigadier Monkton at Pittsburgh, and delivered him General Amherst's dispatches, and my own instructions.

I left Pittsburgh the 20th, at the request of General Monkton, who promised to send his orders after me to Presque Isle, by Mr. Croghan, and to forward Capt. Campbell immediately with a company of the Royal Americans; I got back to Presque Isle the 30th of October, Captain Campbell arrived the day after; Captain Brewer was got there before us, with the Rangers from Niagara, having lost some of the boats, and part of the provisions.

Monckton's orders to Rogers are very detailed and interesting. They are reprinted here in their entirety:

"You will as soon as possible after your return to Presq' Isle with the Rangers you brought with you, to that Post, & the Detachment of the R. A. R. under Capt Cambell, now on their march to join your Detachmt proceed in you Whale Boats, and such Batteaux as Colonel Bouquet Comg at Presqu' Isle may be able to collect for you, taking with you as much Provisions as you can, along Lake Erie to the Detroit, to put in Execution the Instructions you have already received from General Amherst upon your arrival near Detroit, it will be proper for you to Send an Officer forward to the Officer Commanding the French Garrison there, to acquaint him that you are come to take Possession of those Posts, which by the Capitulation of the 8th Septr now belong to the King of Great Britain; and afterwards deliver him with your own Hands the inclosed Letter. When that you have put in Execution your Instructions relative to that Post, I would recommand it to you to leave Capt Cambell there, to keep Possession of it, and do any thing that may be necessary in your Abscence: As you will on your Landing there have many Boats to Spare, you will immediately Send them off with some of your own Detachment either to Niagara, or Presqu' Isle, or both, as you Shall by the Intelligence you may get, find the most practicable to fetch Provisions for the Troops that are to remain: I would likewise recommend it to you to engage Some of the Inhabitants to assist in fetching Provisions as they will doubtless have many Canoes, and Boats, and as there are many Traders at Niagara, & I have ordered others to Presqu' Isle, They will by that means, have an oppirtunity of getting any little necessaries they may want in Exchange for their Skins & Furrs, but they must be told that they are to bring back Provisions for which they will be paid.

"As the Season is now advancing fast, you will yourself with Capt Cambell (whom I must recommend it to you to consult with on all occasions) judge how far it will be practicable for his Detachment to keep Possession of the other Posts this Winter, which will greatly depend on the distance they are from Detroit, the possibility of getting provisions there, and by having a Practicable Communication with him—not but the bringing Off the French Troops from those Posts, and the disarming the Inhabitants residing in these districts will be absolutely necessary as by your Instructions from General Amherst: You have inclosed a Copy of the Oath of Allegiance, which as by General Amherst's Instructions you are to administer to the Inhabitants.

"In my Letters to the officer Commanding the French Troops at Detroit and Michillimakinac , I have in the Strongest manner prest them to procure the releasement of as many Prisoners as they can from the Indians in those Parts, which Prisoners, with the officers and men of the French Troops together with the Arms of the Inhabitants, you will bring off with you:

"In regard to your Return after having performed the Service directed by your Instructions from General Amherst, you yourself will be the best judge of, from the Informations you may get there, and according to the Season of the year.

"As the Inhabitants in a great measure depended on their Guns for their Subsistence, it will be necessary that you leave some few with Captain Cambell for him to give out at Such Times, to Such as may best deserve from their attachment to His Majesty's Government Such an Indulgence. Should you and Captain Cambell think that some of your Rangers may be necessary to be left there, you may in that Case leave a Subb [subaltern] with a Small Party.

"You have also with this a Letter for the Commanding officer of the French Troops at Michillimackinac, which you will likewise deliver him with your own Hands as the former.

"As I am informed that there is a Detachment of an Officer and some of the French Troops of Mr Beletre's Comand at the Shawan Town, you will desire him to Send off an Express to order them up here, that they may be ready to join him to go with him to France; I mention this in the Letter I write to him.

"Mr Dupless is an assistant Engeneer having been taken on French Creek this Summer, you will inquire after him, and procure his releasement; that he may return to his duty.

"You will keep up the Strictest discipline in the Troops under yr Comand, and not Suffer any of the Inhabitants to be disturbed or molested, as they are now become the Subjects of the King of great Brittain: You will by any opportunity acquaint me of your proceedings. The officers Commanding at Presqu' Isle and Niagara will have orders to deliver Provisions to any Boats you may Land, and any other Stores or necessarys they may have and you may want.

"You will communicate these Instructions to Colonel Bouquet Commandg Officer at Presqu' Isle, that he may be informed of the Steps to be taken for Supplying you with Provisions & Stores. Given under my Hand at Fort Pitt this 19th of October 1760" (Bouquet, Volume V, pp. 78-79)

We immediately began to repair the damaged boats; and, as there was an account that a vessel, expected with provisions from Niagara, was lost, I dispatched Capt. Brewer by land to Detroit, with a drove of forty oxen, supplied by Col. Bouquet. Capt. Wait was about the same time sent back to Niagara for more provisions, and ordered to cruise along the north-coast of Lake Eire, and halt about twenty miles to the east of the streight between the Lakes Huron and Erie, till further orders. Brewer had a battoe to ferry his party over the Creeks, two horses, and Capt. Monter with twenty Indians, composed of the Six Nations, Delawares and Shawanese, to protect him from the insults of the enemy Indians.

My order of march over from Presque Isle was as follows:

"The boats to row two deep; first, Major Rogers's boat, abreast of him Captain Croghan; Captain Campbell follows with his company, the Rangers next; and lastly, Lieutenant Holmes, who commands the rear-guard, with his own boat, and that of Ensign Wait's, so as to be ready to assist any boat that may be in distress. Boats in distress are to fire a gun, when Mr. Holmes with the other boats under his command are immediately to go to their relief, take them to the shore, or give such other assistance as he thinks may be best. When the wind blows hard, so that the boats cannot keep their order, a red flag will be hoisted in the Major's boat; then the boats are not to mind their order, but put after the flag as fast as possible to the place of landing, to which the flag-boat will always be a guide.

"It is recommended to the soldiers as well as officers, not to mind the waves of the lake; but when the surf is high to stick to their oars, and the men at helm to keep the boat quartering on the waves, and briskly follow, then no mischief will happen by any storm whatever. Ten of the best steersmen amongst the Rangers are to attend Captain Campbell and company in his boats. It is likewise recommended to the officers commanding in those boats, to hearken to the steersmen in a storm or bad weather, in managing their boats. At evening, (if it is thought necessary to row in the night time) a blue flag will be hoisted in the Major's boat, which is the signal for the boats to dress, and then proceed in the following manner: the boats next to the hindermost, are to wait for the two in the rear, the two third boats for the second two; and so on to the boats leading a-head, to prevent separation, which in the night would be hazardous.

"Mr. Brhreme is not to mind the order of march, but to steer as is most convenient for him to make his observations; he is however desired never to go more than a league a-head of the detachment, and is to join them at landing or encamping.

"On landing, the Regulars are to encamp in the center, and Lieutenant Holmes's division on the right wing with Mr. Croghan's people, Lieut. M'Cormick on the left wing with his division; Mr. Jequipe to be always ready with his Mohegan Indians, which are the picquet of the detachment, part of which are always to encamp in the front of the party; Captain Campbell will mount a guard consisting of one Subaltern, one Serjeant, and thirty privates, immediately on landing, for the security of his own encampment and battoes; Lieutenant Holmes's division to keep a guard of one Serjeant and ten Rangers on the right, and Lieutenant M'Cormick the like number on the left, and likewise to act as Adjutant to the detachment, and the orderly drum to attend him, to be at the Serjeant's call. The general to beat when ordered by the Major, at which time the whole party is to prepare for embarking, the troops half an hour after, when all the guards are to be called in, and the party embark immediately after.

"There is to be no firing of guns in this detachment without permission from the commanding officer, except when in distress on the lake. No man to go without the centries, when in camp, unless he has orders so to do; great care to be taken of the arms, and the officers to review them daily. Captain Campbell will order a drum to beat, for the regulation of his company when landed, at any time he thinks proper for parading his men, or reviewing their arms, & c.

"It is not doubted but due attention will be paid to all orders given.

"Mr. Croghan will, at landing always attend the Major for orders, and to give such intelligence as he may have had from the Indians, throughout the day."

We left Presque Isle the 4th of November, kept a western course, and by night had advanced twenty miles.

The badness of the weather obliged us to lie by all the next day; and as the wind continued very high, we did not advance more than ten or twelve miles the 6th, on a course west-south-west.

We set out very early on the 7th, and came to the mouth of Chogage River; here we met with a party of Attawawa Indians, just arrived from Detroit. We informed them of our success in the total reduction of Canada, and that we were going to bring off the French Garrison at Detroit, who were included in the capitulation. I held out a belt, and told them I would take my brothers by the hand, and carry them to Detroit, to see the truth of what I had said. They retired, and held a council, and promised an answer next morning. That evening we smoked the calamet, or pipe of peace, all the Indians smoaking by turns out of the same pipe. The peace thus concluded, we went to rest, but kept good guards, a little distrusting their sincerity.

The Indians gave their answer early in the morning, and said their young warriors should go with me, while the old ones staid to hunt for their wives and children.

I gave them ammunition at their request, and a string of wampum in testimony of my approbation, and charged them to send some of their sachems, or chiefs, with the party who the drove the oxen along shore; and they promised to spread the news, and prevent any annoyance from their hunters.

We were detained here by unfavorable weather till the 12th, during which time the Indians held a plentiful market in our camp of venison and turkies.

From this place we steered one mile west, then a mile south, then four miles west, then south-west ten miles, then five miles west-and-by-south, then south-west eight miles, then west-and-by-south seven miles, then four miles west, and then southwest six miles, which brought us to Elk River, as the Indians call it, where we halted two days on account of bad weather and contrary winds.

On the 15th we embarked, and kept the following courses; west-south-west two miles, west-north-west three miles, west-by-north one mile, west two miles; here we passed the mouth of a river, and then steered west one mile, west-by-south two miles, west-by-north four miles, north west three miles, west-north-west two miles, west-by-north ten miles, where we encamped at the mouth of a river twenty-five yards wide.

The weather did not permit us to depart till the 18th, when our course was west-by-south six miles, west-by-north four miles, west two miles; here we found a river about fifteen yards over, then proceeded west half a mile, west-south-west six miles and a half, west two miles and a half, north-west two miles, where we encamped, and discovered a river sixteen yards broad at the entrance.

We left this place the next-day, steering north-west four miles, north-north-west six miles, which brought us to Sandusky Lake; we continued the same course two miles, then north-north-east half a mile, north-west a quarter of a mile, north the same distance, north-west half a mile, north by-east one furlong, north-west-by-north one quarter of a mile, north-west-by-west one mile, west-north-west one mile, then west half a mile, where we encamped near a small river, on the east-side.

From this place I detached Mr. Brheme with a letter to Monsieur Beleter [Captain Francois-Marie Piquote de Belestre], the French commandant at Detroit, in these words:

To Capt. Beleter, *or the Officer commanding at* Detroit.

"Sir

"That you may not be alarmed at the approach of the English troops under my command, when they come to Detroit, I send forward this by Lieut. Brheme, to acquaint you, that I have General Amherst's orders to take possession of Detroit, and such other posts as are in that district, which, by capitulation, agreed to and signed by the Marquis de Vaudreuil, and his Excellency Major General Amherst, the 8th of September last, now belong to the King of Great Britain.

"I have with me the Marquis de Vaudreuil's letters to you directed, for your guidance on this occasion, which letters I shall deliver you when I arrive at or near your post, and shall encamp the troops I have with me at some distance from the fort, till you have reasonable time to be made acquainted with the Marquis de Vaudreuil's instructions, and the capitulation, a copy of which I have with me likewise. I am,

Sir,

Your humble servant,

Robert Rogers."

The land on the south-side of Lake Erie, from Presque Isle, puts on a very fine appearance; the country level, the timber tall, and of the best sort, such as oak, hickerie and locust; and for game, both for plenty and variety, perhaps exceeded by no part of the world.

I followed Mr. Brheme on the 20th, and took a course north-west four miles and an half, south-west two, and west three, to the mouth of a river in breadth 300 feet.

Here we found several Huron sachems, who told me "that a body of 400 Indian warriors was collected at the entrance into the great streight, in order to obstruct our passage; and that Monsieur Beleter had excited them to defend their country: that they were messengers to know my business, and whether the person I had sent forward had reported the truth that Canada was reduced." I confirmed this account, and that the fort at Detroit was given up by the French Governor. I presented them a large belt, and spoke to this effect:

"Brothers,

"With this belt I take you by the hand. You are to go directly to your brothers assembled at the mouth of the river, and tell them to go to their towns till I arrive at the fort. I shall call you there as soon as Monsieur Beleter is sent away, which shall be in two days after my arrival. We will then settle all matters. You live happily in your own country. Your brothers have long desired to bring this about. Tell your warriors to mind their fathers (the French) no more, for they are all prisoners to

GARY ZABOLY
©2000

Rogers Meets Pontiac

EXACTLY when and where Major Robert Rogers met the Ottawa war chief, Pontiac, has never been agreed upon by historians. Rogers himself never indicated the date or place, though in his *Journals* he mentions meeting Ottawa leaders at least three times as he led his whaleboat flotilla westward along the southern shore of Lake Erie in November of 1760[1].

Some historians even assert that Rogers never met Pontiac at all on this expedition, that by describing such an encounter in his 1765 book, *A Concise Account of North America*, he was merely capitalizing on the by-then famous name of the great chief to puff up his own role in the events that had taken place. This assertion, however, is itself rather arbitrarily made, and has yet to be supported by any evidence that can contradict Rogers.

Bad weather had frequently plagued the expedition as it neared its destination, French-held Fort Detroit. Sometimes Rogers and his men (mostly Rangers, along with a contingent of Royal Americans) had to camp in the forest and wait more than a few days for more favorable "seas" and skies to return. At the beginning of one of these protracted bivouacs, several Indian chiefs and warriors suddenly entered their camp. They told Rogers that he should advance no further until their great chief, Pontiac, had spoken with him. Pontiac himself soon appeared, and in a very authoritative manner he demanded to know what Rogers' business was here, and how he had dared to enter his territory without gaining the permission of himself, the "king and lord of the country I was in."

Rogers explained that Canada had surrendered, that he had no hostile designs against the Indians, and that he was on his way to take command of Detroit and the other distant French outposts. Pontiac prohibited Rogers from advancing any further by saying "that he stood in the path [the English] travelled in till next morning." However, before leaving, Pontiac asked if Rogers' party needed any supplies. That night the expedition was on high alert for any treachery, but no Indian attack came.

The next day, Pontiac brought a quantity of parched corn and other provisions for Rogers' men, which was paid for. A peace calumet was then smoked, and Pontiac assured Rogers that he could now pass through his country unmolested. If the English were to replace the French, the Ottawa chief said, they must realize that they would nevertheless remain under his authority while garrisoning the posts.

The two leaders met several more times during the expedition's weather-enforced encampment; and Pontiac's influence, according to Rogers, helped break up a planned ambush by a body of Indians that had collected near Detroit.[2]

The scene depicts Pontiac upon his initial meeting with Rogers. No detailed contemporary physical description of the Ottawa chief has survived, although we do have some clues provided by the recollections of those who had known him. For instance, Pierre Chouteau told Francis Parkman that he remembered Pontiac "as a man six feet high, of very commanding appearance, and, whenever he saw him, splendidly dressed."[3] Evidence also suggests that in 1760 Pontiac was in his 40s. Rogers himself noted, in his *A Concise Account of North America,* that Pontiac "puts on an air of majesty and princely grandeur, and is greatly honoured and revered by his subjects."[4] In his conversations with him, Rogers took particular notice of Pontiac's concern that "he was far from considering himself as a conquered prince, and that he expected to be treated with the respect and honour due to a king or emperor, by all who came into his country, or treated with him."[5]

Rogers, at right foreground, wears a surtout coat of green Bath rug. Many of his men wore blanket coats purchased especially for this expedition. One of Rogers' Canadian guides, wearing a white camisole, interprets Pontiac's words. Behind the Frenchman, Royal Artillery Captain Thomas Davies observes the scene. He wears a blue surtout, a cut down hat, and Indian leggings.[6] Davies accompanied the expedition to do what he did best: draw and paint scenes along the way. Royal Engineer Lieutenant Diederick Brehm was also under Rogers' command, his role being to map the route traversed by the party from Montreal to Detroit. (The location of the originals of these works by Davies and Brehm are not known, or even if they have survived to the present day at all).

In the left background are three lesser Ottawa war captains, and in center background stand several men of the expedition, ready for possible action with bayoneted arms. Whaleboats lie at anchor in the fog-shrouded lake.

G.Z.

1. Francis Parkman has Rogers meeting Pontiac at the mouth of the Cuyahoga River on November 7 (*History of the Conspiracy of Pontiac*, The MacMillan Company, New York, 1929, p. 106). John Cuneo, however, suggests that the meeting took place on November 26, near the mouth of the Huron River (*Robert Rogers of the Rangers*, Oxford University Press, New York, 1959, p. 135).
2. *A Concise Account of North America*, by Major Robert Rogers, London, 1765, as excerpted in *The Annual Register*, Vol. 8, December 1765, p. 49.
3. *The Journals of Francis Parkman*, edited by Mason Wade, Harper and Brothers Publishers, New York and London, 1947, Vol. II, p. 415, entry of April 27, 1846.
4. *The Annual Register*, Vol. 8, December 1765, p.49.
5. Ibid., p. 50.
6. Blue surtouts or great coats had been issued to the Royal Artillery Regiment for fatigue duty as early as 1715. Cecil P. Lawson, *A History of the Uniforms of the British Army*, Norman Military Publications, London, 1941, Vol. II, p. 181.

your brothers (the English), who pitied them, and left them their houses and goods, on their swearing by the Great One who made the world, to become as Englishmen for ever. They are now your brothers; if you abuse them, you affront me, unless they behave ill. Tell this to your brothers the Indians. What I say is truth. When we meet at Detroit I will convince you it is all true."

These sachems set out in good temper the next morning, being the 21st; but as the wind was very high, we did not move from this place.

On the 22d we encamped on a beach, after having steered that day north-west six miles, north-north-west four, to a river of the breadth of twenty yards, then north-west-by-west two miles, west-north-west one, west four, and west north-west five; it was with great difficulty we could procure any fuel here, the west-side of the Lake Erie abounding with swamps.

We rowed ten miles the next day, on a course north-west and by west, to Point Cedar, and then formed a camp; here we met some of the Indian messingers, to whom we had spoken two days before: they told us, their warriors were gone up to Monsieur Beleter, who, they said, is a strong man, and intends to fight you, a sachem of the Attawawas was amongst them. All their Indians set out with us. The 24th we went north-west and by north ten miles, and fourteen miles north-east, to a long point; this night sixty of the Indian party came to our camp, who congratulated us on our arrival in their country, and offered themselves as an escort to Detroit, from whence they came the day before. They informed me, that Mr. Bhreme, and his party were confined; and that Monsieur Beleter had set up an high flag-staff, with a wooden effigy of a man's head on the top, and upon that a crow; that the crow was to represent himself, the man's head mine, and the meaning of the whole, that he would scratch out my brains. This artifice, however, had no effect; for the Indians told him (as they said) that the reverse would be the true explanation of the sign.

After we had proceeded six miles north-east, we halted at the request of the Indians, who desired me to call in the chief Captains of the party at the Streight's mouth. I did so, and spent the 26th at the same place, in conciliating their savage minds to peace and friendship.

The morning of the 27th, Monsieur Beleter sent me the following letter by Monsieur Babee.

"Monsieur,

"J'ai recu la lettre que vous m'avez ecrite par un de vos Officiers; comme je n'ai point d'interprete, je ne puis faire la reponse amplement.

L'Officier qui m'a remife la votre, me fait favoir qu'il etoit detache afin de m'anoncer votre arrive, pour prendre possession de cette garison, selon la capitulation fait et Canada, que vous avez conjointement avec un lettre de Monsieur de Vaudreuil a mon addresse. Je vous prie, Monsieur, d'arreter vos troupes a l'entrance de la riviere, jusques a ce que vous m'envoyes la capitulation & la lettre de Monseigneur le Marquis de Vaudreuil, afin de pouvoir y conformer.

Je suis bein supris qu'on ne m'a pas envoye un Officier Francois avec vous, selon la coutume.

J'ai l'honneur d'etre, &c. &c.

De Beleter."

A Monsieur Monsieur *Rogers*,
Major, & commandant le
detachment Anglois."

In English thus.

"Sir,

I received the letter you wrote me by one of your Officers; but as I have no interpreter, cannot fully answer it.

The Officer that delivered me yours, gives me to understand, that he was sent to give me notice of your arrival to take possession of this garrison, according to the capitulation made in Canada; that you have likewise a letter from Mons Vaudreuil, directed to me. I beg, Sir, you'll halt your troops at the entrance of the river, till you send me the capitulation and the Marquis de Vaudreuil's letter, that I may act in conformity thereto.

I am surprised there is no French Officer sent to me along with you, as is the custom on such occasions. I have the honor to be & c. & c.

De Beleter."

To Mr. *Rogers,* Major and
Commander of the English
detachment."

Shortly after a French party, under Captain Burrager, beat a parley on the west-shore; I sent Mr. M'Cormick to know his business, who returned with the Officer and the following letter:

Detroit, le 25me Novembre, 1760.

Monsieur,

"Je vous ai deja marque par Monsieur Burrager les raisons pourquoi je ne puis repondre en detail a la lettre qui m'a ete remise le 22me de courant, par l'Officier que vous m'avez detache.

J'ignore les raisons pourquoi il n'a pas voulu retourner aupres de vous. J'ai envoye mon interprete Huron chez cettre nation, que l'on me dit etre atroupe sur le chemin de les contenir, ne fachant positivement si c'est a vous ou a nous qu'ils en veuillent, & pour leur dire de ma part, qu'ils ayent a se tenir tranquilement; que je favois ce que je devois a mon General, & que de lorsque l'acte de la capitulation seroit regle, j'etois oblige d'obeir. Le dit interprete aordre de vous attendre, & de vous remettre la present. Ne soyez point surpris, Monsieur, si sur le long de la cote vous troverez nos habitans sur leur garde; on leur a annonce qu'il y avoit beaucoup de nations a votre suite, a qui on avois promis le pillage, & que lesdites nations etoient meme determinees a vous le demander; je leur ai permis de regarder, c'est pour votre conversation & surete ainsi que pour la notre, en cas que les dites nations devenoient a faire les insolents, vous seul ne feriez peut-etre pas dans les circonstances presentes en etat de les require. Je me flatte, Monsieur, que si tot que le present vour fera parvenue, vous voudriez bien m'envoyer par quel qu'un de vos Messieurs, & la capitulation la lettre de Monsieur Vaudreuil. J'ai l'honneurd'ettre,

Monsieur,

Votre tres-humble & obeissant serviteur,

Pign. de Beletre."

A Monsieur Monsieur *Rogers,*
Major, commandant le detachment Anglois au bas de
la riviere.

In English thus:

"Sir, Detroit, 25th November. 1760.

"I have already by Mr. Burrager acquainted you with the reasons why I could not answer particularly the letter which was delivered me the 22nd instant by the Officer you sent to me.

"I am entirely unacquainted with the reasons of his not returning to you. I sent my Huron interpreter to that nation, and told him to stop them, should they be on the road, not knowing positively whether they were inclined to favour you or us, and to tell them from me they should behave peaceably; that I knew what I owed to my General, and that when the capitulation should be settled I was obliged to obey. The said interpreter has orders to wait on you, and deliver you this.

"Be not surprised, Sir, if along the coast you find the inhabitants upon their guard; it was told them you had several Indian nations with you, to whom you had promised permission to plunder, nay, that they were even resolved to force you to it. I have therefore allowed the said inhabitants to take to their arms, as it is for your safety and preservation as well as ours; for should these Indians become insolent, you may not perhaps, in your present situation, be able to subdue them alone.

"I flatter myself, Sir, that, as soon as that shall come to hand, you will send me by some of the Gentlemen you have with you, both the capitulation and Monsieur Vaudreuil's letter. I have the honour to be,

Sir,

Your very humble and obedient servant,

To Major Rogers. *Pign. Beletere."*

We encamped the next day five miles up the river, having rowed against the wind; and on the 29th I dispatched Captain Campbell, with Messieurs Burrager and Babee, and their parties, with this letter.

"Sir,

"I acknowledge the receipt of your two letters, both of which were delivered to me yesterday. Mr.

Brheme has not yet returned. The inclosed letter from the Marquis de Vaudreuil will inform you of the surrender of all Canada to the King of Great Britain, and of the great indulgence granted to the inhabitants; as also of the terms granted to the troops of his Most Christian Majesty. Captain Campbell, whom I have sent forward with this letter, will shew you the capitulation. I desire you will not detain him, as I am determined, agreeable to my instructions from General Amherst, speedily to relieve your post. I shall stop the troops I have with me at the hither end of the town till four o'clock, by which time I expect your answer; your inhabitants under arms will not surprise me, as yet I have seen no other in that position, but savages waiting for my orders. I can assure you, Sir, the inhabitants of Detroit shall not be molested, they and your complying with the capitulation, but be protected in the quiet and peaceful possession of their estates; neither shall they be pillaged by my Indians, nor by yours that have joined me.

I am, & c.

R. Rogers."

To Capt. Beletere,
commanding at Detroit.

I landed at half a mile short of the fort, and fronting it, where I drew up my detachment on a field of grass. Here Captain Campbell joined me, and with him came a French officer, to inform me that he bore Monsieur Beletere's compliments, signifying he was under my command. From hence I sent Lieutenants Leslie and M'Cormick, with thirty-six Royal Americans, to take possession of the fort. The French garrison laid down their arms, English colours were hoisted, and the French taken down, at which about 700 Indians gave a shout, merrily exulting in their prediction being verified, that the crow represented the English.

They seemed amazed at the submissive salutations of the inhabitants, expressing their satisfaction at our generosity in not putting them to death, and said they would always for the future fight for a nation thus favoured by Him that made the world.

I went into the fort, received a plan of it, with a list of the stores, from the commanding officer, and by noon of the 1st of December we had collected the militia, disarmed them, and to them also administered the oaths of allegiance.

The oath that was administered to the French inhabitants reads as follows: "I __________ Swear that I Shall be faithful and that I Shall behave my Self honestly, toward His Sacred Majesty George the Second, by the Grace of God King of Great Britain, France, and Ireland, Defender of the faith, and that I will defend him, and his in this Country, with all my Power against his or their Ennemies; and further I Swear to make Known and revail to his Majesty, His General, or their assistants in place present, as much as depends of me all Traitors, or all conspirations that could be formed against his Sacred person, his Country, or his Government." (Bouquet, Volume V, p. 80)

Captain Donald Campbell, of the 60th (Royal American) Regiment, was a very competent and well-liked officer who would be treacherously killed during Pontiac's Uprising in 1763. On December 2, 1760, he wrote a very concise and detailed report of the expedition to Detroit to Colonel Bouquet:

"Major Rogers and his Detachment came safe to this Place the 29th of Novembr We had only the misfortune to loose a man of my Company that fell overboard by some Accident, and some Batteaux drove ashore, and some Boxes of Cartridges damaged. There is noe dependance on the lake at this Season of the year, it is at least a hundred Leagues from this to Presq'isle but People here Say it is still a better Navigation than the North Coast.

"Two days after we left you, we were joined by Some of the principal People of ye Tawa [Ottawa] Nation, who came to make peace with you at presquisle, who returned with us, and then by the Wiandots, whom we were oblidged to humour and give them Provisions as we did not know what Reception we were to have at this Place. they were highly pleased with what we told them; but all this added to the Consumption of our Provisions you know how little we could Spare, but we could not help it and some of its not fit to be made use of.

"Belestre would give noe Credit to the Report of our coming as Friends, but when I brought him the Marquis Vaudreuils Letter, he did every Thing with a good grace, I am certain when you see him you will Not be soe much prejudiced against him besides he is now your Prisoner.

"Your Project of sending the Cattel by land has turned very well, as they have been of great use to us. Mr Navarre will continue to act in his old Employment till he puts in the way of it, he thinks the inhabitants can supply our Detachment with Flour till Next Spring or very Near that time, but how we shall be supplyed with meat, will be the Difficulty. we are still in hopes of 5 Boats from Niagara there is noe dependence on the Lake, they expect it to be Frooze every hour. I believe we could gett some People to goe from this, I noe not how far it would answer, there horses must be wore out before they got there and could not return with a Load. I shall be better Judge of what we want when Capt Crochan [George Croghan] returns, you could gett Indians to undertake it from Pittsburgh.

"We found the Kings Stores here all most empty Some Barrels of Powder and not much of any Thing else, I have not got a Return of it as yet, as Major Rogers took all that on himself he is to give me over every Thing that belongs to the Fort to morrow.

"Majer Rogers is preparing to send to the Posts to bring off the People, he cannot possibly send any of us as the season is too far advanced and a want of Provisions, every body here says he will find great Difficulty to goe himself to Mackilemakinac, even with a Small Detachment they doubt even if its possible to be done.

"We are to have a Treaty with Indians the day after to morrow. I shall a good of Difficulty to Manadge them for the first time they are soe much accustomed to come to the french Commidant for every Thing they want.

"They Inhabitants seem very happy at the Change of Government, but they are in great want of every Thing, it has been a very florishing place before the War, plenty of every Thing;

"The Fort is much better than we expected it is one of the best Stockades I have Seen, but the Commandants houses and what belongs to King in bad repair, we got our People quartered in the Fort for the first time this night; I shall be able to write more about every Thing in a few days I shall be glad to hear from you how soon it is possible" (Bouquet, Volume V, pp. 141-142)

The interval from this time to the 9th was spent in preparing to execute some measures that appeared to be necessary to the service we were upon. I put Monsieur Beletere and the other prisoners under the care of Lieut. Holmes and thirty Rangers, to be carried to Philadelphia; and ordered Capt. Campbell and his company to keep possession of the fort. Lieut. Butler, and Ensign Wait were sent with a detached party of twenty men, to bring French troops from the Forts Miamie and Gatanois.

On December 25, at Philadelphia, Henry Bouquet noted in a letter to General Monckton, "Yesterday arrived from Detroit Lieut holmes of the Rangers escorting the French garrison of the Post, which consists of three officers and 35 Privates Seventeen English Prisoners; The Escort two Off: and 2 Serj. 28 Private." (Bouquet, Volume V, p. 204)

Fort Miamie was located at present day Fort Wayne, Indiana, and Gatanois (actually Fort Ouiatenon) was at present day West Lafayette, Indiana.

Rogers' orders to Lieutenant Butler read as follows:

"By Robert Rogers Esqr Major Commandant of his Majestys Independent Company's of Rangers and Captain of one of the said Company's Commanding his Majestys troops @ Detroit & a.

"To John Buttler Lieut of his Majestys Rangers.

"You are hereby derected to take Under Your Command Ensign Weight of ye Rangers and Eighteen Men of ye said Corps and two Canadians which I send you for Guides and March them to Fort Memamois And when you get near the said Post You are to Acquaint the Commanding Officer there that you are come to take Possession of that Garrison Which by the Capitulation of ye Eight of September Last, Now belongs to the King of Great Britton and afterwards, with your own Hand deliver him the Letter from Mr Beletre-Which you do herewith receive and the Capitulation which you likewise have a Copy of, As soon as the Officer is Made Acquainted with said Letter And Capitulation You will cause him with the French Troops their to Lay down their Arms and afterwards gether in the Arms of the Inhabitance and Adminester to ye Later Oath of Allegiance You will at the same time Aquaint the Inhabitance that as they are Now become the Subjects of his Sacrad Majesty they shall be Protected in Peaicable and Quiet Possession of their Estates And so long as they behave as becometh good and faithfull Subjects Shall protake of all Other Priviledges and Imunities as Granted them by the said Capitulation Already Mentioned.

"As Soon as you have Executed these my Instructions in Regard to the Meamois You will leave Ensign Whight with Parts of your Detachment to Command the Garrison and deliver in his Charge the French Officer And Troops and with the rest of your Troops Proceed to the Fort Vyatanois And in like manner as the former Cause the Troops there to lay down their Arms and administer the Oath of Allegience to ye Inhabitance and gether in their Arms and afterward bring of the French Troops together with such Stores as you may find in the King's Magazine to Fort Meames Where you will take the Command of that Garrison till you can be Reliev'd by some of His Majesty's Troops from Detroit or Pittsburgh.

"if it be possible for you to Subsist a small Party of Your Detachment of which your self will be the best Judge And from thence You are to Detach Ensn Wight to Escort the French Troops to Detroit where he is to deliver them to the Commanding Officer and Receive his Orders.

"I send You A form of the Oath to be Administerd by Inhabitance for the Subsistance of Your Party And defence of the Garrison You will receive A Hundred and Fifty Wight of Powder and Shot Answerab besides forty Days Provisions which is delivered to your Detachment And as it is Absoluttly Nescessary to keep some troops at the Fort Meamois it being Sittuated on the Carrying Place to Les Isle Au noix You will tell the Indians to be Strong and to Hunt for their Brethren the English and bring in Provisions for ye Garrison for which you'll Pay them in Powder and Ball.

"You will Make Your Report from time to time to ye Commanding Officer a Detroit & in so doing this will be your Sufficent Order. Dated at Detroit Decemr ye 7th 1760 (Bouquet, Volume V, pp. 163-164)

I ordered, that, if possible, a party should subsist at the former this winter, and give the earliest notice at Detroit of the enemy's motions in the country of the Illinois. I sent Mr. M'Gee, with a French officer, for the French troops at the Shawanese town on the Ohio. And as provisions were scarce, directed Capt. Brewer to repair with the greatest part of the Rangers to Niagara, detaining Lieutenant M'Cormack with thirty-seven more, to go with me to Michlimakana.

Fort Michilimackinac, at the Straits of Mackinac, present day Mackinaw City, Michigan.

I made a treaty with the several tribes of Indians living in the neighbouring country; and having directed Capt. Wait, just arrived from Niagara, to return again thither immediately, I set out for Lake Huron, and on the night of the 10th encamped at the north-end of the little Lake St. Clair, and the next evening on the west-side of the streight, at the entrance of a considerable river, where many Indians were hunting. We opened

Lake Huron the day following, and saw many Indian hunters on both sides of the mouth of the streights. We coasted along the west-shore of the Lake, about twenty miles north-and-by-west, the next day being the 13th forty, and the 15th thirty-eight miles, passing the cakes of ice with much difficulty. We could not advance at all the 16th, a heavy north-wind sending the cakes of ice on the south-shore in such quantities, that we could find no passage between them. I consulted the Indians about a journey to Michlimakana across by land; but they declared it impracticable at this season without snow-shoes, and to our great mortification we were obliged to return to Detroit; the ice obstructing us so much, that, with the greatest diligence and fatigue, we did not arrive there till the 21st.

> Rogers' failure to reach Michilimackinac that fall was not totally unexpected. As Amherst notes in a letter to William Pitt, Brigadier Monckton suspected it when Rogers departed from Fort Pitt: "I have not received any Account of Major Rogers from the other side of Lake Erie, Br. Genl. Monckton judges, from the time the Major left him, that the Season will not permit to go further than Fort Detroit." (Pitt, Volume II, p. 361)
>
> On December 11, Captain Campbell wrote to Henry Bouquet, "The Major is Sett out for Michillimackinac to bring away the Garrison in our situation it was impossible to send a Garrison. If he passes the bay of Saguinaw before the Frost overtakes him he may get there, if not, he will be oblidged to return.
>
> "The Commandant of Michillimackinac they say is gone with his small garrison, to winter with the Indians, for want of Provisions, he only has a few Soldiers." (Bouquet, Volume V, p. 171)

I delivered the ammunition to Capt. Campbell, and on the 23d set out for Pittsburg, marching along the west-end of Lake Erie, till the second of January 1761, when we arrived at Lake Sandusky.

> Insight into the feelings of the French inhabitants of Detroit for the way they were treated by Rogers and his men is found in a letter from Laurence Eustache Gamelin to Henry Bouquet of December 23, 1760: "Mr. Rogers and his party returned to their province. We were confounded by the good treatment they gave us, and if Detroit were not destitute, even ruined, as you must know, these gentlemen would have found in their hearts everything that gratitude and zeal require." (Bouquet, Volume V, p. 199)

I have a very good opinion of the soil from Detroit to this place; it is timbered principally with white and black oaks, hickerie, locusts, and maple. We found wild apples along the west-end of Lake Erie, some rich savannahs of several miles extent, without a tree, but cloathed with jointed grass near six feet high, which, rotting there every year, adds to the fertility of the soil. The length of Sandusky is about fifteen miles from east to west, and about six miles across it. We came to a town of the Windot Indians, where we halted to refresh.

On January 3d, south-east-by-east three miles, east-by-south one mile and a half, south-east a mile through a meadow, crossed a small creek about six yards wide, running east, travelled south-east-by-east one mile, passed thro' Indian houses, south-east three quarters of a mile, and came to a small Indian town of ten houses. There is a remarkable fine spring at this place, rising out of the side of a small hill with such force, that it boils above the ground in a column three feet high. I imagine it discharges ten hogsheads of water in a minute. From this town our course was south-south-east three miles, south two miles, crossed a brook about five yards wide, running east south east travelled south one mile, crossed a brook about four yards wide, running east-south-east, travelled south-south-east two miles, crossed a brook about eight yards wide. This day we killed plenty of deer and turkies on our march, and encamped.

On the 4th we travelled south-south-east one mile, and came to a river about twenty-five yards wide, crossed the river, where are two Indian houses, from thence south-by-east one mile, south-south-east one mile and a half, south-east two miles, south-south-east one mile, and came to an Indian house, where there was a family of Windots hunting, from thence south-by-east a quarter of a mile, south five miles, came to the river we crossed this morning; the course of the river here is west-north-west. This day killed several deer and other game, and encamped.

On the 5th travelled south-south-west half a mile, south one mile, south-south-west three quarters of a mile, south half a mile, crossed two small brooks running east, went a south-south-west course half a mile, south half a mile, south-east half mile, south two miles, south-east one mile, south half a mile, crossed a brook running east-by-north, travelled south-by-east half a mile, south-south-east two miles, south-east three quarters of a mile, south south-east one mile, and came to Maskongom Creek, about eight yards wide, crossed the creek, and encamped about thirty yards from it. This day killed deer and turkies in our march.

On the 6th we travelled about fourteen or fifteen miles, our general course being about east-south-east, killed plenty of game, and encamped by a very fine spring.

The 7th our general course about south-east, travelled about six miles, and crossed Maskongom Creek, running south, about twenty yards wide. There is an Indian town about twenty yards from the creek, on the east-side, which is called the Mingo Cabbins. There were but two or three Indians in the place, the rest were hunting. These Indians have plenty of cows, horses, hogs, & c.

The 8th, halted at this town to mend our mogasons, and kill deer, the provisions I brought from Detroit being entirely expended. I went a-hunting with ten of the Rangers, and by ten o'clock got more venison than we had occasion for.

On the 9th travelled about twelve miles, our general course being about south-east, and encamped by the side of a long meadow, were there were a number of Indians hunting.

The 10th, about the same course, we travelled eleven miles, and encamped, having killed in our march this day three bears and two elks.

The 11th, continuing near the same course, we travelled thirteen miles and encamped, where were a number of Wiandots and Six Nation Indians hunting.

The 12th, travelled six miles, bearing rather more to the east, and encamped. This evening we killed several beavers.

The 13th, travelled about north-east six miles, and came to the Delaware's town, called Beaver Town. This Indian town stands on good land, on the west-side of the Maskongom River; and opposite to the town, on the east-side, is a fine river, which discharges itself into it. The latter is about thirty yards wide, and the Maskongom about forty; so that when they both join, they make a very fine stream, with a swift current, running to the south-west. There are about 3000 acres of cleared ground round this place. The number of warriors in this town is about 180. All the way from the Lake Sandusky I found level land, and a good country. No pine-trees of any sort; the timber is white, black, and yellow oak, black and white walnut, cyprus, chesnut, and locust trees. At this town I staid till the 16th in the morning to refresh my party, and procured some corn of the Indians to boil with our venison.

On the 16th we marched nearly an east course about nine miles, and encamped by the side of a small river.

On the 17th kept much the same course, crossing several rivulets and creeks. We travelled about twenty miles, and encamped by the side of a small river.

On the 18th we travelled about sixteen miles an easterly course, and encamped by a brook.

In his journal for this date, Amherst reports learning by letter of Rogers' successful occupation of Fort Detroit: "I had letters from Capt Campbell & Col Bouquet informing me that Major Rogers arrived Nov 29th at Detroit with the loss of one man who fell overboard. A deputation from all the Indian Nations met him. Mons Bellestre the commanding Officer of the

Fort would not at first credit that Detroit was included in the Capitulation, but on receiving Mons Vaudreuil's letter he directly gave up the Fort."

"Major Rogers was preparing to bring in the French troops from the other Posts as far as the season would permit. All the inhabitants gave up their arms & took the oath of Allegiance. Mons Bellestre with two officers & 35 privates, the garrison of Detroit, arrived at Pittsburg Dec 24th escorted by Lt Holmes & a Party of Rangers. I ordered them to New York." (Amherst, p. 264)

The 19th, about the same general course, we crossed two considerable streams of water, and some large hills timbered with chesnut and oak, and having travelled about twenty miles, we encamped by the side of a small river, at which place were a number of Delawares hunting.

On the 20th, keeping still an easterly course, and having much the same travelling as the day before, we advanced on our journey about nineteen miles, which brought us to Beaver Creek, where are two or three Indian houses on the west side of the creek, and in sight of the Ohio.

Bad weather prevented our journeying on the 21st, but the next day we prosecuted our march. Having crossed the creek, we travelled twenty miles, nearly south-east, and encamped with a party of Indian hunters.

On the 23rd we came again to the Ohio, opposite to Fort Pitt, from whence I ordered Lieutenant M'Cormack to march the party across the country to Albany, and, after tarrying there till the 26th, I came the common road to Philadelphia, from thence to New York, where, after this long, fatiguing tour, I arrived February 14, 1761.

In a rare firsthand look at Rogers' social side, Captain-Lieutenant Lewis Ourry notes in a February 11 letter from Philadelphia to Henry Bouquet: "Major Rogers, was introduced to one of those polite Assemblies, and went thro' the Ceremony of Saluting all the Ladies; but as soon as Tea was over, he made a Leg, and retreated with the loss of his Heart,/as he told me today/. He is gone to N. York." (Bouquet, Volume V. p. 288)

On February 14, 1761, Amherst noted the completion of Rogers' dangerous and difficult mission in his journal: "Major Rogers & Lt Brehme arrived. They left Fort Detroit Dec 23rd. Rogers had tryed to get to Michillimackinac but the lake began to be so full of ice he was forced to return to Detroit." (Amherst, p. 265)

On February 27, Amherst wrote to Prime Minister Pitt: "On the 4th Instant Monsieur de Bellestre with the Garrison of Detroit arrived here, by his Account there are great Quantities of skins there, about three thousand Packs, as they have had no trade since Niagara was taken, have only disposed of some few to the English at that Place.

"On the 14th Instant Major Rogers arrived here, with the Engineer, I had sent with him to Detroit, he had tryed to get to Michilimackinac but the Season was so far advanced, he was obliged to return, after having proceeded near as far as Saquinaw bay, he left Detroit 23d. Decr and returned by Pittsburg . . . . I send you a Plan of the Fort at Detroit.

"I think it will be necessary to send a small body of Troops that way in the Summer, that all the Out-Posts of the French may be called in, the Country be thoroughly explored, some small Craft built on the Lakes, and Posts fixed for a quiet possession of the whole." (Pitt, Volume II, p. 404)

Thomas Mante's account of Rogers' Detroit Expedition reads as follows: "General Amherst, immediately after the signing of the capitulation at Montreal, made the necessary preparations to take possession of all the places which the French still held in Canada, as equally included in that act. Accordingly, on the 13th of September, Major Rogers embarked with a party of two hundred rangers, another of artillery, commanded by Lieutenant Davis, and Lieutenant Brehem, assistant engineer, to take possession of Detroit, and the posts established on the upper lakes. He was, besides, charged with the delivery of General Amherst's dispatches to General Monckton, who commanded at Fort-Pitt. These dispatches

Major Rogers soon delivered, and after a stay of only few hours, to refresh himself and his men, returned to Presque-Isle. He then proceeded to the Streights that join Lakes Erie and St. Claire; and from thence dispatched Lieutenant Brehem to M. de Beletre, who commanded at Detroit, to acquaint him with the capitulation; and that he had a letter for him from M. de Vaudreuil, with instructions for his conduct on the occasion. Major Rogers, soon after, took possession of the fort in the name of his Brittanic Majesty, and hoisted upon it the British colours. M Beletre and his garrison were ordered to Philadelphia, there to embark for Old France.

"The season was now so far advanced, that snow and ice rendered it impracticable to proceed to Michilimackinack; the Major, therefore, left troops at Detroit, and returned himself to Philadelphia." (Mante, pp. 343-344)

The close of the war brought out another example of Rogers' character and his loyalty to the men who had served with and under him. While trying to provide for his own future, he also did what he could to assist others who were bound to be affected by the inevitable troop reductions. Here are two examples:

On December 23, 1760, Ensign James Gorrell, of Captain Campbell's Company of the 60th at Detroit, wrote to Henry Bouquet in Philadelphia: "As Major Rogers has promised me he will lodge Cash for my Account, to Purchase a Lieutenancy for me in the hands of Mr Nicolson in Market Street Philadelphia . . . . I hope my being here will be no hindrance to my preferment in Case it comes to my turn to purchase." (Bouquet, Volume V, p. 199)

And on March 26, 1761, Rogers wrote the following to Henry Bouquet on behalf of his loyal and trusted Ranger officer, Robert Holmes: "The Bearor Mr Holmes is now on his Journey to join your Regiment in which he is appointed an Ensign As he is a young Gentleman that has served with me in the Ranging Service and for upwards of two Years since he hath been an Officer, hath behaved well and now leaves the said Service with a good Charactre

"I heartily request your Countenance towards him and hope you'll please to favour him with your good Advice on all Occasions and grant him Leave to wait on you for the same." (Bouquet, Volume V, p. 372) Like Captain Campbell, Robert Holmes, while serving as the commander of Fort Miami, was treacherously murdered by Indians during the Pontiac Uprising.

This widespread rebellion was brought on by a number of factors, not the least of which was the frugality of the British in making presents to the Indians, something that they had become well accustomed to under the French. This final quotation, from a letter written by General Monckton to Colonel Bouquet on April 5, 1761, gives a hint of what is to come: "The Indian Expence is Immense, I have Upwards of three Thousand Pounds, to Pay for Rogers's Expedition to Detroit; It is time now that the Indians, should live by their Hunting, & not think that they are always to be receiving Presents." (Bouquet, Volume V, p. 392)

Over time, this attitude would prove to be very costly to the British . . . .

F I N I S.

AN

Hiſtorical ACCOUNT

OF THE

EXPEDITION

AGAINST THE

OHIO INDIANS,

IN THE YEAR MDCCLXIV,

UNDER THE COMMAND OF

HENRY BOUQUET, Eſq.

Colonel of foot, and now Brigadier General in America. Including his Tranſactions with the Indians, Relative to the Delivery of the Priſoners, and the Preliminaries of Peace. With an Introductory Account of the Preceding Campaign, and Battle at Buſhy-Run.

To which are annexed

MILITARY PAPERS,

CONTAINING

Reflections on the War with the Savages; a Method of forming Frontier Settlements; ſome Account of the Indian Country; with a Liſt of Nations, Fighting Men, Towns, Diſtances, and different Routes.

Publiſhed, from authentic Documents, by a Lover of his Country.

D U B L I N.

Printed for JOHN MILLIKEN, at (No 10,) in *Skinner-Row*, MDCCLXIX.

Introduction to *An Historical Account* by Rev. William Smith

THE GENERAL PEACE, concluded between Great-Britain, France and Spain, in the year 1762, although viewed in different lights by persons variously affected in the mother country, was nevertheless universally considered as a most happy event in America.

To behold the French, who had so long instigated and supported the Indians, in the most destructive wars and cruel depredations on our frontier settlements at last compelled to cede all Canada, and restricted to the western side of the Mississippi, was what we had long wished, but scarcely hoped an accomplishment of in our own days. The precision with which our boundaries were expressed, admitted of no ground for future disputes, and was matter of exultation to every one who understood and regarded the interest of these colonies. We had now the pleasing prospect of "entire* security from all molestation of the Indians, since French intrigue could no longer be employed to seduce, or French force to support them."

"Unhappily, however, we were disappointed in this expectation. Our danger arose from that very quarter, in which we imagined ourselves in the most perfect security; and just at the time when we concluded the Indians to be entirely awed, and almost subjected by our power, they suddenly fell upon the frontiers of our most valuable settlements, and upon all our out-lying forts, with such unanimity in the design, and with such savage fury in the attack, as we had not experienced, even in the hottest times of any former war."

Several reasons have been assigned for this perfidious conduct on their part; such as an omission of the usual presents, and some settlements made on lands not yet purchased from them. But these causes, if true, could only affect a few tribes, and never could have formed so general a combination against us. The true reason seems to have been a jealousy of our growing power, heightened by their seeing the French almost wholly driven out of America, and a number of forts now possessed by us, which commanded the great lakes and rivers communicating with them, and awed the whole Indian country. They probably imagined that they beheld "in every little garrison the germ of a future colony," and thought it incumbent on them to make one general and timely effort to crush our power in the birth.

By the papers in the Appendix, a general idea may be formed of the strength of the different Indian nations surrounding our settlements, and their situation with respect to each other.

The Shawanese, Delawares and other Ohio tribes, took the lead in this war, and seem to have begun it rather too precipitately, before the other tribes in confederacy with them, were ready for action.

Their scheme appears to have been projected with much deliberate mischief in the intention, and more than usual skill in the system of execution. They were to make one general and sudden attack upon our frontier settlements in the time of harvest, to destroy our men, corn, cattle, &c. as far as they could penetrate, and to starve our outposts, by cutting off their supplies, and all communication with the inhabitants of the Provinces.

In pursuance of this bold and bloody project, they fell suddenly upon our traders whom they had invited into their country, murdered many of them, and made one general plunder of their effects, to an immense value.

The frontiers of Pennsylvania, Maryland and Virginia, were immediately over-run with scalping parties, marking their way with blood and devastation wherever they came, and all those examples of savage cruelty, which never fail to accompany an Indian War.

*The several quotations in this introduction are taken from the Annual Register, 1763, which is written with great elegance and truth, so far as the author appears to have been furnished with materials.

All our out-forts, even at the remotest distances, were attacked about the same time; and the following ones soon fell into the enemies hands—viz. Le Boeuf, Venango, Presqu' Isle, on and near lake Erie; La Bay upon lake Michigan; St. Joseph's, upon the river of that name; Miamis upon the Miamis river; Ouachtanon upon the Ouabache; Sandusky upon lake Junundat; and Michilimackinac.

Being but weakly garrisoned, trusting to the security of a general peace so lately established, unable to obtain the least intelligence from the colonies, or from each other, and being separately persuaded by their treacherous and savage assailants that they had carried every other place before them, it could not be expected that these small posts could hold out long; and the fate of their garrisons is terrible to relate.

The news of their surrender, and the continued ravages of the enemy, struck all America with consternation, and depopulated a great part of our frontiers. We now saw most of those posts, suddenly wrested from us, which had been the great object of the late war, and one of the principal advantages acquired by the peace. Only the forts of Niagara, the Detroit, and Fort-Pitt, remained in our hands, of all that had been purchased with so much blood and treasure. But these were places of consequence, and we hope it will ever remain an argument of their importance, and of the attention that should be paid to their future support, that they alone continued to awe the whole power of the Indians, and balanced the fate of the war between them and us!

These forts, being larger, were better garrisoned and supplied to stand a siege of some length, than the places that fell. Niagara was not attacked, the enemy judging it too strong.

The officers who commanded the other two deserved the highest honour for the firmness with which they defended them, and the hardships they sustained rather than deliver up places of such importance.

Major Gladwin, in particular, who commanded at the Detroit, had to withstand the united and vigorous attacks of all the nations living upon the Lakes.

The design of this publication, and the materials in my hands, lead me more immediately to speak of the defence and relief of Fort Pitt.

The Indians had early surrounded that place, and cut off all communication from it, even by message. Tho' they had no cannon, nor understood the methods of a regular siege, yet, with incredible boldness, they posted themselves under the banks of both rivers* by the walls of the fort, and continued as it were buried there, from day to day, with astonishing patience; pouring in an incessant storm of musquetry and fire arrows, hoping at length, by famine, by fire, or by harassing out the garrison, to carry their point.

Captain Ecuyer, who commanded there, tho' he wanted several necessaries for sustaining a siege, and the fortifications had been greatly damaged by the floods, took all the precautions which art and judgment could suggest for the repair of the place, and repulsing the enemy. His garrison, joined by the inhabitants, and surviving traders who had taken refuge there, seconded his efforts with resolution. Their situation was alarming, being remote from all the immediate assistance, and having to deal with an enemy from whom they had no mercy to expect.

General Amherst, the commander in chief, not being able to provide in time for the safety of the remote posts, bent his chief attention to the relief of the Detroit, Niagara, and Fort-Pitt. The communication with the two former was chiefly by water, from the province of New-York; and it was on that account the more it easy to throw succours into them. The detachment sent to the Detroit arrived there on the 29th of July, 1763; but Captain Dalyell, who commanded that detachment, and seventy of his men, lost their lives in a rencounter with the Indians near the fort. Previous to this disaster he had passed thro' Niagara, and left a reinforcement there.

Fort Pitt remained all this while in a most critical situation. No account could be obtained from the garrison, nor any relief sent to it, but by a long

*The Ohio and Monongahela, at the junction of which stands Fort Pitt.

and tedious land march of near 200 miles beyond the settlements; and through those dangerous passes where the fate of Braddock and others still rises on the imagination.

Col. Bouquet was appointed to march to the relief of this fort, with a large quantity of military stores and provisions, escorted by the shattered remainder of the 42nd and 77th regiments, lately returned in a dismal condition from the West-Indies, and far from being recovered of their fatigues at the siege of the Havannah. General Amherst, having at that time no other troops to spare, was obliged to employ them in a service which would have required men of the strongest constitution and vigour.

Early orders had been given to prepare a convoy of provisions on the frontiers of Pennsylvania, but such were the universal terror and consternation of the inhabitants, that when Col. Bouquet arrived at Carlisle, nothing had yet been done. A great number of the plantations had been plundered and burnt by the savages; many of the mills destroyed, and the full-ripe crops stood waving in the field, ready for the sickle, but the reapers were not to be found!

The greatest part of the county of Cumberland, thro' which the army had to pass, was deserted, and the roads were covered with distressed families, flying from their settlements, and destitute of all the necessaries of life.

In the midst of that general confusion, the supplies necessary for the expedition became very precarious, nor was it is less difficult to procure horses and carriages for the use of the troops.

The commander found that, instead of expecting such supplies from a miserable people, he himself was called by the voice of humanity to bestow on them some share of his own provisions to relieve their present exigency. However, in 18 days after his arrival at Carlisle, by the prudent and active measures which he pursued, joined to his knowledge of the country, and the diligence of the persons he employed, the convoy and carriages were procured with the assistance of the interior parts of the country, and the army proceeded.

Their march did not abate the fears of the dejected inhabitants. They knew the strength and ferocity of the enemy. They remembered the former defeats even of our best troops, and were full of diffidence and apprehensions on beholding the small number and sickly state of the regulars employed in this expedition. Without the least hopes, therefore, of success, they seemed only to wait for the fatal event, which they dreaded, to abandon all the country beyond the Susquehannah.

In such despondency of mind, it is not surprising, that tho' their whole was at stake, and depended intirely upon the fate of this little army, none of them offered to assist in the defence of the country, by joining the expedition; in which they would have been of infinite service, being in general well acquainted with the woods, and excellent marksmen.

It cannot be contested that the defeat of the regular troops on it this occasion, would have left the province of Pennsylvania in particular, exposed to the most imminent danger, from a victorious, daring, and barbarous enemy; for (excepting the frontier people of Cumberland County) the bulk of its industrious inhabitants is composed of merchants, tradesmen and farmers, unaccustomed to arms, and without a militia law.

The legislature ordered, indeed, 700 men to be raised for the protection of the frontiers during the harvest; but what dependence could be placed in raw troops, newly raised and undisciplined? Under so many discouraging circumstances, the Colonel (deprived of all assistance from the provinces, and having none to expect from the General, who had sent him the last man that could be removed from the hospitals) had nothing else to trust to, but about 500 soldiers of approved courage and resolution indeed, but infirm, and intire strangers to the woods, and to this new kind of war. A number of them were even so weak, as not to be able to march, and sixty were carried in waggons to reinforce the garrisons of the small posts on the communication.

Meanwhile Fort-Ligonier situated beyond the Allegheney-Mountains, was in the greatest danger of falling into the hands of the enemy, before the army could reach it. The stockade being very bad, and the garrison extremely weak, they had attacked it vigorously, but had been repulsed by the bravery and good conduct of Lieutenant Blane who commanded there.

The preservation of that post was of the utmost consequence, on account of its situation and the quantity of military stores it contained, which if the enemy could have got possession of, would have enabled them to continue their attack upon Fort-Pitt, and reduced the army to the greatest streights. For an object of that importance, every risk was to be run; and the Colonel determined to send through the woods, with proper guides, a party of thirty men to join that garrison. They succeeded by forced marches in that hazardous attempt, not having been discovered by the enemy till they came within sight of the Fort, into which they threw themselves, after receiving some running shot.

Previous to that reinforcement of regulars, 20 volunteers, all good woodsmen, who had been sent to Fort-Ligonier by Capt. Ourry, who commanded at Fort-Bedford another very considerable magazine of provisions, and military stores, the principal and centrical stage between Carlisle and Fort-Pitt, being about 100 miles distance from each. This fort was also in a ruinous condition, and very weakly garrisoned, although the two small intermediate posts, at the crossings of the Juniata and of Stony Creek, had been abandoned to strengthen it.

Here the distressed families, scattered for 12 or 15 miles round, fled for protection, leaving most of their effects a prey to the savages.

All the necessary precautions were taken by the commanding officer, to prevent surprize, and repel open force, as also to render ineffectual the enemies fire arrows. He armed all the fighting men, who formed two companies of volunteers, and did duty with the garrison till the arrival of two companies of light infantry, detached as soon as possible from Colonel Bouquet's little army.

These two magazines being secured, the Colonel advanced to the remotest verge of our settlements, where he could receive no sort of intelligence of the number, position, or motions of the enemy. Not even at Fort-Bedford, where he arrived with his whole convoy on the 25th of July, for tho' the Indians did not attempt to attack the fort, they had by this time killed, scalped, and taken eighteen persons in that neighbourhood, and their sculking parties were so spread, that at last no express could escape them. "This (want of intelligence) is often a very embarrassing circumstance in the conduct of a campaign in America. The Indians had better intelligence, and no sooner were they informed of the march of our army, than they broke up the siege of Fort-Pitt, and took the route by which they knew we were to proceed, resolved to take the first advantageous opportunity of an attack on the march."

In this uncertainty of intelligence under which the Colonel laboured, he marched from Fort-Bedford the 28th of July, and as soon as he reached Fort-Ligonier, he determined very prudently to leave his waggons at that post, and to proceed only with the pack horses. Thus disburdened, the army continued their route. Before them lay a dangerous defile at Turtle Creek, several miles in length, commanded the whole way by high and craggy hills. This defile he intended to have passed the ensuing night, by a double or forced march; thereby, if possible, to elude the vigilance of so alert an enemy, proposing only to make a short halt in his way, to refresh the Troops, at Bushy-Run.

When they came within half a mile of that place, about one in the afternoon, (August 5th, 1763) after an harassing march of seventeen miles, and just as they were expecting to relax from their fatigue, they were suddenly attacked by the Indians, on their advanced guard; which being speedily and firmly supported, the enemy was beat off, and even pursued to a considerable distance.

"But* the flight of these barbarians must often be considered as part of the engagement, (if we may use the expression) rather than a dereliction of the field. The moment the pursuit ended, they returned with renewed vigour to the attack.

*The above quotation is from the writer already mentioned, and seems so accurately and elegantly drawn up, from the account of this engagement, sent to his Majesty's ministers, that nothing better can be inserted in its room. There are but one or two small mistakes in it, which are here corrected.

Several other parties, who had been in ambush in some high grounds which lay along the flanks of the army, now started up at once, and falling with a resolution equal to that of their companions, galled our troops with a most obstinate fire.

"It was necessary to make a general charge with the whole line to dislodge them from these heights. This charge succeeded; but still the success produced no decisive advantage; for as soon as the savages were driven out from one post, they still appeared on another, till by constant reinforcements they were at length able to surround the whole detachment, and attack the convoy which had been left in the rear.

"This manoeuvre obliged the main body to fall back in order to protect it. The action, which grew every moment hotter and hotter, now became general. Our troops were attacked on every side; the savages supported their spirit throughout; but the steady behaviour of the English troops, who were not thrown into the least confusion by the very discouraging nature of this service, in the end prevailed, they repulsed the enemy, and drove them from all their posts with fixed bayonets.

"The engagement ended only with the day, having continued from one without any intermission.

"The ground, on which the action ended, was not altogether inconvenient for an encampment. The convoy and the wounded were in the middle, and the troops, disposed in a circle, incompassed the whole. In this manner, and with little repose, they passed an anxious night, obliged to the strictest vigilance by an enterprizing enemy who had surrounded them.

"Those who have only experienced the severities and dangers of a campaign in Europe, can scarcely form an idea of what is to be done and endured in an American war. To act in a country cultivated and inhabited, where roads are made, magazines are established, and hospitals provided; where there are good towns to retreat to in case of misfortune; or, at the worst, a generous enemy to yield to, from whom no consolation, but the honour of victory, can be wanting; this may be considered as the exercise of a spirited and adventurous mind, rather than a rigid contest were all is at stake, and mutual destruction the object: and as a contention between rivals for glory, rather than a real struggle between sanguinary enemies. But in an American campaign every thing is terrible; the face of the country, the climate, the enemy. There is no refreshment for the healthy, nor relief for the sick. A vast unhospitable desart, unsafe and treacherous, surrounds them, where victories are not decisive, but defeats are ruinous; and simple death is the least misfortune which can happen to them. This forms a service truly critical, in which all the firmness of the body and mind is put to the severest trial; and all the exertions of courage and address are called out. If the actions of these rude campaigns are of less dignity, the adventures in them are more interesting to the heart, and more amusing to the imagination, than the events of a regular war.

"But to return to the party of English, whom we left in the woods. At the first dawn of light the savages began to declare themselves, all about the camp, at the distance of about 500 yards; and by shouting and yelling in the most horrid manner, quite round that extensive circumference, endeavoured to strike terror by an ostentation of their numbers, and their ferocity.

"After this alarming preparative, they attacked our forces, and, under the favour of an incessant fire, made several bold efforts to penetrate into the camp. They were repulsed in every attempt, but by no means discouraged from new ones. Our troops, continually victorious, were continually in danger. They were besides extremely fatigued with a long march, and with the equally long action, of preceding day; and they were distressed to the last degree by a total want of water, much more intolerable than the enemy's fire.

"Tied to their convoy, they could not lose sight of it for a moment, without exposing, not only that interesting object, but their wounded men, to fall a prey to the savages, who pressed them on every side. To move was impracticable. Many of the horses were lost, and many of the drivers, stupefied by their fears, hid themselves in the bushes, and were incapable of hearing or obeying orders.

"Their situation became extremely critical and perplexing, having experienced that the most lively efforts made no impression upon an enemy, who always gave way when pressed; but who, the moment the pursuit was over, returned with as much alacrity as ever to the attack. Besieged rather than engaged; attacked without interruption, and without decision; able neither to advance nor to retreat, they saw before them the most melancholy prospect of crumbling away by degrees, and entirely perishing without revenge or honour, in the midst of those dreadful desarts. The fate of Braddock was every moment before their eyes; but they were more ably conducted.

"The commander was sensible that every thing depended upon bringing the savages to a close engagement, and to stand their ground when attacked. Their audaciousness, which had increased with their success, seemed favourable to this design. He endeavoured, therefore, to increase their confidence as much as possible.

"For that purpose he contrived the following stratagem. Our troops were posted on an eminence, and formed a circle round their convoy from the preceding night, which order they still retained. Col. Bouquet gave directions, that two companies of his troops, who had been posted in the most advanced situations, should fall within the circle; the troops on the right and left immediately opened their files, and filled up the vacant space, that they might seem to cover their retreat. Another company of light infantry, with one of grenadiers, were ordered 'to lie in ambuscade,' to support the two first companies of grenadiers, who moved on the feigned retreat, and were intended to begin the real attack. The dispositions were well made, and the plan executed without the least confusion.

"The savages gave entirely into the snare. The thin line of troops, which took possession of the ground which the two companies of light foot had left, being brought in nearer to the center of the circle, the barbarians mistook those motions for a retreat, abandoned the woods which covered them, hurried headlong on, and advancing with the most daring intrepidity, galled the English troops with their heavy fire. But at the very moment when, certain of success, they thought themselves masters of the camp, the two first companies made a sudden turn, and sallying out from a part of the hill, which could not be observed, fell furiously upon their right flank.

"The savages, though they found themselves disappointed and exposed, preserved their recollection, and resolutely returned the fire which they had received. Then it was the superiority of combined strength and discipline appeared. On the second charge they could no longer sustain the irresistible shock of the regular troops, who rushing upon them, killed many, and put the rest to flight.

"At the instant when the savages betook themselves to flight, the other two companies, which had been ordered to support the first, rose 'from the ambuscade,' marched to the enemy, and gave them their full fire. This accomplished their defeat. The four companies now united, did not give them time to look behind them, but pursued the enemy till they were entirely dispersed.

"The other bodies of the savages attempted nothing. They were kept in awe during the engagement by the rest of the British troops, who were so posted as to be ready to fall on them upon the least motion. Having been witnesses to the defeat of their companions, without any effort to support or assist them, they at length followed their example and fled.

"This judicious and successful manoeuvre rescued the party from the most imminent danger. The victory secured the field, and cleared all the adjacent woods. But still the march was so difficult, and the army had suffered so much, and so many horses were lost, that before they were able to proceed, they were reluctantly obliged to destroy such part of their convoy of provisions as they could not to carry with them for want of horses. Being lightened by this sacrifice, they proceeded to Bushy-Run, where finding water, they encamped."

The enemy lost about sixty men on this occasion, some of them their chief warriors; which they reputed a very severe stroke. They had likewise many wounded in the pursuit. The English lost about fifty men and had about sixty wounded.

The savages, thus signally defeated in all their attempts to cut off this reinforcement upon its march, began to retreat with the utmost precipitation to their remote settlements, wholly giving up their designs against Fort-Pitt; at which place Col. Bouquet arrived safe with his convoy, four days after the action; receiving no further molestation on the road, except a few scattered shot from a disheartened and flying enemy.

Here the Colonel was obliged to put an end to the operations of this campaign, not having a sufficient force to pursue the enemy beyond the Ohio and take advantage of the victory obtained over them; nor having any reason to expect a timely reinforcement from the provinces in their distressed situation. He was therefore forced to content himself with supplying Fort-Pitt, and other places on the communication, with provisions, ammunition, and stores; stationing his small army to the best advantage he could, against the approach of winter.

The transactions of the succeeding campaign, will be the subject of the following work, and we shall conclude this introduction, by shewing the sense which his Majesty was pleased to entertain, of the conduct and bravery of the officers and army, on this trying occasion.

Head-Quarters, New-York, Jan. 5, 1764.

ORDERS.

"His Majesty has been graciously pleased to signify to the commander in chief, his royal approbation of the conduct and bravery of Col. Bouquet, and the officers and troops under his command, in the two actions of the 5th and 6th of August; in which, not withstanding the many circumstances of difficulty and distress they laboured under, and the unusual spirit and resolution of the Indians, they repelled and defeated the repeated attacks of the Savages, and conducted their convoy safe to Fort-Pitt.

Signed Moncrief,
Major of Brigade."

To Col. Bouquet,
or officer commanding at Fort-Pitt.

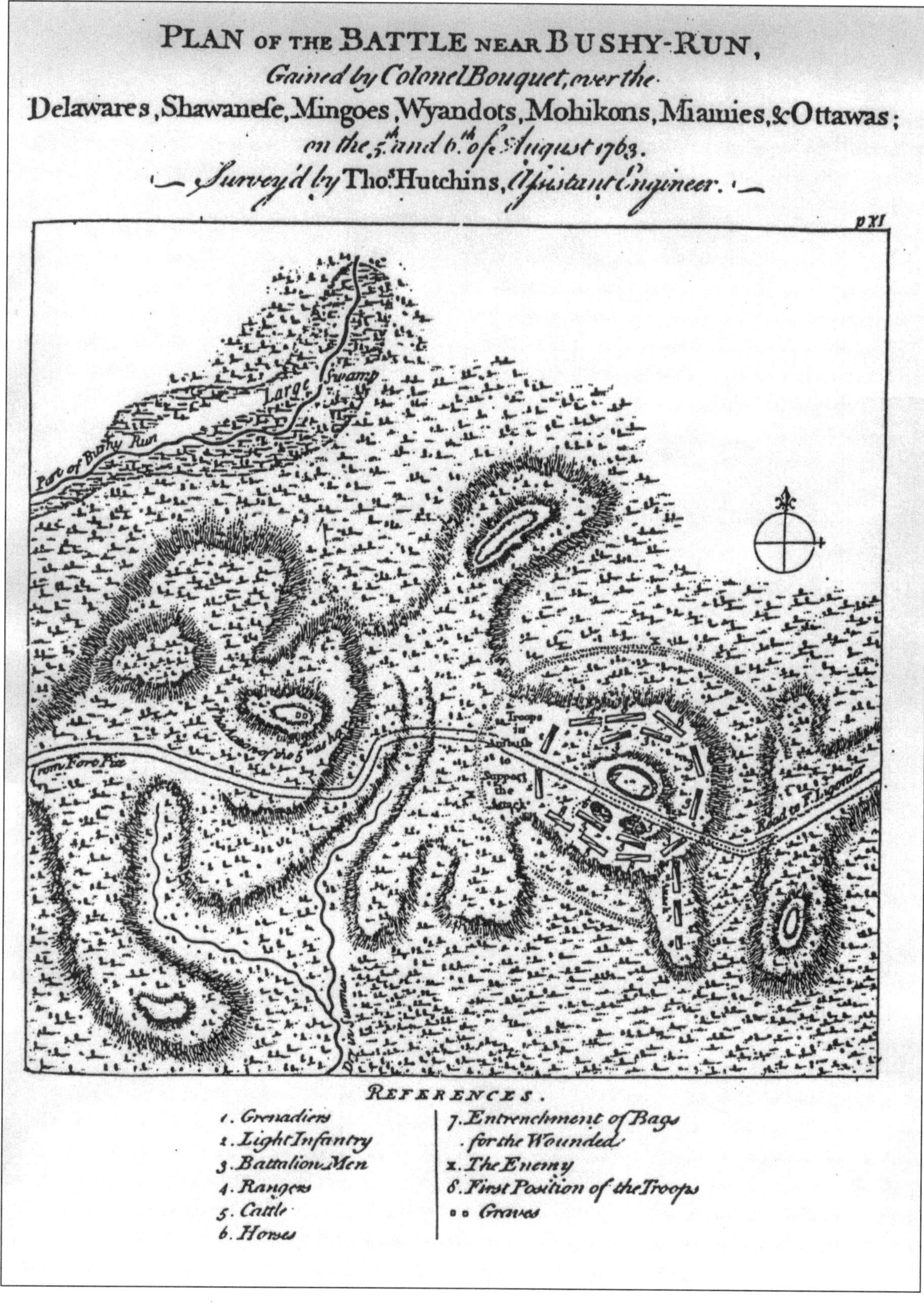

Plan of the Battle Near Bushy Run, by Thomas Hutchins. This map was not included in the Dublin edition of Rogers' Journals, but was a part of Father Smith's separate edition of his *Expedition Against the Ohio Indians.*

An Historical Account of Colonel Bouquet's Expedition Against the Ohio Indians in the Year 1764 by Rev. William Smith

IN the preceding introduction, some account hath been given of the sudden, treacherous and unprovoked attack, made by the Indians upon the frontiers of Pennsylvania, Maryland, and Virginia, soon after the publication of the general Peace, at a time when we were but just beginning to respire from our former calamities, and looked for an approach of quiet on every side. The principal transactions of the campaign 1763 have likewise been briefly recapitulated, and the reader informed by what means the editor became possessed of the valuable papers, which have enabled him to bring the history of this Indian war to a conclusion, and furnished the materials of the following sheets.

Colonel Bouquet, as before mentioned, not having a sufficient number of troops to garrison the different posts, under his command, and at the same time to cross the Ohio and take advantage of the dejection into which he had thrown the enemy, by the defeat at Bushy-Run, was obliged to restrain his operations to the supplying the forts with provisions, ammunition and other necessaries.

In the execution of this service, he received no annoyance from the enemy, for they now saw themselves not only forced to give up their designs against Fort-Pitt; but, retreating beyond the Ohio, they deserted their former towns, and abandoned all the country between Presque-Isle and Sanduski; not thinking themselves safe till they arrived at Muskingam.

Here they began to form new settlements, and remained quiet during the winter. But, in the mean time, having supplied themselves with powder, &c. from the French traders, (and now flattering themselves that the great distance of their settlements would render them inaccessible to our troops) the ensuing spring 1764 presented these savage enemies afresh on our frontiers; ravaging and murdering with their usual barbarity.

To chastize them for their perfidy, General Gage resolved to attack them on two different sides, and to force them from our frontiers; by carrying the war into the heart of their own country. With this view, he destined a corps of troops to proceed under Col. Bradstreet, to act against the Wiandots, Ottawas, Chipwas and other nations, living upon or near the lakes; while another corps, under the command of Col. Bouquet, should attacked the Delawares, Shawanese, Mingoes, Mohickons, and other nations, between the Ohio and the lakes.

These two corps were to act in concert; and as that of Col. Bradstreet could be ready much sooner than the other, he was to proceed to Detroit, Michilimackinac and other places. On his return he was to encamp and remain at Sanduski, to awe, by that position, the numerous tribes of western Indians, so as to prevent their sending any assistance to the Ohio Indians, while Colonel Bouquet should execute his plan of attacking them in the heart of their settlements.

Col. Bouquet's expedition was to proceed altogether by land, and it was on that account attended with great difficulties. His men were to penetrate through a continued depth of woods, and a savage unexplored country; without roads, without posts, and without a retreat if they failed of success. When once engaged in these deserts, they had no convoy, nor any kind of assistance to expect. Every thing was to be carried with them—their ammunition, baggage, tools, stores, and provisions necessary for the troops during the whole expedition. And besides, they were liable to many embarrassments, and difficulties which no prudence could foresee, scarce any caution prevent; so that, in this account, sundry things, which, in the usual method of conducting military operations, might not be thought worthy of a detail, may nevertheless be found highly serviceable to those who may afterwards be employed in this species of war, which is new to Europeans, who must submit to be instructed in it by experience, and in many articles even by the savages themselves.

Part of the 42nd and 60th regiments were ordered on this expedition, and were to be joined by two hundred friendly Indians, and the troops required of Virginia and Pennsylvania. The Indians never came, and the Virginians pleaded their inability to raise men, having already in pay about 700 militia for the defence of their own frontier. In Pennsylvania, a bill for raising 1000 men was passed May 30th; but, with the utmost diligence that could be used, the number could not be compleated till the beginning of August.

On the 5th of that month, the men being assembled at Carlisle, one hundred and eighteen miles to the westward of Philadelphia, Governor Penn, who had accompanied Col. Bouquet to that place, acquainted the two Pennsylvania battalions with the necessity we were laid under of chastising the Indians "for their repeated and unprovoked barbarities on the inhabitants of the Province; a just resentment of which, added to a remembrance of the loyalty and courage of our provincial troops on former occasions, he did not doubt, would animate them to do honour to their country; and that they could not but hope to be crowned with success, as they were to be united with the same regular troops, and under the same able commander, who had by themselves, on that very day, the memorable 5th of August in the preceding year, sustained the repeated attacks of the savages, and obtained a compleat victory over them.—He also reminded them of the exemplary punishments that would be inflicted on the grievous crime of desertion, if any of them were capable of so far forgetting their solemn oath and duty to their king and country, as to be involved in it."

Col. Bouquet then assumed the command of the regular and provincial troops; and the four following days were spent in the necessary preparations for their march; the Colonel giving the most express orders to officers and men to observe strict discipline, and not to commit the least violation of the civil rights or peace of the inhabitants.—He, at the same time, made the most prudent regulations for a safe and commodious carriage of the baggage, taking care to rid himself of all unnecessary incumbrances.

The 13th of August this small army got to Fort Loudoun; but notwithstanding all the precautions taken to prevent desertion, the Pennsylvania troops were now reduced to about 700 men. The Colonel was therefore under a necessity to apply to the government of that province to enable him to compleat their number to the full complement; which was generously granted by a resolve of the Governor and Commissioners August 16th; and the army advancing now beyond the settled parts of Pennsylvania, he made application to the colony of Virginia, where (under the countenance of Governor Fauquier the men wanted were soon raised, and joined) the army at Pittsburgh, about the latter end of September.

Nothing material happened in their march from Fort Laudoun to Fort Pitt, (formally Fort Du Quesne) on the Ohio, three hundred and twenty miles west from Philadelphia; at which place Col. Bouquet arrived the 17th of September.

During this interval, several large convoys were forwarded under strong escorts; and though the enemy continued their ravages all that time on the frontiers, they durst not attack any of those convoys, which all arrived safe at Fort Pitt.

While Col. Bouquet was at Fort Loudoun, he received dispatches by express from Colonel, Bradstreet, dated from Presque-Isle August 14th acquainting him that he (Colonel Bradstreet) had concluded a peace with the Delawares and Shawanese; but Colonel Bouquet perceiving clearly that they were not sincere in their intentions, as they continued their murders and depredations, he determined to prosecute his plan without remission, till he received further instructions from General Gage; who, upon the same principles, refused to ratify the treaty, and renewed his orders to both armies to attack the enemy.

About the time of Colonel Bouquet's arrival at Fort Pitt, ten Indians appeared on the north side of the Ohio, desiring a conference; which statagem the savages had made use of before, to obtain intelligence of our numbers and intentions. Three of the party consented, though with apparent reluctance, to come over to the Fort; and as they could give no satisfactory reason for their visit, they were detained as spies, and their associates fled back to their towns.

On the 20th of September Colonel Bouquet sent one of the above three Indians after them with a message, in substance as follows—"I have received an account from Colonel Bradstreet that your nations had begged for peace, which he had consented to grant, upon assurance that you have recalled all your warriors from our frontiers; and in consequence thereof, I would not have proceeded against your towns, if I had not heard that, in open violation of your engagements, you have since murdered several of our people.

"As soon as the rest of the army joins me, which I expect immediately, I was therefore determined to have attacked you, as a people whose promises can no more be relied on. But I will put it once more in your power to save yourselves and your families from total destruction, by giving us satisfaction for the hostilities against us. And first you are to leave the path open for my expresses from hence to Detroit; and as I am now to send two men with dispatches to Colonel Bradstreet who commands on the lakes, I desire to know whether you will send two of your people with them to bring them safe back with an answer? And if they receive any injury either in going or coming, or if the letters are taken from them, I will immediately put the Indians now in my power to death, and will shew no mercy for the future to any of your nations that shall fall into my hands. I allow you ten days to have my letters delivered at Detroit, and ten days to bring me back an answer."

He added "that he had lately had it in his power, while they remained on the other side of the river, to have put their whole party to death, which punishment they had deserved by their former treachery; and that if they did not improve the clemency now offered to them, by returning back as soon as possible with all their prisoners, they might expect to feel the full weight of a just vengeance and resentment."—

We have been the more particular in our account of this first transaction with the Indians; because the Colonel's firm and determined conduct in opening the campaign, had happy effects in the prosecution of it, and shews by what methods these faithless savages are to be best reduced to reason.

On the 1st of October, two of the Six Nation tribes, an Onondago and Oneida Indian, came to Fort Pitt, and under colour of our ancient friendship with them, and their pretended regard to the English, endeavored to dissuade the Colonel from proceeding with the army. They told him that his force was not sufficient to withstand the power of the numerous nations through whose countries he was to pass, and assured him that if he would wait a little, they would all come and make peace with him; at the same time recommending it particularly to him to send back the two Indians detained as spies. These little arts being clearly made use of to spin out the season till the approach of winter should render it impossible to proceed, they made but little impression. He told them that he could not depend on the promises of the Delawares and Shawanese; and was determined to proceed to Tuscarowas, where, if they had any thing to say, he would hear them.

In the mean time, he was using the utmost diligence to prepare for his march, and was obliged to enforce the severest discipline. One woman belonging to each corps, and two nurses for the general hospital, were all that were permitted to follow the army. The other women in the camp, and those unnecessary in the garrison, were ordered immediately down the country into the settlements. Two soldiers were shot for desertion; an example which became absolutely necessary to suppress a crime which, in such an expedition, would have been attended with fatal consequences, by weakening an army already too small.

Colonel Bouquet, having at length, with great difficulty, collected his troops, formed his maga-

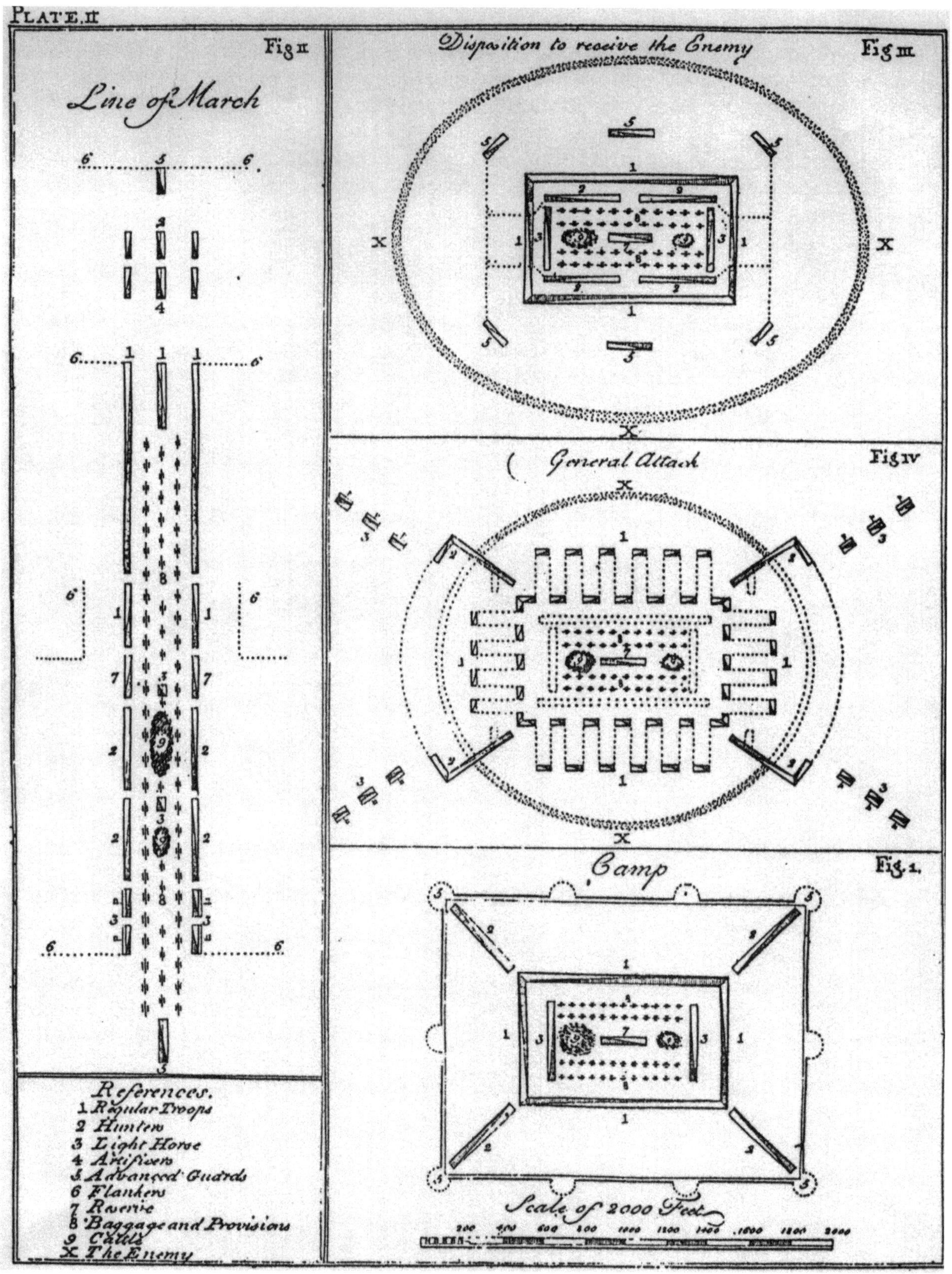

Line of March; Camp; Disposition to Receive the Enemy; and General Attack. This interesting diagram was not included in the Dublin Edition of Rogers' Journals, but was a part of Father Smith's separate edition of his *Expedition Against the Ohio Indians.*

zines, and provided for the safety of posts he was to leave behind him, was ready on the 2d of October to proceed from Fort Pitt, with about 1500 men, including drivers and other necessary followers of the army.

The Colonel, expressing the greatest confidence in the bravery of the troops, told them "he did not doubt but this war would soon be ended, under God, to their own honor, and the future safety of their country, provided the men were strictly obedient to orders, and guarded against the surprizes and sudden attacks of a treacherous enemy, who never dared to face British troops in any open field; that the distance of the enemy's towns, and the clearing roads to them, must necessarily require a considerable time; that the troops in those deserts, had no other supplies to expect but the ammunition and provisions they carried with them; and that therefore the utmost care and frugality would be necessary in the use of them." He published the several penalties against those who should be found guilty of stealing or embezzling any part of them, and ordered his march in the following manner.—

A corps of Virginia* volunteers advanced before the whole; detaching three scouting parties. One of them, furnished with a guide, marched in the center path, which the army was to follow. The other two extended themselves in a line abreast, on the right and left of the aforesaid party, to reconnoitre the woods.

Under cover of this corps, the ax-men, consisting of all the artificers, and two companies of light infantry, followed in three divisions, under the direction of the chief engineer, to clear three different paths, in which the troops and the convoy followed, viz.—

The front-face of the square, composed of part of the 42nd regiment, marched in a column, two deep, in the center path.

The right face of the square, composed of the remainder of the 42nd and of the 60th regiment, marched in a single file in the right-hand path.

The first battalion of Pennsylvanians composed the left face, marching in like manner in the path to the left of the center.

The corps de reserve, composed of two platoons of grenadiers, followed the right and left faces of the square.

The 2nd battalion of Pennsylvanians formed the rear face of the square, and followed the corps de reserve, each in a single file on the right and left hand paths; all these troops covering the convoy, which moved in the center path.

A party of light horse-men marched behind the rear-face of the square, followed by another corps of Virginia volunteers, forming the rear-guard.

The Pennsylvania volunteers, dividing themselves equally, and marching in a single file, at a proper distance, flanked the right and left faces of the square.

This was the general order of march. Nor was less attention paid to particular matters of a subordinate nature. The ammunition and tools were placed in the rear of the first column, or front face of the square, followed by the officers' baggage, and tents. The oxen and sheep came after the baggage, in separate droves, properly guarded. The provisions came next to the baggage, in four divisions, or brigades of pack-horses, each conducted by a horse-master.

The troops were ordered to observe the most profound silence, and the men to march at two yards distance from one another. When the line or any part of it halted, the whole were to face outwards; and if attacked on their march, they were to halt immediately, ready to form the square when ordered. The light horse were then to march into the square, with the cattle, provisions, ammunition and baggage. Proper dispositions were likewise made in case of an attack in the night; and for encampments, guards, communication between the centries, signals, and the like.

Things being thus settled, the army decamped from Fort-Pitt on Wednesday October 3d, and marched about one mile and an half over a rich level country, with stately timber, to camp No. 2. a strong piece of ground, pleasantly situated, with plenty of water and food for cattle.

Thursday October 4th, having proceeded about two miles, they came to the Ohio, at the be-

*These were the men raised in Virginia to compleat the Pennsylvania troops, and were in the pay of the last mentioned province.

ginning of the narrows, and from thence followed the course of the river along a flat gravelly beech, about six miles and a quarter; with two islands on their left, the lowermost about six miles long, with a rising ground running across, and gently sloping on both sides to its banks, which are high and upright. At the lower end of this island, the army left the river, marching through good land, broken with small hollows to camp No. 3; this day's march being nine miles and a quarter.—

Friday October 5th. In this day's march the army passed through Loggs-towns, situated seventeen miles and an half, fifty seven perches, by the path, from Fort-Pitt.

Thomas Nesbitt, of the Crown Point State Historic Site, is a trained surveyor who combines his professional knowledge with his historical interests. He has kindly provided me with the following information about eighteenth-century surveying measurements, so that readers who desire can compute the distances mentioned in the text into modern terms.

- A perch and a rod are the same, and are equal to 16.5 feet, or one quarter of a chain.
- The common unit of surveying measurement in the eighteenth century was the chain.

  One chain is equal to:
  - 66 feet
  - 100 links
  - 4 rods
  - 4 perches
- Therefore, 1 mile is equal to:
  - 80 chains
  - 120 rods or perches
- If these distances do not work out to known modern distances, then consider the possibility that the eighteenth-century measurements were made using Irish rods instead of English rods. The English rod is 16.5 feet, and the Irish rod is 18 feet, which can result in a considerable discrepancy over long distances. Finally, Mr. Nesbitt cautions that even modern distance measurements cannot always be relied on.

This place was noted before the last war for the great trade carried on there by the English and French; but its inhabitants, the Shawanese and Delawares, abandoned it in the year 1750. The lower town extended about sixty perches over a rich bottom to the foot of a low steep-ridge, on the summit of which, near the declivity, stood the upper town, commanding a most agreeable prospect over the lower, and quite across the Ohio, which is about 500 yards wide here, and by its majestic easy current adds much to the beauty of the place. Proceeding beyond Logg's-town, through a fine country, interspersed with hills and rich valleys, watered by many rivulets, and covered with stately timber, they came to camp No. 4; on a level piece of ground, with a thicket in the rear, a small precipice round the front, with a run of water at the foot, and good food for cattle. This day's march was nine miles, one half, and fifty three perches.

Saturday October 6th, at about three miles distance from this camp, they came again to the Ohio, pursuing its course half a mile farther, and then turning off, over a steep ridge, they crossed Big Beaver-creek, which is twenty perches wide, the ford stony and pretty deep. It runs through a rich vale, with a pretty strong current, its banks high, the upland adjoining it very good, the timber tall and young.——About a mile below its confluence with the Ohio, stood formerly a large town, on a steep bank, built by the French of square logs, with stone chimneys, for some of the Shawanese, Delaware and Mingo tribes, who abandoned it in the year 1758, when the French deserted Fort Du Quesne. Near the fording of Beaver-creek also stood about seven houses, which were deserted and destroyed by the Indians, after their defeat at Bushy-run, when they forsook all their remaining settlements in this part of the country, as has been mentioned above.

About two miles before the army came to Beaver-creek, one of our people who had been made prisoner by six Delawares about a week before, near Fort Bedford, having made his escape from them, came and informed the Colonel that these Indians had the day before fallen in with the army, but kept themselves concealed, being surprised at our numbers. Two miles beyond Beaver-creek, by two small springs, was seen the skull of a child, that had been fixed on a pole by the Indians. The Tracts of 15 Indians were this day discovered. The camp No. 5 is seven miles one quarter and fifty seven perches from big Beaver-creek; the whole march of this day being about twelve miles.

Sunday 7th October, passing a high ridge, they had a fine prospect of an extensive country to the right, which in general appeared level, with abundance of tall timber. The camp No. 6 lies at the foot of a steep descent, in a rich valley, on a strong ground, three sides thereof surrounded by a hollow, and on the forth side a small hill, which was occupied by a detached guard. This day's march was six miles sixty-five perches.

Monday 8th October, the army crossed little Beaver-creek, and one of its branches. This creek is eight perches wide, with a good ford, the country about it interspersed with hills, rivulets and rich valleys, like that described above. Camp No. 7 lies by a small run on the side of a hill, commanding the ground about it, and is distant eleven miles one quarter and forty nine perches from the last encampment.

Tuesday October 9th. In this day's march, the path divided into two branches, that to the south-west leading to the lower towns upon the Muskingam. In the forks of the path stand several trees painted by the Indians, in a hieroglyphic manner, denoting the number of wars in which they have been engaged, and the particulars of their success in prisoners and scalps. The camp No. 8. lies on a run, and level piece of ground, with Yellow creek close on the left, and a rising ground near the rear of the right face. The path after the army left the forks was so brushy and entangled, that they were obliged to cut all the way before them, and also to lay several bridges, in order to make it passable for the horses; so that this day they proceeded only five miles, three quarters and seventy perches.

Wednesday 10th. Marched one mile with Yellow-creek on the left at a small distance all the way, and crossed it at a good ford fifty feet wide; proceeding through an alternate succession of small hills and rich vales, finely watered with rivulets, to camp No. 9. seven miles and sixty perches in the whole.

Thursday 11th. Crossed a branch of Muskingam river about fifty feet wide, the country much the same as that described above, discovering a good deal of free stone. The camp No. 10. had this branch of the river parallel to its left face, and lies ten miles one quarter and forty perches from the former encampment.

Friday 12th. Keeping the aforesaid creek on their left, they marched through much fine land, watered with small rivers and springs, proceeding likewise through several savannahs or cleared spots, which are by nature extremely beautiful; the second which they passed being, in particular, one continued plain of near two miles, with a fine rising ground forming a semicircle round the right hand side, and a pleasant stream of water at about a quarter of a mile distant on the left. The camp No. 11. has the abovementioned branch of Muskingam on the left, and is distant ten miles and three quarters from the last encampment.

Saturday 13th. Crossed Nemenshehelas creek, about fifty feet wide, a little above where it empties itself into the aforesaid branch of Muskingam, having in their way a pleasant prospect over a large plain, for near two miles on the left. A little further, they came to another small river which they crossed about fifty perches above where it empties into the said branch of Muskingam. Here a high ridge on the right, and the creek close on the left, form a narrow defile about seventy perches long. Passing afterwards over a very rich bottom, they came to the main branch of Muskingam, about seventy yards wide, with a good ford. A little below and above the forks of this river is Tuscarowas, a place exceedingly beautiful by situation, the lands rich on both sides of the river; the country on the north-west side being an entire level plain, upwards of five miles in circumference. From the ruined houses appearing here, the Indians who inhabited the place and are now with the Delawares, are supposed to have had about one hundred and fifty warriors. This camp No.12. is distant eight miles nineteen perches from the former.

Sunday 14th. The army remained in camp; and two men who had been dispatched by Colonel Bouquet from Fort-Pitt, with letters for Colonel Bradstreet, returned and reported?— "That, within a few miles of this place, they had been made prisoners by the Delawares, and carried to one of their towns sixteen miles from hence, where they were kept, till the savages, knowing of the arrival of the army here, set them at liberty, ordering them to acquaint the Colonel that the head men of the Delawares and Shawanese were coming as soon as possible to treat of peace with them."

Monday 15th. The army moved two miles forty perches further down the Muskingam to camp No. 13, situated on a very high bank, with the river at the foot of it, which is upwards of 100 yards wide at this place, with a fine level country at some distance from its banks, producing stately timber, free from underwood, and plenty of food for cattle.

The day following, six Indians came to inform the Colonel that all their chiefs were assembled about eight miles from the camp, and were ready to treat with him of peace, which they were earnestly desirous of obtaining. He returned for answer that he would meet them the next day in a bower at some distance from the camp. In the mean time, he ordered a small stockaded fort to be built to deposite provisions for the use of the troops on their return; and to lighten the convoy.

As several large bodies of Indians were now within a few miles of the camp, whose former instances of treachery, although they now declared they came for peace, made it prudent to trust nothing to their intentions, the strictest orders were repeated to prevent a surprise.

Wednesday 17th. The Colonel, with most of the regular troops, Virginia volunteers and light horse, marched from the camp to the bower erected for the congress. And soon after the troops were stationed, so as to appear to the best vantage, the Indians arrived, and were conducted to the bower. Being seated, they began, in a short time, to smoak their pipe or calumet, agreeable to their custom. This ceremony being over, their speakers laid down their pipes, and opened their pouches, wherein were their strings and belts of wampum. The Indians present were,

SENECAS	DELAWARES	SHAWANESE
Kiyashuta, chief with 15 warriors	Custalogo, chief of the Wolfe-tribe Beaver, chief of the Turky-tribe, with 20 warriors	Keissinautchtha, a chief, and 6 warriors

Kiyashuta, Turtle Heart, Custaloga and Beaver, were the speakers.

The general substance of what they had to offer, consisted in excuses for their late treachery and misconduct, throwing the blame on the rashness of their young men and the nations living to the westward of them, suing for peace in the most abject manner, and promising severally to deliver up all their prisoners. After they had concluded, the Colonel promised to give them an answer the next day, and then dismissed them, the army returning to the camp.—The badness of the weather, however, prevented his meeting them again till the 20th, when he spoke to them in substance as follows, viz.

"That their pretences to palliate their guilt by throwing the blame on the western nations, and the rashness of their young men, were weak and frivolous, as it was in our power to have protected them against all these nations, if they had solicited our assistance, and that it was their own duty to have chastised their young men when they did wrong, and not to suffer themselves to be directed by them."

He recapitulated to them many instances of their former perfidy—"their killing or captivating the traders who had been sent among them at their own request, and plundering their effects;— their attacking Fort-Pitt, which had been built with their express consent; their murdering four men that had been sent on a public message to them, thereby violating the customs held sacred among all nations, however barbarous;—their attacking the King's troops last year in the woods, after being defeated in that attempt, falling upon our frontiers, where they had continued to murder our people to this day, & c."—

He told them how treacherously they had violated even their late engagements with Colonel Bradstreet, to whom they had promised to deliver up their prisoners by the 10th of September last, and to recall all their warriors from the frontiers, which they had been so far from complying with, that the prisoners still remained in their custody, and some of their people were even now continuing their depredations; adding, that these things which, he had mentioned, were only "a small part of their numberless murders and breaches of faith; and that their conduct had always been equally perfidious.—You have, said he, promised at every former treaty, as you do now, that you would deliver up all your prisoners, and have received every time, on that account, considerable presents, but have never complied with that or any other engagement. I am now to tell you, therefore, that we will be no longer imposed upon by your promises. This army shall not leave your country till you have fully complied with every condition that is to precede my treaty with you.

"I have brought with me the relations of the people you have massacred, or taken prisoners. They are impatient for revenge; and it is with great difficulty that I can protect you against their just resentment, which is only restrained by the assurances given them, that no peace shall ever be concluded till you have given us full satisfaction.—

"Your former allies, the Ottawas, Chipwas, Wyandots, and others, have made their peace with us. The Six Nations have joined us against you. We now surround you, having possession of all the waters of the Ohio, the Missisippi, the Miamis, and the lakes. All the French living in those parts are now subjects to the king of Great-Britain, and dare no longer assist you. It is therefore in our power totally to extirpate you from being a people —But the English are a merciful and generous nation, averse to shed the blood, even of their most cruel enemies; and if it was possible that you could convince us, that you sincerely repent your past perfidy, and that we could depend on your good behaviour for the future, you might yet hope for mercy and peace —If I find that you faithfully execute the following preliminary conditions, I will not treat you with the severity you deserve.

"I give you twelve days from this date to deliver into my hands at Wakatamake all the prisoners in your possession, without any exception; Englishmen, Frenchmen, women and children; whether adopted in your tribe, married, or living amongst you under any denomination and pretence whatsoever, together with all negroes. And you are to furnish the said prisoners with cloathing, provisions, and horses, to carry them to Fort Pitt.

"When you have fully complied with these conditions, you shall then know on what terms you may obtain the peace you sue for."—

This speech made an impression on the minds of the savages, which, it is hoped, will not soon be eradicated. The firm and determined spirit with which the Colonel delivered himself, their consciousness of the aggravated injuries they had done us, and the view of the same commander and army that had so severely chastised them at Bushy-Run the preceding year, now advanced into the very heart of their remote settlements, after penetrating through wildernesses which they had deemed impassable by regular troops—all these things contributed to bend the haughty temper of the savages to the lowest degree of abasement; so that even their speeches seem to exhibit but few specimens of that strong and ferocious eloquence, which their inflexible spirit of independency has on former occasions inspired. And though it is not to be doubted, if an opportunity had offered, but they would have fallen upon our army with their usual fierceness, yet when they saw the vigilance and spirit of our troops were such, that they could neither be attacked nor surprized with any prospect of success, their spirits seemed to revolt from the one extreme of insolent boldness, to the other of abject timidity. And happy will it be for them and for us, if the instances of our humanity and mercy, which they experienced in that critical situation, shall make as lasting impressions on their savage dispositions, as it is believed the instances of our bravery and power have done; so that they may come to unite, with their fear of the latter, a love of the former; and have their minds gradually opened, by such examples, to the mild dictates of peace and civility.

The reader, it is to be hoped, will readily excuse this digression, if it should be thought one. I now resume our narrative. The two Delaware chiefs, at the close of their speech on the 17th, delivered eighteen white prisoners, and eighty-three small sticks, expressing the number of other prisoners which they had in their possession, and promised to bring in as soon as possible. None of the Shawanese Kings appeared at the congress, and Keissinautchtha their deputy declined speaking until the Colonel had answered the Delawares, and then with a dejected sullenness he promised, in behalf of his nation, that they would submit to the terms prescribed to the other tribes.

The Colonel, however, determined to march farther into their country, knowing that the presence of his army would be the best security for the performance of their promises; and required some of each nation to attend him in his march.

Kiyashuta addressed the several nations, before their departure, "desiring them to be strong in complying with their engagements, that they might wipe away the reproach of their former breach of faith, and convince their brothers the English that they could speak the truth; adding that he would conduct the army to the place appointed for receiving the prisoners."

Monday October 22d. The army attended by the Indian deputies, marched nine miles to camp No. 14. crossing Margaret's creek about fifty feet wide —The day following, they proceeded sixteen miles one quarter and seventy seven perches farther to camp No. 15. and halted there one day.

Thursday 25th. They marched six miles, one half and sixteen perches to camp No. 16. situated within a mile of the Forks of Muskingham; and this place was fixed upon instead of Wakautamike, as the most central and convenient place to receive the prisoners; for the principal Indian towns now lay round them, distant from seven to twenty miles; excepting only the lower Shawanese town situated on Scioto River, which was about eighty miles; so that from this place the army had it in their power to awe all the enemy's settlements and destroy their towns, if they should not punctually fulfil the engagements they had entered into —Four redoubts were built here opposite to the four angles of the camp; the ground in front was cleared, a store-house for the provisions erected, and likewise a house to receive, and treat of peace with, the Indians, when they should return. Three houses with separate apartments were also raised for the reception of the captives of the respective provinces, and proper officers appointed to take charge of them, with a matron to attend the women and children; so that with the officers mess houses, ovens, & c. this camp had the appearance of a little town in which the greatest order and regularity were observed.

On Saturday 27th. A messenger arrived from king Custaloga, informing that he was on his way with his prisoners, and also a messenger from the lower Shawanese towns of the like import. The Colonel however, having no reason to suspect the latter nation of backwardness, sent one of their own people, desiring them —"to be punctual as to the time fixed; to provide a sufficient quantity of provisions to subsist the prisoners; to bring the letters wrote to him last winter by the French commandant at Fort Charters, which some of their people had stopped ever since;" adding that, "as their nation had expressed some uneasiness at our not shaking hands with them, they were to know that the English never took their enemies by the hand, before peace was finally concluded."

The day following, the Shawanese messenger returned, saying that when he had proceeded as far as Wakautamike, the chief of that town undertook to proceed with the message himself, and desired the other to return and acquaint the English that all his prisoners were ready, and he was going to the lower towns to hasten theirs.

October 28th. Peter the Caughnawaga chief, and twenty Indians of that nation arrived from Sanduski, with a letter from Colonel Bradstreet, in answer to one which Colonel Bouquet had sent him from Fort-Pitt, by two of the Indians who first spoke to him in favour of the Shawanese, as hath been already mentioned. The substance of Colonel Bradstreet's letter was "that he had settled nothing with Shawanese and Delawares, nor received any prisoners from them —That he had acquainted all the Indian nations, as far as the Illinois, the bay, & c. with the instructions he had received from General Gage, respecting the peace he had lately made; that he had been in Sanduski-lake and up the river, as far as navigable for Indian canoes, for near a month; but that he found it impossible to stay longer in these parts; absolute necessity obliging him to turn off the other way," & c.

Colonel Bradstreet, without doubt, did all which circumstances would permit, in his department; but his not being able to remain at Sanduski agreeable to the original plan, till matters were finally settled with the Ohio Indians, would have been an unfavourable incident, if Colonel Bouquet had not now had the chiefs of sundry tribes with him, and was so far advanced into the Indian country, that they thought it advisable to submit to the conditions imposed upon them.

The Caughnawagas reported that the Indians on the lakes had delivered but a few of their prisoners; that the Ottawas had killed a great part of theirs, and the other nations he had either done the same, or else kept them.

From this time to November 9th, was chiefly spent in sending and receiving messages to and from the Indian towns, relative to the prisoners, who were now coming into the camp one day after another in small parties, as the different nations arrived in whose possession they had been. The Colonel kept so stedfastly to this article of having every prisoner delivered, that when the Delaware kings, Beaver and Custaloga, had brought all theirs except twelve, which they promised to bring in a few days, he refused to shake hands or have the least talk with them, while a single captive remained among them.

By the 9th of November, most of the prisoners were arrived that could be expected this season, amounting to 206* in the whole; besides about 100 more in the possession of the Shawanese, which they promised to deliver the following spring. Mr. Smallman, formerly a major in the Pennsylvania troops, who had been taken last summer near Detroit by the Wyandots, and delivered to the Shawanese, was among the number of those whom they now brought in, and informed the Colonel that the reason of their not bringing the remainder of their prisoners, was that many of their principal men, to whom they belonged, were gone to trade with the French, and would not return for six weeks; but that every one of their nation who were at home, had either brought or sent theirs. He further said that, on the army's first coming into the country, it had been reported among the Shawanese that our intention was to destroy them all, on which they had resolved to kill their prisoners and fight us; that a French trader who was with them, and had many barrels of power and ball, made them a present of the whole, as soon as they had come to this resolution; but that, happily for the poor captives, just as the Shawanese were preparing to execute this tragedy, they received the Colonel's message, informing them that his intentions were only to receive the prisoners and to make peace with them on the same terms he should give to the Delawares.

On this intelligence they suspended their cruel purpose, and began to collect as many of the prisoners as they had power to deliver; but hearing immediately afterwards that one of our soldiers had been killed near the camp at Muskingham, and that some of their nation were suspected as guilty of the murder, they again imagined they would fall under our resentment, and therefore determined once more to stand out against us. For which purpose, after having brought their prisoners as far as Kakautamike, where they heard this news, they collected them all into a field, and were going to kill them, when a second express providentially arrived from Colonel Bouquet, who assured them that their nation was not even suspected of having any concern in the aforesaid murder; upon which they proceeded to the camp to deliver up the captives, who had thus twice so narrowly escaped becoming the victims of their barbarity.

*Virginians	Males,		32
	Females and Children,		58
Pennsylvanians,	Males,		49
	Females and Children,		67
		In all	206

On Friday, November 9th, the Colonel, attended by most of the principal officers, went to the conference-house. The Senecas and Delawares were first treated with. Kiyashuta and ten warriors represented the former. Custaloga and twenty warriors the latter.

Kiyashuta spoke—"With this string of wampum we wipe the tears from your eyes—we deliver you these three prisoners, which are the last of your flesh and blood that remained among the Senecas and Custaloga's tribe of Delawares, we gather together and bury with this belt* all the bones of the people that have been killed during this unhappy war, which the Evil Spirit occasioned among us. We cover the bones that have been buried, that they may be never more remembered—We again cover their place with leaves that it may be no more seen.—As we have been long astray, and the path between you and us stopped, we extend this belt that it may be again cleared, and we may travel in peace to see our brethren as our ancestors formerly did. While you hold it fast by one end, and we by the other, we shall always be able to discover any thing that may disturb our friendship."—

The Colonel answered that "he had heard them with pleasure; that he received these three last prisoners they had to deliver, and joined in burying the bones of those who had fallen in the war, so that their place might be no more known. The peace you ask for, you shall now have. The king, my master and your father, has appointed me only to make war; but he has other servants who are employed in the work of peace. Sir William Johnson is empowered for that purpose. To him you are to apply; but before I give you leave to go, two things are to be settled.

1. "As peace cannot be finally concluded here, you will deliver me two hostages for the Senecas, and two for Custaloga's tribe, to remain in our hands at Fort Pitt, as a security, that you shall commit no further hostilities or violence against any of his majesty's subjects; and when the peace is concluded these hostages shall be delivered safe back to you.

2. "The deputies you are to send to Sir William Johnson, must be fully empowered to treat for your tribes, and you shall engage to abide by whatever they stipulate. In that treaty, every thing concerning trade and other matters will be settled by Sir William, to render the peace everlasting; and the deputies you are to send to him, as well as the hostages to be delivered to me, are to be named and presented to me for my approbation."—

The Colonel, after promising to deliver back two of their people, Capt. Pipe, and Capt. John, whom he had detained at Fort Pitt, took the chiefs by the hand for the first time, which gave them great joy.

The next conference was on November 10th, with the Turkey and Turtle tribes of Delawares, King Beaver their chief and thirty warriors representing the former; that Kelappama brother to their chief** with twenty-five warriors the latter. The Senecas and Custaloga's tribe of Delawares were also present. Their speech and the answer given, were much the same as above; excepting that the Colonel insisted on their delivering up an Englishman, who had murdered one of our people on the frontiers and brought the scalp to them; and they should appoint the same number of deputies and deliver the same number of hostages, for each of their tribes, as had been stipulated for Custaloga's tribe.

November 11. King Beaver presented six hostages to remain with Col. Bouquet, and five deputies to treat with Sir William Johnson, who were approved of. This day he acquainted the chiefs present that as he had great reason to be dissatisfied with the conduct of Nettowhatways, the chief of the Turtle tribe who had not appeared, he therefore deposed him; and that tribe were to chuse and present another for his approbation. This they did a few days afterwards—Smile not, reader, at this transaction; for though it may not be attended with so many splendid and flattering circumstances to a commander, as the deposing an East Indian Nabob or chief; yet to penetrate into the wildernesses where those stern West Indian Chieftains hold their sway, and to frown them

*A belt or string is always delivered when thus mentioned.
**The Chief of the Turtle tribe, for some reason, chose to absent himself.

from their throne, though but composed of the unhewn log, will be found to require both resolution and firmness; and their submitting to it clearly shews to what degree of humiliation they were reduced.

But to proceed. The Shawanese still remained to be treated with, and though this nation saw themselves under the necessity of yielding to the same conditions with the other tribes, yet there had appeared a dilatoriness and sullen haughtiness in all their conduct, which rendered it very suspicious.

The 12th of November was appointed for the conference with them; which was managed on their part by Keissinautchtha and Nimwha their chiefs, with the Red Hawke, Lavissimo, Bensivasica, Eweecunwee, Keigleighque, and forty warriors; the Caughnawaga, Seneca, and Delaware chiefs, with about sixty warriors, being also present.

The Red Hawke was their speaker, and as he delivered himself with a strange mixture of fierce pride, and humble submission, I shall add a passage or two from his speech.

"Brother,

"You will listen to us your younger brothers; and as we discover something in your eyes that looks dissatisfaction with us, we now wipe away every thing bad between us that you may clearly see—You have heard many bad stories of us—We clean your ears that you may hear—We remove every thing bad from your heart, that it may be like the heart of your ancestors, when they thought of nothing but good." [Here he gave a string.]

"Brother; when we saw you coming this road, you advanced towards us with a tomahawk in your hand; but we your younger brothers take it out of your hands and throw it up to God* to dispose of as he pleases; by which means we hope never to see it more. And now, brother, we beg leave that you who are a warrior, will take hold of this chain (giving a string) of friendship, and receive it from us, who are also warriors, and let us think no more of war, in pity to our old men, women and children."—Intimating, by this last expression, that it was mere compassion to them, and not inability to fight, that made their nation desire peace.

He then produced a treaty held with the government of Pennsylvania 1701, and three messages or letters from that government of different dates; and concluded thus —

"Now Brother, I beg We who are warriors may forget our disputes, and renew the friendship which appears by these papers to have subsisted between our fathers."—He promised, in behalf of the rest of their nation, who were gone to a great distance to hunt, and could not have notice to attend the treaty, that they should certainly come to Fort-Pitt in the spring, and bring the remainder of the prisoners with them.

As the season was far advanced, and the Colonel could not stay long in these remote parts, he was obliged to rest satisfied with the prisoners the Shawanese had brought; taking hostages, and laying them under the strongest obligations, for the delivery of the rest; knowing that no other effectual method could at present be pursued.

He expostulated with them on account of their past conduct, and told them—"that the speech they had delivered would have been agreeable to him, if their actions had corresponded with their words. You have spoken, said he, much of peace, but have neglected to comply with the only condition, upon which you can obtain it. Keissinautchtha, one of your chiefs, met me a month ago at Tuscarawas, and accepted the same terms of peace for your nation, that were prescribed to the Senecas and Delawares; promising in ten days from that time to meet me here with all your prisoners—After waiting for you till now, you are come at last, only with a part of them, and propose putting off the delivery of the rest till the spring.—What right have you to expect different terms from those granted to the Delawares, &c. who have given me entire satisfaction by their ready submission to every thing required of them?—But I will cut this matter short with you; and before I explain myself further, I insist on your immediate answer to the following questions —

*Their usual figure for making peace is burying the hatchet; but as such hatchets may be dug up again, perhaps he thought this new expression of "sending it up to God, or the Good Spirit," a much stronger emblem of the permanency and stedfastness of the peace now to be made.

1st. "Will you will forthwith collect and deliver up all the prisoners yet in your possession, and the French living among you, with all the Negroes you have taken from us in this or any other war; and without any exception or evasion whatsoever?"

2d. "Will you deliver six hostages into my hands as a security for your punctual performance of the above article, and that your nations shall commit no farther hostilities against the persons or property of his majesty's subjects?"

Benevissico replied that "they agreed to give the hostages required, and said he himself would immediately return to their lower towns and collect all our flesh and blood that remained among them, and that we should see them at Fort-Pitt* as soon as possible.—That, as to the French, they had no power over them. They were subjects to the king of England. We might do with them what we pleased; though he believed they were all returned before this time to their own country."—

They then delivered their hostages, and the Colonel told them "that though he had brought a Tomahawk in his hand, yet as they had now submitted, he would not let it fall on their heads, but let it drop to the ground, no more to be seen. He exhorted them to exercise kindness to the captives, and look upon them now as brothers and no longer prisoners; adding, that he intended to send some of their relations along with the Indians, to see their friends collected and brought to Fort-Pitt. He promised to give them letters to Sir William Johnson, to facilitate a final peace, and desired them to be strong in performing every thing stipulated."

The Caughnawagas, the Delawares and Senecas, severally addressed the Shawanese, as grandchildren and nephews, "to perform their promises, and to be strong in doing good, that this peace might be everlasting."—

And here I am to enter on a scene, reserved on purpose for this place, that the thread of the foregoing narrative might not be interrupted—a scene, which language indeed can but weakly describe; and to which the Poet or Painter might have repaired to enrich their highest colours of the variety of human passions; the Philosopher to find ample subject for his most serious reflections; and the Man to exercise all the tender and sympathetic feelings of the soul.

The scene I mean, was the arrival of the prisoners in the camp; where were to be seen fathers and mothers recognizing and clasping their once-lost babes; husbands hanging round the necks of their newly-recovered wives; sisters and brothers unexpectedly meeting together after long separation, scarce able to speak the same language, or, for some time, to be sure that they were children of the same parents! In all these interviews, joy and rapture inexpressible were seen, while feelings of a very different nature were painted on the looks of others;—flying from place to place in eager enquiries after relatives not found! trembling to receive an answer to their questions! distracted with doubts, hopes and fears, on obtaining no account of those they sought for! or stiffened into living monuments of horror and woe, on learning their unhappy fate!

The Indians too, as if wholly forgetting their usual savageness, bore a capital part in heightening this most affecting scene. They delivered up their beloved captives with the utmost reluctance; shed torrents of tears over them, recommending them to the care and protection of the commanding officer. Their regard to them continued all the time they remained in camp. They visited them from day to day; and brought them what corn, skins, horses and other matters, they had bestowed on them, while in their families; accompanied with other presents, and all the marks of the most sincere and tender affection. Nay, they did not stop here, but, when the army marched, some of the Indians solicited and obtained leave to accompany their former captives all the way to Fort-Pitt, and employed themselves in hunting and bringing provisions for them on the road. A young Mingo carried this still further, and gave an instance of love which would make a figure even in romance. A young woman of Virginia was among the captives, to whom he had formed so strong an attachment, as to call her his wife. Against all remonstrances of the imminent danger

*It will appear, by the postscript to this account, that the Shawanese have fulfilled this engagement.

to which he exposed himself by approaching to the frontiers, he persisted in following her, at the great risk of being killed by the surviving relations of many unfortunate persons, who had been captivated or scalped by those of his nation.

Those qualities in savages challenge our just esteem. They should make us charitably consider their barbarities as the effects of wrong education, and false notions of bravery and heroism, while we should look on their virtues as sure marks that nature has made them fit subjects of cultivation as well as us; and that we are called by our superior advantages to yield them all the helps we can in this way. Cruel and unmerciful as they are, by habit and long example, in war, yet whenever they come to give way to the native dictates of humanity, they exercise virtues which Christians need not blush to imitate. When they once determine to give life, they give every thing with it, which, in their apprehension, belongs to it. From every enquiry that has been made, it appears—that no woman thus saved is preserved from base motives, or need fear the violation of her honour. No child is otherwise treated by the persons adopting it than the children of their own body. The perpetual slavery of those captivated in war, is a notion which even their barbarity has not yet suggested to them. Every captive whom their affection, their caprice, or whatever else, leads them to save, is soon incorporated with them, and fares alike with themselves.

These instances of Indian tenderness and humanity were thought worthy of particular notice. The like instances among our own people will not seem strange; and therefore I shall only mention one, out of a multitude that might be given on this occasion.

Among the captives, a woman was brought into the camp at Muskingam, with a babe about three months old at her breast. One of the Virginia-volunteers soon knew her to be his wife, who had been taken by the Indians about six months before. She was immediately delivered to her over-joyed husband. He flew with her to his tent, and cloathed her and his child in proper apparel. But their joy, after the first transports, was soon damped by the reflection that another dear child of about two years old, captivated with the mother, and separated from her, was still missing, altho' many children had been brought in.

A few days afterwards, a number of other prisoners were brought to the camp, among whom were several more children. The woman was sent for, and one, supposed to be hers, was produced to her. At first sight she was uncertain, but viewing the child with great earnestness, she soon recollected its features; and was so overcome with joy, that literally forgetting her sucking child she dropt it from her arms, and catching up the new found child in an extasy, pressed it to her breast, and bursting into tears carried it off, unable to speak for joy. The father seizing up the babe she had let fall, followed her in no less transport and affection.

Among the children who had been carried off young, and had long lived with the Indians, it is not to be expected that any marks of joy would appear on being restored to their parents or relatives. Having been accustomed to look upon the Indians as the only connexions they had, having been and tenderly treated by them, and speaking their language, it is no wonder that they considered their new state in the light of a captivity, and parted from the savages with tears.

But it must not be denied that there were even some grown persons who shewed an unwillingness to return. The Shawanese were obliged to bind several of their prisoners and force them along to the camp; and some women, who had been delivered up, afterwards found means to escape and run back to the Indian towns. Some, who could not make their escape, clung to their savage acquaintance at parting, and continued many days in bitter lamentations, even refusing sustenance.

For the honour of humanity, we would suppose those persons to have been of the lowest rank, either bred up in ignorance and distressing penury, or who had lived so long with the Indians as to forget all their former connections. For, easy and unconstrained as the savage life is, certainly it could never be put in competition with the blessings of improved life and the light of religion, by any persons who have had the happiness of enjoying, and the capacity of discerning, them.

Every thing being now settled with the Indians, the army decamped on Sunday 18th November, and marched for Fort Pitt, where it arrived on the 28th. The regular troops were immediately sent to garrison the different posts on the communication, and the provincial troops, with the captives, to their several provinces. Here ended this expedition, in which it is remarkable that, notwithstanding the many difficulties attending it, the troops were never in want of any necessaries; continuing perfectly healthy during the whole campaign; in which no life was lost, except the man mentioned to have been killed at Muskingam.

In the beginning of 1765, Colonel Bouquet arrived at Philadelphia, receiving wherever he came, every possible mark of gratitude and esteem from the people in general; and particularly from the overjoyed relations of the captives, whom he had so happily, and without bloodshed, restored to ther country and friends. Nor was the legislative part of the provinces less sensible of his important services. The assembly of Pennsylvania, at their first sitting, unanimously voted him the following address.

In ASSEMBLY, January 15, 1765, A.M.

To the Honourable HENRY BOUQUET, Esq; Commander in Chief of his MAJESTY's Forces in the Southern Department of AMERICA,

The Address of the Representatives of the Freemen of the Province of Pennsylvania, in General Assembly met.

SIR,

"The representatives of the freemen of the province of Pennsylvania, in general assembly met, being informed that you intend shortly to embark for England, and moved with a due sense of the important services you have rendered to his majesty, his northern colonies in general, and to this province in particular, during our late wars with the French and barbarous Indians, in the remarkable victory over the savage enemy, united to oppose you, near Bushy-Run, in August 1763, when on your march for the relief of Pittsburgh, owing, under God, to your intrepidity and superior skill in command, together with the bravery of your officers and little army; as also in your late march to the country of the savage nations, with the troops under your direction; thereby striking terror through the numerous Indian tribes around you; laying a foundation for a lasting as well as honourable peace with them; and rescuing, from savage captivity, upwards of two hundred of our christian brethren, prisoners among them: these eminent services, and your constant attention to the civil rights of his majesty's subjects in this province, demand, Sir, the grateful tribute of thanks from all good men; and therefore we, the representatives of the freemen of Pennsylvania, unanimously for ourselves, and in behalf of all the people of this province, do return you our most sincere and hearty thanks for these your great services, wishing you a safe and pleasant voyage to England, with a kind and gracious reception from his majesty.

"Signed, by order of the House,
"JOSEPH FOX, Speaker."

The Colonel's Answer was as follows, viz.

To the honourable the Representatives of the Freemen of the province of Pennsylvania, in General Assembly met.

"Gentlemen,

"With a heart impressed with the most lively sense of gratitude, I return you my humble and sincere thanks, for the honour you have done me in your polite address of the 15th of January, transmitted me to New-York by your speaker.

"Next to the approbation of His Sacred Majesty, and my superior officers, nothing could afford me higher pleasure than your favourable opinion of my conduct, in the discharge of those military commands with which I have been intrusted.

"Gratitude as well as justice demand of me to acknowledge, that the aids granted by the legislature of this province, and the constant assistance and support afforded me by the honourable the Governor and Commissioners in the late expedition, have enabled me to recover so many of his Majesty's subjects from a cruel captivity, and be the happy instrument of restoring them to freedom and liberty: To you therefore, gentlemen, is the greater share of that merit due, which you are generously pleased on this occasion to impute to my services.

"Your kind testimony of my constant attention to the civil rights of his majesty's subjects in this Province, does me singular honour, and calls for the return of my warmest acknowledgments.

"Permit me to take this public opportunity of doing justice to the officers of the regular and provincial troops, and the volunteers, who have served with me, by declaring that, under Divine Providence, the repeated successes of his Majesty's arms against a savage enemy, are principally to be ascribed to their courage and resolution, and to their perseverance under the severest hardships and fatigue.

"I sincerely wish prosperity and happiness to the province, and have the honour to be, with the greatest respect, Gentlemen,

"Your most obedient, and most humble servant,

HENRY BOUQUET.

February 4, 1765."

Soon afterwards the Colonel received a very polite and affectionate letter from Governor Fauquier, dated 25th of December, inclosing resolves of the honourable members of his Majesty's Council, and the house of Burgesses, for the colony and Dominion of Virginia.

Those respectable bodies unanimously returned their thanks to him for the activity, spirit and zeal, with which he had reduced the Indians to terms of peace, and compelled those savages to deliver up so many of his Majesty's subjects whom they had in captivity. They further requested the Governor to recommend him to his Majesty's ministers, as an officer of distinguished merit, in this and every former service in which he had been engaged.

The Colonel, in his answer, acknowledged the ready assistance and countenance which he had always received from the Governor and colony of Virginia in carrying on the King's service; and mentioned his particular obligations to Col. Lewis, for his zeal and good conduct during the campaign.

The honours thus bestowed on him, his own modesty made him desirous of transferring to the officers and army under his command; and indeed the mutual confidence and harmony subsisting between him and them, highly redound to the reputation of both. He has taken every occasion of doing justice to the particular merit of Colonel Reid who was second in command; and also to all the officers who served in the expedition, regulars as well as provincials.*

The reader will observe that the public bodies who presented these addresses to the Colonel, not only wished to express their own gratitude, but likewise to be instrumental in recommending him to the advancement his services merited. And surely it is a happy circumstance to obtain a promotion, not only unenvied, but even with the general approbation and good wishes of the public. It ought, however, to be mentioned, that on the first account his Majesty received of this expedition, and long before those testimonies could reach England, he was graciously pleased of his own royal goodness and as a reward of the Colonel's merit, to promote him to the rank of Brigadier General, and to the command of the southern district of America. And as he is rendered as dear, by his private virtues, to those who have the honour of his more intimate acquaintance, as he is by his military services to the public, it is hoped he may long continue among us; where his experienced abilities will enable him, and his love of the English constitution entitle him, to fill any future trust to which his Majesty may be pleased to call him.—

*The Pennsylvania troops were commanded by Lieutenant Colonel Francis, and Lieutenant Colonel Clayton.

POSTSCRIPT .

It was mentioned in the 249th page of this account, that the Shawanese brought only a part of their prisoners with them to Col. Bouquet at Muskingam, in November last; and that, as the season was far advanced, he was obliged to rest satisfied with taking hostages for the delivery of the remainder at Fort-Pitt, in the ensuing spring.

The escape of those hostages soon afterwards, as well as the former equivocal conduct of their nation, had given reason to doubt the sincerity of their intentions with respect to the performance of their promises. But we have the satisfaction to find that they punctually have fulfilled them. Ten of their chiefs, and about fifty of their warriors, attended with many of their women and children, met George Croghan, Esq; deputy agent to Sir William Johnson, at Fort-Pitt, the 9th of last May; together with a large body of Delawares, Senecas, Sandusky and Munsy Indians; where they delivered the remainder of their prisoners, brightened the chain of friendship, and gave every assurance of their firm intentions to preserve the peace inviolable for ever.

There is something remarkable in the appellation they gave to the English on this occasion; calling them Fathers instead of Brethren.

Lawaughqua, the Shawanese speaker, delivered himself in the following terms.—

"Fathers, for so we will call you hence-forward; listen to what we are going to say to you.

"It gave us great pleasure yesterday to be called the children of the great King of England; and convinces us your intentions towards us are upright, as we know a Father will be tender of his children, and they are more ready to obey him than a Brother. Therefore we hope our Father will now take better care of his children, than has heretofore been done.—

"You put us in mind of our promise to Col. Bouquet; which was to bring your flesh and blood to be delivered at this place. Father, you have not spoke in vain—you see we have brought them with us,—except a few that were out with our hunting parties, which will be brought here as soon as they return.

"They have been all united to us by adoption; and altho' we now deliver them up to you, we will always look upon them as our relations, whenever the Great Spirit is pleased that we may visit them.

"Father, We have taken as much care of them, as if they were our own flesh and blood. The are now become unacquainted with your customs and manners; and therefore, we request you will use them tenderly and kindly, which will induce them to live contentedly with you.

"Here is a belt with the figure of our Father the King of Great-Britain at one end, and the Chief of our nation at the other. It represents them holding the chain of friendship; and we hope neither side will slip their hands from it, so long as the Sun and Moon give light."

The reader will further remember that one of the engagements which the different Indian Tribes entered into with Colonel Bouquet, was to send deputies to conclude a peace with Sir William Johnson. This has also been punctually fulfilled; and we are assured that Sir William "has finished his congress greatly to his satisfaction, and even beyond his expectations." Thus every good consequence has ensued from this important expedition, which our fondest wishes could have induced us to expect from the known valour and spirit of the able commander who had the conduct of it; and we now have the pleasure once more to behold the temple of Janus shut, in this western world!

Reflections on the War with the Savages of North America.

THE LONG CONTINUED RAVAGES of the Indians on the frontiers of the British colonies in America, and the fatal overthrows which they have sometimes given our best disciplined troops, especially in the beginning of the late war, have rendered them an object of our consideration, even in their military capacity. And as but few officers, who may be employed against them, can have opportunities to observe the true causes of their advantages over European troops in the woods, it is with the utmost pleasure that I now proceed to lay before the public the following valuable papers, which I mentioned* to have been communicated to me by an officer of great abilities and long experience, in our wars with the Indians.

As scarce any thing has yet been published on a subject now become of the highest importance** to our colonies, these papers will undoubtedly be an acceptable present to the reader, and the remarks contained in them may be more and more improved by the future care and attention of able men, till perhaps a compleat system is at length formed for the conduct of this particular species of war.

SECTION I.

OF THE TEMPER AND GENIUS OF THE INDIANS.

The love of liberty is innate in the savage; and seems the ruling passion of the state of nature. His desires and wants, being few, are easily gratified, and leave him much time to spare, which he would spend in idleness, if hunger did not force him to hunt. That exercise makes him strong, active and bold, raises his courage, and fits him for war, in which he uses the same stratagems and cruelty as against the wild beasts; making no scruple to employ treachery and perfidy to vanquish his enemy.

Jealous of his independency and of his property, he will not suffer the least encroachment on either; and upon the slightest suspicion, fired with resentment, he becomes an implacable enemy, and flies to arms to vindicate his right, or revenge an injury.

The advantages of these savages over civilized nations are both natural and acquired. They are tall and well limbed, remarkable for their activity, and have a piercing eye and quick ear, which are of great service to them in the woods.

Like beasts of prey, they are patient, and deceitful, and rendered by habit almost insensible to the common feelings of humanity. Their barbarous custom of scalping their enemies, in the heat of action; the exquisite torments often inflicted by them on those reserved for a more deliberate fate; their general ferocity of manners, and the successes wherewith they have often been flushed, have conspired to render their name terrible, and some times to strike a pannic even into our bravest and best disciplined troops.

Their acquired advantages are, that they have been inured to bear extremes of heat and cold; and from their infancy, in winter and summer, to plunge themselves in cold streams, and to go almost naked, exposed to the scorching sun or nipping frosts, till they arrive to the state of manhood. Some of them destroy the sensation of the skin by scratching it with the short and sharp teeth of some animal, disposed in the form of a currycomb, which makes them regardless of briars and thorns in running thro' thickets. Rivers are no obstacles to them in their wild excursions. They either swim over, or cross them on rafts or canoes, of an easy and ready construction.

In their expeditions they live chiefly by hunting, or on wild fruits and roots with which the woods supply them almost every where.

They can bear hunger and thirst for several days, without slackening, on that account, their perseverance in any proposed enterprize.

*See the introduction.
**It will appear by the account of Indian tribes and towns annexed to these papers, that the enemies we have to deal with are neither contemptible in numbers or strength.

By constant practice in hunting, they learn to shoot with great skill, either with bows, or fire-arms; and to steal unperceived upon their prey, pursuing the tracts of men and beasts, which would be imperceptible to an European. They can run for a whole day without halting, when flying from an enemy, or when sent on a message. They steer, as if by instinct, thro' trackless woods, and with astonishing patience can lie whole days motionless in ambush to surprize an enemy, esteeming no labour or perseverance too painful to obtain their ends.

They besmear their bodies with bear's grease, which defends them against rains and damps, as well as against the stings of Muskitoes and Gnats. It likewise supples their limbs, and makes them slippery as the ancient gladiators, who could not be held fast when seized in fight.

Plain food, constant exercise, and living in the open air, preserve them healthy and vigorous.

They are powerfully excited to war by the custom established among them, of paying distinguished honours to warriors.

They fight only when they think to have the advantage, but cannot be forced to it, being sure by their speed to elude the most eager pursuit.

Their dress consists of the skins of some wild beast, or a blanket, a shirt either of linen, or of dressed skins, a breech clout, leggins, reaching half way up the thigh, and fastened to a belt, with mokawsons on their feet. They use no ligatures that might obstruct the circulation of their blood, or agility of their limbs. They shave their head, reserving only a small tuft of hair on the top; and slit the outer part of the ears, to which, by weights, they give a circular form, extending it down to their shoulders.

They adorn themselves with ear and nose rings, bracelets of silver and wampum, and paint their faces with various colours. When they prepare for an engagement they paint themselves black, and fight naked.

Their arms are a fusil, or rifle, a powder horn, a shot pouch, a tomahawk, and a scalping knife hanging to their neck.

When they are in want of fire-arms, they supply them by a bow, a spear, or a death hammer, which is a short club made of hard wood.

Their usual utensils are a kettle, a spoon, a looking glass, an awl, a steel to strike fire, some paint, a pipe and tobacco-pouch. For want of tobacco, they smoke some particular leaves, or the bark of a willow; which is almost their continual occupation.

Thus lightly equipped do the savages lie in wait to attack, at some difficult pass, the European soldiers, heavily accoutred, harassed by a tedious march, and encumbered with an unwieldy convoy.

Experience has convinced us that it is not our interest to be at war with them; but if, after having tried all means to avoid it, they force us to it, (which in all probability will often happen) we should endeavour to fight them upon more equal terms, and regulate our manoeuvres upon those of the enemy we are to engage, and the nature of the country we are to act in.

It does not appear from our accounts of Indian wars, that the savages were as brave formerly as we have found them of late; which must be imputed to their unexpected successes against our troops on some occasions, particularly in 1755; and from the little resistance they have since met with from defenceless inhabitants.

It is certain that even at this day, they seldom expose their persons to danger, and depend entirely upon their dexterity in concealing themselves during an engagement, never appearing openly, unless they have struck their enemies with terror, and have thereby rendered them incapable of defence—From whence it may be inferred that, if they were beat two or three times, they would lose that confidence inspired by success, and be less inclined to engage in wars which might end fatally for them. But this cannot reasonably be expected, till we have troops trained to fight them in their own way, with the additional advantage of European courage and discipline.

Any deviation from our established military system would be needless, if valour, zeal, order and good conduct, were sufficient to subdue this lightfooted enemy. These qualities are conspicuous in our troops; but they are too heavy, and indeed too valuable, to be employed alone in a destructive service for which they were never intended. They require the assistance of lighter corps, whose dress, arms and exercises, should be adapted to this new kind of war.

This opinion is supported by the example of many warlike nations, of which I beg leave to mention the following.

The learned Jesuit* who has obliged the world with a treatise on the military affairs of the ancient Romans, tells us, from Shallust,** that this wise nation, our masters in the art of war, were never hindered even by the pride of empire, from imitating any foreign maxim or institution, provided it was good; and that they carefully adopted into their own practice whatever they found useful in that of their allies or enemies; so that by receiving some thing from one, and some from another, they greatly improved a system even originally excellent.

My good friend and Grand Rapids police department chaplain, Father Dennis Morrow, is fluent in Latin. He graciously looked over the Latin footnotes that follow and advised me that the Latin basically repeats what is already written in English. Therefore, I have not had these footnotes translated).

The defeat of Antony and Crassus by the Parthians, of Curio by the Numidians, and many other instances, convinced the Romans that their legions, who had conquered so many nations, were not fit to engage light-troops, which, harassing them continually, evaded all their endeavours to bring them to a close engagement; and it is probable that if Julius Caesar had not been assassinated, when he was preparing to march against the same Parthians, to wipe off the reproach of the former defeats, he would have added to his legions a greater number of light troops, formed upon the principles and method of that nation, and have left us useful lessons for the conduct of a war against our savages.

That he did not think the attack of irregular troops contemptible, appears clearly in several parts of his commentaries, and particularly in the African war. The various embarrassments he met with from the enemy he had then to deal with, necessarily call to our mind many similar circumstances in the course of our wars with the Indians; and the pains he took to instruct his soldiers to stand and repel the skirmishes of the nimble Africans, may furnish instruction to us in our military operations against the savage Americans.

We are told that while Caesar was on his march "to Scipio's*** quarters, the enemy's horse and light-armed infantry, rising all at once from an ambuscade, appeared upon the hills, and attacked his rear. His legions forming themselves, soon beat the enemy from the higher ground. And now thinking all safe, he begins to pursue his march. But immediately the enemy break forth from the neighbouring hills; and the Numidians, with their light-armed foot, who are wonderfully nimble, always mixing and keeping equal pace with the cavalry in charging or retiring, fall afresh on the Roman foot. Thus they frequently renewed the charge, and still retired when he endeavored to bring them to close engagement. If but two or three of his veterans faced about and cast their piles with vigour, two thousand of the enemy would fly, then returning rally again, making it their business to harass his march, and to press

*Vid Joannis Antonii Valtrini Lib. de re milit. Vet. Rom.

**Neque enim Romanis superbia unquam obstitit, quo minus aliena instituta, si modo proba fuissent, imitarentur; et quod ubique apud focios vel hostes idoneum visum esset, cum studio domi exsequerentur —Aliaque ab aliis accepta, ipsi longe facere meliora quae quidem digna statuissent.

***Labienus, Afraniusque cum omni equitatu, levique armatura, ex infidiis adorti agmini Caesaris extreino se offerunt, atque ex collibus primis exsistunt.—Primo impetu legionum equitatus, levis armatura hostraum nullo negotio loco pulsa et dejecta est de celle. Quum jam Caesar existimasset hostes pulsos deterritosque finem lacessendi facturos, et iter coeptum pergere coepisset; iterum celeriter ex proximis collibus erumpunt; atque in Caesaris legionarios impetum faciunt Numidae, levisque armaturae, mirabili velocitate praediti; qui inter equites pugnabant, et una pariterque cum equitibus accurrere et refugere consueverant. Hoc saepius facerent, &c —Caesaris autem non amplius tres, aut quatuor milites veterani, si se convertissent, et pila viribus contorta in Numidas infestos conjecissent, amplius duorum millium numero ad unum terga vertebant; ac rursus ad aciem passim, conversis equis, se colligebant, atque in spatio consequebantur, et jacula in Legionarios conjiciebant.

Caesar contra ejusmodi hostium genera copias fuas, non ut imperator exercitum veteranum,victoremque maximis rebus gestis, sed ut lanista tirones gladiatores condocefacere: quo pede sese reciperent ab hoste, &c.—Mirifice enim hostium levis armatura anxium exercitum ejus atque sollicitum habebat: quia et equires deterrebat proelium inire, propter equorum interritum; quod eos jaculis interficiebat; et legionarium militem defatigabat, propter velocitatem. Gravis enim armatura miles simul atque ab his insectatus constiterat, in eosque impetum fecerat, illi veloci curfu facile periculum vitabant.

upon his rear, following at some distance, and throwing their darts at the legions.

"Caesar, having so subtil an enemy to deal with, instructed his soldiers, not like a general who had been victorious in the most arduous exploits, but as a fencing-master* would instruct his scholars; teaching them with what pace to retreat from the enemy, and how to return to the charge; how far to advance, and how far to retire; and likewise in what place and manner to cast their piles. For their light armed infantry gave him the greatest uneasiness, deterring his troopers from meeting them, by killing their horses with their javelins, and wearying his legions by their swiftness. For whenever his heavy-armed foot faced about and endeavoured to return their charge, they quickly avoided the danger by flight."

But without going back to the ancients, we have seen this maxim adopted in our days. Marshall de Saxe finding the French army harassed by the Hussars and other Austrian light troops, formed also several corps of them of different kinds; and the king of Prussia in his first war introduced them into his army, and has augmented and employed them ever since with success. We have ourselves made use of them in the two last wars in Europe: But the light troops wanted in America must be trained upon different principles. The enemies we have to deal with, are infinitely more active and dangerous than the Hussars and Pandours; or even the Africans above-mentioned. For the American savages, after their rapid incursions, retreat to their towns, at a great distance from our settlements, through thickety woods almost impenetrable to our heavy and unwieldy corps, composed of soldiers loaded with cloaths, baggage and provisions, who, when fatigued by a long march, must be a very unequal match to engage the nimble savage in woods, which are his native element.

Another unavoidable incumbrance, in our expeditions, arises from the provisions and baggage of the army, for which a road must be opened, and bridges thrown over rivers and swamps. This creates great labour, retards and weakens the line of march, and keeps the troops tied to a convoy which they cannot lose sight of, without exposing it to become a prey to a vigilant enemy, continually hovering about to seize every advantage.

An European, to be a proper judge of this kind of war, must have lived some time in the vast forests of America; otherwise he will hardly be able to conceive a continuity of woods without end. In spite of his endeavours, his imagination will betray him into an expectation of open and clear grounds, and he will be apt to calculate his manoeuvres accordingly, too much upon the principles of war in Europe.

Let us suppose a person, who is entirely unacquainted with the nature of this service, to be put at the head of an expedition in America. We will further suppose that he has made the dispositions usual in Europe for a march, or to receive an enemy; and that he is then attacked by the savages. He cannot discover them, tho' from every tree, log or bush, he receives an incessant fire, and observes that few of their shot are lost. He will not hesitate to charge those invisible enemies, but he will charge in vain. For they are as cautious to avoid a close engagement, as indefatigable in harassing his troops; and notwithstanding all his endeavours, he will still find himself surrounded by a circle of fire, which, like an artificial horizon, follows him every where.

Unable to rid himself of an enemy who never stands his attacks, and flies when pressed, only to return upon him again with equal agility and vigour; he will see the courage of his heavy troops droop, and their strength at last fail them by repeated and ineffectual efforts.

He must therefore think of a retreat, unless he can force his way thro' the enemy. But how is this to be effected? his baggage and provisions are unloaded and scattered, part of his horses and drivers killed, others dispersed by fear, and his wounded to be carried by soldiers already fainting under the fatigue of a long action. The enemy, encouraged by his distress, will not fail to encrease the disorder, by pressing upon him on every side, with redoubled fury and savage howlings.

*Lanista, in Latin, is an instructor of gladiators, which in English can only be translated a Fencing-master.

He will probably form a circle or a square, to keep off so daring an enemy, ready at the least opening to fall upon him with the destructive tomahawk: but these dispositions, tho' a tolerable shift for defence, are neither proper for an attack, nor a march thro' the woods.—

This is not an imaginary supposition, but the true state of an engagement with the Indians, experienced by the troops who have fought against them. Neither is there any thing new or extraordinary in this way of fighting, which seems to have been common to most Barbarians.*

What is then to be done to extricate our little army from impending destruction?

This is a problem which I do not pretend to resolve. But as every man would, in similar circumstances, determine himself some way or other, I will propose my own sentiments, founded upon some observations which I believe invariable in all engagements with savages.

The first, that their general maxim is to surround their enemy.

The second, that they fight scattered, and never in a compact body.

The third, that they never stand their ground when attacked, but immediately give way, to return to the charge.

These principles being admitted, it follows—

1st. That the troops destined to engage Indians, must be lightly cloathed, armed, and accoutred.

2d. That having no resistance to encounter in the attack or defence, they are not to be drawn up in close order, which would only expose them without necessity to a greater loss.

And, lastly, that all their evolutions must be performed with great rapidity; and the men enabled by exercise to pursue the enemy closely, when put to flight, and not give them time to rally.

These remarks will explain the reasons of the alterations proposed in the formation of a corps of troops, for the service of the woods. It is not, however, to be expected that this method will remove all obstacles, or that those light troops can equal the savages in patience, and activity; but, with discipline and practice, they may in a great measure supply the want of these advantages, and by keeping the enemy at a distance afford great relief and security to the main body.

SECTION II.

GENERAL IDEA OF AN ESTABLISHMENT OF LIGHT TROOPS, FOR THE SERVICE OF THE WOODS.

I shall only venture a few notions suggested by experience upon this subject, chiefly with a view to recommend it to the consideration of persons capable of proposing a proper method of forming such an establishment: and, in order to be better understood, I will suppose a corps of 500 men to be raised and disciplined for the woods, besides two troops of light horse, to which a company of artificers might be added. The fittest men for that service would be the natives of America bred upon the frontiers, and inlisted between the age of 15 and 20 years, to be discharged between 30 and 35.

CLOATHING.

The cloathing of a soldier for the campaign might consist of a short coat of brown cloth, lappelled, and without plaits; a strong tanned shirt, short trowsers, leggins, mokawsons or shoe packs, a sailor's hat, a blanket, a knapsack for provisions, and an oiled surtout** against the rain. To this might be added, in winter quarters or time of peace, three white shirts and stocks, with a flannel waistcoat.

*Vid. Caef. Comm. lib. V. de bello Gallico, et lib. II. de bello civili.

**The following Watch-coat was contrived by an officer, whose name I do not remember. But instead of the oiled linen to be put under the hat, a cap might perhaps answer better. He writes as follows, viz.

"As the Indian war will require frequent incursions into a wild country, where a man sick or wounded, is in several respects more detrimental to the service than a man killed, every thing that may contribute to the health of the men is of moment.

"In this view, I propose a sort of surtout, to preserve men, in a great measure, both from wet and cold.

"Take a large checked shirt, of about half a crown sterling per yard, for it should be pretty fine; cut off the wrist-bands, and continue the opening of the breast down to the bottom; sew up the sides from the gussets downwards; rip out the gathers in the fore parts of the collar as far as the shoulder straps, and resew it plain to the collar.

"The shirt will then become a sort of watch-coat like a bed-gown, with very wide sleeves.

"Take a quantity of linseed oil; and boil it gently till one half is diminished, to which put a small quantity of litharge of gold, and when it is well incorporated with the oil, lay it on with a brush upon the watch-coat, so that it shall be every where equally wet. [Continued next page]

ARMS.

Their arms, the best that could be made, should be short fusils and some rifles, with bayonets in the form of a dirk, to serve for a knife; with powder horns and shot pouches, small hatchets and leathern bottles for water.

EXERCISES.

The soldiers being raised, cloathed, and formed into companies under proper officers, must, before they are armed, be taught to keep themselves clean, and to dress in a soldier-like manner. This will raise in them a becoming spirit, give them a favourable opinion of their profession, and preserve their health. The first thing they are to learn is to Walk well, afterwards to Run; and, in order to excite emulation, small premiums might from time to time be given to those who distinguish themselves. They must then run in ranks, with open files, and wheel in that order, at first slowly, and by degrees increase their speed: this evolution is difficult, but of the utmost consequence to fall unexpectedly upon the flank of the enemy. They are to disperse and rally at given signals; and particular colours should be given to each company, for them to rally by; the men must be used to leap* over logs and ditches, and to carry burthens proportioned to their strength.

When the young soldiers are perfect in these exercises, they may receive their arms, with which they are to perform the former evolutions in all sorts of grounds. They will next be taught to handle their arms with dexterity; and, without losing time upon trifles, to load and fire very quick, standing, kneeling, or lying on the ground. They are to fire at a mark without a rest, and not suffered to be too long in taking aim. Hunting and small premiums will soon make them expert marksmen.

They ought to learn to swim, pushing at the same time their cloaths, arms, and ammunition before them, on a small raft; and to make use of snow shoes. They must then be set to work, and be taught to throw up an intrenchment, open a trench, make fascines, clays and gabions; likewise to fall trees, square logs, saw planks, make canoes, carts, ploughs, hand and wheel barrows, shingles and clap-boards, casks, batteaus and bridges, and to build log houses, ovens, &c.

By example and practice, the most ingenious among them will soon become tolerable good carpenters, joyners, wheelwrights, coopers, armourers, smiths, masons, brickmakers, saddlers, taylors, butchers, bakers, shoemakers, curriers &c.

LIGHT HORSE and DOGS.

I said that, to compleat this establishment, they should have two troops of light horse, supposed of 50 men each, officers included. The men are to perform the same exercises as the foot, and afterwards be taught to ride, and particularly to be very alert at mounting and dismounting with their arms in their hands, to gallop through the woods up and down hills, and leap over logs and ditches.

The horses ought to be bought up on the fron-

[Continued from previous page]

"I suppose the watch-coat, hung in a garret, or other covered place, and so suspended by crooked pins and packthreads in the extremities of the sleeves and edges of the collar, that one part shall not touch another. In a short time, if the weather is good, it will be dry; when a second mixture of the same kind should be laid on with a brush as before. When the second coat of painting is dry, the grease will not come off, and the surtout is an effectual preservative from rain; it is very light to carry, and being pretty full on the back, it will not only keep the man dry, but also his pack and ammunition.

"The sleeves are left long and wide to receive the butt end of a firelock (secured) and to cover it below the lock. The coat is double breasted to be lapped over, according to which side the rain drives. A man will be kept dry by one of these surtouts as far as the knees. If, from the vicinity of the enemy, it is improper to make fires at night, he may place his pack on a stone, and, sitting upon it, change his shoes and leggins, and, if he pleases, wrap his blanket round his legs and feet, then drawing the watch-coat close to his body, it will keep him warm, as no air can pass through it, and, leaning against the trunk of a tree, he may pass a tolerable night, both warm and dry.

"It would be of service to have a small piece of the same oiled linen to put under the hat or cap to carry the rain down to the watchcoat or surtout, otherwise whatever wet soaks through the hat or cap, will run down the neck, and thereby, in some measure, defeat the design of the watch-coat.

"Perhaps it might be useful to mix some dark or greenish colour with the oil of the second coating, to make the watch-coat less remarkable in the woods."

*Vegetius gives us an account of many similar exercises, which the Romans found necessary to establish among their military. Miles sylvam caedebat, aestivis temporibus natabat, ad palum dimicabat, saltabat, currebat. Exempla hujus exercitationis crebra sunt apud Livium. Sic ille de Scipione Africano, 3 decad. lib. VI. "Primo die legiones in armis IV. millium spatio decurrerunt. Secundo die arma curare et tergere ante tentoria jussit. Tertio die sudibus inter se in modum justae pugnae concurrerent, praepilatisque missilibus jaculati sunt. Quarto die quies data. Quinto iterum in armis decursum est."—Quibus porro modis obviam eatur elephantis. Veget. lib. III. cap. 24.

tiers, where they are bred and used to feed in the woods, and are strong and hardy. They are to be thoroughly broke, made to stand fire, to swim over rivers, &c. their saddles and accoutrements very simple, strong and light. The number of horses might be reduced to one half, in time of peace, tho' they would be of little expence, as they might be bred and maintained without charge in the military settlement. This corps should be equipped as the foot, having only a short rifle in lieu of a fusil, and a battle ax with a long handle, the only sort of arms they should make use of in the charge.

Every light horse man ought to be provided with a Blood-hound which would be useful to find out the enemies ambushes, and to follow their tracts; they would seize the naked savages, or at least give time to the horse men to come up with them; they would add to the safety of the camp at night by discovering any attempt to surprize it.

ARTIFICERS.

The company of artificers should be composed of the most useful tradesmen, and ought to be maintained at all time for the instruction of the soldiers, the use of the settlement, or the service of the army, during the campaign. It will now be time to draw forth this military colony and remove them to the ground laid out for that use in the woods, and at a good distance from the inhabitants. The nature of this settlement will hereafter be more particularly described.

Necessity creating industry, our young soldiers will soon provide themselves with the most useful articles, and in a couple of years be able to raise provisions for themselves.

While the greatest part would be employed in clearing the ground, fencing, ploughing, sowing, planting, building and making utensils and houshold furniture, others might hunt with their officers, and remain a fortnight or a month out of the camp, without other provisions than a little flour, and what they could procure by hunting and fishing: then to be relieved, and the whole trained up in that way.

The military exercises must still be kept up and practiced, and great care taken to inculcate and preserve purity of manners, obedience, order and decency among the men, which will be found much easier in the woods than in the neighbourhood of towns.

In order to make this military establishment more generally useful; I would propose that the soldiers should only receive a very small part of their pay; leaving the remainder in the military chest.

Their accounts should be settled every year, and when their services should intitle them to their discharge, I could wish that each of them had 200 acres of land given him, in a district appropriated for that purpose; and receiving then the whole ballance of pay due to them, they would be enabled to compleat their settlement. This institution appears not only practicable, but easy, if attended to with patience, assiduity and firmness. The plan I would propose is as follows.

Method of forming such SETTLEMENTS upon the Frontiers, as might support themselves during an Indian War.

Let us suppose a settlement to be formed for one hundred families, composed of five persons each, upon an average.

Lay out upon a river, or creek, if it can be found conveniently, a square of one thousand seven hundred and sixty yards, or a mile for each side.

That square will contain—	640 acres
Allowing for streets and public uses	40
To half an acre for every house -	50
To one hundred lots at five and half acres	550
	640 acres

The four sides of the square measure 7040 yards, which gives to each house about 70 yards front to stockade, and the ground allowed for building will be 210 feet front and about 100 feet deep.

An acre of ground will produce at least 30 bushels of Indian corn. Therefore, two acres are sufficient to supply five persons, at the rate of twelve bushels each person. Two other acres will be a pasture for cows and sheep, another acre for hay, to be sown with red clover. The remaining half acre may be laid out for a garden.

Round the town are the commons, of three miles square, containing, exclusive of the lots above-mentioned, 5120 acres. On three sides of the town, five other Squares will be laid out of three square miles, containing 5760 acres each, one of which is reserved for wood for the use of the Settlement; the other four to be divided into 25 out-lots or plantations, of about 230 acres each, so that in the four Squares there will be one hundred such plantations, for the 100 families.

Another township may be laid out joining this, upon the same plan, and as many more as you please upon the same line, without losing any ground.

Thus the town, A, has its commons, its woodland, and its 4 squares marked No.1. each containing 25 plantations of 230 acres, as proposed above. In like manner, the other towns, B, C, D, have their appurtenances respectively marked.

Let us now suppose this plan accomplished, and such corps as these fully settled, trained and disciplined, in the manner above-mentioned; I would ask whether any officer, entrusted with an expedition against the savages, would not chuse to have them in his army? I may safely answer for those who have been employed in that service, that they would prefer them to double the number of the best European troops. And when they had served the time limited, namely from their 15th to their 35th year, what vast satisfaction would it be to pay over to them their share of savings from the public chest; and, as a reward of their faithful toils, to vest them and their heirs with their several plantations, which they would now be enabled to cultivate as their own? This prospect would engage many people to enter their sons, in such corps; and those veterans, when thus discharged, would not only be the means of forming and animating others by their example, but in case of a war would still bravely maintain the property they had so honourably acquired, and be the greatest security of the frontier where they are settled.

THE following is a rough ſketch of the whole.

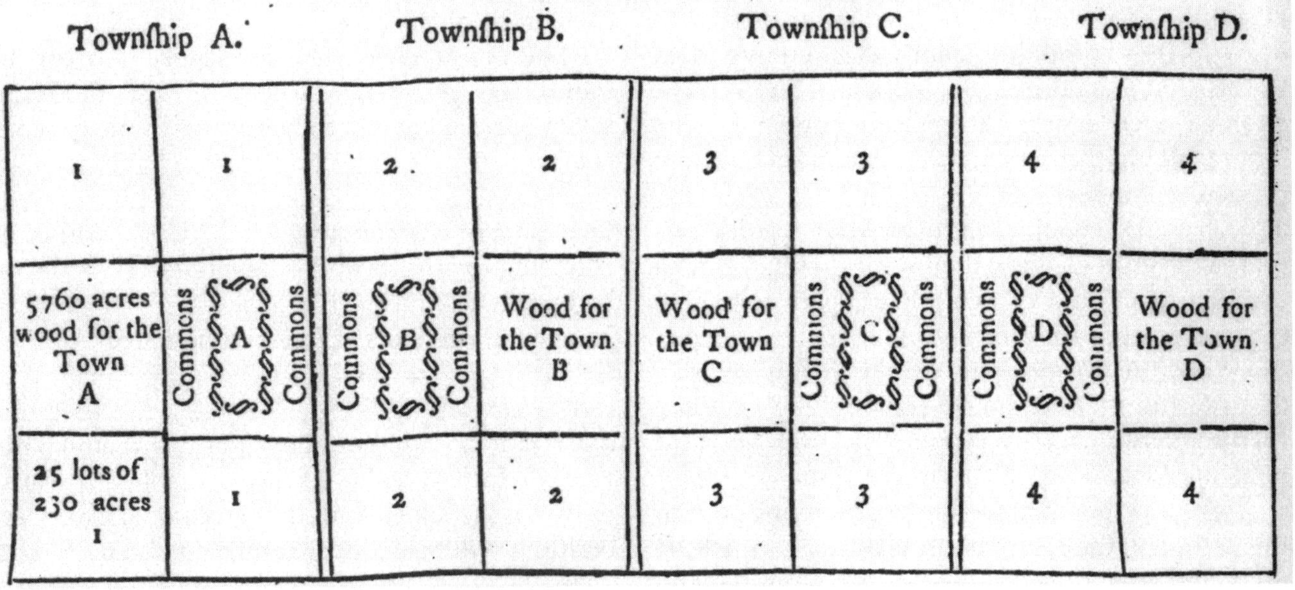

Townſhip A.		Townſhip B.		Townſhip C.		Townſhip D.	
1	1	2	2	3	3	4	4
5760 acres wood for the Town A	Commons A Commons	Commons B Commons	Wood for the Town B	Wood for the Town C	Commons C Commons	Commons D Commons	Wood for the Town D
25 lots of 230 acres 1	1	2	2	3	3	4	4

Plan of a frontier settlement. This sketch was originally published in both Father Smith's separate edition of his Expedition Against the Ohio Indians and the Dublin edition of Rogers' Journals.

PREPARATIONS FOR AN EXPEDITION IN THE WOODS AGAINST SAVAGES.

It is not practicable to employ large bodies of troops against Indians; the convoys necessary for their support would be too cumbersome, and could neither be moved with ease, nor protected. It would be better to fit out several small expeditions, than one too unwieldy: I will therefore suppose that a corps intended to act offensively shall not exceed the following proportions.

Two regiments of foot	900
One battalion of hunters	500
Two troops of light horse	100
One company of artificers	20
Drivers and necessary followers	280
In all	1800

The first article to provide is the provisions, and next the carriages.

The daily ration of a soldier in the woods should consist of one pound and a half of meat (which requires no carriage) and one pound of flour, with a gill of salt per week.

Upon that allowance 1800 men will require for six months or 182 days - -	327,600 lb. Flour.
Allowing one fourth for accident - - - - -	81,900
For six months	409,500 lb. Flour.
Meat for the same time with a fourth part more for accidents, or 2048 beeves at 300 lb. each	614,400 lb. Meat.
Salt for 26 weeks - - - - -	182 Bushels.

The above quantity would serve the whole campaign, but one half would be sufficient to penetrate from the last deposite into the heart of the enemy's country: therefore we shall compute the carriages for this last quantity only.

Every horse carries about 150 lb. neat weight, therefore, to carry flour for three months or 204,750 lb. will require 1365 horses.

Horses for flour - - - - - - - - - - -	1365
For 91 bushels of salt - - - - - - -	46
Ammunition - - - - - - - - - - - - -	50
Tents - - - - - - - - - - - - - - - - - - -	50
Tools - - - - - - - - - - - - - - - - - - -	50
Hospital - - - - - - - - - - - - - - - - -	20
Officers baggage and staff - - - -	150
	1731

To reduce this exorbitant number of horses, and the great expence attending it, I would propose, for such parts of the country as would admit of it, to make use of carts drawn each by four oxen, and carrying about 1300 lb or six barrels of flour. The above quantity of 204, 750 lb. will then be carried by 160 carts drawn by 640 oxen

Spare oxen with the army - - - - -	384
The number of oxen wanted - - -	1024

This method would not be as expeditious as the carriage by horses, and would require more time and attention in cutting the road, and bridging the swampy places, &c. but, on the other hand, what an expence would be saved! and by killing the oxen in proportion as the flour is used, and abandoning the carts, the convoy is daily reduced, and the grass near the encampment will not be so soon consumed, which is not the case with horses, which must equally be fed though unloaded. This is an object of consequence, particularly near the end of the campaign, when the scarcity of fodder obliges to move the camps every day, and to place them in low and disadvantageous grounds.

I would therefore incline for the use of carts, and they could be made before hand by the hunters and their artificers.

The oxen should be bought in the provinces where the farmers make use of them in their works. One or two soldiers would drive the cart and take charge of the four oxen.

There are few rivers in North-America deep in summer, and which these carts with high and broad wheels, could not ford; but if the contrary shou'd happen, the carts, provisions and baggage, may be rafted over, or a bridge built. In a country full of timber, and with troops accustomed to work, no river will stop an army for a long time.

By the above method, 3 or 400 horses would be sufficient to carry the baggage, ammunition, tents, tools, &c.

EXPLANATION OF THE FOUR PLANS, PLATE II. [See page 240]

Representing the different positions of our army in the woods.

ENCAMPMENT.

The camp (Fig. 1) forms a parallelogram, of one thousand by six hundred feet. Eight hundred men of the regular troops (1) encamp on the four sides, which gives twenty-four feet to each tent, containing six men. The light-horse (3) encamp within the parallelogram. The reserve (7) in the center.

The provisions, ammunition, tools and stores (8) and the cattle (9) are placed between the two troops of light horse and the reserve. The hunters (2) encamp on the outside diagonally at the four angles, being covered by redoubts (5) formed with kegs and bags of flour or fascines. Besides these four redoubts, another is placed to the front, one to the rear, and two before each of the long faces of the camp, making in all ten advanced guards of 22 men each, and 7 centries, covered if possible by breast works of fascines or provisions. Before the army lay down their arms, the ground is to be reconnoitred, and the guards posted, who will immediately open a communication from one to the other, to relieve the centries, and facilitate the passage of rounds.

The centries upon the ammunition, provisions, head quarters, and all others in the inside of the camp are furnished from the reserve. The officers, except the staff and commanders of corps, encamp on the line with their men.

The fires are made between the guards and camp, and put out in case of an attack in the night.

LIINE of MARCH, Plate II. Fig. II.

Part of the hunters (2) in three divisions detaching small parties (5, 6) to their front and to their right and left, to search the woods and discover the enemy.

The artificers and axe-men (4) to cut a road for the convoy, and two paths on the right and left for the troops.

One hundred and fifty of the regular troops (1) in two files, who are to form the front of the square; these march in the center road.

Two hundred and fifty regulars (1) in one file by the right hand path; and 250 (1) by the left hand path, are to form the long faces.

These are followed by 150 regulars (1) in two files, who are to form the rear of the square.

The reserve (7) composed of 100 regulars in two files.

The rest of the hunters (2) in two files.

The light horse (3.)

The rear guard (5) composed of hunters, follows the convoy at some distance and closes the march. The scouting parties (6) who flank the line of march, are taken from the hunters and light horse, and posted as in plan (Fig. 2) some orderly light horsemen, attend the General and field officers who command the guard divisions, to carry their orders. Two guards of light horse take charge of the cattle (9)

The convoy (8) proceeds in the following order.

The tools and ammunition following the front column.

The baggage.

The cattle.

The provisions.

The whole divided into Brigades, and the horses two a breast.

DEFILES.

In case of a defile, the whole halt until the ground is reconnoitred, and the hunters have taken possession of the heights. The center column then enters into the defile, followed by the right face; after them the convoy; then the left and rear face, with the reserve, the light horse, and the rear guard.

The whole to form again as soon as the ground permits.

DISPOSITION TO RECEIVE THE ENEMY, Fig. (3)

The whole halt to form the square or parallelogram, which is done thus. The two first men of the center column stand fast at two yards distance. The two men following them, step forward and post themselves at two yards on the right and left. The others come to the front in the same manner, till the two files have formed a rank, which is the front of the square.

The rear face is formed by the two file-leaders turning to the center road, where having placed themselves at two yards distance, they face outwards, and are followed by their files, each man posting himself on their right or left, and facing towards the enemy the moment he comes to his post.

As soon as the front and rear are extended and formed, the two long faces, who have in the mean time faced outwards, join now the extremities of the two fronts, and close the square.*

TO REDUCE THE SQUARE.

The right and left of the front, face to the center, where the two center men stand fast. Upon the word "march" these step forward and are replaced by the two next, who follow them, and so on; by which means, that front becomes again a column. The rear goes to the right about, and each of the two center men leads again to the side paths followed by the rest.

While the troops form, the light horse and each division of the convoy take the ground assigned to them within the square, as if they were to encamp; and the horses being unloaded, two parallel lines will be formed, with the bags and kegs of provisions, to cover the wounded and the men unfit for action. The hunters take post on the most advantageous ground on the out side, and skirmish with the enemy, till the square is formed; when, upon receiving their orders, they retire within the square, where they take their posts as in Fig. (3)

The small parties of rangers (5) who have flanked the line of march, remain on the outside, to keep off the enemy and observe their motions.

When the firing begins the troops will have orders to fall on their knees, to be less exposed till it is thought proper to attack.

The four faces, formed by the regular troops, are divided into platoons *chequered*. One half, composed of the best and most active soldiers, is called the first Firing, and the other half the second Firing.

The eight platoons at the angles are of the second Firing, in order to preserve the form of the square during the attack.

It is evident that, by this disposition, the convoy is well covered, and the light troops, destined for the charge, remain concealed; and as all unexpected events during an engagement are apt to strike terror, and create confusion, among the enemy, it is natural to expect that the savages will be greatly disconcerted at the sudden and unforeseen eruption, that will soon pour upon them from the inside of the square; and that, being vigorously attacked in front and flank at the same time, they will neither be able to resist, nor, when once broke, have time to rally, so as to make another stand. This may be effected in the following manner.

GENERAL ATTACK, Fig. IV.

The Regulars (1) stand fast.

The hunters (2) sally out, in four columns, thro' the intervals of the front and rear of the square, followed by the light horse (3) with their bloodhounds. The intervals of the two columns who attack in the front, and of those who attack in the rear, will be closed by the little parties of rangers (5) posted at the angles of the square, each attack forming in that manner, three sides of a parallelogram. In that order they run to the enemy (X) and having forced their way through their circle, fall upon their flanks; by wheeling to their right and left, and charging with impetuosity. The moment they take the enemy in flank, the First Firing of the regular troops march out briskly and attack the enemy in front. The platoons detached in that manner from the two short faces,

*These evolutions must be performed with celerity.

proceed only about one hundred yards to their front, where they halt to cover the square, while the rest of the troops who have attacked pursue the enemy, till they are totally dispersed, not giving them time to recover themselves.

The sick and wounded, unable to march or ride, are transported in litters made of flour bags, through which two long poles are passed, and kept asunder by two sticks, tied across beyond the head and feet to stretch the bag. Each litter is carried by two horses—

These remarks might have been extended to many other cases that may occur in the course of a campaign or of an engagement, but it is hoped this sketch will be sufficient to evince the necessity of some alteration in our ordinary method of proceeding in an Indian War.

APPENDIX I.

CONSTRUCTION OF **FORTS** AGAINST INDIANS.

AS we have not to guard here against cannon, the system of European fortification may be laid aside, as expensive, and not answering the purpose. Forts against Indians, being commonly remote from our settlements, require a great deal of room to lodge a sufficient quantity of stores and provisions, and at the same time ought to be defensible with one half of their compleat garrisons, in case of detachments or convoys.

I am therefore of opinion that a square or pentagon, with a block-house of brick or stone* at every angle, joined by a wall flanked by the block-houses, would be the best defence against such enemies. A ditch from seven to eight feet deep might be added, with loop holes in the cellars of the block-houses six feet from the ground, to defend the ditch.

Along the inside of the curtains the traders might build houses and stores, covered as well as the block-houses with tiles, or slate, to guard against fire arrows. There will remain a specious area for free air and use, in which as well as in the ditch, gardens might be made and well dug.

The powder magazines might be placed in the center of the area, keeping only a small quantity of cartridges in each block-house for present use.

The garrisons of such forts would be free from surprizes, even if they had no centries, for nothing can get at them, while the doors are well bolted and barred.

SOME REASONS FOR KEEPING POSSESSION OF OUR LARGE FORTS IN THE INDIAN COUNTRY.

As these forts have been one of the causes of the last war and are a great eye-sore to the savages, they have bent their chief efforts against them; and therefore, while thus employed, they have been less able to distress our settlements. Our forts keep the Indian towns at a great distance from us. Fort-Pitt has effectually driven them, beyond the Ohio, and made them remove their settlements at least 60 miles further westward. Was it not for these forts, they would settle close on our borders, and in time of war infest us every day in such numbers as would over-power the thin inhabitants scattered on our extensive frontier. The farmer unable to sow or reap would soon fall back on our chief towns, or quit the country for want of bread. In either case, what would be the fate of the large towns burthened with the whole country, and deprived of subsistance and of the materials of trade and export?

The destruction of these forts being, in time of war, the chief aim of the savages, they gather above them to distress the garrisons, and to attack the convoy; thereby giving us an opportunity to fight them in a body, and to strike a heavy blow, which otherwise they would never put in our power, as their advantage lies in surprizes, which are best effected by small numbers. Experience has convinced them that it is not in their power to break those shackles, and therefore it is not probable that they will continue a check upon them, and

*Experience has demonstrated that fortifications made of wood decay very soon, and are on that account of considerable expence.

save the difficulty and expence of taking post again and their country. Our forts are likewise the proper places for trade, which being closely inspected, it will be easy for us to limit their supplies, to such commodities as they cannot turn against us, and to put a speedy stop all just causes of complaints, by giving immediate redress.

A few forts, with strong garrisons, I should judge to be more service than a greater number weakly guarded. In the last war we lost all our small posts; but our more considerable ones, Detroit and Fort-Pitt, resisted all the efforts of the savages, by the strength of their garrisons.

APPENDIX II.

THE following Paper was written by an Officer well acquainted with the places he describes; and is thought worthy of a place here, as every thing is material which can encrease our knowledge of the vast countries ceded to us, and of the various nations that inhabit them.

Account of the French Forts ceded to Great Britain in Louisiana.

The settlement of the Illinois being in 40 degrees latitude, is 500 leagues from New-Orleans by water and 350 by land.

The most proper time of the year for going there, is the beginning of February. The waters of the Mississippi are then high, and the country being overflowed, there is less to fear from the savages, who are hunting in that season.

The encampments should be on the left of the river, as the enemies are on the right, and cannot have a sufficient number of crafts to cross if their party is large.

They generally attack at day-break, or at the time of embarking.

The inhabitants might bring provisions half way, if they were allowed good pay.

The Delawares and Shawanese lie near Fort Du Quesne,* which is about 500 leagues from the Illinois. The Wiandots and ottawas, (who are at the Detroit) are about 250 leagues from the Illinois by land. And the Miamis about 200 by land.

Nevertheless as intelligence is carried very fast by the Savages, and as all the nations with whom we are at war, can come by the Ohio,** we must be vigilant to prevent a surprize.

The mouth of the Ohio, in the Mississippi, is 35 leagues from the Illinois.

Thirteen leagues from the Mississippi, on the left of the Ohio, is Fort Massiac, or Assumption, built in 1757, a little below the mouth of the river Cherokee.*** It is only a stockade, with four bastions and eight pieces of cannon. It may contain 100 men. In four days one may go by land, from this fort to the Illinois.

It is of consequence for the English to preserve it, as it secures the communication between the Illinois and Fort-Pitt.

Fort Vincennes, which is last post belonging to Louisiana, is upon the river Ouabache,† 60 leagues from its conflux with the Ohio. It is a small stockade fort, in which there may be about 20 soldiers. There are also a few inhabitants. The soil is extremely fertile, and produces plenty of corn and tobacco.

The distance from this fort to the Illinois, is 155 leagues by water. And it may be travelled by land in six days.

The nation of savages living at this post is called Pianquicha. It can furnish 60 warriors.

Altho' we do not occupy Fort Vincennes at present, yet it would be of the utmost consequence for us to settle it, as there is a communication from it with Canada, by going up the Ouabache.

From this post to the Ouachtanons is 60 leagues, and from thence to the Miamis (still going up the Ouabache) is 60 leagues further; then there is a portage of six leagues to the river Miamis, and you go down that river 24 leagues to Lake Erie.

*So the French formerly called what is now Fort Pitt.

**Part of the navigation of the Ohio, from Fort-Pitt is described as follows, viz. That the difficult part of the river is from Fort-Pitt about 50 or 60 miles downwards. There are 52 islands between Fort-Pitt and the lower Shawanese town on Scioto; and none of them difficult to pass in the night, but one at the mouth of Muskingham, occasioned by a number of trees lying in the channel. From the lower Shawanese Town to the falls, there are but 8 or 9 islands. At the falls, the river is very broad, with only one passage on the east side, in which there is water enough at all seasons of the year to pass without difficulty. Below the falls, the navigation is every way clear, down to the Missisippi.

***River Cherokee falls into the Ohio about 800 miles below Fort-Pitt. This river is in general wide and shoal up to the south mountain, passable only with bark canoes, after which it grows very small.

†Ouabache or Wabash empties itself into the Ohio about 60 miles above the Cherokee river, on the opposite or west side.

Mr. Daubry went by that rout in 1759 from the Illinois to Venango,* with above 400 men, and two hundred thousand weight of flour.

Thirty-five leagues from the mouth of the Ohio, in going up the Missisippi, on the right, is the river Kaskasquias. Two leagues up this river, on the left, is the settlement of the Kaskasquias, which is the most considerable of the Illinois.

There is a fort built upon the height on the other side of the river, over against Kaskasquias; which, as the river is narrow, commands and protects the town.

I don't know how many guns there may be, nor how many men it may contain. There may be about 400 inhabitants.

The Illinois Indians, called Kaskasquias, are settled half a league from the town; and are able to turn out 100 warriors. They are very lazy and great drunkards.

Six leagues from Kaskasquias, on the bank of the Missisippi, is Fort Chartres, built of stone, and can contain 300 soldiers. There may be 20 cannon at most, and about 100 inhabitants round Chartres.

The Illinois Indians at that place, who are called Metchis, can furnish 40 warriors.

Between the Kaskasquias, and Fort Chartres, is a small village, called *La Prairie du Rocher* (the Rock Meadow) containing about 50 white inhabitants; but there is neither fort nor savages.

Near Fort Chartres is a little village, in which is about a score of inhabitants. Here are neither savages nor fort.

Fifteen leagues from Fort Chartres, going up the Missisippi, is the village of the Casquiars. There is a small stockade fort; I don't know if there is any cannon. There may be about 100 inhabitants.

The Illinois Indians living near this village are called Casquiars, and can turn out 60 warriors.

I compute there are about 300 Negroes at the Illinois.

The country of the Illinois is fertile, producing good wheat and corn. All kinds of European fruit succeed there surprizingly well, and they have wild grapes with which they make tolerable wine. Their beer is pretty good.

There are mines of lead, and some salt. They make sugar of maple, and there are stone quarries.

APPENDIX III.

ROUT from Philadelphia to Fort-Pitt

	Miles	Qrs.	Per.
From Philadelphia			
to Lancaster	66	0	38
to Carlisle	55	0	00
to Shippensburgh	22	0	00
to Fort Loudoun	24	3	00
to Fort Littleton	17	3	00
to the crossing of			
the Juniata	18	3	00
to Fort Bedford	14	3	00
to the crossing of	29	0	39
Stoney creek	20	1	43
to Fort Ligonier	56	0	00
to Fort Pitt			
	324	2	40

This Appendix III in Rogers' Dublin edition is not included in the separate Rev. Smith edition of *Bouquet's Expedition.* Rogers' Appendix IV is the same as Appendix III in Smith.

*By the above paper the rout is given up the Missisippi, part of the Ohio, and up the Ouabache to Fort Vincennes, and likewise to the Illinois. Again from Vincennes and the Ouachtanons by water, on the westerly communication to the Miamis portage, then by water down that river by the easterly rout into the Lake Erie, proceeding as far as Presqu' Isle, then by the 15 m. portage into Buffalo or Beef river, lately called French creek, then down the same to Venango on the Ohio. In order therefore, to carry this rout still further, we shall continue it from Venango to the mouth of Juniata in Susquehannah, which brings it within the settled parts of Pennsylvania, viz.

From Venango to Licking creek, 10 miles. To Toby's creek, 13. To a small creek, 1. To the parting of the road, 5. To a large run, 3. To Leycaumeyhoning, 9. To Pine Creek, 7. To Chuckcaughting, 8. To Weeling Creek, 4. To the crossing of ditto, 4. To a miry swamp, 8. To the head of Susquehanna, 10. To Meytaunign creek, 18. To Clear Field creek, 6. To the top of Allegheny, 1. To the other side, ditto, 6. To Beaver dams, 5. To Franks Town, 5. To the Canoe place, 6. To the mouth of Juniatta, 100. Total 239 miles.

APPENDIX IV.

Number of Indian Towns, situated on and near the Ohio River, and its branches, with their distances from Fort-Pitt, and the distances of the principal branches from each other at their conflux with the Ohio.

	Distance from one another	Distance from Ft. Pitt.
From Fort Pitt		
First ROUT about N.N.W.	Miles	Miles
to Kushkuskies Town on Big Beaver-Creek		45
up the east branch of Beaver Creek to Shaningo	15	60
up ditto to Pematuning	12	72
to Mohoning on the West branch of Beaver Creek	32	104
up the branch to Salt Lick	10	114
to Cayahoga River	22	146
to Ottawas town on Cayahoga	10	156
From Fort Pitt		
Second ROUT W.N.W.		
to the mouth of Big Beaver-Creek		25
to Tuscarawas	91	116
to Mohickon John's Town	50	166
to Junundat or Wyandot town	46	212
to Fort Sandusky	4	216
to Junqueindundeh	24	240
From Fort Pitt		
Third ROUT about W.S.W.		
to the Forks of the Muskingham		128
to Bullet's Town on Muskingham	6	134
to Waukatamike	10	144
to King Beaver's Town on the heads of Hochocking	27	171
to the lower Shawanese Town on Sioto River	40	211
to the Salt Lick town on the heads of Sioto	25	236
to the Miamis fort	190	426

	Distance from one another	Distance from Ft. Pitt.
By water from Fort Pitt		
Fourth ROUT down the Ohio; general course about S.W.		
to the mouth of Big Beaver Creek		27
to the mouth of Little Beaver Creek	12	39
to the mouth of Yellow Creek	10	49
to the two Creeks	18	67
to Weeling	6	73
to Pipe Hill	128	85
to the long Reach	30	115
to the foot of the Reach	18	133
to the mouth of Muskingham river	30	163
to the little Canhawa river	12	175
to the mouth of Hockhocking river	13	188
to the mouth of Letort's creek	40	228
to Kiskeminetas	33	261
to the mouth of big Canhawa or new river	8	269
to the mouth of big Sandy creek	40	309
to the mouth of Sioto river	40	349
to the mouth of big Salt Lick river	30	379
to the Island	20	399
to the mouth of little Mineamie or Miammee* river	55	454
to the big Miammee or Rocky river	30	484
to the Big Bones**	20	504
to Kentucky River	55	559
to the Falls of the Ohio	50	609
to the Wabash, or Ouabache	131	740
to Cherokee River	60	800
to the Missisippi	40	840

N.B. The places mentioned in the first three Routs are delineated in the foregoing map, by an officer who has an actual knowledge of most of them, and has long served against the Indians. The fourth Rout down the Ohio was given by an Indian trader, who has often passed from Fort-Pitt to the Falls; and the distances he gives of the mouths of the several rivers that fall into the Ohio may be pretty certainly depended on. Our maps hitherto published are very erroneous in placing some of those rivers.

*These rivers, called Little and Great Mineamie or Miammee, fall into the Ohio between Sioto and the Ouabache, and are different from the Miamis river, which runs into the west end of lake Erie, below the Miamis fort.
**So called from Elephant's bones said to be found there.

APPENDIX V.

Names of different Indian Nations in North-America, with the numbers of their Fighting Men; referred to in the Note, page 255.

The following list was drawn up by a French trader, a person of considerable note, who has resided many years among the Indians, and still continues at Detroit, having taken the oaths of allegiance to the King of Great Britain. His account may be depended on, so far as matters of this kind can be brought near the truth; a great part of it being delivered from his own personal knowledge.

	Warriors
Conawaghrunas, near the falls of St. Louis	200
St. Lawrence Indians	
Abenaquis,	350
Michmacs,	700
*Amalistes,	550
*Chalas,	130
living towards the heads of the Ottawa river	
Nipissins,	400
Algonquins,	300
Les Tetes de Boule, or Round Heads, near the above	2500
Six Nations, on the frontiers of New-York, &c.	1550
Wiandots, near lake Erie	300
near the Lakes Superior and Michigan	
Chipwas,	5000
Ottawas,	900
Messesagues, or River Indians, being wandering tribes, on the lakes Huron and Superior,	2000
Powtewatamis, near S. Joseph's and Detroit	350
near Puans bay	
Les Puans,	700
Folleavoine, or Wild-Oat Indians	350
South of Puans bay	
*Mechecouakis,	250
Sakis,	400
Mascoutents,	500
Ouisconsins, on a river of that name, falling into Missisippi on the east-side	550
far north, near the lakes of the same name	
Christinaux,	3000
Assinaboes, or Assinipouals	1500
Blancs** Barbus, or White Indians with Beards	1500
towards the heads of Missisippi	
Sioux, of the meadows	2500
Sioux, of the woods	1800
Missouri, on the river of that name	3000
*Grandes Eaux	1000
south of Missouri	
Osages,	600
Canses,	1600
Panis blancs,	2000
Panis piques,	1700
Padoucas,	500
Ajoues, north of the same	1100
Arkanses, on the river that bears their name, falling into Missisippi on the west side	2000
Alibamous, a tribe of the Creek,	600
Unknown, unless the author has put them for tribes of the Creeks	
*Ouanakina	300
*Chiakanessou	350
*Machecous	800
*Caoitas	700
*Souikilas	200
Miamis, upon the river of that name, falling into Lake Erie	350
Delawares (les Loups) on the Ohio	600

[*Editor's note: The explanation for the tribes marked by a single asterisk is given in the paragraph following this table.]
**They live to the north-west, and the French, when they first saw them, took them for Spaniards.

Shawanese on Sioto	500
on the Ouabache	
Kickapoos	300
Ouachtenons	400
Peanquichas	250
Kaskasquias, or Illinois in general, on the Illinois river	600
*Pianria	800
Catawbas, on the frontiers of North-Carolina	150
Cherokees, behind South-Carolina	2500
Mobile and Missisippi	
Chickasaws	750
Natchez	150
Chactaws	4500
	56,500

The above list consists chiefly of such Indians as the French were connected with in Canada and Louisiana. Wherever we knew the names by which the different nations are distinguished, by the English, we have inserted them. But the orthography is yet very unsettled, and the several nations marked with an * asterism are unknown to us, and therefore they are left as they stand in the original list.

So large a number of fighting men may startle us at first sight; but the account seems no where exaggerated, excepting only that the Catawba nation is now almost extinct. In some nations which we are acquainted with, the account falls even short of their numbers; and some others do not appear to be mentioned at all, or at least not by any name known to us.

Such, for instance, are the Lower Creeks, of whom we have a list according to their towns. In this list their warriors or gunmen are 1180, and their inhabitants about 6000. Thus a comparative judgement may be formed of the nations above-mentioned; the number of whose inhabitants will (in this proportion to their warriors, viz. 5 to 1) be about 283,000.

F I N I S.

JOURNAL

OF THE

SIEGE OF DETROIT,

BY

Major ROBERT ROGERS

Introduction

MAJOR ROGERS arrived at Detroit on the 29th of July, 1763, with the Detachment under the Command of Capt. Dalyel, and shared in the gallant but unfortunate Sortie made under the Command of that Officer a few Days after, in which the Leader and many of his Men perished. The Information contained in the following Narrative is entirely from hearsay, and only brings down the Chain of Events to the 4th of July, although dated nearly a Month later. It is probable that Maj. Rogers began to write an Account of the Siege soon after his Arrival, and that this was only partly finished when the sailing of two Vessels offered a convenient Opportunity for sending it to Sir William Johnson. At the Close of the Volume of Journals published by Major Rogers in 1765, is an Advertisement of a second Volume to contain, among other Things, an Account of the Indian Wars in America subsequent to 1760. Subscriptions were solicited and the Book was promised within a limited Time, but from some Cause unknown, it was never printed. It is reasonable to infer that the following Pages were intended to form a Portion of the Book, and that this Fragment, now first printed, may be the only Part that has been preserved. It was found among the Manuscripts of Sir William Johnson in the New York State Library.

F.B.H. [Franklin B. Hough]

JOURNAL
OF THE
SIEGE OF DETROIT.

A JOURNAL of the Siege of Detroit, taken from the Officers who were then in the Fort, and wrote in their Words in the following Manner, viz:

The 6th of May; when we were privately informed of a Conspiracy formed against us by the Indians, particularly the Tawa* Nation, who were to come to council with us the next Day, and massacre every Soul of us. On the Morning of that Day, being Saturday the 7th of May, fifteen of their Warriors came into the Fort and seemed very inquisitive and anxious to know where all the English Merchants Shops were.

At 9 o'Clock the Garrison were ordered under Arms and the Savages continued coming into the Fort till 11 o'Clock, diminishing their Numbers as much as possible by dividing themselves at all the Corners of the streets most adjacent to the Shops. Before
12 o'Clock they were three hundred Men, at least three times the Number equal to that of the Garrison; but seeing all the Troops under Arms, and the Merchants Shops shut, imagined prevented them from attempting to put their evil Scheme into execution that Day.

Observing us thus prepared, their Chiefs came in a very condemned like Manner, to Council, where they spoke a great deal of Nonsense to Major Gladwine and Capt. Campbell, protesting at the same Time the greatest Friendship imaginable to them, but expressing their Surprise at seeing

*Ottawa

all the Officers and Men under Arms. The Major then told them that he had certain Intelligence that some Indians were projecting Mischief, and on that Acct he was determined to have the Troops always under Arms upon such Occasions: That they being the oldest Nation, and the first that had come to Council, needed not to be astonished at that Precaution as he was resolved to do the fame to all Nations.

At 2 o'Clock they had done speaking, went off seemingly very discontented and crossed the River half a League from the Fort, where they all encamped about 6 o'Clock that Afternoon. Six of their Warriors returned and brought an old Squaw Prisoner, alledging that she had given us false Information against them. The Major declared she had never given any kind of Advice. They then insisted upon naming the Author of what he had heard in regard to the Indians, which he declined to do, but told them it was one of themselves, whose Name he promised never to reveal; whereupon they went off and carried the old Woman Prisoner with them. When they arrived at their Camp, Pondiac their greatest Chief seized on the Prisoner and gave her three Strokes with a Stick on the Head, which laid her flat on the Ground, and the whole Nation assembled around her and called repeated Times kill her, kill her.

Sunday the 8th, Pondiac and several other of the principal Chiefs came into the Fort, at 5 o'Clock in the Afternoon and brought a Pipe of Peace with them of which they wanted to convince us fully of their Friendship and Sincerity, but the Major judging that they only wanted to caggole us would not go nigh them nor give them any Countenance, which obliged Capt. Campbell to go and speake with them, and after smoaking with the Pipe of Peace and assuring him of their Fidelity, they said that the next Morning all the Nation would come to Council where every thing would be settled to our Satisfaction, after which they would immediately disperse, and that that would remove all kind of Suspicion.

Accordingly on Monday Morning the 9th, six of their Warriors came into the Fort at 7 o'Clock and upon seeing the Garrison under Arms went off without being observed. About 10 o'Clock we counted fifty-six Canoes, with seven and eight Men in each, crossing the River from their Camp, and when they arrived nigh the Fort, the Gates were shut, and the Interpreter went to tell them that not above fifty or sixty Chiefs would be admitted into the Fort, upon which Pondiac immediately desired the Interpreter in a peremptory Manner to return directly and acquaint us that if all their People had not free Access into the Fort none of them would enter it: that we might stay in our Fort, but he would keep the Country, adding that he would order a Party instantly to an Island where we had twenty-four Bullocks, which they immediately killed. Unluckily three Soldiers were on the Island and a poor Man with his Wife and four Children which they all murthered except two Children, as also a poor Woman and her two Sons, that lived about half a Mile from the Fort.

After having thus put all the English without the Fort to death, the [they?] ordered a Frenchman who had seen the Woman and her two Children killed and scalped, to come and inform us of it, and likewise of their having murthered Sir Robert Davers, Captain Robertson and a Boat's Crew of six Persons two Days before, being Saturday the 7th of May, near the Entrance of Lake Huron, for which Place they set out from hence on Monday the 2d Inst. in order to know if the Lakes and Rivers were Navigable for a Schooner which lay here to proceed to Michilimackinac. We were then fully persuaded that the Information given us was well founded, and a proper Disposition was made for the Defense of the Fort, although our Number was but small, not exceeding one hundred and twenty, including all the English Traders, and the Works were nigh Mile in Circumference.

On Tuesday the 10th, very early in the Morning, the Savages began to fire on the Fort, and Vessels which lay opposite to the east and west Sides of the Fort.* About 8 o'Clock the Indians called a Parley and ceased firing, and half an Hour after, the Waindotes Chiefs came into the Fort, on their way to a Council where they were called by the Tawas and promised us to endeavor

*The Channel of Detroit River opposite the Fort, ran but a few Degrees South of West, although its general Course is nearly South.

to soliciate and persuade the Tawas from committing further Hostilities. After drinking a Glass of Rum they went off at three o'Clock that Afternoon. Several of the Inhabitants and four Chiefs of the Tawas, Waindotes and Chippawas and Pottawattomes came and acquainted us, that most of all the Inhabitants were assembled at a Frenchmans House about a Mile from the Fort, where the Savages proposed to hold a Council, and desiring Captain Campbell and another Officer to go with them to that Council, where they hoped with their Presence and Assistance further Hostilities would cease, assuring us at the same Time that come what would; that Capt. Campbell and the other Officers that went with him, should return whenever they pleased. This Promise was assertained by the French as well as the Indian Chief, whereupon Captain Campbell and Lieutenant McDougal went off escorted by a Number of the Inhabitants and the four Chiefs, they first promised to be answerable for their returning yt [that] Night.

When they arrived at the House already mentioned they found the French and Indians assembled, and after counceling a long while, the Waindotes were prevailed on to sing the War Song, and this being done, it was next resolved that Captain Campbell and Lieutenant McDougall should be detained Prisoners, but would be indulged to lodge in a French House till a French Commandant arrived from the Ilenoes, that next Day five Indians and as many Canadians would be dispatched to acquaint the Commanding Officer of the Ilonies that Detroit was in their Possession and require of him to send an Officer to Command, to whom Captain Cample and Lieutenant McDougall would be delivered. As for Major Gladwin he was summoned to give up the Fort and two Vessels, &c., the Troops to ground their Arms, and they would allow as many Battoes and as much Provision as they judged requesite for us to go to Niagara: That if these Proposals were not accepted of, they were a thousand Men, and storm the Fort at all events, and in that Case every Soul of us should be put to the Torture. The Major returned for Answer, that as soon as the two Officers they had detained were permitted to come into the Fort, he would after consulting them give a positive Answer to their Demand, but could do nothing without obtaining their Opinion.

On Wednesday the 11th, several Inhabitants came early in the Morning into the Fort, and advised us by way of Friendship to make our Escape aboard the Vessels, assuring us that we had no other Method by which we could preserve our Lives, as the Indians were then fifteen hundred fighting Men, and would be as many more in a few Days, and that they were fully determined to attack us in an Hours time. We told the Mons'rs that we were ready to receive them, and that every Officer and Soldier in the Fort would willingly perish in the Defense of it, rather than condescend or agree to any Terms that Savages would propose. Upon which the French went off as I suppose to communicate what we had said to their Allies, and in a little afterwards the Indians gave their usual Hoop, and five or six hundred began to attack the Fort on all Quarters. Indeed some of them behaved extremely well and advanced very boldly in an open plain exposed to our Fire, and came within sixty Yards of the Fort, but upon having three Men killed and above a dozen wounded, they retired as briskly as they advanced, and fired at three hundred Yards Distance till seven oClock at Night, when they sent a Frenchman into the Fort with a Letter to the Major, desiring a cessation of Arms, that Night, and proposing to let the Troops with their Arms aboard the Vessels, but insisting upon our giving up the Fort, leaving the French Auxilliary all the Merchandize and officers Effects, and had even the Insolence to demand a Negro Boy belonging to a Merchant to be delivered to Pondiack.

The Major's Reply to these extraordinary Propositions was much the same as to the first.

Tuesday the 12th, five Frenchmen and as many Indians were sent off for the Ilinoes with Letters wrote by a Canadian agreable to Pondiacs Desire. On the 13th we were informed by the Inhabitants that Mr. Chapman, a Trader from Niagara, was taken Prisoner by the Waindotes, with five Battoes loaded with Goods.

The 21st, one of the Vessels was ordered to sail for the Niagara; but to remain till the sixth of June at the Mouth of the River in order to advert the Battoes which we expected daily from Niagara.

Upon the 22d we were told that Ensign Paully who commanded at Sandusky was brought Prisoner by ten Tawas, who reported that they had prevailed after long Consultation with the Waindotes who lived at Sandusky to declare War against us; that some Days ago they came early of a Morning to the Block House, and murthered every Soul therein, consisting of twenty seven Persons, Traders included; that Messrs. Callender and Prentice, formerly Captains in the Pennsylvania Regt were amongst that Number, and that they had taken one hundred Horses loaded with Indian Goods, which with the Plunder of the Garrison was agreed to be given the Waindotes before they condescended to join them; that all they wanted was the Commanding Officer.

On the 29th of May, we had the Mortification to see eight of our Battoes in the Possession of the Enemy, passing on the opposite Shore, with several Soldiers Prisoners in them. When the foremost Battoe came opposite the Sloop, she fired a Gun, and the Soldiers aboard called at those in the Battoe, that if they passed the Savages would kill them all, upon which they immediately seized on two Indians and threw them overboard with him and tomahawked him directly, they being near the Shore and it quite shoal. Another Soldier laid hold of an Oar, and struck that Indian upon the Head, of which Wound he is since dead. Then there remained only three Soldiers, of which two were wounded, and although fifty Indians were on the Bank not sixty Yards, firing upon them, the three Soldiers escaped aboard the Vessel, with the Battoe loaded with eight Barrels of Provisions and gives the following Account of their Missfortune, viz:

That two Nights before, about 10 o'Clock, they arrived about six Leagues from the Mouth of the River where they encamped. That two Men went a little from the Camp for Firewood to boil their Kettle, when one of the two was seized on by an Indian, killed and scalped in an Instant. The other Soldier ran directly and alarmed the Camp, upon which Lieutenant Cuyler immediately ordered to give Ammunition to the Detachment, which consisted of one Serjeant and seventeen Soldiers of the Royal Americans, three Serjeants and seventy-two Rank and File of the Queens Independent Company of Rangers. After having delivered their Ammunition, and a Disposition made of the Men, the Enemy came close to them without being observed, behind a Bank and fired very smartly on one Flank which could not sustain the Enemys Fire and they retired precipitately and threw the Whole in Confusion. By that Means the Soldiers embarked aboard the Battoes with one, two and three Oars in each Battoe, which gave an Opportunity to the Savages of taking them all except the two Battoes that escaped with Mr. Cuyler to Niagara.

Sunday the 5th of June, we were acquainted that Fort Maimes was taken, that Ensign Holms who commanded there had been informed by two Frenchmen who arrived there the preceding Day of Detroits being attacked by the Indians, which he would hardly believe, but threatened to imprison the French for that Report, that an Indian Woman had betrayed him out of the Fort by pretending that another Woman was very sick, and begged of him to come to her Cabin to let blood of her, and when he had gone a little Distance from the Fort was fired on and killed.

> Ensign Holmes is Robert Holmes, the former lieutenant in Rogers' Rangers, now commissioned in the 60th (Royal American) Regiment.

The Serjeant hearing the Report of the firing ran to see what it was, and was immediately taken Prisoner. The Soldiers shut the Gates and would have probably defended the Fort if one Walsh, a Trader who had been taken Prisoner a few Days before, had not advised them to open the Gates, alledging that if they did not comply the Indians would set Fire to the Fort and put them to death; whereas, if they opened the Gates, they should be well treated. Whereupon the Gates were opened, and the Soldiers grounded their Arms.

On the 10th of June we heard that Ensign Schlosser the Commanding Officer at Saint Josephs was taken Prisoner and that all the Garrison (except three Men) were massacred. That the Indians came on the 25th of May with a Pretence to Council, and as soon as the Chiefs had shaken Hands with Mr. Schlosser, they seized on him, gave a Shriek and instantly killed ten Men.

The 12th we were told that Lieut. Jenkins and all the Garrison of Owat'anon, consisting of a Sergeant and eighteen Men were taken Prisoners and carried to the Ilonies.

The 18th a Jesuit arrived from Michillimakenac and brought a Letter from Captain Etherinton and Lieutenant Lessley, with an Account of their being taken Prisoners. That Lieutenant Jamet and twenty-one Soldiers. [had been killed?—incomplete sentence in original edition] That on the 2nd the Indians were playing Ball as usual nigh the Fort, where Captain Etherington and Lieut. Lessley happened to be looking at them, but were suddenly seized on and carried into the Woods. At the same Time the Savages had purposely thrown their Ball into the Fort, as if that had happened by Accident, and followed it directly into the Fort, where a Number of their Women had Tomahawks and Spears concealed under their Blankets, which they delivered them and put the whole Garrison to death, except thirteen Men.

The 30th we were informed that the Blockhouse at Presque Isle was burned, that Ensign Christie and all his Garrison, which consisted of twenty-nine Men were taken Prisoners except six Men, who it was believed made their escape to La Beuf.

On the Night of the 2d Instant [should probably read "Captain Campbell" here, but it is missing in the original edition] and Lieut. McDougall were lodged at the House I have already mentioned, about two Miles from the Fort, and made a Resolution to Escape, when it was agreed on between them that McDougall would set off first, which he did and get safe into the Fort, but you know it was much more dangerous for Captain Campbell than for any other Person by Reason that he could neither run nor see, and being sensible of that failing I am sure prevented him from attempting to escape.

The 4th a Detachment was ordered to destroy some Breastworks and Entrenchments the Indians had made a Quarter of a Mile from the Fort, and about twenty Indians came to attack that Party, which they engaged but were drove off in an Instant with the Loss of one Man killed (and two wounded) which our People scalped and cut to Pieces. Half an Hour after the Savages carried the Man they had lost before Captain Campbell, striped him naked, and directly murthered him in a cruel Manner, which indeed gives one Pain beyond Expression, and I am sure cannot miss but to affect sensibly all his Acquaintences, although he is now out of the Question.

The Indians likewise reported that Venango and Le Beuf is taken by the Savages.

Dated at Detroit 8th Augt 1763.

To Sir William Johnson.

Lieutenant Jehu Hay, of the 60th or Royal American Regiment, in his diary entry for July 2, gives this account of the fate of Captain Donald Campbell, also of the 60th:

"At three o'clock this morning Lieut. McDougall with an Albany trader arrived at the fort, having made their escape from the Indians . . . .

"This morning Mr. [Pierre] Labutte came into the fort and informed us that as soon as the Chippewas were informed that we had killed the son of their great chief, they went to Pondiac and told him that he was the cause of all their ill luck, that he caused them to enter into the war and did nothing himself, that he was very brave in taking a loaf of bread or a beef from a Frenchman who made no resistance, but it was them that had all the men killed and wounded every day. For that reason they would take that from him which he intended to save himself by in the end; then went and took Capt. Campbell, stripped him, and carried him to their camp, where they killed him, took out his heart and ate it reeking from his body, cut off his head, and the rest of the body they divided into small pieces . . . ." (Hay, pp. 215-216)

* * * * *

Regrettably, Rogers' *Journal of the Siege of Detroit* ends not only before the termination of the siege, but also before the Battle of Bloody Run, which was to be Rogers' last, and one of his most heroic, fights with Indians.

To flesh out the story, here is Thomas Mante's account of the Battle of Bloody Run. It is followed by Rogers' own brief personal account of the action, and then a very vivid one from the *Gentleman's Magazine*..

Thomas Mante's Account of the Battle of Bloody Run

Captain Ecuyer, who commanded in this fort, [Fort Pitt] wanted almost as many necessaries to sustain a regular siege, as the Indians did to form one. Besides, his works had been greatly damaged by the overflowing of the neighboring rivers: but he, with great judgment, employed every method to conquer these inconveniences; and, seconded by those who had fled to him for protection, took every possible step, not only to maintain his post, but repulse the enemy.

Sir Jeffrey Amherst now commanded in America; but he was a commander almost without any troops to obey him. The finest army, for its numbers, in the whole world; that army which had conquered the French territories in this quarter of the globe, was now quite melted down by the West-India service, insomuch that there scarce remained a sufficiency of effective men for the common garrison duty. Besides, the shattered remains of the seventy-seventh and eightieth regiments were at this very time actually reduced or disbanded, and ordered for England to be discharged there. But considering the critical situation of affairs, and the necessity there was of putting an immediate stop to the horrid cruelties which the savages were every where committing, he thought it his duty to detain them; and sending invalids to the nearer garrisons to relive such troops as were more fit for active service, he ordered the forty-second and part of the seventy-seventh regiment to Fort-Pitt. The fifty-fifth was at Ontario, the forty-sixth at Niagara, and the eightieth at Detroit.

The fewness of his troops put it out of the General's power to think so soon of re-establishing the more distant posts; He, therefore, for the present, confined his whole attention to Fort-Pitt, Niagara, and Detroit.

A small body, therefore, was hastily collected for the relief of Detroit, and another for the reinforcement of the garrison of Niagara. These troops were commanded by Captain Dalyell, who, having left those destined for Niagara, proceeded to

Detroit, where he arrived on the evening of the 30th of July 1763. Pondiac, a celebrated Indian chief, with the numerous tribes in the vicinity of that place, had for some time been closely blockading it by land; and by means of conference allowed him within the fort, had surprised the garrison, were it not for vigilance of the very able officer who commanded there. Suspicion is the best guard against such insidious foes; and Major Gladwin had the good sense to draw this conclusion from their former conduct in similar circumstances. Accordingly, before he admitted the Indians into the place, he put the garrison under arms, and made such other dispositions, as totally defeated their treacherous design. Had they succeeded in their deep-laid scheme, of putting him first to death, every man of them must have fallen a victim to the resentment of this troops. Pondiac had sagacity enough to perceive this. He harangued, as usual, on a belt, white on one side, and green on the other; and began his discourse on the white side. The turning the belt was to be the signal, in case circumstances proved favorable, for opening the tragedy by the murder of Major Gladwin; but Pondiac thought better of the matter, and never made use of it.

Many of the French had inlisted under the banners of Pondiac; and one of them became his secretary. It was a thing without precedent, for such a multitude of Indians to keep the field so long. Their strong propensity to roving, and the difficulty of providing them with subsistence, had hitherto hindered their chiefs from undertaking any affair which required time and numbers to achieve it. But on this occasion, the influence of Pondiac kept them together, whilst the address of his secretary procured them provisions. To accomplish this, he issued formal orders to the neighbouring inhabitants, in the name of the French king, for what flour and cattle was wanted; and before Captain Dalyell's arrival, had gone so far as to summon Major Gladwin to surrender his fort to that monarch.

Had Captain Dalyell brought nothing but provisions with him to Detroit, his coming there might have been reckoned a very essential service; for, by the time he reached it, the garrison was reduced to the greatest straits. But this was not enough to satisfy his martial ardour. He unhappily considered the Indians as a very despicable foe, and despised them accordingly. As soon, therefore, as he became acquainted with their situation, he supposed that it could be no difficult matter, not only to make them abandon their present design, but so effectually chastise them, as to prevent their attempting any thing like it for the future.

It was in vain that Major Gladwin, who knew better, endeavoured to persuade the Captain from their dangerous undertaking. All his arguments were looked upon by him as no better than so many contrivances to prevent his reaping a large harvest of military glory. The Major, therefore, considering, that, as Captain Dalyell was Sir Jeffrey's aid de camp, he might reasonably supposed best acquainted with his sentiments; he therefore permitted him to make the attempt with two hundred and fifty men. To give him more was impossible, without risking the loss of the place, should any accident happen to those he gave.

With this force, Captain Dalyell sallied out, about half an hour after two in the morning of the 31st of July; taking the great road by the river-side, whilst two boats, in the nature of the row-gallies, and a pateraro in each of them, rowed up the river, with orders to keep close to the shore, and up with the line of march, in order to take off the killed and wounded, and cover a retreat in case of accident. About a mile and a half from the fort, the Captain ordered his men to form into platoons; and, if attacked in front, to defend themselves by street-firing. About a mile farther, the advanced guard, commanded by Lieutenant Brown, was fired upon by the enemy from under the cover of their works, and had several men killed and wounded. Some of the balls reached to the main body, and threw the men into some confusion; but they soon recovered. Captain Grey then returned to the enemy's fire on the front of their works, as the quarter where most execution might be expected, it being still to dark to distinguish objects. Captain Grant, being in the rear, was now likewise fired on from

GARY ZÁBOLY
© 2000

Ambush at Bloody Run

THE realities of forest warfare had not made Robert Rogers a stranger to ambush. He had survived many ambushes during the French and Indian War, and had also inflicted many of the same upon the enemy. For such "guerilla" fighters ambush was, in fact, the preferred method of initiating combat.

On July 31, 1763, Rogers found himself again caught in the middle of yet another major ambush, this time one planned and executed by Chief Pontiac, commanding a body of over 400 warriors composed mainly of his own Ottawas and their Chippewa and Huron allies. The recipients of this deadly surprise were 247 men led by Captain James Dalyell, aide de camp to General Amherst and only recently arrived at besieged Fort Detroit with a reinforcement of Regulars, along with some 20 new Ranger recruits under Major Rogers.

Dalyell, like the similarly doomed Captain William J. Fetterman 103 years later in the hills of Wyoming, was confident that a little show of force against Indians was better than *no* offensive action, and, despite the disapproval of Detroit's commandant, Major Henry Gladwin, he organized a column for a surprise night attack on Pontiac's encampments east of the fort. After 2 a.m. on the morning of the 31st, Dalyell's men marched out of the fort, in column of twos, each man stripped to his waistcoat and armed with a bayoneted musket, fusil, or carbine, and a "sword" (probably a short hanger).

Twenty-five men of the 55th Regiment of Foot comprised the advance guard, which tramped ahead of the main body by 20 yards. The main body was a mix of soldiers from the 55th, 60th, and 80th regiments, as well as Rogers' handful of Rangers; and the rear guard was under the command of a captain of the 80th. Among the leading elements of the column were a couple of local Frenchmen, acting as guides. To their right, in the Detroit River, two large bateaux, armed with swivel guns, endeavored to keep pace with the men, but were gradually being outdistanced.

Over a mile and a half east of the fort, Parent's Creek debouched into the river, and not far from the shallow, grass-choked mouth of the creek stood a narrow wooden bridge some 75 feet long. West of the creek, the land immediately surrounding the road was treeless. To the left of the road stood houses, fields and orchards of the French inhabitants; and across the creek a ridge rose abruptly, topped with more houses and fields, fences and wood piles.[1] Among these ready- made "entrenchments" Pontiac's warriors waited, unseen despite the presence of the moon.

By the time Dalyell's men had reached the bridge, they were marching in platoons (perhaps six across). The advance guard, under Lieutenant Archibald Brown of the 55th, had nearly reached the center of the bridge, with the main body just stepping onto it, when the ridge on the opposite shore exploded with muzzle blasts and arrows, "which killed and wounded the greatest Part of the advanced Guard," wrote a participant; "the Fire we returned in Platoons, and soon after received a Fire from our left flank."[2]

The column was thus halted and thrown into sudden confusion; but Captain Dalyell sprang into action to ward off panic, bellowing orders and getting the wavering lines re-formed, as well as collecting a detachment for a charge across the bridge. The charge was made, but the Indians had dispersed from their "entrenchments" and scattered to take cover at a distance, while other Indians continued to pepper the column from cover in positions west of the creek.

After a while Dalyell, wounded in the thigh, and unable to engage the enemy in close combat, led a retreat back across the bridge; and, realizing that increasing numbers of the Indians were pressing his flank, ordered a general withdrawal. Most of the dead and wounded men were placed in the bateaux, and rowed back to the fort, as the column began a desperate fighting retreat. Along the way Dalyell, while attempting to rescue a fallen sergeant of the 55th wounded during a charge against an enemy position, was himself shot dead. Captain James Grant of Gage's Light Infantry (80th Regiment) now took command of the column, while Major Rogers and a number of men drove a party of Indians from the house of settler Jacques Campeau. More than 200 Indians quickly besieged the house; but the diverting fire they received from its windows enabled the rest of the column to hasten its withdrawal.

Eventually the two armed bateaux returned from the fort, the fire from their swivels covering the withdrawal of Rogers and his men from the house. By eight a.m., nearly six hours after marching out of its gates, the harried survivors of the ambush at Parent's Creek began staggering back into Detroit. The 55th had suffered the most in killed (13) and wounded (28). In toto, including the men who later died of their wounds at the fort, Dalyell's command had sustained 21 killed and 47 wounded.[3] Dalyell's body had been left behind during the retreat; and, recognizing him as the leader of the attempted surprise attack, the Indians tore his heart out and wiped it across the faces of several English prisioners. They also scalped and disemboweled him, and cut off one arm and one leg.[4]

The illustration depicts the scene as it might have looked a minute or two after the opening Indian salvos on the advanced guard: the dead and dying men of the 55th on the bridge; platoons at the head of the bridge directing their fire at the enemy positions on the ridge; and the main column in a somewhat confused condition. Rogers, at lower left, shouts for the rest of the men to come up, while Captain Dalyell, in an officer's undress frock coat, orders hesitating soldiers to keep advancing.

In right foreground are three men of Gage's Light Infantry. Their leather caps sport ostrich plumes,[5] and they wear brown Indian-style leggings and moccasins. Beyond them, men of the Royal Americans (60th Regiment), dressed mostly in brown marching gaiters and wearing either tricorns or jockey caps, advance towards the contingent of the 55th at the bridge.

Parent's Creek would forever after be known as "Bloody Run," its waters that night grown red with blood seeping down the banks, or between the planks of the bridge, or from bodies that had fallen into it.

G.Z.

1. The geography of the area is very clearly defined, to scale, in a British watercolor map painted in 1763. See color reproduction of same in *The Frontiersmen*, by Paul O'Neill, Time- Life Books, Alexandria, Virginia, 1977, pp. 102-103.
2. Letter from Detroit, August 8, 1763, in *The New York Mercury*, September 5, 1763 (also published in the October 1763 issue of *The Gentleman's Magazine*.) This contains many details of the battle found nowhere else. The manner of firing platoons here was known as "street firing," with those who had discharged their weapons retiring down the sides of the column to reload and reform at the end of it.
3. List of killed and wounded in *Ibid*.
4. *Diary of the Siege of Detroit*, J. Munsell, Albany, New York, 1860, p. 57, 61.
5. Ostrich feathers commonly decorated the caps of many ranger and light infantry units from the mid-eighteenth century up through the early years of the nineteenth. The Thomas Davies painting of General Amherst's camp at the head of Lake George in 1759, now in the collection of the Fort Ticonderoga Museum, clearly shows a green-clad Ranger sporting a feather attached to the left side of his cap, as well as a brown-clad man, evidently one of Gage's men, wearing a cap similarly decorated. Almost certainly these caps did not have crowns decorated with tufts of hair, as some modern historians and artists have suggested.

some houses and fences, about twenty yards from his left; upon which he faced about his own and Captain Hopkin's company, and gave a full discharge on those places from whence he had been fired upon. The enemy seeming to retire in consequence of this ready and resolute return of their salute, Captain Dalyell ordered Captain Grant to take possession of those houses and fences from which it had been given; and Captain Grant, having immediately executed these orders, found, in one of the houses, two men, who informed him, that the enemy were about three hundred strong; and being withal, perfectly well apprized of the garrison's design, intended to get between the sallying party and the fort, to cut off their retreat.

As soon as Captain Dalyell was made acquainted with this superiority of the enemy, and the use they intended to make of it, he concluded it was high time to think of a retreat; and to cover this march, ordered Captain Grant to take post in an orchard. By this time the Indians began an heavy firing on his rear, from the fences and cornfields which lay behind it, and he himself was one of the first who fell on the occasion. Captain Grant, being informed by Lieutenant Macdougal of Captain Dalyell's death, and likewise, that Captain Grey was too severely wounded to act, assumed the command, which, by these events, devolved upon him; and continuing the retreat, took possession of the houses, barns, and fences, in the way to the fort. But Captain Rogers, having been hard pressed by the enemy, from behind a house in which he had taken post, was obliged to wait for one of the row-gallies to cover this retreat. When the boat arrived, and had dispersed the savages by a few discharges, Captain Rogers lost no time in embracing the opportunity to come off; and his and several other small bodies, into which the salliers had separated, having joined again without any confusion, they continued their march back to the fort in good order. It must not be forgot, that Captain Grant, by the able manner in which he conducted this dangerous retreat, acquired to himself particular honour. Besides Captain Dalyell, we lost one serjeant, and eighteen rank and file killed; Captain Grey, Lieutenants Duke and Brown, one drummer, and thirty-eight rank and file wounded.

Though the issue of this sally did great honour to Major Gladwin's foresight, it proved extremely disadvantageous to the English affairs; not so much, indeed, by their loss in men, as by the fresh spirits with which it inspired the Indians. (Mante, pp. 484-489)

Robert Rogers' Account of the Battle of Bloody Run

Rogers gallantly covered the British retreat from the Jacques Campeau house, which he had secured with a force of thirty men and two officers. He later wrote:

Here I stood them, for about two Hours, with only the Loss of two Men; they were in Number 200 at least, and they kept up a very brisk fire through the Windows of the House, which were very large; but I fortified them with Beaver Skins as there were many in the House, as also the Chamber, beating the Boards off the Roof, and making a Breast-Work of them and Skins." At about 8:00 am, "the two Rowboats came up, one with a 3 Pounder in her Bow she immediately threw in a Shower of Round and Grape to the Right and Left of the House, to a Barn and some Defiles which were there, and drove the Enemy back, with the Help of our Small-arms. This gave us an Opportunity of making our Retreat to the Fort, where we arrived at Half past 8. (Cuneo, *Robert Rogers*, p. 166)

Ironically, the commander of the boat with the three pounder that came to Rogers' aid was Diedrich Brehm, the engineer officer who had scouted with him on so many occasions during the French & Indian War. (The *Gentleman's Magazine*, October 1763, p. 487, and Peckham, p. 207)

The *Gentleman's Magazine* Account of the Battle of Bloody Run

This day arrived an express from Sir Jeffery Amherst, commander in chief of his Majesty's forces in North America, dated *New York, Sept. 3*, with the following advices:

Detail of the Action of the 31st of July, commanded by Capt. Dalyell, against the Indian Nations, near Fort Detroit, [the Straits.]

On the evening of the 30th of July, Capt. Dalyell, aid-de-camp to General Amherst, being arrived here with the detachment sent under his command, and being fully persuaded that Pontiac, the Indian chief, with his tribes, would soon abandon his design, and retire, insisted with the commandant that they might be easily surprised in their camp, totally routed, and driven out of the settlement; and it was thereupon determined that Capt. Dalyell should march out with 247 men. Accordingly, we marched about half an hour after two in the morning, two deep, along the great road by the river side, two boats up the river along shore, with a pattetaro in each, with orders to keep up with the line of march, to cover our retreat, and take off our killed and wounded; Lieut. Bean, of the Queen's Independents, being ordered with a rear guard to convey the dead and wounded to the boats. About a mile and a half from the fort we had orders to form into platoons, and, if attacked in the front, to fire by street firings.

A pattetaro was a small cannon.

Street firing was a technique used in narrow and confined areas. The soldiers were formed in a column, with a designated number abreast. The front rank would fire a volley, then fall back to the rear of the column and reload. The next rank would then fire and fall back to reload in the same fashion. The other ranks would do likewise, resulting in an almost continuous volley being directed at the enemy. This could be done from a stationary position, or while advancing or retiring, and was a very effective tactic.

We then advanced, and in about a mile farther, our advanced guard, commanded by Lieut. Brown of the 55th regiment, had been fired upon so close to the enemy's breast works and cover, that the fire, being very heavy, not only killed and wounded some of his party, but reached the main body, which put the whole into a little confusion; but they soon recovered their order, and gave the enemy, or rather their works, it being very dark, a discharge or two from the front, commanded by Capt. Gray. At the same time the rear, commanded by Capt. Grant, were fired upon from a house, and some fences, about 20 yards on his left; on which he ordered his own and Capt. Hopkin's companies to face to the left, and give a full fire that way.

This was the infamous Captain Joseph Hopkins, who would later desert to the French and figure prominently in Rogers' court-martial while commandant at Fort Michilimackinac. He commanded a company of the Queen's American Rangers during Pontiac's Uprising.

After which, it appearing that the enemy gave way every where, Capt. Dalyell sent orders to Capt. Grant to take possession of the above-said houses and fences, which he immediately did, and found in one of the said houses two men, who told him, the enemy had been there long, and were well apprized of our design. Capt. Grant then asked them the numbers: They said above 300; and that they intended, as soon as they had attacked us in the front, to get between us and the fort; which Capt. Grant told Capt. Dalyell, who came to him when the firing was over. And in about an hour after he came to him again, and told Capt. Grant he was to retire, and ordered him to march in the front, and post himself in an orchard. He then marched, and about half a mile further on his retreat he had some shots fired on his flank, but got possession of the orchard, which was well fenced; and just as he got there he heard a warm firing in the rear, having, at the same time, a firing on his own post, from the fences and the corn field behind it. Lieut. McDougal, who acted as Adjutant to the detachment, came up to him, Capt. Grant, and told him that Capt. Dalyell was killed, and Capt. Gray very much wounded, in making a push on the enemy, and forcing them out of a strong breast-work of cord wood, and an intrenchment which they had taken possession of; and that the command then devolved upon him. Lieut Bean immediately came up and told him, that Capt. Rogers had desired him to tell Capt. Grant that he had taken possession of a house, and that he had better retire with what numbers he had, as he, Capt. Rogers, could not get off without the boats to cover him, he being hard pushed by the enemy from the enclosures behind him, some of which scoured the road thro' which he must retire. Capt. Grant then sent Ensign Pauli with 20 men back to attack a party of the enemy which annoyed his own post a little, and galled those that were joining him from the place where Capt. Dalyell was killed, and Capt. Gray, Lieuts. Brown and Luke were wounded, which Ensign Pauli did, and killed some of the enemy in their flight. Capt. Grant at the same time detached all the men that he could get, and took possession of the inclosures, barns, fences, &c. leading from his own post to the fort, which posts he reinforced with the officers and men as they came up. Thinking the retreat then secured, he sent back to Captain Rogers, desiring he would come off; that the retreat was quite secured, and the different parties ordered to cover one another successively, untill the whole had joined; but Capt. Rogers not finding it right to risque the loss of more men, he chose to wait for the armed boats, one of which appeared soon, commanded by Lieut. Brehm, whom Capt. Grant had directed to go and cover Capt. Rogers's retreat, who was in the next house: Lieut. Brehm accordingly went, and fired several shots at the enemy: Lieut Abbott, with the other boat, wanting ammunition, went down with Capt. Gray. Lieut. Brown and some wounded men returned also, which Capt. Grant supposes the enemy seeing, did not wait her arrival, but retired on Lieut. Brehm's firing, and gave Capt. Rogers with the rear, an opportunity to come off: So that the whole from the different posts joined without any confusion, and marched to the fort in good order, covered by the boats on the water side, and by our own parties on the country side, in view of the enemy, who had all joined, and were much stronger than at the beginning of the affair, as was afterwards told us by some prisoners that made their escape; many having joined them from the other side of the river, and other places. The whole arrived at the Fort about eight o'clock, commanded by Capt. Grant, whose able and skillful retreat is highly commended.

"Return of killed and wounded of the several detachments near Detroit, July 31, 1763.

"55th Regiment. 1 Serjeant, 13 rank and file, killed. Captain Gray, 2 Lieutenants, (Duke and Brown,) 1 drummer, 28 rank and file, wounded.

"Royal Americans. 1 killed, 1 wounded.

"80th Reg. 2 killed, 3 wounded.

"Queen's Rangers. 2 killed, 3 wounded.

"Total 19 killed, 42 wounded.

(The *Gentleman's Magazine,* October 1763, pp. 486-487)

Robert Rogers Launches the Northwest Passage Expedition from Fort Michlimackinac

IT is six o'clock in the morning of Wednesday, September 17, 1766. The place: Fort Michilimackinac, main entrepot of the western fur trade, strategically located on the straits connecting lakes Huron and Michigan. Built by the French in 1715, and reconstructed and expanded in the years since, it is now under British control. Major Robert Rogers is its commandant; and on this morning he is at last sending off his long-dreamed-of expedition in search of the elusive Northwest Passage. The leadership of the exploration party he has assigned to Captain James Tute, one of his Ranger officers during the French and Indian War. James Stanley Goddard is second in command and secretary to the detachment, Joseph Reaume its interpreter, Andrew Stewart its commissary, and Augustus Ange, L'Orange and Gabriel Loring *engages.* They had been preceded fifteen days before by Jonathan Carver, the expedition's surveyor and mapmaker, who had instructions to wait for them at the Falls of St. Anthony on the Mississippi.

Once united, the entire party would then winter on the river among the Sioux. In the spring, they were to travel to the foothills of the Rocky Mountains, where they would spend another winter; and, in the spring of 1768, seek to discover "the Northwest Passage from the Atlantic into the Pacific Ocean, if any such Passage there be, or for the Discovery of the Great River Ourigan that falls into the Pacific Ocean about the Latitude Fifty."[1]

Rogers at this moment in his 35 years of life was at the summit of his career. Far-famed for his Ranging exploits of the previous decade and for the authorship of three books published recently in England, *A Concise Account of North America, Journals of Major Robert Rogers,* and the play, *Ponteach: Or the Savages of America; A Tragedy,* he had in 1765 petitioned King George III and his ministers for the command of the post at Michilimackinac, crucial as it would be for the launching of his expedition. He was not only granted the appointment, but also received a captain's commission in the 60th Regiment of Foot (the Royal Americans), and was given superintendency over the adjacent Indian nations, and thus personal control of the trade in that region. On October 17, 1765, Rogers kissed the hand of the king in court.[2]

Incentive for Rogers and Tute and their explorers was a prize of 20,000 pounds sterling for the discovery of the Passage.

James Stanley Goddard reported a "light Breese from the North East" as he left the fort "in a Bark Canoe" that September morning.[3] They were to pose as traders, not explorers,[4] although they only "had a Canoe of Goods with them not quite full."[5]

The illustration depicts Rogers on the 50-foot stretch of wharf that extended from the shore, the fort itself about another 50 feet south of the shore. He wears for the occasion a full dress captain's uniform of the 60th, and a dark blue caped cloak. His wife, Elizabeth, stands next to him in a hat of beaver and a short, fur-trimmed cloak, fashionable attire during the reigns of the two Georges, and not unbefitting her role as wife of the Governor of Michilimackinac.[6] Despite—or perhaps, because of—several career-enforced separations from her husband during their five-year marriage, Elizabeth has willingly accompanied Robert to his far-distant billet, the area still a wilderness, and only one year removed from the end of a major Indian war that had begun with the massacre of the British garrison at this very post.

Nearby stands Captain Frederick Spiesmaker, 2nd Company, 2nd Battalion of the 60th, and second in command at the fort. He is dressed in a blue surtout coat with brass buttons and yellow binding, worn both for fatigue duties and cool weather. Two sentries at the gate also wear surtouts. An Ottawa family watches the embarkation as well, the child smoking a pipe, an unusual anthropological observation found in a contemporary sketch of members of this tribe by George Townshend, in the collection of the Courtauld Institute of Art, London.

Captain Tute wears a blanket coat, common to voyageurs, farmers, and soldiers of Canada, and

GARY ZABOLY ©1996

adopted by the English long before their conquest of New France. His otterskin cap is also typical of a fur trader,[7] as were calico shirts, parti-colored sashes, breechclouts, leggings, and moccasins. The Canadian at the bow of the canoe wears a stocking cap characteristic of his countrymen, a short, white, sweater-like garment as depicted in a 1754 painting of a canoeist on the St. Lawrence River,[8] and smokes a "micmac" pipe, many examples of which have been uncovered in archaeological digs at the fort.[9]

The canoes are of Chippewa manufacture, and are equipped with short sails, and rolls of bark for repair. Such a canoe, with mast attached, can be seen in an 1817 watercolor of the Straits of Mackinac.[10] Larger fur brigade *canots du nord* and *canots de maitre* were also paddled on the Great Lakes and interior rivers, some examples of which can be seen beached for overnight shelters in the background.

Unfortunately, unlike Lewis and Clark 40 years later, Rogers' expedition was sadly underfinanced and undermanned, and thus ill-equipped to fulfill his grand dream. Tute, Carver and company returned to Michilimackinac on August 30, 1767, professing an inability to continue due to lack of provisions.

In 1772 and 1775, despite a series of career, marital and monetary problems that all but ruined his reputation, Rogers made two more attempts to obtain royal funding for a Northwest Passage expedition; but no monies ever appeared for the former petition, and the beginning of the American Revolution forestalled the latter permanently, as things turned out, for Rogers.

G. Z.

1. Major Rogers' Instructions to Captain James Tute, 12th September 1766, in *Treason? At Michilimackinac: The Proceedings of a General Court Martial held at Montreal in October 1768 for the Trial of Major Robert Rogers*, edited by David A. Armour, Mackinac Island State Park Commission, Mackinac island, Michigan. Revised edition of 1972, p. 50.
2. John R. Cuneo, *Robert Rogers of the Rangers*, Oxford University Press, New York, 1959, p. 180.
3. Ibid., p. 193.
4. Rogers' letter to Tute, July 15, 1767, Armour, *Treason? At Michilimackinac*, p. 54.
5. Armour, p. 56.
6. Elisabeth McClellan, *History of American Costume, 1607-1870*, Tudor Publishing Company, New York, 1969. Reprint of 1904 edition, p. 167.
7. For example, four years earlier, a deserter from Gage's 80th Light Infantry left Fort William Augustus (formerly Fort Levis) on the St. Lawrence, dressed in "an Otter Skin Cap, which he stole from a Sergeant, with an intention to disguise himself and pass as an Indian trader." *The New-York Mercury*, August 30, 1762.
8. Anonymous wood plaque painting, in J. Russell Harper, *Painting In Canada: A History*, 1966, p. 17.
9. Eugene T. Petersen, *France At Mackinac: A Pictorial record of French life and culture, 1715-1760*, Mackinac Island State Park Commission, Mackinac Island, Michigan (n.d.), p. 17.
10. Reproduced in *The American Heritage History of the Great West*, by the Editors of American Heritage, American Heritage Publishing Co., Inc., New York, 1965, p. 113.

Gary Zaboly © 2000

The Grand Council at Michlimackinac, July 2, 1767

IN his role as "Captain Commandant" of Fort Michilimackinac, Major Robert Rogers sought to transcend the prescribed limitations of his authority in the region by engaging not only in heightened trade with the Indians, but also as a mediator between tribes that had long been enemies of one another. When Rogers was not personally visiting the outlying villages, he beckoned Indian leaders to come to the fort itself, to receive presents, discuss trade, and confer about shaky tribal relations.

On July 2, 1767, "a Grand Council was Held outside the Fort,"[1] in Rogers' own words, attended by chiefs of the Menominee, Winnebago, Sauk, Fox, Sioux, Chippewa. Ottawa and Missisauga: a congregation that would have made Sir William Johnson himself proud to have conceived and supervised.

The council began with a number of speeches and replies made by the attendees; and since the mood appeared to be leaning towards the "peace and Amity" Rogers had been hoping for, he soon "lighted the Calumet or Pipe of Peace which was smoaked with the Formality usual on such occasions by the Chiefs of all the Tribes and Nations, who gave one another the Strongest assurances of Friendship and Love, Promised to forgive and forget all past injuries and Affronts, to keep down and restrain the Fire of their young Warriors and use their utmost endeavours to prevent mischief on all sides for the future...Some Refreshments were distributed and the Council concluded to the mutual Satisfaction of all Parties."[2] Presents were distributed the next day.

In his *Concise Account of North America*, Rogers himself describes the calumet: "The bowl of this pipe is made of a kind of soft red stone. . .the stem is of cane, elder, or some kind of light wood, painted with different colours."[3] At peace councils a wing or a row "of eagle's feathers" was attached to the pipe by "a cord of porcupine twine and dangling, multi-colored ribbons," in the words of Captain Pierre Pouchot.[4]

Added Rogers: "the calumet. . .in all treaties is considered as a witness between the parties, or rather as an instrument by which they invoke the sun, and moon to witness their sincerity, and to be, as it were, guarantees of the treaty between them."[5]

Once the calumet was lit, and the ceremony had begun, it was passed from chief to chief for each to take a ritualistic puff. This ceremony might have taken place under a "shade" of pine branches held by upright posts, a not uncommon structure for such lengthy councils held under the hot summer sun. Such shades, or "booths," were also built for councils with Indians west of the Mississippi far into the nineteenth century.

The eastern wall of stockaded Fort Michilimackinac can be seen in the background, with part of the tribal encampments nearby, and the Straits of Mackinac beyond. In the far left background is part of the fort's garden, and several of its stables.

Rogers holds aloft the calumet to begin the ceremony; and his words are translated to the seated chiefs by interpreters. Officers of the 60th Regiment, as well as a white trader, sit at a table and observe the proceedings near a barrel full of post-council "refreshments," perhaps rum or brandy.

G.Z.

1. "Rogers' Michilimackinac Journal," edited by William L. Clements, reprinted from the *Proceedings of the American Antiquarian Society for October 1918*, Worcester, Massachusetts, published by the Society, 1918, p. 36.
2. Ibid., p. 36
3. "Customs, Manners &c. of the Indians in North America extracted from Major Rogers' *Account* of North America," as excerpted in *The Universal Magazine*, London, December 1765, p. 314.
4. Captain Pierre Pouchot, *Memoirs on the Late War in North America Between France and England*, translated by Michael Cardy, edited and annotated by Brian Leigh Dunnigan, Old Fort Niagara Association, Inc., Youngstown, New York, 1994, p. 473.
5. Rogers, *Universal Magazine*, p. 314.

Rogers' Rangers and Their Uniforms: Fact to Legend, Legend to Misconceptions

A Critical Study by Gary Zaboly

ANY ATTEMPT to describe the uniform of the Ranger companies under the command of Major Robert Rogers during the French and Indian War must be accompanied with one caveat: no evidence has been found to indicate that their uniform ever remained the same, in terms of pattern, fabric and color, from one year of their existence to the next. When the phrase, "the Ranger uniform" is written or spoken, one must be careful to distinguish the particular year, campaign and sometimes company under consideration, and not assume that there was a standard "uniform" for more than any one year of the war.

The first major scholarship—and until recently the *only* real scholarship—to explore into the subject area of the uniforms of Rogers' Rangers was done by Burt Garfield Loescher in his 1946 book, *The History of Rogers: Rangers, Volume I: The Beginnings, Jan. 1755-April 6, 1758,* published by the author in San Francisco. This volume remains a goldmine of information, not only in what it offers the student concerning the uniforms, weapons and accouterments of the Rangers, but also in its narrative history of the corps, accompanied by numerous footnotes and appendices supporting and augmenting the main text. Additional new information on the Rangers' uniforms was offered in Loescher's *Genesis: Rogers' Rangers, The First Green Berets: The Corps & The Revivals, April 6, 1758-December 24, 1783,* published by the author in San Mateo, California, in 1969, and recently reprinted by Heritage Books, Inc., of Bowie, Maryland.

Historians and novelists prior to Loescher generally offered sketchy, frequently inaccurate descriptions of Ranger uniforms based on scattered fragments of evidence, occasional oral traditions, legends, and more often mere guesswork. In his classic 1884 work, *Montcalm and Wolfe,* Francis Parkman, despite intensive research into hundreds of sources concerning the war as a whole, could offer only the following about the dress of Rogers' men:

> These rangers wore a sort of woodland uniform, which varied in the different companies, and were armed with smooth-bore guns, loaded with buckshot, bullets, or sometimes both."[1]

In 1885, Joseph B. Walker, in *Life and Exploits of Robert Rogers, The Ranger,* a lecture given to the New England Historic and Genealogical Society, came a little closer to the mark when he described his concept of a typical Ranger under Rogers:

> Stand such a man in a pair of stout shoes or moccasins; cover his lower limbs with leggins and coarse small clothes; give him a close-fitting jacket and a warm cap; stick a small hatchet in his belt; hang a good-sized powder-horn by his side, and upon his back buckle a blanket and a knapsack stuffed with a moderate supply of bread and raw salt pork; to these furnishings add a good-sized hunting knife, a trusty musket and a small flask of spirits, and you have an average New Hampshire Ranger of the Seven Years' War.[2]

A number of nearly forgotten novels have featured Robert Rogers and his Rangers, among them G. A. Henty's *With Wolfe In Canada, The Winning of a Continent* (1887). The protagonist, James Walsham, goes on a scout with Rogers, but none of the

GARY ZABOLY
©1997

Rangers' attire, save for moccasins, is described. As for weapons, their preference is "a well-finished rifle." Later he ventures into enemy country to the north with some independent "scouts" dressed "in hunting shirt and leggings. . . .His cap was made of squirrels' skins, which would pass equally well on both sides of the frontier."[3]

Western illustrator Frederic Remington, almost as prolific in his writings as he was in his drawings and paintings, made a rare foray east of the Mississippi in 1897 in his *A Rogers' Ranger In the French and Indian War, 1757-1759,* a slim volume based on his *Harper's Monthly* article, *Joshua Goodenough's Old Letter.* This was pure fiction presented as an actual memoir, and it was so convincingly contrived and worded that it actually fooled many subsequent historians. Remington wrote and illustrated another fake "memoir," supposedly written by a Frenchman recalling his adventures in the wilds of seventeenth-century Canada, called *The Spirit of Mahongui.* Both *Goodenough* and *Mahongui* appeared in the collection of Remington stories, *Crooked Trails,* first published in 1898.

"Joshua Goodenough" recalls the Rangers of 1757 as being "dressed in the fashion of those times in skin and grey duffle hunting frocks." After the Battle on Snowshoes, he writes, the enemy Indians hacked Ranger prisoners to death after finding a scalp "in the breast of a man's hunting frock."[4]

Another writer of boys' books, G. Waldo Browne, wrote several titles dealing with wilderness warfare in the eighteenth century, including *With Rogers' Rangers* (1907). In this novel's first chapter, a small band of scouts led by Robert Rogers slinks through a 1754 New Hampshire forest seeking "reds":

> All three were dressed in the favourite suit of the woodsman of that day,—small-clothes of the coarse cloth spun at home and covered with buckskin leggings and hunting-shirt or sort of tunic, both garments frilled and ornamented in a fantastic manner with edgings of the same material and porcupine quills. Their feet were encased in moccasins of Indian pattern, while their heads were protected with the oft-described coonskin caps of that day. . . . About their rugged bodies were girthed strong belts from which were suspended stout, serviceable knives and hatchets. Over their shoulders were hung two sashes, crossing each other upon the back and breast, carrying bullet-pouches, powder-horns, wipers, and pickers for their firearms and steel for striking fire.[5]

They soon meet up with "The Woodranger" a man "a little over fifty," his clothing (as well as his character) clearly patterned after Natty Bumppo's in Cooper's *The Last of the Mohicans:*

> His garb was that of a woodsman, a pair of tight-fitting buckskin pantaloons, frilled up and down the seams, a hunting-frock of the colour of the green wood, fringed along the sleeves and around the bottom with yellow, and girthed closely about the waist by a wide belt, so the garment could not flutter as he moved through the forest. A cap made of the skin of the silver fox, shorn of its fur for summer wear, with the long tail hanging down his shoulders, covered his head. Upon his feet he wore a pair of Indian moccasins, which were ornamented with Porcupine quills.[6]

They later join William Johnson's expedition to Lake George in 1755, after which Rogers' Rangers become the army's main scouting arm. The description of their dress in Chapter XXII is a paraphrasing of Joseph B. Walker's description of Ranger dress in his 1884 lecture, and for this reason will not be quoted here.[7]

Kenneth Roberts' concept of the uniform for Rogers' Rangers in his now classic 1937 novel, *Northwest Passage,* consisted of a "hunting smock of greenish buckskin," buckskin leggings, and a glengarry cap of green wool with two short ribbons hanging in back.[8] When *Saturday Evening Post* illustrator Matt Clark was assigned the job of illustrating the serialized debut of *Northwest Passage* in that magazine, he wrote a letter to Roberts with specific questions about the Ranger uniform, one of which asked if the Scotch bonnets they wore had poms or not. Roberts replied that they were glengarries, which had the benefit of not catching on twigs, and which could be used as "water dippers."[9] (It is significant that Roberts left no known notes regarding his sources for his concept of Ranger wear). The 1940 MGM movie version of the novel fully adopted the green buckskins and "glengarry" caps,[10] as did the 1953 low-budget film *Fort Ti*, and the 1958 NBC television series *Northwest Passage.*

The novelist John Jennings tried to capitalize on Roberts' success by rushing to print his own historical novel, *Next To Valour,* in 1939, which also featured Rogers and his Rangers, though they were not the book's main focus. Midway through the novel, Rogers appears wearing a knee-length green buckskin coat and a feathered jockey cap.[11] Some thirty-five pages later, John Stark is described wearing a suit of fringed, "deep green" buckskin, and a "small Scotch cap."[12]

Although James Fenimore Cooper's Hawkeye is not a Ranger, but rather an impromptu scout for the British army in 1757, in *The Last of the Mohicans* (1826), his attire bears mentioning here. As noted earlier, the dress of G. Waldo Browne's "Woodranger" clearly evolved from Natty Bumppo's:

> He wore a hunting-shirt of forest green, fringed with faded yellow, and a summer cap of skins which had been shorn of their fur. . . . His moccasins were ornamented after the gay fashion of the natives, while the only part of his underdress which appeared below the hunting-frock, was a pair of buckskin leggings, that laced at the sides, and which were gartered above the knees with the sinews of a deer.[13]

Oddly, although there have been perhaps a dozen filmed versions of *Mohicans*, none of them have ever costumed Hawkeye in the dress Cooper so carefully described. The latest version, in 1992, actually sends Daniel Day-Lewis capless into the forest, and constantly running through it with his long hair never catching on any thickets or branches. His fringeless linen or tow shirt is left in its undyed natural state. That the producers of this film decided to so radically depart from Cooper's concept of Hawkeye's dress is perhaps not so surprising, when one considers how Bumppo himself was here transformed from a thinking man of the woods—whose philosophies ranged from decrying civilization's relentless inroads to empathizing with the decline of the "red" race—into a shallow character better suited to a paperback romance novel.

Green hunting shirts during the French and Indian War also appear in Cooper's 1845 novel, *Satanstoe: Or, The Littlepage Manuscripts.* In chapter twenty, Cornelius Littlepage and several friends join General Abercromby's expedition against Fort Carillon in 1758. He describes their campaign outfit:

> Each of us had a coatee, made of common cloth; but we all carried hunting-shirts, to be worn as soon as we entered the woods. These hunting-shirts, green in color, fringed and ornamented garments of the form of shirts to be worn over all, were exceedingly smart in appearance, and were admirably suited to the woods. It was thought that the fringes, form and color, blended them so completely with the foliage as to render them in a manner invisible to one at a distance, or at least undistinguished. They were much in favor with all the forest corps of America, and formed the usual uniform of the riflemen of the woods, whether acting against man or only against the wild beasts.[14]

This nineteenth-century concept of white men of the French and Indian War in upstate New York ranging through the woods in green, fringed hunting shirts is one that passed on into the works of many twentieth-century novelists, as already related. But Cooper's chronology, in terms of the attire, is actually twenty years too early. His reference to "the usual uniform of the riflemen of the woods" is not insignificant, for such fringed hunting shirts, although there are vague hints that they *might* have existed earlier, did not begin to appear in appreciable numbers anywhere until the early 1770s, concurrently with the rise of the rifle-armed frontiersmen of the Middle Atlantic and Southern colonies. Such shirts virtually exploded onto the scene during the Revolution, when they became Washington's favored dress because of their low cost and durability for those in his army who lacked real uniforms. In fact they were worn during that war in a wide variety of colors, often with differently colored fringes serving as a kind of facings.

In *Satanstoe* Cooper not only dresses his French and Indian War British woodsmen in green hunting shirts, but he also arms *all* of Rogers' Rangers with rifles. In Chapter XXIII, the skirmish of July 6, 1758 that began with the killing of Lord George Augustus Howe is described by Cornelius Littlepage. He describes the closing scenes of the engagement:

> Among the provincials was a partisan of great repute, of the name of Rogers. This officer led a party of riflemen on our left flank, and he drove in the enemy's skirmishers, along his own front, with rapidity, causing them to suffer a considerable loss."[15]

Thus, Rogers' men are all "Hawkeyes" in a sense. However, while rifles *were* issued to the ten best marksmen of each of the Regular British regiments under Abercromby in 1758,[16] there is no direct evidence yet found to indicate that all of the men under Rogers' command carried them in that campaign.

The prototype for Hawkeye's dress was probably seen by Cooper himself in New York State in the first two decades of the nineteenth century. "Green frocks with Yellow fringe" were in fact the uniforms the governor of the state ordered for the New York Rifle Corps when it was formed in 1809, a uniform that lasted until the end of the War of 1812.[17] Doubtless this uniform hearkened back to rifle dress worn during the Revolution by men of New York and other colonies, keeping, as it were, a proud tradition alive. When Cooper heard tales in Otsego County from such old-time hunters as David Shipman (born in 1740, and said to be Cooper's model for Leatherstocking), whose French and Indian War service, if any, is unknown, but who is definitely known to have served in the Revolution, he must have learned of all the green-garbed "woodsmen" present on the New York frontier in those days. If Cooper assumed that such green garb was of the fringed hunting shirt variety, and that it was common in the 1750s as well as the 1770s, it is an assumption that can be easily understood, and forgiven by historians.

What facts *are* known about the uniforms of Rogers' Rangers, from their inception in 1755 through their final days of service in the early 1760s? And what especially are we to make of the oft-quoted and rather scanty reference, in the letter-book of an Albany merchant's agent, to an order for their uniforming in early 1758?

Robert Rogers first appears on the Lake George war front during the campaign of 1755, when he captained the first "Ranging" company of Colonel Joseph Blanchard's First New Hampshire Regiment. The outfitting of the Rangers probably duplicated in many ways that of the rest of the regiment; and, as no uniform had been issued by New Hampshire to its soldiers that year, it can be surmised that modified civilian or hunting garb was worn. (This entire regiment, in fact, was considered a kind of body of woods-rangers rather than typical Provincial militia). Upon recruitment, allowances were advanced to those lacking muskets or blankets; but the regiment was found to be still vastly undersupplied when it arrived in Albany in August.[18]

Major General William Johnson's Provincial army was already on the march, and before the New Hampshire men could join it they had to be equipped with "small brass kettles (one to five men) [as well as additional] Blankets. . .shirts, jackets, shoes, stockings, caps, briches, axes and hatchets," and one tent for each of the ten companies.[19] No doubt their appearance helped inspire an eyewitness description of the soldiers under Johnson as "raw Country Men. . .most of them came with nothing more than a Wastecoat, 2 Shirts and one Blanket...Without Sword or Bayonet."[20] Following their significant role in the routing of Dieskau's French and Indians at Lake George on

September 8, the New Hampshire men acquired considerable plunder in the twelve hundred packs abandoned by the enemy's Indians and Canadian militia.[21] Among the items picked up were the tumplines attached to most of those packs. Indian tumplines had long since been in use among New England rangers, too, possibly for at least half a century before this battle; and the men under Rogers' command would continue to use them throughout the rest of the war.[22]

Enormous logistical difficulties, and the onset of winter, brought Johnson's campaign to a close, and most of the army was disbanded. Robert Rogers, however, along with forty-two hardy volunteers from his company and the rest of the regiment, stayed on to continue ranging out of newly-built Fort William Henry, as well as augmenting its small garrison.[23] Watchcoats, blankets, and many other cold weather necessities were in short supply.[24] But some relief for the northern posts did arrive in the form of civilian gifts, such as the 55 coats sent up from Albany.[25] From Philadelphia came "1339 warm Waistcoats, 1000 Pair of milled Stockings, and 332 Pair of Knit Mittens."[26]

Company commissary William Taylor sold a number of clothing items to Rogers' men, on credit, in December 1755. These items were: 19 great coats, 26 jackets, 54 checked and plain shirts of either wool or linen, 24 pairs of shoes, 24 pairs of milled hose, 18 pairs of breeches, 11 milled caps, 8 striped vests, 11 stockings, and 1 blanket. No color is given to any of these.[27]

In March of 1756, Commander-in-Chief William Shirley awarded Rogers a commission as captain of "His Majesty's Independent Company of Rangers," to be composed of sixty privates, three sergeants, an ensign, and a lieutenant. "Ten Spanish dollars were allowed to each man towards providing cloaths, arms and Blankets," in Rogers' own words.

In London on January 25, 1756, Lord Loudoun heard from New York Independent captain John Rutherford his suggestions on equipping the "Wood Men" of America to serve as partisans in the forest against the Canadians and Indians. Of them all, Rutherford said, "the best [are] from New Hampshire." He proposed that they be equipped with "Light Arms. . .Indian Knives and Hatchets." On the general condition of the Rangers with Johnson, Rutherford added that "At Present they Cloath themselves and are very Raged by which they catch colds." He proposed clothing them: "The French do it with French Blankets and Indian Stockings brought from home which come up middle thigh without Britches. The Shoes are made of Deerskin ready Dressed." In general, Rutherford noted how thick the forests were, and that even Regulars needed to adapt themselves, and their uniforms, to the new country. "No man can go thro without Indian Stockings and all wounds in the Legs are Dangerous from the Climat [sic] and vermin which breed Maggots in the Wounds."[28]

The relatively un-uniformed condition of Rogers' own Ranging company continued throughout 1756. In fact, it became something of an event when it was reported that "a Number of Officers at Albany, made a Collection and presented Capt. Rogers with a handsome Suit of Cloaths," as reported in the *Boston Gazette* of March 1, 1756. However, this was somewhat refuted in the *New-York Mercury* of March 29, 1756, which noted, "The Present that was presented to Capt. Rogers, was not a Collection from the Officers there; but a free Gift of the Inhabitants of that City and County."

The "ten Spanish dollars allowed each Ranger towards providing cloaths, arms and blankets" that same month probably did little to ensure uniformity of dress among the privates since no uniform was specified. Still, it is almost unarguable that Rogers—if he did not personally buy the clothing for them—would have instructed the Rangers to keep camouflage in mind when they made their purchases at Albany merchants' shops and in sutlers' stores at the forts and camps. Green and brown were the most sensible colors for wearing in the woods; and, judging by the green uniforms later worn by Rogers' men, it is no great leap of logic to assume that green would have been favored during these earlier years, too. If green clothing or cloth was in short supply, there were alternatives. A plain shirt of linen or tow for summer wear, for instance, could be dyed ("painted" is a frequently used contemporary term).

"Paint shirts" were sometimes distributed as gifts to Indians.[29] Or plain shirts were given to them, which they colored according to their tastes. In 1757, Peter Williamson noted that "the better Sort" among the Delawares and Shawnee "have Shirts of the finest Linen they can get, and to these some wear Ruffles; but these they never put on till they have painted them with various Colours, which they get from the Pecone Root, and Bark of Trees, and never pull them off to Wash, but wear them, till they fall in Pieces." Even their blankets "they paint with various Figures; but particularly the Leaves of Trees, in order to deceive their Enemies when in the woods."[30] This certainly sounds very similar to the leafy patterns on contemporary U.S. Army and Ranger camouflage dress.

"Tanned shirts" were probably in a number of cases synonymous with "painted shirts." During the Revolution, tanned shirts were described as being shirts made of "Ticklenbergh or tow cloth, that is stout"and put into a tanvat until they had turned the color of a "fallen dry leaf." They could be worn cut open in front, like a frock coat, and wrapped over the chest with a belt or sash.[31] During the Revolution, however, these were usually made with capes, and fringed. No hard evidence for this type of "rifle shirt" being worn during the French and Indian War/Pontiac period has been found; but further research may someday suggest that it was.

One slight suggestion, for a prototype at least, may lie in Willam Smith's *Reflections On the War With the Savages Of North-America*, written at the tag end of Pontiac's War. In this, Smith makes recommendations for "Light Troops" going into the field against the Indians. Among other items of clothing, he notes that "a strong tanned shirt" should be worn. That "tanned" and "painted" might indeed suggest the same thing is verified in a letter written "from the camp at Wachalamacqui, King Casteloga's Capital, 130 miles from Fort Pitt, on November 20, 1764," describing the "expedition against the savages" that had left Fort Pitt on October 3—the very same expedition, led by Colonel Bouquet, described by Smith in his book. In this anonymous letter, published in the *Scots Magazine* of January 1765 (p. 49), the Virginian riflemen are described; and they might have provided Smith with the source for his recommendation of "strong tanned shirt." Among Bouquet's forces, reads the letter, are:

> 400 Virginian volunteers, all armed with rifles, and excellent marksmen, and dressed *alamode de sauvages*, with painted shirts and fur-caps stained with paint.

Could these Virginians have been wearing tanned shirts cut in front and worn gown-style, as other Virginia riflemen did just ten years later, at the Battle of Point Pleasant? Or were the 1764 riflemen wearing plain English shirts that had been simply dyed or tanned? That it was described as a type of "savage" dress is important. Fighting the Indians in the woods by not only utilizing their native tactics but also by approximating their dress seems to have become the only effective answer. Even in the long settled communities, "savage" attire had become somewhat fashionable among certain soldiers. In 1762, an account of a militia exercise in New Haven, Connecticut, recorded an accident among the soldiers, some of whom were "dress'd in an Indian dress."[32] Ten years later, among the militia of Charlestown, on the outskirts of Boston, "were a Number dressed in the true Indian Taste, who exhibited the Indian Art of War with great Activity, and to the great Diversion of the Spectators."[33]

There are actually many accounts of white men dressed like Indians all throughout the eighteenth century: some undoubtedly referred to a near-naked look (breechclouts, leggings and moccasins), others to a matchcoat mantle, and others to a shirt. When and where the fringed "rifle shirt" of the 1770s was first worn remains uncertain, and an area that cries out for more research and analysis. The earliest reference to a "hunting shirt" I have been able to find comes from an account of the May 16, 1771 Battle of the Alamance, in North Carolina. In the wake of the battle, the property of the frontier "Regulators" was picked up, "consisting of hunting shirts, Wallets of Dumplings, Jackets, Breeches, Powder-Horns, Shot-Bags, &c."[34]

Checked shirts, too, could be dyed with a dark green color and made waterproof with linseed oil, as William Smith was informed by a nameless officer (see footnote in the attached Appendix by Smith, *Reflections On the War With the Savages Of North America*, for the full description).

In fact Major James Burd of Pennsylvania recommended in 1757 that the province's soldiers sent into the woods to engage Indians ought to be each supplied with "a green Shirt, a green Jacket, a Green Blankett, and a green Cloth Capp. . .our being dress'd intirely in green, would be of great Service to us, and would prevent in some Measure our Party's from being Discovered Upon a March."[35]

Thus, green was seen as a purely sensible color choice for men campaigning in the woods; and for Rogers' Rangers, in their early days, it must surely have been no less preferred a color. It also might have been the color choice for the two independent companies of rangers raised in 1756 by Massachusetts Governor William Shirley, captained respectively by Thomas Speakman and Humphrey Hobbs. In April 1756, Shirley wrote to Major General John Winslow that each man of these companies was to receive "A good Hunting Coat Vest & Breeches, a pair of Indian Stockings, Shoes, and a Hatchet."[36] No color was indicated, but clearly this was *not* an osnaburg frock, as some historians have interpreted it.[37] Because "97 1/2 yards Osnabrigs" were distributed to each of the two companies, some have assumed that the bolts of this cloth, a kind of coarse linen, were therefore made into the "hunting coats, vests and breeches" ordered by Shirley.

In truth, osnaburg had a wide variety of uses for eighteenth-century military men. It was made into tents, haversacks, shot pouches, wallets, knapsacks, and sometimes even leggings.[38] It was also used for shirts, and for "small clothes" such as breeches and waistcoats, and often drawers. Sometimes it was used as a lining. It was made into sacks and bedding, and short petticoat "kilts" or trousers for sailors. Working frocks were made of it, especially for farmers, carpenters, woodcutters and wagoners; and during the Revolution it was very popular because it was cheap, and easily could be made into *hunting shirts* and *hunting frocks*; but never—in 1756 at least—was it made into the kind of "hunting coat" Shirley was referring to. In 1756, a *hunting coat* was a horse of a different color. Still, the confusion among historians is an understandable one, since the terms seem almost synonymous.

Almost, but not quite. In the course of my research into the dress of Rogers' Rangers, I consistently failed, for many years, to encounter any primary evidence describing a "hunting coat" of the mid-eighteenth century, as mentioned by William Shirley. Then, in the mid-1980s, while scanning numerous issues of colonial newspapers in order to extract information on a variety of related subjects, I stumbled across the very first reference I had seen, other than Shirley's, to a contemporary "hunting coat." It was published some eleven years after Shirley wrote his letter to Winslow, and appeared in the *Maryland Gazette* of October 1, 1767:

> Ran away from the Kingsbury Furnace Mine-bank, near Baltimore, three indentured servants, one of whom was William Hatton. . .[he] had on, an old red Jacket, an old green short Hunter's Coat, with Pockets under the arms, and yellow Metal Buttons.

Clearly this was no fringed hunting shirt or frock, but a type of hunting garment not uncommon in England and Europe. The upper pockets were generally used to carry loose ball for quick loading during the hunt. In fact, British light infantry at Quebec in 1759 had two such pockets, made of leather, sewed to just below the breast area, for balls and flints, with a flap of red cloth to secure the contents in case of the soldier falling. British light infantry sent to the West Indies in the 1760s also wore these upper pockets. Captain George Scott, in a letter to Lord Loudoun in

February 1758, recommended that Ranger coats be made with pockets sewn on the inside of the breast of the coat.

In the *Pennsylvania Chronicle* of June 19, 1769, we have another example of a hunting coat, worn by James Havard, a runaway from west New Jersey: "a blue lapelled hunting coat, bound with binding lighter than the coat."

The *Royal Gazette*, a New York Tory newspaper, on October 9, 1779, listed several stolen items in an advertisement, including, "One suit of green broad cloth cloaths, with gilt oval buttons; One suit of light coloured silk jean, with solid silver buttons, and a laurel engraved round them. One suit of nankeen cloaths; the above cloaths made short fit for shooting."

Sufficient examples of such hunting coats exist in eighteenth-century art, especially in the works of George Stubbs, Arthur Devis, Thomas Gainsborough, and Benjamin West, to suggest the look of the above quoted examples, as well as the possible cut and pattern of those worn by Hobbs' and Speakman's companies. Some of these paintings even show upper-breast pockets on the coats. Hunting dress was readily available through many civilian merchants and tailors. For instance, Patrick Audley of New York City advertised in newspapers dating from 1753 through 1761 his ability to make "gentlemen's laced and plain clothes, [and] hunting dresses."[39]

What we have, then, for these two companies in 1756 are coats with metal buttons, possibly double-breasted, possibly with binding, maybe even upper-breast pockets, and most likely short in length. Most "hunting coats" had collars, usually in a contrasting shade or even a different color from the body of the coat; however, some collarless types *were* made. As for the main color of the coats for Hobbs' and Speakman's men, again, it might have been green; but as of yet it remains unknown, and one can only speculate and theorize.

After the first Battle on Snowshoes against the French and Indians on January 21, 1757, several miles northwest of Ticonderoga, private Ranger Thomas Brown, of Speakman's company, was captured by the Indians. All he says about his uniform *per se* is that his captors went to "searching my Pockets" where "they found some money," and that one of them "cut thro' my Cloaths" with a cutlass. He also talks of having a blanket, snowshoes, tomahawk, "gun" and "shoes."[40]

The summer of 1757 found the companies of Hobbs and Speakman, following the deaths of those captains earlier in the year, under the new command of captains Charles Bulkeley and John Stark, respectively. All were now under the overall command of Robert Rogers, and, along with Captain John Shepherd's and Rogers' own company, had been sent as part of the British expedition against Louisbourg, led by Lord Loudoun. In July, at Halifax, British captain John Knox penned a sketch of these companies in their warm-weather campaign outfit:

> A body of rangers, under the command of Captain Rogers, who arrived with the other troops from the southward, march out every day to scour the country; these light troops have, at present, no particular uniform, only they wear their cloaths short, and are armed with a firelock, tomahock, or small hatchet, and a scalping knife; a bullock' horn full of powder hangs under their right arm, by a belt from the left shoulder; and a leathern, or seal's skin bag, buckled round their waist, which hangs down before, contains bullets, and a smaller shot, of the size of full-grown peas: six or seven of which, with a ball, they generally load; and their Officers usually carry a small compass fixed in the bottoms of their powderhorns, by which to direct them, when they happen to lose themselves in the woods.[41]

Once again, "short" clothing is indicated, *a la* short hunting coats and vests, or jackets, coats, waistcoats and possibly even shirts that have been deliberately trimmed. Knox does not mention headgear, but the fact that the companies are reported as having "no particular uniform" suggests a probable variety—leather jockey caps, knit caps, Scotch bonnets, and felt hats cut down to brims about two inches wide.

One thing to keep in mind here is that although Knox says these four companies had "no particular uniform," he might in fact be referring to them as a body of companies without *matching* uniforms. That is, each of Rogers' companies might indeed have worn their own *company* uniform, if they had them. We know for certain that Bulkeley's and Stark's companies, formerly Hobbs' and Speakman's, still must have had much of their "hunting coat, vest and breeches" garb in evidence, which would have given those companies some semblance of uniformity. Thus, the different cut and pattern, and possibly even different color and color shade, of each company would still qualify to define the entire "body of rangers" as having "no particular uniform." It might help to note here that Lord Loudoun in January 1758, ordered Rogers to raise five new companies, and he stressed that they "must be uniform in every company." This would seem to suggest that most of the old Ranger companies were indeed uniformed differently from one another.

The company of John Shepherd is a unique case at this time. Of the four Ranger companies under Rogers' command this one seems to have been the least likely to be wearing items of any uniformity, since it was originally part of the New Hampshire Regiment of 1756, which had not been uniformed by their province. Thus, the effects of three of these Provincials-turned-Rangers, who died either in Halifax or en route back to New York, make up a hodgepodge of clothing and gear (as recorded by Ranger sergeant Moses Kelsey, also of Shepherd's):

> Account of effects of Thomas Chase died 13 175- at Halefax
> One New French gun marked TC
> One Coton and Linen Shirt
> One frock asinbrgs
> One pare of asinbrgs Trousers[42]
> One powder horn one boolet pouch
> One pare of yarn Stockins
> One Betel [Bottle]
> Fifteen Spanish mild [milled] dolers
> One gray Jacket two pare of Stockins
> Two pare of Britchis
> One Striped Jacket one Shirt
> An old hat and Cap
> These things are kept in Charge with John Holon
> Newcastel August 23rd 1757
>
> Isaac Grifin died on his pashis [passage] from Halifax and Left the Things following:
> One Coat
> One Striped [?]
> One pare of Britches
> One Cotin and Linin Shirt
> Two pare of yarn Stockins
> One old felt hat
> One gun marked IG 1757
> One powder horn and Bolet pouch
> Forty one Spenesh mild dolors
>
> Sgt. Job Lieby
> One gun
> One Coat
> One blew Jeaket
> One Red pare of britches
> One pare of Sleve Butens Silver
> Three pare of Stockins
> One flask One pare of Lather Britchis
> One Tow Shirt one hat
> One pare of shoes
> One Chist [Chest]
> Died at hallefix August the 13th 1757.[43]

These, then, were among the items of dress Knox had observed on some of the Rangers at Nova Scotia. Knox's details of weapons and accouterments, in his overall description of Rogers' men, are also unique, and later, he provides us with even more. In his entry for October 10, 1757, he notes that a scouting party of Regulars and Rangers discovered an abandoned enemy camp, in Nova Scotia, finding therein "a small leather bag of balls and buck-shot, also a firelock, which, by the marks, appeared to have formerly belonged to a man of the ranging company."[44] (Clearly, the Rangers' "leathern, or seal's skin bag" was *not* a small cartridge box or "belly box"). In

May 1758, another detachment near Nova Scotia's Fort Edward chased off an enemy party and found in its wake "a pair of large silver buckles, which they got some time before from a Serjeant of rangers who fell into their hands."[45]

Hunting coats and even vests would have been too much to bear on the hottest summer days, so they were no doubt dispensed with in such weather, and shirts were worn loose by the Rangers. Near South Bay on July 9, 1757, Massachusetts Provincial soldier Rufus Putnam, doing temporary Ranger duty near South Bay, noted:

> This night we encamped as well, but the gnats and mosquitoes were a great trouble to us, having no blankets; and I had nothing but a shirt and Indian stockings, and no man can tell what an affliction those little animals were."[46]

The revolutionary influence of Rogers' Rangers on usually inflexible British army conventions in so many areas was already being felt in 1757; in fact, some British officers began to imagine, however unwisely, that their own men could outperform the homegrown American woodsmen in forest scouting and warfare. Plans were set in motion for Colonel Thomas Gage to organize a regiment of "light infantry," or British "rangers" as they were called at this early stage of the game.[47] After a conversation with Major General Edward Webb, Lord Loudoun penned in his journal on November 23, 1757, a preliminary list of "Cloaths talkt of for Rangers:"

> a Match coat Different Colour from those
> the French get
> Woolen Wastcoat
> Britches
> Shirt and Roller
> Stockings
> Shoes
> Indian Stockings
> For Accouterments
> Horn and Bag for Bullets
> Tomahock
> Blanket

The "Match coat" noted here is often an elusive term when it is used in the eighteenth century. Generally it referred to a small blanket, usually of stroud or duffles, or else of animal skins, that the Indians would wear about them much the way Highlanders wear their plaids: belted around their waists and draped over one shoulder. However, Loudoun's "Match coat" is decidedly meant to describe a different thing entirely. The reference to the French suggests that it was intended to resemble in style, if not in color, the *capot* worn by Canadian militiamen, Marines, *coureur de bois* and *voyageurs*. These were fashioned from a variety of fabrics, and came in a number of colors, often with binding on the edges. Sometimes they were cut from a white trade blanket, hence the term "blanket coat." It was also a popular item among the Indians. It was made in several ways: with buttons, with laces for tying, or without either and intended to be wrapped around and held with a belt or a sash. Sometimes there was just one button, holding it together near one side of the wearer's neck.

That it was called a "matchcoat" by Webb and Loudoun is interesting; but, in fact, while "matchcoat" most often referred to a blanket worn like a cloak, sometimes it *was* made into coats with sleeves. For example, take the case of the runaway servant in 1770 Baltimore reported in an advertisement as wearing "a Matchcoat Blanket Coat."[48] John Josselyn in 1673 noted that the New England Indians purchased from the English "a sort of Cloth called trading cloth of which they make Mantles, Coats with short sleeves, and caps for their heads which the women wear."[49] Thus, "matchcoats" can indeed describe either a mantle or a coat. In 1677, Robert Plot wrote that the Indians of Virginia and New England took "Duffields. . .otherwise called Shags, and by the Merchants, Trucking-cloth. . .to apparel themselves with them, their manner being to tear them into Gowns of about two Yards long, thrusting their Arms through two Holes made for that Purpose, and so wrapping the rest about them as we our Loosecoats."[50] In the 1770s, Indians were still wearing these, as tourist Patrick M'Robert noted. Their "clothing," he wrote, "is generally a skin or blanket, made with sleeves like a short jockey-coat, and tied about the waist with a belt."[51]

That Loudoun was referring to a coat-like garment was later confirmed in his diary entry dated November 24, 1757, in which he recorded information received from Major John Spittal of the 47th Regiment, who had served in Nova Scotia. Loudoun wanted to know how the Rangers there, during "Governor Shirley's War" in the late 1740s, had been clothed and accoutered. According to Spittal, the several companies of independent rangers (including John Gorham's) had received clothing sent from England, in the form of:

> A Brown Match Coat with Brown Buttons
> A Brown Wastcoat
> Sheepskin Britches
> Shoes and Stockings as the Troops
> Shirts and Rollers

After the war, these companies were clothed in "French Cloathing that were taken at Sea and bought from the Captain very cheap."

Elsewhere, Loudoun, while describing the dress of the Virginia Provincial troops, makes yet another reference to "match coats" worn by white soldiers. On December 28, 1755, George Washington wrote to Captain William Cocke of the Virginia Regiment that "I have found it impracticable to procure Clothes for your men. I think none so proper for Rangers as Matchcoats; therefore would advise you to procure them."[52] Loudoun himself, in his entry of November 13, 1757, described information he had received about this regiment:

> The Virginia Troops good [sic] Cloathed in Blue faced with Red and Looping besides which each man buys for himself a Match Coat, which is made of a thick Flannel. . .They die [sic] it brown with Hickory Bark and make the Match Coat short.

Evidence found in other sources, such as the Bouquet Papers, points to men of the Virginia regiment wearing blankets, flannel waistcoats, flannel jackets, and blanket coats while on the march to Fort Duquesne in 1758. Thus, the terms blanket, waistcoat, jacket, and blanket coat, in the eyes of some writers of the 1750s, might sometimes be synonymous with "match coat."

At other times the term "watchcoat" also seems to have been interchanged with "matchcoat" on the frontier, especially if the "watchcoat" had been made of "trucking cloth" like duffle or stroud.

Gage's Light Infantry were initially dressed, in 1758, in "dark brown short coats" with dark brown linings (linings were not necessarily *facings*), and no lace.[53] The exact cut and pattern of the coat is not known, though one suspects it might have been a "matchcoat" style—at least matchcoat as Lord Loudoun understood it. This remains a moot point, however.

Unfortunately, when Loudoun ordered Robert Rogers to expand his Ranger corps with an additional five companies, including one composed of Indians, in January 1758, he did not describe in his diary either their uniforms or their accouterments; nor did Rogers. Loudoun instructed Rogers, as the Ranger leader notes in his *Journals,* that "Your men. . .are likewise to provide themselves with good warm cloathing, which must be uniform in every company, and likewise with good warm blankets. And the company of Indians to be dressed in all respects in the true Indian fashion." Out of the advance of "one month's pay for each of the said five companies" was to be drawn the cost of the uniforms and arms.

By March 4, all five companies were raised and deemed ready for service. However, only one company—Captain Moses Brewer's Mohegan Indians from Connecticut—joined the Rangers at Rogers' Island. The other four "white" companies, captained by James Rogers, John McCurdy, Jonathan Brewer, and William Stark, were ordered to go directly to Boston after they were recruited in New England, and from thence to join General Amherst's thrust against Louisbourg. These companies remained in the Nova Scotia/St. Lawrence theaters for the duration of the war. So in early 1758 there were probably none of the new green uniforms on Rogers' Island except perhaps those worn by the white officers of the Mohegan company. Loudoun's orders that the "good warm cloathing. . .must be uniform in every company" referred only to these new companies, *not* Rogers' old ones.

Of course, it is fairly obvious that any new uniform Rogers ordered for these new Rangers would have reflected the pattern he had already adopted for some of those companies long since established and billeted on Rogers' Island. One additional clue that Rogers' companies on the island were not given new uniforms at this time is that over three months later, in April 1758, Rogers was apparently, and finally, considering ordering fresh uniforms for them. How long a gap existed since their last uniforming is not known. It must be remembered that just nine months earlier Captain John Knox had written that the four Ranger companies in Nova Scotia under Rogers "had no particular uniform." Evidently by April 1758 this was still the case, and each company was dressed somewhat differently from the next. That Rogers was thinking about finally giving *all* his men clothing that would be "uniform in every company" is suggested in agent John MacComb's letter to his New York employers, the clothiers and merchants Gregg and Cunningham. MacComb, writing from Albany on April 22, 1758, was both describing the uniforms Rogers had ordered in January (from other firms), as well as touching upon the new uniform order the Ranger leader seems to have been considering at this time. The pertinent part of this letter is printed here as originally written, grammar and punctuation unchanged:

> The Close that Rogers had made for his people are chiefly of Green Bath Rug & low priced green Cloths with wt. Mettle Buttons, & white Silver lace Hats, some of them Silver laced, cord or looping on their Jackets, all lin'd with Green Serge—I aprehend it would be runing a very great risque, the ordering such a great quantity of Cloths without a Certainty of gettin them disposed of. Mr. Forsey made the greatest qty. of any one, Kenedy & Lyle, & Preble & Wiles made a fiew also.
>
> If you intended such a thing, I think the best way would be to consult with the Major about that Matter, but you know best. . .I believe a parcel of Scotch Bonnets would sell well, as the Rangers who can get them wear nothing else when they go out.[54]

The inference is very plain: a future order was being *considered* with Gregg and Cunningham. By June 14, 1758 the order had still not been made, since MacComb wrote to his employer,

> Major Rogers was here the other day, he says he expects to be removed into the Regulars soone, on which acct he will not engage for any clothing for his men, he is satisfyed he would have them on better terms they coming from you, than he had heretofore. He promised he would write you on that matter.[55]

Does MacComb's letter of April 22 provide any clues as to the physical construction of the uniforms Rogers ordered for the four new "white" companies? Historians have interpreted "Green Bath Rug" as the essential fabric used in making them, and that these uniforms were worn all year round. They have also interpreted "Green Bath Rug" as a kind of "frieze," or rough wool, used for making uniform jackets and vests.[56] However, nothing could be further from the truth, in terms of the kind of clothing for which "Green Bath Rug" would have been used.

In many years of trying to interpret MacComb's description of Rogers' January 1758 order, I was never able to come across any reference to "Bath Rug" being used for any items of eighteenth-century clothing, let alone uniforms. But persistence paid off; long hours spent perusing Colonial newspapers soon solved the riddle for me in the 1980s (just as they had in explaining the "hunting coat" question). In the October 5, 1767 issue of *Weyman's New-York Gazette,* I came across the following advertisement:

Just imported by ADAM GILCHRIST, In the Ship Hope, Capt. Davies from London, best Superfine Cloaths, viz.. . . .superfine buff Shagg. . .Naps, Bath Rugg for Surtouts.

All at once, MacComb's mysterious reference to "Green Bath Rug" seemed solved at last: it was used, according to this, to make the short greatcoats known as "surtouts," worn during rainstorms as well as in wintertime. Still, this was only one reference, and additional confirmation was needed. The latter was found in yet another advertisement, in the *New-York Journal or General Advertiser* of October 16, 1766, reporting a stolen "new-Fashioned Bath-Rug Surtout Coat." In the same paper's issue of December 29, 1768, an ad noted the theft of "an old brown Bath Rug Great Coat."

Nowhere did I find "Bath Rug" or even "Rug" used for a uniform jacket or waistcoat as was previously thought. "Rug" in the eighteenth century was a coarse, nappy, weighty wool used mainly for surtouts, greatcoats, watchcoats, cloaks, nightgowns, mantles, and bed coverlets: all rather heavy items of apparel.[57] It was not a "rug," viz, carpet, in the modern sense of the word; and "Bath" simply refers to the city in England in which it and other coating materials were manufactured. It came in several textures: "superfine," "thrumbed," "shaggy" or heavily "fringed" all over, and "spotted."[58] Color-wise, it was most often green. In fact, Albany merchants' shops in the 1750s sold green and spotted rug on a fairly consistent basis.[59] Coarse "rug" mantles were also still being worn by some rural Irish men and women as late as the early eighteenth century.[60]

Almost unarguably, then, Rogers' Rangers had been wearing green surtouts or else gown-like coats of "Bath Rug" or of just plain "rug" in winter weather prior to 1758. Such overcoats were not new to them, when one is reminded of the "19 great coats" issued to Rogers' men in December of 1755. The accompanying illustration depicts a group of Rangers on Rogers' Island circa 1758. John Stark stands above three Rangers about to leave on a scout. He wears a double-breasted surtout coat of green Bath Rug, with a short cape.

The Ranger at lower right wears a green coat of tiny shorn loops of rug, giving it a shaggy resemblance to dyed fur, or to a covering of fringes. It has a small cape, or collar, similar to those on some greatcoats of the time, used to protect the lower part of the face in cold weather.[61]

In the background, two Rangers are on a wood-cutting detail. One wears a loose rug "gown" with a hood, and a knit stocking cap. Such gowns were not uncommon even in England. One London citizen described a ghost he had seen in a dream, wearing "a long, dangling Rug Gown, bound round his Loins with a broad Leather Girdle."[62] Rug gowns were also worn by "poor people" in eighteenth-century hospitals, and by watchmen.[63] The other Ranger wears a cloak made of shaggy rug, also hooded.[64]

Three types of rug coats are shown in the drawing because any one of them might have been considered a "surtout" by Rangers. They were warm and resistant to moisture, and it is almost certain that they would have been worn in camp in the winter, and no doubt on sentry duty, though their use in the field has not yet been verified.[65] Both British and Provincial troops wore surtouts, often as a kind of fatigue dress, or worn over their uniforms to keep them clean while on duty, or simply for warmth in cold weather. Most of these coats seem to have been "blue with yellow metal buttons" (i.e., brass buttons). William Smith, in his treatise on carrying the war to the Indians, recommended that the clothing of "light troops" include "an oiled surtout against the rain."

That "surtouts" could refer to not just one but several types of garments, according to eighteenth-century eyes, is verified in a number of places. A deserter from Colonel Seth Warner's Green Mountain Rangers in 1776 was described as wearing a "blanket surtout coat."[66]

In London in 1716, the surtout was also known as "a greatcoat, joseph, or wrap-rascal," the latter being sometimes a gown-like item and at other times a coat with buttons and cape.[67] Thus, "surtout" was mostly used to refer to an overcoat, but at other times it could mean a blanket coat, a gown, and even an oiled shirt cut into a gown. Once again, the flexibility of eighteenth century terminology must always be kept in mind.

MacComb's letter also mentions "low pric'd green Cloths with wt. [white] Mettle Buttons. . . some of them Silver laced, cord or looping on their Jackets, all lin'd with Green Serge." At the second Battle on Snowshoes on March 13, 1758, Captain Henry Pringle, a volunteer from the 27th Regiment of Foot, notes that his comrade Lieutenant Boyle Roche had thrown off his "green jacket." Pringle mentions his own coat, two waistcoats, a blanket, a silk handkerchief, and a "furred cap." These are important details, especially regarding the two waistcoats, or "jackets." Troops on winter campaign frequently wore two waistcoats. One of them would likely have been their regimental or company waistcoat, whether it was green, red, blue, or buff. Flannel and striped or spotted "swanskin" were fabrics often used for "under-waistcoats"—viz., waistcoats for added warmth to be worn *under* the uniform waistcoat or jacket.

Consider, for example, the "swanskin half-thicks fit for soldiers' winter waistcoats" advertised in the *New-York Mercury* of November 27, 1758, or the double-breasted kind, also made for soldiers, sold via the *Boston Post-Boy* of April 16, 1759. During King George's War, Quakers in London donated for the use of English troops "Woolen Waistcoats to double over the Breast and Belly, long enough to be under their Waistbands, to be worn under their other Cloaths."[68] Witney and duffle were also used for "under-jackets" or "under-waistcoats," and they generally had sleeves.

In addition to the "green jacket" mentioned by Pringle at the Battle on Snowshoes of March 13, 1758, the French-allied Indians also found on the battlefield a discarded "officer's jacket."[69] Another French account says that Robert Rogers "left on the field of battle, his coat, and even the order he received from his general."[70] This almost certainly indicates a laced coat or jacket long and heavy enough to be considered a short "coat."

Jabez Fitch, a Connecticut Provincial stationed on Rogers' Island in the winter of 1757-58, provides evidence for the type of shirts worn by the Rangers. On January 20, 1758, he notes that, at "Captain Durkee's blockhouse. . .we overhalled the stores and found a vast number of flaning [flannel] shurts shoes stockings mild [milled] caps and many larg pieses of Cloath cheefly Striped and Checkd Flaning." More than a month later, on February 24, he saw Major Rogers at the blockhouse, who "bought a number of shurts there &c."[71] Flannel shirts seem to have been a Ranger staple readily adopted by other units. During the Revolution, Dr. Benjamin Rush opined that American soldiers ought to wear more flannel:

> The Roman soldiers wore flannel shirts next to their skins. This was one among other causes of the healthiness of the Roman armies. During the last war in America, Gen. (then Col.) Gage obliged the soldiers of his regiment [the 80th] to wear flannel shirts from an accidental want of linen, and it was remarkable during a sickly campaign on the Lakes not a single soldier belonging top the said regiment was ever seen in any of the military hospital.[72]

The Ranger jackets, or coats, of 1758 were probably short and double-breasted (in imitation of some "hunting coats"), as were the waistcoats. The lapels were no doubt long enough to be buttoned at the waist, which would provide extra warmth in wintertime: a stipulation even Major George Scott, a Regular officer assigned to command light troops in Nova Scotia, had pointed out in a clothing proposal for Rangers to Lord Loudoun in February of 1758.[73] The sleeves might have been plainly cuffed and buttoned, or cut in a "slash," marine fashion, with three buttons, as shown in the drawing. The green serge lining might have been revealed on cuffs, falling collars (if collars they had), as well as the lapels of the coats, although it must be remembered that "lined" does not necessarily mean "faced" in every case.

At upper right in the illustration is another captain, sans overcoat, wearing a wig tied *en solitaire*, and a silver-laced dress uniform coat, with silver shoulder knot. His shirt is of fine linen, and sports ruffles. His laced green jockey cap is based on the one seen in Captain Thomas Davies' oil painting of General Amherst's camp at the southern end of Lake George in 1759, now in the collection of the Fort Ticonderoga Museum. This captain also wears a Ranger's green breeches, and carries a straight, silver-hilted sword.

At left foreground stands a Ranger private in a visored winter cap of beaverskin, with a "cape" that was buttoned or laced under the chin.[74] He has a sleeved waistcoat of spotted swanskin under his green jacket. A striped white blanket is wrapped around him in Indian fashion; in extreme cold weather or blizzard conditions it could be draped over his head and shoulders. His sealskin bullet bag hangs outside on a belt for quick access; his blanket mittens are stuffed into the latter. On his back is a pack of a rolled bearskin containing provisions and miscellaneous items for the trail, tied and carried with a tumpline worn over one shoulder. The bearskin when unraveled also served as a mattress. His feet are encased in warm moosehide shoepacks, or high-flapped moccasins; and metal ice-creepers are strapped onto them. His musket, its barrel cut and stock dressed down to make it lighter, is protected in a gun case of bearskin. A wooden stopple in the muzzle keeps the barrel dry.

The second figure from the left wears a private's green jacket of a "low-priced green cloth" such as ratteen or frieze, with two upper outside pockets for balls and flints. The jacket is double-breasted, with two rows of white metal buttons, and two buttons below to close the "skirt" of the jacket. He has a green waistcoat; a striped flannel waistcoat under it; and a checked shirt. A silk handkerchief is tied around his neck. He wears buckskin breeches, leggings of green ratteen tied with a red garter,[75] a Scotch bonnet, and deerskin moccasins. His canteen, filled with diluted rum, is covered with cloth, and the blade of his tomahawk sits in a leather case. A greased "lock cover" protects the mechanisms of his carbine. His powder-horn is carried with a quilled and beaded strap of Indian make, while the tumpline of his pack is plain and undecorated.

Captain John Stark, aside from his Bath Rug surtout, wears a white silver-laced black felt hat, with silver button and loop holding a green cockade. He has buff-colored gloves, drawers of canvas or wool, leather buskins, and shoes. A cutlass with a green sword knot rises from a vent in his coat. His waistcoat is silver laced. A spotted handkerchief is wrapped around his neck.

The Ranger at lower right, aside from his shaggy surtout, wears another kind of fur cap typical of the period, made of bearkskin or wolfskin. He also wears fur gloves with the hair on the inside. His powder horn hangs by a webbed strap, and his similarly-made, quill-patterened tumpline is Iroquoian in origin. Ice skates and snowshoes hang from his pack. A small leather bag in front, on its own belt, contains balls and buckshot. His tomahawk is covered with a buttoned leather case, and the other half of the double-frogged belt suspension carries a short bayonet. His musket is carried in a long gun case made of a stroud blanket, with a decorative "list" edge. His leggings are of dark blue stroud, edged with binding. A deerskin knapsack, with the hair on, carries extra items.

The background of the scene depicts Fort Edward's western walls, the iced-over Hudson River, and, at right, the big blockhouse and one of the Ranger huts on Rogers' Island.

Tumplines were used by the Rangers all throughout the war; and in fact they were distributed to almost all of General Abercromby's troops when his army was "Rangerized" in the late spring and early summer of 1758. A sutler's account book in the Huntington Library reveals John Stark's purchase of a "Muttoomp Line" (along with a "Coat," "Blanket," and "2 Shirts") in 1759.[76]

During the remaining years of the war—until the 1763 Treaty of Paris—the uniforms of the Rangers serving under Major Robert Rogers' direct command present an intriguing problem for the researcher, because variations in their tailoring continue to appear in the scattered bits of documentation that have thus far been found. No consistent pattern seems to prevail except for the main color—green—and in fact it almost seems as if the companies continued to be differently uniformed, without ever receiving a single, unifying attire for the corps as a whole.

There was never any one pattern for the uniform being produced by any one vendor working with the same fabrics. By late 1759, for instance, Thomas and Benjamin Forsey, the clothiers who had made most of the uniforms for the Louisbourg-bound companies in January 1758, were no longer in business.[77] New uniforms were being made for the sometimes scattered companies at different times and evidently by different clothiers; and due to a variety of exigencies ready-made items of clothing were no doubt bought for some of them. No contemporary document, in fact, ever specifies the "uniform of Rogers' Rangers" as, for instance, "the uniform of the 42nd Highlanders" or "the uniform of the New York Provincials" might be mentioned. Always it is simply a "Ranger's waistcoat," or a "Ranger's jacket," or "Ranger cloaths": terms that almost seem generic. Certainly the implication is that "Ranger" clothing was different enough from Regular and Provincial uniforms to allow such a distinction to be easily made; but there were no "Rogers' Rangers uniform" references ever made. Ranger dress, it seems, continued as "no particular uniform," as Knox wrote in July of 1757.

The fact is that "Rogers' Rangers" was a term used to describe the various companies of Rangers serving under Rogers' direct command—a corps, not his own "regiment." (Rogers was never a "Colonel" of a regiment during the French and Indian War). The men he led were a collection of short-term independent Ranger companies. Rogers was merely the ranking Ranger officer in the northern New York region; and in fact he often acted as a kind of "task force" commander leading detachments drawn from various Ranger, Provincial and Regular units. When Rogers had been ordered by Lord Loudoun in January 1758 to raise five new companies, he did arrange for their recruitment and uniforming; but once they were sent to Nova Scotia they fell under the overall command of Major George Scott. Rogers could continue to recommend officers for commissions in the companies, but he never commanded any of them personally (unless individual Rangers later re-enlisted in other companies); nor was he responsible for the re-uniforming most of them underwent in mid-1759.

From 1759 onward "Ranger" clothing seems to have existed in a variety of styles and fashions, and sometimes even colors. In mid-June of that year, a servant ran off from his master, who placed the following notice in *Weyman's New-York Gazette* of July 2:

> Run-away about a fortnight ago, from John Lavenue, inn holder at Albany, an English servant man, named John Exelby. . .[he] had a Ranger's green waistcoat on, with his hat cut in the form of a jockey cap.

The jockey cap is a significant item. Referring back to Thomas Davies' view of Amherst's Lake George camp that same year, 1759, the green-clad figure in the painting, who might very well represent one of Rogers' Rangers, wears a green jockey cap bound with white or yellow. It is decorated with what seems to be a black ostrich feather: a not uncommon touch for jockey caps in both civilian and military circles. Jockey caps in various colors *were* available in merchants' shops during this period; they were often made of velvet or cloth. In the *Boston Evening-Post* of December 17, 1753, we

Facing page: Detail from Captain Thomas Davies' *View of the Lines at Lake George, 1759*. exhibited at the Royal Academy in 1774, it may have been painted years earlier, or perhaps executed in the early 1770s from Davies' on-the-scene sketches and watercolors. While Davies' Revolutionary War sketchbook exists, his French and Indian War sketchbook has not yet been found, so a precise identification of these two foreground figures cannot be made. They might represent a typical Ranger and a Stockbridge Indian under Rogers' command; there is also the possibility that Davies was portraying Robert Rogers himself, along with "Captain Jacobs." In any case, the details, outside of the green jockey cap, confirm much that has already been concluded about the attire of both Rogers' Rangers and the Stockbridge Indians. Courtesy the Fort Ticonderoga Museum.

find one merchant selling "stript [sic], scarlet and green Sham-Velvet Caps." The *Boston Gazette* of June 28, 1756, advertised "green & crimson velvet caps." In the *New-York Mercury* of December 17, 1764, "black, green and blue jockey caps" were announced for sale. However, purchasing green jockey caps bound with lace sufficient for a number of Ranger companies would more likely have been a special commission for a hatter, or several hatters, considering the numbers needed.

Rangers wearing green jockey caps also appear three years after the Amherst campaign. Joseph Hopkins, who was a sergeant-major with Rogers' Rangers in 1759, formed his own unit in late 1761, "the Queen's Royal Independent Company of American Rangers."[78] Diarist Hannah Callender saw them in Philadelphia on July 2, 1762, and briefly described their appearance:

> The Queen's company are here at the Barracks. Their clothing is romantic green with yellow buttons, button holes and green caps dressed with feather and flowers. In front of the cap is Latin Per Sylvas."[79]

The adverb "romantic" used here to describe green is curious. Did the Rangers' uniforms remind young Hannah of romance novels, or of colorful tales of medieval England, such as those of Arthur and Robin Hood? Or did she use the word "romance" as it relates to Nature, indicating a general impression of the green of the woods?

The jacket or short coat worn by the figure in Davies' painting is of a middle shade of green, with green cuffs of a slightly darker green, and perhaps even lapels (the figure is rather small, and the details are nebulous). There seem to be at least ten buttons on the left side of the coat. His waistcoat is green, as are his breeches and leggings. The flaps of the latter are tightly sewn, giving an irregularly-bunched effect. Garters with a touch of red tie them below the knees. A powder horn on a whitish strap—probably woven like a tumpline from hemp or the inner bark of certain trees (see footnote 22)—hangs from his left shoulder. It is not clear if he has a bullet pouch hanging in front from a waistbelt, so vague are the details. His footwear is also indistinct.

The fact that what might be a Stockbridge Indian lounges next to this green-clad figure, and that they both stand on the road near the Ranger encampment that was posted on it—viz., south of the main camp—tends to point to the figure as being a Ranger rather than a green-clad British Light Infantryman or some other unit (and there is no evidence for green uniforms on the British Light Infantry with Amherst in 1759).

Were jockey caps the rule for Rangers in 1759, as opposed to the "Scotch bonnets" MacComb mentions that they favored during the winter of 1757-58? Jockey caps were worn by Gorham's Rangers, Dunn's Rangers of New Jersey, Gage's 80th Regiment of Light Armed Infantry; and Major George Scott himself recommended them for Ranger headgear in the proposal he had sent to Lord Loudoun in February of 1758.[80]

So it is entirely possible that many of the Rangers serving under Rogers in 1759 wore jockey caps, too, as the Davies painting shows, and as Exelby wore during his escape perhaps in an attempt to disguise himself as a Ranger. No evidence has ever been found to substantiate, as some historians have claimed, that only Ranger *officers* wore jockey caps. They were worn by men of all ranks, at least in the field.[81]

Scotch bonnets were no doubt still being worn by many, and as we shall see, blue bonnets became the headgear for the Ranger companies in Nova Scotia in 1759. But in merchants' and sutlers' shops from New York to Albany and north to the British forts, not only were "Scotch bonnets" sometimes available, but also "Kilmarnock caps and bonnets" (*Weyman's New-York Gazette* March 19, 1759). The Scottish Kilmarnock bonnet was somewhat broader-topped than the "Scotch bonnet," and the "Kilmarnock cap" was almost like the later glengarry cap of nineteenth-century Highland regiments. In *Weyman's New-York Gazette* of September 6, 1784, a merchant sold "Kilmarnock caps, Crimson and green mock velvet ditto." If green Kilmarnock bonnets or caps were available for purchase by any of the companies serving under Rogers, would the Rangers have preferred *them* over blue bonnets?

The question intrigues; but taking the argument a step further, there might also have been *green* "Scotch bonnets" available for sale now and then; and the most elementary logic dictates that the green-clad Rangers would probably have preferred green headgear if it was available. I recall a battle re-enactment at Crown Point in 1980 between recreated Ranger and French forces. At the beginning of the "engagement" the Rangers came slinking down a tree-clad hill to surprise the enemy in the flank. Even though the trees were in full foliage, I could still make out the red poms and the light-to-middle blue bonnets plunging down the slope, and I then realized that the Rangers of the 1750s, in the field at least, would never have worn bonnets this particular shade of blue, and especially not with red poms on them.

Were green bonnets among the "Scotch bonnets various colors" being offered by a merchant in the *Boston Gazette* dated March 4, 1765? If green Scotch bonnets *were* among the available items being sold in New York and New England merchant shops of the 1750s-60s, would Rogers' men have preferred them over the traditional blue ones? Color choice here would have been strictly pragmatic—and sane. It is not insignificant that Adjutant John Parker of the New Hampshire Regiment lost "a Green Cap" to Montcalm's pillaging Indians after the surrender of Fort William Henry; and a number of others of the regiment lost "worsted caps," color not specified.[82] However, "green worsted caps" *were* being sold by merchants during the war, such as Albany's Rowland de Paiba, who in the *New-York Mercury* of December 27, 1756 advertised "green, scarlet, stript [striped], single and double worsted caps." Former New Hampshire soldier Samuel Blodgett, now also a merchant, offered for sale in *The Boston Post-Boy* of April 16, 1759, "mill'd and worsted Caps. . .for the campaign." It must also be remembered that commissary William Taylor sold "11 milled caps" to Rogers' company in December 1755.

Many nightcaps of the period were also made of milled and worsted wool; and when worn flat might be considered a kind of pseudo-Scotch bonnet. In 1760 Colonel John Goffe gave an order to his New Hampshire regiment that, "as it is observed a number of the men accustom themselves to wear woolen night caps in the day time, he allows them hats. They are ordered for the future not to be seen in the day time with anything besides their hats on their heads, as ye above mentioned custom of wearing night caps must be detrimental to their health."[83]

Before closing the case for green as a color choice for Ranger headgear—when it was available—we must also not forget Major James Burd's 1757 suggestion that Pennsylvania troops engaging Indians in the woods wear "a green Cloth Capp."[84] Unless the blue Scotch bonnets being worn by some of Rogers' men were of a dark blue, simple life-and-death logic dictates that they would *not* have worn bright shades of colors easily detected by enemy parties bent on ambush, scalps, torture and captives.

In the *New-York Mercury* of July 30, 1759, the following advertisement was posted that clearly illustrates out the wide range of clothing worn by Rangers serving under Rogers:

> Taken up, and now in the Goal at Goshen, in Orange County, a Negro Man named (as he says) Jacob; has a Scar from his Chin under his under Lip; has the Negro Mark with a Cut on each Cheek in his own Country;[85] has had the Small-pox, and a little pitted with it; has a Scar on his right Wrist, he says it was shot with a Ball; is five Feet seven Inches and a Half high, is about 25 or 30 Years old, has a green Jacket lined with red, Buckskin Breeches,[86] blue Indian Stockings, fine white Shirts, with Chitterlings;[87] has a Gun iron mounted, spotted Silk Handkerchief; he says he was in Rogers's Rangers three Years, and was at the Battle of Ticonderoga; that he belonged formerly to one Daniel McCoy, in New York, who lived near the Old-Sly, and that his Master had

given him free for serving three Years in the Rangers, and that Mr. Livingston's Negro Wench Rose, had his Freedom Paper; he is a spry able Fellow, he has been found in many Lies, and has been charged with Pilfering. Whosoever owns the said Negro may have him upon paying the Charges.

EBENEZER KEELER.

A search for additional information on this possible black Ranger was not successful; but clearly his garb is Ranger-like. Indian stockings of blue strouds were often worn by Rangers as well as Indians. A "green Jacket lined with red" might at first seem odd for one of Rogers' Rangers to be wearing, but one must again remember that "lined" does not necessarily mean "faced." However, there may be some significance in noting that the uniforms Robert Rogers ordered for his Loyalist King's Rangers in 1782 were green coats faced with red, and green breeches.[88] Jacob's jacket, then, might indicate some kind of precedence among the Rangers, (although some Pennsylvania Provincial companies wore green jackets with red facings). As for his race, there were more than a few black and mulatto (as well as Native American) soldiers among both the Rangers and the Provincial troops; nor did Rogers have any qualms about again recruiting men of these backgrounds when he organized his Queen's Rangers in 1776.

Meanwhile, the four companies raised in January of 1758—James Rogers', Moses Hazen's (formerly James McCurdy's), Jonathan Brewer's, and William Stark's—were, in mid-1759, en route from Nova Scotia to the St. Lawrence with General James Wolfe. They comprised four of the six Ranging companies serving in a corps commanded by Major George Scott, the other two captained by Joseph Gorham and Benoni Danks.

Before leaving Halifax in May, Captain John Knox of the 43rd Regiment of Foot made an observation that clearly indicated that the original green uniforms and surtouts of a year and a half earlier had been done away with. He wrote (speaking, it is to be assumed, of all six Ranger companies):

> The rangers have got a new uniform clothing; the ground is of black ratteen or frieze, lapelled and cuffed with blue; here follows a description of their dress; a waistcoat with sleeves; a short jacket without sleeves; only armholes and wings to the shoulders (in like manner as the Grenadiers and Drummers of the army), white metal buttons, linen or canvas drawers, with a blue skirt or petticoat of stuff, made with a waistband and one button; this is open before and does not quite extend to their knees; a pair of leggins of the same colour with their coat, which reach up to the middle of the thighs (without flaps) and from the calf of the leg downward they button like spatterdashes; with this active dress they wear blue bonnets, and I think, in great measure resemble our Highlanders."[89]

Who was responsible for this new Ranger uniform in the Nova Scotia/St. Lawrence theater? As a color for concealment, only a very dark blue would have sufficed for the bonnets, facings and the "petticoat" or kilt they wore. Some of the companies of British Rangers in Nova Scotia in the early 1750s, at one point in their existence, had been "completely cloathed in blue Broad Cloth."[90] which was generally indigo in color.[91] So blue—dark blue—had already been worn by Rangers of the region, and not just in surtout form (like clerk Lawrence Elkins of Moses Brewer's Mohegan company). The blue bonnets of 1759 were a departure for Gorham's men, at least: they had worn leather caps in previous years and would wear them in later years, too. We may never know who designed the new uniforms for the Rangers with Wolfe in 1759. They in no way resembled any of the recommendations for Ranger dress Major George Scott himself had made to Lord Loudoun in early 1758, so even though he was leader of the Rangers at Quebec, crediting him with this change may be premature.

Back at the Lake George front, General Amherst had moved his army north and captured the French forts of Carillon and St. Frederic. Rogers was sent off on September 13, 1759, from

Crown Point, on his epic St. Francis expedition. Indian stockings, tumplines, moccasins, footings (extra soles for moccasins), hatchets, leather cases and belts were among the items Rogers issued to his Rangers and the other volunteers (drawn from Provincial and Regular units) on this trek.[92] Relics found decades later along the line of the Rangers' retreat from St. Francis, stretching from the St. Francis River south to the Connecticut River, indicated a number of other items carried by the Rangers (assuming that these were relics of Rogers' expedition). Compiled from a host of sources, including nineteenth-century local histories of the towns along the route, these relics were: knapsacks, a snuff-box, pistols, musket barrels, a bayonet, a leather ribbon, a powder horn, ball pouches, sword blades, clasp-knives, a small copper kettle, a hatchet, buttons, silver knee and shoe buckles, Indian moccasins, beads, and miscellaneous loot from the Abenaki mission church at Odanak, including a pair of golden candlesticks, an incense vessel, wampum, a statue of a saint, even silver chandeliers. Not yet found is a solid silver statuette of Our Lady of Chartres, taken from the altar, supposedly weighing ten pounds.

Deserters were quite frequent among the armies in eighteenth-century America, and the ranks of the Rangers proved no exception. In late September of 1759,

> the body of a Man was found in the River near Dunstable; it is thot it had been drowned sometime; the Body was naked, excepting a Pair of Indian Stockings on his Legs, and Moggasons on his feet: by which it is thot it is probable he was one of the men lately deserted from the Rangers.[93]

The river mentioned here would have been the Merrimack, the town Dunstable, in northern Massachusetts. The *Boston News-Letter* of August 2, 1759 named a number of men reported deserting from Captain Jonathan Burbank's Ranger company at Lake George on July 13, including "Thomas Chamberlain and John Harrad, both of Dunstable," so the body might have been either that of Chamberlain or Harrad. The details of dress are perhaps more valuable for what they neglect to mention: does the fact that only moccasins and leggings are indicated mean that the Ranger might have worn an Indian-style breechclout instead of breeches?

Breechclouts worn by New England and New York frontiersmen of the French and Indian War period may seem unlikely to many, especially to those who conceive that even the wildest frontiersmen of that time and place still had enough British gentlemen's blood in them to refrain from wearing such savage garb. This conception is a mistake, judging by the evidence. The Rangers were nothing like the hunters of England and Scotland chasing stags in the greenwood and heather. The Rangers were men who engaged in a savage, unconventional brand of warfare, which included ambush, hand-to-hand combat with knife and tomahawk, scalping fallen enemies, shooting enemy wounded and enemy prisoners on occasion, sometimes setting fire to enemy dwellings in which people still remained alive (as at St. Francis). They were prone to frostbite, hypothermia, arthritis, scurvy, dysentery, and other ailments derived from engaging in wilderness campaigning, often in enemy country and without fires to warm them at night. When food ran out they resorted to eating tree bark, leaves, roasted leather, amphibians, and even the flesh of their fallen comrades.[94] They wholly adopted many Native American techniques, tools and articles of clothing, such as ways of fire-making and tracking and hunting, snowshoes, tumplines, bark huts, brush shelters, matchcoat mantles, bearskin mattresses, moccasins, shoepacks, leggings, fur caps of Indian design, breechclouts, and at times even warpaint and hair styles, because these things had been time-tested for centuries, and in the eighteenth century there were no more suitable substitutes at hand.

Hearken back to Rufus Putnam's memoir noting his having "nothing but a shirt and Indian stockings," which also suggests a breechclout, while on a South Bay scout. Then there is the case of a Ranger named Morison, who went to spy on

Ticonderoga in the early summer of 1759 with an Indian and a half-breed "in the breech-clouts of Indians."[95] An important distinction must also be drawn between Rangers and the Light Infantry units of the time, a distinction perhaps best exemplified by contemporary chronicler John Entick, in his description of the British forces at Louisbourg in 1758:

> The Rangers are a body of irregulars, who have a more cut-throat, savage appearance; which carries in it something of natural savages: the appearance of the light infantry has in it more of artificial savages.[96]

Over a year before this was written, in fact, there were reports of spies among the British in Halifax in the form of "French Indians dressed like Rangers [who] walk the streets."[97] How would French Indians have disguised themselves as "Rangers"? Adding a cap, or a jacket, to their usual garb of moccasins, leggings, breechclout and blanket? Robert Rogers himself is said to have gone through the village of St. Francis the night before he attacked it, to "reconnoiter the Town. . . and was spoken to several Times by the Indians, but was not discovered, as he was dress'd like one of them."[98] Some historians have doubted that Rogers would have ever done such a seemingly foolish thing, and so it is rarely mentioned in histories dealing with his activities. However, the oral traditions of the Odanak (St. Francis) Abenakis include at least two separate accounts of strange men walking through the village that night and telling some of the women and children to hide because there would be an attack in the morning.[99] It must be remembered that General Amherst's orders to Rogers included the command that no women or children were to be killed; and evidently Rogers attempted to ensure that this order was obeyed by disguising himself as an Indian and delivering the message personally (along with Lieutenant Turner and Ensign Avery and possibly a Stockbridge Indian), to the Abenaki noncombatants. When, in 1775, Rogers was rumored to have again disguised himself as an Indian and walked through an American army camp to spy on it, it was not thought unusual for him.[100]

Conversely, Canadian partisans sometimes did the same thing, as evinced in this account concerning the activities of Joseph Marin:

> Extract of a Letter from a Gentleman at New-York, dated September 4, 1759: "Mons. Morin. . .says that 12 Days before he was taken at Niagara, he was in Pittsburgh fort, a whole day, in Disguise, drest & painted as a friend Indian, treated well by the English, and shewn every part of the fort."[101]

There is also the case of Captain Quinton Kennedy of the 44th Regiment of Foot, who joined Gage's 80th Light Infantry Regiment in 1759. Three years earlier, it seems, he had "gone Indian," judging by one report in the *Scots Magazine* of November 1756 (p. 559):

> Lieutenant Kennedy has married an Indian squaw, whose tribe has made him a king. General Abercrombie gave him a party of highlanders joined with a party of Indians to go a-scalping, in which he had some success. He has learned the language, paints and dresses like an Indian, and it is thought will be of service by his new alliance. His wife goes with him, and carries his provisions on her back.

Kennedy, in fact, was assigned by General Amherst, at Crown Point in 1759, to deliver a message to General Wolfe at Quebec; and he went with one white man, Lieutenant Hamilton, and four Indians, all in Indian dress and paint, through the heart of Abenaki country. Their disguise was uncovered by an Abenaki hunting party, and they were seized. This enraged Amherst so much that he immediately ordered Rogers out against St. Francis. (Two years later, in the war with the Cherokees, Kennedy continued to lead both Indians and white men dressed and painted like Indians).

On the northern frontier at this time, it seems that white men dressed as Indians were not all that novel or exotic. William Johnson and his white officers often dressed like the Iroquois contingents they led into battle. For instance, one observer present the night before the 1758 Battle of Carillon noted that "I met Sir William Johnson, with about 300 Indians, and Whites disguised in Indian dresses."[102] Even the New York Dutch bush-lopers went scouting and raiding against the French with Iroquois war parties. When the French partisan leader La Corne captured a group of six in 1747, seemingly all Indians, he soon discovered that one of them was actually "a Dutchman [who] spoke Indian like themselves. . . [he was]dressed like an Indian, wearing even a scalp-lock".[103]

In 1760 the last active campaigns of the war in the north took place. On March 30, in Lebanon, Connecticut, two Rangers on a rare recruiting furlough decided to desert:

> Deserted from a Recruiting Party of Rangers, lying at Lebanon, belonging to an Independent Company commanded by Captain Joseph Wait, on the 30th Day of March last, two Soldiers belonging to the Company, viz., John Thomson. . .he had on a great Coat, callicoe Waistcoat, with a Sword.—and John Watson. . .with short yellow Hair had on a short green Waistcoat, with a Striped Silk one under it, and a pair of Orange colour'd Cloth Breeches. . .15 Dollars Reward for each. . .
>
> WILLARD STEVENS, Lieutenant."[104]

Clearly these were soldiers of the company—one of them is even wearing a sword—not new recruits. The "Striped Silk" waistcoat brings to mind the "8 striped vests" William Taylor sold to Rogers' men in 1755. Watson also wears "a short green Waistcoat" with "Orange colour'd Cloth Breeches." Whether the orange breeches were part of a dress uniform, or just a new pair worn to replace an old one of a different color, can only be surmised.[105] Still, this is further evidence indicating that all-green outfits were not necessarily mandatory for Rangers on all occasions. Two deserters from Captain Israel Putnam's Connecticut Ranger company in July 1760 wore "brown colour'd Coats," and one of them wore "a green Waistcoat."[106]

Earlier, in January of 1760, British Engineer Lieutenant John Montresor led a party from Quebec southeastward to Maine, carrying messages and exploring the country along the way. Accompanying him were ten Rangers of Captain Moses Hazen's company. Almost inevitably the party began to run out of provisions, and the winter wilderness afforded too little to sustain them, so they resorted to broiling "their Moccasins[107] and Bullet Pouches, snow-shoe Netting and Strings," and, the following day, "their Leather Breeches."[108]

From 1761 we have additional scraps of evidence that point to a continuing disparity of Ranger dress. At Crown Point on May 26 of that year, Joseph Fish "Deserted from His Majesty's Inniskilling [27th] Regiment of Foot. . .[he] went off in a blanket coat, red breeches, and green waistcoat; has served in the Rangers."[109] The red breeches would seem to be part of his Regular's garb, although when we recall the orange breeches of Ranger John Watson in 1760, and the red lining of Jacob's jacket in 1759, we are left with questions about the color red and the Rangers; and so far there has been little consistency in Ranger dress throughout the years except for the nearly ubiquitous "green waistcoat." (If red was worn at all by the Rangers, it might have been on strictly non-field occasions).[110]

Another former Ranger wearing "red breeches" who deserted in 1761 was David Hughes. In this case, too, the red breeches were probably part of the uniform of the Massachusetts regiment he was absconding from; but clearly his coat was not:

> Deserted from His Majesty's Service on the 22nd of July, David Hughes, formerly belonged to Major Rogers, a private soldier in Colonel Thwing's regiment and Captain Edward Blake's Company. . .a green Coat with green plush Lappells, Cuffs and Collar, with white metal buttons, a white waistcoat, and red breeches.[111]

At first glance the phrase "formerly belonged to Major Rogers" would seem to indicate that he had been one of Rogers' Rangers, or more specifically, one of Rogers' own company. However, what this phrase might really mean is revealed in an ad published in the *Boston Weekly News-Letter* of October 5, 1765, over four years later:

> If David Hughes, formerly belonging to Major Rogers, and Servant to him, be living, and will apply to Richard and Samuel Draper Printers in Boston, he may hear of about 60 pounds Sterling that was left him by a Relation that died in England, and of whom he can obtain it.

In the eighteenth century, servants were often identified as belonging to a particular master by their livery—in effect, a uniform. Sometimes this "uniform" would be the master's cast-off clothing; and if the master had once been, or still was, a soldier, then it might be the latter's actual regimentals.[112] Thus, David Hughes might have been wearing Rogers' own "undress" (sans lace) uniform coat of the previous year or even earlier; or perhaps Hughes was wearing his own coat if he had actually served in the Rangers. The "green plush Lappells, Cuffs and Collar" are vastly different from the green serge lining of the January 1758 uniforms. Serge was generally firmly woven, fine and smooth-textured.[113] Plush was a thick wool velvet, though even shinier than velvet; and often it was made in a "hair" form with goats' or camels' hair.[114] It was sometimes used to face saddle seats.[115] Breeches, jackets, waistcoats, winter jackets and hunting coats were made of it.[116] Thomas Gainsborough's 1755 portrait of Robert Andrews and his wife, in the collection of the National Gallery, in London, has Andrews wearing a "cloth-colored," double-breasted hunting coat, with plain cuffs that do not seem to have buttons on them, and a velvety green falling collar that might indeed be plush. Benjamin West's 1758 portrait of fifteen-year-old Thomas Mifflin shows the latter in a dark blue hunting coat and a brass-buttoned green waistcoat that, also judging by its texture, might be plush.

Intriguingly, three years after Hughes' desertion, a "Mulatto Servant Man, named Jacob Jones," ran away from one John Peirce of Concord, Chester County, Pennsylvania, a short distance west of Philadelphia. The report in *The Pennsylvania Gazette* of November 15, 1764 notes that Jones "hath been about three Years in the Army, and had two Passes, one from Major Rogers." His connection with Rogers is not spelled out, though his attire suggests a possible Ranger association:

> [He] had on a good green double breasted Coat, with a small Cape, and yellow Metal Buttons, a good black Hat Plush Jacket without Sleeves.

Could Jones have been a former Ranger, and could he have been wearing an old Ranger coat? Did his plush jacket match the plush lapels, collars and cuffs of Hughes's coat, as facings and jacket/waistcoat often did?[117] On the other hand, a number of Pennsylvania companies wore green coats with green lapels during the French and Indian War, so the argument for Jones' coat being a Ranger one rests on inconclusive ground.

Plush and Major Rogers and his Rangers again come into the picture in 1762, when Robert Rogers' brother James put the following advertisement in *The Boston Weekly Post-Boy* of November 22, 1762:

> Ran away from me the Subscriber at Londonderry, in the Province of New Hampshire, on the 18th of September, a Negro Man Servant named Prince about 40 Years of Age, about 5 feet 5 Inches high, speaks good English, had on when he went away a green Coat, blue plush Breeches, diaper Jacket, several pair of thread Stockings with him; he looks very serious and grave, and pretends to be very religious: He is the property of Major Rogers and has been several Years to the Westward, and pretends to be free.

Prince had first run away from Major Rogers

in 1760,[118] and one must wonder if the Ranging life with his active and famous master had proved too much for him.

Evidence for a uniform for the few Rangers raised by Rogers during Pontiac's War has not been found.

In *Weyman's New York Gazette* of July 22, 1765, "a parcel of Rangers Cloaths" was advertised as being ready for sale, along with, incredibly, "a parcel of cutlasses, French Cuttoes, silver tipt, Scalping Knives and Tomahawks"![119]

Not only Ranger clothing but Regular uniforms were also sold after—and sometimes during—the French and Indian War. These generally became servants' dress.[120] The following, from 1770, might be such Ranger-related attire:

> Ran-away from Samuel Gilbert of Littleton, an indentured Servant boy named Samuel Gilson. . . . He went away in Company with a short thick set Fellow, who wore a green Coat and a green Jacket double-breasted, also a pair of Indian green Stockings."[121]

In none of these quotes is "the uniform of Rogers' Rangers" mentioned. In truth, "Rogers' Rangers" was a term used to describe any number of disparate Ranger companies that fell under his command at any given time. They became his corps, not his "regiment." Green remains the most common color, but no evidence exists for all of the companies attached to him ever being unified in a consistent single pattern, or even the same fabric or shade of green. At rare times two or more companies seem to have enjoyed common uniforms, such as Hobbs' and Speakman's in 1756 and the four companies raised in early 1758; but this infrequent, piecemeal approach was evidently the only way some of the men ever achieved any uniformity of appearance. Ranger coats with linings of green serge, green plush, and even red cloth were recorded at various times, further exemplifying the lack of continuity in dress throughout the war. But theirs was not a unique case: the history of other Ranging and light infantry units as well as many Provincial regiments also reflect such almost annual variations in attire.

Considering the exigencies of time, money, and the availability of proper fabrics during the frontier campaigns in North America, it should not be surprising that maintaining precise consistency in color shade and tailoring, year after year, proved to be, for Rogers' Rangers and many others, a practical impossibility.

There are no verifiably authentic likenesses of Robert Rogers. In the Appendix to his *Robert Rogers of the Rangers*, "Portraits of Robert Rogers," John R. Cuneo clearly pointed out the facial similarities of the series of "rebel officers," in mezzotint form, published in London in 1776 by Thomas Hart.[122] One of them is supposed to be Rogers (before it became known that he had joined the British and not the American side in the Revolution). However, not only do most of the faces in the series resemble one another, but all the uniforms look alike, too. The result is that "Robert Rogers" wears virtually the same coat, with the same buttoning, sleeves and lace, as General David Wooster and General Charles Lee. The only items that might be considered Ranger-related in the print are the beaded jockey cap, powder horn and its strap, beaded hunting bag and bandolier, and leggings. However, all of these items, as well as the details seen in the two background Indians, are obviously copied from Benjamin West's epic painting of 1770, *The Death of General Wolfe.*

Some historians have considered the green-clad figure in West's canvas to represent one of Rogers' Rangers of 1759. Others have suggested it could be Rogers himself.[123] Elsewhere there is some reason to believe that West might have intended the figure to portray Colonel William Howe, commander of the Light Infantry at Quebec, although no documentation exists to confirm green as the color of any of the light infantry companies at Quebec, as some of them had been attired in 1758 at Louisbourg.[124] There is a fourth possibility, also: that he could be one of the officers of William Johnson's "Indian Department," who were known, at least in later years, to be clothed in green.[125] On the figure's powderhorn, "Sr. William Johnson's" is indicated next to an engraving of the "MOHAWK RIVER." (The figure is too young and slender to represent Johnson himself).[126]

A final possibility exists, too: that West indeed intended to represent an American Ranger, but only generically. Associating him, in terms of proximity, with the foreground Indian (who also seems more symbolic than tribally identifiable), West might have been attempting an allegorical statement about the American Colonies' role in the war, since all the other figures depict British officers, aides, soldiers and sailors. Like so much else about "Rogers' Rangers," and the variety of clothing and uniforms they wore, we are left with much to conjecture about, and with just a few particles of truth sifted laboriously from the deep trenches of history.

1 Francis Parkman, *Montcalm and Wolfe,* Vol. I, Little, Brown, and Company, Boston, edition of 1901, p. 448.

2 Joseph B. Walker, *Life and Exploits of Robert Rogers, The Ranger,* A Paper Read Before the Members of the New England Historic-Genealogical Society, November 5, 1884, John N. NcClintock and Company, Boston, 1885, Boston, p. 4.

3 G. A. Henty, *With Wolfe In Canada,* Walker and Company, New York, reprint of 1961, p. 105, 145.

4 Frederic Remington, *A Rogers' Ranger In the French and Indian War, 1757-1759,* Harper & Brothers, New York, 1897, p. 2, 9.

5 G. Waldo Browne, *With Rogers' Rangers,* A. Wessels Company, New York, 1907, p. 15.

6 Ibid., pp. 23-24.

7 Idem, p. 221

8 Kenneth Roberts, *Northwest Passage,* Doubleday & Company, Inc., Garden City, New York, 1937, p. 77.

9 Kenneth Roberts, *I Wanted To Write,* Doubleday & Company, Inc., Garden City, New York, 1949, p. 322.

10 The glengarry cap actually does not predate the Napoleonic period, although the Kilmarnock cap, which *was* worn in the eighteenth century, resembles it in many ways. The latter was also available in many colors, including green, in some of Albany's merchant shops during the French and Indian War.

11 John Jennings, *Next To Valour,* The MacMillan Company, New York, 1939, p. 414.

12 Ibid., pp. 448-449.

13 James Fenimore Cooper, *The Last of the Mohicans, A Narrative of 1757,* Charles Scribner's Sons, New York, 1919, p. 21.

14 James Fenimore Cooper, *Satanstoe, or The Littlepage Manuscripts, A Tale of the Colony,* D. Appleton and Company, New York, 1888, p. 324.

15 Ibid., p. 373.

16 See illustration and caption for *The Renovated 55th.*

17 H. Charles McBarron and Frederick P. Todd, *New York Rifle Corps, 1809-1815,* Plate no. 81 in the Military Uniforms in America series, The Company of Military Historians. In Chapter 13 of *The Pioneers,* old Natty Bumppo recalls that "When I went with Sir William [Johnson] agin the French, at Fort Niagara, all the rangers used the rifle." Once again, Cooper seems to be relying on wishful romantic thinking than actual documentation.

18 *Provincial Papers of New Hampshire, From 1749 to 1763,* Manchester, New Hampshire, Volume VI, p. 362, 431.

19 Ibid., p. 431.

20 Peter Wraxhall to Henry Fox, September 27, 1755, *Military Affairs In North America, 1748-1765,* edited by Stanley Pargellis, Hamden, Connecticut, 1969, p. 141, 143.

21 Theordore Atkinson to John Tomlinson, 9 December 1755, *Provincial Papers of New Hampshire,* Vol. VI, p. 440. Robert Rogers was scouting along the Hudson River at the time of the battle.

22 For a more detailed look at tumplines, see Gary S. Zaboly, "The Use of Tumplines in the French and Indian War," *Military Collector & Historian,* Vol. XLVI, No. 3, Fall 1994, p.109.

23 William Johnson to Governor Sir Charles Hardy of New York, October 13, 1755, *The Papers of Sir William Johnson,* Edited by James Sullivan, Vol. II, p. 190.

24 Officers' report to a council of war, October 11, 1755, *Johnson Papers,* Vol. II, pp. 178-179.

25 Burt Garfield Loescher, *The History of Rogers' Rangers, Vol. I: The Beginnings, Jan. 1755-April 6, 1758,* San Francisco, 1946, p. 271.

26 "Letter from Governore Shirley to a Gentleman" of Philadelphia, Boston, February 4, 1756, *The Boston Evening-Post,* March 15, 1756.

[27] List of clothing supplied to Rogers' company, December 1755, New Hampshire State Archives, William Taylor's deposition of June 2, 1762, Court Case 03847, New Hampshire State Archives.

[28] "Memorandum from Major Rutherford, 1756, LO 770, the Loudoun Papers, The Huntington Library, San Marino, California.

[29] "We gave the King and Great Men some Clothes, and Paint Shirts," Journal of Christopher Gist, entry of February 19, 1751, at the "Twigtwee [Miami] Town," in Louis Preston Summer, *Annals of Southwest Virginia, 1769-1800.*

[30] Peter Williamson, quoted in Cumming, Hiller, Quinn and Williams, *The Exploration of North America, 1630-1776,* G.P. Putnam's Sons, New York, 1974, p. 67.

[31] See 1775 description on the tanning of hunting shirts by Silas Deane, in H. Charles McBarron Jr. & Frederick P. Todd, uniform plate, "Associators of the City and Liberties of Philadelphia," *Military Uniforms In America: The Era of the American Revolution, 1755-1799,* Presidio Press, San Rafael, California, 1974, p. 104.

[32] *The New Hampshire Gazette,* June 25, 1762.

[33] *The Boston Evening-Post,* October 14, 1772.

[34] *The Boston Gazette,* June 17, 1771. The "wallets" were probably leather or canvas bags.

[35] Pennsylvania State Archives, *Papers of the Provincial Council, Executive Correspondence,* microfilm roll B-7, frame 839, quoted in Albert W. Haarmann, "American Uniforms During the French and Indian War," *Military Collector and Historian,* Vol. XXXII, No. 2, Summer 1980, p. 62. Adopting green for forest concealment was hardly rocket science. White men had long since learned this from the Indians. For instance, in 1704, on the Connecticut River, an Englishman and five Mohegan Indian allies scouted out the location of an enemy Indian stockade. After nine days of travel, they discovered fresh tracks. "Here we made a halt," reads the account by Caleb Lyman, "to consult what methods to take; and soon concluded to send out a spy, with green leaves for a cap and vest, to prevent his own discovery, and to find out the enemy." Samuel Penhallow, *The History of the Wars of New-England with the Eastern Indians,* J. Harpel, Cincinnati, 1859, p. 31.

[36] LO 1090, Huntington Library.

[37] E.g., Loescher in Vol. I, p. 278. In fact, it is a misconception that is hard to die: see Gerry Embleton's interpretation of a man of Hobbs' or Speakman's in a " 'hunting coat' of Osnaburg," p. 41, *Military Illustrated, Past and Present,* No. 39, August 1991.

[38] John MacComb, Albany agent for merchants Gregg and Cunningham, wrote to them on September 25, 1757 that he had "to make 1500 Bags for W. Coventry. You'll therefore please send me 20 ps. [pieces—i.e., bolts] Ozenbrigs." John MacComb's Letter-Copy book.

[39] See Audley's advertisements in *The New York Mercury* of December 31, 1753 and *Weyman's New York Gazette* of July 6, 1761.

[40] "A Narrative of Thomas Brown," in Russell P. Bellico, *Chronicles of Lake George: Journeys In War and Peace,* Purple Mountain Press, Fleischmanns, New York, 1995, pp. 49-50.

[41] Captain John Knox, *An Historical Journal of the Campaigns in North America for the Years 1757, 1758, 1759, and 1760,* Toronto, 1914, Vol. I, p. 34.

[42] An ozenbrig (or osnaburg) frock and a pair of ozenbrig trousers was a typical combination worn by soldiers of the 1750s on work detail or other "fatigue" assignments, not by woodsmen hunting French and Indians. Even in Nova Scotia, the Rangers would have had ditches and latrines to dig, huts to build, wood to gather, etc. By way of example, in Halifax in 1751 a new British brig was launched, and *The New York Evening Post* of July 8, 1751 reported that "the Carpenters that built her were dressed in clean white Frocks and Trowsers, clean white Shirts, Gold laced Hats".

[43] "The Journal of Moses Kelsey," *The Granite State Magazine,* II.

[44] Knox, *An Historical Journal,* p. 79.

[45] Ibid., p. 170.

[46] *Journal of General Rufus Putnam, 1757-1760,* E.C. Dawes. Ed., Joel Munsell's Sons, New York 1886. Oddly, *A Dictionary of American English* (University of Chicago, 1938) quotes Putnam as writing that he had "nothing but a Shirt and *Breech-Clout*".

[47] For example, this newspaper report: "London, May 3, Lieutenant-Colonel Thomas Gage is appointed colonel of a regiment of rangers in America." *Boston Post-Boy,* July 24, 1758.

[48] *The Maryland Gazette,* February 8, 1770.

[49] John Josselyn, *An Account of Two Voyages To New-England,* London 1674, reprint Boston, Massachusetts, 1865, p. 92.

[50] Florence M. Montgomery, *Textiles In America, 1659-1870,* W.W. Norton & Co., New York, 1984, p. 228.

[51] Patrick M'Robert, *A Tour Through Part of the North Provinces of America,* Edinburgh, 1776 (Arno, 1968).

[52] *The Writings of George Washington From the Original Manuscript Sources, 1745-1799,* John C. Fitzpatrick, ed., Vol 1.

[53] Eric I. Manders, Brian Leigh Dunnigan, John R. Elting,

The Company of Military Historians, *Military Uniforms In America* plate no. 613, "80th Regiment of Foot, 1757-1764".

54 John MacComb's Letter Copy Book, Ms. # 10106, New York State Library.

55 Ibid.

56 See, for example, Burt G. Loescher, *The History of Rogers' Rangers*, Vol. I, p. 280; John R. Cuneo, *Robert Rogers of the Rangers*, pp. 74-75; Gerry Embleton and Philip Haythornthwaite, *Military Illustrated, Past and Present*, No. 39, August 1991, p. 45.

57 See various definitions of "Rug" in *A New Oxford Dictionary*, Oxford, 1888; Samuel Johnson's *Dictionary*; Florence M. Montgomery, *Textiles In America, 1650-1870*, pp. 335-336.

58 *The New Hampshire Gazette*, September 25, 1767.

59 See for example ads by Thomas and Benjamin Forsey in *The New-York Mercury* of October 24, 1757, and Shipby and Henry, in the same paper's issue of November 7, 1757. Even Gregg and Cunningham sold "Ruggs & Coatings" in New York City: see their ad in *Weyman's New-York Gazette*, December 5, 1757.

60 Aileen Ribeiro, *Dress in Eighteenth Century Europe*, p. 81. See also references in the *Oxford English Dictionary.*

61 In *The American Weekly Mercury* of March 20, 1733, a highwayman was reported wearing "a dark Rug Coat, close button'd, with the Cape about the Face."

62 *The Boston Evening-Post*, July 30, 1739.

63 Definitions under "Rug-Gown," *A New Oxford Dictionary.*

64 In *The New-York Gazette and Weekly Mercury* of October 6, 1777, a merchant announced for sale, "For LADIES and GENTLEMEN'S wear...rugs for long cloaks".

65 "A blue Surtout Coat, with Brass Buttons," was worn by Lawrence Elkins, a company clerk deserting from Moses Brewer's company on July 2, 1759 (*Boston Post-Boy*). A Ranger of Joseph Waite's company wore "a great Coat" when he deserted in 1760 (*New London Summary*, May 9, 1760).

66 *The Connecticut Courant*, April 29, 1776.

67 Aileen Ribeiro, *Dress In Eighteenth Century Europe*, p. 26.

68 *The New-York Evening Post*, March 10, 1746.

69 *Documents Relative to the Colonial History of the State of New York*, E.B. O'Callaghan, ed., Albany, 1858, Vol. 10, p. 838.

70 Ibid., p. 839.

71 *The Diary of Jabez Fitch in the French and Indian War*, Rogers Island Historical Association, Glens Falls, New York, 1968, p. 44, 50.

72 Dr. Rush's instructions to officers "for Preserving the Health of Soldiers," *The Spirit of 'Seventy-Six: The Story of the American Revolution As Told by Participants*, edited by Henry Steele Commager and Richard B. Morris, Bonanza Books, New York, 1983, p. 837.

73 Huntington Library, California, Loudoun Papers, LO6927, Scott to Loudoun, 13th Feb. 1758. Scott's proposals for Rangers' dress actually were written nine months after Colonel James Prevost had written a very similar proposal, covering the same essential items of wear—cap, coat, cloak, and so on—in a letter to Lord Loudoun dated May 12, 1757. One wonders who was the *first* to come up with these ideas! *Military Affairs In North America, 1748-1765: Selected Documents From the Cumberland Papers In Windsor Castle*, Stanley Pargellis, ed., Archon Books, New York, 1969, pp. 337-340.

74 Ten years earlier, an English expedition to Hudson Bay required that each man wear "a large Beaver Cap, double, to come over the Face and Shoulders." *The Boston Evening-Post*, December 28, 1747. Such caps can be seen on winter hunters in eighteenth century European art (e.g., "The Bear Hunt" by Carlo Van Loo), and even on LaPotherie's sketch of a Canadian hunter in 1722, though the flaps are rolled or folded up. In November of 1756, information was received at Fort Johnson that French-allied Indians were "employed in making beaver Caps with Capes for the officers, two caps for a French blanket." E.B. O'Callaghan, *Documents Relative to the Colonial History of the State of New York*, Vol. 7, p. 240.

75 On September 8, 1758, John MacComb wrote to Philip DeVismie, New York merchant, "Have you any low priced green Rateens fit for making Leggins of, this you'll please advise me immediately by post." In 1759, the Royal Americans in Albany wore green leggings with red garters; and the garters on the "Ranger" in Thomas Davies' 1759 view of Lake George seem to be red.

76 Reuben Allin, Leaf from "A Commissary's account" book, 1759, BR Box 257 (13).

77 Burt G. Loescher, *Genesis: Rogers Rangers, The First Green Berets*, San Mateo, California, 1969, p. 262, ftn. 88.

78 Their name as recorded in *Weyman's New-York Gazette*, May 31, 1762.

79 "Extracts from the Diary of Hannah Callender," *The Pennsylvania Magazine of History and Biography*, Vol. XII, 1888, pp. 455-456.

80 Huntington Library, Loudoun Papers, LO6927. Scott to Loudoun, 13th Feb. 1758.

81 A Boston merchant had the following advertisement

printed in the March 14, 1757 issue of *The Boston Gazette:* "To be Sold by William Winter...a Parcel of Leather Caps, very convenient for Soldiers."

Even after the war, jockey caps were often worn by men doing outdoor work. Captain Samuel Holland, Surveyor General of the Province of Quebec beginning in 1764 and of the Northern District of America, wrote from Louisbourg to the Board of Trade, in London, on November 10, 1766, while describing his survey of Cape Breton: As a Mark of Distinction and Attachment to the Right Honourable Board, I have agreed with the Gentlemen and Privates of my Party to wear a green Uniform, with Leather Caps, which last are much more convenient, and less troublesome than Hats, in our Excursions thro' Woods, and by Water, and In Front of the Caps we beg Leave of their Lordships, to have embossed the Emblem and Motto of Trade and Plantations. Perhaps not without significance is the fact that Holland had served with Amherst at Louisbourg in 1758, where he saw the British Light Infantry companies dressed in green and blue jackets. *Public Archives of Nova Scotia,* Publication No. 2, Halifax, 1935, p. 46.

82 *State of New Hampshire, Miscellaneous Provincial and State Papers, 1725-1880,* Vol. XVIII, compiled and edited by Isaac W. Hammond, Manchester, New Hampshire, 1890, p. 481. Not insignificantly, some of the New Hampshire troops are recorded as having also lost green jackets, which, along with the green caps, suggests that in 1757 this regiment was probably largely uniformed in that color.

83 *Manchester Historic Association Collections,* Vol. I, part III, 1900, p. 268.

84 Albert W. Haarmann, "American Uniforms During the French and Indian War," *Military Collector and Historian,* Vol. XXXII No. 2, Summer 1980, p. 62.

85 These marks, according to *The Dictionary of American English,* indicate "a mark or scar identifying a slave as being from a particular part of Africa." *The Georgia Gazette* of July 5, 1769 more specifically noted that one runaway slave "has his country marks thus III on each cheek." Another runaway had "three long Cuts from his Temple downwards on each side his Face" (*New England Weekly-Journal,* August 2, 1731). In *The Newport Mercury* of February 22, 1768, the country of origin is indicated, the runaway having "a large Guinea Mark on each cheek".

86 Durable buckskin breeches were common among troops—Ranger, Provincial and Regular—in the field during the war, substituting, when they were available, for the usual colored cloth breeches of the company or regiment.

87 Frills or pleating on the front of a shirt.

88 Burt G. Loescher, *Genesis: Rogers' Rangers,* p. 185.

89 Captain John Knox, *An Historical Journal,* Vol. I, p. 307. None of Rogers' companies at lakes George and Champlain were ever recorded as wearing this peculiar getup. In warm weather they were often ordered to march "in their waistcoats," but no documentation has been found to indicate that they were *sleeved* waistcoats.

90 From a recruiting ad in *The Boston Weekly News-Letter,* October 4, 1750. These companies were captained, variously, by John Gorham, William Clapham, and Francis Bartelo.

91 See eighteenth century samples of blue broadcloth, in color, in Plates D-100A and D-102B in Florence M. Montgomery, *Textiles In America, 1650-1870.*

92 Burt G. Loescher, *Genesis, Rogers' Rangers,* p. 56.

93 *The Boston News-Letter,* October 4, 1759.

94 See Gary S. Zaboly, "Trail Food In Eighteenth Century America," 3-part series focusing mainly on Ranger provisions and their hunting and foraging methods, in *Muzzleloader,* Nov./Dec. 1993 and Jan./Feb. and Mar./April 1994.

95 *The Journals of Francis Parkman,* edited by Mason Wade, Harper & Brothers, 1947, Vol. I, p. 262.

96 John Entick, *The General History of the Late War,* London, 1764, Vol. 3, p. 227.

97 Loudoun's diary, January 7, 1757.

98 *The Boston Gazette,* November 26, 1759.

99 Gordon Day, "Rogers' Raid In Indian Tradition," *Historical New Hampshire, Vol. XVII, June 1962, pp. 11-14.*

100 Letter of George Washington to Major General Philip Schuyler, 18 December 1775, in William Cutter, *The Life of Israel Putnam,* Kennikat Press, New York, p. 369.

101 *North Carolina Gazette,* October 18, 1759.

102 *Lloyd's Evening-Post,* September 22, 1758.

103 *Documents Relative To the Colonial History of the State of New York,* E. B. O'Callaghan, ed., Vol. X, p. 81, 108.

104 *The New-London Summary,* May 9, 1760.

105 Eighteenth century dyes were far from being colorfast. Long exposure to rain and shine, for instance, might eventually turn the "lobster"-colored uniform of the Regulars almost orange—perhaps even as orange as Ranger Watson's breeches.

106 *The New-London Summary,* July 11, 1760.

107 According to a report in *The Pennsylvania Gazette* of March 6, 1760, they ate "the Tops of their Shoes," which probably referred to the high flaps of shoepacks.

108 "Lt. John Montresor's Journal of an Expedition in 1760

Across Maine from Quebec," *New England Historical and Genealogical Register,* January 1882, p. 30.

109 *The Boston News-Letter,* June 8, 1761.

110 Curiously, Ranger commissary William Taylor ordered for himself "2 pairs of red breeches" in December 1755 while he provided Rogers' men with other clothing. NH State Archives, Court Case 03847.

111 *The Boston Post-Boy and Advertiser,* July 27, 1761.

112 Anne Buck, *Dress In Eighteenth Century England,* Holmes & Meier Publishers Inc., New York, 1979, p. 105, 108.

113 Florence M. Montgomery, *Textiles In America, 1650-1870,* pp. 344-45.

114 *Encyclopaedia Britannica,* Edinburgh, 1771, p. 484.

115 *The American Weekly Mercury,* June 16, 1743.

116 Florence M. Montgomery, *Textiles In America, 1650-1870,* pp. 325-326. Anne Buck's *Dress in Eighteenth Century England,* p. 136, shows a red hair-plush waistcoat ca. 1780-1800, double-breasted with metal buttons. A blue plush hunting frock ca. 1762 is shown in Joseph Wright's painting of Francis Burdett, p. 80, Aileen Ribeiro, *A Visual History of Costume: The Eighteenth Century,* B. T. Batsford Ltd., London and Drama Book Publishers, New York, 1986.

117 Could this jacket have been like the "green Plush Jacket, the Button Holes workt or turn'd forward with the same stuff," worn by a runaway servant reported in *Weyman's New York Gazette* of November 23, 1761?

118 As reported in *The Boston Weekly Post-Boy* of April 28, 1760, which noted only that he was "meanly dressed."

119 A "Negro" runaway from Newark, New Jersey, was dressed in "a short Rangers Coat, gray or blue, and a red Watch-coat." *The New-York Gazette and Weekly Mercury,* May 22, 1769.

120 Gary S. Zaboly, "Civilian Servants in Military Uniforms, French & Indian War Period," *Military Collector and Historian,* Vol. XLI, No. 2, Summer 1989, pp. 79-80.

121 *The Boston Gazette,* January 8, 1770.

122 John R. Cuneo, *Robert Rogers of the Rangers,* Oxford University Press, 1959, pp. 282-283.

123 Although West completed the first of several oil versions of *The Death of General Wolfe* in 1770, his earliest known preliminary sketch was made in 1765. Robert Rogers first visited London that year; but no evidence exists to support the seemingly credible surmise that Rogers might have posed for this figure in his old Ranger garb.

124 The Marquess of Sligo, "Key To Figures in 'The Death of Wolfe'," *The Canadian Historical Review,* Vol. III, September 1922, pp. 272-278.

125 Some of them might have worn green much earlier. On June 9, 1755, William Johnson ordered from Albany merchants Colden and Kelly "green thin Velvit" and "green Allapaca or other green light Stuff" to both face and line a "lapelled Coat," although the color of the coat itself is not specified. *The Papers of Sir William Johnson,* edited by James Sullivan et al., 1921-57, Vol. I, p. 571. In November 1756, "100 Cheap Green Waste Coats with white Mettle Buttons" were on a list of goods Johnson ordered from London. Ibid., p. 898. When the Mohawk chief Joseph Brant visited London in 1776, he was described by a Captain Snyder as wearing "a short green coat, with two silver epaulets, and a small laced round hat," in addition to blue leggings and breechclout and beaded moccasins. Carolyn Thomas Foreman, *Indians Abroad, 1493-1938,* University of Oklahoma Press, Norman, Oklahoma, 1943, p. 95.

126 Some Benjamin West scholars contend that the figure resembles West's later full-length portrait of a red-coated man with beaded Indian leggings, sitting next to a standing Indian, and generally thought to represent Guy Johnson, Sir William Johnson's nephew. However, although Guy Johnson actually did not visit London until the winter of 1775-76, William Johnson's son, John Johnson, *was* in London between 1765 and 1767, and some theorize that it was he who commissioned it. The red coat is definitely of pre-Revolutionary tailoring, and thus more likely to be John Johnson. Since the sitter has not been conclusively identified, possibilities continue to be discussed, including the fairly unlikely one that he might be Robert Rogers himself. See Helmut von Erffa and Allen Staley, *The Paintings of Benjamin West,* A Barra Foundation Book, Yale University Press, New Haven & London 1986, pp.523-525.

Appendix: Portraits of Major Robert Rogers

Robert Rogers was one of the most widely known men of his age, but there still remains a great deal of mystery about him. Charles Townshend was an English politician whose brother Colonel Roger Townshend was killed at Ticonderoga in 1759. Charles befriended Rogers while he was in England, and in 1765 he remarked, "Major Rogers marches thro' the prints in a thousand various Shapes,"* yet surprisingly, no accurate likenesses of Rogers are known to exist. Two imaginary ones dating from 1776 are reproduced here.

Major Robert Rogers, Commander in Chief of the Indians in the Back Settlements of America, published by Thomas Hart, London, October 1, 1776. Courtesy of the William L. Clements Library, the University of Michigan, Ann Arbor.

The Hart mezzotint is the most commonly reproduced image of Rogers. It is a part of a series of prints of military leaders published at the outset of the Revolutionary War. All of the images in the series bear significant similarities to one another in both facial features and uniform details, but have little resemblance to the people that they are supposed to represent. For a look at the similarities in these portraits, see the National Portrait Gallery's *The Dye Is Now Cast: The Road to American Independence 1774-1776*. At least three other portraits of Rogers, based heavily on Hart's mezzotint, were published about this same time. None of these can be seriously considered authentic.

Major General Rogers. Courtesy of the William L. Clements Library, the University of Michigan, Ann Arbor.

This portrait is also unreliable. It appeared in the *Hibernian Magazine* for September, 1776, and is described simply as "An elegant Likeness of that Officer, engraved from an original Drawing." At the time of publication, the accompanying article lamented how Rogers had been forced to side with the rebels because of the way he had been treated by the British government. (See p. 20). T.T.

*Cuneo, Rogers, p. 178. For Cuneo's discussion of the portraits of Robert Rogers, see his Appendix, pp. 281-283. By "prints," Townshend was most likely referring to newspapers, as they were commonly referred to at that time.

Bibliography

NOTE: In addition to citing the sources used in the preparation of this book, this bibliography is intended to assist other researchers in identifying and locating important books and documents. In some cases, more than one edition of an entry is cited, in order to document its publishing history. At times additional comments are added to explain the uniqueness of a work.

The abbreviation *B.F.T.M.* is used throughout for the *Bulletin of the Fort Ticonderoga Museum.* *D.H.S.N.Y.* refers to the *Documentary History of the State of New York,* and *D.R.C.H.S.N.Y.* is *Documents Relating to the Colonial History of the State of New York.*

Amherst, Jeffery. *The Amherst Expedition Against Ticonderoga, 1759: Extracts from the General Orders of the Army.* In *B.F.T.M.*, Volume VI, Number 3, January 1942, pp. 88-105.

Amherst, Jeffery. *The Journal of Jeffery Amherst, Recording the Military Career of General Amherst in America from 1758 to 1763.* Edited and with an introduction and notes by J. Clarence Webster, M.D. The Ryerson Press, Toronto, and the University of Chicago Press, Chicago, 1931.

Anderson, Fred. *Crucible of War: The Seven Years' War and the Fate of Empire in British North America 1754-1766.* Alfred A. Knopf, New York, 2000.

Anonymous. *Attack and Repulse at Ticonderoga, July 1758.* An anonymous letter, believed written from the camp at Lake George during the retreat from Ticonderoga, published in the *B.F.T.M.*, Volume VII, Number 1, January 1945, pp. 15-18.

Anonymous, and T. D. Seymour Bassett, editor. *A Ballad of Rogers Retreat, 1759.* Believed written about 1760. Republished in *Vermont History,* Volume 46, 1978, pp. 21-23.

Armour, Dr. David A. *Colonial Michilimackinac.* Mackinac State Historic Parks, Mackinac Island, Michigan, 2000.

__________________, editor. *Treason? At Michilimackinac: The Proceedings of a General Court Martial held at Montreal in October 1768 for the Trial of Major Robert Rogers.* The Mackinac Island State Park Commission, (now Mackinac State Historic Parks), Mackinac Island, Michigan, 1967; revised 1972.

Arnot, Hugh. *A Journal or Proceedings of the Army Under the Command of Majr. Genl. Abercromby from June ye 17th Untill July ye 9th Campaign 1758.* Reprinted in *"Like Roaring Lions Breaking from Their Chains": The Highland Regiment at Ticonderoga,* Nicholas Westbrook, editor. In the *B.F.T.M.*, Volume XVI, Number 1, 1998, pp 16-91.

Baldwin, Jeduthan. *Extracts from the Diary of a Revolutionary Patriot: The Journal of Captain Jeduthan Baldwin.* December 1, 1755 to May 4, 1756. Reprinted in the *Journal of the Military Service Institute,* Vol. XXXIX, July-August 1906, pp. 123-130. This issue covers Baldwin's French and Indian War exploits; his Revolutionary War journal was reprinted in the next issue.

Beattie, Daniel J. and Maarten Ultee, editor. *The Adaptation of the British Army to Wilderness Warfare, 1755-1763.* In *Adapting to Conditions: War and Society in the Eighteenth Century.* The University of Alabama Press, 1986, pp. 56-83.

Bellico, Russell P. *Chronicles of Lake Champlain: Journeys in War and Peace.* Purple Mountain Press, Fleischmanns, New York, 1999.

__________________. *Chronicles of Lake George: Journeys in War and Peace.* Purple Mountain Press, Fleischmanns, New York, 1995.

__________________. *Sails and Steam in the Mountains: A Maritime and Military History of Lake George and Lake Champlain.* Purple Mountain Press, Fleischmanns, New York, 1992, revised 2001.

Bird, Harrison K. Jr. *The Uniforms of Robert Rogers' Rangers.* In *B.F.T.M.,* Volume VIII, Number 2, July 1948, pp. 65-71.

B.F.T.M. See the *Bulletin of the Fort Ticonderoga Museum.*

Black, Robert W. *Rangers in Korea.* Ivy Books, New York, 1989.

Bosse, David. *The Maps of Robert Rogers and Jonathan Carver.* Published in The *American Magazine and Historical Chronicle,* by the William L. Clements Library, University of Michigan, Ann Arbor, Michigan, Vol. 2, No. 1, Spring-Summer 1986, pp. 45-61.

Boston News-Letter, No. 2058, February 7, 1760. Original in the William L. Clements Library, University of Michigan, Ann Arbor, Michigan.

Bougainville, Louis-Antoine de, and Edward P. Hamilton, ed. *Adventures in the Wilderness: The American Journals of Louis Antoine de Bougainville, 1756-1760.* University of Oklahoma Press, Norman, 1964.

Bouquet, Henry. *The Papers of Henry Bouquet, December 11, 1755–July 1765.* Edited by Donald H. Kent, Louis M. Waddell, and Autumn L. Leonard. The Pennsylvania Historical and Museum Commission, Harrisburg. Published in six volumes: 1951, 1972, 1976, 1978, 1984, 1994.

Bray, George A. III. *The Delicate Art of Scalping.* In *Muzzleloader Magazine,* May/June 1986, pp. 54-56.

Brehm, Diedrick, et al. *A New Description of Fort Ticonderoga.* Reprinted in the *B.F.T.M.,* Volume XI, Number 1, December 1962, pp. 35-48.

Brown, Charlotte. *The Journal of Charlotte Brown, Matron of the General Hospital with the English Forces in America, 1754-1756.* Reprinted in *Colonial Captivities, Marches, and Journeys.* Edited under the auspices of the National Society of the Colonial Dames of America, by Isabel M. Calder. The MacMillan Company, New York, 1935.

Brown, Thomas. *The Narrative of Thomas Brown.* Boston, 1760. Reprinted several times, including as part of *Scalps and Tomahawks: Narratives of Indian Captivity,* edited by Frederick Drimmer, Coward-McCann Inc., New York, 1961, which was reprinted as *Captured by the Indians: 15 Firsthand Accounts, 1750-1870,* Dover Publications Inc., New York, 1985. There is also a very nice recent but undated facsimile reprint by Ye Galleon Press, Fairfield, Washington.

Bulletin of the Fort Ticonderoga Museum. Long standing publication of Fort Ticonderoga. Articles referenced are listed under their individual authors, with the specific *Bulletin* issue also cited.

Cadieux, Pierre B., and Real Fortin. *Les Constructions Militaires Du Haut-Richelieu,* Editions Mille Roches, 1977. Pages 18-19 translated from the French by Albert Smith of Saint Jean, Quebec; personal letter to the author, June 1988.

Carver, Jonathan. *Travels Through the Interior Parts of North America in the Years 1766, 1767, and 1768.* London, 1781. Facsimile reprint by Ross & Haines, Inc. Minneapolis, Minnesota, 1956.

Champion, Henry. *The Journal of Colonel Henry Champion from Colchester to Ticonderoga.* Reprinted in *The Champion Genealogy: History of the Descendants of Henry Champion of Saybrook and Lyme, Connecticut,* by Francis Bacon Trowbridge. Printed for the author, New Haven, 1891. (Note: apparently Champion was only a captain at the time he kept this journal).

Charlevoix, Pierre de. *Journal of a Voyage to North America.* Originally published in 1744; republished by Readex Microprint Corporation, New Canaan, Connecticut, 1966, two volumes.

Cleaveland, Rev. John. *Journal of Rev. John Cleaveland: June 14, 1758-October 25, 1758.* Original in the collections of Fort Ticonderoga. Published in the *B.F.T.M.,* Volume X, Number 3, 1959, pp. 192-233.

Cobb, Samuel. *The Journal of Captain Samuel Cobb, May 28, 1758-October 29, 1758.* In the *B.F.T.M.,* Volume XIV, Number 1, 1981, pp. 12-31.

Cognets, Louis des, Jr. *Amherst and Canada.* Privately published by the author, Princeton, New Jersey, 1962.

Connecticut Gazette, New Haven, April 3, 1756. Original in the collections of George A. Bray III. Copy in the author's collection.

Crown Point Foundation. *18th Century Crown Point Maps.* Crown Point Foundation and the New York State Council on the Arts, New York, New York, 1971.

Cuneo, John R. *Rangers Life on Rogers Island.* In *Exploring Rogers Island, Fort Edward, N.Y.* Publication Number Two, Rogers Island Historical Association, Fort Edward, New York, 1969.

____________. *Robert Rogers of the Rangers.* (Cited in footnotes as *Cuneo).*

-Oxford University Press, New York, 1959, hardcover

-Richardson & Steirman, New York, 1987, hardcover

-Fort Ticonderoga Museum, Ticonderoga, NY, 1988, trade paperback. The cover of this edition is a beautiful reproduction of the *View of the Lines at Lake George, 1759,* by Captain Thomas Davies, Royal Artillery. This painting, from the Fort Ticonderoga Museum Collection, contains what may be the only contemporary sketch of a Rogers' Ranger.

____________. Unpublished personal research notes for *Robert Rogers of the Rangers.* Original in the collections of the William L. Clements Library, the University of Michigan, Ann Arbor, Michigan. (Cited in footnotes as "Cuneo: *Notes*"). Copy in the author's collection. There are no page numbers in the original manuscript. Therefore, for the purposes of my citations, I have added my own numbers. The page titled "Abbreviations in Notes and Bibliography" is page number one, and each page is numbered sequentially thereafter.

Dann, John C., editor. *North West Passage Revisited.* Published in The *American Magazine and Historical Chronicle,* by the William L. Clements Library, University of Michigan, Ann Arbor, Michigan, Vol. 2, No. 1, Spring-Summer 1986, pp. 18-35.

Day, Gordon M. *Oral Tradition as Compliment.* In

Ethnohistory, The American Society for Ethnohistory, Volume 19, Number 2, Spring 1972, pp. 99-108.

____________. *Rogers' Raid in the Indian Tradition.* In *Historical New Hampshire,* The New Hampshire Historical Society, Volume XVII, June 1962, pp. 3-17.

Dibble, Ebenezer. *Diary of Ebenezer Dibble.* Copied and communicated by T. S. Woolsey. Connecticut Society of Colonial War Proceedings, Volume 1, 1903, pp. 313-329.

D.H.S.N.Y. See O'Callaghan, E. B., *Documentary History of the State of New York.*

D.R.C.H.S.N.Y. See O'Callaghan, E. B., *Documents Relating to the Colonial History of the State of New York.*

Entick, Rev. John, M.A. *The General History of the Late War, Containing Its Rise, Progress and Event, in Europe, Asia, Africa, and America.* London, 1763.

Fitch, Jabez Jr. *The Diary of Jabez Fitch, Jr. in the French and Indian War 1757.* The Rogers Island Historical Association, Glens Falls, New York, 1968.

Forbes, John. *Writings of General John Forbes Relating to His Service in North America.* Compiled and edited by Alfred Procter James, Ph.D. The Collegiate Press, Manasha, Wisconsin, 1938.

Ford, Worthington Chauncey. *British Officers Serving in North America 1754-1774.* Compiled from the "Army Lists." Originally published in the *New England Historical and Genealogical Register for 1894.* David Clapp & Son, Boston, 1894. Facsimile reprint by the Kings Arms Press & Bindery, Oldwick, New Jersey, 1999.

Frazier, Patrick. *The Mohicans of Stockbridge.* University of Nebraska Press, Lincoln, 1992.

French, Jonathan. *Journal of Jonathan French.* March 14 to October 20, 1757. Original manuscript in the William L. Clements Library, University of Michigan, Ann Arbor, Michigan.

Fuller, Archelaus. *Journal, May-November 1758.* In the *B.F.T.M.,* Volume XIII, Number 1, December 1970, pp. 5-17.

Gage, Thomas, et al. *The Gage Papers, American Series 1: 1755-February 1759.* Original manuscripts in the collections of the William L. Clements Library, University of Michigan, Ann Arbor, Michigan.

Gage, Thomas, et al. *The Gage Papers, American Series 2: March-July 1759.* Original manuscripts in the collections of the William L. Clements Library, University of Michigan, Ann Arbor, Michigan.

Galvin, John R. *The Minute Men.* Hawthorn Books, Inc., New York, 1967.

Gavit, William. *The Gavit Letters, 1759.* In the *B.F.T.M.,* Volume IX, Number 4, Fall 1983, pp. 217-219.

General Orders of 1757, Issued by the Earl of Loudoun and Phineas Lyman in the Campaign Against the French. Books for Libraries Press, Freeport, New York, 1970. Lyman also spelled his name Phinehas.

Gentleman's Magazine, London, March 1758. Original copy in the author's collection.

Gentleman's Magazine, London, September 1758. Copy of quoted material in the author's collection.

Gentleman's Magazine, London, October 1758. Copy of quoted material in the author's collection.

Gentleman's Magazine, London, May 1759. Original in the collections of Fort Ticonderoga. Copy of quoted material in the author's collection.

Gentleman's Magazine, London, October 1763. Copy of quoted material in the author's collection.

Goodrich, Josiah. *The Josiah Goodrich Orderbook.* Published in the *B.F.T.M.* in two parts:

-Part I: May 22-June 30, 1759 in Volume XIII, No. 6, Fall 1980, pp. 412-431.

-Part II: July 1-25, 1759 in Volume XIV, Number 1, Summer 1981, pp. 39-61.

Harper, J. R. *78th Fighting Fraser's in Canada: A Short History of the Old 78th Regiment or Fraser's Highlanders 1757-1763.* The Society of the Montreal Military and Maritime Museum, The Fort, St. Helen's Island, Montreal. Published by DEV-SCO Publications, Ltd., Laval, Quebec, Canada, 1966.

Hawks, John. *Orderly Book and Journal of Major John Hawks, on the Ticonderoga-Crown Point Campaign, Under General Jeffrey Amherst 1759-1760.* The Society of Colonial Wars in the State of New York, printed by H.K. Brewer & Co., New York, 1911.

Hay, Jehu. *Lieut. Jehu Hay's Diary: Under Siege in Detroit, 1763.* Original manuscript in the Clements Library, University of Michigan, Ann Arbor, Michigan. Reprinted in *The Lakeside Classics: Narratives of Colonial America 1704-1765.* Edited by Howard H. Peckham. The Lakeside Press, R.R. Donnelley & Sons Company, Chicago, 1971.

Haynes, Dr. Thomas. *Memorandum of Collonial French War A.D. 1758-.* Original manuscript in the collections of Fort Ticonderoga. Reprinted in the *B.F.T.M.,* in three parts:

-Part I: Volume XII, Number 1, 1966, pp. 72-78.

-Part II: Volume XII, Number 2, 1966, pp. 150-160.

-Part III: Volume XII, Number 3, 1967, pp. 193-203.

Henderson, James. *James Henderson's Journal from May 28, 1758 to Nov. 7, 1758 and from May 2, 1759 to Dec. 3, 1759.* Reprinted in *The First Half Century of the Society of Colonial Wars in the Commonwealth of Massachusetts, 1893-1943,* Publication No. 11, Boston, 1944.

Henshaw, William. *The Orderly Book of Lieut. William Henshaw.* Reprinted in *Manuscript Records of the French and Indian War in the Library of the American Antiquarian Society.* Published by the Society, Worcester, Massachusetts, 1909. Facsimile reprint by Heritage Books Inc., Bowie, Maryland, 1992, pp. 180-254.

Hervey, William. *Journals of the Hon. William Hervey, in North America and Europe, from 1755 to 1814; with Order Books at Montreal, 1760-1763: With Memoir and Notes.* Suffolk Green Books No. XIV, Bury St. Edmund's: Paul & Matthew, Butter Market, 1906.

Hibernian Magazine: or, Compendium of Entertaining Knowledge. September, 1776. Original in the William L. Clements Library, University of Michigan, Ann Arbor, Michigan. Copy of quoted material in the author's collection.

Hodge, Samuel Jr. *Orderly Book of Samuel Hodge, Jr., of Dover, N.H., 1760.* Reprinted in *Vineland Historical Magazine* in three parts:

-Part I: Volume 18, Number 3, pp. 300-305.

-Part II: Volume 18, Number 4, pp. 353-356.

-Part III: Volume 19, Number 1, pp 28-30.

Houlding, J. A. *Fit for Service: The Training of the British Army, 1715-1795.* Clarendon Press, Oxford, 1981.

Jackson, H. M. *Rogers' Rangers, A History.* Privately published, 1953.

Johnson, Samuel. *A Dictionary of the English Language.* Times Books, London, 1979. Originally published in 1755.

Kalm, Peter, and Adolph B. Benson, editor. *Peter Kalm's Travels in North America: The English Version of 1770.* Dover Publications, New York, 1987.

Knox, John, and Arthur G. Doughty, editor. *An Historical Journal of the Campaigns in North America for the Years 1757, 1758, 1759, and 1760.* Published in three volumes by the Champlain Society, Toronto, 1914; reprinted by Greenwood Press, New York, 1968.

Laurent, Joseph, Abenaki Chief. *New Familiar Abenakis & English Dialogues: The First Ever Published on the Grammatical System.* Leger Brousseau, Quebec, Canada, 1884.

Lery, Gaspard-Joseph Chaussegros de. *Diary, May 8th to July 2nd, 1756.* Published in the *B.F.T.M.*, Volume VI, Number 4, July 1942, pp. 128-144.

Lewis, Theodore B. *Major Robert Rogers: Commandant of Michilimackinac.* In the *B.F.T.M.*, Volume XIII, Number 3, 1972, pp. 227-240.

Lock, John D. *To Fight with Intrepidity . . . The Complete History of the U.S. Army Rangers 1622 to Present.* Pocket Books, New York, 1998. Republished in hardcover by Fenestra Books, Tucson, Arizona, 2001.

Loescher, Burt Garfield. *The History of Rogers' Rangers, Volume I: The Beginnings: January 1755-April 6, 1758.* Published by the author, San Francisco, California, 1946.

____________. *The History of Rogers' Rangers, Volume II: Genesis: Rogers' Rangers—The First Green Berets, The Corps and the Revivals: April 6, 1758-December 24, 1783.* Published by the author, San Mateo, California, 1969.

____________. *The History of Rogers' Rangers, Volume III: Officers and Non-Commissioned Officers.* Published by the author, Burlingame, California, 1957.

London Chronicle: or, Universal Evening Post, from July 29, to August 1, 1758. Original in the collections of Fort Ticonderoga. Copy of quoted material in the author's collection.

London Chronicle: or, Universal Evening Post, from September 19, to September 21, 1758. Original in the collections of Fort Ticonderoga. Copy of quoted material in the author's collection.

London Chronicle: or, Universal Evening Post, from November 23, to November 25, 1758. Original in the collections of Fort Ticonderoga. Copy of quoted material in the author's collection.

London Chronicle: or, Universal Evening Post, from May 8, to May 10, 1759. Original in the collections of George A. Bray III. Copy of quoted material in the author's collection.

London Magazine, London, October 1758. Copy of quoted material in the author's collection.

London Morning Post and Fashionable World, May 25, 1795.

Lossing, Benson J. *The Pictorial Field-Book of the Revolution; or, Illustrations, by Pen and Pencil, of the History, Biography, Scenery, Relics, and Traditions of the War for Independence.* Two volumes. Harper & Brothers, Publishers, New York, 1859.

Lyman, Phinehas [also spelled Phineas]. *Phinehas Lyman's Order Book, May 2-November 18, 1757.* Original manuscript in the collections of the Clements Library, the University of Michigan, Ann Arbor, Michigan. Lyman was the colonel of a Connecticut Provincial Regiment.

Lyon, Lemuel, and Abraham Tomlinson, editor. *Military Journal for 1758.* Reprinted in *The Military Journals of Two Private Soldiers 1758-1775,* pp. 11-45. Reprint of the 1854 edition by Books for Libraries Press, Freeport, New York, 1970.

MacLeod, D. Peter. *The Canadian Iroquois and the Seven Years' War.* The Canadian War Museum Historical Publication No. 29, Dundurn Press, Toronto, 1996.

Mante, Thomas. *The History of the Late War in North-America and the Islands of the West- Indies, Including the Campaigns of MDCCLXIII and MDCCLXIV Against His Majesty's Indian Enemies.* W. Strahan and T. Cadell, London, 1772. Reprinted by Research Reprints, Inc., New York, 1970.

Matheney, Christopher. *In Defense of Major Robert Rogers, or An Answer to His Critics Regarding His Actions at the First and Second Battles on Snowshoes.* Unpublished essay written for the completion of the requirements of the Senior Ranger Program of Jaeger's Battalion, Rogers' Rangers, 1999. Copy in the author's possession.

Mayo, Lawrence Shaw. *Jeffery Amherst.* Longmans, Green and Company, New York, 1916.

McCulloch, Lt. Col. Ian, CD, editor. *"Believe Us, Sir, This Will Impress Few People!": Spin- Doctoring, 18th Century Style.* In the *B.F.T.M.*, Volume XI, Number 1, 1998, pp 92-107.

______________________. *Buckskin Soldier: The Rise and Fall of Major Robert Rogers.* In *The Beaver*, April/May 1993, pp. 17-26.

______________________. *Men of the 27th Foot: Two Portraits. B.F.T.M.*, Volume XI, Number 2, 1999, pp. 128-151.

______________________. *"Within Ourselves . . ." The Development of British Light Infantry in North America During the Seven Years' War.* In *Canadian Military History*, Volume 7, Number 2, Spring 1998, pp. 41-55.

Miller, Lillian B. *The Dye Is Now Cast: The Road to American Independence, 1774-1776.* The Smithsonian Institution Press, Washington, DC, for the National Portrait Gallery, 1975.

Moerman, Daniel E., editor. *"Herbs, Plants, and Shrubs that possess uncommon Virtues": Robert Rogers on the Dyes and Medicines of the American Indian.* Published in The *American Magazine and Historical Chronicle*, by the William L. Clements Library, University of Michigan, Ann Arbor, Michigan, Vol. 2, No. 1, Spring-Summer 1986, pp. 36-44.

Moneypenny, Alexander. *Orderly Book.* Original in the collections of Fort Ticonderoga. Published in the *Bulletin of the Fort Ticonderoga Museum* in the following segments:

-March 23-June 29, 1758, Volume XII, Number 5, December 1969, pp. 328-357.

-June 30-August 7, 1758, Volume XII, Number 6, October 1970, pp. 434-461.

-August 8, 1758-October 26, 1758, Volume XIII, Number 1, December 1970, pp. 89-116.

-October 27, 1758-May 6, 1759, Volume XIII, Number 2, June 1971, pp. 151-184.

-July 15-August 3, 1759, Volume II, Number 6, July 1932, pp. 219-25.

Morris, Samuel. *The Journal of Samuel Morris—1758.* Original in the William L. Clements Library, University of Michigan, Ann Arbor, Michigan.

Munroe, Edmund. *Orderly Book of Ensign Edmund Monroe.* Reprinted in the *New England Historical and Genealogical Register*, Volume XVI, July 1862, pp. 217-220. (Note: at the time he kept the orderly book, Munroe was the sergeant-major of Rogers' Rangers).

New Hampshire Gazette, October 6, 1758

New York Mercury # 380, Monday, November 26, 1759. Original in the William L. Clements Library, University of Michigan, Ann Arbor, Michigan.

Obomsawim, Elvine. Taped interview, transcribed in *A History of the Abenaki People IV: Major Rogers and the English—Abenaki Invisibility.* University of Vermont Instructional Development Center, Burlington, 1977.

O'Callaghan, Edmund Bailey, editor. *The Documentary History of the State of New York. (D.H.S.N.Y.)* Weed, Parsons & Co., Albany, 1849-1851. The entire four volume series is published on CD-Rom by the Fine Books Company, Abilene, Texas.

O'Callaghan, Edmund Bailey, editor. *Documents Relating to the Colonial History of the State of New York, Procured by John Romeyn Brodhead. (D.R.C.H.S.N.Y.)* Weed, Parsons & Co., Albany, 1856. The full fifteen volumes published on CD-Rom by LeGrand J. Weller, Abilene, Texas.

Padeni, Scott A. *Forgotten Soldiers: The Role of Blacks in New York's Northern Campaigns of the Seven Years' War.* In the *B.F.T.M.*, Volume XVI, Number 2, 1999, pp. 152-169.

Pargellis, Stanley, editor. *Military Affairs in North America 1748-1765: Selected Documents from the Cumberland Papers in Windsor Castle.* Archon Books, Hamden Connecticut, 1969; originally published by the American Historical Association, 1936.

Parker, John. *New Light on Jonathan Carver.* Published in The *American Magazine and Historical Chronicle*, by the William L. Clements Library, University of Michigan, Ann Arbor, Michigan, Vol. 2, No. 1, Spring-Summer 1986, pp. 4-17.

Parkman, Francis. *Montcalm and Wolfe: The Decline and Fall of the French Empire in North America.* Collier-Macmillan Ltd., London, 1962. Published in many other editions.

Peckham, Howard H. *Pontiac and the Indian Uprising.* Phoenix Book: The University of Chicago Press, Chicago and London, 1961. First published in 1947; numerous other editions have been printed.

Pennsylvania Gazette, April 6, 1758. Original copy in the collections of Fort Ticonderoga.

Pierce, Ken. *A History of the Abenaki People IV: Major Rogers and the English—Abenaki Invisibility.* University of Vermont Instructional Development Center, Burlington, 1977.

Pitt, William, and Gertrude Selwyn Kimball, editor. *Correspondence of William Pitt When Secretary of State with Colonial Governors and Military and Naval Commissioners in America.* Two volumes. The MacMillan Company, New York & London, 1906. Reprinted by Kraus Reprint Co., New York, 1969.

Pomeroy, Seth, and Louis Effingham de Forest, editors. *The Journals and Papers of Seth Pomeroy, Sometime General in the Colonial Service.* Publication Number 38 of The Society of Colonial Wars in the State of New York. The Tuttle, Morehouse & Taylor Company, New Haven, Connecticut, 1926.

Pouchot, Pierre, with Michael Cardy, translator, and Brian Leigh Dunnigan, editor. *Memoirs of the Late War in North America Between France and England.* Old Fort Niagara Association, Inc., Youngstown, New York, 1994. Originally published in Switzerland in 1781.

Richards, Frederick B., *The Black Watch at Ticonderoga.* Heritage Books, Inc., Bowie, Maryland, 1999.

Quaife, Milo M. *Detroit Biographies: Robert Rogers.* In *Michigan History Magazine*, Volume 35, Number 2, 1951, pp. 139-150.

Roberts, Kenneth. *Northwest Passage.* Special two volume, limited edition of 1050 copies. Volume I is the novel itself. Volume II is an appendix containing research material that Roberts compiled while working on this famous book. Doubleday, Doran & Company, Inc., Garden City, New York, 1937.

Roby, Luther, editor. *Reminiscences of the French War; Containing Rogers' Expeditions with the New-England Rangers Under His Command as Published in London in 1765; with notes and illustrations. To Which is Added and Account of Maj. Gen. John Stark; with Notices and Anecdotes of Other Officers Distinguished in the French and Revolutionary Wars.*

-Original edition published by Luther Roby, Concord, New Hampshire, 1831.

-Reprinted in slightly different form by The Freedom Historical Society, Freedom, New Hampshire, 1988.

-The version of Rogers' *Journals* reprinted in this work is slightly abridged from Rogers' original editions.

Rogers, Mary Cochrane. *A Battle Fought on Snowshoes, March 13, 1758.* Published by the author (Robert Rogers' great-great granddaughter) Derry, New Hampshire, 1917. It contains an account of the battle, biographical information, review of Rogers' books, a muster roll of Bulkeley's Company, and other miscellaneous information.

Rogers, Robert. *A Concise Account of North America.* Various editions:

-London, 1765.

-Germany, 1767.

-Johnson Reprint Corporation, New York, 1966.

Rogers, Robert. *Journals of Major Robert Rogers.* Various editions:

-London, J. Millan, 1765.

-Dublin, R. Acheson, 1769.

-Dublin, J. Potts, 1770.

-Joel Munsell's Sons, Albany, 1883, published an edition with an introduction and notes by Franklin B. Hough.

-Corinth Books, Inc., distributed by the Citadel Press, New York, 1961. With an introduction by Howard H. Peckham.

-University Microfilms, Inc., Ann Arbor, Michigan, 1966.

-Readex Microprint Corporation, New Canaan, Connecticut, 1966.

-Dresslar Publishing, Bargersville, Indiana, 1997. Republished the Dublin edition as *Warfare on the Colonial American Frontier: The Journals of Major Robert Rogers & An Historical Account of the Expedition Against the Ohio Indians in the Year 1764, Under the Command of Henry Bouquet, Esq.*

-Also see Luther Roby: *Reminiscences of the French War.*

Rogers, Robert. *Journal of Robert Rogers the Ranger on His Expedition for Receiving the Capitulation of Western French Posts (October 20, 1760 to February 14, 1761).* Edited by Victor Hugo Paltsits. Reprinted in the *Journal New York Public Library*, April 1933, pp. 261- 276.

Rogers, Robert. *Journal of the Siege of Detroit.* Published in *Diary of the Siege of Detroit in the War with Pontiac*, pp. 123-135. Edited and with notes by Franklin B. Hough, Albany, New York, 1860.

Rogers, Robert. Letter (voucher) to Thomas Gage regarding pay of the Rangers, March 1, 1760. Original in the collections of the William L. Clements Library, the University of Michigan, Ann Arbor, Michigan; copy in the author's possession.

Rogers, Robert. Letter to Thomas Gage regarding the court-martial of Lieutenant Samuel Stephens, April 1, 1760. Original in the collections of the William L. Clements Library, the University of Michigan, Ann Arbor, Michigan; copy in the author's possession.

Rogers, Robert. *Michilimackinac Journal.* Published in the *Proceedings of the American Antiquarian Society,* Worcester, Massachusetts, 1918. Edited and with an introduction by William L. Clements.

Rogers, Robert. *Ponteach, or the Savages of America: A Tragedy.* Various editions:

-London 1766.

-Caxton Club, Chicago, 1914. Contains an introduction and a biography of Robert Rogers by historian Allan Nevins.

-Lenox Hill Publishing and Distributing Company, New York, 1971. The Lenox Hill edition is a reprint of the Caxton Club edition.

Rogers Robert. *Report of Scout to Fort Ticonderoga, March 3, 1759.* Original in the collections of the William L. Clements Library, the University of Michigan, Ann Arbor, Michigan; copy in the author's possession.

Rogers, Robert J. U. E. *Rising Above Circumstances: The Rogers Family in Colonial America.* Sheltus & Picard Inc., Bedford, Quebec, Canada, 1999.

Silcox, James H. Jr. *Rogers and Bouquet: The Origins of American Light Infantry.* In *Military Review,* December 1985, pp. 62-74.

Skinner, Henry, and Gary S. Zaboly, editor. *A Royal Artillery Officer with Amherst: The Journal of Captain-Lieutenant Henry Skinner, 1 May-28 July 1759.* In *B.F.T.M.,* Volume XV, Number 5, 1993, pp. 363-387.

Simcoe, John G. *Simcoe's Military Journal: A History of the Operations of a Partisan Corps Called the Queen's Rangers Commanded by Lieut. Col. J. G. Simcoe, During the War of the American Revolution.* Bartlett & Welford, New-York, 1844. Reprinted by Arno Press, Inc., 1968.

Smith, Joseph. *Journal of Joseph Smith of Groton.* Welcome A. Smith Esq., Norwich, Connecticut, 1896.

Smith, George. *An Universal Military Dictionary.* Limited Edition Military Series, Museum Restoration Service, Ottawa, Ontario, Canada, 1969. Originally published by J. Millan, London, 1779.

Smith, William, Rev. *An Historical Account of the Expedition Against the Ohio Indians in the Year 1764, Under the Command of Henry Bouquet, Esq.* This work by Father Smith was also reprinted as a part of the Dublin edition of Rogers' *Journals,* and Robert Rogers is sometimes erroneously credited with being the author.

-Philadelphia, William Bradford, Philadelphia, Pennsylvania, 1765.

-London, 1766.

-Amsterdam, 1769. Published in French, translated by C. G. F. Dumas.

-Robert Clarke & Co., Cincinnati, Ohio, 1868. This edition contains a preface by Francis Parkman, as well as Parkman's translation of Dumas' *Biographical Sketch of General Bouquet.*

-Readex Microprint Corporation, New Canaan, Connecticut, 1966.

Spicer, Abel; Russell P. Bellico, editor. *Journal for 1758,* reprinted in *Chronicles of Lake George: Journeys in War and Peace.* Purple Mountain Press, Ltd., Fleischmanns, New York, 1995, pp. 91-119. Originally printed in *The History of the Descendants of Peter Spicer,* compiled by Susan Spicer Meech and Susan Billings Meech, F.H. Gilson, Boston, 1911, pp. 390-406. Excerpts and page numbers quoted in this text are from Dr. Bellico's version.

Starbuck, David R., Ph.D. *The Great Warpath: British Military Sites from Albany to Crown Point.* University Press of New England, Hanover and London, 1999.

Stark, Caleb, *Memoir and Official Correspondence of Gen. John Stark, with Notices of Several Other Officers of the Revolution; Also a Biography of Capt. Phinehas Stevens, and of Col. Robert Rogers, with an Account of His Services in America During the "Seven Years' War."*

-Published by G. Parker Lyon, Concord, New Hampshire, 1860.

-Facsimile reprint, with a new introduction and preface by George Athan Billias, Gregg Press, Boston, Massachusetts, 1972.

Steele, Ian K. *Betrayals: Fort William Henry & the "Massacre."* Oxford University Press, New York, 1990.

________________. *Warpaths: Invasions of North America.* Oxford University Press, New York, 1994.

Steele, Russell V. *Backwoods Warfare: The Rangers and Light Infantry in North America—Their Leaders, Uniform and Equipment.* In *B.F.T.M.,* Volume VII, Number 6, July 1947, pp. 24-36.

Stott, Earl, et al. *Exploring Rogers Island, Fort Edward, N.Y.* Publication Number Two, Rogers Island Historical Association, Fort Edward, New York, 1969.

Simes, Thomas. *The Military Medley: Containing the Most Necessary Rules and Directions for Attaining a Competent Knowledge of the Art: To Which Is Added an Explanation of Military Terms, Alphabetically Digested.* London, 1768. Reprinted by the Kings Arms Press and Bindery, Oldwick, New Jersey, 1990.

Titus, Timothy D. *An Illustrated History of Crown Point State Historic Site.* New York State Office of Parks, Recreation, and Historic Preservation, 1994.

Todish, Timothy J. *America's FIRST First World War: The French & Indian War 1754-1763.* Dickinson Press, Grand Rapids, Michigan, 1982; Eagle's View Press, Ogden, Utah, 1988; Purple Mountain Press, Fleischmanns, New York, 2002.

________________. *Crown Point on Lake Champlain.* In *Muzzleloader Magazine*, July/August 1984, pp. 45-49.

________________. *Fortress Louisbourg: The Gibraltar of North America.* In *Muzzleloader Magazine,* May/June 1987, pp. 34-39.

________________. *Michilimackinac: Land of the Great Turtle.* In *Muzzleloader Magazine*, March/April 1983, pp. 16-20.

________________. *Rangers at Fort Edward.* In *Muzzleloader Magazine*, July/August 1990, pp. 54-58.

________________. *Rendezvous on the Ouabache: Fort Ouiatenon and the Feast of the Hunter's Moon.* In *Muzzleloader Magazine,* September/October 1991, pp. 39-42.

________________. *The 1758 Attack on Ticonderoga.* In *Muzzleloader Magazine*:

Part I, November/December 1999, pp. 54-61.

Part II, January/February 2000, pp. 41-50.

________________. *Triumph and Tragedy: The Siege of Fort William Henry.* In *Muzzleloader Magazine*:

Part I, November/December 1992, pp. 36-40.

Part II, January/ February 1993, pp. 31-36.

Van Shaick, Goose. *Orderly Book, May 24–October 27, 1758.* Original in the collections of Fort Ticonderoga.

Walker, Anthony, Colonel, U.S.M.C. Retired. *The Woods Fighters: Rogers' Rangers in the Wilderness War, 1755-1760.* Seafield Press, Newport, Rhode Island, 1994.

Walker, Joseph B. *Life and Exploits of Robert Rogers, the Ranger: A Paper Read Before the Members of the New England Historic-Genealogical Society, at Their Monthly Meeting in Boston, November 5, 1884.* John N. McClintock and Company, Boston, 1885.

Wallace, R. F. H., editor. *Regimental Routine and Army Administration in North America in 1759: Extracts from Company Order Books of the 42nd Royal Highland Regiment.* From the *Journal of the Society for Army Historical Research,* Volume 30, Number 121, Spring 1952.

Webster, Robert. *Robert Webster's Journal of Amherst's Campaign, April 5th to November 23rd, 1759.* Original in the collections of the Fort Ticonderoga Museum. An edited version of this journal was published in *B.F.T.M.*, Volume II, Number 4, July, 1931.

Westbrook, Nicholas, editor. *"Like Roaring Lions Breaking Their Chains": The Highland Regiment at Ticonderoga.* In *B.F.T.M.*, Volume XVI, Number 1, 1998, pp 16-91.

Wells, Phillip. *Journal of a Scout Performed by Phillip Wells, January 23-February 7, 1759.* Original manuscript in the *Gage Papers, American Series 1: 1755-February 1759,* in the collections of the William L. Clements Library, University of Michigan, Ann Arbor, Michigan.

Wilson, Commissary. J. Watts de Peyster, editor. *Commissary Wilson's Orderly Book—Expedition of the British and Provincial Army Under Maj. Gen. Jeffrey Amherst Against Ticonderoga and Crown Point, 1759.* J. Munsell, Albany, New York, and Trubner Co., London, 1857. The exact identity of Commissary Wilson is unclear. On March 9, 1757 a David Wilson became the Quartermaster of the 43rd Regiment of Foot, but in 1759 this regiment was serving in the northern theater, and was not a part of Amherst's Campaign. David Wilson may have been on detached service, or could have changed regiments, but no proof of this has been discovered.

Wood, Lemuel. Russell P. Bellico, editor. *Journal for 1759*, reprinted in *Chronicles of Lake George: Journeys in War and Peace.* Purple Mountain Press, Ltd., Fleischmanns, NY, 1995, pp. 121-145. Originally published by *The Essex Institute Historical Collections,* Volume 19, 1882, pp. 61-80 & 143-192, and Volume 20, 1883, pp. 156-60. Excerpts and page numbers quoted in this text are from Dr. Bellico's version.

Wolfe, Major General James. *Instructions to Young Officers and a Placart to the Canadians.* London, 1768. Museum Restoration Service Edition, Ottawa, Ontario, Canada, 1967.

Zaboly, Gary. *The Battle on Snowshoes.* In *American History Illustrated,* December, 1979, pp. 12-24.

________________. *Wilderness Commandos: The Dress, Weapons, and Accouterments of Rogers' Rangers.* In *Muzzle Blasts,* June, 1978, pp. 7-14

Zarzynski, Joseph W., and John Farrell, edited by David R. Starbuck. *Recent Underwater Archaeological Surveys at Lake George, New York.* In *Archaeology of the French & Indian War: Military Sites of the Hudson River, Lake George, and Lake Champlain Corridor.* Adirondack Community College, Queensbury, New York, 1995.

Index

To make this index more informative and usable, as much as possible all persons are listed by their full name and the highest rank attained during the war.

For most military figures, their primary unit affiliation is also given.

In situations where there is more than one person with the same name, (i.e. the Stark and Brewer brothers and the two Captain Jacobs), every effort has been made to correctly identify the specific person being referred to.

Although the connection is frequently obvious, various spellings (and misspellings) of names and places are also often recognized.

Where a page number is followed by a lower case "n," it indicates that the reference is in a footnote at the bottom of the page. The abbreviation "ftn." indicates a numbered footnote in Gary Zaboly's text.

To further assist the reader, major index entries have been broken down by campaign year, and in some instances, into additional subgroups.

Purple Mountain Press, established 1973, and Harbor Hill Books, acquired 1990, are publishing companies committed to producing the best books of regional and maritime interest, including Timothy J. Todish's *America's FIRST First World War: The French and Indian War, 1754-1763*. For a free catalog write Purple Mountain Press, Ltd., P.O. Box 309, Fleischmanns, NY 12430-0309; or call 845-254-4062, or fax 845-254-4476, or email purple@catskill.net. http://www.catskill.net/purple.

About the editor/annotator

TIM TODISH, a native of Grand Rapids, Michigan, has had a nearly lifelong interest in Rogers' Rangers and the French and Indian War. He is a graduate of Michigan State University with a degree in Management.

While still in college, Todish became interested in black powder shooting and historical reenacting, which still occupies much of his time. He is the Adjutant of the French and Indian War reenactment group Jaeger's Battalion, Rogers' Rangers.

Now retired from the Grand Rapids Police Department with over twenty-seven years of service, Todish works as an independent historical writer and consultant, specializing in the French and Indian War and Alamo periods. He provided background information and worked as an extra in the 1992 movie *The Last of the Mohicans,* and also served as the Technical Advisor and appeared as an extra in the award winning History Channel documentary *Frontier: Legends of the Old Northwest.* In addition, he has also done consulting for such productions as the Learning Channel show *Archeology,* and the PBS series *Anyplace Wild.* Todish has written articles for a number of historical publications, and is on the Special Features Staff and is a regular contributor to *Muzzleloader Magazine.*

He has written a number of historical articles for such magazines as *The Journal of the Forces of Montcalm & Wolfe, Living History, Smoke & Fire News* and *F&I War.* His books include *America's FIRST First World War: The French & Indian War, 1754-1763* (first issued in hardcover by Dickinson Brothers, Grand Rapids, Michigan, in 1982 and in paperback by Eagle's View Publishing Company, Ogden, Utah, in 1988, this book has been revised for a second edition in 2002 for Purple Mountain Press, Fleischmanns, New York) and, *Alamo Sourcebook 1836: A Comprehensive Guide to the Alamo and the Texas Revolution* (with Terry Todish, and original art by Ted Spring).

About the artist

GARY ZABOLY developed a very early interest in American colonial and frontier history.

His education included courses in drawing and painting at the High School of Art and Design and the Art Students League. Some of the books he has illustrated include the award-winning *Texian Iliad,* by Stephen L. Hardin, *Rising Above Circumstances: The Rogers Family in Colonial America,* by Robert J. Rogers, *Blood of Noble Men: The Alamo Siege and Battle, An Illustrated Chronology,* by Alan C. Huffines, *On the Prairie At Palo Alto,* by Charles M. Haecker and Jeffrey G. Mauck, as well as two upcoming books by eminent Rogers Ranger historian Burt Garfield Loescher.

His artwork is on permanent display at the Alamo, in San Antonio, in the form of wayside signs placed around the site depicting its appearance in 1836, and in illustrations on the outdoor exhibit, the Wall of History. Additional works of his reside in the collections of the Lake George Historical Association, the Aztec Club of 1847, the Fort Ticonderoga Museum, and the Montana Historical Society, among others.

He is a Fellow of the Company of Military Historians, a member of the Friends of Fort Ticonderoga, the New York Historical Society, the Alamo Society, and a founding board member of the Alamo Battlefield Association.

His work, both illustrated and written, has appeared in some sixty books and magazine articles, some of the latter published in *The Alamo Journal, American History Illustrated, The Bulletin of the Fort Ticonderoga Museum, French and Indian War Quarterly, Military Collector and Historian, Muzzle Blasts, Muzzleloader, Old West and True West.* His artwork has also been sold through galleries, private commissions, and in print form, as well as illustrating a number of historical television documentaries.

He lives with his wife, Cora, on a bluff overlooking the Hudson River in Riverdale, New York